D1480543

NO TURNING BACK

NO TURNING BACK

The Beginning of the End of the Civil War: March–June 1864

Don Lowry

HIPPOCRENE BOOKS
New York

For information, address:
HIPPOCRENE BOOKS, INC.
171 Madison Avenue
New York, NY 10016

ISBN 0-87052-010-5

Library of Congress Cataloging-in-Publication Data is available.

Printed in the United States of America.

"Whatever happens, there will be no turning back."

—Ulysses S. Grant to Abraham Lincoln

CONTENTS

PART TWO—THE WILDERNESS

PART THREE—
SPOTSYLVANIA

PART FOUR—THE ROAD SOUTH

PREFACE

Several things led to the writing of this book. I could say that it goes back to the unmarked day in my childhood when my older brother fed my curiosity about the American Civil War by presenting me with a paperback copy of Fletcher Pratt's one-volume history of the conflict. Or at least it goes back to my high school days when I discovered Bruce Catton's Army of the Potomac trilogy. The desire to write something on the subject is at least that old. After college and six years in the air force I started to write a history of the war, only to discover how little I really knew. The project was abandoned in favor of making a living.

In addition to twenty years of further reading and research on the war, there were three main reasons why my writing finally assumed the present form. First was the decision to follow a strictly chronological approach. Too often in my reading did I find that authors skipped back and forth in time—in order to avoid shifting geographically—until all sense was lost of how events on different fronts affected each other.

Second was the choice of the campaign of 1864 as a starting place, where the chronological approach seemed even more appropriate because it was Grant's desire to combine all Union forces for the first time into one coordinated campaign. This choice was triggered by my discovery some years ago of Edward Steere's excellent study of the otherwise little-understood battle of the Wilderness and by William Glenn Robertson's more recent book on Butler's Bermuda Hundred operations (see Appendix C). I wanted to explore how the two campaigns effected each other. It was sheer luck on my part that William D. Matter's study of the battle of Spotsylvania came out just as I was getting started.

The third, and perhaps most crucial, factor was the acquisition of a home computer that put the actual work of organizing facts, writing, and revising within reach of my talents and time. All those who have made this powerful tool available and affordable to writers like myself have my profound gratitude.

All quotes in the text are presented with the same spelling and punctuation as found in the sources noted. For instance, the correct spelling of Spotsylvania is with one T, but if the source spelled it with two T's I have left the second T in.

Some may say that I have been overly dependent in my research on secondary sources, but it has not been my intention to dig up new facts, merely to arrange them in a chronological narrative. No one is responsible for any errors or omissions in the present work but myself. I would like to thank Kevin Pollock, Gregory J. W. Urwin, Betty Johnston, Mary L. Suggs and especially my wife Julie for their encouragement along the way, and my editor, Tanjam Narasimhan, for polishing some of the rough edges off the text.

I make no apologies for the fact that my sympathies are with Lincoln, Grant, and the Union cause. I am most heartily glad that they won. I respect the Confederate soldiers and most of their leaders, but not their cause. However, my feelings are consistent with this remark made by Lincoln: "Let us therefore study the incidents of this [war], as philosophy to learn wisdom from, and none of them as wrongs to be revenged."[1]

---

1. Roy P. Basler, ed. *The Collected Works of Abraham Lincoln* (New Brunswick, 1953), vol. 8, 101.

PART ONE

TAURUS RISING

"He doesn't ask me to do impossibilities for him, and he's the first general I've had that didn't."

—Abraham Lincoln

CHAPTER ONE

The Uncommon Common Man

8–10 March 1864

In the Blue Room of the White House, President Abraham Lincoln was shaking hands with a vast procession of men and women. "His face wore a general expression of sadness," one observer noted, "the deep lines indicating the sense of responsibility which weighed upon him; but at times his features lighted up with a broad smile, and there was a merry twinkle in his eyes as he greeted an old acquaintance and exchanged a few words with him in a tone of familiarity."

It was the evening of 8 March 1864, almost three years since the beginning of the Civil War, and the Lincolns were holding a routine Tuesday evening reception. Army Captain Horace Porter, just quoted above, was there that night. He recorded that Lincoln was in evening dress, but that his turned-down collar was a size too large for him and that his necktie was awkwardly tied. The president's height of six feet four inches, very uncommon at that time, enabled him to see over the heads of most of his visitors, so perhaps he was one of the first to notice an ordinary-seeming officer approach.

"At about half-past nine o'clock," Porter noted, "a sudden commotion near the entrance to the room attracted general attention, and, upon looking in that direction, I was surprised to see General Grant walking along modestly with the rest of the crowd toward Mr. Lincoln. . . . Although these two historical characters had never met before, Mr. Lincoln recognized the general at once from the pictures he had seen of him. With a face radiant with delight, he advanced rapidly two or three steps toward his distinguished visitor, and cried out: 'Why, here is General Grant! Well, this is a great pleasure, I assure you,' at the same time seizing him by the hand, and shaking it for several minutes with a vigor which showed the extreme cordiality of the welcome."[1]

Major General Ulysses S. Grant was, at that moment, perhaps the most famous and most popular man in the United States. Yet Captain Porter was probably the only person in that throng of Washington dignitaries and hangers-on who had ever laid eyes on him before. Porter had been serving on the staff of General George H. Thomas at Chattanooga, Tennessee when Grant had won his most recent victory there the previous November.

Actually, Grant had been one of the North's first heroes in the Civil War. His capture of Confederate Forts Henry and Donelson in February 1862 had been the first major victory for Union forces, and his famous reply to the Confederate commander's request for terms had turned an obscure brigadier into a household name as Unconditional Surrender Grant. That victory had brought him a second star, but when his forces had been surprised at the subsequent battle of Shiloh, even though he had driven back the attacking Southerners he had temporarily been eclipsed by his superior, Henry Wager Halleck. Old Brains, as Halleck was known, had left his desk in St. Louis to take the field for a methodical, grinding advance on the Rebel railroad junction of Corinth, Mississippi.

Grant had been relegated to the superfluous job of second-in-command of Halleck's accumulated forces and had only been talked out of resigning by General William T. Sherman, who had himself survived an earlier fall from grace. But when Halleck had been called to Washington in the summer of 1862 to become general-in-chief, Grant had slowly emerged from obscurity again. First he had engineered a pair of defensive victories at Corinth and nearby Iuka while other Union generals were being driven back to Kentucky and Maryland. However, General William S. Rosecrans, then Grant's subordinate on the spot, had received most of the credit. Then in the spring of 1863 Grant had executed a daring and brilliantly improvised campaign to cut off, beseige, and capture Vicksburg, the main Southern bastion on the Mississippi River. That previously impregnable fortress had surrendered on the Fourth of July 1863, the same day that Robert E. Lee had begun his retreat from Gettysburg in distant Pennsylvania, and Grant had suddenly become a hero again.

When Rosecrans, then commanding the Union forces that had captured Chattanooga, had been defeated at the battle of Chickamauga that September, it had been the highly successful Grant who had been called upon to set things right. He had been put in command of most of the Union forces between the Appalachian Mountains and the Mississippi. Given the choice between retaining Rosecrans in command at Chattanooga, where he had retreated and was currently beseiged, or replacing him with Thomas, Grant had chosen Thomas. Then, although on crutches from injuries suffered recently when his horse had fallen with him, he had made his way into the beleaguered city to take personal command. Grant had brought up Sherman with part of his old army as well as reinforcements sent from the east, cleared Rebel forces from Thomas's supply line, and driven the Southern army of General Braxton Bragg from a formidable position back to the hills of Georgia. Thus Grant had turned what appeared to be developing into the Union's worst defeat of the war into one of its most resounding victories.

The president had once said that if the general took Vicksburg, "Why Grant is my man and I am his the rest of the war."[2] Chattanooga had reconfirmed and strengthened the general's place in Lincoln's esteem, and the nation's. After Chattanooga, Congress had revived the three-star rank of lieutenant general, previously held only by George Washington. It was now up to the president to decide whom to promote to that rank, but there was no doubt in anyone's mind that Congress hoped and Lincoln intended for the three stars to be pinned on none other than Grant. Those three stars would make him the army's senior officer and thus the general-in-chief. The bill had passed through Congress on 26 February, and Grant's nomination had been sent in on 1 March and confirmed on the second. The next day the general had received telegraphic orders to report to Washington to receive his commission.

Grant arrived in Washington on the eighth accompanied only by two staff officers and his 14-year-old son Fred, who had just recovered from a near-fatal illness contracted while campaigning with his father in Mississippi. Somehow the officers sent to meet him at the railroad station missed him, perhaps because they were looking for a conquering hero instead of ordinary Sam Grant. Author Richard Henry Dana (*Two Years*

Before the Mast) happened to be at Willard's Hotel when Grant checked in and saw that "a short, round-shouldered man, in a very tarnished major-general's uniform, came up. . . . He had no gait, no station, no manner, rough, light-brown whiskers, a blue eye and rather a scrubby look withal. A crowd formed aorund him; men looked, stared at him, as if they were taking his likeness. . . .

"I joined the starers," Dana wrote his wife. "I saw that the ordinary, scrubby-looking man, with a slight seedy look, as if he was out of office and on half-pay and nothing to do but hang around the entry of Willard's, cigar in mouth, had a clear blue eye, and a look of resolution, as if he could not be trifled with, and an entire indifference to the crowd about him. Straight nose, too. Still, to see him talking and smoking . . . in that crowd, in such times—the generalissimo of our armies, on whom the destiny of the empire seemed to hang!"[3]

If Dana disapproved of the crowd that surrounded Grant, the general was embarrassed by it, as by all public attention. He attempted to dine quietly alone with Fred in the hotel but was recognized and subjected to three cheers from his fellow diners. After dinner he found, on his return to his rooms, a special invitation to come by the White House. He left Fred at the hotel and walked the two blocks with a Pennsylvania congressman for his first meeting with Lincoln.

"The President," Porter observed, "who was eight inches taller, looked down with beaming countenance upon his guest. Although their appearance, their training, and their characteristics were in striking contrast, yet the two men had many traits in common, and there were numerous points of resemblance in their remarkable careers. Each was of humble origin, and had been compelled to learn the first lessons of life in the severe school of adversity. Each had risen from the people, possessed an abiding confidence in them, and always retained a deep hold upon their affections. Each might have said to those who were inclined to sneer at his plain origin what a marshal of France, who had risen from the ranks to a dukedom, said to the hereditary nobles who attempted to snub him in Vienna: 'I am an ancestor; you are only descendants.' "

The president and the general conversed briefly and then Mr. Lincoln introduced his distinguished guest to Secretary of State Henry Seward, who led him to where Mrs. Lincoln was conversing with some of the other women. She was delighted to take charge of the popular guest, but the other visitors were so curious to catch a glimpse of the general that they soon got completely out of hand. Seward succeeded in maneuvering Grant through the crowd into the much larger East Room, where the people could circulate more freely, but even this did not solve the problem. The large throng surged and swayed and crowded until concern was felt for the safety of the ladies, and cries of "Grant, Grant," were followed by cheer after cheer. Seward finally persuaded the shy general to climb upon a couch so that he could be seen by more of the people. "The little, scared-looking man who stood on a crimson-covered sofa was the idol of the hour," one newsman related. However, the sight of him only made the crowd noisier and more excited, and a rush was made to shake his hand. The president sent word that he and Secretary of War Edwin Stanton would await the general in one of the smaller rooms, but it took an hour, and the help of several officers and White House ushers, for the general to make his way there.

When Grant finally rejoined the president, Lincoln informed him that he would present his commission at a ceremony the next day and that he would be expected to reply to a short speech. Knowing that the general was no public speaker, and to help him in framing his reply, Lincoln gave him a copy of his own speech and indicated a couple of points he hoped the general would cover.

That second meeting the next day proved to be more decorous if not less embarrassing to Grant, who hated speaking in public. Nevertheless, in the presence of the cabinet, General Halleck, some of Grant's staff officers, and Fred, the general was formally presented the commission which placed upon him the president's and the nation's trust and hope for victory in a war that had already lasted far longer, and cost far more in lives and treasure, than either side had ever expected. The president's oath to preserve, protect and defend the Constitution of the United States left him no room for any peace with the Southern states that did not involve their return to the Union. And, as the Confederate government refused to discuss peace on any terms but independence, there was nothing for Lincoln to do but fight until he either won, or was replaced in office. And he had just about a year left before the end of his term. That year, and with it the future of the country, were now entrusted to Ulysses S. Grant.

Not quite 42 years of age at that time, Grant was to most of his contemporaries and to history, somewhat of an enigma. The uncommon common man, someone called him. Gentle and quiet in personal habits and so repulsed by the sight of blood that he could eat meat only if it had been charred almost to a cinder, he nevertheless came to be considered a butcher of his own men, supposedly only capable of winning battles by piling up corpses until one side ran out of men. This was not true. The key to the man was his determination. In his memoirs he confessed that all his life he had an aversion to retracing his steps. If he found he had taken a wrong turn he would resort to any device to avoid turning

around. Thus he had tried every way to get at Vicksburg until he had
finally captured it, and so he would eventually force his way into the
Confederate capital. In the process, "like Grant took Richmond" became
a common expression for unswerving tenacity.

He was born Hiram Ulysses Grant on 27 April 1822, his parents' first
child. Devotees of astrology will note that he was thus a Taurus by sun
sign, and whatever the merits or shortcomings of that pseudo-science, he
was a Taurus if ever there was one, the word being almost synonymous
with stubborn. He hated his father's Ohio leather tanning business because of his aversion to the sight of blood but nonetheless had not been
eager to take up the appointment his father had secured for him to West
Point. Typically, however, he had stuck it out to graduate 21st in the 39-
man class of 1843. His only distinction at the academy had been in
horsemanship. A clerical mistake there had changed his name to Ulysses
Simpson Grant, and his classmates had turned his new initials into "Uncle
Sam," which at least was better than "Hug," and soon he had become just
plain "Sam" to his friends.

Higher-placing graduates had taken up all the lieutenants' vacancies in
the cavalry, which he would have preferred, so he had been commissioned
in the 4th Infantry and stationed at Jefferson Barracks near St. Louis.
There he had met his future bride, Julia Dent, sister of his West Point
roommate, a scion of the lessor Missouri aristocracy. A lieutenant and
regimental quartermaster during the Mexican War, of which he disapproved, Grant had earned considerable notice for his conspicuous
coolness under fire. He had been promoted to captain and had married
Julia, but had then been sent to a lonely post in California where the gold
rush had so inflated prices that he could not afford to have his family join
him. Some said that his reputation as a man who could not hold his liquor
dated from this separation. At any rate, he resigned his commission to get
home again, but had so little success in civilian life that he had eventually
been forced to take a position in his father's hated leather business, by
then relocated to Galena, Illinois.

That move had turned out to be fortuitous in a way he could never have
foreseen. When the Confederates fired on Fort Sumter and Lincoln called
for volunteers, Grant, like former officers all over the North, had offered
his services to the overworked War Department. He received no answer,
but the governor of Illinois had used him to help enroll the state's
volunteers and had then finally appointed him colonel of an infantry
regiment. However, Galena, a lead-mining community in northwestern
Illinois, was also the home of Congressman Elihu Washburne, a friend
and supporter of Lincoln. He had considered that his district was entitled

to a brigadier general's star to hand out and that Grant, whose father and brothers were still in business in Galena, was just the man to pin it on. Throughout the war Grant continued to benefit from the sponsorship of Washburne. It was Washburne who had introduced the bill to restore the grade of lieutenant general.

Grant himself, however, had never shown any political tendencies during the war. If he had, he might never have been promoted to lieutenant general. The same prominence that had led to Grant's promotion had also led to his name being bandied about as a potential presidential nominee in that election year of 1864, even though nobody was quite sure whether he was a Democrat or a Republican. Grant later confessed to having voted for Buchanan, a Democrat, in 1856, instead of the Republican Fremont, who had been a captain in the army and a controversial figure in California. He explained that he had not known Buchanan, whereas he had known Fremont.

But Lincoln intended to stand for reelection in 1864 himself and did not want to raise up any rivals for either the nomination or the election. Washburne had sent Russell Jones, Federal marshall for Chicago and an acquaintance of both Grant and Lincoln, around to the White House for a friendly chat. He just happened to ask if the president would like to know whether Grant was interested in the presidency. Lincoln admitted to some curiosity on that subject, whereupon Jones had produced a letter from Grant to himself in which he had denied all interest in the office, saying, "I already have a pretty big job on my hands, and my only ambition is to see this rebellion suppressed. Nothing could induce me to think of being a presidential candidate, particularly so long as there is a possibility of having Mr. Lincoln re-elected."

"My son," Lincoln had said, "you will never know how gratifying that is to me. No man knows, when that Presidential grub gets to gnawing at him, just how deep it will get until he has tried it; and I didn't know but what there was one gnawing at Grant."[4]

After receiving his commission, Grant left the White House and went off to inspect the defenses of Washington, an impressive ring of earthworks completely surrounding the city and its Virginia suburbs across the Potomac River. That evening he dined with Secretary of State Seward, despite the misgivings of his own chief of staff, John A. Rawlins, who had been a young lawyer in Galena before the war. Rawlins had suffered the pains of having an alcoholic father, and was now Grant's self-appointed conscience when it came to drink. "Where I am wine is not drunk by those with whom I have any influence," he wrote his wife.[5]

The next day, 10 March, Grant went with Secretary of War Stanton to

Mathew Brady's portrait gallery on Pennsylvania Avenue to have his picture taken. While the general was sitting for the camera, one of Brady's assistants fell through a skylight overhead, throwing lethal shards of broken glass all around him. Grant glanced up casually, with "a barely perceptible quiver of the nostril," but displayed no other emotion. Brady called the general's calm reaction "the most remarkable display of nerve I ever witnessed."[6] Later Grant took a military train down into Virginia to visit what promised to be his biggest problem of command, the Army of the Potomac.

The Army of the Potomac was the Union's largest and best known force. It had been forged by General George B. McClellan in the early days of the war from the wreckage of the defeat at Bull Run and the vast outpouring of volunteers that had followed that disaster. McClellan had been a great organizer and inspirer of troops, but unfortunately was exceedingly cautious. His paranoia had soon widened to encompass the administration because the president and the secretary of war dared to disagree with his policies or to withhold from him all the reinforcements to which he felt entitled. McClellan's shortcomings had eventually necessitated his removal, which in turn had brought to the surface a great roil of political intrigue in and around that army. McClellan had his supporters among politicians in and out of office and among the officers of the army he had trained. These men could not see his faults and had viewed his downfall almost as treason on the part of the administration. His successor, Burnside, also had many shortcomings and had also been removed, as was the next, Hooker, until the Army of the Potomac had become a force led by officers as much concerned with internal politics and old grievances as with finding some way to defeat the wily Robert E. Lee.

Lincoln had finally given command of the Army of the Potomac to Major General George Gordon Meade, who had been appointed in the midst of Lee's move north into Pennsylvania in the summer of 1863, while Grant had been besieging Vicksburg. Meade had quickly taken hold of the reins of command and had done a commendable job of cutting short the invasion of the North by taking a threatening stand at Gettysburg and there turning back Lee's efforts to destroy his army. But, to Lincoln's everlasting regret, Meade had lacked the killer instinct to turn Lee's retreat to Virginia into a war-winning rout. Since that time, Meade and Lee had maneuvered back and forth in northern Virginia but had fought no great battles. Lincoln had resigned himself to getting no victories from the Army of the Potomac and had taken comfort in the progress of Grant in the West. But now that Grant was assuming the overall command, the president hoped that something could be done about Robert E. Lee.

1. Horace Porter, *Campaigning With Grant* (New York, 1897), 18.
2. T. Harry Williams, *Lincoln and His Generals* (New York, 1952), 272.
3. W. E. Woodward, *Meet General Grant* (New York, 1928), 176.
4. Bruce Catton, *Grant Takes Command* (Boston, 1968), 111–112.
5. Ibid., 128.
6. Shelby Foote, *The Civil War: A Narrative* (New York, 1974), vol. 3, 8–9.

CHAPTER TWO

"He Is Not An Ordinary Man"
10–26 March 1864

We Americans of the twentieth century are used to having our wars fought in someone else's country on some other continent far, far away. They are, after all, noisy, dirty affairs apt to entirely disrupt the normal course of business. But in 1864 the unpleasantness was a good deal closer to home. From Alexandria, just south of Washington, Grant's train chugged along through less than sixty miles of war-torn Virginia countryside, passing numerous sites of previous battles large and small to bring the new lieutenant general to Brandy Station, the headquarters of the Army of the Potomac. But, even as he started on his new duties that tenth day of March, two distant events were already working against him. That same day, three small divisions of his old Army of the Tennessee were leaving Vicksburg to join what was scheduled to be a brief side show up the Red River from Louisiana to Texas, and in the much nearer Shenandoah Valley of Virginia, politically influential Major General Franz Sigel was taking command of the little backwater Department of West Virginia.

To honor the arrival of the new general-in-chief, Meade had turned out a regiment of zouaves—infantry wearing baggy red trousers, white leggings, and turbans in imitation of the crack North African regiments of the French army—as well as a military band. Unfortunately for them,

Grant arrived after dark in the middle of a pouring rain. Furthermore, he was entirely tone deaf. He once said that he only knew two tunes: One was "Yankee Doodle" and the other wasn't.[1] But the lieutenant general had not come to look at honor guards or to listen to music. He had come to see Meade.

Tall, dour, irrascible Major General George Gordon Meade was born in Spain of Philadelphia gentry on diplomatic duty. He was six years older than Grant and had graduated from West Point eight years ahead of him, ranking nineteenth in a class of 56, high enough to be originally commissioned into the artillery. He had resigned a year after graduation to become a civil engineer but reentered the service in 1842 and fought in the Mexican War in the elite position of topographical engineer. With the coming of the Civil War he was made a brigadier general of volunteers and commanded a brigade in the unique Pennsylvania Reserve Division, a force the governor of Pennsylvania had recruited in excess of what the War Department had required of his state in those innocent days before the defeat at Bull Run. After that disaster, the division joined McClellan's new Army of the Potomac, and Meade fought through all of that force's campaigns and battles. By the time McClellan had fought his last battle, at Sharpsburg, Maryland, Meade had advanced to the command of a division, and when Lee humiliated Hooker at Chancellorsville, Meade was in command of a corps. When two senior corps commanders declined appointment as Hooker's successor, Meade was given the job. It was dropped on him in the middle of the movement to intercept Lee's invasion of Meade's home state.

After defeating Lee's attempts to destroy the Army of the Potomac at Gettysburg, Meade conducted a cautious pursuit of the retreating Confederates, exhorting his troops to "drive from our soil every vestige of the presence of the invader," by which he meant herd the Rebels back to Virginia. When Lincoln learned of this he exclaimed, "Drive the invader from our soil! My God! Is that all?" Meade had failed to grasp the central point of the entire war: that Virginia, too, was "our soil" unless, of course, the Confederates won the war. Later, after he had regained his sense of humor about the subject, Lincoln told Meade that his pursuit of Lee had reminded him of "an old woman trying to shoo her geese across a creek." Lee had been trapped by the rain-swollen, bridgeless Potomac but had built a semi-circle of earthworks and faced Meade down until the river fell and he was able to slip away. "Your golden opportunity is gone," Lincoln had told Meade, "and I am distressed immeasurably because of it."[2]

Throughout the rest of 1863 Meade and Lee had maneuvered back and forth between Washington and the Rapidan River, inflicting minor defeats on each other and each sending detachments to the West, but neither was able to find an opening worth the risk of an all-out attack. Lincoln at first was tempted to remove Meade, who asked to be relieved whenever he felt the president or Halleck was criticising him—which was often—but Lincoln could find no one better with whom to replace him. Grant, when informally approached, had begged to be spared the job, preferring to stay in the more familiar West and realizing that to bring in a new commander from outside the Army of the Potomac would only have increased the dissension in its officer corps. But that was before he had been promoted and given responsibility for the entire war. Thus, as Meade emerged from his tent to welcome the lieutenant general, the question on Grant's mind was what to do with the Army of the Potomac and with George Meade. By the time he left for Washington the next day, he had decided about Meade at least, if not the army.

"I had known General Meade slightly in the Mexican war," Grant said in his memoirs, "but had not met him since until this visit. I was a stranger to most of the Army of the Potomac, I might say to all except the officers of the regular army who had served in the Mexican war. There had been some changes ordered in the organization of that army before my promotion. One was the consolidation of five corps into three, thus throwing some officers of rank out of important commands. Meade evidently thought that I might want to make still one more change not yet ordered. He said to me that I might want an officer who had served with me in the West, mentioning Sherman specially, to take his place. If so, he begged me not to hesitate about making the change. He urged that the work before us was of such vast importance to the whole nation that the feeling or wishes of no one person should stand in the way of selecting the right men for all positions. For himself, he would serve to the best of his ability wherever placed. I assured him that I had no thought of substituting any one for him. As to Sherman, he could not be spared from the West."

Nothing Meade could have said would have made a better impression on his new boss. "This incident gave me even a more favorable opinion of Meade than did his great victory at Gettysburg the July before," Grant said, adding that, "It is men who wait to be selected, and not those who seek, from whom we may always expect the most efficient service."[3] So Meade would stay. Besides, Grant would have had the same problem as Lincoln had. Who would be any better? The radical Republicans of Congress' Joint Committee on the Conduct of the War would have preferred to have Hooker back, because he was a hard-war general who had no sympathy for slavery or rebels, not a kid-gloves respecter of private property such as McClellan and Meade. But it is unlikely that

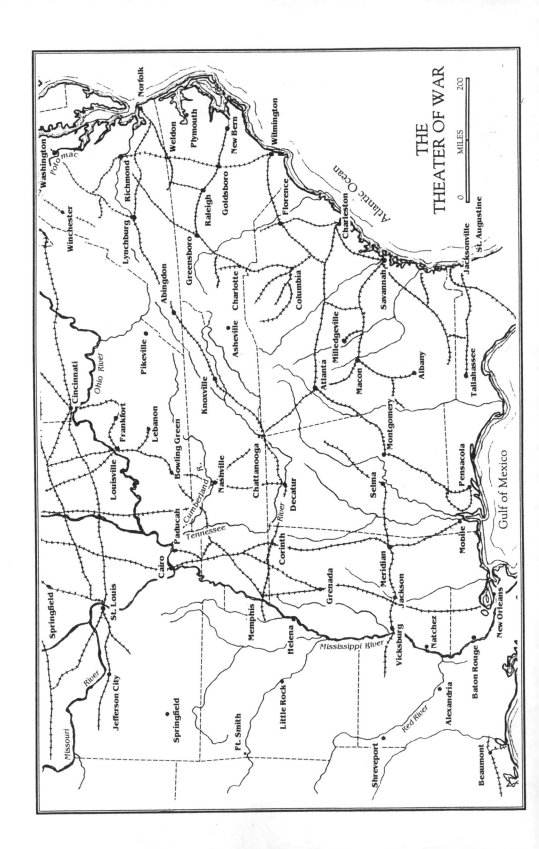

THE THEATER OF WAR

MILES
0   200

Grant would even have considered reinstating Hooker. Like Fremont, he knew Hooker.

In the end, Grant's answer to the question of what to do about Meade was tied up with another problem: what to do with himself. His predecessors as general-in-chief, Scott, McClellan, and Halleck, had all been headquartered in Washington, but Grant had originally thought to remain in the West. He certainly did not relish the idea of being subjected to more scenes such as the one at the White House. Nor did he want to be where every politician with a plan, a demand, or a favorite general could get at him. But he saw now that the president, and the people, obviously expected him to do something about the Confederacy's annoyingly successful General R. E. Lee, whose Army of Northern Virginia was encamped just across the Rapidan River from Meade's forces. It was evident that if Meade could have done anything about Lee on his own he would have done so during the previous nine months. Meade, on the other hand, possibly took this chance to tell Grant how hard it had been fighting Lee with Halleck, Stanton, and Lincoln all looking over his shoulder giving him contrary instructions and reminding him that he was responsible for the defense of the nation's capital.

Grant found a typically straight-forward, no-nonsense solution to all these problems: he would make his own headquarters with the Army of the Potomac. This would keep him out of Washington and away from the crowds and the politicians, yet close enough for easy communication with Stanton and Lincoln. It would at the same time protect Meade from interference by the authorities in Washington, and allow Grant to provide the drive and killer instinct to the Army of the Potomac that Meade and his predecessors never had. In a way, it looked as if Grant were voluntarily placing himself at the head of the Army of the Potomac, the very position that he had once begged Halleck not to give him. But as lieutenant general and general-in-chief he would have certain advantages, both within that army and without—advantages that he would not have had as merely another major general in the series of commanders inflicted on that unhappy force. For one thing, he could take charge without removing the army's present commander, which would offend that officer's supporters inside and outside of the army and stir up all those who would have preferred some other to take his place. For another, Grant's third star lent him an air of authority that would come in handy both in getting the officers of that army to obey his orders, and in keeping the administration from interfering with them.

As a corollary to this decision, Grant found the perfect employment for his predecessor as general-in-chief, Major General Henry Wager Halleck. Born a year before Meade, Halleck had graduated from West Point four years behind him and four ahead of Grant, rating third in the class of 1839. He had a "brilliant career as a soldier, teacher, writer and lawyer. He taught at West Point, became an expert on fortifications, published books on legal and military subjects, fought in Mexico, served as secretary of state of California, and established himself as the leading lawyer in gold-rush San Francisco."[4] The aging Winfield Scott, hero of the War of 1812 and conqueror of Mexico, had hoped to hang on to the position of general-in-chief until Halleck could arrive from California to take his place, but he was pushed into retirement by the ambitious McClellan too soon for that. Halleck had to settle for the second-biggest job, com-mander of the Union forces in the Mississippi Valley. He was sent out to St. Louis to replace Fremont, who had overstepped his authority by proclaiming an end to slavery in Missouri, compromising the Lincoln administration's efforts to placate the border slave states that had so far sided with the North.

Halleck was a good administrator who found much to do in straighten-ing out the mess left behind by the inefficient Fremont. He was fortunate to have at his disposal a number of talented subordinates and the navy's hastily constructed river gunboat fleet. One of those subordinates had been U.S. Grant, commanding Union forces at Cairo, Illinois where the Ohio and Mississippi rivers converge. When Grant and the gunboats captured Forts Henry and Donelson, opening the way into Tennessee by means of the Cumberland and Tennessee rivers, and General John Pope and the gunboats took New Madrid, Missouri, and Island Number 10 in the Mississippi, opening that river nearly to Memphis, it was Halleck who received much of the credit. He received command of all Union forces between the Appalachians and the Rockies as his reward. He sent Grant up the Tennessee to encamp at a bend in the river near the key railroad junction of Corinth, Mississippi with orders to await the arrival of Pope from the Mississippi and General Don Carlos Buell from Nashville. However, the Confederate commander in the West, Albert Sidney Johnston, decided not to wait for those forces to amass and attacked the unprepared Grant in what became known as the battle of Shiloh. Grant was able to hold on the first day, and Buell arrived in time to help him counterattack on the second, and drive off the slain Johnston's successor, P. G. T. Beauregard.

Halleck then took the field for the first and only time, conducting a creeping, overcautious advance on Corinth, which Beauregard evacuated just in time to save his own forces from capture. Meanwhile, McClellan had taken his Army of the Potomac from Washington down to the Virginia Peninsula east of Richmond, the Confederate capital. It was an unsuccessful attempt to get in behind the main Rebel army in the East, then commanded by Joseph E. Johnston (no kin to Albert Sydney). McClellan, stripped of his title as general-in-chief upon leaving Washington, conducted a seige of Yorktown that coincided with Halleck's of Corinth and was eluded by Johnston as Halleck was by Beauregard. As he approached Richmond, McClellan's forces had to straddle the swampy Chickahominy River. First Johnston attacked the southern wing, picking up a wound that lost him his command, and then his successor, R. E. Lee, attacked McClellan's northern flank and drove him to huddle under the protection of the gunboats in the James River. Meanwhile Pope had been sent east to form a new Army of Virginia out of forces that McClellan had left behind when embarking for the Peninsula. And Halleck was ordered to Washington to become general-in-chief after all.

The first job Lincoln had handed him was to decide what to do with McClellan and the Army of the Potomac. Could they still make a campaign from where they were, or should they be brought back to Washington to start all over again? Halleck went down to talk to McClellan and found that general unwilling to move from his camp without reinforcements that Halleck knew could not be provided. Since he was not asked about the desirability of replacing McClellan and it was obvious that the latter could not or would not do anything useful where he was, Halleck recommended bringing the Army of the Potomac back to northern Virginia. But that was just what Lee had been waiting for. As soon as he heard that McClellan's forces were returning north, he took out after Pope, caught him, and thrashed him at the second battle of Bull Run. After that, Halleck increasingly avoided taking responsibility for operations in the field, confining himself to handling the paperwork in Washington, and offering advice to Lincoln when asked for it and to the commanders of armies and departments when directed by Lincoln to do so.

Now Grant's decision was that Halleck would go right on doing just that. Only his title would change. He would be known as the Chief of Staff of the Army (not to be confused with Rawlins, who was chief of staff to General Grant). Halleck would serve as a channel of communication between Lincoln and Grant and between Grant and the commanders of armies and departments, other than Meade. Halleck had a talent for translating Lincoln's and Stanton's civilian ideas into terms their officers could understand and, especially, for translating the generals' technical jargon into language the two civilians could grasp. Most importantly, he would free Grant from the routine paper work and housekeeping, thus allowing the lieutenant general to concentrate on strategy and the coordination of his various field forces. Meade would serve a similar function of handling the more mundane areas of army command so that Grant could concentrate on the operations of the Army of the Potomac.

Grant's trip to meet Meade had been a big disappointment to the public in Washington. It had been advertised that he would accompany the president to Grover's Theater that evening, where Edwin Booth, the famous actor, was playing Shakespeare's Richard III. The theater had been elaborately decorated in Grant's honor, sporting a banner painted with the words "Unconditional Surrender." Despite the rain storm, the house was packed. Even standing room was sold out. President and Mrs. Lincoln as well as Secretary of State Seward were there, but the owner of the theater had to go on stage and explain to the audience that military duties had called the new lieutenant general out of town. He promised however that the general would attend Booth's performance as Hamlet the next night.[5] But the audience was destined to be disappointed again. Grant returned to Washington on the eleventh and conferred with Lincoln that afternoon at the White House but declined all further social engagements, including a dinner that the first lady was planning for him. "I appreciate the honor Mrs. Lincoln would do me," he said, "but time is very important now. And really, Mr. Lincoln," he added, "I have had enough of this show business."[6] He left that very evening on a westbound train. He would make stops for inspection along the way, but he was headed for a rendezvous with his most trusted subordinate, Major General William T. Sherman.

"I was much pleased with Grant," Meade wrote to his wife, "and most agreeably disappointed in his evidence of mind and character. You may rest assured he is not an ordinary man."[7]

---

1. Foote, *The Civil War*, 3:9.
2. T. Harry Williams, *Lincoln And His Generals*, 265, 270–271.
3. Ulysses S. Grant, *Personal Memoirs of U.S. Grant*, (New York, 1886), vol. 2: 116–117.
4. Patricia L. Faust, ed., *Historical Times Illustrated Encyclopedia of the Civil War* (New York, 1986), 332.
5. Margaret Leech, *Reveille in Washington* (New York, 1941), 313.
6. Foote, *The Civil War*, 2:12.
7. Ibid., 11.

CHAPTER THREE

"A Mere Demonstration Will Not Be Sufficient"

13–18 March 1864

On 13 March 1864, two days after Grant left the Army of the Potomac and headed back toward the West, those three divisions of his old army, the ones that had left Vicksburg three days before, reached Simsport, Louisiana. This force of 10,000 men, called Detachment, Army of the Tennessee, and commanded by Brigadier General Andrew Jackson Smith, consisted of the Provisional Division, 17th Army Corps, under General T. Kilby Smith, and two divisions under General J. A. Mower called the Right Wing, 16th Army Corps. They were all veterans of the Vicksburg campaign and had just returned from an expedition under Sherman to break up Rebel railroads and industries in central Mississippi where, in Sherman's words, they had cut "a swath of desolation fifty miles broad

across the State of Mississippi which the present generation will not
forget."[1]

A. J. Smith's men, Sherman's Gorillas they called themselves, accompanied by Admiral David Dixon Porter's gunboat fleet, had taken transports southward down the Mississippi to the mouth of the Red,
northwest a short way up the Red to the Atchafalaya, and southward just
a little way up the Atchafalaya to Simsport, where they disembarked.
From there they marched northwestward overland through bayeau-
crossed prairie to attack Fort De Russy, which defended the Red River
approach to Alexandria, Louisiana. Meanwhile the gunboats and transports went back down the Atchafalaya and up the Red to attack the fort
from the river side. Late on the fourteenth the gunboats signaled their
presence and distracted the Confederates by opening fire, whereupon
Smith's infantry charged and captured the fort, its eight heavy guns and
two field pieces, and its garrison of 260 Rebels for the cost of 38 Union
casualties. Thus was auspiciously begun a campaign that not only failed in
reaching its objective but seriously upset the strategy that Grant was only
then beginning to work out for the spring campaigns of all the Union
forces.

As soon as the fort fell Porter, whose fleet of thirteen ironclads and
seven other gunboats was the most formidable force that had ever been
collected in western waters, proceeded on up the Red with some of
Smith's troops on transports, while the rest of the infantry set to work to
destroy Fort De Russy for good. Porter arrived off Alexandria (population 600) on the fifteenth, and T. Kilby Smith's division landed on the
sixteenth to occupy the town one day ahead of the schedule previously
arranged between Sherman and Major General Nathaniel Banks, commander of the Union army's Department of the Gulf.

Early in the war, Union forces had invaded the Mississippi Valley not
only from the north but also from the south. David Porter, then only a
commander, had conceived the plan to capture New Orleans, the South's
largest city and most important port. He sold the idea to Secretary of the
Navy Welles, who appointed Porter's foster brother, David Farragut, to
command a naval force to run past the forts guarding the lower Mississippi to reach the city. Farragut did just that on 24 April 1862, shortly
after the Union victories at Shiloh and Island No. 10. Farragut took his
fleet of ocean-going men-of-war up the Mississippi all the way to and past
Vicksburg, but that city sat high on a bluff and was not intimidated by the
ships' guns. Having no soldiers to take and hold the place, Farragut
eventually returned to the gulf. Meanwhile the army had moved in to
hold down the conquest farther south. In this case the army was repre-

sented by Major General Benjamin Franklin Butler, a prominent Massachusetts Democrat and militia officer.

Butler had already proven valuable to the Lincoln administration. His
influence on other northern Democrats in support of the war, and the
Republican president running it, was perhaps his greatest contribution. In
addition, his prompt action in occupying Baltimore in May of 1861 had
been decisive in preventing Maryland from joining its fellow slave states
and in keeping open the rail lines between Washington and the North. In
August of that year he had led a successful amphibious expedition to
capture Forts Hatteras and Clark in North Carolina. He had then returned to Massachusetts to recruit and organize a force to operate in the
gulf. After occupying New Orleans, he sent forces up the river to take
Vicksburg, but by then the Confederates had reinforced that city enough
to hold it until Grant finally beseiged it a year later. The army settled for
occupying Baton Rouge, the state capital, and repulsed a prompt Confederate counterattack, led by former United States vice president John C.
Breckinridge. But the city was later evacuated, and by the time Butler had
occupied the La Fourche district, a fertile area west of New Orleans, he
had stretched his available forces about as far as they would go.

Butler's job in Louisiana had been primarily that of administering the
conquered area, for which he had shown considerable talent. Eventually,
however, he had so aggravated the entire South and so embarrassed his
government in Europe with such actions as hanging a man for pulling
down the United States flag, confiscating $800,000 from the Dutch consul
on the charge that it was intended for purchasing war supplies for the
South, and issuing his famous "Woman Order," that he had been recalled
in December of 1862. The "Woman Order" stated: "As the officers and
soldiers of the United States have been subjected to repeated insults from
the women (calling themselves ladies) of New Orleans, in return for the
most scrupulous non-interference and courtesy on our part, it is ordered,
that hereafter, when any female shall, by word, gesture, or movement,
insult or show contempt for any officer or soldier of the United States, she
shall be regarded and held liable to be treated as a woman of the town
plying her avocation."[2] He was nicknamed "Spoons" for allegedly stealing silverware from Southern homes, but after the "Woman Order" he
was best known to the South as Beast Butler.

He had been replaced by another Massachussetts political general,
Nathaniel P. Banks, who had been a prominent Democratic congressman
before shifting to the new Republican party. His election as the first
Republican Speaker of the House of Representatives in 1856 had taken a
month and a half of bitter and protracted struggle to overcome the

obstructionism of the poor-loser Democrats.[3] He had later served as governor of his state from 1858 to 1861. His military career before coming to Louisiana had been less fortunate than Butler's, however. When Mc-Clellan had taken his Army of the Potomac down to the Peninsula in the spring of 1862 Banks had been in command of a force left to control the northern end of the Shenandoah Valley. Banks and Fremont, who had been allowed a second chance after being removed from Missouri and given a small command in West Virginia, had been among the Union generals outmarched and outsmarted by Confederate general Stonewall Jackson during his famous Shenandoah Valley campaign that spring.

When General Pope had come east that summer after participating in Halleck's slow advance on Corinth, it had been to unify the forces of Banks, Fremont, and Irwin McDowell in order to prevent a repetition of Jackson's exploits. But soon thereafter Jackson had defeated Banks again at Cedar Mountain, and Lee had come north after driving McClellan from the gates of Richmond to defeat Pope at the second battle of Bull Run. Pope had been exiled to Minnesota to fight Indians, and his forces had been combined with the Army of the Potomac. But when McClellan had marched off to face Lee for the last time at Antietam, Banks had been left behind to command the defenses of Washington. Then had come the appointment to succeed Butler.

Banks had brought with him to Louisiana a sizable number of rein-forcements and orders to move up the Mississippi and link up with Grant's forces coming down that river. Baton Rouge had promptly been reoccupied, but Banks had then discovered that, since Farragut's passage up to Vicksburg and back, Port Hudson, a bit further upriver, had been fortified, with 21 heavy guns bearing on the river and a garrison of 12,000 men protecting it. The Confederates had held the stretch of the river between that place and Vicksburg, further north, and Banks could only communicate with Grant by the most roundabout means: by ship through the gulf, around Florida and up the east coast, thence by tele-graph to Cairo and then by boat down the Mississippi. Deeming this newly discovered obstruction too big to attack, Banks had determined to find a way of getting around it by means of the Red River. Farragut had managed to get two ships past Port Hudson's guns to take control of the Mississippi between that point and the mouth of the Red. Then Banks had moved slowly all the way up the Teche to Alexandria, driving the smaller force of Confederate general Richard Taylor, son of President Zachary Taylor, before him. Taylor had then retreated up the Red toward Shreveport and, while Grant was moving to besiege Vicksburg, Banks had turned downriver to Simpsport, crossed the Atchafalaya and moved to Bayou Sara, where the advance of his army crossed the Mississippi and moved against the rear of Port Hudson while other of his forces had come up the Mississippi to join them there. When word had arrived that Vicksburg had surrendered, the smaller Confederate garrison at Port Hudson had bowed to the inevitable and had followed suit.

Both Grant and Banks had wanted to make the gulf port of Mobile, Alabama their next objective, but Lincoln and Halleck had cast their eyes in the opposite direction. While the United States was embroiled in its Civil War, imperial France had taken advantage of a dispute over unpaid claims to land a force in Mexico and interfere in the civil war going on in that country. Lincoln was powerless to enforce the Monroe Doctrine while fighting the Rebels, especially with the Confederacy in firm control of Texas. He therefore desired Banks to establish a Union presence in Texas as soon as possible. "However," one of Banks' staff officers wrote, "it did not take long to realize that to march an army three hundred miles across a barren country, with no water in the summer and fall, and plenty of water but no road in the winter and spring, was really not to be thought of, especially when the column would have to guard against an active enemy on its flank and rear during the march and to meet and overcome another at its end."[4]

So the direct move westward from New Orleans was out. The best route, because it offered the relative security of a gunboat-patroled, steamboat-operated supply line, appeared to be up the Red River through Alexandria and Shreveport and on into northeast Texas. But the Red was a very seasonal river and its water level would not be high enough to float the Union gunboats and transports until March. Meanwhile Banks utilized the power of the navy's gulf squadron to capture a number of isolated points along the Texas coast, starting with Brownsville at the mouth of the Rio Grande and working east. He had also received the 13th Corps of Grant's, now Sherman's, Army of the Tennessee, as a permanent reinforcement and arranged for the loan of A. J. Smith's force when the Red should rise. It was to be a three-pronged offensive, with Banks bringing his main force along the Teche again to Alexandria, where he was to meet Smith and Admiral Porter coming up the Red not later than 17 March. The third prong would march overland from Little Rock, Arkansas under Major General Frederick Steele, commander of the Department of Arkansas.

Missouri had been one of the most active areas in the early days of the Civil War, where Grant, Halleck, Pope, and many another Federal general had gained their first experience. But eventually the Confederates, except for numerous bands of guerillas and bushwhackers, had been driven southward into Arkansas. Many of the Southern troops from that area had been sent east of the Mississippi as part of A. S. Johnston's con-

centration for the attack on Grant at Shiloh. Although they arrived too late to fight in that battle, they had participated in Beauregard's defense of Corinth against Halleck's snail-paced advance, and they had made up the forces that Grant and Rosecrans bested in defense of that town and nearby Iuka in the fall of 1862.

Meanwhile, Union forces had moved into northeast Arkansas, basing themselves at Helena on the Mississippi, and the Confederates eventually fell back to Little Rock. Grant had been given authority over the forces at Helena and had brought Steele's division from there in time to take part in the entire Vicksburg campaign. Later more forces had been brought from there and from Missouri to help in the siege of that town. After Vicksburg fell, Steele had been sent back to Helena to organize a drive on Little Rock with forces taken from Grant's army and with others sent down from Missouri. He had marched southwestward against the Arkansas capital with twice as many men as were defending it, and the Southerners had eventually withdrawn without a fight on 10 September 1863. Halleck had then ordered Steele to hold the line of the Arkansas River and wait until Banks was ready to cooperate with him in a campaign against Shreveport and the Red River Valley.

Steele had been a West Point classmate of Grant's, graduating below him, ranking 30th out of 39. Unlike Grant, he had not left the army before the war, and had risen to the rank of major in the regular army before transfering to the volunteers. All of his Civil War service had been in the Missouri and Arkansas area until his division had been added to Sherman's corps of Grant's army for the Vicksburg campaign. In January 1864 his Arkansas expedition had been separated from Sherman's (formerly Grant's) Army of the Tennessee to become the Department of Arkansas, a separate part of Grant's Military Division of the Mississippi and co-equal with Sherman, Thomas' Army of the Cumberland, and the Department of the Ohio, then under John G. Foster. Steele had been asked by Halleck to start moving south on 1 March in order to prevent Confederate forces in southern Arkansas from acting against Banks on the Red, but when A. J. Smith arrived at Alexandria on the sixteenth, Banks was himself running a week late, and Steele had not yet moved at all. The latter had, instead, responded to Halleck that the best he could do would be a demonstration against Arkadelphia or Hot Springs. He could undertake an all-out campaign to the Red River only "against my own judgement and that of the best-informed people here. The roads are most if not quite impracticable; the country is destitute of provision." He stayed at Little Rock awaiting a reply, which came, but not from Halleck. A telegram shot back from Nashville saying, "Move your force in full cooperation with General N. P. Banks' attack on Shreveport. A mere demonstration will not be sufficient." It was signed, "U. S. Grant Lieutenant General."[5]

Grant had returned from Washington to Nashville, where he had made his headquarters since his victory at Chattanooga. On 17 March, the day after A. J. Smith reached Alexandria, Sherman arrived in Nashville at Grant's summons. After returning to Vicksburg from his Mississippi expedition, he had gone down to New Orleans to see Banks and had arranged the details of lending A. J. Smith's detachment to him. Then he had gone back up to Vicksburg to arrange the organization and transportation of that force, and then continued on to Memphis, where he had received Grant's dispatch to hurry to Nashville by the seventeenth. As General Grenville Dodge recalled, it was on that occasion that he, Grant and Sherman and a few other generals went to the theater to see a performance—a rather poor performance as he remembered it—of Hamlet. It will be recalled that Grant had not had time to see Hamlet with Lincoln before leaving Washington. But perhaps it was not so much a matter of time as of location. In Washington he was a crowd-drawing celebrity. In Nashville, a Southern city under occupation since his victory at Fort Donelson had opened the Cumberland River to Union gunboats, he was just another Yankee officer. After the play the group of generals went looking for a restaurant where they could find some oysters, one of Grant's favorite delicacies. After scouring the city, they finally found such a place and they sat around talking informally and enjoying the stew until they were ejected by the proprietress who, not recognizing her guests, rather angrily informed them that General Grant's curfew regulations required her to close at midnight.

The next day the generals gathered at Grant's headquarters, and Dodge remembered that, in response to Sherman's questions, Grant described the Army of the Potomac as "the finest army he had ever seen, far superior to any of ours in equipment, supplies and transportation." After explaining that he planned to make his headquarters with that army and turn his command in the West over to Sherman, Grant discussed his intention of taking several of his generals east with him, but Sherman objected so strongly to losing them that Grant finally agreed to take only Major General Philip Sheridan, a division commander in Thomas' army who had made a very good impression on him at Corinth and Chattanooga.[6] At any rate, on the eighteenth of March Sherman assumed command of the Military Division of the Mississippi, and Grant, having closed out his headquarters, prepared to take a train back to Washington.

But first he invited Sherman to witness a ceremony at which Grant was to receive a fancy sword from the mayor of Galena, his pre-war home. In his memoirs, Sherman described how the mayor gave a polished speech and handed Grant the resolutions of the city council engrossed on parchment with ribbon and seal. Then, he continued, "General Grant said: 'Mr. Mayor, as I knew that this ceremony was to occur, and as I am not used to speaking, I have written something in reply.' He then began to fumble in his pockets, first his breast-coat pocket, then his pants, vest, etc., and after considerable delay he pulled out a crumpled piece of common yellow cartridge-paper, which he handed to the mayor. His whole manner was awkward in the extreme, yet perfectly characteristic, and in strong contrast with the elegant parchment and speech of the mayor. When read, however, the substance of his answer was most excellent, short, concise, and, if it had been delivered by word of mouth, would have been all that the occasion required."[7]

1. Shelby Foote, *The Civil War*, 3:30.
2. Mark Mayo Boatner, III, *The Civil War Dictionary* (New York, 1959), 945.
3. Allan Nevins, *Ordeal of the Union* (New York, 1947), vol. 2, 412–416.
4. Richard B. Irwin, "The Red River Campaign," in *Battles and Leaders of the Civil War* edited by Robert Underwood Johnson and Clarence Clough Buel (New York, 1887), vol. 4, 346.
5. Foote, *The Civil War*, 3:62.
6. Catton, *Grant Takes Command*, 137–138.
7. William T. Sherman, *Memoirs of Gen. W. T. Sherman* (New York, 1891), vol. 1, 429–430.

CHAPTER FOUR

"The Beginning of the End"

19–26 March 1864

Years after the war, Sherman returned to the Burnet House, a hotel in Cincinnati, and showed a friend the room in which he and Grant had planned the campaign of 1864. Grant had asked Sherman to ride along on the train with him as far as Cincinnati so they could discuss what to do in their spring offensives. But the noise of the cars made it impossible to carry on a conversation, so they fell silent. At Cincinnati, Sherman's wife met the train, and that also delayed the two generals' talk. Finally they found a room at the hotel where they consulted their maps and outlined the strategy that would win the war. "Yonder began the campaign," Sherman told his friend after the war. "We finally settled on a plan. . . . He was to go for Lee and I was to go for Joe Johnston. That was his plan. No routes prescribed. . . . It was the beginning of the end."[1]

Like Grant, William Tecumseh Sherman had been born in Ohio. He was two years older than Grant and had graduated from West Point three years ahead of him. When Sherman was nine his father had died, leaving eleven children. As his mother could not provide for them all, the older ones had been farmed out to relatives and friends. "Cump," as he was known, had been raised by his father's friend Thomas Ewing, a prominent senator and cabinet member, and he had eventually married Ewing's daughter Ellen. Sherman's younger brother John had followed in their foster father's footsteps and became a Republican senator from Ohio. Tecumseh had graduated sixth in the 42-man West Point class of 1840 and had been commissioned in the artillery. He had seen little action in the Mexican War but, like Grant, had been stationed for a while in California. He had resigned his commission in 1853 and had tried several civilian occupations, including banking, law, and real estate, in various parts of the country before becoming the superintendent of the Louisiana State Seminary of Learning and Military Academy near Alexandria, Louisiana. But when Louisiana had seceded from the Union he had resigned that position, and after Fort Sumter was fired on he had returned to the regular army as colonel of the new 13th Infantry.

Sherman had commanded a brigade at the first battle of Bull Run, after which he had been promoted to brigadier general of volunteers and sent to Kentucky as second-in-command under General Robert Anderson, who had been the commander of Fort Sumter. When Anderson had become ill, Sherman had succeeded to his command, but the strain of trying to accomplish anything with untrained volunteers had worn him down also. When he had told the secretary of war that he would need 200,000 troops, the newspapers had said he was crazy. He had been ordered to turn his command over to Buell and report to Halleck, then still in St. Louis, for orders. After a number of minor assignments he seemed to have regained his poise and had been given command of one of Grant's divisions in time for the battle of Shiloh. He had soon become Grant's most trusted subordinate and best friend in the army. He had commanded a corps during the Vicksburg campaign, and when Grant had been given command of all the western forces Sherman had succeeded him as head of the Army of the Tennessee. Now, with Grant moving up once more to become general-in-chief, Sherman would again succeed him, becoming the new commander of the Military Division of the Mississippi. That command had been created in the fall of 1863 to give Grant control of all Union forces from the Appalachians to Arkansas exclusive of Banks' Department of the Gulf and the Department of Missouri, to which Rosecrans had been exiled.

The basic military building block of the Civil War was the regiment, usually of infantry or cavalry but sometimes of heavy artillery or engineers. In the twentieth century, recruits join "the army" and are assigned to a unit. In the nineteenth century a recruit joined a regiment, which was raised by a state government, not the Federal or Confederate, and he remained in that regiment to the end of his enlistment. It theoretically contained about a thousand men, but it began to lose strength the minute it was organized. Only the most cursory physical examinations were made to weed out the unfit before the rigors of campaigning did the job, and no regular arrangements were made for providing replacements to keep units up to strength. The Confederacy introduced the draft in 1862 and the Union in 1863. Drafted men were then used to feed reinforcements to established units, but almost never in quantities sufficient to make up for the losses to combat and disease. By the spring of 1864 it was a rare regiment indeed that could field more than 500 men, while many were down to half that or less. Regiments were supposed to be commanded by colonels, usually appointed by the governor of the state in which the unit was raised, often for purely political reasons or as a reward for rounding up enough recruits to form the regiment.

The next step up the military hierarchy was the brigade, composed of two or more regiments, but ideally four. Both sides tended to increase the number of regiments in their brigades as the war went on in order to keep the total strength up to 2,000 men or so. Two or more brigades made up a division. Union divisions usually averaged about three brigades, while Confederate divisions were often larger. The larger armies of both sides grouped their divisions in army corps, or corps for short. Only two Confederate armies were large enough to need this step in the chain of command. The Federal government organized its forces throughout the country into a series of corps, eventually numbered from 1 through 25, some of which included all the forces in a given army or department.

Before the war, when the entire United States Army contained fewer than 17,000 men, the country had been divided into a number of geographic departments. Both sides continued to use this system throughout the war, with the field armies being merely the movable forces of the various departments. For instance, Grant's old Army of the Tennessee was technically the Department of the Tennessee. Only the Army of the Potomac existed, ever since the Peninsula campaign, as a non-geographic entity. The Confederates were sometimes rather vague about the boundaries between their departments and were not always consistent with names, but they, too, stuck to the geographic system.

Sherman's new command, the Military Division of the Mississippi, was one step higher up the military ladder than a department. It was, at that time, the only headquarters of that level on either side. One of its components was Steele's Department of Arkansas, which corresponded geographically with that state, or as much of it as Steele could control. Its troops constituted the 7th Army Corps. Another component was what had been first Grant's and then Sherman's Department of the Tennessee, which was now being turned over to Major General James B. McPherson. Geographically this covered a bit of northeast Louisiana opposite Vicksburg, as much of Mississippi as could be controlled, that part of Tennessee and Kentucky west of the Tennessee River, what little of northern Alabama was under Union control, and southern Illinois around Cairo.

It was divided into three corps. Sherman's old 15th Corps, now under General John A. Logan, was stationed in northern Alabama along the upper Tennessee River. The 16th Corps, commanded by Stephen A. Hurlbut with headquarters at Memphis, was scattered all over, and outside, the department. It contained the garrison units in western Tennessee and Kentucky, Mower's two divisions, called the Right Wing, serving with A. J. Smith in Banks' Red River campaign, and the Left Wing, consisting of two divisions under Dodge, stationed near the 15th Corps. McPherson had been the commander of the 17th Corps, with headquarters at Vicksburg, before being appointed to replace Sherman as commander of the Army of the Tennessee. Besides garrisons in and around that town and Kilby Smith's provisional division with A. J. Smith, most of the 17th Corps was temporarily stationed at Cairo.

Grant and Sherman had always been much freer about moving divisions or smaller units around between the corps of the Army of the Tennessee than other army commanders had been. Sherman had just reorganized its forces somewhat, partly to provide the 10,000 troops who were his contribution to the Red River campaign, and partly to accommodate the government's policy of providing "veteran furloughs" to reenlisting units. Most of the regiments in the Union army had originally signed up for three years, and in early 1864 all those units that had been formed at the beginning of the war were approaching the end of their enlistments. The Union cause could not afford to lose these experienced soldiers, so the government went to great lengths to encourage these men to reenlist. One device used was to promise that every unit in which a certain minimum percentage of men reenlisted would be given a leave to go home before the spring campaign.

"This was a judicious and wise measure," Sherman wrote in his memoirs, "because it doubtless secured the services of a very large portion of the men who had almost completed a three-years enlistment, and were therefore veteran soldiers in feeling and in habit. But to furlough so many of our men at that instant of time was like disbanding an army in the very midst of battle."[2] To complicate matters, any men who had been added to those units at later dates, and had thus not yet served their three years, were not entitled to the furlough. To cover the entire problem as best he could, Sherman had transfered most of the reenlisting ("veteranizing" it was called) regiments into two divisions of the 17th Corps, which were then sent to Cairo, where the non-veterans would await the return of the reenlisted men from their leaves. These divisions would, by the time the campaign began, be commanded by General Frank Blair, who was currently serving in Congress and who was the brother of Lincoln's postmaster general.

Another department in Sherman's new command was the Department of the Cumberland. (Note that most Federal departments were named after major rivers in or bordering their territories.) This was the force that Sherman had inherited from Anderson and turned over to Buell, although under the latter it was known as the Army of the Ohio. When Rosecrans had replaced Buell, the name had reverted to Cumberland. When Grant had been given the newly created Military Division of the Mississippi, after Rosecrans' defeat at Chickamauga, the secretary of war had given him the choice of keeping Rosecrans or having Thomas in his place. Grant was not terribly fond of Thomas, but greatly preferred him to Rosecrans, whom he had found it almost impossible to work with during the defense of Corinth and Iuka. This department covered the central half of Tennessee and what little of northern Georgia the Union held. At Chickamauga it had consisted of the 14th, 20th and 21st Corps, a small Reserve Corps and a Cavalry Corps. Due to losses at that battle, the Reserve Corps was merged into the 14th, and the 20th and 21st were combined and designated the 4th, a number that had been abandoned in the East some time before. Two small corps that had been sent west by Meade in response to the defeat at Chickamauga, the 11th and 12th, were together commanded by Hooker, Meade's predecessor in command of the Army of the Potomac, but were now officially part of Thomas' department.

The remaining component of Sherman's new command was the Department of the Ohio. This was the second organization to bear that name, and was created in August of 1862 as a rear area garrison department. After losing command of the Army of the Potomac to Hooker, Burnside had been sent West with his old 9th Corps to take over this department. He went on to achieve one of Lincoln's fondest desires in the spring of 1863. While the Confederates were concentrating against Rosecrans' drive on Chattanooga, he occupied eastern Tennessee, a hotbed of Union sentiment in the heart of the South. He then fought off a Rebel attempt to recapture Knoxville while Grant was defeating Bragg at Chattanooga. Burnside was replaced shortly thereafter by John G. Foster and he in his turn by John M. Schofield, who had until then been commanding in Missouri. Besides the 9th Corps, which was about to be returned to

the East, Schofield had only the 23rd Corps and some cavalry. Geographically, the department consisted of Kentucky, except that small portion
west of the Tennessee River, and Burnside's eastern Tennessee conquests.

   Grant's plans for the spring had progressed, by the time of his discus-
sions with Sherman in that Cincinnati hotel room, at least to these main
points: Grant would tackle Lee and go for the Confederate capital at
Richmond. Sherman, as his successor in the West, would undertake the
campaign Grant had intended to make himself until convinced that he
would have to go to the East. The primary focus of that campaign would
be to advance with as large a force as could be accumulated and supplied
from Chattanooga into the mountains of northern Georgia to capture the
crucial railroad junction and industrial center, Atlanta. But it is doubtful
whether Grant expected even the capture of Richmond and Atlanta to end
the rebellion. There were two basic ways he could win the war. The short
way would be to completely destroy the two major Confederate armies.
But in three years of war no major army of either side had been destroyed, or even come close to being destroyed, in the open field. Grant
had captured sizable forces at Fort Donelson and at Vicksburg by besieging them with their backs to unfordable rivers. And that was the only wat
likely to destroy either major Rebel army: force them into the defense of
some major objective, surround them and starve them into submission.
But without a major river or some other impassable terrain to help
contain them, either army was probably too big to surround with the
forces available to the Union. The longer way to win the war was to
destroy the South's material capacity, and the human will to sustain its
armies—to supply them with food, ammunition and replacements.
   Grant's plans for the West were more advanced than for the Virginia
theater because he had been responsible for that area longer. His capture
of Vicksburg had given the Federal government control of the Mississippi
River, and that control had split the Confederacy into two unequal parts.
It was almost impossible for Rebel forces west of the river to affect events
east of the river, and vice versa. The navy's blockade of the Atlantic and
gulf coasts severely limited Southern imports of weapons, ammunition,
and other critical supplies. Now the gunboats on the Mississippi shut off
the eastern part of the Confederacy from those few imports that made
their way into Texas by way of Mexican ports. Grant wanted to cut the
eastern Confederate states in two again, but unfortunately there was not
another Mississippi River where it was needed. However, if Southern
railroads could be blocked or disrupted so badly that the Confederate
government was unable to repair them, the South would not be able to
transport enough food from where it was grown, and its armies would

starve. If its means of producing weapons and ammunition could be destroyed, its armies could not continue to fight. And any Union threat against a critical point in the Southern supply system might serve to pin one of its armies to its defense. That army could then be defeated or captured along with the objective, as had happened at Fort Donelson and at Vicksburg. The key points to threaten were Richmond in the East and Atlanta in the West.

As an adjunct of the drive on Atlanta, Grant still had hopes for an early move from New Orleans against Mobile, the South's only remaining major port on the gulf coast. Unfortunately for his plans, Halleck had already sent Banks, who commanded the Department of the Gulf, off up the Red River in exactly the opposite direction. Grant had fired off instructions to Banks to proceed no farther than Shreveport, to garrision that place with Steele's help, and to start getting ready to move on Mobile as soon as possible. It was Grant's desire for Banks to take Mobile and move up the Alabama River to take Selma, with its important munitions works, as well as Montgomery, the state, and original Confederate, capital. With Atlanta and Montgomery in Federal hands, the South's eastern seaboard would have no railroad connection with Mississippi, Louisiana or Alabama.

Out on the Red River that nineteenth of March things were still going well. The advanced unit of Banks' own forces, a division of 4,600 cavalry and mounted infantry under Brigadier General Albert L. Lee, reached Alexandria that day. Two days later, A. J. Smith sent Mower's infantry and one brigade of Lee's cavalry 23 miles farther up the Red to Henderson's Hill to clear the way across a stream called Bayou Rapides. That night, in a heavy rain storm, Mower skillfully surprised the only Confederate cavalry in the area, the 2nd Louisiana, capturing almost the entire regiment, 250 men and 200 horses, plus all four guns of an accompanying battery of artillery, with only trifling losses to the Union forces. That was a heavy blow to Taylor, still the Rebel commander in northern Louisiana, since it deprived him of his means of scouting the Federal forces. Taylor retreated upriver to Natchitoches, and Mower returned to Alexandria. That same day a force of 4,000 men under Brigadier General John M. Thayer, known as the Frontier Division, left Fort Smith on the western border of Arkansas headed south for a rendezvous with Steele's main column of 8,000 men, which left Little Rock two days later. Another force of 2,000, mostly cavalry, was based on Pine Bluff with orders to divert attention to itself from the other columns while keeping a close watch on the Confederate troops at Camden, where Rebel Major General Sterling Price was known to headquarter. Steele headed his main column south-

west toward Rockport and Arkadelphia with the intention of striking the
upper Red well above Shreveport so that he could then march downstream to take that city in reverse, while Banks was approaching from the
opposite side.[3]

That same day, Grant returned to Washington, this time accompanied
by his wife Julia and their six-year-old son, Jess. Their other children were
staying in St. Louis with a cousin of Julia. They found a boarding house
for little Jess and for his mother, who was suffering from an eye infection,
and Grant had a few conferences with Halleck and Lincoln, but he did
not intend to stay in town for long.[4]

Sixty miles south of Washington, four brigades of Lee's Confederate
army engaged in a giant snowball fight that day. The famous Stonewall
Brigade of Virginians and Stafford's Louisiana brigade, both of Allegheny
Johnson's Division, challenged Dole's Georgians and Ramseur's North
Carolina brigade, both of Rodes' Division. The Georgians at first declined on account of unfamiliarity with snow but eventually decided to
join in. The two sides molded a supply of ammunition, formed lines of
battle, sent out skirmishers to the front and had at it. The Louisianians,
also unaccustomed to the sport, were driven back across a field to the
position of their Virginia allies whose commander, General James A.
Walker, shouted for his men to charge. The Stonewall Brigade responded
with enthusiasm, but Walker was singled out by the Georgians, and both
he and his horse were soon transformed into a mass of white fluff. The
Virginians were then forced to give ground, but as the Georgians pressed
forward the Louisiana brigade emerged from some woods to surprise
them with a flank attack. The Georgians and Carolinians were pursued
over the snow-covered hills until darkness finally called a halt to the
struggle, and the Stonewall Brigade celebrated another victory with an
ear-splitting Rebel yell.[5]

The next day, 24 March, the day that Banks finally arrived at Alexandria and Mower paraded his captured Rebel cavalrymen and guns
through that city, another loose thread of Grant's half-formed plans
started to unravel. The Federal commander of a small post guarding
Union City in northwest Tennessee surrendered his post and his regiment, the 7th Tennessee Cavalry, to what he presumed was overwhelming
force. Only later was it discovered that he had mistaken logs with wheels
attached for enemy cannon; and that the man who had sent him a note
under a flag of truce ending: "If you persist in defense, you must take the
consequences. N. B. Forrest, Major General, Commanding," was actually only the colonel of the Confederate 7th Tennessee Cavalry, sent out
by Forrest to gobble up his Federal counterpart's 481 men and 300 horses,

plus their arms and supplies.[6] Forrest's name alone was obviously worth at least a brigade in that part of the country.

A self-made millionaire businessman and slave-trader before the war, Forrest had originally enlisted as a private but had later raised a battalion of cavalry at his own expense. He had escaped with his men from Fort Donelson rather than join the surrender ordered by his superiors, and he had commanded the rear guard on the Confederates' retreat from Shiloh. His force had continued to grow as he began a series of raids on Union garrisons and supply lines that kept Federal control of west and central Tennessee in doubt for most of the war. A man of no formal education, military or otherwise, Forrest had become famous for doing the unexpected, the audacious, and the unconventional. After quarreling with General Bragg, then commander of the Army of Tennessee, when ordered to turn over his troops to another officer, he had been sent to northern Mississippi to command what he called "the Cavalry Department of West Tennessee and North Mississippi," and to recruit a new force to contest control of that area with the Federals. During Sherman's recent Meridian campaign, Forrest had defeated and turned back a Union cavalry force twice the size of his own as it was moving south from Memphis to join Sherman.

The afternoon following the surrender of Union City, Forrest and one of his two divisions rode into Paducah, Kentucky. This Federal supply depot was strategically located at the junction of the Tennessee and Ohio rivers. The garrison retreated into its earthworks, which were supported by two gunboats patrolling the river. Forrest sent in his usual demand: "If you surrender you shall be treated as prisoners of war, but if I have to storm your works you may expect no quarter." This time it did not work, and a couple of dozen of his men were lost in an unsuccessful and overexuberant attack on the fortifications. But what he really wanted was in the unprotected depot, where he captured large amounts of clothing and medical supplies to go with the several hundred horses and about fifty prisoners that he rounded up outside the earthworks. After destroying everything useful that he could not carry off, including a government steamboat and a number of bales of cotton, he withdrew around midnight. At Mayfield he stopped to give furloughs to his three Kentucky regiments with orders to go home, get new clothes and new horses, and meet him at Trenton, Tennessee a week later, orders that every man obeyed. They obviously did not feel the same as one of his Mississippi soldiers from the upper-crust plantation class, who wrote, "Forrest may be, and no doubt is, the best cavalry officer in the West, but I object to a tyrannical, hot-headed vulgarian's commanding me."[7]

As Forrest's cavalry was riding into Paducah, Banks' infantry and artillery were finally marching into Alexandria. Actually, it took both the 25th and the 26th for them to come in, and right behind them came a courier with orders from Grant. In a message which the lieutenant general had written from Nashville eleven days before, Banks was glad to find that he was ordered to go against Mobile after all. As for the current expedition up the Red, Grant said that if Banks could capture Shreveport by 25 April he should do so. He should then leave Steele to defend the place and return downriver with his own forces to get ready for the advance on Mobile and return A. J. Smith's divisions to Sherman for the advance on Atlanta. On the other hand, if he did not think he could take Shreveport by the 25th, he should return Smith to Vicksburg by the tenth, "even if it should lead to the abandonment of the expedition."[8]

Unfortunately for Grant, for Sherman, and especially for Banks, the latter decided to press on to Shreveport.

---

1. James Lee McDonough and James Picket Jones, *War So Terrible* (New York, 1987), 14–15.
2. Foote, *The Civil War,* 3:31.
3. Ibid., 64–65.
4. Catton, *Grant Takes Command,* 140.
5. James I. Robertson, Jr., *The Stonewall Brigade* (Baton Rouge, 1963), 217.
6. Foote, *The Civil War,* 3:106.
7. Ibid., 106–107.
8. Ibid., 31–32, and Irwin, "The Red River Campaign," 350.

CHAPTER FIVE

"The Very Man I Want"

26 March—7 April 1864

On the 26th of March, Grant abandoned the Washington office that had been prepared for him and proceeded to Culpeper Court House, a little town about six miles south of Meade's headquarters at Brandy Station. There he would make his own headquarters until the army moved, although he would make weekly trips back to Washington for consultations. Meade had found a plain brick house for him near the railway station, and a number of tents were soon pitched in the yard for additional accommodations. Naturally the newspapers made much of the fact that Grant's headquarters were closer to the enemy than Meade's, but then Meade was never on good terms with the newspapermen.

Orders began to issue forth immediately. One fired off that same day went to Major General Quincy A. Gillmore, commander of the Department of the South. His command, also known as the 10th Corps, had tried to batter its way into Charleston harbor for most of 1863, but with little success. Since the attempt had been given up, he had recently informed Halleck that he could spare 10,000 men for service elsewhere and requested that he be sent with them. Now Gillmore was told to ready all surplus men for transfer, although his request to accompany them was still under consideration.[1]

Out on the Red River the next day, Banks began marching his forces out of Alexandria, headed upstream toward Shreveport, about 120 miles to the northwest. Accompanying him with one of his divisions was Major General William B. Franklin, another classmate of Grant's and the commander of the 19th Corps, and Brigadier General Thomas Ransom with two divisions from the 13th Corps, as well as A. L. Lee's cavalry. Another division of the 19th Corps was left behind to hold Alexandria. A. J. Smith's Gorillas, who had not brought many supply wagons along, took to the transports to accompany Admiral Porter's fleet, which headed upriver two days later.

The river, however, was not cooperating. The annual rise, which normally began around the first of the year, had not yet started. Perhaps it was just a coincidence, but this had happened twice before, in 1846 and 1855.[2] There may have been a nine-year cycle. Porter must have wondered how, if he got his boats up the river, he would get them back down again. But he had promised to take his gunboats wherever the sand was wet, so he concentrated now on just getting up the river. However, the Red was so low that getting above the rapids at Alexandria was proving difficult. The leading gunboat, the *Eastport,* hung on the rocks for nearly three days, and the hospital steamer *Woodford* following her was wrecked. So it was not until 3 April that the last of Porter's 13 gunboats and 30 transports succeeded in making the passage. Seven gunboats and the larger transports were left below the rapids.[3]

In Arkansas, Steele finally reached Arkadelphia that same day, the 29th, after averaging only ten miles a day over a week of marching through bottomlands that had to be corduroyed for the wagons. But there was no sign of Thayer's column from Fort Smith, so he waited for three days in hopes of receiving some news.

Also on that day, one of Grant's favorite officers, Major General E. O. C. Ord, stepped off a train at Cumberland, Maryland with a letter from the lieutenant general to Major General Franz Sigel. Grant had plans for fitting Sigel's little command into his grand design for the spring. He wanted two columns to advance from West Virginia at the same time as he was moving against Lee. Sigel was to assemble a force of 8,000 infantry, 1,500 cavalry and three batteries of artillery at Beverly with Ord in command. At Grant's signal, this force would advance on Covington, Virginia where it would destroy as much as possible of the Virginia & Tennessee Railroad, an important east-west link. He was then to proceed to Lynchburg to attack its supply depot. The second prong of the attack would be under the command of Brigadier General George Crook, who was to assemble a force of cavalry at Charleston, West Virginia and advance against the same railroad about 100 miles further south, hit the South's main salt works at Saltville and the lead mines at Wytheville, and then turn northeast down the Shenandoah Valley to the important rail-road terminus of Staunton. It was believed that if Crook could have even one full day to damage these essential facilities he could put them out of order for the duration of the war.[4]

Sigel was another general more important for his political connections than for any military ability. He was born in Baden, Germany and graduated from the military academy at Karlsruhe. He was minister of war during the unsuccessful revolution of 1848 and was forced to flee Germany, settling eventually in St. Louis, where he was a leader of the large German immigrant community there. At the beginning of the Civil War he raised a regiment of infantry and was soon promoted to brigadier general, and eventually major general, during the early operations in Missouri. He was then transferred to the East, where he replaced Fremont after the latter resigned over being subordinated to Pope, who was junior to him. Sigel's force became a corps in Pope's Army of Virginia and, after Second Bull Run, it was redesignated the 11th Corps. Poor health forced him to give up that command, but now he was feeling better and this new job had been found for him because his influence with the German immigrants made him too important to ignore. Grant had little faith in Sigel's military ability and thus assigned the major tasks in the latter's department to more trusted officers. As a sort of after thought, he gave Sigel himself a job so that he would be too busy to interfere with Ord or Crook. Sigel was to assemble a supply train and enough troops to protect it, and move southward up the Shenandoah Valley to meet Crook and Ord at Staunton and resupply them for the move against Lynchburg.

Ord was older than both Grant and Sigel and had graduated from West Point in 1839. He had commanded one of the three brigades of the Pennsylvania Reserve Division while Meade commanded one of the others, and then had his own division in the 1st Corps. After being promoted to major general, he had been transferred to Grant's Army of the Tennessee, where he had commanded a division at the defense of Corinth. He then took over the 13th Corps near the end of the Vicksburg campaign, going with it to Banks' department after the fall of that city. Crook was a younger man, graduating from West Point in 1852. His early Civil War service had been in West Virginia, participating with a division from that area in McClellan's Antietam campaign. He had then been placed in command of a cavalry division in Rosecrans' Army of the Cumberland, fighting at Chickamauga before being transferred back to West Virginia.

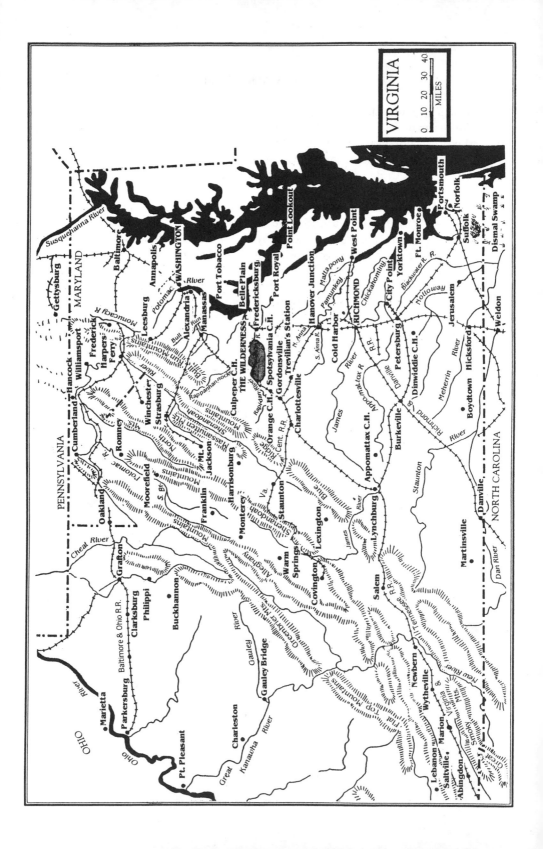

Two days later, another of Grant's favorites arrived in Washington. He was one officer that Grant did take from the West, besides Sheridan. Perhaps Sherman didn't mind losing this one. He did not say. His name was William Farrar Smith or, more commonly, W. F. Smith. However, there were so many Smiths even in the officer corps of the small, pre-war regular army that most of them acquired nicknames early on. At West Point someone noticed that his hair was thinning and hung the name "Baldy" on him. He was stuck with the sobriquet for life even though, as he complained, he often had more hair than those who called him this. Complaining, as it turned out, was one of the things he did best. Smith had graduated from West Point two years behind Grant, fourth in a class of 41, and was commissioned in the engineers. He had commanded an infantry regiment, the 3rd Vermont, at First Bull Run and had worked his way up through the ranks of the Army of the Potomac to command the 6th Corps under Burnside at the battle of Fredericksburg. After that battle, he and Franklin had written a letter directly to Lincoln objecting to Burnside's leadership and offering a plan of campaign of their own. Lincoln had been sympathetic, but Congress had taken umbrage at his bypassing normal channels and had refused to confirm his promotion to major general.

Smith had eventually been transferred to the West, where he became the chief engineer of the Army of the Cumberland. He had been in that position when Grant came to Chattanooga to get that army out of the fix Rosecrans had gotten it into, and it had been Smith who devised the plan that opened the supply line into the beseiged city. Grant had been very impressed by this and other evidence of capacity and had made him chief engineer of his Military Division of the Mississippi, urging the Senate to confirm his promotion after all. As Grant wrote in his memoirs, "I found a decided prejudice against his confirmation by a majority of the Senate, but I insisted that his services had been such that he should be rewarded. My wishes were now reluctantly complied with, and I assigned him to command of one of the corps under General Butler. I was not long in finding out that the objections to Smith's promotion were well founded."[5] But that was written after the fact. At the time of Grant's promotion to lieutenant general there was even talk that he might want Smith appointed commander of the Army of the Potomac. By the time Smith arrived in Washington on 31 March, Grant had already confirmed Meade in that job, but then the rumor was that he would replace Ben Butler.

That officer, it will be remembered, had been removed from command at New Orleans, and after sitting on the shelf for almost a year, at the end of 1863 had been sent to take command of the Department of Virginia and

North Carolina. This was an amalgamation of two departments that had previously been separate. The new combined department included several lodgements on the coast of North Carolina plus garrisons in southeast Virginia around Norfolk, Suffolk, and Yorktown and at Fortress Monroe, a formidable pre-war fortification at the tip of the Virginia Peninsula that Federal forces had held since before the war. Smith had talked to Grant about a plan to concentrate a good-sized force in Butler's department to attack Richmond from the south, up the James River, while Meade kept Lee busy further north. But Butler was too powerful politically to be dislodged from his new command unless he made some drastic mistake.

At any rate, after conferring with Smith at Washington on the 31st, Grant assigned him to Butler, and the two of them plus Rawlins, Congressman Washburne, Mrs. Grant and Lieutenant Colonel Comstock, one of Grant's aides, took ship for Fortress Monroe, which they reached on the morning of the first of April. As Butler, whom Comstock described as "sharp, shrewd, able, without conscience or modesty—overbearing. A bad man to have against you in a criminal case,"[6] was too influential to remove and too inexperienced militarily to run such a campaign on his own, Grant was apparently giving him the best military man he had available in Smith. Basically, the plan was to gather as large a field force as possible from among Butler's garrisons and put them under Smith, bring up Gillmore's excess troops from South Carolina and, in concert with Grant's and Meade's drive from the north, move up the James to cut the rail lines into Richmond and threaten that city from the south while preparing a supply base in close proximity to the Confederate capital from which the Army of the Potomac could operate in the future, if necessary.

Before outlining his own plans, Grant asked Butler for his ideas. Butler's thoughts were similar to his own, especially in recommending the Bermuda Hundred peninsula between the James and Appomattox rivers as an excellent base. But he was told that his suggestion that the Army of the Potomac be brought immediately to the James would never be accepted by Lincoln and Stanton, who would fear for the safety of Washington. As finally outlined in Grant's written instructions to Butler, Smith would command the forces gathered from Butler's own department, the 18th Corps, and Gillmore would command the 10th Corps brought up from his Department of the South. When Grant gave the word, Butler would move up the James with the help of the navy and take City Point, on the south bank of the James near its junction with the Appomattox. Richmond would be his ultimate objective with an eye to cooperation with the Army of the Potomac as it approached from the north. He should also plan a cavalry raid against the railroad that ran between Petersburg, Virginia and Weldon, North Carolina.

That same first day of April, Steele left Arkadelphia without having heard anything of Thayer's column which was to have met him there. Steele's supplies were limited, and he could not afford to wait any longer. As his forces moved down the old military road that led to Washington, Arkansas they began to run into opposition from Confederate cavalry hovering around the flanks and the rear of their column. Price, the Rebel commander for Arkansas, had only cavalry to harass Steele's march because he had been ordered to send his two small divisions of infantry to the Red River to reinforce Taylor.

Both Price and Taylor belonged to the Trans-Mississippi Department of the Confederate army, commanded by General Edmund Kirby Smith, whose headquarters were at the very town of Shreveport for which Banks and Steele were marching. Unlike the Federal army, which had only one lieutenant general, the Southern army had several, as well as a few full generals, the four-star rank. This Smith, styled Kirby Smith, was in the same West Point class as Baldy and seven years behind A. J. He had resigned as major of the 2nd U.S. Cavalry to join the Confederacy and commanded a brigade at First Bull Run. He was promoted to major general and sent to command the Department of East Tennessee, from which he invaded Kentucky in the fall of 1862 in conjunction with Bragg's Army of Tennessee. Even though that invasion was ultimately turned back, he was then promoted and sent to command the Trans-Mississippi which, ever since the fall of Vicksburg and Port Hudson had cut the Confederacy in two, was becoming known as Kirby-Smithdom, an almost-separate nation.

Smith had been quick to see that Banks and Steele were planning an expedition against him, but his own resources for meeting it were very slim. Nevertheless, he had ordered his third district commander, John Magruder in Texas, to send all movable forces to Shreveport, and Price to send all his infantry there. Taylor was ordered to fall back to the same point, delaying Banks as much as possible until the reinforcements arrived. Price, meanwhile, was to slow Steele's progress with his cavalry until Banks could be dealt with. Then all would turn on Steele.

On the third of April, as Grant was leaving Fortress Monroe and the last of Porter's gunboats pulled out of Alexandria, Banks' main force was at Natchitoches, about half the way to Shreveport, and A. J. Smith's force was four miles farther on at Grand Ecore. Banks was joined that day by 1,500 black troops, veterans of Port Hudson known as the Corps d'Afrique, who partially made up for the loss of the 3,000-man Marine Brigade, a force of mounted infantry attached to the fleet, who were being sent off because of an outbreak of smallpox among them. There was one more new arrival that Banks would just as soon have done without. That was Brigadier General John M. Corse, one of Sherman's inspector-generals. He had been sent by Sherman with orders for the return of A. J. Smith's men by 10 April. Sherman's letter to Banks explained that, "Forrest, availing himself of the absence of our furloughed men and of the detachment with you, has pushed up between the Mississippi and Tennessee Rivers, even to the Ohio. He attacked Paducah, but got the worst of it, and he still lingers about the place. I hope that he will remain thereabouts till General A. J. Smith can reach his destined point, but this I can hardly expect; yet I want him to reach by the Yazoo a position near Grenada, thence to operate against Forrest, after which to march across to Decatur, Alabama. You will see that he has a big job, and therefore should start at once. . . . I leave Steele's entire force to cooperate with you and the navy, but, as I before stated, I must have A. J. Smith's troops now as soon as possible."[7] But Banks was within four days' march of Shreveport, and he decided to go on.

On that same third of April, Steele's column was attacked by John S. Marmaduke's division of Price's cavalry. The head of Steele's column was crossing the Little Missouri at Elkin's Ferry when Marmaduke launched a heavy attack on the main body of the Union column farther back at Okolona. He was beaten off, but at the cost of time and the consumption of more rations. With no railroad and no river to keep him supplied through the thinly populated area of southern Arkansas, Steele's force could only eat what it had brought along with it, and what it had brought would have to last until it made connection with Porter's fleet.

The fourth of April saw another unprepossessing officer from the West arrive in Washington. This time it was Major General Philip Henry Sheridan, ordered east to take command of the Cavalry Corps of the Army of the Potomac. Captain Horace Porter saw him there. "He had been worn down almost to a shadow by hard work and exposure in the field; he weighed only a hundred and fifteen pounds, and as his height was but five feet six inches, he looked anything but formidable as a candidate for a cavalry leader. He had met the President and the officials at the War Department that day for the first time," Porter continued, "and it was his appearance on this occasion which gave rise to a remark made to General Grant the next time he visited the department: 'The officer you brought on from the West is rather a little fellow to handle your cavalry.'

To which Grant replied, 'You will find him big enough for the purpose before we get through with him.' "[8]

Sheridan, the son of Irish immigrants, was brought up in Ohio and graduated from West Point, ranked 34th in the 52-man class of 1853, ten years after Grant. He had been a captain on Halleck's staff during the advance on Corinth before being commissioned colonel of the 2nd Michigan Cavalry Regiment and assigned to command a small cavalry brigade. He was so impressive in that capacity that he was promoted to brigadier general and given an infantry division in Buell's army. He distinguished himself at the battles of Perryville and Stones River, winning his second star. At Chattanooga he played a prominent part in the decisive charge up Missionary Ridge that broke the Confederate line, and his division was the only element of the Federal forces that retained enough cohesion to pursue the routed Southerners.

The Cavalry Corps had been formed about a year before as part of the general reorganization of the Army of the Potomac that was Hooker's great contribution to the cause. It had initially been commanded by George Stoneman during the Chancellorsville campaign, then by Alfred Pleasonton through the Gettysburg campaign and until a few days before Sheridan's arrival. Under Pleasonton the Cavalry Corps had stood up to the Southern cavalry of Jeb Stuart for the first time. By the battle of Gettysburg it had established itself as at least the equal of the vaunted Rebel cavaliers. But in order to improve the morale and efficiency of the cavalry, Pleasonton had needed to take away the numerous escorts attached to every corps and division commander in the infantry; and fight Meade's tendency to use the cavalry for such unglamorous and wasteful duties as guarding wagons and performing picket duty for the infantry. In the end, Pleasonton had stirred up too much resentment within the army and especially in George Meade.[9] It is doubtful that Meade suspected that he was clearing the way for a cavalry commander who not only shared Pleasonton's views on the proper use of the mounted arm, but also had enough influence with the new general-in-chief to override Meade's objections. Grant had told Lincoln that he wanted "the very best man in the army" to command the cavalry in his upcoming campaign. Halleck, who was present, asked, "How would Sheridan do?" to which Grant replied, "The very man I want."[10]

The same day that Sheridan reached Washington, Grant was writing his old friend Sherman a letter marked "private and confidential." In it he outlined his plans as follows: "It is my design, if the enemy keep quiet and allow me to take the initiative in the spring campaign, to work all parts of the army together, and somewhat towards a common centre. For your information I now write you my programme, as at present determined upon.

"I have sent orders to Banks, by private messenger, to finish up his present expedition against Shreveport with all dispatch; to turn over the defence of Red River to General Steele and the navy, and to return your troops to you and his own to New Orleans; to abandon all of Texas, except the Rio Grande, and to hold that with not to exceed four thousand men; to reduce the number of troops on the Mississippi to the lowest number necessary to hold it, and to collect from his command not less than twenty-five thousand men. To this I will add five thousand men from Missouri. With this force he is to commence operations against Mobile as soon as he can. It will be impossible for him to commence too early.

"Gillmore joins Butler with ten thousand men, and the two operate against Richmond from the south side of the James River. This will give Butler thirty-three thousand men to operate with, W. F. Smith commanding the right wing of his forces and Gillmore the left wing. I will stay with the Army of the Potomac, increased by Burnside's corps of not less than twenty-five thousand effective men, and operate directly against Lee's army, wherever it may be found.

"Sigel collects all his available force in two columns, one, under Ord and Averell, to start from Beverly, [West] Virginia, and the other, under Crook, to start from Charleston [West Virginia] on the Kanawha, to move against the Virginia and Tennessee Railroad.

"Crook will have all cavalry, and will endeavor to get in about Saltville, and move east from there to join Ord. His force will be all cavalry, while Ord will have from ten to twelve thousand men of all arms.

"You I propose to move against Johnston's army, to break it up and to get into the interior of the enemy's country as far as you can, inflicting all the damage you can against their war resources.

"I do not propose to lay down for you a plan of campaign, but simply lay down the work it is desirable to have done and leave you free to execute it in your own way. Submit to me, however, as early as you can, your plan of operations.

"As stated, Banks is ordered to commence operations as soon as he can. Gillmore is ordered to report at Fortress Monroe by the 18th inst., or as soon thereafter as practicable. Sigel is concentrating now. None will move from their places of rendezvous until I direct, except Banks. I want to be ready to move by the 25th inst., if possible. I know you will have difficulties to encounter in getting through the mountains to where supplies are abundant, but I believe you will accomplish it.

"From the expedition from the Department of West Virginia I do not calculate on very great results; but it is the only way I can take troops from there. With the long line of railroad Sigel has to protect, he can spare no troops except to move directly to his front. In this way he must get through to inflict great damage on the enemy, or the enemy must detach from one of his armies a large force to prevent it." Grant closed by quoting, uncredited, the expression Lincoln had used when this plan had been explained to him: "In other words, if Sigel can't skin himself he can hold a leg while some one else skins."[11]

Grant's plans for Sherman called for him to assemble as many men as possible in northern Georgia and northern Alabama for an advance on Atlanta, but all such forces would, as they advanced, be dependent for supplies on the railroad running down from Nashville to Chattanooga. However, Sherman found the capacity of these lines "so small," he wrote in his memoirs, "especially in the number of locomotives and cars, that it was clear that they were barely able to supply the daily wants of the armies then dependent on them, with no power of accumulating a surplus in advance. We could not attempt an advance into Georgia without food, ammunition, etc.; and ordinary prudence dictated that we should have an accumulation at the front, in case of interruption to the railway by the act of the enemy, or by common accident."

On the sixth of April he issued an order limiting the use of the railroads to transporting supplies for the army, forbidding their use for civilian traffic of any form. He further required the commanders of garrisons within thirty miles of Nashville to haul out their own supplies in wagons. Troops destined for the front could no longer ride the rails. They would have to march. Beef cattle would also have to use their own legs to reach the front. "This was a great help," Sherman wrote, "but of course it naturally raised a howl. Some of the poor Union people of East Tennessee appealed to President Lincoln, whose kind heart responded promptly to their request. He telegraphed me to know if I could not modify or repeal my orders; but I answered him that a great campaign was impending on which the fate of the nation hung; that our railroads had but a limited capacity, and could not provide for the necessities of the army and of the people too; that one or the other must quit."

By these means Sherman had about doubled his daily accumulation of stores at the front, but even that was not enough. So he called in his quartermaster, commissary chief, and transportation chief to calculate just what was needed. When they discovered that they still did not have enough cars or locomotives, he ordered all trains arriving in Nashville from Louisville to be held for the run to Chattanooga. "As soon as Mr. Guthrie, the President of the Louisville & Nashville Railroad, detected that we were holding on to all his locomotives and cars," Sherman said, "He wrote me, earnestly remonstrating against it, saying that he would not be able with diminished stock to bring forward the necessary stores from Louisville to Nashville. I wrote to him, frankly telling him exactly how we were placed, appealed to his patriotism to stand by us, and advised him in like manner to hold on to all trains coming into Jeffersonville, Indiana . . . in a short time we had cars and locomotives from almost every road at the North; months afterward I was amused to see, away down in Georgia, cars marked 'Pittsburg & Fort Wayne,' 'Delaware & Lackawanna,' 'Baltimore & Ohio,' and indeed with the names of almost every railroad north of the Ohio River."[12]

Out on the Red River that same sixth of April, the second anniversary of the battle of Shiloh, two Confederate generals met to discuss another combination of forces with the similar purpose of meeting another Federal advance before it could make an attack. Dick Taylor had been fuming for days about having to give up the greater part of Louisiana—his district and his home state—without a fight. He knew he was outnumbered by five or six to one, but he had been threatening to bring on a battle anyway, rather than retreat any farther. Mild-mannered Kirby Smith let him rant but returned to Shreveport without making a decision. He had begun to worry that perhaps he had chosen the wrong Yankee column to fight first. After all, Steele was the West Pointer, "bold, ardent, vigorous," in Taylor's words, while Banks was only a bumbling amateur. Meanwhile, Brigadier General Thomas Green's cavalry joined Taylor that day from Texas, bringing the total Confederate force to about 9,000 men. Another 4,500 men from Arkansas were only 25 miles away, but Kirby Smith had not yet decided whether to send them on or start them back the way they had come.

That was the day that Steele, with most of his column finally across the Little Missouri, finally received word of the missing division from Fort Smith. Thayer had been delayed by bad roads but hoped to reach Steele in a day or two, or three. It was also the same day that Banks' column left Natchitoches on the final leg of its march to Shreveport. T. Kilby Smith's division remained on the transports while 1700 cavalry patrolled the north bank of the river. Lee and the rest of his cavalry led the main column along the south bank, followed by Ransom's two divisions of the 13th Corps, Emory's division of the 19th, and the Corps d'Afrique. A. J. Smith followed with Mower's two divisions the next day, marching on their own feet now. Grover's 2nd Division of the 19th Corps was left to hold Natchitoches.

That seventh of April, Grant brought one more of his favorite officers into the game. Brigadier General James Harrison Wilson had been Grant's chief engineer during the Vicksburg campaign, in a way making him Baldy Smith's predecessor. In January he had been transferred to Washington in the hope that he could bring some efficiency to the recently established Cavalry Bureau of the War Department. "No more efficient or better appointment could be made for the place," Grant had said when Halleck had asked for Wilson.[13] His transfer had been made with the understanding that it would only be for about 60 days, after which he was to return to Grant. When he was not busy lobbying for Grant's promotion to lieutenant general or for Baldy Smith's appointment to command the Army of the Potomac, Wilson did make some improvements in the Union cavalry.

First of all he clamped down, with some success, on the contractors who sold sub-standard horses to the government, but perhaps his major contribution was to get the Spencer repeating carbine approved as the standard cavalry weapon. Military small arms had been undergoing a period of rapid development since the percussion cap had replaced the flintlock as the standard means of igniting the gunpowder shortly before the war with Mexico. Then a French captain named Minié had invented a way to combine the accuracy and range of a rifle with the ease of loading and higher rate of fire of the smoothbore musket, producing the rifled musket. Practical breech-loading rifles and carbines (short rifles) began to appear at about the same time. They used various expedients for opening the breech, or rear, of the barrel to allow the bullet and powder to be loaded there, and thus to avoid the long trip down the barrel from the muzzle.

While the rifled, muzzle-loading musket was the standard infantry weapon of both sides, the Union cavalry had been issued with every imaginable type of breech-loading carbine, some good, some barely functional. The Spencer was the next logical step, a repeating carbine. It was one of the first weapons to use a self-contained metal cartridge that included the bullet, the powder, and the primer all in one package. Seven cartridges could be loaded into a tube in the butt of the carbine, and after each round was fired the trigger guard was levered forward and back to expel the empty cartridges and load new ones into the breech. It was similar to the later Winchester of Western movie fame, except that the hammer still had to be cocked by hand rather than as part of the levering action. The Spencer was capable of a sustained rate of about 15 shots a minute, compared to around 7 or 8 for a breechloader and about 3 for a muzzleloader.[14] Only a few Union cavalry regiments had received these weapons by the spring of 1864 but their effect, both upon the enemy and upon the users' morale, was considerable.

Now Grant had a new job for Wilson, who was only 27 years old and an 1860 graduate of West Point. He was given command of the 3rd Division of the Cavalry Corps of the Army of the Potomac and was replaced at the Cavalry Bureau by his assistant, Colonel August V. Kautz. As head of the 3rd Division, Wilson replaced General Hugh Judson Kilpatrick. Better known as "Kill-Cavalry," he was a year older than Wilson, but had graduated from West Point a year later, in the class of 1861. Kilpatrick had taken over command of the division just as it had been transferred from the defenses of Washington to the Army of the Potomac, only days before the battle of Gettysburg. He was vain and reckless, but he had provided aggressive leadership where it was needed most. However, he had just suffered a mighty blow to his oversized ego.

Kilpatrick had been appointed by Lincoln himself, probably at his own secret and roundabout, out-of-channels suggestion, to lead a large cavalry raid in late February and early March. Its object had been to free thousands of Union prisoners of war being held in Richmond, and to spread thousands of copies of Lincoln's proclamation offering amnesty to any Rebels who would renew their allegiance to the Federal government. But the raid had ended as a dismal failure, leaving Kilpatrick ripe for a transfer. He was sent West to join the forces Sherman was accumulating for his drive into Georgia.

Other moves were also necessary to clear the way for Wilson's appointment to command the 3rd Division. Both brigade commanders in the division were senior to Wilson on the list of brigadier generals. So Henry Davies was transferred to the 2nd Division, and George Custer and his entire brigade were moved to the 1st Division, being replaced by Colonel George H. Chapman and his brigade. It was obvious that Grant had his eye on the cavalry, as he had sent two of his favorite officers to that corps.

---

1. William Glenn Robertson, *Back Door To Richmond* (Newark, 1987), 18.
2. Foote, *The Civil War*, 3:33.
3. Irwin, "The Red River Campaign," 350.
4. Grant, *Memoirs*, 2:133.
5. William C. Davis, *The Battle of New Market* (New York, 1975), 19–20.
6. Robertson, *Back Door To Richmond*, 18–23.
7. Sherman, *Memoirs*, 2:13–14.
8. Porter, *Campaigning With Grant*, 23–24.
9. Stephen Z. Starr, *The Union Cavalry in the Civil War*, (Baton Rouge, 1981) vol. 2, 73–74.

10. Foote, *The Civil War,* 3:135.

11. Grant, *Memoirs,* 2:130–132.

12. Sherman, *Memoirs,* 2:10–12.

13. Starr, *Union Cavalry,* 2:68.

14. W. Eugene Sloan, "Goodbye To The Single-Shot Musket," *Civil War Times Illustrated* 23, (3, May 1984).

CHAPTER SIX

"You Have Saved The Army"

7–10 April 1864

On the same day that Wilson was ordered to the Army of the Potomac, one of General Robert Lee's favorite officers, Lieutenant General James Longstreet, was ordered by the Confederate War Department to return with his corps to Virginia and report to Lee. Longstreet, a Georgian, had graduated from West Point one year before Grant and had been a close enough friend to attend his wedding. He had commanded a brigade at the first battle of Bull Run and was then promoted to major general. During the Peninsula campaign he had won Lee's confidence and had been given command of one of the two wings of the Army of Northern Virginia, the other belonging to Stonewall Jackson. Following the Second Bull Run and Antietam campaigns the Confederate Congress finally legalized the use of corps in the Rebel army and established the grade of lieutenant general to stand between the existing major general and general. Long-street became the senior lieutenant general in the Southern army and his wing became the 1st Corps of the Army of Northern Virginia, with Jackson's wing as the 2nd Corps.

That was how Lee's army had been organized for its great defensive victory at Fredericksburg in December of 1862. However, Longstreet had been sent with two of his divisions to southeast Virginia early in 1863 and had missed Lee's and Jackson's great counter-punch victory at Chancellorsville in May. Jackson had been killed in that battle, and Lee's army had then been reorganized from two corps of four divisions each, into three corps of three divisions each. Two of Jackson's division commanders, Richard Ewell and A. P. Hill, had been promoted to lieutenant general. Ewell had succeeded to the 2nd Corps, from which Hill's Division had been taken and combined with Richard Anderson's from the 1st Corps to form the nucleus of a new 3rd Corps for Hill. A third division had been formed from two of the six brigades of his old division plus two brigades of reinforcements and was commanded by Henry Heth. The Army of Northern Virginia had fought the Gettysburg campaign with that organization, but in September of 1863, partly at his own insistence, Longstreet had again been detached, this time with his entire corps.

Pickett's Division, which had suffered heavy losses at Gettysburg, had been dropped off in southeast Virginia, but Longstreet and the other two divisions had gone on to Georgia to reinforce Bragg's Army of Tennessee. Bragg, with those and other reinforcements, had soundly defeated Rosecrans at the battle of Chickamauga. Longstreet had played the key role by exploiting an accidental hole in the Federal line to defeat and scatter half of Rosecrans' army. The Federals had fallen back to Chattanooga and Bragg had followed them, taking up commanding positions on the ridges which dominated their supply lines into the town. But, following Baldy Smith's plan, Grant, the new Union commander, had reestablished a secure supply line. Then Bragg had made his greatest error. He had detached Longstreet, sending him off into east Tennessee to attempt the recovery of Knoxville, which had fallen to Burnside while the Confederates were concentrating on Rosecrans.

However, Longstreet's force had been insufficient to retake Knoxville, and in his absence Grant had driven Bragg from Lookout Mountain and Missionary Ridge. Bragg's retreat into northern Georgia had left his army separated from Longstreet's corps by the Union forces. When Grant had sent Sherman to the support of Burnside at Knoxville, Longstreet had retreated northward until he finally came to rest at Bristol, on the border between Tennessee and Virginia. There he had spent the winter, plotting various ways to undertake an offensive that would regain something: middle Tennessee, eastern Kentucky, anything. But no practical combination of forces could be found, let alone supplied, for any such project.

And anyway Longstreet had displayed no particular talent for independent command. Meanwhile there was growing evidence that Grant planned to undertake a major campaign against Lee as soon as the spring rains stopped and the muddy roads dried in Virginia. Lee would be needing every soldier he could find.

Out on the Red River that day, 7 April, A. J. Smith led Mower's two divisions out of Grand Ecore as the tail of Banks' thirty-mile-long column, while Porter headed upstream again with six light-draft gunboats and the transports carrying T. Kilby Smith's small division. A. L. Lee's cavalry, at the head of the strung-out Federal column, finally encamped seven miles beyond Pleasant Hill after having had to fight its way forward against Green's Texas horsemen most of the day. At about 10 p.m. Ransom, at Pleasant Hill, received an order from Franklin, who was in overall charge of the column, to send at least a brigade of his infantry to the cavalry's support. His two 13th Corps divisions had marched all day through pine woods in the midst of a heavy storm. Now they were asked to march another eight miles by night. The road was poor and had diverged too far from the river for the Federals to receive any aid from their fleet. Ransom sent Colonel Frank Emerson's 1st Brigade of Colonel William Landram's 4th Division, which reached Lee's camp on the morning of the eighth. Lee had resumed his advance and he soon ran into a strong line of Confederate skirmishers. His cavalry was forced to dismount and Emerson's infantry had to deploy into battle line to drive the Rebels before them. It was exhausting work in the muggy heat.

Union Colonel William Heath of the 33rd Missouri remembered that Ransom "was apprehensive of an attack by superior numbers from early in the morning. . . . He seemed to 'feel it in the air.' So impressed was he with the imprudence of advancing . . . he halted his column and asked General Banks for permission to await the arrival of the center within proper supporting distance, saying to him frankly that he felt he was then, 'in the presence of the enemy in superior force.' "[1] But Banks insisted on continuing the advance. He had been made to understand, by Grant and Sherman, that time was of the essence.

About noon, Lee's cavalry and Emerson's infantry approached Sabine Cross Roads, where the path which they had been following emerged from the pine woods into a large clearing. There they found a strong line of Southern cavalry and infantry barring their way. Lee still insisted on pushing ahead and the Confederates again gave ground, but the Federals found an even larger Rebel force at the edge of the next woods. Colonel Landram, Emerson's division commander, fired off a hasty note to Ransom: "My men have skirmished and marched through the bushes and thickets for eight or nine miles, making, in all, a march of fifteen or sixteen miles. They have no water and are literally worn out. Can you have them relieved soon? General Lee insists on pushing ahead. . . ." Ransom had already sent ahead Landram's other brigade, Vance's, but it was delayed by Lee's train of 300 wagons blocking miles of the road. Now Ransom followed in person. He passed the wagons and Vance's marching troops and arrived at the head of the column at about 1:30 p.m. to find the troops there confronted by a superior force of Rebels. He placed his infantry on the right of the Union line and Lee's cavalry on the left, supported by a battery of artillery, and waited for reinforcements.

On the Confederate side, Taylor was juggling units while waiting impatiently either for the Arkansas infantry to arrive, or for the Federals to make an attack. About 3 p.m. Banks himself reached the front of the Union column. He sent back orders for the rest of his units to hurry forward, but no more Union troops had arrived by the time Taylor at last unleashed the attack he had been aching to launch for days. About 4 p.m. he ordered Mouton's Louisiana infantry to charge, supported by two brigades of dismounted Texas cavalry. Despite the surprise and the blood-curdling shriek of the rebel yell, Landram's exhausted infantry delivered a blistering fire that cut down Mouton and broke the first wave of Southerners in confusion. However, they rallied and came on again, like "infuriated demons." Before the day was over not only Mouton but four of his colonels had been killed, and more than a third of the men in his division were casualties. But unit by unit, Taylor's forces took up the assault, altogether outnumbering Landram's and Lee's men by about two to one. Soon they overlapped Lee's left flank, and the Union line began to unravel and head for the rear.

Ransom put together a second line built around an Illinois battery of six light rifled cannon and Vance's infantry, but Ransom was soon hit in the left knee by a Minié bullet and carried from the field. Franklin arrived on the scene at the head of Cameron's division of the 13th Corps, which had taken two hours to march five miles through the mud and bypass Lee's wagons. They were just in time to be swept away in a general retreat as the Rebels broke the final Union stand. When the Federals reached Lee's wagons, still blocking the road, all order was lost. Lee, who had previously been denied permission to keep his wagons further back in the column, said the retreat found that "most of them were turned around; but a great many of them were in ruts, against trees, the mules shot, etc., and we lost some artillery there by reason of it."[2] The Confederates captured 20 guns, along with numerous prisoners and 156 wagons.

About then a courier caught up with Taylor bearing a letter written that morning by Kirby Smith saying, "A general engagement now could not be given with our full force. Reinforcements are moving up—not very large, it is true. . . . Let me know as soon as you are convinced that a general advance is being made and I will come to the front."

"Too late, sir," Taylor smiled. "The battle is won."[3]

Three miles in rear of the original site of the battle, Emory's division of the 19th Corps, marching to reinforce the front, met the routed column pressing in great disorder for the rear. Emory's men forced their way through the confused mass of fugitives and wagons, and formed line in a good position to check the pursuit. A Federal lieutenant remembered a "moving sea of wagons, guns, caissons, riderless cavalry horses, ambulances with their freight of moaning, dying humanity," suddenly brought to a halt in a heap by the roadblock.[4] Taylor soon came up and drove in Emory's skirmishers to take possession of a small stream which they had been defending, in order to provide his troops with drinking water, but he could not budge the main Union battle line before darkness ended the day's fight. Banks ordered a withdrawal to Pleasant Hill where he would find A. J. Smith's veterans and water for his own men and could consolidate his forces for the expected second round the next day. The withdrawal began at 10 p.m., made up mostly of "men without hats or coats, men without guns or accoutrements, cavalrymen without horses and artillerymen without cannon, wounded men bleeding and crying at every step, men begrimed with smoke and powder, all in a state of fear and frenzy," as one participant described them, and Banks the most dejected of them all.[5]

When daylight revealed that Emory had evacuated his position, Taylor started his whole force in pursuit, led by Green's Texas cavalry and the two infantry divisions from Arkansas that had arrived too late for the first day's battle. It was afternoon by the time the Confederates came upon the Union battle line at Pleasant Hill, where Emory's division had joined A. J. Smith's two to form a defense while the rest of the Federal army continued downriver toward Grand Ecore. The troops from Arkansas, two small divisions under Brigadier General Thomas J. Churchill, were so tired from having marched 45 miles since the previous morning that Taylor halted his entire force for a two-hour rest. Then he formed his men into line of battle, with two brigades of cavalry on the left of the road and what had been Mouton's division, now Polignac's, in support. To the right of the road he placed J. G. Walker's Texas infantry, with Churchill's Arkansas and Missouri divisions to his right and three regiments of cavalry covering the far right flank. Two more brigades of cavalry were sent to turn the Federals' right and seize the road to Blair's Landing on the river.

At 5 p.m. Churchill started the advance. His two divisions, determined to make up for what they had missed the day before, struck Banks' left-most brigade, part of Emory's division, with irresistable fury. The Union brigade commander fell dead, and his regiments were outflanked and crushed. Churchill's elated troops wheeled to their left like a huge swinging door, flanking each Federal unit in turn while Walker advanced against their front. However, just as things looked darkest for the Federals, A. J. Smith hurried his Gorillas over from the Union right and outflanked Churchill in turn. The Rebels were brought to a sudden halt and began to give way one regiment at a time as each in turn was taken end-on. They made a brief stand in the cane along the banks of a creek, but point-blank volleys and hand-to-hand combat drove them out, and panic began to set in.

Now it was the Southerners' turn to run and the Federals' to cheer. Walker was carried from the field with a bullet in the groin, and his Texans joined the rout, streaming for the rear. Polignac's Louisiana division formed a line to discourage pursuit as darkness began to fall, but the rest of the Confederates fell back about six miles to the nearest water in a good imitation of the Union retreat of the night before. Banks found A. J. Smith in the gathering darkness and gratefully shook his hand. "God bless you," he exclaimed. "You have saved the army."[6]

Banks had been considering all day the possibility of returning to the offensive, and this defensive success confirmed his resolve to the point of sending off orders to Lee to turn the supply wagons around and bring them back to Pleasant Hill. But when he conferred with Franklin, Emory and one of his brigade commanders, Dwight, they convinced him that the safer course was to continue downriver to regain the protection of the fleet and a secure supply line, differing only on the exact spot at which to make the connection. Banks decided to accept the advice of these West Pointers, choosing Grand Ecore as the army's next destination. A. J. Smith was furious when he learned of this loss of nerve and proposed to Franklin that the latter arrest Banks and take charge of a rapid advance on Shreveport, but Franklin would have no part of mutiny.

Ten miles to the west, Taylor was roused from sleep at about 10 p.m. by Kirby Smith, who had ridden all day from Shreveport after learning early that morning of Taylor's unauthorized attack at Sabine Cross Roads. Now he discovered that another battle had been fought without his orders, and lost, and that Taylor was getting ready to start a third. Kirby Smith pointed out the threat of Steele descending on Shreveport from the north while its defenders were all with Taylor, not to mention the possibility that Porter might land the troops from the transports there at any moment. Taylor still insisted that Banks was the proper target and that the others would back off when they learned of his defeat, but Kirby Smith demurred and finally issued a peremptory order for the infantry to march for Shreveport the next day, leaving Taylor only Green's 3,000 Texas cavalry and Polignac's Louisiana infantry, now down to 2,000 men. So dawn would see the two armies, each having won one battle and each having lost one, march off in opposite directions.

Far away to the north on the same day as the fight at Pleasant Hill, Thayer's Frontier Division finally caught up with Steele's main column and began crossing the Little Missouri. Unfortunately for Steele, they brought with them very little to eat and 4,000 more mouths to feed. So he ordered his headquarters to send out a supply train, "using, if necessary, every wagon and mule at Little Rock."[7] The supplies were to meet him, if they could get through, at Camden, for which point he now determined to turn aside. In the meantime, he began diversionary skirmishing with Price's cavalry in his front. This had now grown to six brigades, a total of about 6,000 men, or fully half the strength of Steele's entire force, including Thayer.

In Virginia on that ninth of April, blissfully ignorant of the turn of events in Louisiana and Arkansas, Grant presented Meade with a letter marked "For Your Perusal Alone." It was the equivalent of the one he had sent to Sherman, and it outlined the same plans for Banks, Sigel, and Butler. But it went on to reveal the state of his planning for the Army of the Potomac: "Lee's army will be your objective point," he said. "Wherever Lee goes, there you will go also. The only point upon which I am now in doubt is, whether it will be better to cross the Rapidan above or below him. Each plan presents great advantages over the other with corresponding objections. By crossing above, Lee is cut off from all chance of ignoring Richmond and going north on a raid. But if we take this route, all we do must be done whilst the rations we start with hold out. We separate from Butler so that he cannot be directed how to cooperate. By the other route Brandy Station can be used as a base of supplies until another is secured on the York or James rivers.

"These advantages and objections I will talk over with you more fully than I can write them.

"Burnside with a force of probably 25,000 men will reinforce you. Immediately upon his arrival, which will be shortly after the 20th inst., I will give him the defence of the road from Bull Run as far south as we wish to hold it. This will enable you to collect all your strength about Brandy Station and to the front.

"There will be naval co-operation on the James River, and transports and ferries will be provided so that should Lee fall back into his intrenchments at Richmond, Butler's force and yours will be a unit, or at least can be made to act as such." He went on to direct that Meade reduce the

baggage of all levels of command, and to begin to arrange for the supplies
that would be needed for either contingency, whether he decided to cross
the Rapidan to Lee's left or to his right.[8]

The following day, while Taylor's and Banks' armies were marching
away from each other along the Red River, Admiral Porter first learned
that Banks was retreating instead of advancing. The next morning
T. Kilby Smith, whose division was riding the transports with the fleet,
received written orders to return to Grand Ecore, where the main Union
column was starting to intrench. There Banks ordered a pontoon bridge
thrown across the Red River so that a strong detachment could be placed
on the northern bank. Then he sent orders to New Orleans for reinforcements to be forwarded to him from there and from Texas.

That same day, at his Nashville headquarters Sherman was writing an
answer to Grant's outline of his general plan. After acknowledging receipt
of his friend and superior's letter he commented, "That we are now all to
act on a common plan, converging on a common centre, looks like
enlightened war."

Up to that time there had been little coordination among the various
Federal commands, and the Confederates had taken advantage of that fact
by repeatedly shifting forces from quiet fronts to more active ones. That
had been the deciding factor, or nearly so, in several major battles, from
First Bull Run to Shiloh, the Virginia Peninsula, Vicksburg, Chickamauga, and even now, on the Red River. Grant wanted to make sure that
each Union commander kept the Rebels in his front too occupied when
they were to be sent as reinforcements somewhere else, and too busy to
conduct offensives or raids of their own. That is why he, with Meade's
and Burnside's forces, would endeavor to keep the South's most dangerous army, under Lee, locked in mortal combat, preventing its interference with Sherman or any of the other Northern armies. Sherman was
to do likewise with the Rebels' other large force under Joseph Eggleston
Johnston.

"Like yourself," Sherman continued, "you take the biggest load, and
from me you shall have thorough and hearty cooperation. I will not let
side issues draw me off from your main plans in which I am to knock Jos.
Johnston, and to do as much damage to the resources of the enemy as
possible. I have heretofore written to General Rawlins and to Colonel
Comstock (of your staff) somewhat of the method in which I propose to
act. I have seen all my army, corps, and division commanders, and have
signified only to the former, viz., Schofield, Thomas, and McPherson,
our general plans, which I inferred from the purport of our conversation
here and at Cincinnati." He went on to outline a plan of campaign that he

later had to modify considerably, then stated, "I will ever bear in mind that Johnston is at all times to be kept so busy that he cannot in any event send any part of his command against you or Banks.

"If Banks can at the same time carry Mobile and open up the Alabama River, he will in a measure solve the most difficult part of my problem, viz., 'provisions.' But in that I must venture. Georgia has a million of inhabitants. If they can live, we should not starve. If the enemy interrupt our communications, I will be absolved from all obligations to subsist on our own resources, and will feel perfectly justified in taking whatever and wherever we can find.

"I will inspire my command, if successful, with the feeling that beef and salt are all that is absolutely necessary to life, and that parched corn once fed General [Andrew] Jackson's army on that very ground."[9]

---

1. James T. Hufstodt, "Ransom at the Crossroads," *Civil War Times Illustrated*, 19 (8, December 1980): 9–17.
2. Starr, *Union Cavalry*, 3:497.
3. Foote, *The Civil War*, 3:45.
4. Hufstodt, "Ransom at the Crossroads."
5. Foote, *The Civil War*, 3:46.
6. Ibid., 50.
7. Foote, *The Civil War*, 3:67.
8. Grant, *Memoirs*, 2:134–137.
9. Sherman, *Memoirs*, 2:27–29.

CHAPTER SEVEN

"If Slaves Will Make Good Soldiers"

12–17 April 1864

High on a bluff overlooking the east bank of the Mississippi, 40 miles north of Memphis, sat a semi-circle of earthworks known as Fort Pillow. It had originally been built by the Rebels to guard the river approaches to the town and was named after a Confederate general. But by the morning of 12 April 1864, it had been in Union hands for almost two years. Sherman had actually ordered it to be evacuated when he was preparing for his march across Mississippi a couple of months before, but General Stephen Hurlbut, headquartered in Memphis in command of the 16th Corps, had retained a small garrison there to encourage the enlistment of black soldiers from the area. On the twelfth of April the fort was manned by 262 members of the 6th U.S. Colored Heavy Artillery Regiment and of Battery D, 2nd U.S. Colored Light Artillery, and by 295 men of the 13th Tennessee Cavalry. The latter were white Union sympathizers, or what the Confederates called "homemade Yankees." Also present were an unknown number of women and children.

At daylight that morning the 1500 men of two brigades of Forrest's Rebel cavalry under Brigadier General James R. Chalmers began investing the land side of the fort. The original Confederate trace of about two miles had already been reduced twice, and now there were but 125 yards of earthworks set on the edge of the bluff with the drop to the river at its rear and a six-foot-deep, twelve-foot-wide ditch on the other three sides. The Federals had six light cannon (two 6-pounder guns, two 12-pounder howitzers, and two 10-pounder Parrott rifles) and the support of a gunboat, the *New Era,* one of a class of small, lightly armored riverboats known as tinclads, carrying six 24-pounder howitzers. But Chalmers had posted his men, dismounted, in the cover of the old Rebel earthworks and had put sharpshooters on hills around the little fort to keep the Federals' heads down. One of these picked off the Union commander, Major Lionel F. Booth of the heavy artillery regiment, around 9 a.m., and Major William F. Bradford of the 13th Tennessee took over.

Forrest himself arrived on the scene around 10 a.m. and soon spotted a fatal weakness in the Union position. He ordered Chalmers to advance his men to the foot of the slope on which the fort stood, to within an average of about a hundred yards of the Federals. That was dangerously close range against artillery and troops armed with rifled muskets. They made it. "Not, however, without considerable loss," reported Forrest, who had three horses shot from under him that day. But once the Rebels reached the slope, they were safe. The Union earthworks were about four feet thick at the top, so the cannon could not be depressed enough to fire on the Confederates at the foot of the slope, nor could riflemen fire on them without climbing up on top of the parapet and thus exposing themselves to the Southern sharpshooters.

The gunboat kept up a supporting fire all morning but with little effect, and at about 1 p.m. it ran out of ammunition. Forrest, too, was suffering from an ammunition shortage, but at about 3 p.m. his wagons arrived with more and, confident that he could take the fort by assault "with less loss than to have withdrawn under fire,"[1] he sent in his usual demand for surrender. It included the customary threat: "Should my demand be refused, I cannot be responsible for the fate of your command."[2]

Bradford asked for an hour to consult with his officers and with the captain of the *New Era.* Forrest, noticing three more steamboats ascending the river, feared the Yankee was stalling in hope of receiving help from that quarter, but allowed him twenty minutes. The Federals evidently did hope for help, or else thought that the Confederates were trying to bluff them as they had the defenders of Union City. At any rate, the officer delivering Bradford's reply expressed doubt about Forrest's presence. The answer Bradford had sent said, "Negotiations will not attain the desired object." Forrest identified himself to the officers who brought the note and told them he demanded "an answer in plain, unmistakable English: Will he fight or surrender?" The answer Bradford sent back said simply, "I will not surrender."[3] Forrest turned to his bugler and ordered him to sound the charge.

While the sharpshooters laid down a covering fire, the dismounted cavalry ran forward in two waves, into the muddy ditch. The second wave, with the help of the first, climbed up to a narrow ledge between the top of the ditch and the bottom of the parapet and then turned to pull up the men of the first wave. "So far as safety was concerned," one of Forrest's captains wrote, "We were as well fortified as they were; the only difference was that they were on one side and we were on the other of the same fortification."[4] At a signal, the sharpshooters stopped firing, and the troops on the ledge swarmed up and over the parapet, firing their weapons into the defenders and reportedly screaming racial epithets. The Federal troops and the women and children were driven down the bluff to the river where, unaware that the *New Era* had expended all its ammunition, they evidently expected the gunboat to either protect them or take them on board. Many even went out into the river, but as they descended the bank an enfilading fire was poured into them by Confederates who had worked their way around to the flank. Some of the defenders tried to surrender, but the Rebels reportedly refused to accept prisoners and were heard to shout, "No quarter!"[5] and "Kill them, God damn them; it is General Forrest's orders."[6]

"In less than twenty minutes from the time the bugles sounded the charge," Forrest reported, "firing had ceased, and the work was done. One of the Parrott guns was turned on the gun-boat. She steamed off without replying."[7] A Confederate sergeant later wrote home about how "the poor, deluded negroes would run up to our men, fall upon their knees and with uplifted hands scream for mercy, but were ordered to their feet and then shot down."[8] Forrest reported that "the river was dyed with the blood of the slaughtered for two hundred yards. The approximate loss was upward of five hundred killed, but few of the officers escaping. My loss was about twenty killed. It is hoped that these facts will demonstrate to the Northern people that negro soldiers cannot cope with Southerners."[9] Of the 295 whites in the fort, 168 (about 60 percent) were taken alive, despite the well-known hatred of the Confederates for their "Tory" neighbors. But of the 262 black soldiers in the garrison, only 58, about 20 percent, were taken prisoner. The rest were either dead or too badly wounded to be moved. It has been claimed ever since that Forrest, a post-war leader of the Ku Klux Klan, not only did not order a massacre—as the battle was quickly labeled by the North—but did all he could to stop it.

But he had threatened any Federal garrison that defied him with just such an outcome too many times for his protestations of innocence to deserve much credence. Confederate refusal to treat former slaves, or any blacks, as prisoners of war was also well known.

Forrest claimed that he had made several attempts to contact the Federal boats in order to turn over the unmovable wounded to them, but could not induce them to communicate with him. Perhaps this was a result of his well-deserved reputation for trickery. At any rate, he also turned his attention to enforcing the Confederate draft laws in western Tennessee. He sent out agents with orders to "sweep the country, bringing in every man between the ages of eighteen and forty-five. Take no excuse, neither allow conscripts to go home for clothes or anything else; their friends can send them."[10]

That same day, down on the Red River, Green's Texas cavalry and three cannon posted in ambush on a bluff near Blair's Landing attacked Admiral Porter's gunboats and transports as they were descending the river to rejoin Banks. In the brisk fight that followed, the Confederates were driven off and Green was killed. The next day, 13 April, Porter and T. Kilby Smith returned to Grand Ecore, although it would be two more days before all the gunboats arrived. The water level, which had never risen very far, was now falling again and the vessels were heading down to Alexandria as fast as they could cross the bar.

Northward on the Little Missouri that April thirteenth, another brigade of Confederate cavalry arrived to help block Steele's advance. This was Colonel Tandy Walker's brigade of Choctaws from the Indian Territory (Oklahoma), old enemies of Thayer's Frontier Division. But Steele, after three days of skirmishing to give the impression that he would advance at any moment, instead slipped off eastward toward Price's former headquarters town of Camden, Arkansas, forty miles away. When Price discovered where Steele was heading he sent Marmaduke's division of Missouri cavalry to get in front of him and block his progress, while Fagan's and Maxey's divisions were to overtake him from the rear.

Also on 13 April, General Abraham Buford, one of Forrest's brigade commanders, unsuccessfully tried to bluff the Union commander of the garrison of Columbus, Kentucky on the Mississippi River, with a demand that concluded with the threat: "Should I be compelled to take the place, no quarter will be shown to the negro troops whatever; the white troops will be treated as prisoners of war."[11] The next day, Buford's brigade rode into Paducah again. As before, the defenders fell back into their fortifications, and under a flag of truce Buford sent in the customary threat, allowing the Union commander one hour to arrange for the removal of noncombatants before he attacked. The Federal commander, Colonel Stephen G. Hicks of the 40th Illinois Infantry, accepted the hour of grace and then added, "After that time come ahead; I am ready for you."[12] Without waiting for the hour to expire, the Rebels withdrew after gathering up some horses the Paducah newspapers had been boasting that they missed on their previous visit.

By the time Forrest himself rode into Jackson, Tennessee that day, he had received an order from Lieutenant General Leonidas Polk, commander of the Confederate Department of Alabama, Mississippi and East Louisiana. Polk directed him to return immediately to Mississippi, where his forces would be combined with those of Major General Stephen D. Lee, Polk's chief of cavalry, in order to meet a large Federal raid which was expected to be launched soon from Decatur, Alabama. Forrest obeyed the order, although he replied that, "No such raid will be made from Decatur or any point west of there." As it turned out, he was absolutely right. He wrote to President Jefferson Davis the next day that he felt the proper use of his and S. D. Lee's cavalry would be a move into middle Tennessee and Kentucky, "which could create a diversion of the enemy's forces and enable us to break up his plans."[13] In other words, he wanted to attack Sherman's supply line which stretched all the way from Louisville through Nashville to Chattanooga.

The fourteenth of April was also the day that Longstreet arrived at Charlottesville from Bristol. He had not received the order to return to Virginia until the eleventh, and the railroad was only able to transport 1500 of his men per day. Longstreet had hoped that his men would be transported from Charlottesville to Petersburg, in his old stomping grounds of southeast Virginia, but instead they were marched northeast to Gordonsville, where the strategic Orange & Alexandria Railroad from the Shenandoah Valley met the Virginia Central, which ran southeastward to Richmond. There his men went into camp somewhat southwest of Lee's army. Observers noticed a significant decline in the numbers and equipment of the 1st Corps over the seven months since its departure for the West.

Out on the Red River the next day, the fifteenth, the last of Porter's gunboats reached Grand Ecore, but eight miles downriver that same day the largest of the ironclads, the *Eastport*, hit a mine (known in those days as a torpedo) and sank in the shallow water. And 125 miles to the north, Steele's column pushed through Marmaduke's cavalry to reach Camden. It was on the next day, the sixteenth, that Kirby Smith headed north from

Shreveport to engage Steele. He took with him the two divisions of
infantry that Churchill had recently brought down from Arkansas plus
Walker's division of Texas infantry. On the seventeenth, Steele was writing
to Halleck to explain why he had turned aside from the direct route to
Shreveport. "Our supplies were nearly exhausted," he said, "and so was
the country. We were obliged to forage from five to fifteen miles on either
side of the road to keep our stock alive."[14]

Grant's plans for West Virginia were also going wrong that day. Ord
and Sigel had rubbed each other the wrong way. Sigel resented having a
teacher's pet imposed on him, taking away his troops for an expedition in
his own department and leaving him almost completely out of the picture.
Was he the department commander or not? "All dispositions were made in
such a manner as if I did not exist at all," he complained.[15] Ord, never
particularly known for tact, was perhaps too inclined to exploit his special
commission from Grant and too disinclined to afford Sigel any way to
save face in an awkward situation. He complained that the troops Sigel
had sent him were 1,500 short of the 8,000 Grant had ordered. When
Sigel was then asked to prepare to meet Ord with supplies at some point
in the campaign he replied "in so many words, I don't think I shall do
it."[16] Ord threw up his hands and asked Grant to relieve him of command
of the West Virginia expedition. His wish was reluctantly granted on 17
April, and Lieutenant Colonel Orville Babcock of Grant's staff arrived at
Sigel's headquarters that day to consult on a new plan. They decided to
use the forces Ord would have led to beef up Crook's column, which was
to raid the East Tennessee & Virginia Railroad, and Sigel's own column
which would push up the Shenandoah.

That same seventeenth of April, a new Federal commander took over
the District of West Tennessee, the area that had been receiving so much
attention from Forrest lately. Major General Cadwallader Colden Washburn replaced Major General Stephen A. Hurlbut. This Washburn was,
despite the difference in spelling, a younger brother of Congressman
Elihu B. Washburne, Grant's political sponsor. He too had served in
Congress, and then he had raised and taken command of the 2nd Wisconsin Cavalry. His early war service had been in the Missouri-Arkansas area
until, having risen to major general, he had been given command of a
provisional corps of reinforcements at Vicksburg, where Sherman had
seen him in action.

Hurlbut had also been a Republican politician in pre-war Illinois, one
to whom Lincoln had given a star. Along with Sherman, he had commanded a division at Shiloh and soon had been given his second star.

During the Vicksburg campaign he had, again like Sherman, commanded a corps, the 16th. His corps, however, had not taken the field as a unit. Instead it had served as the garrison force for west Tennessee while the rest of the Army of the Tennessee campaigned down the Mississippi. Some of its troops had been sent off to various other tasks—Mowers two divisions with A. J. Smith were in the 16th Corps, as were Dodge's two divisions which were then preparing to take part in Sherman's plunge into northern Georgia—but Hurlbut himself had remained at Memphis most of the time. He seemed to have found his niche as a rear area occupation commander. However, Forrest had turned Hurlbut's particular part of the Union rear into another front and Sherman, evidently unhappy with the way his old comrade was letting the Rebels run loose in his district, appointed Washburn to take his place. It remained to be seen whether this would make much of a difference.

Also on 17 April, Grant was making changes in which Forrest's recent actions might have played some part. On that date the Federal general-in-chief ordered the indefinite suspension of the exchange of prisoners with the Confederate army. There were at least three reasons behind this move: the ill-treatment of black prisoners by the South, the improper return to duty of Rebels previously captured, and grand strategy. When Benjamin Butler had been appointed to command the Federal Department of Virginia and North Carolina in December of 1863 he had also been named a special agent for prisoner exchange. Despite the fact that the Confederate government officially considered Butler an outlaw because he was among the Union generals who recruited former slaves, the Rebel commissioner, Judge Robert Ould, had met with him to work out an acceptable procedure. Ould did agree to treat all free negroes as prisoners of war. The 54th Massachussetts, for instance, then serving in South Carolina, was made up mostly of free blacks from the northern states. But the ultimate stumbling block was the treatment of former slaves.

The issue went to the heart of the differences between the North and the South. So far as the Confederate States were concerned slaves, including those who had run away and joined the Union army, were not men but movable property, like horses. They must be returned to their lawful owners if possible. In recent months a number of Confederate generals had gotten into trouble by proposing that slaves be recruited into the Confederate army, in order to overcome its disadvantage in manpower. As General Howell Cobb, the former governor of Georgia who had served as chairman of the Confederate constitutional convention had commented, "If slaves will make good soldiers, our whole theory of slavery is wrong."[17]

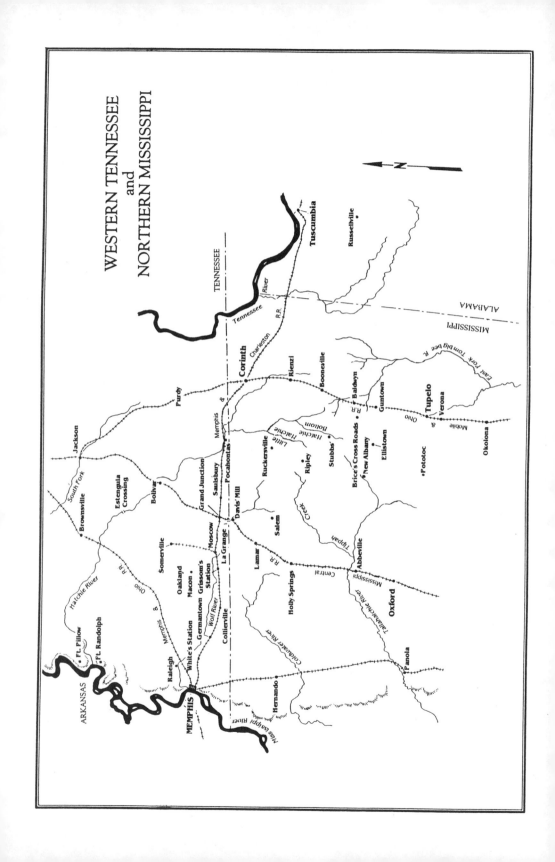

Confederate legal thought saw officers like Butler as instigators of servile insurrection, always the South's greatest dread. "The Federal Government," proclaimed an editorial in the *Richmond Enquirer*, "has planted itself insolently upon the demand that our runaway negroes, when taken in arms against their masters, shall be treated as prisoners of war, and shall be exchanged against white men. Confederates have borne and forborne much to mitigate the atrocities of war; but this is a thing which the temper of the country cannot endure."[18]

To the United States, however, black soldiers were men and entitled to the same considerations as prisoners of war as were white soldiers (although they did not receive equal pay). The Federal government could not condone mistreatment of its soldiers and expect to recruit any more blacks. "The law of nations knows no distinction of color," said the Federal War Department's instructions to its armies in the field, "and if any enemy of the United States should enslave and sell any captured persons of their Army, it would be a case for the severest retaliation, if not redressed upon complaint." As for the form of retaliation, the instructions proclaimed: "The United States cannot retaliate by enslavement; therefore death must be the retaliation for this crime against the law of nations."[19] In other words, the North was threatening to kill Southern prisoners in retaliation for the enslavement of Union prisoners.

The arrangements for exchange had already broken down because the Federal government suspected that thousands of prisoners, captured when Vicksburg and Port Hudson surrendered and then released on parole—their signed promise not to fight again until properly exchanged—had been returned to the ranks without such exchange. The Confederates, of course, denied any such impropriety. Now the issue of former slaves had brought negotiations to a deadlock.

Anyway, Grant had also decided that there was a strategic reason for discontinuing the exchange of prisoners. The North had a much larger white population than the South, and could also recruit the black population of both sections. Union soldiers captured by the Rebels could be replaced by new troops, but the Confederate army already had every man that its recruiters and conscription agents could reach. "Every man we hold," Grant said, "when released on parole or otherwise, becomes an active soldier against us. . . . If a system of exchange liberates all prisoners taken, we will have to fight on until the whole South is exterminated."[20]

Down in Georgia just then, the same General Cobb who doubted that slaves could make good soldiers was already having a hard time finding food for all the prisoners being sent to the new camp at Andersonville. Grant's resolve would cost those Union soldiers who were or who would become prisoners, as well as the Confederates in Federal hands, extreme suffering, but it would contribute to the shortening of the war and to the ultimate victory. Every Federal soldier in a Southern prison camp was another mouth for the Confederate government to feed when it had all it could do to keep its own soldiers fed. And every Union prisoner in the South represented one Rebel in the North kept out of the Confederate ranks. Thinner Southern ranks meant a shorter war, and ultimately every month or week that the war could be shortened meant thousands of Federal and Confederate soldiers who would not be killed or maimed by battle or disease.

---

1. Anonymous, "The Capture of Fort Pillow," in *Battles and Leaders*, 4:419.
2. Foote, *The Civil War*, 3:109.
3. Anonymous, "The Capture of Fort Pillow," 419.
4. Foote, *The Civil War*, 3:109.
5. Ibid., 110.
6. Dudley Taylor Cornish, *The Sable Arm* (Lawrence, Kansas, 1957) 175.
7. Anonymous, "The Capture of Fort Pillow," 419.
8. Foote, *The Civil War*, 3:112.
9. Grant, *Memoirs*, 2:138.
10. Foote, *The Civil War*, 3:112.
11. Starr, *Union Cavalry*, 3:409, n. 49.
12. Ibid., 408–409.
13. Foote, *The Civil War*, 112.
14. Ibid.
15. Davis, *The Battle of New Market*, p. 21.
16. Ibid.
17. Foote, *The Civil War*, 2:955.
18. Cornish, *The Sable Arm*, 170.
19. Ibid., 166.
20. Faust, ed., *Historical Times Encyclopedia*, 604.

CHAPTER EIGHT

Iron Ships and Wooden Men

17–20 April 1864

On 17 April 1864, Confederate brigadier general R. F. Hoke with three brigades of veteran infantry, began to invest the Union fortifications at Plymouth, North Carolina on the south bank of the Roanoke River, close to where it empties into Albemarle Sound. Farther up the river that same day an ironclad gunboat christened the CSS *Albemarle*, was launched from the riverside cornfield where it had been built. She promptly set off downstream on her maiden voyage, with fitters still working on her armor and machinery, to assist Hoke's land forces. Wooden Federal gunboats were not going to disrupt this operation, as they had previous ones, if she could help it.

Both the Federal and Confederate governments recognized Richmond, the Southern capital, as marking the approximate boundary between two different theaters of operations, one to the north where Lee and Meade confronted each other, the other to the south in tidewater Virginia and the North Carolina sounds. The James River and the smaller Elizabeth River flow together into a broad tidal estuary known as Hampton Roads. There, at the tip of the historic peninsula between the York and the James, sat Fortress Monroe, a strongpoint built before the war to control access to these waters and the lands they drained. Federal troops had held this post since before the war, and as a foothold on the lower peninsula this force was soon expanded into the Department of Virginia.

It was in Hampton Roads that the first battle of ironclad ships had occurred, for on the south side of the roads lay Norfolk, Virginia, site of one of the pre-war navy's largest bases. Secessionists had seized the base in the early days of the conflict, although much of it had been burned before the Southerners could take possession. One victim of the flames had been a steam-and-sail-powered man-of-war known as the *USS Merrimack*. It had burned to the water line, but the Confederates had raised what was left of it and used its hull and balky engines as the basis of a radically designed ironclad gunboat and ram, renamed the *CSS Virginia*. The day after it had sortied from the Elizabeth River to terrorize the wooden ships of the Union blockading squadron it had encountered the even more innovative *USS Monitor*, the first ship to use a revolving gun turret. Neither ship had been able to sink the other, but the *Monitor* had prevented the *Merrimack/Virginia* from further depredations against the wooden fleet while the Rebel ship had discouraged any Union advance up the James toward Richmond.

Less than a month later, McClellan had landed the Army of the Potomac at Fortress Monroe to begin his ill-fated Peninsula campaign. When the Confederates had finally evacuated Yorktown they had also marched out of Norfolk. Lincoln himself, on a visit to the field at the time, had directed the occupation of the latter city by forces of the Department of Virginia, even as McClellan had been moving up the Peninsula toward Richmond. With its base about to be occupied by the Federals and the water level in the James too low to allow the *Virginia* to go upstream to Richmond, the Confederate crew had destroyed their powerful ironclad to prevent it from falling into Union hands.

When the Army of the Potomac had returned to northern Virginia, one division had been left behind to hold the eastern end of the Peninsula, including Yorktown, and had eventually been added to the Department of Virginia. Over the years the Union foothold on both sides of the lower James had been gradually strengthened and expanded. In the spring of 1863 Longstreet had been sent to the area to gather supplies for the Confederacy and to see what he could do about recovering some of the lost ground. He had conducted a half-hearted siege of Suffolk, but to no avail. It had only caused him to miss out on the battle of Chancellorsville. During the Gettysburg campaign Union forces had made a feeble demonstration up the Peninsula toward Richmond, but nothing much had come of that either.

South of Norfolk, along the coast of North Carolina, a series of low, narrow islands separates the Atlantic Ocean from Albemarle and Pamlico sounds. Benjamin Butler's capture of Fort Hatteras in 1861 had opened a way into this internal coast for Union forces, and Ambrose Burnside had led an expedition in early 1862 that had captured Roanoke Island, New Berne, Plymouth, Beaufort and Washington, North Carolina. But when McClellan had retreated from before Richmond, Burnside had been sent with most of his forces, newly designated the 9th Corps, first to Fortress Monroe and then to Fredericksburg. From there they had reinforced Pope during the Second Bull Run campaign and then had been attached to the Army of the Potomac through Burnside's defeat at Fredericksburg. Then both Burnside and the 9th Corps had been sent west. Meanwhile, the Union lodgements on the coast of North Carolina had settled into a quiet routine of occupation. The Federal forces had been too small to make further conquests, and the Confederates had usually been too busy elsewhere to spare forces to recapture the positions lost.

In December of 1862 the Federals had advanced from New Berne for a raid on the Wilmington and Weldon Railroad at Goldsboro. In March of 1863 Longstreet, during his brief sojourn in command south of the James, had sent Major General D. H. Hill to retake New Berne, but he had been repulsed by Union gunboats sent up the Neuse River from Pamlico Sound. Shortly thereafter Hill had besieged Washington, North Carolina while Longstreet had been giving the same treatment to Suffolk, Virginia, but neither place had been recaptured. Late in January 1864 Major General George E. Pickett, Confederate commander in southern Virginia and North Carolina where he and his decimated division had been sent after Gettysburg, had received orders from Lee to make another try at recapturing New Berne.

With 13,000 troops divided into three unequal forces commanded by Brigadier General Seth Barton, Colonel James Dearing and Brigadier General Robert Hoke, Pickett had planned a three-prong attack. Barton had been sent across the Trent River to attack New Berne from the southwest; Dearing, with a smaller force, had advanced from the northeast to capture Fort Anderson directly across the Neuse from New Berne; and Pickett, with Hoke's division-sized force, had moved against the town from the northwest. The Confederate navy had cooperated by sending a force of fourteen cutters down the Neuse to attack the Union gunboats. Despite a promising beginning, including the capture and scuttling of the Federal gunboat *Underwriter*, the plan had failed when both Barton and Dearing found the enemy's defenses too strong to attack. About all the Rebels had gotten out of the campaign were 22 former Confederates Hoke had captured wearing Federal uniforms. After a drumhead court martial they had all been hanged as deserters.

Then a new plan was devised by General Bragg. Long before his defeat by Grant at Chattanooga, Braxton Bragg had lost the support of most of his subordinates. He had a tendency to throw away the fruits of victory and was, as Grant phrased it, "naturally disputatious." In his memoirs, Grant told an anecdote from Bragg's days in the pre-war army that illustrates Bragg's personality: "On one occasion, when stationed at a post of several companies commanded by a field officer, he was himself commanding one of the companies and at the same time acting as post quartermaster and commissary. As commander of the company he made a requisition upon the quartermaster—himself—for something he wanted. As quartermaster he declined to fill the requisition, and endorsed on the back of it his reasons for so doing. As company commander he responded to this, urging that his requisition called for nothing but what he was entitled to, and that it was the duty of the quartermaster to fill it. As quartermaster he still persisted that he was right. In this condition of affairs Bragg referred the whole matter to the commanding officer of the post. The latter, when he saw the nature of the matter referred, exclaimed, 'My God, Mr. Bragg, you have quarrelled with every officer in the army, and now you are quarrelling with yourself!' "[1]

There was one individual, however, with whom Bragg got along quite well, and that was Jefferson Davis, president of the Confederacy. Davis was an 1828 graduate of West Point who had served as colonel of a Mississippi volunteer infantry regiment during the Mexican War and had been secretary of war in the Franklin Pierce administration. Consequently, he considered himself something of a military genius. In fact, he had accepted the presidency of the Confederacy very reluctantly because he had hoped to become a great general instead. He was also "prideful, stubborn, doctrinaire, and often narrow-minded," and "tended toward cronyism in his appointments."[2] He was quick to take offense at any hint of disloyalty or disagreement with his own opinions (he seemed to equate the two), and equally inclined to reward those who agreed with him or who showed other signs of loyalty. He continually quarreled with his vice president, the Confederate Congress, governors of the Southern states, and almost all of his leading generals, especially Joseph E. Johnston and P. G. T. Beauregard. The two major exceptions were R. E. Lee, who was always properly deferential toward his president, and Braxton Bragg. Perhaps he saw in Bragg a kindred spirit of hair-splitting correctitude, or maybe he just took pleasure in befriending the man who was famous for quarrelling with everyone else.

At any rate, Davis had sustained Bragg in command of the Army of Tennessee long after everyone else thought he would have to go. And even when he finally did remove Bragg, after Chattanooga, he did not send him into military oblivion. Instead Davis kicked him upstairs as his personal military advisor, a job once held by Lee and analogous to that held by Halleck in the Union army. One of the first projects Bragg undertook after settling into his new job was to devise a plan for redeeming Southern fortunes in his native North Carolina. Fortunately for him, help was at hand from the miniscule Confederate States Navy.

The *CSS Albemarle* followed the general layout of the *Merrimack/Virginia*. That is, from the water line up she consisted of a sloping ironclad casemate that protected the gun deck. She was smaller than her famous predecessor and carried only two guns, one rifled cannon of 6.4-inch bore at each end of the casement, fore and aft. Each was on a pivot so that it could fire out of any of three gunports, starboard, port, or abeam. And she was sheathed in two layers of two-inch iron. The Roanoke River had many twists and turns up where the *Albemarle* was launched. That fact had served to keep the Union gunboats from interfering with her construction but together with the speed of the current, it also forced the ironclad to come down the river stern first, dragging a heavy chain behind her to aid in negotiating sharp turns.

On the following day, 18 April, General R. E. Lee was ordering his units along the Rapidan to send all excess baggage to the rear and prepare for action. Out on the Red River Nathaniel Banks received instructions that Grant had written weeks before, urging that he "start at the earliest possible moment" his campaign against Mobile.[3] The next day Banks ordered his forces to retreat to Alexandria.

Up in Arkansas on 18 April a train of 198 heavily loaded wagons sent out by Steele with an escort of about 1,000 men of infantry and cavalry and a battery of four guns, was bringing in supplies that had been rounded up—or plundered, as the Rebels saw it—from the surrounding area. The Federals were fifteen miles out of Camden at a place with the ominous name of Poison Springs when they were attacked by over 3,000 Confederate cavalry under Generals Marmaduke and Maxey. The four guns and 170 of the wagons were captured, and the rest burned.

Among the Union soldiers was the 1st Kansas Colored Regiment from Thayer's Frontier Division, and among the Confederates were Tandy Walker's Choctaws, who were delighted at this opportunity to take revenge on a unit that had helped plunder their own area of the frontier in the past. Out of the 182 black casualties at Poison Springs 117 were killed. The commander of the Kansas regiment claimed this high percentage was due to the "murder on the spot" of a number of his wounded men by the Choctaws. Steele learned that afternoon of the attack at Poison Springs, but then a scout came in from the Red River with the even worse news of Banks' defeat at Sabine Cross Roads and retreat to Grand Ecore. Of course he did not know that Banks was already retreating further down river, but he could see that the defeat made it likely that Kirby Smith would now send even more forces against his own hungry troops at Camden.

Also on 18 April, another of the Confederacy's full generals was being given a new job. Pierre Gustave Toutant Beauregard was reassigned from the Department of South Carolina, Georgia, and Florida to the Department of North Carolina and Cape Fear—which he immediately renamed the Department of North Carolina and Southern Virginia—making him the direct opponent of Ben Butler. Beauregard, a Louisianian of French descent, had been the South's first military hero. He had commanded the Rebel forces that had started the war by firing on the small Federal garrison of Fort Sumter in Charleston harbor. That bloodless victory and his success at Bull Run had earned him an overblown reputation and promotion to full general, placing him in the company of officers like Lee and the two Johnstons who had outranked him considerably in the old army.

He had graduated from West Point in 1838, ranked second in a class of 45, and had served with Lee as an engineer on Winfield Scott's staff in the Mexican War. After Sumter he had commanded the South's main army in northern Virginia until he had been reinforced by Joseph E. Johnston just in time for the first battle of Bull Run. He had then been sent to help Albert Sidney Johnston in the West and had succeeded to the command of the western army when that Johnston was killed at Shiloh. After evacuating Corinth, Mississippi in the face of Halleck's ponderous advance, he had reported himself sick and had lost his command to Bragg. He had eventually been returned to Charleston, where he was still immensely popular, to defend that town and the southern Atlantic coast in general. He had successfully prevented all of Union General Quincy Gillmore's attempts, aided by the U.S. Navy, to enter Charleston harbor, and now he was being called on to defend the area south of Richmond from the attack the Confederates presumed that Butler, and possibly Burnside, was preparing.

Beauregard, like Davis, had an exalted opinion of his own military genius which, along with his Gallic temper and acerbic tongue, kept him in constant conflict with his president. Not surprisingly, he did not get along with Bragg, either. Due to his early rise, he had been promoted about one rank above his true abilities. Nevertheless, Davis' choices for the command were limited. The present commander, Pickett, with at least some of his troops, was about to be returned to Lee's army, while most of the troops in Beauregard's old department were about to be shifted to

North Carolina, and a senior general would be needed there. All the other full generals except Bragg already held critical positions and it was too early to return Bragg to the field. Besides, Beauregard had seniority over Bragg as a full general, and Davis was a stickler for such military niceties, even when they worked against one of his favorites. But before Beauregard could take command of his new department, dramatic events had already begun happening there.

Early that morning, the eighteenth, Hoke's infantry had tried to storm one of the earthworks guarding Plymouth but had been repulsed. In the afternoon Rebel artillery opened fire on the town and its breastworks, and then the fight became general. But the two largest of the four Federal wooden gunboats in the Roanoke, the *Miami* and the *Southfield,* opened a crossfire on the Confederates that repulsed three attacks and caused them to fall back out of range about 9 p.m.

That night, ten hours behind schedule due to stops for repairs, the *CSS Albemarle* came to anchor about three miles above Plymouth and a mile or so upriver from a Union battery on a bluff. These guns guarded an area of the river where torpedoes, sunken vessels, piles, and other obstructions had been placed by the Federals when they learned that a Rebel ironclad was being constructed upriver. The ship's builder, Mr. Gilbert Elliott, who was on board as a volunteer aide to Captain J. W. Cooke, decided to have a look at what the ironclad was up against. He set off in the dark in a small boat with a pilot and two seamen. They took along a pole to make soundings and discovered that, due to spring freshets of record proportions, ten feet of water covered the obstructions. The *Albemarle,* Elliott knew, drew nine feet of water. "With muffled oars, and almost afraid to breathe, we made our way back up the river, hugging the northern bank," Elliott recorded, "and reached the ram about 1 o'clock, reporting to Captain Cooke that it was practical to pass the obstructions provided the boat was kept in the middle of the stream."[4]

Meanwhile Cooke had turned the ironclad around and cleared her for action. He had learned that the army had been attacking Plymouth all day but had withdrawn, evidently because of the Union gunboats. So as soon as he heard Elliott's report, Cooke aroused his men, gave the order to get up steam, slipped the cables, and started off downriver. The obstructions were safely passed at about 4 o'clock on the morning of the nineteenth, despite a few shots from the battery on the bluff. "Protected by the iron-clad shield," Elliott wrote, "to those on board the noise made by the shot and shell as they struck the boat sounded no louder than pebbles thrown against an empty barrel."[5]

Not long afterwards the Confederates spotted two Federal steamers coming up the river toward them in the dark. These were the Miami and the *Southfield,* both of a class of fast, sidewheel steamboats known as double-enders because they had rudders both fore and aft so they could get about in narrow waters without turning around. Commander C. W. Flusser, USN, was in command of these two boats. He had lashed them loosely together with long spars and chains in hopes of trapping the Rebel ironclad between them so that she could not be used as a ram, while the Federals would toss explosives down her smokestack. However, Cooke ran the *Albemarle* close to the southern shore and then, without firing a shot, turned suddenly toward the Union vessels.

Both wooden gunboats opened fire as soon as their guns could be brought to bear. They fired exploding shells from 9-inch smoothbore guns and 100-pounder rifles but the only damage done to the ironclad was to put dents in her casemate. With extra momentum from the current, the *Albemarle,* still disdaining to return fire, struck the *Miami* a glancing blow and then rammed the side of the *Southfield* near her boilers. The wooden boat sank rapidly, taking part of her crew with her. For a minute it looked like she would also take both the *Miami* and the ironclad down, but the Union boat managed to cut her connections with the *Southfield* in time. However, the *Albemarle's* bow had run so far into her victim's hull that it was pressed low enough for water to pour into her gun ports in great volume. But when the *Southfield* hit the bottom of the river she turned over on her side. This released the ram's bow and allowed her to return to an even keel.

Meanwhile the *Miami* continued to fire at the ironclad from point-blank range. Commander Flusser was killed by flying pieces of one of his own shells that rebounded from the *Albemarle,* and several members of the Federal gun crews were wounded also. Next, Union sailors tried to board the ram but were fought off by Confederates crowded onto the top of the casemate, firing muskets that were loaded and passed up to them by fellow crewmen below. Finding that she could neither board the ironclad nor damage it with gunfire, the *Miami* finally moved off. She was too fast for the *Albemarle* to catch and ram, but a couple of parting shots from the Rebels' guns helped speed the wooden boat on her way.

The ironclad, which had suffered only one casualty, a seaman hit by a pistol ball, could now turn the tables on the Union soldiers at Plymouth, who until now had received only help from the river, not hindrance. After patching up his riddled smoke stack, Captain Cooke steamed past Plymouth that afternoon and in conjunction with Hoke's artillery began a bombardment that continued until well after dark. "This terrible fire had to be endured without reply," reported the Federal commander, "as no man could live at the guns."[6]

The next day, while the *Albemarle* poured shot and shell into the

Union fortifications, General Hoke's troops attacked again. The Confederate losses were high. According to Elliott, just one of the three brigades lost 500 men killed and wounded in a charge against the breastworks covering the eastern end of the town. But despite the stiff resistance of the Federals the works were carried, and when it became obvious that further resistance was useless, the Union commander surrendered. Hoke became the proud captor of 2,834 soldiers, 30 guns and a great quantity of supplies. He was promoted to major general as of that date, 20 April 1864.

"The ram will probably come down to Roanoke Island, Washington, and New Bern," Major General John J. Peck, the Federal district commander, informed Ben Butler, the commander of the Department of Virginia and North Carolina, that day. "Unless we are immediately and heavily reinforced, both by the army and navy, North Carolina is inevitably lost."[7]

---

1. Grant, *Memoirs*, 2:86–87.
2. Faust ed., *Historical Times Illustrated Encyclopedia*, 208.
3. Foote, *The Civil War*, 3:55.
4. Gilbert Elliott, "The First Battle of the Confederate Ram 'Albemarle,'" in *Battles and Leaders*, 4:626–627.
5. Ibid.
6. Foote, *The Civil War*, 3:115.
7. Ibid., 116.

CHAPTER NINE

"Going Out To Fight For the Flag"

21–29 April 1864

"I am sorry to see the people settling down to the belief that this year will end the war," Sherman wrote on 21 April in a letter to Phil Ewing, his foster brother. "That is impossible," he said. "Full 300,000 of the bravest men of this world must be killed or banished in the South before they will think of peace, and in killing them we must lose an equal or greater number, for we must be the attacking party. Still we as a nation have no alternative or choice. It must be done whether we want or not."[1] He had a good point. The war was far from being won that spring of 1864, and many good men would yet go under the sod before it was over. The real question was whether the North was willing to pay the butcher's bill. Sherman was correct that the Federals had to be the attacking party. The Confederate government still controlled most of the South, and if the United States wanted it back, it would have to take it by force. He was also right that the attacking party would have the higher losses. That had already been the case in wars before the advent of the rifled musket which, with its far greater range and accuracy than the smoothbore, had further enhanced the advantage of the defense. The growing tendency of both sides to entrench every position they expected to stay in for very long was also increasing the defense's edge.

Out on the Red River, where Admiral Porter's fleet was struggling to get back downstream, the outcome was looking very doubtful. The largest ironclad in his fleet, the *USS Eastport,* had been started by the Confederates, captured by the Federals at Cerro Gordo, Tennessee and completed by them at Mound City, Illinois. The expedition up the Red was her first but, as mentioned earlier, she had struck a torpedo eight miles below Grand Ecore on 15 April and had sunk in the shallow river. However her captain, Lieutenant Commander S. L. Phelps, was determined to save her. After six days of strenuous effort, he finally succeeded in sealing off the leak and, with two steampump boats which Porter brought to his assistance, she was refloated on 21 April. But after proceeding about forty miles downriver, she grounded again.

That same day a dispatch that had been sent down the Red and up the Mississippi to Cairo, Illinois, and from there by telegraph, reached Grant at Culpeper, Virginia. It was thus that the bad news of Banks' defeat had finally come to the general-in-chief. The next day, Grant telegraphed Halleck to say that he thought Banks ought to be removed from command of the Department of the Gulf. Lincoln, however, was not eager to dismiss such a politically important general in an election year. He had Halleck reply that the president wanted to wait for more details on the Red River disaster before taking any action.

Somewhat farther south, P. G. T. Beauregard was also busy on the telegraph that 22nd of April. He had reached Weldon, North Carolina that day to take over his new department but had received no instructions from Richmond. He fired off telegrams to Bragg requesting a map of his new command, a definition of the limits of his department, and an estimate of the forces at his disposal. He officially assumed command the next day. Beauregard's area of responsibility included all of North Carolina east of the mountains and that part of Virginia south of the James and Appomattox rivers. Pickett, the former commander, had been reduced to a district commander within Beauregard's department, holding with only a few men both Petersburg, Virginia and the line of the Blackwater River between that city and the Federals at Suffolk. A single regiment was located at Weldon. Two more were guarding the important port of Wilmington. Two hundred men guarded the vital railroad at Goldsboro. Three regiments of infantry held the just-reconquered

Plymouth, and two more were guarding prisoners at Tarboro. There was a force the size of a small division menacing New Berne, and Hoke's three brigades were now moving toward Washington, North Carolina.

It was on the 23rd of April that General Corse returned to Sherman after delivering the latter's message to Banks. Sherman realized from what Corse told him that A. J. Smith and his troops were not going to be available for the start of the campaign in Georgia, let alone for chasing Forrest on their way east. That same day Sherman was reporting to the secretary of war about the capture of Fort Pillow. "I know well the animus of the Southern soldiery," he said, "and the truth is they cannot be restrained. The effect will be of course to make the negroes desperate, and when in turn they commit horrid acts of retaliation we will be relieved of the responsibility. Thus far negroes have been comparatively well behaved, and have not committed the horrid excesses and barbarities which the Southern papers so much dreaded." He went on to suggest that, instead of setting guidelines on how to respond to Rebel atrocities, they should "let the soldiers affected make their rules." He explained that, "the Southern army, which is the Southern people, cares no more for our clamor than the idle wind, but they will heed the slaughter that will follow as the natural consequences of their own inhuman acts."[2]

Out in Louisiana, Taylor was pursuing Banks' entire army down the Red with only Polignac's 2,000 Louisiana infantry and the Texas cavalry division, which had been augmented by a fresh brigade and was now commanded by John A. Wharton, in place of the late Thomas Green. But he was not content to merely follow the Union column. Twice Banks' route crossed the Cane River, a tributary of the Red. At the second crossing, 36 miles below Natchitoches, Hamilton Bee, one of Wharton's brigade commanders, whose late brother had given Stonewall Jackson his nom de guerre, had taken up a position to block the road while the rest of the army harrassed the rear of the Federal column. But Brigadier General Richard Arnold, who had replaced A. L. Lee as Banks' chief of cavalry, discovered the ambush and scouted out alternate crossings of the Cane. On 23 April Emory, now commanding the 19th Corps in the absence of the wounded Franklin, sent two brigades of his own corps, supported by Cameron's small division of the 13th Corps, to ford the Cane three miles upstream and turn Bee's left flank while Emory himself kept the Confederates' attention to their front and right. The plan worked to perfection. The assault of one of the flanking brigades drove Bee out of a strong position and the Rebels retreated thirty miles. "He displayed great personal gallantry, but no generalship," Taylor said of Bee and removed him from his command.[3]

Up in Arkansas that same 23 April, Steele at last heard from Banks in a dispatch written a week earlier at Grand Ecore, before he had decided to retreat farther downriver. He had proposed that if Steele marched on to join him on the Red, the two could still achieve their objective. "I am confident we can move to Shreveport without material delay," Banks had written, "and that we shall have an opportunity of destroying the only organized rebel army west of the Mississippi." Steele replied that "owing to contingencies, it is impossible for me to say definitely that I will join you at any point on Red River within a given time." Among the contingencies Steele had to consider was Price's Rebel army. "We have been receiving yesterday and today rumors of reinforcements sent by Kirby Smith to Price at this point, and of a contemplated attack," Steele added. "It is said that 8000 infantry have arrived."[4]

As a matter of fact, Kirby Smith himself had arrived outside Camden three days before with his three small divisions of infantry from Louisiana. With them and Price's cavalry he hoped to capture Steele and his entire command, but to do that he would have to flush nim out of his entrenchments. As a beginning, he opened an artillery bombardment of the Camden defenses that same 23rd of April. Meanwhile he dispatched James F. Fagan's cavalry division, reinforced by Jo Shelby's brigade, to raid Steele's supply lines all the way back to Little Rock if necessary.

Fagan crossed to the north bank of the Ouachita River on 24 April and received reports from scouts that a large Federal wagon train with a strong escort had left Camden two days before, headed for Pine Bluff to get supplies. Fagan was determined to catch these wagons before they could get across the Saline River at Mount Elba, so he pushed his troopers on a forced march of 45 miles to reach a crossroads five miles from the river that night. There he learned that the Union wagons had made camp a few miles to the west. He also learned that the train consisted of 240 government wagons as well as a number belonging to refugees, sutlers, and cotton speculators, escorted by three regiments of infantry and one of cavalry with a combined strength of 1,440 (less than half of Fagan's numbers), and a battery of six guns. Fagan sent Shelby's Missourians ahead to block the road to Mount Elba and posted his own men near Mark's Mill, where they could attack the flank and rear of the Federal column as it came along the road the next morning.

Shortly after dawn on the 25th, the Union wagons reached Fagan's position but the Federal infantry, after recovering from the initial surprise, put up a better fight than the Rebel cavalryman had anticipated. It took four hours of heavy combat, some of it hand-to-hand, and Shelby had to be called on to join in, but the Federals finally surrendered regiment by regiment. Fewer than 150 Union troops escaped. Three hundred wagons, the six cannon, and 1,300 men were captured and carried off to the north as Fagan continued to head for the Arkansas River. That night a handful of fugitives from the column reached Camden, and Steele called a council of war to consider what course his army should follow. Other than starve, there only seemed to be two choices: surrender or retreat. The council unanimously recommended the latter.

On 25 April, Banks and the head of his column reached Alexandria, where he met General David Hunter bearing orders from Grant to definitely bring the Red River expedition to an end. Banks would have been glad to comply, but Porter's fleet could not retreat any farther. The river at Alexandria had fallen six feet since the gunboats and transports had gone upstream a month before. For a mile and a quarter bare rocks were showing above the surface. The channel held only three feet four inches of water, and had narrowed in some places to a mere thread. Unless the army stayed to protect the navy, the boats might all be captured by the Rebels.

Also on the 25th, Burnside's 9th Army Corps marched through Washington, D.C. on its way to reinforce the Army of the Potomac. It was 25,000 strong—four divisions of infantry, four regiments of cavalry, and fourteen batteries of artillery. It was an organization with a unique history. The 9th Corps had originally been formed out of troops from the Union lodgements in North and South Carolina sent back north under Burnside after McClellan met defeat on the Peninsula. Two of its divisions had fought in the second battle of Bull Run, and the entire corps had been present at Antietam and Fredericksburg. By then Burnside had been appointed to replace his old friend McClellan in command of the Army of the Potomac.

Ambrose Everett Burnside had graduated from West Point in 1847, four years after Grant, one after McClellan. Before the war he had invented a breechloading carbine which was still being used by the army, although he had lost his share in the company that produced it before the war began. He had reentered the service as colonel of a Rhode Island infantry regiment and, like Sherman, had commanded a brigade at the first battle of Bull Run. His expedition to North Carolina had earned him a second star and a reputation for ability in independent command.

He looked the part of a great general. He was tall, amiable, and wore distinctive side whiskers that flowed into his mustache, contrasting with his clean-shaven chin and bald head. That style of whiskers came to be known by a reversal of his name into "sideburns." But he was not up to the command of a force as large as the Army of the Potomac and had sense enough to know it. Twice he had refused offers of the job, but his sense of duty had obliged him to obey when he had been ordered to succeed McClellan. He had shown some promise at first by devising a scheme to get between Richmond and Lee's army (then along the upper Rappahannock River) by shifting rapidly to Fredericksburg, where he planned to cross the river on pontoon bridges before Lee could catch up with his sudden shift. The plan had gone awry when someone forgot to make sure that the pontoons were forwarded to the right place.

Burnside had then demonstrated a dangerous stubborn streak by persisting in a good plan long after it had gone bad. By the time his army had crossed, Lee's troops had been entrenched in very strong positions. But the more things went wrong the more Burnside had been determined to butt straight ahead, eschewing all maneuver and strategem. When that did not work he had sulked and had complained to Lincoln, rightly enough, about uncooperative subordinates (with Baldy Smith at the top of the list), and then had finally tried maneuvering. He had ordered a march back upstream to cross the river to Lee's left, but rains came and turned the dirt roads to quagmires, and it was all his army could do to struggle back to its camp across from Fredericksburg and go into winter quarters. Burnside had then been replaced with Hooker and sent west to command the Department of the Ohio. Most of his old 9th Corps had gone with him but was soon diverted to reinforce Grant at Vicksburg. When it finally returned to Burnside in the summer of 1863, he had led it and the 23rd Corps across the mountains of eastern Kentucky and Tennessee to take Knoxville and liberate the Union-supporting population of east Tennessee. He had successfully defended his conquest from Longstreet that winter, but his overly shrill calls for help had not endeared him to Grant, who had rushed Sherman to his relief only to find he had not been in as much trouble as he had indicated.

Soon after that Burnside had been sent, again with his 9th Corps, to Annapolis, Maryland. This was a good, central location from which they could be sent just about anywhere along the coast via Chesapeake Bay, or inland by railroad. The regiments that had veteranized had been sent home on leave, while newly raised units had been brought in to add to the corps' strength. It had now been completely reorganized into four divisions, each with two brigades of infantry and two batteries of artillery. There was also one provisional brigade of dismounted cavalry and heavy artillery regiments serving as infantry, four unbrigaded regiments of cavalry, and six batteries of reserve artillery. The new 4th Division was made up entirely of United States Colored Troops, regiments of black soldiers with white officers, all determined, since hearing about Fort Pillow, to fight to the death. Now Burnside and his troops were being sent into northern Virginia to guard the Army of the Potomac's supply line and allow Meade to concentrate his force for the upcoming movement forward. Since Burnside was senior to Meade, his corps would not officially become part of that army again but would be directly subordinate to Grant himself.

The city of Washington had been an armed camp for three years by the time the 9th Corps marched down Fourteenth Street that day. All through the spring units, groups of replacements, and individual soldiers were seen heading south in a steady stream, while the sick and unfit of Meade's army and many civilians—sight-seers, sutlers, officers' wives and newspaper correspondents lacking the proper passes—were coming north from the Rapidan. But the 9th Corps was the largest body of troops to pass through the city in a very long time. Spring was new, the trees and the grass were turning green, and, although rain had fallen the night before and more rain threatened, it was a good day for a parade. Burnside stood beside President Lincoln on the balcony of Willard's Hotel to review the troops as they marched by. Not far away a Confederate spy named Frank Stringfellow was making a careful estimate of Burnside's strength. A reporter for the *Boston Journal* noted the enthusiasm that swept through the black troops as they paraded past the man who had signed the Emancipation Proclamation. These were, he said, men who were "for the first time shouldering arms for their country; who till a year ago never had a country, who even now are not American citizens, who are disinfranchised—yet they are going out to fight for the flag!"[5] The soldiers eventually marched on over the Potomac into Virginia, the veterans and the recruits, the cowards and the heroes, the white and the black, as well as two companies of Indian sharpshooters. Many of them would never return.

In West Virginia that day, Sigel arrived at Martinsburg, near the northern end of the Shenandoah, to inspect the units he would be leading personally up the valley. He did not like what he found. The artillery seemed to be all right, but he found the cavalry "in a wretched condition," and two regiments of Ohio infantry that had been captured by Lee's army the summer before and recently exchanged, he considered to be "entirely useless."[6] The only unit in which he had much faith was the 34th Massachussetts, which was regarded by his other troops as a bunch of barbarians.

In North Carolina, Beauregard was writing to Bragg to complain about the scattered nature of the forces in his new department. Knowing that Butler was receiving reinforcements at Hampton Roads and that Burnside was gathering another force at Annapolis, possibly for a return to the scene of his early triumphs in North Carolina, the Confederate wanted to deploy his units in such a way as to be able to counter any Federal offensive. He did not directly ask to be allowed to cancel the expeditions against New Berne and Washington—Bragg's own projects—but his disapproval was evident. He proposed to divide his department into three military districts: one, under Pickett with headquarters at Petersburg, would extend from the James to the Roanoke; a second, with no commander specified, from there to the Neuse River; and the third, under Major General W. H. C. Whiting, already commanding at Wilmington, from the Neuse to Cape Fear. Then, before this letter could reach Richmond, he telegraphed to ask for several units from his old command in South Carolina to be sent to reinforce him. He had received a report that day that up to 60,000 Union troops were concentrated on the Virginia Peninsula, many having recently arrived by sea. Beauregard suggested that Petersburg might be at least an intermediate objective of Butler's force and asked, "Are we prepared to resist him in that direction? Can the forces of this Dept. be concentrated in time?"[7]

From the 21st to the 25th of April, Commander Phelps had worked day and night to save his ship, the *Eastport*, aground in the shallow Red River, but the army had marched away and the rest of the fleet was also having to head downriver. Since the ironclad could not be saved in time, Phelps gave the order to blow her up. A ton and a half of powder was used, but when the electric detonator failed, Phelps himself applied a slow match and jumped over the side into a waiting launch. A large fragment of the iron hull just missed him. The remaining gunboats, the tinclads *Cricket, Juliet,* and *Fort Hindman,* had gone about twenty miles when the Rebels opened fire on them with twenty pieces of artillery. The *Cricket,* in the five minutes she was under fire, was struck 38 times and lost 12 men killed and 19 wounded out of a crew of 50. Among the wounded was the pilot, but Admiral Porter took his place and got the little boat through the gauntlet of fire. The remainder of the squadron, under Phelps, turned back upstream except for the two pumpboats, which were destroyed. Phelps waited until the next day, as the last of Banks' army was marching into Alexandria, to run the batteries with the remainder of the squadron. This was done with the loss of fifteen killed and wounded on the *Juliet,* and seven more on the *Fort Hindman.*

At Camden, Arkansas the 26th was given over by Steele to preparations for departure and the destruction of everything useful that couldn't be taken along. After dark, even as drums were beating taps to fool the Confederates into thinking that all was normal within the Union lines, the loaded wagons began to cross the Ouachita on a pontoon bridge. They were all across by midnight, followed by the infantry, and then the engineers silently took up the bridge. It was well after sun-up when the Rebels discovered that their quarry had fled, and it was midmorning by the time they marched into Camden. Marmaduke's cavalry swam their horses across the river, and Maxey's troopers listened to a speech by Kirby Smith thanking them for their service in Arkansas before they departed to return to Indian Territory to meet a reported invasion from Missouri. Meanwhile Price began the construction of a raft for ferrying Walker's and Churchill's infantry across, but that took all night.

That day, 27 April, Sigel was holding a grand review of his little army at Martinsburg, West Virginia. But as the various units marched out onto the parade ground all order began to disappear. No one seemed to know where they were supposed to be, and the review degenerated into utter confusion. The experience was not an auspicious beginning to the campaign. The next day, Sigel's last unit finally arrived. His force was divided into two divisions, one of infantry and one of cavalry, each consisting of two brigades. There were also five batteries of artillery. Altogether there were 9,000 men and 28 guns.

That same day, the 28th, Grant was notifying Butler of his intention to have the Army of the Potomac advance on the fourth of May. Butler was directed to move the night of the fourth and get as far up the James River as possible by daylight. Reinforcements, he was told, were being collected in Washington which could be sent to him if Lee should fall back into the defenses of Richmond. Sherman was being directed to be ready to move by the fifth, and Sigel was directed to move in conjunction with the others. Sherman was moving his headquarters forward that day from Nashville to Chattanooga in preparation for the coming campaign.

At 8 a.m. the next day, 29 April, Sigel's column set out up the Shenandoah Valley, already three hours behind schedule. This pleasant, prosperous valley lay between the Alleghenies to the west and the Blue Ridge to the east. As the Shenandoah River flows northeastward along the western foot of the Blue Ridge, to travel in that direction would be to go downstream, or down the valley, and to move southwestward would be to go upstream, or up the valley. It was an area of divided loyalties. The large, slave-dependant, cash-crop plantations of the tidewater area were rare there. Medium-sized family farms were far more common, and many of the families had originally come down from Pennsylvania. At the northeast corner of the valley, where the Shenandoah flowed into the Potomac as the latter cut its way through the mountains, was the hilly little town of Harpers Ferry. As the site of a Federal arsenal, it had been the object of John Brown's famous raid in 1859. He had seized the arsenal with the expressed object of arming the slaves of the area and instigating a revolt. Instead, he had been bottled up by armed citizens and captured by a couple of companies of marines from the barracks at Washington led by then U.S. Army colonel R. E. Lee.

In 1861, Joe Johnston had commanded a small Confederate army in the upper valley that had slipped away from its Union counterpart and had used the railroad to join Beauregard at Manassas and there defeat the Federals in the first battle of Bull Run. Thomas J. "Stonewall" Jackson had been the next Rebel commander in the Shenandoah. He had been an 1846 graduate of West Point and a former professor at the Virginia Military Institute. Closed-mouthed, eccentric, and a devout Presbyterian, he had turned a few suggestions from Lee into a brilliant campaign that had defeated three Federal forces and kept any of them from reinforcing McClellan at the gates of Richmond or accomplishing anything else for a couple of months. He had then shown up at Richmond in time to join in Lee's offensive which had led to McClellan's withdrawal from the Peninsula.

The Shenandoah proved to be a great asset to the Confederacy, both as a breadbasket for the Southern army and as a position of immense strategic value. A Confederate army advancing down the valley was moving toward the Baltimore & Ohio Railroad, a vital Federal connection with the West, as well as toward the critical, poorly defended Union heartland of eastern Pennsylvania, Baltimore, Philadelphia, and New York, not to mention the back door to Washington. On the other hand, a Federal force moving up the valley was getting no closer to Richmond at all while getting steadily farther from its sources of supply. Furthermore, a Confederate force in the lower valley was a threat to the flank of any Union army east of the Blue Ridge. Lee had used the Shenandoah as a protected supply corridor for his army during both the Antietam and Gettysburg campaigns. During the former he had sent most of his army to capture a large Federal garrison at Harpers Ferry, and during the latter his 2nd Corps, under Ewell, had gobbled up a sizable Union force at Winchester.

Now Sigel's little army, made up mostly of troops who had never done anything but garrison rear-area backwaters, was heading up the famous valley—famous for Federal defeats—and despite a number of Union sympathizers lining the road to cheer them on, the Northern soldiers were apprehensive. "We are in for business now," said a private in the 18th Connecticut.[8] The weather had turned suddenly warm after months of winter, and the troops were not used to long marches. Soon they began to throw away extra clothing and equipment to lighten their load, while the hard macadam surface of the Valley Turnpike was making their feet sore.

It took them eleven hours to march eleven miles. That same day, Halleck was writing to Sherman: "It seems but little better than murder to give important commands to such men as Banks, Butler, McClernand, Sigel and Lew Wallace, and yet it seems impossible to prevent it."[9]

1. Joseph H. Ewing, "The New Sherman Letters," *American Heritage* 3 (5, July–August 1987): 37.
2. Cornish, *The Sable Arm*, 174.
3. Foote, *The Civil War*, 3:58–59.
4. Ibid., 70–71.
5. Noah Andre Trudeau, *Bloody Roads South* (Boston, 1989), 19.
6. Davis, *The Battle of New Market*, 22–23.
7. Robertson, *Back Door to Richmond*, 48–49.
8. Davis, *The Battle of New Market*, 24.
9. Catton, *Grant Takes Command*, 147.

CHAPTER TEN

"The Fault Is Not With You"

29 April–2 May 1864

On 29 April, General Lee arrived at Mechanicsville, Virginia to visit his 1st Corps, newly returned from its seven-month sojourn in the West. Longstreet had his 10,000 men turned out for the commanding general's inspection. "Guns were burnished and rubbed up, cartridge boxes and belts polished, and the brass buttons and buckles made to look as bright as new," one participant recalled. "Our clothes were patched and brushed up, so far as was in our power, boots and shoes greased, the tattered and torn old hats were given here and there 'a lick and a promise,' and on the whole I must say I think we presented not a bad-looking body of soldiers."[1]

The men were extremely glad to be away from Braxton Bragg, unfriendly east Tennesseans, and the unlucky West in general, and especially to be back with the undefeated Lee, respectfully known among them as Marse (for "master") Robert. The citizen soldiers on both sides in the Civil War were spared the kind of discipline maintained in the regular army, and they were not afraid to show their feelings. Longstreet's men cheered Lee wildly as they passed in review. "General Lee must have felt good in getting the welcome extended to him by those who had been lost to him so long," one of those soldiers wrote. "The men hung around him and seemed satisfied to lay their hands on his gray horse or to touch the bridle, or the stirrup, or the old general's leg—anything that Lee had was sacred to us fellows who had just come back. And the General—he could not help from breaking down . . . tears traced down his cheeks, and he felt that we were again to do his bidding."[2]

"Does it not make the General proud," a chaplain asked a colonel on Lee's staff, "to see how these men love him?" But the colonel replied, "Not proud. It awes him."[3]

As for the enemy, Longstreet, who had known Grant at West Point, told his visitors, "We must make up our minds to get into line of battle and to stay there, for that man will fight us every day and every hour till the end of the war."[4]

Just what Lee was going to do with Longstreet's force was a subject of some concern among Federal generals. The possibility of another Confederate thrust down the Shenandoah was always to be considered. But Grant had already told Halleck that Burnside's corps would be available to oppose any move Longstreet might make toward the Valley. That very day, the 29th, Grant was writing to Halleck that he probably would advance by his own left to the east of Lee unless something came up to change his mind, like a move by Lee around his right, toward the Shenandoah. At any rate he would move on 4 May, attempting to turn Lee by one flank or the other. "Should Lee fall back within his fortifications at Richmond without giving battle, I will form a junction with Butler and the two forces will draw supplies from the James River," he said. "My own notions about our line of march are entirely made up, but as circumstances beyond my control may change them, I will only state that my intention will be to bring Butler's and Meade's forces together."[5]

Out on the Red River that day, the 29th, the chief engineer of the 19th Army Corps, Lieutenant Colonel Joseph Bailey, approached Banks with a scheme for saving Admiral David Porter's fleet, presently trapped by the low water in the river. Bailey had been a lumberman in Wisconsin before the war and had used wing dams to raise the water level in sluggish streams so that he could float logs to market. He was confident that he could build similar dams, extending out from each bank on the Red, to raise the water between them high enough and for long enough to get the gunboats and transports over the rapids at Alexandria. "I wish I was as sure of heaven as I am that I can save the fleet," he said.[6] Banks was skeptical, even though Bailey had used the same means to float a couple of transports captured in a creek near Port Hudson the previous summer. This was a much wider stream with a much swifter current, but Banks took the engineer to see Admiral Porter and explain about his dams. "If damning would get the fleet off, we would have been afloat long ago," Porter quipped.[7] But since the army was willing to do most of the work, and there was no other plan to consider, he was willing to give it a try.

In Arkansas, Steele's column was marching as hard as it could for Little Rock. His men were doing their best to maintain their head start over the pursuing Rebels gained by their night-time withdrawal from Camden, but the men were weak from days of short rations. Moreover, it was raining and the roads were turning to mud. Before nightfall on the 29th, Marmaduke's Rebel cavalry had caught up with the tail of the Federal column. But by then the head of the column had reached the Saline River at Jenkins Ferry and the Union engineers were already busy laying their pontoon bridge and corduroying the approaches on both sides of the stream. The work continued after dark, and Steele's chief engineer reported that "the rain came down in torrents, putting out many of the fires, the men became exhausted, and both they and the animals sank down in the mud and mire, wherever they were, to seek a few hours' repose."[8]

By 7:30 on the morning of the 30th, the first of Kirby Smith's infantry had caught up with the Union troops that were guarding the road to the pontoon bridge. "An intercepted dispatch from General Sherman to General A. J. Smith, directing the immediate return of his force to Vicksburg, removed the last doubt in my mind that Banks would withdraw to Alexandria as rapidly as possible, and it was hoped the falls would detain his fleet there until we could dispose of Steele, when the entire force of the department would be free to operate against him," Kirby Smith wrote after the war. "I confidently hoped, if I could reach Steele with my infantry, to beat him at a distance from his depot, in a poor country, and with my large cavalry force to destroy his army."[9]

Price, in charge of the leading Confederate infantry, committed his units as fast as they arrived, but the Federals had built themselves log breastworks in the edge of a wood overlooking a rain-soaked cornfield. The Union flanks were protected by a creek on one side and a swamp on the other. One brigade of Churchill's Arkansans charged as best they could up the muddy road and through the wet cornfield, but they met a murderous fire that drove them back. Then Churchill sent in a second brigade, but with no better result. Meanwhile, Price ordered Parson's newly arrived Missouri division into line of battle. Reinforced by Churchill's remaining brigade and supported by a battery and a half of artillery, they advanced across the muddy cornfield. The Union line had just been replenished with fresh troops, including the large 2nd Kansas

Colored Infantry, and they met this new threat with a withering fire, while Federal units that had crossed to the far side of the creek on the north flank raked the Southerners with an enfilading fire. The black troops then charged the Rebel artillery shouting, "Remember Poison Springs!" and captured three guns at bayonet point. About 150 Rebels were killed or mortally wounded, while the 2nd Kansas Colored lost only 15 men killed and 55 wounded. One Confederate prisoner was taken alive, by mistake. The Kansas regiment's white colonel had him sent to the Southern lines with a warning to his compatriots about the cost of massacring black soldiers.

Farther south the Confederate right made better progress, driving the Yankees from their breastworks and entering the woods beyond the cornfield, but Union reserves rushed to the spot, counterattacked, and drove the Southerners back again. By that time Kirby Smith had arrived, as had Walker's division of Texas infantry. He sent them in to the attack, but the Federal fire cut down all three of the division's brigade commanders, and the Texans also had to fall back. It was about 12:30 by then, and the Union wagons and cavalry had crossed the river. The infantry now followed unmolested, taking the three captured guns with them. As soon as they were across the river, the bridge was cut loose and set on fire, since there were no more rivers to cross on the way to Little Rock. Besides, the mules were too worn down to haul the pontoons any farther. The Confederates had no bridge with which to cross nor much inclination to do so. Fagan's raiding cavalry soon arrived, having made a wide circuit through Arkadelphia, which put his men on the wrong side of the river for a pursuit too. Anyway the Rebels seemed content to see Steele's army march away undestroyed.

The afternoon of the 29th, Horace Porter, who had witnessed Grant's first meeting with Lincoln, had arrived at Culpeper Court House to take up a position as one of Grant's aides de camp. He had been trying to join Grant's staff ever since the latter had come to Washington. The general-in-chief was agreeable, but Secretary of War Edwin McMasters Stanton had insisted that Porter continue his duties at the War Department. Porter had finally gone to see the secretary about it. "A Frenchman once said that during the Revolution, while the guillotine was at work, he never heard the name Robespierre that he did not take off his hat to see whether his head was still on his shoulders; some of our officers were similarly inclined when they heard the name of Stanton," Porter wrote. "However, I found the Secretary quite civil, and even patient, and, to all appearances, disposed to allow my head to continue to occupy the place where I was in the habit of wearing it. Nevertheless, the interview ended without his having yielded. I certainly received a very cold bath at his hands, and to this day I never see the impress of his unrelenting features upon a one-dollar treasury note without feeling a chill run down my back."[10]

However, on 27 April Porter had learned that the lieutenant general's request for his services had been granted, and two days later, bumped up two grades to lieutenant colonel, he reported for duty at the plain brick house in the little Virginia town where the general-in-chief of all the armies made his headquarters. The next morning, the 30th, Grant chose Porter to accompany him on a ride over to Meade's headquarters. "As we rode along," Porter recorded, "he began to speak of his new command, and said: 'I have watched the progress of the Army of the Potomac ever since it was organized, and have been greatly interested in reading the accounts of the splendid fighting it has done. I always thought the territory covered by its operations would be the principal battle-ground of the war. When I was at Cairo, in 1861, the height of my ambition was to command a brigade of cavalry in this army.'"

The conversation turned to Chattanooga for a while and then Grant "spoke of his experiences with Mr. Lincoln, and the very favorable impression the President had made upon him. He said: 'In the first interview I had with the President when no others were present, and he could talk freely, he told me that he did not pretend to know anything about the handling of troops, and it was with the greatest reluctance that he ever interfered with the movements of army commanders: but he had common sense enough to know that celerity was absolutely necessary; that while armies were sitting down waiting for opportunities to turn up which might, perhaps, be more favorable from a strictly military point of view, the government was spending millions of dollars every day; that there was a limit to the sinews of war, and the time might be reached when the spirits and resources of the people would become exhausted. He had always contended that these considerations should be taken into account, as well as purely military questions, and that he adopted the plan of issuing his "executive orders" principally for the purpose of hurrying the movements of commanding generals; but that he believed I knew the value of minutes, and that he was not going to interfere with my operations. He said, further, that he did not want to know my plans; that it was, perhaps, better that he should not know them, for everybody he met was trying to find out from him something about the contemplated movements, and there was always a temptation "to leak." I have not communicated my plans to him or to the Secretary of War,'" Grant said.

"When we reached General Meade's camp," Porter related, "that officer, who was sitting in his quarters, came out and greeted the general-in-chief warmly, shaking hands with him before he dismounted. General

Meade was then forty-nine years of age, of rather a spare figure, and graceful in his movements. He had a full beard, which, like his hair, was brown, slightly tinged with gray. He wore a slouched felt hat with a conical crown and turned-down rim, which gave him a sort of Tyrolese appearance. The two commanders entered Meade's quarters, sat down, lighted their cigars, and held a long interview regarding the approaching campaign. I now learned that, two days before, the time had been definitely named at which the opening campaign was to begin, and that on the next Wednesday, May 4, the armies were to move."[11]

Washburn, the new commander at Memphis, wired Sherman on 30 April that he was dispatching that same day an expedition to intercept Forrest, who was thought to be on his way back to Mississippi. After sending downriver to Vicksburg for reinforcements and scraping every other barrel available, he had been able to put together a force of 3,500 cavalry, 2,000 infantry, a battery of field artillery and four little mountain howitzers, all under the command of the department's chief of cavalry, Brigadier General Samuel Sturgis. Washburn was "confident that they will whip . . . Forrest and drive him from the State."[12] Forrest left Jackson, Tennessee the next day, heading south.

In Richmond, that final day of April was a routine one for Confederate president Jefferson Davis, at least until lunch time. His wife, less than two months short of delivering her fifth child, had just brought in a tray of food from home, for if left to himself he would neglect to eat. But before the meal could be set before him a servant rushed in with word that his five-year-old son, Joe, had fallen from a balcony of the Confederate White House. Father and mother rushed home to find the boy unconscious, with both legs broken and his skull fractured. Apparently the youngster had climbed a plank left by some carpenters while they were eating their lunch, and had fallen thirty feet to a brick-paved courtyard. He had been found by his seven-year-old brother, Jeff, Jr. When a neighbor arrived, she found little Jeff kneeling down by his fallen brother, and he called out to her in distress, "I have said all the prayers I know how, but God will not wake Joe!"[13] The younger boy died soon after his mother reached him.

A friend of the family came to the house that evening with Mrs. Davis's sister to find that "every window and door of the house seemed wide open, and the wind blowing the curtains. It was lit up, even in the third story . . . As I sat in the drawing room, I could hear the tramp of Mr. Davis's step as he walked up and down the room above, but not another sound. The whole house was as silent as death." Before she left she saw the young body laid out upstairs "white and beautiful as an angel, covered with flowers." As she walked home she met General Wade Hampton, who walked on with her, telling her of a discussion he had had with General Lee. But she wrote that, "I could see or hear nothing but little Joe and the broken-hearted mother and father, and Mr. Davis's step still sounded in my ear as he walked that floor the livelong night."[14] At the boy's funeral the next day people saw that the president, erect and awe-inspiring in his self-discipline, had new streaks of gray in his hair and that his blind left eye looked even blinder.

At the other White House, the one in Washington, that final day of April, President Lincoln was writing a letter to General Grant: "Not expecting to see you again before the Spring campaign opens, I wish to express, in this way, my entire satisfaction with what you have done up to this time, so far as I understand it. The particulars of your plans I neither know, or seek to know. You are vigilant and self-reliant; and, pleased with this, I wish not to obtrude any constraints or restraints upon you. While I am very anxious that any great disaster, or the capture of our men in great numbers, shall be avoided, I know these points are less likely to escape your attention than they would be mine. If there is anything wanting which is within my power to give, do not fail to let me know it."[15]

Around this time, one of Lincoln's personal secretaries, William O. Stoddard, returned to duty after an illness and found the president relaxing on a sofa "looking as if he did not care two cents for the past, present or future." Lincoln was in a mood to chat, and eventually the subject came around to General Grant, whom Stoddard had not yet seen. The secretary wanted to know what kind of man Grant was. The president replied that he was "the quietest little fellow you ever saw." But what about his ability as a general, Stoddard asked. Lincoln sat up and pointed a finger at his secretary and said, "Stoddard, Grant is the first General I've had! He's a general!" Naturally, Stoddard wanted him to explain.

"I'll tell you what I mean," Lincoln said. "You know how it's been with all the rest. As soon as I put a man in command of the army he'd come to me with a plan of campaign and about as much as say, 'Now, I don't believe I can do it, but if you say so I'll try it on,' and so put the responsibility of success or failure on me. They all wanted me to be the general. It isn't so with Grant. He hasn't told me what his plans are. I don't know, and I don't want to know. I'm glad to find a man who can go ahead without me."

But how would he do against Lee, Stoddard wanted to know. Lincoln ignored the question, having warmed to his subject, and as he "put on his story-telling expression," he continued with his own point: "You see, when any of the rest set out on campaign they'd look over matters and pick out some one thing they were short of and that they knew I couldn't hope to give them and then tell me they couldn't win unless they had it; and it was most generally cavalry."

Lincoln began to laugh silently and went on: "When Grant took hold I was waiting to see what his pet impossibility would be, and I reckoned it would be cavalry as a matter of course, for we hadn't horses enough to mount even what men we had. There were fifteen thousand or thereabouts up near Harper's Ferry, and no horses to put them on. Well, the other day, just as I expected, Grant sent to me about those very men; but what he wanted to know was whether he should disband them or turn 'em into infantry. He doesn't ask me to do impossibilities for him, and he's the first general I've had that didn't."[16]

Of course, there never had been any 15,000 dismounted cavalry at Harpers Ferry—1,500, maybe. Stoddard must have gotten the figure wrong. But Lincoln was right about his general. Grant answered the president's letter on the first day of May: "Your very kind letter of yesterday is just received. The confidence you express for the future, and satisfaction with the past, in my military administration is acknowledged with pride. It will be my earnest endeavor that you, and the country, shall not be disappointed.

"From my first entrance into the volunteer service of the country, to the present day, I have never had cause of complaint, have never expressed or implied a complaint, against the Administration, or the Sec. of War, for throwing any embarrassment in the way of my vigorously prossecuting what appeared to me my duty. Indeed since the promotion which placed me in command of all the Armies, and in view of the great responsibility, and importance of success, I have been astonished at the readiness with which every thing asked for has been yielded without even an explanation being asked. Should my success be less than I desire, and expect, the least I can say is, the fault is not with you."[17]

On the morning of 1 May, a brigade of troops from Butler's Army of the James landed at the village of West Point, where the Pamunkey and Mattapony rivers join to form the York. This had been McClellan's main supply base during the Peninsula campaign, and Butler had sent these troops up the York as a diversion, in hopes of confusing the Confederates about his ultimate intentions. Baldy Smith, typically, derided the idea.

May Day was also the day Sigel resumed his march up the Shenandoah Valley. He had spent the previous day in camp at the little town of Bunker Hill giving his inexperienced troops a bit more drill and thinking about what to do next. Then on the first of May he set out to march his men another eleven miles to the town of Winchester, site of many previous battles, large and small. One of his infantrymen recorded that there was "perhaps not a mile of the whole route over which we passed along which there could not be seen a soldier's grave."[18] They reached Winchester about 4:30 that afternoon. Many of them had been captured there the previous June by Lee's army as it headed toward Pennsylvania. Many of their dead comrades were still lying where the victorious Rebels had thrown them, barely covered with dirt. The sight put a gloom over the men, despite the pleasant weather and the beauty of the valley. To make matters worse, the wagons carrying their rations were delayed for some reason, and the men were hungry.

The same day that Sigel marched out of Bunker Hill, Confederate partisans rode in. Lieutenant Colonel John Singleton Mosby had, since early 1863, caused such havoc in supposedly conquered regions of northern Virginia, especially the counties just east of the Blue Ridge, that the area was coming to be known as "Mosby's Confederacy." His men would assemble secretly, attack some sleepy garrison or poorly protected supply column and then blend into the civilian population when the Yankees came looking for them. "About May 1st, with a party of 10 men, I captured 8 of Sigel's wagons near Bunker Hill, in the Valley, but was only able to bring off the horses attached (34 in number) and about 20 prisoners," he recorded. "The horses and prisoners were sent back, while with another detachment of 20 men who had joined me I proceeded to Martinsburg, which place we entered that night, while occupied by several hundred Federal troops, and brought off 15 horses and several prisoners."[19]

Other than such partisans as Mosby's, the only Rebel soldiers in the Shenandoah Valley just then were Brigadier General John D. Imboden and his brigade of cavalry. They had never been outside the Valley and nearby West Virginia except during the previous summer, when they had arrived at Gettysburg just in time to escort Lee's wagons on the retreat back to Virginia. Much farther south was the Confederate Department of Western Virginia, with headquarters at the little town of Dublin, on the Virginia & Tennessee Railroad. It had been commanded since early March by Major General John C. Breckinridge, who had been vice president of the United States in the Buchanan administration, preceding Lincoln's. When the Democratic party had split into northern and southern wings in 1860, thus allowing the Republicans to elect a president for the first time ever—which in turn had led to Southern secession and the war—Breckinridge had been the Southern wing's candidate for president. He had no formal military education, but had served in the Mexican War. He had commanded a division at Shiloh and had then led an unsuccessful attempt to recapture Baton Rouge, Louisiana. His division had been sent to menace Nashville while Bragg and Kirby Smith had been invading Kentucky in the fall of 1862, then had joined the former for the battle of Stones River. He had served under Joseph E. Johnston during the Vicksburg campaign, and had returned with his division to the Army of Tennessee for the battles of Chickamauga and Chattanooga. Like many others, he had quarreled with Bragg and had been sent, without his division, to his present assignment.

He was a tall, handsome, charming Kentuckian of about Grant's age, fond of his bourbon and a spellbinding orator, and this was his first independant command. It included all of southwestern Virginia and any parts of West Virginia and Kentucky that could be taken. To guard all that area, which included such vital targets as the railroad, the salt works at Saltville, and the lead mines at Wytheville, he had three small brigades of infantry, one of which was brand new to his department, and one brigade and various smaller units of cavalry. On 1 May he received a telegram from Lee indicating that the Federals in West Virginia, believed to be under General Averell, were headed Breckinridge's way. Lee's authority over Breckinridge was nebulous but the Shenandoah, at least, was traditionally within Lee's command. Now that general was urging Breckinridge to cooperate with Imboden to meet the threats to their respective areas. "It will be impossible to send any reinforcements to the Valley from this army," he said.[20]

Actually there were two Federal columns getting ready to advance against Breckinridge, besides Sigel's own force in the lower (northern) Valley. Both Union forces came under Brigadier General George Crook, commander of the Kanawha District, part of Sigel's Department of West Virginia. Crook had a force of about 6,000 men, mostly infantry, under his personal direction at Gauley Bridge, where the Kanawha and New rivers converged about seventy miles almost due north of Breckinridge's headquarters at Dublin. His other force, of about 2,000 cavalry, was under Averell, and was gathering about 45 miles farther west at Logan, West Virginia. The latter was to go after the salt works and lead mines and then follow the railroad northeast to join up with Crook. Meanwhile, that officer would move against Dublin and the nearby railroad bridge over the New River. The combined forces would then move north through Lexington to Staunton, where Sigel was supposed to meet them with supplies. Crook's infantry set out on its march through the Alleghenies on the second of May.

That same day, down in North Carolina, Hoke's Rebel brigades began their investment of the Federal garrison at New Berne. The weather was not so fair out in west Tennessee, where Sturgis's Union force from Memphis was struggling through muddy roads and over rundown bridges toward Bolivar, Tennessee in the hope of intercepting Forrest. Because he was running behind schedule, Sturgis sent Colonel Joseph Kargé ahead with 700 picked cavalry, to seize the crossings of the Hatchie River. However, when Kargé got there, he found that Forrest had already arrived with his own advance guard of about 300 men, and they held him off long enough for the Confederate wagons and unarmed men to cross to the east side of the river. Then Forrest destroyed the bridge to keep the Federals from following the wagons and marched south toward Ripley with his main body before Sturgis could bring up the main Union column. All Sturgis could do was to follow the Rebels south.

1. Douglas Southall Freeman, *Lee's Lieutenants* (New York, 1944), 3, 341.
2. Douglas Southall Freeman, *R.E. Lee* (New York, 1935), 3, 267.
3. Foote, *The Civil War*, 3:122.
4. Edward Steere, *The Wilderness Campaign* (New York, 1960), 45.
5. Ibid., 29.
6. Foote, *The Civil War*, 3:78.
7. Ibid.
8. Ibid., 3:74.
9. E. Kirby Smith, "The Defense of the Red River," in *Battles and Leaders*, 4:372.
10. Porter, *Campaigning With Grant*, 23.
11. Ibid., 26–29.
12. Starr, *Union Cavalry*, 3:412–413.
13. Mary Boykin Chestnut, *A Diary From Dixie* (Boston, 1945), 405.
14. Ibid.
15. Basler, ed., *Abraham Lincoln*, 7:324.
16. Catton, *Grant Takes Command*, 176–177.
17. Basler, ed., *Abraham Lincoln*, 7:324–325.
18. Davis, *The Battle of New Market*, 33.
19. Charles Wells Russell, ed., *The Memoirs of Colonel John S. Mosby* (Bloomington, Indiana, 1959), 272–273.
20. Davis, *The Battle of New Market*, 26.

PART TWO

THE WILDERNESS

"It was as though Christian men had turned to fiends, and hell itself had usurped the place of earth."

Horace Porter

CHAPTER ELEVEN

"Grant Will Cross By One of Those Fords"

2–4 May 1864

In Virginia that second day of May, Lee was holding a conference with all his corps and division commanders on top of Clark's Mountain, which rises some 600 feet above the flat lands of northeastern Virginia. The Confederates had a lookout and signal station there to watch the Yankee camps on the other side of the Rapidan River, and unusual volumes of smoke had been observed north of the river. The countryside below was in the full green bloom of spring, but no crops were raised there anymore. All the farmers had long since moved away to avoid the violence of battle and the depredations of marching armies.

At 57 years of age, Lee was a father figure to the assembled officers. Lee had been considered the best soldier and the handsomest man in the pre-war army, and he was still a striking figure although his thinning hair and close-trimmed beard had turned grey since the beginning of the war and were now becoming white. He was the youngest son of a Revolutionary War cavalry leader known as Light Horse Harry, but spiritually he was the heir of George Washington. In fact, his wife was the daughter of Washington's adopted son, Martha's grandson by her first marriage. Abstemious and austere in his personal habits, Lee was the very embodiment of the West Point motto, "Duty, Honor, Country," except that in his case, despite service in the regular army that had taken him to New York, St. Louis, Texas and other places, "country" to Lee meant "Virginia."

Early in the war he had been known as the King of Spades because he had ordered his soldiers, free-born white men all, to perform manual labor digging entrenchments. He had also been called Granny Lee because of his supposed timidity, but after he had driven McClellan away from Richmond in seven days of bloody attacks, all such thoughts were dismissed. Even before that, an officer on Lee's staff had told a friend, "If there is one man in either army, Confederate or Federal, head and shoulders above every other in audacity, it is General Lee! He will take more desperate chances, and take them quicker than any other general in this country, North or South"[1] Lee's audacity was built on a fatalistic religious faith. "I know in whose powerful hands I am," he once wrote, "and on Him I rely and feel that in all our life we are upheld and sustained by Divine Providence."[2] At the outbreak of the war he had been asked by a bishop whether he thought the South could win. "I am not concerned with results," he had answered. "God's will ought to be our aim, and I am contented that His designs should be accomplished and not mine."[3] Man might propose, but God would dispose, and all a soldier could do was his duty.

He was an extremely tactful man which, together with his sense of duty, record of success, and complete lack of interest in politics, allowed him to get along with President Davis. When a subordinate let him down, Lee did not reprimand him or punish him, but took the blame upon himself. Often this served to shame the delinquent into better performance. It certainly earned Lee the loyalty of his officers. If a subordinate proved to be lacking in capacity—and Lee was a very good judge of military talent—he found some way to quietly transfer him out of the Army of Northern Virginia. This improved the efficiency of his own forces, but meant that the rest of the Confederate armies and departments accumulated his incompetent cast-offs.

Lee's successes had come partly from boldness, and from his selection of the right men for the right jobs within his own army, and partly from his understanding of his opponents, most of whom he had known in the pre-war army. Two key appointments had stood him in especially good stead. His reliance on Stonewall Jackson as his strong right arm, his executive officer, had been complete. Lee and Jackson had made an ideally complementary pair. The other key appointment was that of Jeb Stuart to command his cavalry. In the early days of the war the Southern cavalry, natural horsemen, had been far superior to the Yankees. And Stuart knew how to get the most out of them to accomplish the primary purpose of the mounted arm: to serve as the eyes and ears of the army. Therefore Lee had possessed the invaluable advantage of having much better information about his opponents' forces and their movements than the Federals had about his.

He disliked having to write detailed orders and loathed paperwork in general. His style was to study the enemy, plan the bold stroke, give brief, general, verbal instructions to his corps commanders, and then leave the actual details of the operation to them—and to God the final outcome. He seldom took a direct hand in the actual conduct of the fighting. This had worked well with Jackson and Stuart, and to some extent with Long-street, although Lee had always seen fit to give the latter more direct supervision than the other two. But since the death of Jackson at Chancellorsville almost a year before, this hands-off approach had led to problems.

With the return of the 1st Corps, Lee's Army of Northern Virginia was again organized much as it had been for the Gettysburg campaign the previous summer, except that Stuart's cavalry was now divided into three small divisions instead of a single large one, and Longstreet's 1st Corps was short one division since Pickett was still in southern Virginia and North Carolina. Longstreet was then 43, a Georgian in an army dominated by Virginians. Lee called him his War Horse. His men called him Old Pete. He was large and stolid, somewhat slow and methodical, ambitious for independent command and sometimes prone to argue with Lee's judgement, but he was an excellent tactician, quite capable of handling a corps on his own. His 1st Corps contained about 10,000 infantrymen.

Lee's 2nd Corps, with about 20,000 bayonets in three divisions, was commanded by a Virginian, Richard Stoddert Ewell, 47, known to his men as Old Baldhead. Dick Ewell, if it were possible, was even more eccentric than the late Stonewall Jackson had been. Sometimes he seemed to think he was a bird and cocked his head to one side and talked in a high, chirping voice. He had lost a leg in the Second Bull Run campaign and had just returned to duty when he was named to succeed Jackson the previous summer. He had been an excellent division commander, but he did not quite have what it took to be a first-rate corps commander. He was indecisive and preferred to be told exactly what to do. During the winter lull Ewell had married a well-propertied widow who was happy to oblige on the domestic front. In military matters, Ewell was under the influence of one of his division commanders, Jubal Early.

Another Virginian, Ambrose Powell Hill, 38, commander of the 22,000-man 3rd Corps, had also been an outstanding division commander, but he too seemed to find the responsibility of corps command too much for him. Both Hill's and Ewell's problems reflect the tendency of any hierarchical organization to promote people until they finally reach a job they cannot handle. Lee had doubted that either of them could fill Stonewall Jackson's place, which is at least one reason why he promoted both instead of just one of them and why he rearranged his army into three corps after Jackson's death. Little Powell Hill was an emotional, impulsive, sensitive man who apparently suffered from an ulcer. As a division commander he had found relief from stress in the direct action of combat, but as a corps commander his responsibilities were greater while his involvement in action was diminished, and with each crisis he became more and more ill. He was neither eccentric nor colorful, except for a habit of wearing a red fireman's shirt in combat. He was always cheerful, informal and courteous and was well-liked, but he was essentially a loner. His one close friend in the army, General Dorsey Pender, who had succeeded to the command of Hill's division, had been killed at Gettysburg. Ever afterwards Hill carried a hint of melancholy in his gaze.

It had been a winter of discontent for Lee. The rains had immobilized both armies, and the lack of forage for the horses had forced him to spread out his cavalry and artillery units over what little pasture was available for grazing at that time of year. So the aggressive, audacious general was forced to sit and watch the gradual strengthening and awakening of his enemy across the river. He would have preferred to seize the initiative and force the Federals to respond to his own moves, not vice versa. But since the Federals had brought Burnside's 9th Corps forward he knew he was outnumbered, although he did not realize it was by a factor of almost two to one. He had defeated such odds before, but only after the larger Union force had committed itself to some venture that put it where Lee could get at it a piece at a time.

After Lee had studied the landscape and the Union camps spread out below Clark's Mountain through his field glasses and had commented that "those people," his name for the enemy, were going to move soon, he turned to the young soldier in charge of the signal station. "Sergeant," he asked, "do you keep a guard on watch at night?" When the answer was negative he replied, "Well, you must put one on."[4] That the Federals must move soon was obvious. Where they would go was less certain. Grant was a new, unfamiliar opponent, but it was obvious that, as the North's man of the hour, the pressure must be on him to strike a blow.

The Rapidan River, which separated the two armies, was a tributary of the larger Rappahannock, joining it some twenty miles east of Clark's

Mountain. The Rapidan-Rappahannock combination formed a barrier to the advance of the Union forces, the first of several river lines that the Federals would have to cross. Moreover, the land on the southern side of the Rapidan, roughly from Clark's Mountain eastward to the junction with the larger river, was covered by a thick stand of second-growth timber known as the Wilderness. It was a thinly populated area whose original forest had been cut down to provide firewood for small-scale mining operations. The woods were growing back in a tangle of small trees, bushes, and brambles, all but impenetrable in places and limiting visibility almost everywhere. Such terrain would restrict the movements of the advancing Federals and severely handicap their powerful artillery—the one arm in which the Southerners conceded Northern superiority. Lee's generals could not help but remember that it was in the eastern edge of the Wilderness around a little crossroads called Chancellorsville that they, except for Longstreet, had defeated the Army of the Potomac almost exactly one year before.

Ewell's 2nd Corps was now stationed in the western fringe of the Wilderness, just east of Clark's Mountain. Hill's 3rd Corps was farther southwest around the little town of Orange Courthouse, and Longstreet's 1st Corps was still farther southwest near Gordonsville. This disposition, centered well to the west of Meade's deployment, protected the Orange & Alexandria and Virginia Central railroads—vital arteries of supply—from a move around Lee's left, and it seemed to be inviting, even forcing, the Federals to march to his right into the heart of the Wilderness. Now Lee pointed a gloved hand eastward beyond the camps of Ewell's three divisions to the center of that jungle, where two roads ran down from the Federal camps to a pair of river crossings known as Germanna Ford and Ely's Ford. "Grant will cross by one of those fords," he said.[5] He did not elaborate or explain this prediction, but it soon proved true enough. Even as Lee spoke, Meade's staff was issuing written orders that would put the Army of the Potomac in motion at midnight of May 3–4 toward not one but both of those crossings.

Late that afternoon (2 May) a storm burst over the camps of Ben Butler's Army of the James around Yorktown and Gloucester. High winds ripped tents from their moorings while driving rain and hail pelted the soldiers thus suddenly bereft of cover. Men drenched to the skin fought to secure the tarpaulins that covered supplies. Teamsters and artillerymen sought to recapture horses that had broken loose. Then, as suddenly as it had come, the storm died down, leaving the Federals in a sea of mud strewn with flattened tents.

But even that did not dampen the spirits of the troops. One colonel among the 10th Corps units recently brought up from South Carolina wrote his wife the next day: "I have an altogether different feeling from that which used to possess me when I received marching orders in some cases down South. I have not the horrible feeling that we are to be wasted."[6] However, those in the know higher up were not so sanguine. A reporter for the *New York Times* who had attached himself to Baldy Smith's headquarters was writing to his managing editor that same day: "The expedition is aimed at Richmond and is intended primarily to divert Lee from Grant. It is looked upon, I believe, as of a desperate character— a sort of forlorn hope ready to be used up in the case of bringing Lee down this way. The chances are considered about even against and for its success. Ten days probably will tell the story."[7] Meanwhile, Butler's infantry units were told to be ready to embark the next day. The artillery units were already loading onto barges. Newspaper war correspondents were advised to be ready by the evening of 4 May "for a start somewhere."[8]

The third of May was a busy day on most fronts. In South Carolina, two brigades of Confederate infantry were beginning a long train ride toward Richmond. In West Virginia, Crook's Federal column, having left Gauley Bridge the day before, was now toiling up the New River valley into the Allegheny Mountains. Out in Arkansas, Steele's forces finally slogged their way through muddy roads to the relative safety and comfort of their entrenchments at Little Rock. His recent opponent, Kirby Smith, was issuing orders that would take his three Confederate infantry divisions back to Louisiana for another crack at Banks. And the latter's soldiers were busy constructing Bailey's dams in an effort to save Admiral Porter's fleet.

Within General John Imboden's brigade of cavalry, which was all the Confederates had with which to oppose Sigel's advance up the Shenandoah, was a company of partisan rangers commanded by Captain John H. McNeill. These were local men who knew the back roads and hiding places of the area as no Northern invader could ever know them. Some of his men were also deserters from regular Confederate units who happened to prefer the life of guerillas. Imboden had, in fact, recently court-martialed McNeill for refusing to turn such men over to him, but the partisan leader was released because his services were needed in the impending campaign. The general and the captain put their heads together and decided to out-Mosby Mosby with an even more daring raid against an even more sensitive target, Sigel's primary defensive responsibility, the Baltimore & Ohio Railroad. After dark on May third,

McNeill and sixty men left his camp heading north. That same day, word reached both General Lee and the Confederate authorities at Richmond of Sigel's advance up the Valley.

The night shift that Lee had ordered for the signal station on Clark's Mountain reported that evening that shadows could be seen repeatedly moving in front of the enemy's campfires, indicating that the Federals were on the move in the dark, but the direction of their march could not be determined. Lee ordered Ewell to prepare to march to the east at daylight—toward the fords where he had predicted Grant would cross—but he did not alert Hill or Longstreet. Lee had already ordered the latter to extend in the opposite direction, just in case Grant crossed him up and moved to the west after all.

Over on the other side of the Rapidan, Grant's senior staff officers gathered in the little front room of the headquarters at Culpeper to receive their final instructions. For some time the general sat writing last-minute orders. "After he had finished he turned his back to the table, crossed one leg over the other, lighted a fresh cigar, and began to talk of the momentous movement which in a few hours was to begin," Horace Porter remembered. "He said: 'I weighed very carefully the advantages and disadvantages of moving against Lee's left and moving against his right. The former promised more decisive results if immediately successful, and would best prevent Lee from moving north to make raids, but it would deprive our army of the advantages of easy communication with a water base of supplies, and compel us to carry such a large amount of ammunition and rations in wagon-trains, and detach so many troops as train guards, that I found it presented too many serious difficulties; and when I considered especially the sufferings of the wounded in being transported long distances overland, instead of being carried by short routes to water, where they could be comfortably moved by boats, I had no longer any hesitation in deciding to cross the Rapidan below the position occupied by Lee's army, and move by our left. This plan will also enable us to cooperate better with Butler's forces, and not become separated too far from them. I shall not give my attention so much to Richmond as to Lee's army, and I want all commanders to feel that hostile armies, and not cities, are to be their objective points.' . . . During the discussion that evening he rose from his seat, stepped up to a map hanging upon the wall, and with a sweep of his forefinger indicated a line around Richmond and Petersburg, and remarked: 'When my troops are there, Richmond is mine. Lee must retreat or surrender.' "[9]

Meade's chief of staff, the very capable Major General Andrew A. Humphreys, had worked out the initial movement in great detail, and at midnight of 3–4 May the Army of the Potomac began to move toward the Rapidan in two columns. That army, like Lee's, consisted of three corps of infantry and one of cavalry. Throughout most of 1863 it had contained seven corps of infantry but the two smallest, the 11th and 12th, had been sent west the previous September, and in March, just before Grant arrived, Meade had ordered the remaining five to be consolidated into three, primarily because he could not seem to find five generals capable of commanding corps to his satisfaction. By the time the reorganization was effected Grant had taken over, and many of the troops assumed he was to blame. It was an unpopular move, because the men had strongly identified with their old units.

The 1st Corps, which had opened both the battles of Antietam and Gettysburg for the Federals, was discontinued. Its popular and capable commander, John F. Reynolds, Meade's good friend, had been killed at Gettysburg. His successor, John Newton, had proved disappointing and had been sent west to command a division under Sherman. The 1st Corps' three divisions were consolidated into two and transferred to the 5th Corps, whose three old divisions were also consolidated into two. The new, enlarged 5th Corps, containing 24,000 infantrymen, was now commanded by Major General Gouverneur Kemble Warren, an 1850 graduate of West Point and pre-war officer of engineers. He had begun the war as the lieutenant colonel of the 5th New York, a famous zouave unit, and worked his way up to brigade command. He had then been made the chief engineer of the Army of the Potomac, and in that capacity had become one of the heroes of Gettysburg when he had taken the initiative to order troops to the far left of the Union line just in time to prevent Longstreet's men from capturing a key eminence known as Little Round Top. Since then he had commanded the 2nd Corps while its regular commander, Major General Winfield Scott Hancock, recovered from a severe wound received at Gettysburg.

The 2nd Corps' three divisions had also been consolidated into two, and two divisions of the 3rd Corps were transferred in so that the 2nd Corps now had four divisions and about 25,000 men. Hancock was finally sufficiently recovered from his wound to resume command of the corps. He was an 1840 graduate of West Point, three years ahead of Grant, and had commanded a brigade and then a division before taking over the 2nd Corps shortly before Gettysburg.

The 3rd Corps had been discontinued and its 3rd Division, made up of former garrison units that had reinforced the army from the Shenandoah after Gettysburg, had been transferred to the 6th Corps, whose original three divisions had also been consolidated into two. Major General John

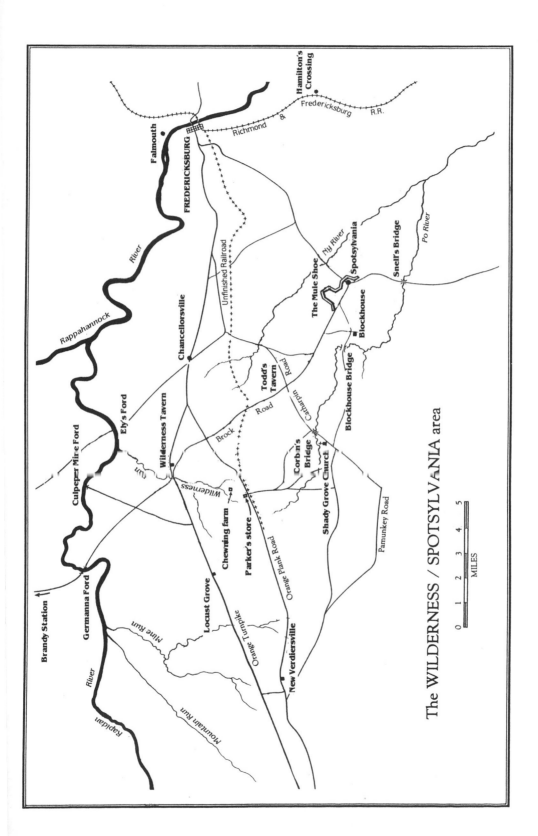

The WILDERNESS / SPOTSYLVANIA area

Sedgwick, the commander of the 6th Corps (now 20,000 men) had been in that position since before Chancellorsville. He had graduated from West Point in 1837, only two years after Meade. Highly competent, if unspectacular, Sedgwick was the best-loved of all the senior officers in the Army of the Potomac despite, or because of, his insistence on discipline. His troops called him Uncle John. He was an affable bachelor, with an insatiable penchant for games of solitaire.

Hancock, who was eleven years younger, was a hard-hitting, very capable commander, and a born leader of men. He was a handsome man of inspiring bearing who, as if by magic, always managed to be wearing a clean white shirt, even when everyone else was bedraggled from hours in the saddle and begrimed with mud, dust or gunsmoke. One of Meade's staff officers said that Hancock was a "very great and vehement talker but always says something worth hearing."[10] Warren, six years younger than Hancock, was brilliant and sensitive, but a bit on the slow and cautious side and inclined to become too involved in detail. The Cavalry Corps, of about 12,000 troopers, was, of course, commanded by Sheridan. He was a year younger than Warren and a driving, smash-'em-up, extremely capable commander, but brand new to both corps command and the Army of the Potomac.

In the first few minutes of 4 May, Wilson's 3rd Cavalry Division, escorting a section of the Cavalry Corps' bridge train, left its camp and led the way down the road toward Germanna Ford. Warren's infantry followed with their own bridge train, while Sedgwick's corps, in the rear, did not take up the march until daylight. Brigadier General David McMurtrie Gregg's 2nd Cavalry Division started down the road to Ely's Ford at 2 a.m. with another section of the Cavalry Corps' bridge train, followed by Hancock's 2nd Corps and the reserve artillery of the army. Brigadier General Alfred T. Torbert's 1st Cavalry Division, the corps' largest, was assigned to stay on the north side of the river for the first day to guard the rear of the immense train of 4,300 supply wagons. Part of the train would follow Hancock and part take a third ford in between the two main crossings. At about 2 a.m. Wilson's advance splashed across the 200-foot-wide river and drove off a picket of the 1st North Carolina Cavalry. At 5:50 a.m., Wilson notified Warren that his last cavalry unit was across the river and a bridge built on canvas pontoons was almost ready. Warren's infantry began crossing at 7 a.m., by which time their own wooden pontoon bridge was also completed. Wilson then sent his cavalry down the road into the Wilderness to cover the infantry's advance.

1. It is interesting to note that the Confederate officer quoted, Col. Joseph Ives, still spoke of North and South as "this country," not "these countries." Freeman, *R. E. Lee,* 2:92.

2. J. F. C. Fuller, *Grant and Lee* (Bloomington, Indiana, 1957), 110.

3. Ibid.

4. Freeman, *Lee's Lieutenants,* 3:344.

5. Clifford Dowdey, *Lee's Last Campaign* (New York, 1960), 32.

6. Robertson, *Back Door To Richmond,* 55.

7. Ibid.

8. Ibid., 56.

9. Porter, *Campaigning With Grant,* 36–37.

10. Mark Mayo Boatner, III, *The Civil War Dictionary* (New York, 1959), 372.

CHAPTER TWELVE

"The Trip Will Undoubtedly Be Prolonged"

4 May 1864

As the sun evaporated the morning mist, the Confederate signal station on Clark's Mountain could see long columns of Union infantry and artillery moving to the east toward the fords of the Rapidan. A flag-signal warning was wig-wagged to Ewell's headquarters, and word reached Lee, farther west, at about 9 a.m. He sent an order to A. P. Hill to start two of his divisions toward the Wilderness and leave the other behind to guard the wagon trains. Longstreet was also ordered to prepare to move out.

There were four main east-west routes into, and through, the Wilderness. The Orange Plank Road wound from Lee's headquarters at Orange Court House eastward toward Fredericksburg on the Rappahannock, following the low ridge between the small streams that flow north into that river and the Rapidan, and those that flow southeast to form the York. A straighter road, the Orange Turnpike, roughly paralleled that route along slightly lower ground a bit farther north. South of the Orange Plank Road were two more round-about routes. One started out as the

Old Fredericksburg Road and ran southeast before turning northeast and then east, by which time it was known as the Catharpin Road. Eventually, at a place called Shady Grove Church, it turned northeast again and connected with the Orange Plank Road a few miles west of Fredericksburg. The fourth route, the Pamunkey Road, dipped to the southeast from the Orange Plank Road a bit east of Orange Court House, crossed the Old Fredericksburg Road at Jackson's Shop, and gradually bore east and then northeast before connecting with the Catharpin Road at Shady Grove Church. From there its name changed to the Shady Grove Road and it ran on eastward to Spotsylvania Court House and passed to the south of Fredericksburg.

Ewell's corps, except for one brigade sent across the Rapidan to see if the Federals were really gone and three separate regiments left to hold the old positions, headed southeast from the river toward a crossroad with the Orange Turnpike called Locust Grove. Meanwhile, Hill formed two of his divisions on the Orange Plank Road and marched eastward, preceded by Stuart and part of his cavalry. Hill's other division, under R. H. Anderson, took position to cover the army's rear, just in case.

Longstreet was ordered to follow Hill's route but, typically, he countered with the proposal that he take the Old Fredericksburg-Catharpin route, which he said was shorter and "would at the same time relieve the Plank Road of the pressure of troops and trains."[1] Lee assented and was seemingly impressed with Longstreet's suggestion that Grant might be trying to draw the Confederates eastward toward Fredericksburg while all or part of Butler's forces moved up the York River to join the Union brigade at West Point, putting them in the rear of any attempted Rebel stand at Fredericksburg. Longstreet, after all, knew Grant better than anyone else in Lee's army. There was also the possibility that the Federals might turn westward, as they had under Meade the previous December. That maneuver had ended in a standoff along the banks of Mine Run, a small stream that ran northward into the Rapidan. In either case, the 1st Corps might come in handy on a road to the south of the current position of both armies. So as Lee faced eastward toward the Union army's new position, Ewell would be on his left along the Orange Turnpike, Hill in the center on the Orange Plank Road, and Longstreet on his right on the Catharpin Road. Ewell would be the farthest east, closest to the enemy, Hill farther back, and Longstreet a day's march behind.

The plans that Humphreys had drawn up for the Army of the Potomac were designed to do four things: to cross the Rapidan before Lee could effectively interfere; to put the Federals in a position from which they threatened to interpose between Lee and Richmond; to put the army where it could turn Lee's southern flank should he choose to hold his old positions along Mine Run; and to protect the immense train of supply wagons on which the Army of the Potomac was now dependent. Guarding the trains constrained the army to a slower march through the Wilderness than was desirable for the purposes of the other three objectives because the 4,300 wagons could not negotiate the poor roads as quickly as the troops themselves. In fact, it would be late the next day before all of them even got across the Rapidan.

Wilson's horsemen cautiously followed the Germanna Plank Road southeastward until they reached its junction with the Orange Turnpike in a clearing near a roadside hostel called Wilderness Tavern. Patrols were sent westward along the turnpike toward Locust Grove, where shots were exchanged with Rebel pickets, and farther southeast down the Brock Road to Todd's Tavern. Around noon, Griffin's 1st Division at the head of Warren's 5th Corps reached the same Orange Turnpike intersection, and the cavalry moved out again, following a wagon track due south up the valley of another small tributary of the Rapidan called Wilderness Run.

Shortly before noon, Grant and Meade, with their respective staffs, crossed the river at Germanna Ford. Grant rode his big bay horse Cincinnati up the bluff and took over a deserted old gabled farmhouse overlooking the ford for his headquarters. Meade's tent was pitched nearby. Accompanying Grant was a civilian in black clothes that the soldiers took to calling the general's private undertaker, but in reality was Congressman Elihu B. Washburne, Grant's political sponsor. He had come along to see for himself the fruits of his labor in getting Grant to his present position. The general sat down on the front steps of the old house, lit one of his endless chain of cigars, and silently watched Sedgwick's men march over the bridge.

The common soldiers of the Army of the Potomac did not yet know quite what to make of the lieutenant general. They doubted the significance of his western victories. Until he had proven himself against the Confederates' first team he was just another general. As more than one of their officers had already said to Grant or his staff, "You don't know Bobby Lee!"[2] The enlisted men were not particularly enthusiastic about him, but they had come to respect him. One veteran summed Grant up pretty well after seeing him for the first time: "He looks as if he meant it." One of Meade's staff officers described the same quality in the general-in-chief: "Grant wears an expression as if he had determined to drive his head through a brick wall and was about to do it."[3] There was one thing that Grant had done which had certainly been a big hit with the veteran infantrymen. He had taken oversized, pampered heavy artillery regiments, used to living in comfortable barracks in Washington, and made foot-slogging infantrymen out of them. This amused the old soldiers no end. Misery always loves company.

After watching the soldiers march past for a while, Grant finally spoke to his staff officers. "Well, the movement so far has been as satisfactory as could be desired," he said. "We have succeeded in seizing the fords and crossing the river without loss or delay. Lee must by this time know upon what roads we are advancing, but he may not yet realize the full extent of the movement. We shall probably soon get some indications as to what he intends to do." A newspaper correspondent then asked Grant how long it would take him to reach Richmond, which had defied the best efforts of Union commanders for three years. "I will agree to be there in about four days," the general replied to the reporter's amazement. "That is," Grant added dryly, "if General Lee becomes a party to the agreement; but, if he objects, the trip will undoubtedly be prolonged." Around 1 p.m. a courier came over from Meade's headquarters with the transcript of a Confederate signal from Clark's Mountain that a Union signal station had decoded. "That gives just the information I wanted," Grant exclaimed after reading it. "It shows that Lee is drawing out from his position, and is pushing across to meet us."[4] He immediately sent word for Burnside to abandon the railroad line to Washington and to make forced marches for Germanna Ford.

About that same time, Meade was informed that a large force of Rebel cavalry which had wintered around Fredericksburg was now concentrating just south of that town at Hamilton's Crossing. This prompted the army commander to order that Torbert's big 1st Cavalry Division should cross the river the next morning and join Gregg's 2nd Division on the army's eastern flank. Sheridan was to take personal command of the combined force and protect the wagon train from those Confederate horsemen.

At 2 p.m. Wilson's troopers reached the Orange Plank Road at Parker's Store, and Wilson sent the 5th New York Cavalry Regiment westward to scout toward Mine Run. Other patrols were sent toward the Catharpin and Pamunkey roads. Meanwhile, Griffin's infantry turned west on the Orange Turnpike and advanced a little over a mile before halting to establish a strong picket line to protect the western flank of the moving army. "An ominous silence was our only welcome," a captain from New York remembered. Some Pennsylvanians scouted around and reported that "No other idea of the country can be given save that it was a forest apparently without limit, with clearings so few and their space so contracted as scarcely to be considered as breaking the solemn monotony of tree, chaparral and undergrowth."[5]

Warren's next division, Crawford's 3rd, the Pennsylvania Reserve Division in which Meade had once commanded a brigade, briefly followed Wilson's cavalry south but soon stopped and made camp in the fields of a plantation owned by a Major Lacy. Warren's other two divisions soon came up and went into bivouac nearby. At 3:05 p.m. Warren reported that his men "were almost all in camp and washing their feet."[6] The leading division of Sedgwick's 6th Corps, Getty's 2nd, followed Warren's troops across the Rapidan but halted on the Germanna Plank Road near another little stream called Flat Run about two and a half miles northwest of Wilderness Tavern. There it was soon joined by Wright's 1st Division. Finally, Rickett's 3rd Division crossed the pontoon bridge at 6 p.m. and took position to guard the crossing until Burnside's 9th Corps should arrive the next day. Gregg's 2nd Cavalry Division had crossed the Rapidan at Ely's Ford before dawn. Confederate pickets immediately carried the news to Major General Fitzhugh Lee, Robert E. Lee's nephew, whose Rebel cavalry division was the force gathering around Hamilton's Crossing. Around 6:30 a.m., when Hancock's infantry reached the ford, Gregg's troopers pushed ahead past Chancellorsville (a one-house village) to Aldrich's farm, where the Catharpin Road joined the Orange Plank Road. Patrols were sent out in all directions, toward Hamilton's Crossing, Spotsylvania Court House and beyond Shady Grove Church. Hancock's leading division, the 1st, under Barlow, arrived at Chancellorsville around 9:30 that morning and went into camp along the Orange Plank Road. The rear of the 2nd Corps crossed over the pontoons at Ely's Ford at 1:10 p.m., and by 3 p.m. all four of Hancock's divisions were in camp around the burned-out Chancellor house.

This early halt of the Union infantry was a necessary part of Humphrey's plan, in order to give the numerous wagons time to get over the river and to keep them from getting so far behind the infantry that they might fall prey to a sudden dash by the redoubtable Rebel cavalry or to one of Lee's bold flanking movements through the cover of the screening Wilderness. Otherwise, most of the infantry could easily have marched clear of the confining woods before dark, well before Lee could have done anything about it.

The Rebels, having started later, were still marching when the Federals went into camp. It was about sunset when Ewell's advance reached Locust Grove, and his three divisions bivouacked along and south of the turnpike. Heth's division of Hill's 3rd Corps marched through New Verdiersville about the same time and encamped along the Orange Plank Road. Wilcox's Division of the same corps encamped just west of the little town. Lee, who had ridden with Hill all day, had his tent pitched across the road from the Rhodes house about halfway between the two divisions. He always avoided using any houses for his headquarters for fear of bringing reprisals down on the property should it later fall into the enemy's hands. Not long afterwards a dispatch arrived from Longstreet saying that his 1st Corps would camp that night about halfway between Mechanicsville, its starting point, and where Lee was at the moment. He hoped to reach Richard's Shop on the Catharpin Road by noon the next day.

At 8 p.m. an order was drafted for forwarding to Ewell: "General Lee will be found in the woods opposite this house (Rhodes') to-night. He wishes you to be ready to move on early in the morning. If the enemy moves down the river, he wishes you to push on after him. If he comes this way, we will take our old line. The general's desire is to bring him to battle as soon now as possible."[7]

"Just the orders I like," Ewell exclaimed when he received this directive early the next morning, "go straight down the road and strike the enemy wherever I find him."[8]

Confederate president Jefferson Davis telegraphed an order to Beauregard that fourth day of May to cancel Hoke's attack on New Berne, North Carolina unless immediate success was certain and to prepare to return the troops to Virginia. In Petersburg, George Pickett was preparing that day to relinquish command of his district and to proceed to Hanover Junction, between Richmond and Fredericksburg, where the units of his old division were to reassemble, protecting Lee's supply line from Butler's troops at West Point. Now that it was almost too late, Davis was finally giving in to Lee's requests for the return of all his detached units. Beauregard, for his part, was already angling for a transfer north of the James to reinforce Lee for the big battle presumably forthcoming. He telegraphed that same day to Major General Daniel Harvey Hill, another victim of a quarrel with Bragg who was not only temporarily without an assignment but had even lost his promotion to lieutenant general because Davis had declined to send his name to the Confederate senate for confirmation. Hill, no kin to A. P. Hill but a brother-in-law of the late Stonewall Jackson, had commanded a division under Lee at Antietam, then the defenses south of the James, and most recently a corps at Chickamauga. He had applied to Beauregard to serve unofficially on the creole's staff. "I would be glad to have you as volunteer aide," Beauregard lamented, "but see no prospect now, of active operations in this Dept. for me, Burnside having joined his forces with Meade."[9]

On the Virginia Peninsula and just across the York at Gloucester, some of Butler's units were awakened as early as 2:30 that morning of 4 May, but few had embarked on their transports until 10 a.m., most not until after noon. It was discovered that the loading facilities on the Gloucester side were inadequate, and the lines of soldiers were growing terribly long. One of the problems was that the 10th Corps had no commander to arrange the order of loading. Quincy Gilmore had remained in South Carolina so long to oversee the shipping of his units north from there that Butler and Grant had even considered delaying the entire operation. He finally arrived during the loading on the fourth. As evening came on, Butler began to prod his dilatory subordinate: "Having waited for your army corps from Port Royal I am not a little surprised at waiting for you here. Push everything forward."[10] But at least the men already on board were entranced by the scene of hundreds of boats forming line in the broad tidal river. "As twilight faded into darkness," a young soldier in the 118th New York wrote, "lights appeared on the transports and these, rocking and changing, seem like so many loose stars playing over the river to cheer our departure. Playing bands, men cheering and singing; busy tugs coughing through the fleet bearing orders; neighing horses and noise of escaping steam; soldiers shouting from steamer to steamer—but not a responsible word as to our destination."[11]

At Fortress Monroe, Ben Butler, his staff and his signal corps detachment went on board his headquarters ship, the *Greyhound*. And after dark the troops up at West Point, having apparently misled the Confederates after all, despite Baldy Smith's derision, quietly boarded boats and joined the others down the York.

Over on the south side of the James at Portsmouth, Butler's chief of cavalry issued final orders for an early departure the next morning on a move into enemy country. Butler, probably at Baldy Smith's suggestion, had originally asked for Smith's friend James Wilson to command his cavalry, but Grant had already decided to give that officer a division in the Army of the Potomac and instead gave Butler Wilson's successor as head of the Cavalry Bureau, Colonel August V. Kautz. Since the latter was outranked by the commanders of Butler's cavalry regiments, Grant promoted him to brigadier general.

Kautz had been born in Germany but was brought to the United States as an infant. He had been raised in the same small Ohio town where Grant had spent his own childhood but, with six years difference in their ages, they had not been friends. Kautz served as a private in the Mexican War and then went to West Point, graduating in the class of 1852. Like Grant, he served in the 4th Infantry on the Pacific Coast, but the two did not serve together. Kautz fought on the Peninsula as a captain in the 6th Cavalry and was later appointed colonel of the 2nd Ohio Cavalry. Now he had under his command at Portsmouth a small cavalry division of four regiments totaling 1,750 men. Colonel Simon Mix's 1st Brigade consisted of the 3rd New York Cavalry and half of the 1st District of Columbia Cavalry. The latter regiment was armed with a weapon even more potent than the Spencer: the Henry repeating rifle. This was the true forerunner of the Winchester. It held fifteen self-contained metallic cartridges in a tube under the barrel, and pushing the lever below the trigger forward and back not only expelled an expended cartridge and loaded a new one, but also cocked the hammer at the same time. It was the finest rifle available during the entire war. Colonel Samuel Spear's 2nd Brigade of Kautz's division contained eleven companies of the 11th Pennsylvania Cavalry and would be joined by the 5th Pennsylvania along the way.

Joseph E. Johnston, down in Georgia, was telegraphing Richmond for reinforcements on the fourth of May, because scouts had been reporting for three days that Sherman's forces were stirring and preparing to advance against him. As a matter of fact, Confederate reinforcements were already on the way. With almost all of Sherman's units now concentrated near Chattanooga, and Banks effectively neutralized out on the Red River, the Confederates could spare troops from Mobile and central Mississippi.

Indeed, two of Sherman's three armies were advancing that day. Sherman had originally intended to send McPherson's Army of the Tennessee southeast from northern Alabama to Rome, Georgia and on to cut the railroad between Atlanta and Johnston's army at Dalton. But, with A. J. Smith's troops still out on the Red River with Banks and the 17th Corps not yet returned from veteran furlough, McPherson's force was deemed too small to operate independently. Instead, Sherman had it brought to the Chattanooga area to reinforce Thomas' Army of the Cumberland. Meanwhile, most of Schofield's even smaller Army of the Ohio was moving down from east Tennessee to take position on Thomas' left.

In southwestern Virginia that day, 4 May, Breckinridge was just getting ready to move out and meet the Union forces approaching his command from beyond the Alleghenies when he received a telegram that said: "Information received here indicates the propriety of your making a junction with General Imboden to meet the enemy on his movements toward Staunton. Communicate with General R. E. Lee and General Imboden." It was signed "Jefferson Davis."[12] He also received an order from Bragg to send a cavalry brigade to east Tennessee. His own plans thrown completely awry, the former vice president immediately fired off a wire to General Lee for instructions. To go to the aid of Imboden would be very difficult, he pointed out. His men were from 36 to 60 miles away from the Virginia Central Railroad, which was the only good route to

Staunton, Sigel's presumed objective. Marching all the way would, of course, be even slower.

That message must have crossed with one from Lee informing him that the president had given Lee command over him and that Imboden had been ordered to report to Breckinridge. "I trust you will drive the enemy back," Lee concluded.[13] Word came in from Imboden that he was calling out the local reserves—old men and boys—and that Sigel's column contained 7,000 men. Thus just as his own department was being threatened by a large enemy force, the Kentuckian was being ordered to face about in a new direction and move more than a hundred miles over bad roads and one rickety railroad to "drive back" another enemy force that was also considerably larger than his own and Imboden's units combined. Breckinridge wired back to Lee for more information on Union movements and proposed to join Imboden's cavalry and reserves against Sigel with his two infantry brigades while he left his own cavalry—ignoring Bragg's order to send part of it off in the opposite direction—to hold his own department against the advancing Federals. All he could do then was wait for Lee's answer.

Meade's troops spent a gloomy night in the Wilderness after halting early on the afternoon of 4 May. Their mood changed from cheerfulness and expectancy as they marched on that bright spring day to somber reflection and foreboding after darkness overtook them in the woods. The tops of the pine trees began to sway and sigh as a breeze came up, and the forest dampened sounds into a strange and sinister silence, accentuated occasionally by the mournful cry of the whippoorwills and the plaintive hooting of an owl. The usual campfire talk and singing were absent that night, for the Wilderness carried "a sense of ominous dread," one New Yorker remembered, "which many of us found it almost impossible to shake off."[14]

The common soldiers of the Army of the Potomac considered themselves to be as good at fighting as their Rebel counterparts man for man, but they had come to expect defeat as a matter of course after a steady diet of it for three years. Sergeant Will Owen of the 20th Maine had recently written to his sister: "We have men enough and they will fight if our leading men will do what is right. It is no use for men to say that it has been impossible to settle this up before. I know that there has been men and money enough and now with this Grand Army of Volunteers if we are defeated it will be with mismanagement, nothing else. The Army is now most old and tried soldiers and veterans. They know how to fight and expect to. What will then defeat us? Mismanagement?"[15]

In the camps of Hancock's 2nd Corps around Chancellorsville that night the men found many reminders of the year before, when another promising campaign had gone bad in these entangling woods because their leaders had once again been outgeneraled by Bobby Lee. There were even grimmer souvenirs than the burned-out shell of the Chancellor house, for many of the casualties had been buried in shallow graves in the fields where these men now camped, and rain and wind had begun to expose some of their bones. One of Hancock's soldiers prodded a skull with his foot and turned to his comrades. "This is what you are all coming to," he exclaimed, "and some of you will start toward it tomorrow."[16]

1. Steere, *The Wilderness Campaign*, 75.
2. Ibid., 28.
3. Catton, *Grant Takes Command*, 159.
4. All three quotes in this paragraph are from Porter, *Campaigning With Grant*, 43.
5. Both quotes from Trudeau, *Bloody Roads South*, 35.
6. Ibid., 51.
7. Steere, *The Wilderness Campaign*, 81.
8. Ibid.
9. Robertson, *Back Door To Richmond*, 54.
10. Ibid., 57.
11. Ibid, 57–58.
12. Davis, *The Battle of New Market*, 27.
13. Clifford Dowdey and Louis H. Manarin, eds., *The Wartime Papers of R. E. Lee* (New York, 1961), 718–719.
14. Bruce Catton, *A Stillness at Appomattox* (New York, 1957), 62.
15. John J. Pullen, *The 20th Maine* (New York, 1957), 185.
16. Catton, *A Stillness at Appomattox*, 62.

CHAPTER THIRTEEN

"Apparently a Complete Surprise"

5 May 1864

Franz Sigel, still ensconced at Winchester drilling his little army, decided to hold a mock battle on 5 May, as further training for his troops. The regimental officers had been up all the previous night studying their manuals of tactics, but it did not seem to help. One problem was that most of Sigel's staff officers, like himself, were German and unable to deliver orders in intelligible English. Between them and the inexperienced division and brigade officers every unit in the command was soon moving back and forth in complete disorder, some advancing, some retreating, some charging imaginary enemies. The 116th Ohio, after marching back and forth for a while, was ordered to make a charge and was then forgotten. The troops advanced so far that they failed to hear recall sounded. Eventually mounted staff officers had to be sent to bring them back. Night finally brought an end to the frustrating, humiliating exercise and the exhausted men all returned to their camps—except, that is, for the 34th Massachusetts, which no one had remembered to call in from the skirmish line.

"Thus endeth the first lesson," the chaplain of the 116th Ohio commented. "Yes, by God!" his colonel rejoined, "and a h—l of a lesson it was, too." Another of Sigel's men complained that "there was never anything seen half so ridiculous, and it bred in everyone the most supreme contempt for General Sigel and his crowd of foreign adventurers." To make matters worse, Sigel ordered the operation to be repeated the next day. Upon hearing that, the colonel of the 34th Massachusetts turned his regiment over to his lieutenant colonel, saying, "I've lost all interest in it and the service; I won't serve under such fools; and you are a fool if you do."[1]

At dawn on that fifth of May, Captain John McNeill and his Rebel partisans were at a crossroads outside the town of Piedmont in northern West Virginia, or northwestern Virginia as the Confederates still considered it. After Virginia had seceded from the Union, the almost slaveless, Union-loving, mountainous western counties had in turn seceded from the state. They were admitted to the Union in 1863 as the new, separate state of West Virginia.

It was a situation that had forced both the Federal and Confederate governments into inconsistent positions. Although the Confederacy would never have existed had not Southern politicians insisted that each state had the right to withdraw from the Union whenever it felt like doing so, neither the Confederate government nor the state of Virginia would concede that counties had the same right to separate from their states. The Federal government under the Republican administration, on the other hand, had denied the right of states to secede but found it useful to back the secession of the western counties of Virginia from their state. Neither government was willing to let ideological consistency get in the way of political and military expediency. However, the issue well illustrated the ultimate question raised by secession: where would it end? If the South could set up shop on its own, why not the West Coast, or the state of Kentucky, or the city of New York, or any little town that wanted to feel important, or the 500 block of Main Street? That way would lead to the balkanization of North America: a collection of petty states perpetually wrangling over borders, tariffs, navigation of the rivers—the very situation that the Constitution had been designed to avoid.

Anyway, McNeill ordered the telegraph wires leading out of Piedmont cut, then sent Captain John T. Peerce with ten men along one road toward Bloomington, Maryland, while he and the rest of his small command followed the other road toward Piedmont. Outside the town, which was on the Baltimore & Ohio Railroad, McNeill stopped the first westbound train that came by, and sent a lieutenant and two men into Piedmont on the engine under a flag of truce, to demand the surrender of the small Union garrison. The Federals, from the 6th West Virginia Infantry, were reluctant at first but were persuaded when McNeill and the rest of his men rode in and started shooting. What the Rebel commander did not know was that his approach had been spotted, and word had already been telegraphed to a larger Union garrison five miles south at New Creek when the wire was cut.

McNeill had fire set to the Baltimore & Ohio roundhouse, machine shops, and storage sheds, destroyed nine engines found standing in the yards and sent six others, unmanned but under full steam, careering down toward New Creek so that they would smash into anything on the tracks along the way. Then he set fire to over 75 freight cars. The smoke served as a beacon for the 75 men and one cannon dispatched from New Creek as soon as the telegraph had brought word of the raiders' presence. The Federals quickly reached McNeill's outposts, opened fire with their cannon, and killed one Confederate, causing the partisans to withdraw hastily toward Bloomington, Peerce having sent word that the line of retreat was open in that direction.

Peerce had, meanwhile, stopped two eastbound freight trains and turned their contents over to the citizens of the town. Then, forewarned of what was coming, he ambushed a troop train and captured 115 Federal soldiers who had weapons but no ammunition with which to resist. Peerce was busy destroying the trains he had captured when McNeill and the main body rode in, not far ahead of their pursuers. They tried to burn the bridge over the North Fork of the Potomac River, which formed the border between the two states, but they didn't have time. So, after paroling their prisoners, the Confederates rode off into the mountains.

The raid had accomplished all that Imboden had hoped it would. The physical damage would soon be repaired, although at the cost of hundreds of thousands of dollars. But more importantly, the Baltimore & Ohio complained loudly to Secretary of War Stanton, who in turn voiced his displeasure to Franz Sigel. The latter received word of the raid late that same day, after his sham battle had fizzled. He considered himself blameless, since he had marched away from the railroad on direct orders from General Grant, and had advised the governor of West Virginia to call out the militia to guard the Baltimore & Ohio in his absence. Nevertheless, he ordered 500 cavalry to go after McNeill's 60, thus weakening his own advance even as the Confederates were beginning to concentrate what little force they could find to send against him.

At 5 a.m. that same morning, after nine hours of suspense, Breckinridge received an answer to his telegram to Lee. That general said

that he could not be sure that Staunton was the threatened point, but it
seemed that all the Federal forces once sent west—for Ord's aborted
offensive—had returned to the east and were now advancing up the
Valley. "These are the forces I wish you to meet, or by some movement to
draw back before they get on my left," Lee continued. "Imboden reports
Sigel with 7,000 men approaching Front Royal. Communicate with him,
and try and check this Valley movement as soon as possible."[2]

Breckinridge began firing off orders to his subordinates. His infantry
brigades were to start marching the next morning for Jackson's River
Depot on the Virginia Central Railroad, where trains would be ready by
the time they arrived to pick them up one at a time. While Breckinridge
was packing his own saddlebags for the ride north, word arrived from
Imboden that Sigel had reached Winchester, which put him closer to
Staunton than Breckinridge's forces. The Kentuckian and his staff put
their essentials onto a pack mule and set out that evening for the town of
Narrows to confer with Brigadier General Gabriel C. Wharton, one of his
brigade commanders. That same day, Averell's 2,000 Union horsemen left
Logan Courthouse, about seventy miles north of Saltville, like his superior, Crook, headed straight for the area Breckinridge was stripping of
defenders.

That same afternoon, 5 May, the *USS Miami*, which had survived the
encounter with the *CSS Albermarle* a couple of weeks before, along with
an army transport and two smaller ships, the *Commodore Hull* and the
Ceres, was sent to lay torpedoes in the mouth of the Roanoke River to
keep that Rebel ironclad from moving into the sound for which it was
named. But as the Federal ships neared the buoy marking the river's
mouth, the Confederate ram was seen to be coming out. It was accompanied by a steamer called *Cotton Plant* loaded with troops and towing
several launches, and another known as *Bombshell*, a former Union boat
which the Southerners had sunk at Plymouth and later raised. The Confederates were trying to get into the sounds to go down to help Hoke's
troops take New Berne. When the two sides caught sight of each other,
Cotton Plant and its troops were sent back to a place of safety while the
Federal ships outran the ram to join the rest of the force guarding the
sound, before turning to fight.

By 3:10 p.m. the Union squadron had formed two columns and was
advancing to meet the *Albemarle*. The main column consisted of the
double-enders *Mattabesett*, *Sassacus*, and *Wyalusing* and the smaller
Whitehead, while the *Miami* formed a supporting column with the
smaller *Ceres*, *Commodore Hull* and *Seymour*. The *Miami* carried a
torpedo which its commander hoped to explode under the enemy ram

and some of the other Union ships carried strong nets with which to foul her propeller. At 4:40 p.m. the *Albemarle* opened the battle with a shot from her forward gun that struck the *Mattabesett*'s bow, wounding six men in the crew of the forward 100-pounder pivot rifle. The ram headed straight for that ship, but the more nimble Union vessel maneuvered to avoid a head-on collision, delivering a broadside from two large rifles and four 9-inch smoothbores at a range of 150 yards as the two ships passed each other. The *Sassacus* followed suit but, as the ship's surgeon wrote, "the guns might as well have fired blank cartridges, for the shot skimmed off into the air, and even the 100-pound solid shot from the pivot-rifle glanced from the sloping roof into space with no apparent effect."[3]

But the Union ships began to circle around behind the ironclad, and the *Mattabesett* fired her forward rifle and howitzers into the unarmored *Bombshell*, which surrendered and was ordered to follow in the Federals' wake. The *Sassacus* then came up and also fired into the *Bombshell*, unaware that it had already surrendered. When the mistake was discovered, the *Bombshell* was ordered to pass astern and anchor, but was almost run down by the *Wyalusing* as it came up. However, that ship also learned of the surrender and backed engines just in time. As the ironclad came round in a half-circle the three double-enders were following a larger circle around it. Then the *Sassacus* saw her chance. Her captain, Lieutenant Commander Francis A. Roe, ordered his engineer to give her all the steam she could carry and he cut sharply across the circle and headed straight for the *Albemarle*'s broadside. His ship's bow was shod with a bronze beak weighing three tons, and he intended to turn the tables on the Confederates and ram the ram.

The *Sassacus*' surgeon recorded that "with full steam and open throttle the ship sprang forward like a living thing."[4] The guns ceased firing and the crew was ordered to lie down, then the wooden ship struck the ironclad at what Roe estimated as ten knots. The shock of the collision extinguished the lights inside the *Albemarle*'s iron-sheathed casemate, and the Rebel monster heeled over with water washing over her after deck. "Through the starboard shutter, which had been partly jarred off by the concussion," the surgeon wrote, "I saw the port of the ram not ten feet away. It opened, and like a flash of lightning I saw the grim muzzle of a cannon, the gun's-crew naked to the waist and blackened with powder; then a blaze, a roar and the rush of the shell as it crashed through, whirling me round and dashing me to the deck."[5]

Roe continued to pour on the steam in hopes of forcing the ironclad under, while firing three 100-pound, iron shots from one of his pivot guns at the ironclad from point-blank range. All three shattered against the monster's side, showering the *Sassacus* with fragments. By then, the two vessels had swung alongside each other bow to stern, and the *Albemarle's* aft gun was brought to bear. It sent an exposive shell crashing through the Federal ship's wooden side, smashing into her starboard boiler. As the *Sassacus* filled with steam and screaming scalded men, she dropped astern of the Confederate ram. Her guns continued to fire, but the shot bounced off the ironclad's casemate into the air like so many marbles.

The Federal ships were now in great confusion and in considerable danger of firing into each other, and it took some time to bring order to the squadron. The *Miami* was told to try her torpedo, but she steered badly and was unable to get into position; while the *Wyalusing* mistakenly signalled that she was sinking. Then the *Mattabesett* steamed in close, firing as rapidly as possible and, after passing the Rebel ship, attempted to lay a net in her path, but it was torn and lost before properly positioned. The Federal ship then turned and steamed past the ram in the other direction, firing its other broadside as shot from the ironclad mortally wounded two men and did considerable damage to the wooden vessel. By then it was growing dark, and the signal was given to cease firing. The *Albemarle* returned the way it had come, followed watchfully at a respectful distance by the *Commodore Hull* and the *Ceres*. The bronze beak of the *Sassacus* had been twisted and almost entirely torn away, while the *Albemarle* had suffered no discernable damage except for a riddled smokestack. However, she had proven so unwieldy that her captain decided that it was impossible to steam down into Pamlico Sound to help Hoke take New Berne after all.

Just as the sun came up on that morning of 5 May, another violent thunderstorm had hit the mass of ships assembled off the Virginia Peninsula. It was a dramatic beginning to an important day but it had soon blown over, leaving a warm, pleasant morning. Ben Butler had hoped to start moving shortly after midnight but, thanks partly to Gillmore, he was already running late. At 4 a.m. Butler signaled Admiral Samuel P. Lee to send the navy's gunboats on upstream while he hurried the army transports. Finally, at 6 a.m., the head of the fleet began to move. Brigadier General Charles Graham's three army gunboats were already well upstream, followed by the navy's wooden gunboats and then its ironclad monitors, each towed by two small gunboats. Then came the fleet of transports carrying the Army of the James. "It was a motley array of vessels," Baldy Smith remembered. "Coasters and river steamers, ferry-boats and tugs, screw and side-wheel steamers, sloops, schooners, barges, and canal-boats raced or crawled up the stream toward the designated landing."[6]

Smith's 18th Corps, leading the way, consisted of three divisions totalling 16,978 infantrymen and 1,012 artillerymen, plus the 1st New York Mounted Rifles. Bringing up the rear was Gillmore's 10th Corps, also consisting of three divisions, totalling 16,812 infantry and 1,114 artillerymen, plus the 1st Battalion of the 4th Massachusetts Cavalry and eight companies of the 1st New York Engineers. The troops were in a festive mood as they glided effortlessly off to war. The bands began to play, and the soldiers gazed at the passing scenery or watched Butler steaming up and down the column of transports on the *Greyhound* waving his cap and roaring, "Forward!" as he came abreast of each boat. His enthusiasm was infectious and many of the troops broke into cheers.

The fleet steamed past the old wreckage of the victims of the *Merrimac/Virginia*, then up the broad tidal river past the ruins of the vine-covered church at Jamestown, where American history had first begun. Occasionally, large plantations came into view, some of the oldest and richest in the country. The pastures were green and the fields were full of corn and cotton. Slaves were occasionally seen gesticulating as if asking to be taken away, and several times the soldiers on the ships caught sight of long lines of the 1st and 2nd U.S. Colored Cavalry paralleling the river on the northern bank. Abandoned Confederate earthworks were visible, and as the hours passed and the broad river narrowed, Rebel signal stations were easily discerned.

There were a few key points along the shore from which a hostile force could easily dispute the use of the river. Since the Federal army would depend on the river for supplies, Butler's plan included the occupation of these places. Brigadier General Edward Hinks' division of the 18th Corps consisted entirely of black regiments. Part of Wild's 1st Brigade of that division was now dropped off at the first of these, a bluff on the north bank known as Wilson's Wharf. A few miles farther upstream the rest of the brigade was left to occupy the site of an old Confederate fortification known as Fort Powhatan. The *USS Atlanta* and two gunboats were also left to protect the river supply line.

In mid-afternoon the advance elements approached the confluence of the James and its principal tributary, the Appomattox River. A large Rebel flag could be seen flying on the bluff on the south bank where the little port town of City Point lay. Hinks, sent with his other brigade to occupy the site, found several navy warships halted just out of range of the bluff. When he asked why the navy had stopped, he was told that Admiral Lee was transferring his flag from a wooden gunboat to an ironclad before risking an engagement. Appalled at such timidity and aware that the army gunboats were already lying off the town, Hinks ordered his transport forward, perhaps encouraged by the sight of the *Greyhound* racing toward him. Hinks' transport pulled up at the wharf, and black troops advanced up the bluff to capture a Confederate signal detachment as it frantically signalled news of the Federals' landing to a station nearer to Petersburg. The Rebel flag was soon replaced by the stars and stripes, and Union signalmen took over the Confederate platform to communicate with the fleet, which was pushing on a mile and a half up the James to Bermuda Hundred Landing.

Ships' boats had to be used to disembark Smith's two white divisions there because the shallow water prevented a close approach to the beach. While the troops were ferried ashore, the army gunboats chased a Rebel steamer upstream and the navy began to drag the river for torpedoes. After Smith's first units fanned out to protect the landing, the 9th New Jersey was detailed to construct a makeshift dock from old canal boats and scrap lumber brought along for the purpose. As darkness fell, the transports lined up to unload their troops and cargo, and all night long soldiers who had temporarily lost their land legs stumbled off into the night to find a place to camp. At 9 p.m. Butler sent off a message to Grant and Secretary of War Stanton that said: "No opposition thus far. Apparently a complete surprise."[7]

At 11:30 that morning Beauregard again rejected D. H. Hill's offer to serve on his staff for there still did not appear to be much prospect of action in his department. He kept his options open, however, by saying that he would telegraph back should things change. Not long after sending that note, the telegraph in Beauregard's headquarters began to rattle off a message from George Pickett up at Petersburg. The latter reported that his scouts had sighted a Union fleet coming up the James River. Without waiting for further details, Beauregard sent an order to Hoke to call off the attack at New Berne and bring his force to Weldon. Then a telegram was fired off to Whiting, in command of the southern district of the department, authorizing him to use all available railroad trains to hasten Hagood's South Carolina infantry brigade, which had previously been ordered to Richmond. He also gave Pickett permission to go outside of the chain of command and call directly upon the War Department for assistance if necessary.

Less than an hour after Pickett's first message another arrived, asking for troops. Beauregard authorized Pickett to halt Hagood's Brigade when it reached Petersburg and ordered Pickett to remain in command at that city instead of moving to reinforce Lee as he had been ordered. At 12:35 p.m. Beauregard advised Bragg that Pickett had placed the head of the Federal fleet in sight of City Point and informed him of the orders that he had given Pickett regarding Hagood's South Carolinians. As further messages from Pickett kept him apprised of Butler's progress, Beauregard

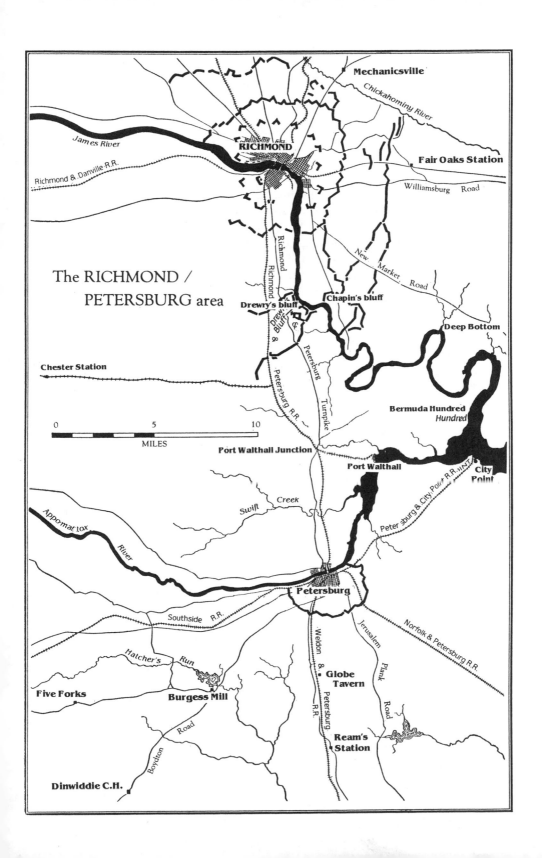

The RICHMOND /
PETERSBURG area

Mechanicsville

Chickahominy River

James River

RICHMOND

Fair Oaks Station

Richmond & Danville R.R.

Williamsburg Road

Richmond

New Market Road

Drewry's bluff

Chapin's bluff

Drew. Bluff

Deep Bottom

Richmond & Petersburg

Chester Station

Petersburg R.R.

Petersburg Turnpike

Bermuda Hundred
Hundred

0   5   10
MILES

Port Walthall Junction

Port Walthall

City
Point

Petersburg & City Point R.R.

Swift Creek

Appomattox River

Petersburg

Southside R.R.

Norfolk & Petersburg R.R.

Hatcher's Run

Weldon & Petersburg R.R.

Jerusalem Plank Road

Globe
Tavern

Five Forks

Burgess Mill

Road

Ream's
Station

Boydton

Dinwiddie C.H.

began to gather up his units. A regiment from Kinston was ordered north and three more were directed to Weldon. Another telegram was fired off to Hill, telling him to come on. At 4:30 that afternoon Beauregard advised Pickett that Bragg had forbidden the halting of Hagood's Brigade. It must be sent on to Richmond.

Without those South Carolinians, all Pickett had to defend Petersburg were the 31st North Carolina of Thomas Clingman's brigade, the Washington Artillery Battalion of New Orleans, which had wintered there since being dropped off by Longstreet on his way west in the fall, and the poorly armed local reserves and militia. The rest of his troops were guarding the Blackwater line against the Federals around Norfolk and Suffolk. A train was sent down there to pick up General Clingman and another of his regiments and return them to the city, but it was nearly 6 p.m. before it arrived.

Pickett fired off numerous reports to Richmond about the advance of the Federal fleet and his own weakness, but could elicit no response. That evening he telegraphed Adjutant General Cooper, "Have you received any telegrams from me to-day? I have sent a great many and received no answers. Have you any guards or any force between this city and Richmond? The enemy have landed at Bermuda Hundred. Unless you guard the railroad they will cut off communication. Reply at once."[8] Those were bold words for a major general to address to the highest-ranking officer in the army, but Pickett was desperate and frustrated and probably very sorry that he had not taken an earlier train to Hanover Junction and left this crisis to someone else. He got no answer to this message either. About 9:30 p.m. another one came from Beauregard but it said, "Have no troops to send . . . Do the best you can, with what you have." This was followed half an hour later by another in which Beauregard stated, "Am unfortunately too unwell to go to Petersburg tonight: but will do so tomorrow evening or next day."[9] The only help he had to offer was to dispatch his new volunteer aide, Harvey Hill, to confer with Pickett, but the responsibility for defending the city would still rest with the latter.

At sunrise on the fifth, August Kautz had led three regiments of Union cavalry and two guns of the 8th New York Battery out of Portsmouth, Virginia and by the time they had cleared Suffolk they had picked up the 5th Pennsylvania Cavalry to bring the force's strength up to 2,500 troopers. After a halt to rest the men and horses and await the return of scouts, Kautz marched on toward a crossroads known as Andrews Corners, apparently threatening to force a crossing of the lower Blackwater. They rested there about three hours, but at midnight the troopers were ordered back into the saddle, this time heading northeast, parallel with the river.

1. All three quotations in this paragraph are from Davis, *The Battle of New Market*, 41–42.

2. Dowdey and Manarin, eds., *Wartime Papers of R. E. Lee*, 719.

3. Edgar Holden, "The 'Albemarle' and the 'Sassacus,'" in *Battles and Leaders*, 4:628.

4. Ibid., 629.

5. Ibid.

6. William Farrar Smith, "Butler's Attack On Drewry's Bluff," in *Battles and Leaders*, 4:207.

7. Robertson, *Back Door To Richmond*, 62.

8. Ibid., 68.

9. Ibid.

CHAPTER FOURTEEN

"If He Is Disposed To Fight"

5 May 1864

At five o'clock on the morning of 5 May, about the same time that Kautz was leading his horsemen out of Portsmouth, his former Cavalry Bureau boss, James Wilson, was leading his own troopers out of their bivouac around Parker's Store, at the junction of the Orange Plank Road and the country lane which they had followed through the Wilderness the day before. Now they took the same track on southward toward the Catharpin Road, except for the 5th New York Cavalry, which was left at Parker's Store to watch the Orange Plank Road and to serve as a connecting link with Warren's infantry that was expected to follow.

About eight miles west of there as the crow flies, Lee was having breakfast with Brigadier General Armistead L. Long, his former military secretary who was now the commander of the artillery of the 2nd Corps. "In the course of the conversation that attended the meal," Long recalled, "he expressed himself surprised that his new adversary had placed himself in the same predicament as 'Fighting Joe' had done the previous Spring. He hoped the result would be even more disastrous to Grant than that which Hooker had experienced. He was, indeed, in the best of spirits, and expressed much confidence in the result—a confidence which was well founded, for there was reason to believe that his antagonist would be at his mercy while entangled in these pathless and entangled thickets, in whose thickets disparity of numbers lost much of its importance."[1] To Lee it no longer mattered much whether Grant was headed upriver or down. Grant's army was now within Lee's reach on his side of the river, while blinded and hamstrung by the Wilderness. All Lee had to do was to keep the enemy in sight while he concentrated his forces.

The Confederate army was moving in seven different columns that morning. Northeast of Lee's headquarters tent, Dick Ewell was happily leading his 2nd Corps eastward on the Orange Turnpike in search of an enemy to fight, and here at New Verdierville Stuart was leading part of his cavalry eastward on the Orange Plank Road, followed by A. P. Hill and two of his divisions. Seven miles to the southwest, Brigadier General Tom Rosser's Laurel Brigade of cavalry was riding eastward through Richard's Shop along the Catharpin Road, headed toward Shady Grove Church. Nineteen miles east of Rosser, Fitzhugh Lee and his cavalry division, whose presence near Fredericksburg the day before had caused Meade such concern for the protection of his vast wagon train, was moving westward by a route that would take him through the little county seat of Spotsylvania Court House, skirting the Yankees to the south to rejoin the main body of the army. To the west of R. E. Lee's headquarters, R. H. Anderson's infantry division was hastening toward the Orange Plank Road to rejoin Hill's 3rd Corps, having fulfilled its mission of guarding the army's rear. To the southwest, Longstreet's two divisions were across the North Anna River and moving toward the Catharpin Road. And far to the southeast, R. D. Johnston's brigade of Ewell's corps was about midway on its 66-mile forced march to rejoin the army from detached duty near Hanover Junction. Lee probably hoped that Pickett was also headed for Hanover Junction to reassemble his diversion from its four brigades scattered around southern Virginia and North Carolina.

It was evidently Lee's purpose to use Ewell's three divisions and Hill's two as well as Stuart's cavalry to follow, observe, and delay the Union army from the west. Meanwhile he would bring up Anderson and Longstreet, perhaps for a move around the Federals' southern flank aided by Fitzhugh Lee's cavalry and R. D. Johnston's infantry brigade, and maybe even Pickett. It does not seem to have occurred to Lee that Grant was also contemplating a move around the southern flank. But Humphreys' original plan for the Army of the Potomac was designed to cope with Lee's strong defensive position along Mine Run, should he choose to occupy it again, by sending Sedgwick and Warren west on the Orange Plank and Catharpin roads respectively while Hancock, the army's hardest-hitting corps commander, was brought down to the Pamunkey Road for a move against Lee's southern (right) flank. Yet both Grant and Lee were flexible. Like two boxers feeling each other out, what they did would depend on what they thought the other was doing, or trying to do.

Unknown to each other, both generals hoped to fight a decisive battle north of Richmond. Neither wanted the campaign to end in a seige of Richmond—Lee because he knew it would ultimately end in Union victory, Grant because it would take too long. Furthermore, since Grant wanted to fight as soon as possible, he seemed to assume that Lee would try to avoid a fight and fall back to a good defensive position behind the next river. And since Lee wanted to fight as soon as possible so he could turn his attention to other problems, like Butler and Sigel, he evidently assumed that Grant was trying to avoid him and to get down to Fredericksburg and as far toward Richmond as he could before Lee could stop him. That is why Lee was glad to find "those people" still within the confines of the Wilderness this morning. Now all he had to do was snap at their heels until they finally, reluctantly turned to fight, by which time he hoped to have all his forces assembled.

At 5 a.m. that day Warren's Union 5th Corps began to move from its camps near Wilderness Tavern down the side road toward Parker's Store on the Orange Plank Road, where Wilson left the 5th New York Cavalry before moving the rest of his division farther south. The infantry column was led by Brigadier General Samuel W. Crawford's 3rd Division, the Pennsylvania Reserves, followed by Brigadier General James S. Wadsworth's 4th Division and Brig. Gen. John C. Robinson's 2nd Division, while Griffin's 1st Division was to bring up the rear from its position a short way west on the Orange Turnpike. Just as Warren was leaving his headquarters camp to join the column a staff officer galloped up with word from Griffin that Rebels were advancing in force on his pickets. "I do not believe that Warren ever had a greater surprise in his life," another staff officer recorded, but noted that he did not let it show. "Tell Griffin to get ready to attack at once," was Warren's cool response.[2] He then sent a message to Meade advising the army commander of this development which he passed off as a mere demonstration to annoy his column. He said that he would continue his advance but leave Griffin in place for now.

At 6:20 a.m. Warren sent an order to Griffin to push out a force at once to see what the enemy had out there. At 7 a.m. Griffin passed the order on to Brigadier General Joseph J. Bartlett and his 3rd Brigade. Bartlett directed one of his colonels to take two regiments and find out whether the enemy's force consisted of cavalry or infantry, and what his intentions were. The colonel in turn moved the two regiments up to the picket line at about 8 a.m. and then ordered each of them to send out two companies as skirmishers. As they moved forward and engaged the Confederate skirmishers, they discovered that a strong enemy infantry force was present and was busy throwing up earthworks.

Meade had left Germanna Ford at dawn while Grant had stayed behind so he could talk with Burnside when the latter arrived there. The army commander was moving toward Wilderness Tavern with Humphreys and the rest of his staff when he was met by a messenger from Warren with word that Confederate infantry was on the turnpike in force, about two miles from the tavern. A few minutes later Meade arrived at Warren's headquarters on the turnpike and there he ordered the corps commander to halt his column and attack the enemy with his whole force. At the same time, about 7:30 a.m., he sent word to Hancock, whose 2nd Corps was marching southwest from Chancellorsville down a track known as the Catherine Furnace Road, to halt at Todd's Tavern. Warren was also sending off orders: to the commanders of his three marching divisions to halt, face west, and form a line that would connect with Griffin's left. Meanwhile Meade sent word to Grant that he was suspending Humphrey's original plan until he could see what came of Warren's attack. "I think the enemy is trying to delay our movement, and will not give battle, but of this we shall soon see. For the present I will stop here, and have stopped our trains."[3]

Sedgwick's 6th Corps had not been ordered to halt so, while Rickett's 3rd Division stayed to guard the ford, his lead division, Getty's 2nd, slowly advanced to Wilderness Tavern, and Wright's 1st followed to the intersection of the Germanna Plank Road with a track called the Culpeper Mine Road that ran southwest to cross the Orange Turnpike about two and a half miles west of the tavern. It was just west of the latter intersection that Ewell's 2nd Corps of Lee's army was even then deploying on a north-south line facing east. Earlier that morning Brigadier General John M. Jones' brigade, at the head of Ewell's column, had driven in Griffin's pickets, leading the Federals to alter their plans. Then, having discovered the Federals' location, Jones fell back about two miles and took position at this junction while keeping his skirmishers engaged. Around 8 a.m. Ewell sent word to Lee that his advance elements were within sight of the enemy near Wilderness Tavern, and requested instructions.

Before this news reached Lee but at about the same hour, that general, who was again riding with Hill along the Orange Plank Road, heard the sharp report of a rifle fire to the southeast, indicating that Rosser's Laurel Brigade of cavalry was engaged on the Catharpin Road. Stuart immediately rode off with all the troopers at hand to join in the fun. Wilson had reached the Catharpin Road near Craig's Meeting House after leaving his 1st Brigade about a mile behind at the crossing of a small east-west stream called Robertson Run. He then sent one squadron of the 1st Vermont, which he considered his best regiment, westward on the Catharpin Road. The squadron had only gone about half a mile when it ran into the head of Rosser's Confederate brigade. The Virginians charged the Vermonters and drove them back to the meeting house, where Union reinforcements joined the fight. Rosser's troopers then dismounted to seek cover in the woods on both sides of the road, but Wilson's men also dismounted and, with the firepower of their seven-shot Spencer carbines, drove the Confederates back down the road for two miles.

Meanwhile, with the Southern cavalry gone from the Orange Plank Road ahead, Hill sent Kirkland's infantry brigade from Heth's Division out to form the point of his column. At around the same time, Lieutenant Colonel John Hammond, commander of Wilson's 5th New York Cavalry, was moving his regiment westward along the same road to reinforce his advanced detachment about two miles west of Parker's Store. Here Kirkland's Rebel infantry, with a four-gun battery in support, ran into the Union cavalry. Hammond's troopers had also recently been rearmed with Spencer carbines, and they threw up a hail of lead as they slowly gave ground in the face of an entire corps.

It was about 8 a.m. when the halt order caught up with Crawford's Pennsylvania Reserve Division at the head of Warren's infantry column. By that time it had advanced to within a mile of Parker's Store and Crawford reported that, from the sound of it, the cavalry was engaged in brisk fighting nearby. Meanwhile Warren had himself ridden down the road to confer with General Wadsworth, whose 4th Division was behind Crawford's, and urge him to quick action. With a sweep of his arm Warren indicated the deep woods to the west and said, "Find out what is in there."[4] Major Roebling of Warren's staff was sent on down the road to give Crawford the details of the attack order while Warren returned briefly to his headquarters before riding out along the turnpike to confer with Griffin. Warren was already gone by 9 a.m. when Crawford's dispatch about the cavalry fight on the Plank Road reached corps headquarters. For some reason its significance was not recognized either there or at army headquarters, where it was received about fifteen minutes later.

Crawford and Major Roebling, however, were concerned about the sound of heavy firing they could hear gradually approaching on the

Orange Plank Road. Crawford had stopped on a cleared plateau around Chewning's farm, which seemed too good a defensive position to abandon until it was known what was going on just south of them. The 13th Pennsylvania Reserve Regiment, a famous sharpshooter outfit better known as the Pennsylvania Bucktails, was formed in line of battle to cover the road to Parker's Store, and four other regiments were deployed to cover its flanks. The division's other five regiments were held in reserve.

Meanwhile, Major Roebling went down the road to investigate the firing and soon discovered that Hammond's 5th New York Cavalry had been fighting A. P. Hill's infantry all morning. Hammond had deployed his entire regiment, except for a few men to hold the horses, as dismounted skirmishers, a thin line of troops normally thrown out in front of a line of battle to protect the larger force from surprises. Kirkland's Brigade at the head of Hill's infantry column had found it necessary to stumble through the thickets on both sides of the road and repeatedly threaten Hammond's flanks in order to make any progress, for the troopers' repeating carbines had convinced the Rebels that they faced at least a brigade of Union infantry. Nevertheless, by 9 a.m. Kirkland's Confederates had forced the troopers beyond the Parker's Store crossroads, and Crawford's attempts to reconnoiter toward the Orange Plank Road met strong resistance.

Sometime soon after Kirkland had driven Hammond's troopers beyond Parker's Store, probably around 9 a.m., Ewell's new son-in-law, Major Campbell Brown, brought Lee that general's report that Union infantry were still at Wilderness Tavern. He sent Brown back with instructions for Ewell to regulate his own advance by the sound of firing at the head of Hill's column in order to keep the two corps even with each other, and cautioned him not to bring on a general engagement. Lee obviously assumed that the Federals there were the rear guard of a column that, like the Yankees on the Orange Plank Road, would soon retire eastward, for it would be impossible for Ewell to both keep up with Hill and avoid a battle if the Federals on the turnpike refused to move.

At Germanna Ford, Grant was still impatiently awaiting the arrival of General Burnside when a courier brought him Meade's message concerning his decision to halt his advance and attack the Confederates lurking in the woods to the west on the Orange Turnpike. At 8:24 a.m. Grant replied, approving of Meade's aggressive intent: "Your note giving movement of the enemy and your dispositions received. Burnside's advance is now crossing the river. I will have Rickett's division relieved and advance at once, and urge Burnside's crossing. As soon as I can see Burnside I will go forward. If any opportunity presents itself for pitching into a part of Lee's army, do so without giving time for dispositions."5 At 9 a.m., Meade answered that "Warren is making his dispositions to attack, and Sedgwick to support him." As for Lee, Meade added, "if he is disposed to fight this side of Mine Run at once, he shall be accommodated."6

However, Grant had grown tired of waiting for Burnside, so at 8:40 a.m. he left an order for that general to place one of his 9th Corps divisions on the ridge south of the Rapidan to cover the crossing and to follow Sedgwick's 6th Corps with the rest of his divisions. It then took until around 10 a.m. for Grant to catch up with Meade near Wilderness Tavern. After a brief conference, the two took position on a knoll in the open ground near the Orange Turnpike and Germanna Plank Road intersection, where they both made their headquarters throughout the impending battle.

Almost four hours had passed since Warren had ordered Griffin to find out what was west of him on the turnpike. Over two and a half hours had passed since Meade had ordered Warren to attack whatever was out there with his entire force. But no attack had yet been made. Griffin's division had, with difficulty, been formed in line of battle in the woods, but by then Warren had been ordered to use his entire corps for the attack. So, while they waited for the other divisions to flounder through the thickets and over small streams to extend the line, Griffin's troops began to chop down trees to their front in order to clear a field of fire, piling up the logs to form a breastwork. As it turned out, only Wadsworth's 4th Division came forward to extend Griffin's line. The 3rd Division had not even tried, for Crawford had decided that he dare not abandon the plateau around the Chewning farm in the face of the Rebel threat advancing along the Orange Plank Road. Robinson's 2nd Division had been too late to join the front line before Wadsworth connected with Griffin, so it was formed in reserve behind the other two.

The lieutenant general had arrived just in time to share with his army commander the shock of a message from Crawford and Roebling that the Confederates were at Parker's Store and had cut the infantry off from Wilson's 3rd Cavalry Division. On the heels of this information came one of Meade's staff officers with word that he had heard firing on the Culpeper Mine Road, connecting the Germanna Plank Road with the Orange Turnpike. The two reports taken together indicated that the Rebels were working their way around both flanks of Warren's line of battle even while it was still struggling to form itself in the infernal thickets that gave the Wilderness its name. Moreover, the Confederates on the southern flank also posed a dire threat to Wilson's small cavalry division, while any Rebels that might be lurking on the northern flank were in a position to threaten the wagons still crossing over Culpeper Mine Ford and lumbering off to the southeast. The woods were full of small tracks and byways that the Southerners had familiarized themselves with over the months, and by which small parties might easily slip past Sedgwick's marking columns for a raid on the wagons.

Grant immediately set to work to get things moving before the Confederates could cause further trouble. He knew that previous opponents of Lee had come to grief by stopping to think or to reconnoiter while the wily old Rebel maneuvered against their rear or flank. The obvious way to keep Lee from pulling a stunt like that again was to keep him too busy with defense to execute any bold maneuver. Grant thus gave orders for Warren to attack along the Orange Turnpike without further delay and without regard for his flanks; for Brigadier General Horatio G. Wright's 1st Division of the 6th Corps to advance down the Culpeper Mine Road, clearing it of any Rebels and connecting with Griffin's northern flank; for Getty's 2nd Division of the 6th Corps, minus one brigade attached to Wright, to proceed from Wilderness Tavern to the Brock Road-Orange Plank Road intersection and attack down the Orange Plank Road toward Parker's Store; and for Hancock's 2nd Corps to march northward on the Brock Road from Todd's Tavern to support Getty's attack. While Meade and his staff were sending out these orders to the various commands Grant lit another cigar, sat down on a stump, took out his penknife, and began to silently whittle on a stick. The only sign that he was inwardly seething over the maddening unresponsiveness of the Army of the Potomac was that he failed to remove his brand new pair of yellow thread gloves, thus ruining them, apparently without noticing. It would take still another two and a half hours before Warren's attack went in.

Not long after 11 a.m., Lee received word from Ewell that Federal troops could be seen crossing the turnpike from north to south along the Germanna Plank Road. These were members of Getty's division. Again Lee ordered his 2nd Corps commander to conform to Hill's movements and not to bring on a battle until Longstreet arrived. He still saw no contradiction in those two instructions. Evidently neither Lee nor Ewell had any idea that most of Warren's corps was in the woods between Ewell and the troops that were visible on the Germanna Plank Road. At 12:15 p.m., Lee heard heavy firing break out farther up the Orange Plank Road. The head of Hill's column had apparently run up against something big. After several crashing volleys, silence returned.

Union brigadier general George Washington Getty had led his 2nd Division of the 6th Corps away from Wilderness Tavern at about 10:50 a.m. He took the Germanna Plank Road southeast to where it was crossed by a lesser track called the Brock Road, then followed that due south until it crossed the Orange Plank Road. While his three infantry brigades trudged along, he and his staff rode ahead to have a look at what they were getting themselves into. As they approached the Orange Plank Road they could see Union cavalrymen galloping past the intersection. These were troopers of the 5th New York. One of them slowed enough to shout that Rebel infantry was following, and in force. A few musket shots to the west added emphasis to the trooper's warning, and Getty sent an aide to fetch his column at the double-quick. Then he posted himself, his officers, and his orderlies across the road facing west, to buy time with a show of force.

One of the staff officers remembered that "soon a few gray forms were discerned far up the narrow Plank Road moving cautiously forward, then a bullet went whistling overhead, and another and another, and then the leaden hail came faster and faster over and about the little group until its destruction seemed imminent and inevitable. But Getty would not budge. 'We must hold this point at any risk,' he exclaimed, 'our men will soon be up.' In a few minutes, which seemed like an age to the little squad, the leading regiment of Wheaton's brigade, the 1st, came running like greyhounds along the Brock Road until the first regiment passed the Plank Road, and then, at the command 'Halt!' 'Front!' 'Fire!', poured a volley into the woods and threw out skirmishers in almost less time than it takes to tell it. Dead and wounded rebel skirmishers were found within thirty yards of the crossroads, so nearly had they gained it, and from these wounded prisoners it was learned that Hill's corps, Heth's division in advance, supported by Wilcox's Division, was the opposing force."[7]

Around noon, Sheridan finally learned from Humphreys that Wilson's 3rd Cavalry Division had been cut off from the infantry of Warren and Sedgwick. He replied that he was ordering Gregg's 2nd Cavalry Division to proceed by way of the Catharpin Road and Todd's Tavern to Shady Grove Church, from which place it was to open communication with Wilson. Torbert's 1st Division had finally reached Chancellorsville, where Sheridan would keep it to protect the wagons in Gregg's absence.

Also about noon, Stuart and his reinforcements joined Rosser on the Catharpin Road just as Wilson's troopers, who had been driving Rosser westward with the firepower of their Spencers, were beginning to run low on ammunition. There had been no sign of Warren's infantry which should already have reached Parker's Store, nor of Hancock's, which should have been reaching Shady Grove Church. No communication had come from either Sheridan or Meade all morning, so Wilson did not know that both infantry columns had been halted. He called off the pursuit of Rosser and ordered Colonel George H. Chapman, commander of his 2nd

Brigade, to hold his front line with a strong picket and to place the rest of his troops in an open field a half-mile to the rear. A mile even farther to the east, Wilson posted his two batteries of horse artillery and his personal escort, which consisted of about fifty troopers of the 8th Illinois Cavalry. The rest of his small division (except for the 5th New York), Colonel Truman H. Bryan's 1st Brigade, was still back at Robertson's Run, north of Craig's Meeting House.

Around 1 p.m. Chapman discovered that Rosser had been reinforced and that the Rebels were preparing to advance. Considering the odds against him and his dwindling supply of ammunition, Wilson ordered Chapman to fall back past Craig's Meeting House and reform behind Bryan's 1st Brigade. Just then the Confederates came swarming out of the woods to the west and Chapman's two and a half regiments could not stop them. The led horses became unmanageable and broke loose, and the dismounted troopers soon followed them eastward in a disorganized mass. Stuart's Rebels followed in hot pursuit until they came upon Wilson's two horse batteries and his little escort detachment. The twelve light field pieces poured a staggering fire into the Confederates, and at the crucial moment Lieutenant William W. Long of the 8th Illinois Cavalry led his fifty men in a mounted charge down the road, buying Chapman's fleeing troopers enough time to get away. After crossing Robertson Run they reformed behind Bryan's 1st Brigade. Here Wilson learned from Bryan that the enemy had taken the Parker's Store junction and had cut him off from Warren's infantry. The Southern cavalry was pushing on eastward on the Catharpin Road, thus also cutting Wilson off from the head of Hancock's column, if it was still coming that way. So he took the only course remaining open to him and marched eastward on a byroad that led along the northern bank of Robertson Run, paralleling Stuart's Confederates who were moving along the southern bank about a mile away.

Out on the turnpike, the men who would have to lead the Federal infantry attack, Griffin and his brigade commanders, were convinced that the Rebels were stronger in their front than the higher-ups seemed to realize. Suspecting that the Southerners were also preparing to attack, and confident in the strength of his own position, Griffin wanted to take the defensive, and the more Warren exhorted him to move the more stubborn he became. Warren, meanwhile, was receiving the biting end of Meade's famous temper. When Griffin sent a staff officer to Warren with one final appeal, he met the general just after he had left the little knoll where Grant and Meade had their headquarters. "He answered me," the officer related, "as though fear was at the bottom of my errand. I remember my indignation," he added.[8]

Unable to talk his superiors out of the attack down the Orange Turnpike, Griffin finally ordered his three brigades out from behind their breastworks around noon to advance through the tangled woods. Wadsworth's men accompanied them, extending their line to the south. After moving half a mile through dwarf pines and matted underbrush, many of the units had become intermixed, and one entire brigade had been squeezed out of the line because Wadsworth's units were moving at a slightly different angle from Griffin's on their right. Finally the Federals came to the edge of a large clearing, the fields of a family named Sanders, and here Griffin called a halt to reform. The clearing was about 400 yards wide with a dry streambed cutting across it from north to south. On the far side of this clear field of fire, just inside the opposite tree line, was Ewell's main line of battle.

---

1. Steere, *The Wilderness Campaign*, 84.
2. Ibid., 96.
3. Ibid., 102.
4. Ibid., 112.
5. Ibid., 107.
6. Ibid., 104.
7. Ibid., 137.
8. Ibid., 133.

CHAPTER FIFTEEN

"We Fought Them Fiercely"

5 May 1864

At around 1 p.m. the sun suddenly flashed on thousands of fixed bayonets as the front line of Griffin's and Wadsworth's divisions stepped out of the edge of the woods and, with a cheer, began to advance. On the Union right, north of the turnpike, the first line of Brigadier General Romeyne B. Ayres' 1st Brigade of Griffin's division chased the Rebel skirmishers out of the draw that slanted across the field, then drove them up the opposite slope toward Ewell's main line in the edge of the next woods. As the Federals crossed the gully, a tremendous crossfire struck them from the front and from the right, where Ewell's line overlapped their own. While Warren and Ewell both deployed seven brigades in their lines, and the Federals slightly outnumbered the Rebels, most of the Union brigades were formed in two lines, with two of their seven brigades in support behind the other five. Therefore, Ewell's newly formed line, which was doubled only near the center, was about twice as long as Warren's.

The 140th New York was on the left of Ayres' front line, near the turnpike, and the withering Confederate fire caused it to crowd farther to its left. The rest of Ayres' front line, on the other hand, consisted of seven small battalions of the regular army and they inclined to the right,

although their superb discipline allowed them to maintain perfect alignment until the right end of their line became entangled in saplings and
vines at the north end of the field. About then Captain George B.
Winslow, commander of Battery B, 1st New York Light Artillery,
brought two of his guns galloping down the turnpike, crossed the gully
and swung them into action. They immediately began to fire salvos of
tree-shattering solid shot that sent branches and splinters smashing into
Rebels and New Yorkers indiscriminately.

All this was witnessed by the three volunteer regiments in Ayres'
second line while they too reformed after reaching the eastern edge of
Sanders' field. Then the second line also went down the slope to the gully,
where they met a storm of Minie balls. Many men fell, some to rise and
stagger to the rear with bleeding wounds or smashed limbs, others never
to rise again. But the line pressed up on the slope. The 146th New York, a
zouave regiment, held the left of this second line, and its colonel led it
into the gap in the first line caused by the separation of the 140th and the
regulars, while the other two regiments of the second line followed the
regulars off to the right. The regulars had been brought to a halt by the
fire of two and a half Rebel brigades to their front and right, so the two
right-hand regiments of Ayres' second line, the 91st and 155th Pennsylvania, passed over them in an attempt to reach the Confederate works.
But the withering crossfire also broke the Pennsylvanians' line, and both
they and the regulars went streaming back across the field in disordered
clumps, over the gully and back up the first slope to the eastern edge of
the field, where they rallied behind two Massachussetts regiments of
Colonel Jacob B. Sweitzer's 2nd Brigade which had been in reserve
behind the first two lines.

Unaware of what was happening on their right, the 140th and 146th
New York charged into the woods on the west side of the field, firing on
the run, and were met by the close-range fire of three Virginia regiments.
"Closing with the enemy, we fought them fiercely with bayonet, as well
as bullet," a captain in the 146th wrote. "Up through the trees rolled
dense clouds of battle smoke, circling about the green of the pines and
mingling its fleecy billows with the white of the flowering dogwoods."
Beneath the smoke, grim, desperate men ran back and forth, firing,
shouting, and stabbing with bayonets. They quickly became disoriented
in the dense woods. "Many dashed directly into the enemy's fire in a
belief they were going to the rear," the same captain remembered. "Officers lost control of their companies and utterly bewildered, rushed
hither and thither, looking for their men." The right end of the 146th's
line was surrounded and captured when the Pennsylvanians and regulars
retreated, but the Rebels had troubles of their own, and soon disappeared

from that part of the field. "We ceased fire when not a rebel opposed us and we seemed successful," the captain recorded.[1]

Just to the south of Ayres' brigade in the Federal attack formation was Brigadier General Joseph J. Bartlett's 3rd Brigade of Griffin's division, also formed in two lines, with the 1st Michigan out ahead as skirmishers. With Brigadier General Lysander Cutler's famous Iron Brigade of Wadsworth's 4th Division pacing them on the left, the three regiments of Bartlett's front line charged across the open field. Bartlett's second line, composed of the 118th Pennsylvania and the 20th Maine, followed in support. "The bugle sounded the 'Charge' and advancing to the edge of the field, we saw the first line of battle about half way across it, receiving a terribly fatal fire from an enemy in the woods on the farther side," a lieutenant in the 20th Maine remembered. "This field was less than a quarter of a mile across, had been planted with corn the year before, and was now dry and dusty. We could see the spurts of dust started up all over the field by the bullets of the enemy, as they spattered on it like the big drops of a coming shower you have so often seen along a dusty road."[2]

Bartlett's and Cutler's men ran across the field, supported by Griffin's other brigade, Colonel Jacob B. Sweitzer's 2nd, and struck the six Virginia regiments of Confederate brigadier general John M. Jones' brigade which constituted the right flank of Major General Edward "Allegheny" Johnson's division. Assaulted in front and seeing their flank threatened by Wadsworth's other two brigades extending the Union line to the south, Jones' men gave ground and quickly. Jones was killed trying to stay the rout, and his aide-de-camp, the son of Major General Jubal Early, fell at his side. The Federals pushed on into the woods where, as Sergeant Will Owen, who had written his sister about mismanagement, recalled, "the balls were cutting the little limbs of the trees so they fell like leaves in Autumn."[3] About twenty yards into the woods, Owen was hit in the right leg. He got up and hobbled to the rear, his fighting done for the summer, while his regiment pressed on.

The 20th Maine passed through the disordered ranks of the 83rd Pennsylvania, one of the front-line regiments, as the clatter of musketry swelled around them. It sounded strange to them, because it lacked the bass accompaniment of artillery familiar from other battles. It sounded, one soldier said, like a boy with a stick pressed against a picket fence running faster and faster until the rattle merged into a continuous roar. The bitter odor of gun smoke was soon joined by the sweeter, but just as ominous, smell of wood smoke as muzzle blasts set the dry leaves and small twigs on fire and the numerous little blazes spread to bushes and trees, fanned by a strong wind.

This was the only part of Ewell's defense that had the support of a

second line, for Major General Robert E. Rodes had formed his division
south of the turnpike with his left brigade, the five Alabama regiments of
Brigadier General Cullen Battle, behind Jones' Virginians. His other two
brigades extended this second line off to the south. However, the sudden
disruption of Jones' line had given the Alabamans little time to prepare
and, being back in the woods, they could not see what was happening to
their front. They fired a quick volley at the advancing Federals and then
also fell back in disorder through the thickets. Doles' Brigade of Georgians, to the right of Battle's, was also disrupted and pushed back as
Bartlett and Cutler continued to advance.

After pressing on through the thickets for about half a mile with its
right flank on the turnpike, the 20th Maine came to a second open field.
The regiment's commander, Major Ellis Spear, was just reforming his men
in the field when a murderous volley struck them from the right and rear.
At first they thought other Union troops were firing on them by mistake,
but they soon discovered that Rebels were swarming around their right in
great numbers. The smoke, the thickets, and the noise had completely
hidden the fact that most of Ayres brigade had retreated, and Ewell's two
left-most brigades had pursued them into Sanders' field. Bartlett had also
outrun his flanking units to the south, thus exposing that flank too. The
Iron Brigade had been slowed by its encounter with Doles' Georgians,
while to its left Colonel Roy Stone's 3rd Brigade of Wadsworth's division
had encountered almost impenetrable marshy ground around a small
stream called Mill Branch. The left-flank brigade, Brigadier General
James C. Rice's 2nd, meanwhile edged to its right, toward where Stone
should have been. This exposed its left to the fire of Brigadier General
Junius Daniel's brigade of North Carolinians, holding the southern flank
of Ewell's line.

When the 20th Maine discovered that it was flanked, it tried a maneuver
which had been effective at Gettysburg, where it had been on the left
flank of the entire army: Captain Walter G. Morrill formed his Company
B, and some fragments of other regiments that had become attached to the
20th, at right angles to the rest of the regiment, facing the turnpike. It
worked for a few minutes, but then Morrill was knocked down by a
bullet in the face. He got up and tied a handkerchief around his head and
went on fighting, but his bleeding became so bad that his men took him to
the rear and the rest of the regiment and the brigade soon followed. Most
of the men got back through the woods to their own breastworks,
although some of them had to charge Confederates from the rear to get
through. One small group led by a lieutenant from the 20th Maine
brought in 32 prisoners captured along the way. General Bartlett was seen
galloping out of the woods all alone, his elaborate uniform torn, blood

running down his face, and bullets flying all around him. As his horse jumped the twelve-foot ditch in the middle of Sanders' field it was struck in mid-leap, turned a somersault in the air and fell dead on top of the general. Remarkably, Bartlett survived both the fire and the fall and got up to continue his escape on foot.

When the Federals broke through the center of his line, Dick Ewell galloped back down the turnpike to where his other division, under Major General Jubal Early, was held in reserve. The corps commander slid to a halt so close to Brigadier General John B. Gordon that the latter braced himself for the pain of Ewell's wooden leg slamming into his own knee, but it missed by a fraction of an inch. Ewell ordered Gordon to form his brigade of Georgians on the right of the turnpike, check the enemy and save the corps' artillery, which was then retreating along the road. "I moved my brigade by the right flank," Gordon reported, "and formed at right angles to the road with as much expedition as the nature of the ground and the fire from the enemy's artillery and advancing infantry would admit. Some of my men were killed and wounded before the first regiment was placed in position. As soon as the formation was completed I ordered the brigade forward."[4]

The Confederates' luck was in. Gordon's six regiments happened to advance right into the gap in the Union line caused by Stone's floundering in the marsh. The young Rebel general deployed two of his regiments in a thin line to protect his front, and wheeled another to his left, against Cutler's southern flank, and the other three to his right against Rice's right flank. Unexpectedly assailed on both flanks, Rice's five regiments began to retire and then broke into a rout. The colonel of the 56th Pennsylvania managed to rally about 350 men on a slight elevation and prepared to slow the Confederate pursuit, but General Wadsworth soon rode up and, judging the colonel's force too small to be effective, ordered him to withdraw. The Federals fell back all the way to the Lacy house before stopping to reorganize.

Other than the two New York Regiments of Ayres' brigade, that left only Cutler's Iron Brigade facing the enemy, and when Gordon's left-most regiment struck their southern flank and the forces that had routed Ayres and Bartlett closed in on their right, they too broke and fled toward the rear. Their retreat took them right through the four supporting Maryland regiments of Colonel Andrew Denison's 3rd Brigade of Brigadier General John C. Robinson's 2nd Division of the 5th Corps, which was the only part of that division to join in the attack. Robinson's other two brigades had been held back at Lacy's as the corps reserve.

The Maryland Brigade had only joined the Army of the Potomac after

Gettysburg, and it still was not considered a completely reliable outfit. Perhaps their border-state origins also made the Marylanders suspect. But they managed to survive the shock and confusion of seeing the crack Iron Brigade turn and run. Then they stood up to the pursuing Confederates. Arrangements were being made to pivot the brigade's left flank when it was discovered that Rebels were on their right rear. The 4th Maryland fell back twenty yards and opened fire on these Southerners while the other three regiments retreated. The 4th then fell back another thirty yards, where its colonel reported to the brigade commander. By his order, the 4th fell back, preserving its alignment in the thickets, and joined the rest of the brigade at the reserve line of breastworks.

One of Gordon's regiments, the 61st Georgia, followed the retreating Federals cautiously through the woods, ambushed the 7th Pennsylvania Reserve regiment, part of one of Crawford's brigades belatedly sent to join the attack. After a sudden point-blank volley from the Rebels, 271 surviving Pennsylvanians surrendered, and only forty got away. The rest of Colonel William McCandless' 1st Brigade of Crawford's division, after wandering in the woods, reached the Lacy house without serious incident.

Meanwhile, the two New York zouave regiments of Ayres' brigade had found the respite caused by Bartlett's success to their left, ended by Brigadier General George "Maryland" Steuart's brigade of Virginians and North Carolinians returning to the fray. The three Virginia regiments lapped around the right flank of the 146th New York, while the two North Carolina regiments attacked the left of the 140th. A captain of the 146th went back to the edge of the woods to check the unit's rear. "We were not only flanked but doubly flanked," he said. "Rebel troops covered the field we had just crossed. We were in a bag and the strings were tied."[5]

The two regiments of New Yorkers ran back across Sanders' field under a murderous Confederate fire, some taking temporary refuge in the gully and others hiding behind dead artillery horses in the road before continuing their flight to the rear. As if they did not have enough problems, the forest fires then reached the edge of the clearing, where the dry grass and weeds burst into flames that swept across the field, fanned by the wind. Federals and Confederates forgot their differences long enough to work together to rescue wounded men lying in the fire's path. The flames not only threatened to burn these men, but to set off the ammunition in their cartridge boxes. "The almost cheerful 'Pop! Pop!' of cartridges gave no hint of the dreadful horror their noise bespoke," wrote one participant. "Swept by the flames, the trees, bushes, and logs which Confederates had thrown up as breastworks now took fire and dense clouds of smoke rolled across the clearing, choking unfortunates who were exposed to it and greatly hindering the work of rescuers. The clearing now became a raging inferno in which many of the wounded perished. The bodies of the dead were blackened and burned beyond all possibility of recognition, a tragic conclusion to this day of horror."[6] But it was far from over yet.

As Steuart's men chased the two zouave units across the open field, a lieutenant of the 1st North Carolina spotted the two Federal cannon that had accompanied the advance and led a detachment in a charge straight for them. As the gunners engaged in fierce hand-to-hand combat with the Rebels, several zouaves stopped running long enough to help the artillerymen. "It was claw for claw and the Devil for us all," wrote one Confederate.[7] But the guns were captured. The Carolinians then continued their pursuit but were surprised to find vast numbers of Federals retreating out of the woods behind them, and took refuge in the ditch. Behind the fleeing Yankees came Battle's Alabama brigade, and one of its colonels promptly laid claim to the abandoned cannon. The North Carolinians broke cover to dispute his right to the guns, and during the ensuing argument were reinforced by the rest of their regiment and other units of Steuart's Brigade. The heated debate might have resulted in a war between North Carolina and Alabama had not the Federals mounted a counterattack. As it turned out, the guns remained in no-man's land until the next day.

The Union force that counterattacked the North Carolinians and Alabamans was part of the two brigades of Robinson's 2nd Division of the 5th Corps that had been held in reserve. They replaced the two Massachussetts regiments behind which Ayres' regulars had rallied, while those and the rest of Griffin's division fell back to the reserve trenches. Wadsworth's three brigades were reformed in the open ground around the Lacy house, and Crawford's Pennsylvania Reserves, after reluctantly giving up the Chewning house plateau, formed on Warren's extreme left. Mindful of Lee's injunction not to bring on a full-scale battle, Ewell called off the pursuit of the repulsed Federals and reestablished his defensive position.

Meanwhile, Wright's division of the Union 6th Corps had been struggling down the Culpeper Mine Road in an attempt to connect with Griffin's right. However, it was so difficult to deploy in the thickets on both sides of the road, let alone to advance in the face of stiff resistance from the 1st North Carolina Cavalry and skirmishers from Ewell's infantry, that the main attack was over before Wright's five brigades were in position. By then Ewell had sent Hays' and Pegram's brigades of Early's

Division to the left end of his line to face Wright. Eventually, as Wright's division deployed north of the turnpike, Robinson's two fresh brigades were aligned just south of and parallel to the pike and facing south so as to connect Wright with Griffin's division.

Meanwhile Griffin, a hard-case former artilleryman who was especially upset over losing those two guns, blamed his superiors for forcing him to advance against his better judgement and without secure flanks. After seeing his men safely to their position, he rode back to army headquarters on the knoll in the northwest corner of the intersection of the Germanna Plank Road and the Orange Turnpike. There he burst in on Meade, Grant, and their staffs. His face flushed with anger and his eyes darkly bloodshot, Griffin demanded to know why his division had not been supported. When he received no answer from the startled assemblage he exclaimed, with appropriate expletives, that he had driven Ewell's forces three-quarters of a mile but that Wadsworth's division on his left had broken and that Wright's 6th Corps division had never come up on his right. With both flanks exposed his men had been cut to pieces and compelled to retreat.

Meade, who perhaps secretly shared the younger man's anger over being hurried before his preparations were completed, did not respond with his own famous temper but heard his division commander out and tried to soothe him, although with little success. Griffin finally ran out of steam, or gave up, and rode off to rejoin his command. Rawlins denounced the man's behavior as mutinous, while Grant, who had not quite caught Griffin's name, stood up and began buttoning his coat as if preparing to stand on his dignity, asking Meade, "Who is this General Gregg? Why don't you arrest him?" Meade also stood up, towering over his shorter commander. He reached down and helped Grant with his buttons like a parent with a small child and said, "It's not Gregg but Griffin, and it's only his way of talking."[8]

Down on the Orange Plank Road, Getty's Union division and Heth's Confederate division had reached a standoff. "My skirmish line was unable to drive the enemy's skirmishers any further," Heth remembered, "they halted, and the division came up, line of battle was formed. All was quiet for an hour or more."[9] Meanwhile, Hancock was on his way to the same area. At about 9 a.m. he had received Meade's 7:30 a.m. order to suspend his march toward the Catharpin Road and halt his column at Todd's Tavern. By then his advance, Brigadier General John Gibbon's 2nd Division, was already beyond Todd's Tavern and had to be recalled, while the other three divisions of the 2nd Corps were stopped there and along the Catherine Furnace Road. At 11:40 a.m. Hancock received Meade's order of 10:30 a.m. to move up the Brock Road to the Orange Plank Road. He set off with his staff in advance of his troops and upon his arrival consulted with Getty, while his chief of staff, Lieutenant Colonel C. H. Morgan, rode on to report to Meade.

At noon Meade sent orders for Hancock to support Getty in an attempt to clear the Orange Plank Road as far as Parker's Store, but somehow this message went astray. It was not until Morgan reported to army headquarters around 1:30 p.m.—just about the time word arrived that Warren's attack had been repulsed—that Meade realized that Hancock did not know that he was expected to attack. The exasperated army commander fired off another note to Hancock urging immediate action but did not seem to realize that only the headquarters of the 2nd Corps had reached the Orange Plank Road and that the troops were still strung out along the way, some of them still on the other side of Todd's Tavern. Meanwhile, Hancock learned from Getty that the latter was facing two divisions of A. P. Hill's corps. In the face of that much force, Getty had ignored his orders to attack and had entrenched instead. All his efforts to establish communication with Warren's left had failed, and he expected to be attacked at any moment.

Shortly after 2 p.m. Hancock's infantry came swinging up the Brock Road with Major General David Birney riding at the head of the column. He was told to form his 3rd Division in line on the left of Getty's 6th Corps division and start entrenching. An hour later Brigadier General Gershom Mott's 4th Division arrived and was told to entrench on Birney's left. Meanwhile, at 2:40 p.m. a rider arrived with Meade's dispatch of 1:30 p.m. ordering the 2nd Corps to attack. Just as Hancock was reading this, another messenger appeared with Meade's lost order written at noon. Hancock acknowledged receipt of both dispatches and added, "I am forming my corps on Getty's left, and will order an advance as soon as prepared. The ground over which I must pass is very bad—a perfect thicket. I shall [form] two divisions with brigade front. General Getty says he has not heard of Warren's left, probably because he has not advanced far enough."[10]

While Warren and Ewell had been slugging it out on the turnpike, and Hill and Getty had been facing each other on the Orange Plank Road, the cavalry had not been idle. At 2:45 p.m. Gregg, commander of the Union 2nd Cavalry Division, arrived at Todd's Tavern and reported to Sheridan that he had found Chapman's brigade of Wilson's division nearby and that "General Wilson is falling back to this point."[11]

After Wilson had sent Chapman's disorganized brigade down the side road leading east, followed by Bryan's intact command, he detailed Colo-

nel W. H. Brinton's 18th Pennsylvania Cavalry to cover the rear, and he
and his headquarters escort rode at the head of that regiment. As it turned
out, the side road connected with the Catharpin Road just north of where
it crossed the Po River on Corbin's Bridge. Chapman's brigade turned
into the Catharpin Road and proceeded to Todd's Tavern, where he was
found by Gregg, who learned from him of Wilson's plight.

Meanwhile, Bryan's brigade also turned into the Catharpin Road, but
just as Wilson and his escort reached the junction, a squadron of Rebel
cavalry came over the ridge just south of the Po. When they spotted the
Federals they charged over the bridge and up the northern bank. However, the 18th Pennsylvania smashed into them just in time to save Wilson.
Three times the fight see-sawed back and forth before Colonel Brinton
ordered his troopers to fall back towards Todd's Tavern with the Confederates right behind. At a bend in the road they came upon two
regiments which Gregg had sent out to help, one deployed on each side of
the road.

As the tail of Wilson's column cleared the way, one squadron of the 1st
New Jersey Cavalry charged the head of the Rebel column with drawn
sabers, broke its formation and drove it back on its supports. The Confederates counterattacked and sent the squadron galloping back to its own
supports, meanwhile unlimbering a battery of horse artillery. As soon as
the retreating squadron was out of the field of fire, the rest of the Union
regiment delivered a volley of carbine fire that knocked many Rebels out
of the saddle and sent the rest galloping back down the hill. Then the
Jersey troopers charged down the slope in pursuit, and the Southerners
fell back over the bridge and withdrew to the west. Sheridan had Gregg
and Wilson construct breastworks at Todd's Tavern and later sent Chapman's brigade northwest on the Brock Road to connect with Hancock's
infantry.

A mile or so west of where Getty's division was being reinforced by
Hancock was the home of the Widow Tapp. Lee, Hill and Jeb Stuart were
conferring in a nearby grove of trees in an elevated field. Hill was sick
again, as he usually was when combat threatened. The three had heard the
firing to the north along the turnpike but, perhaps because of the lack of
artillery fire, had not recognized it for the major battle that it was.
However, Lee was concerned about the two-mile gap between Ewell's
forces on the turnpike and Hill's on the Orange Plank Road. Just then, as
if to illustrate the problem, a skirmish line of Union infantry came out of
some pines within easy musket range of the high-ranking conference.
Both groups eyed each other in surprise, and then the Federals faded back
into the trees without firing a shot, not realizing how close they had come

to winning the war right then and there. Lee promptly ordered Wilcox's Division to move into the woods between the two roads to connect the left of Heth's Division, on the Orange Plank Road, with the right of Ewell's forces on the Turnpike.

Around 3 p.m. one of Lee's staff officers came to Heth and said the commanding general was anxious for him to occupy the Brock Road-Plank Road intersection if he could do so without bringing on a general engagement. Heth, the only officer in the army that Lee called by his first name—besides his own son and nephew—replied sensibly that the Federals held the road in strength and he had no way of knowing in advance whether or not they could be driven from it, let alone whether that would bring on a general engagement. But he told the staff officer to tell General Lee, "I am ready to try if he says 'attack.' "[12]

By that time, Wright's division of the Federal 6th Corps had pushed down the Culpeper Mine Road and connected with Robinson's division of the 5th Corps. Ewell had countered this threat by sending Early with two of his brigades to extend the left of his line to the north. Then suddenly Maryland Steuart's Confederate brigade broke cover and charged Wright's southernmost brigade, which was commanded by a talented young colonel named Emory Upton. The Yankees held their own in burning woods on ground that was already strewn with the dead and wounded from Warren's charge earlier in the day. Then all three of Wright's brigades, supported by the one borrowed from Getty earlier, counterattacked and drove the Confederates back to their main line, which ran northwestward along a low flat ridge from the northwest corner of Sanders' field toward the little stream called Flat Run. When the Federals struck the Rebel breastworks the regiments of the various brigades were already becoming intermingled, and they were repulsed. But they came back for more, and the battle raged on indecisively. A Wisconsin soldier in the 6th Corps recorded that, being unable to see their enemies, the Federals "soon began to fire by ear-sight."[13] Confederate brigadier general Leroy A. Stafford, commander of a Louisiana brigade in Allegheny Johnson's division, was among the mortally wounded.

Over on the Rebel left there was another Louisiana brigade, a crack outfit in Early's Division. Back in 1862 it had been commanded by Dick Taylor who was now, in 1864, out on the Red River giving Banks a hard time. The brigade now belonged to Brigadier General Harry Hays. As soon as he got his unit into position on the left of Ewell's line he sent it forward, without waiting for Pegram's Brigade which was supposed to come up on his own left. He advanced until stiffening resistance brought his regiments to a halt. Of the supports he had expected, only the 25th

Virginia of Jones' Brigade showed up. When the Rebels ran into Brigadier General David A. Russell's Union brigade, the Virginians moved up to the left of Hays' line to take on Russell's supports, the brigade borrowed from Getty and commanded by Brigadier General Thomas H. Neill. Two of Neill's regiments held off the Virginians while five companies of the 5th Wisconsin, which had been detached as skirmishers on the far right, slipped through the woods and surrounded them. Three hundred Virginians and their colors were captured. Up against such heavy odds, Hays had to fall back. As a result, the fighting on that part of the field, which had lasted about an hour, died down.

At about 2:15 p.m. Meade had informed Warren that Brigadier General James Ricketts' 3rd Division of the 6th Corps, on the Germanna Plank Road, had been ordered to report to Warren. He also told the 5th Corps commander, mistakenly, that "Hancock is up at the Orange Plank road and will attack immediately. Getty will be brought to your support, if necessary, as soon as Hancock is ready. Hancock will endeavor to connect with your left."[14] At the same time, Meade sent a dispatch informing Hancock of Warren's repulse and that, since Crawford's division had been called in from the Chewning house plateau, the exact position of Warren's left flank was not yet known. There was no mention that Getty was half-promised to Warren, nor that Warren had been told that the 2nd Corps commander would "attack immediately."

Hancock received that note about 3 p.m.—just when Wright was colliding with Ewell—and immediately replied that he would be attacking with the divisions of Mott, Birney, and Getty, two in front and the other in support, with the objective of pushing the enemy back to Parker's Store. However, the rider carrying this dispatch to army headquarters had not had time to reach Meade before the latter sent Lieutenant Colonel Theodore Lyman of his staff down to the Plank Road with orders for Hancock and Getty attack at once, ready or not. He delivered the order to Getty first, assuring him that the 2nd Corps would support him. Then he went to Hancock and delivered orders for him to join in Getty's attack. Meade had also seen fit to specify the formation he wanted Hancock to use: one 2nd Corps division on each side of Getty, and Hancock's other two divisions in reserve—thus showing that he didn't understand that only two of Hancock's divisions had reached the vicinity of the Orange Plank Road. He did add, "or such other dispositions as you may think proper,"[15] but Hancock felt bound to comply with the army commander's stated wishes. About 4 p.m., after receiving Hancock's last two messages, Meade directed Warren to "make dispositions to renew the attack, if practicable. General Hancock has just been heard from and will soon attack. You will have one brigade of Ricketts' besides Robinson and Crawford, who have not been engaged."[16]

Meade made two mistakes in this message: first, he only ordered Warren to make dispositions, not to actually attack; second, he left it up to Warren to decide whether even that was "practicable."

Warren did not attack.

---

1. Steere, *The Wilderness Campaign*, 160.
2. Pullen, *The 20th Maine*, 193.
3. Ibid., 194.
4. Steere, *The Wilderness Campaign*, 168–169.
5. Ibid., 173.
6. Ibid., 174.
7. Ibid.
8. Ibid., 182–183.
9. Trudeau, *Bloody Roads South*, 62.
10. Steere, *The Wilderness Campaign*, 189.
11. Ibid., 269.
12. Freeman, *Lee's Lieutenants*, 3:352.
13. Trudeau, *Bloody Roads South*, 65.
14. Steere, *The Wilderness Campaign*, 187.
15. Ibid., 190.
16. Ibid., 195.

CHAPTER SIXTEEN

"Like Fire in a Canebrake"

5 May 1864

Down on the Orange Plank Road Getty, a mere division commander, was not about to ignore an order straight from army headquarters. His skirmishers stepped off at just about 4 p.m. and immediately drew fire from Heth's Rebel pickets. Getty had his three brigades (one was with Wright) each deployed in two lines. Colonel Lewis A. Grant's crack 2nd Brigade of five Vermont regiments had formed with its right touching the Orange Plank Road, Brigadier General Frank Wheaton's 1st Brigade with its left on the right of the road, and Brigadier General Henry L. Eustis' 4th Brigade of New Englanders to the right (north) of Wheaton. A battery of light artillery from the 2nd Corps went into position at the Brock Road-Orange Plank Road intersection in support.

In order to comply with Meade's desire to have one 2nd Corps division deployed on each side of Getty's 6th Corps division, Hancock ordered Birney to move from his position on Getty's left, by the rear of the latter's advancing division, to redeploy on his right and then advance. At the same time, Mott was to advance at an oblique angle until his right flank connected with Getty's left. Meanwhile, until the 2nd Corps divisions caught up, both of Getty's flanks would be "in the air," as the expression went.

The two divisions available to Hancock for the attack just happened to have been the two transferred to him in Meade's recent consolidation from the old 3rd Corps. Each consisted of only two brigades. Back in 1862 they had been considered two of the best divisions in the Army of the Potomac, but that was mostly due to the fighting qualities of their commanders, who at that time had been Joe Hooker and Phil Kearny. Kearny was killed in the Second Bull Run campaign and Hooker had moved on to corps and army command. Meanwhile the two divisions had taken a real pounding at Gettysburg, and Birney and especially Mott were by no means considered the fighters that Hooker and Kearny had been.

The seven brigades of Getty, Birney, and Mott would be met initially by the four brigades of Harry Heth's Division of A. P. Hill's corps. Heth had three brigades deployed in a single northwest-southeast line across the Orange Plank Road, with Kirkland's Brigade in reserve behind the center. A single cannon positioned in the road just behind Kirkland's Brigade was the Rebels' only artillery support, but it was later reinforced by two more guns. Heth had about 6,700 infantry, while Getty alone had 7,200 and Birney and Mott would add another 9,700. The odds, of course, were unknown to either side at the time. Hancock did not know that Wilcox was not yet deployed beside Heth, nor could he be sure that Anderson or even Ewell was not lurking in the woods just ahead.

The advancing Federals would not only have to force themselves through the thickets but would also have to negotiate several small streams which ran down from the slight rise followed by the Orange Plank Road. Getty's main-line regiments followed their skirmishers forward, with each company deployed in a narrow column so they could thread their way through the difficult terrain. After they had advanced about half a mile over a series of low ridges and intervening marshy swales, the increasing volume of musketry to their front indicated that the skirmishers had found the Rebels' main line of battle, and the little company columns swung forward into line, closed ranks, and charged forward.

Murderous volleys from the Confederate defenses brought the Yankees to a halt at about fifty-yards range. "As soon as the first volleys were over," Colonel Grant of the Vermont Brigade (no kin to the lieutenant general) recalled, "our men hugged the ground as closely as possible and kept up a rapid fire; the enemy did the same. The rebels had the advantage of position, inasmuch as their line was partially protected by a slight swell of ground, while ours was on nearly level ground. The attempt was made to dislodge them from that position, but the moment our men rose to advance, the rapid and constant fire of musketry cut them down with such slaughter that it was found impracticable to do more than maintain our then present position."[1]

Because Heth's Division was formed in a single line, while Getty's brigades were each in two or more lines, the Confederates again overlapped the Union flanks, as was the case earlier, up on the turnpike. Colonel Grant, upon discovering this problem on the Federal left, managed by some skillful maneuvering—one of his regiments had to crawl into position—to rearrange his five regiments from two lines and a reserve facing southeast into one line that curved back to face south. Getty believed himself to be up against A. P. Hill's entire corps and considered his own advance as a spoiling attack intended to forestall a Rebel assault until Hancock could get his troops into position. Both Getty and Colonel Grant expected a Confederate counterattack to hit their left flank at any moment, so Getty called on Birney for support. This request arrived while the two 2nd Corps divisions were in the process of executing their difficult realignment onto Getty's two flanks.

Birney responded by suspending the motion of his large 1st Brigade so that he could use it as a general reserve for the three attacking divisions, after sending three of its regiments to Colonel Grant's immediate support. One of these went toward the right of Colonel Grant's brigade, but the other two were placed behind his left-most regiment, the 5th Vermont. "I went to Major Dudley, commanding the 5th Vermont," Colonel Grant recorded, "and called his attention to the fact that the position of the enemy in his front was less protected than it was in front of the rest of the brigade and asked him if he could, with the support of the two regiments in his rear, break the enemy's line. 'I think we can,' was the reply of the gallant major. I went to the commanders of these two regiments, and asked them to support the Fifth in its advance. The men rose with a cheer and answered, 'We will.' The order for the charge was given, and all advanced in good style, and the enemy partially gave way. The two near regiments were thrown into some confusion and soon halted and laid down, and Major Dudley, finding his regiment far in advance, and exposed to a flank fire, wisely did the same."[2] One of the support regiments, the 20th Indiana, captured the colors of the 55th Virginia.

In the breastworks along the Brock Road south of Getty's original position, Mott's two brigades formed up in two lines while the division's skirmishers were sent to clear the Rebel pickets from the area to be advanced over, and develop the Confederates' main line. Colonel Robert McAllister, commanding Mott's 1st Brigade, on the division's right, remembered that "in the advance the Eighth New Jersey Volunteers was on my right, and in coming up they found themselves in rear of the left regiment of the Sixth Corps [5th Vermont], who were engaging the enemy. The Eighth New Jersey laid down, but soon the troops in front gave way and the Eighth received the fire from the enemy. The Fifth [New Jersey] on its left, gave way and carried back with it a portion of the Eighth, leaving Captain Stelle with a small portion of the regiment and the colors." Meanwhile, the process of advancing in company columns by the right oblique through the woods had caused the regiments to crowd too closely together, and when they tried to deploy into line they became entangled with each other as well as with the thickets. "After moving a short distance the line of battle passed over the skirmish line and commenced firing," McAllister wrote. "On receiving the enemy's fire, to my great astonishment, the line began to give way on the left."[3] In its retreat the division's first line passed over the second, which stood up to the pursuing Rebels for fifteen or twenty minutes before it, too, melted away, falling back to the safety of the breastworks the men had built along the Brock Road.

Lieutenant Colonel Lyman returned to 2nd Corps headquarters around 5 p.m. to serve as Meade's eyes and ears on the Orange Plank Road. "Report to General Meade," Hancock told him, "that it is very hard to bring up troops in this wood, and that only a part of my Corps is up, but I will do as well as I can." Then Lyman saw an officer ride up and report to Hancock: "Sir! General Getty is hard pressed and nearly out of ammunition." "Tell him," Hancock replied, "to hold on and General Gibbon will be up to help him." Another officer rode up: "General Mott's division has broken, sir, and is coming back." "Tell him to stop them, sir!!" Hancock roared. But even as he spoke, a crowd of soldiers came out of the woods retreating into the Brock Road. Hancock rode among them calling out, "Halt here! Halt here! Form behind this rifle-pit. Major Mitchell, go to Gibbon and tell him to come up on the double quick!"[4]

To the north of Mott's retreating Federals were the remaining regiments of the brigade which Birney had left as a reserve, and these now advanced by the left flank to restore the situation. The historian of one of these regiments, the 124th New York, wrote that "a wild storm of bullets, which rattled through the brush, patted against the trees, and hissed and whistled through the air. [We] halted to rectify our line . . . Strengthened by many of Mott's men [we] moved forward . . . and opened a counter-fire, which turned the tide of battle here. The Confederates slowly and steadily retired. [We] passed over Confederate dead and wounded, then began to take prisoners, singly and in twos and threes. We could seldom see the enemy's battle-line because of the denseness of the foliage; but powder flashes from the opposing lines often told that they were but a few yards apart . . . [We] halted on the east edge of a swale, or low piece of ground, which was covered with the most dense growth of saplings I ever saw."[5]

An officer of the 11th North Carolina of Kirkland's Confederate reserve brigade remembered that as his regiment advanced over the Rebel front-line troops their brigade commander "sneered sardonically: 'Go ahead; you'll soon come back.' And sure enough we did. We struck as he had done the Federal line behind intrenchments, from which in vain we tried to dislodge it, and recoiled, lying down in turn behind MacRae's line. I fancy he smiled sardonically then."[6]

Meanwhile, Birney's other brigade, his 2nd, commanded by Brigadier General Alexander Hays, marched up the Brock Road and formed line of battle beyond the Orange Plank Road. Then, with the 1st United States Sharpshooters acting as the brigade's skirmishers, Hays' troops plunged into the woods to support Getty's right. Thrashing blindly through the thickets covering alternating ridges and swales, his regiments one by one ran into ambushing volleys from the Mississippi/North Carolina brigade of Brigadier General Joseph R. Davis, the Confederate president's nephew, delivered at a range of about forty yards. Many Federals fell, but those who did not held steady and returned a deadly fire that announced they were not intimidated. Hays rode up and down, straightening his line as coolly as if on parade, until he was shot through the head and carried to the rear. His senior colonel took over, and his men continued the fight. "The slaughter is fearful," a Michigan color sergeant remembered, "men fall on every side, and my flag is receiving its share of bullets. Charge after charge is made on both sides. Sometimes we drive the enemy, and then they rally and drive us."[7]

Soon Brigadier General John Gibbon's 2nd Division of Hancock's 2nd Corps came marching up, Colonel Samuel S. Carroll's 3rd Brigade in the van. "It was a welcome sight," Lyman wrote, "to see Carroll's brigade come along that Brock road, he riding at their head as calm as a May morning. 'Left face—prime—forward,' and the line disappeared in the woods to waken the musketry with double violence."[8]

Carroll's brigade was one of the best in the army. He formed his men on the right, or north, of the Orange Plank Road and advanced with his left touching that highway. Gibbon's next brigade, Brigadier General Alexander Webb's 1st, formed line of battle in the Brock Road to help drive off the Confederates who were pursuing Mott's division. Brigadier General Joshua Owen's 2nd Brigade marched on behind Webb to the Orange Plank Road, where he formed his regiments with their right flank on the road and they stepped off to join Carroll. The sun was beginning to set as word reached Getty's troops that help was on the way, and they began to fire off the ammunition they had been hording during the prolonged battle. Then Carroll's brigade passed over Wheaton's troops and struck the Confederates a violent blow. Two of Heth's brigades were hard pressed. Colonel Carroll was wounded but refused to leave the field while the battle raged. However, his and Owen's brigades were stopped by a strong Rebel counterblow that was so sudden that the staff officer who carried orders for the withdrawal of Colonel Grant's Vermont Brigade was captured.

Meanwhile, up on the northern flank of the two armies, things heated up again around 5 p.m. That is when Brigadier General Truman Seymour's 2nd Brigade of Ricketts' 3rd Division of Sedgwick's 6th Corps arrived to reinforce Wright's division. Seymour could have arrived much earlier except that Ricketts had been the victim of conflicting orders from Grant and Meade. He had been covering the crossing at Germanna Ford when Burnside's troops began to arrive, and Grant had ordered him forward. Then he received orders from Meade to block the roads leading around the army's right flank. In the face of conflicting orders, Ricketts stood fast and requested clarification. Meade had passed word of this development to Grant before the two had come together that morning but Grant had waited until they met before resolving the matter by confirming Meade's orders. Finally, around 1:30 p.m., Ricketts was relieved by some of Burnside's troops, and his two brigades were called in and positioned at the intersection of the Germanna Plank Road and the Culpepper Mine Road. From there Seymour was later sent to help Wright, and the other brigade to reinforce Warren. About 6 p.m., after receiving word that Hancock's last two divisions were going to join the fight down on the Orange Plank Road, Meade ordered Warren to renew the attack along the turnpike immediately, and Sedgwick to renew Wright's attack at once.

Rickett's division was somewhat of a second-rate, stepchild outfit. It had been made up of garrison units from the Shenandoah and West Virginia the previous summer and sent to reinforce the Army of the Potomac after the losses taken at Gettysburg. At first it formed a new 3rd Division for the old 3rd Corps. Then, in the recent reorganization it had been transferred to the 6th Corps.

Seymour formed his five regiments into two lines on gently rolling ground covered with trees. He had reconnoitered the Confederate position and satisfied himself that his right overlapped the Rebel line, which he planned to outflank and roll up while Wright and Warren kept the Southerners' attention to their front. He had failed, however, to detect Brigadier General John Pegram's Virginia brigade deploying on the Confederate left. So, in fact, the Rebel line overlapped his own, and it was backed by a sizable contingent of artillery.

Colonel J. Warren Keifer, later to become Speaker of the House of Representatives but then commander of the 110th Ohio and in charge of Seymour's front line, recalled that his troops charged forward in gallant style, pressing the enemy back about a half-mile, until they came upon the enemy on the slope of a hill, entrenched behind logs hurriedly thrown together. Keifer discovered that Wright's troops had not kept pace on his left and that the Southerners overlapped both his flanks. He called a halt and sent this information to Seymour, but back came orders to attack. Feeling sure that his information had not reached the brigade commander he delayed, but when a second order to attack came, he felt he had to obey. So at about 7 p.m. "the line was advanced to within 150 yards of the enemy's works," he recorded, "under a most terrible fire from the front and flanks. It was impossible to succeed; but the two regiments, notwithstanding, maintained their ground, and kept up a rapid fire for nearly three hours, and then retired under orders for a short distance only."[9] Keifer was wounded at about 8:30 p.m. by a bullet passing through both bones of his left forearm, but he did not relinquish command until darkness brought an end to the fight at about 9 p.m. Neill's brigade on Seymour's left had also attacked and suffered heavy losses. Wright's own brigades had not left their positions but supported the attack with heavy firing. Warren did not attack at all, possibly with Grant's approval, although some of his force was used in a different direction.

Around 2:30 that afternoon Confederate major general Cadmus Wilcox had been ordered to take his 3rd Corps division into the woods to connect Heth's left with Ewell's right. He had marched his four brigades off through the Widow Tapp's fields under the eyes of General Lee himself. The last two brigades had been dropped off at the Chewning house plateau, from which Wilcox reported that he could see Federal troops around Wilderness Tavern, moving toward the Confederate right. But Wilcox and his first two brigades had pushed on over Wilderness Run to the thickets where Wadsworth had formed his Union division earlier in the day for the attack on Ewell. Then Wilcox had ridden on ahead of his troops and found Brigadier General John Gordon, who had almost collided with Ewell's wooden leg earlier that day and whose brigade still formed the right flank of the Rebel 2nd Corps' line. The conference of these two generals had been broken up at about 4 p.m., just as the rear of Wilcox's column had been passing Lee back in the Widow Tapp's fields, when the sound of an immense volume of musketry had torn through the brush in which Heth's Division lay.

Wilcox had hurried south to where he had left the head of his own forces and had been met by a courier from Lee with orders for him to bring these men back to the Orange Plank Road; Heth was under violent attack and needed support. The army commander had already ordered the two rear brigades recalled from the Chewning plateau. That order had arrived around 5 p.m., and the two brigades had formed column and marched rapidly back across the Widow Tapp's fields. The leading brigade, the South Carolinians of Brigadier General Samuel McGowan, had turned into the Orange Plank Road, forcing ambulances bearing Heth's wounded out of the way, and hastened to the front despite shells bursting among them from a few Union guns that had been dragged forward.

Now Wilcox had only the sound of firing to go by in determining where to send his brigades. Just then the firing seemed to be hottest on the Confederate right so the second brigade, Brigadier General A. M. Scales' North Carolinians, was sent in that direction while McGowan's regiments formed line of battle across the road. These passed over Heth's front line and raised the high-pitched Rebel yell, which was answered by a murderous volley. Some of Heth's men, unaware that friendly forces were now to their front, answered that with a volley of their own that struck McGowan's men from the rear. Then when the latter's right flank regiment stopped to return the Yankee volley it was blasted by Union artillery and driven back. The next regiment in the line held its ground, and the other three continued to advance. It was probably these troops who struck Carroll's front line a hard blow. They drove the artillerymen from their guns and took many prisoners, but a fierce counterattack brought the Rebels to a halt, and a threat to their flank forced them to retire, allowing the gunners to return to their cannon.

Scales' Brigade reached the south flank of Heth's line in time to prevent it being turned, but failed to connect with McGowan's right. The latter, with Federals working onto both flanks, was subjected to a withering crossfire. One witness described McGowan's front as "the shortest, most huddled, most ineffective line-of-battle ever seen."[10] Scales' North Carolinians were forced to fall back by pressure on their front and right, but McGowan's South Carolinians stayed and absorbed tremendous punishment.

Meanwhile, Hancock's remaining division, Brigadier General Francis Barlow's 1st, had finally arrived on the field and, after pausing to throw up more breastworks, was ready to advance. The fate of the battle now hung on a race between these four Federal brigades and the remaining two Confederate brigades of Wilcox's Division. A third party to the race was the setting sun. One of Barlow's brigades was left behind as a reserve, but the other three moved out through the woods toward Hill's right flank.

On the Confederate side, Brigadier General Edward Thomas's four Georgia regiments were sent to bolster Davis' Mississippians just in time to obviate a suicide charge. One tenth of the 340 men of the lone North Carolina regiment belonging to Davis's Brigade were dead, and almost half of them were wounded. The next day 157 dead Yankees were counted in front of their position.

Wilcox's other brigade, the last such unit left to the Rebels on the Orange Plank Road front, was composed of five North Carolina regiments and was commanded by 31-year-old Brigadier General James Lane. Hill himself directed Lane to the support of Scales' shaken regiments on the far right. The gathering dusk deepened the gloom under the trees and the powder smoke, and the musketry sounded to one soldier "like fire in a canebrake."[11] After floundering through the thickets and marshes Lane's left-flank regiment, the 7th North Carolina, which had been told that McGowan's friendly troops were still up ahead, was suddenly hit by a blast of Union fire from a small ridge 75 yards to its front and left. The Federals followed that up with an advance, and demands that the Rebels surrender, emphasizing their point with another volley. The 7th broke and fled for the rear. Then, before Lane could do anything to help his left, his right was suddenly struck by two brigades of Barlow's division. Lane turned first two companies and then an entire regiment to face this threat, but they were no match for all those Yankees, and the whole brigade followed the 7th back over the swampy swales and little ridges to where the other Confederates were holding on.

Harry Heth surveyed the line of intermingled, disorganized, fought-out units from his own and Wilcox's divisions and lamented, "I should have left well enough alone." Cavalry commander Jeb Stuart and Colonel Venable of Lee's staff were on hand to assess the situation. Venable spoke for every Confederate on this part of the field when he murmured, "If night would only come."[12] But before it did, Hill and his ulcer had one more crisis to face. An excited courier brought him word that another whole division of Yankees was pushing through the woods which Wilcox had abandoned between the Orange Plank Road and the turnpike, and was approaching Hill's left flank.

The movement of Wilcox's brigades returning over the Widow Tapp's open fields had been reported to Meade by Warren's 5th Corps headquarters: "Our signal officers report a heavy column of the enemy's infantry moving in a field this side of the Plank Road and going toward General Hancock."[13] This information reached Meade and Grant as they were already on their way to visit Warren in search of reinforcements to send to the 2nd Corps. General Wadsworth, whose troops had reformed in the fields near Warren's headquarters after their rout by Ewell, pleaded to be allowed to redeem his division's reputation by being given this second chance.

Wadsworth was the silver-haired, 56-year-old son of one of New York state's wealthiest land-owners. He had been a prominent politician in his home state but had declined a major general's commission early in the war to serve as a volunteer staff officer. Later he had accepted a brigadier general's star, but had taken time off to run for governor of New York. When he was defeated, he returned to his division. Both he and his troops had been in the 1st Corps until the recent consolidation, and his division contained some of the best units in the army, including the famous Iron Brigade of western units. It took about an hour for Meade's staff to produce orders for Wadsworth. Reinforced by Baxter's 2nd Brigade of Robinson's 2nd Division of the 5th Corps, also former 1st Corps troops, he was to attack southward and take Hill in the flank. Robinson pleaded for permission to accompany his one brigade, and this was granted. The Federals moved out in two lines of battle plus a reserve at about 6 p.m., advancing cautiously for fear of running into another ambush in the thick woods. It took them over an hour to approach Hill's flank.

That Confederate had no reserves and could not spare a single, exhausted regiment from his line facing Hancock. All he had with which to meet this Federal juggernaut was the corps' provost guard, the 125 men of the 5th Alabama Battalion who were guarding prisoners to the rear of the line. The prisoners were turned over to whatever noncombatants could be found, and the Alabamans were spread out in a skirmish line and told to charge forward and raise a Rebel yell as if they were being followed by a strong line of battle. Firing as fast as they could and screaming their heads off, they crashed through the woods until they brought Wadsworth's front line units to a halt, convinced that they faced a large Confederate force. Colonel Roy Stone's horse reared in fright, throwing him to the ground, and his brigade panicked and broke for the rear. But his men were met by the lowered bayonets of Cutler's Iron Brigade in the second line and stopped in their tracks. Stone's officers restored order in the gathering dusk, and the advance was resumed, pushing the 125 Alabamans—or what was left of them—steadily back through the woods until darkness brought the Federals to a halt around 9 p.m., about a half-mile north of the Orange Plank Road. At last throughout the Wilderness the firing gradually died away to the occasional shots of nervous pickets, the moaning of the wounded, and the mournful cries of the whippoorwills. Darkness and the Wilderness had saved A. P. Hill's corps. The sun had won the three-way race.

Not long after Grant and his staff had finished their evening meal,

Meade walked over from his headquarters and the two generals sat by the campfire and, with Grant's staff and Congressman Washburne, discussed the day's events and made their plans for the next morning. Horace Porter remembered Grant saying, "As Burnside's corps, on our side, and Longstreet's, on the other side, have not been engaged, and the troops of both armies have been occupied principally in struggling through thickets and fighting for position, to-day's work has not been much of a test of strength. I feel pretty well satisfied with the result of the engagement; for it is evident that Lee attempted by a bold movement to strike this army in flank before it could be put into line of battle and be prepared to fight to advantage; but in this he has failed."[14]

Sometime before 8 p.m. Grant issued orders for a general attack all along the line to be launched at 4:30 the next morning, and Meade passed these orders on to his corps commanders. But Sedgwick, Warren, and Hancock, gathered at army headquarters for a conference, asked that the attack be delayed by an hour and a half due to the dense thickets, the fatigued condition of the men, and the need for some daylight in which to form their units and bring up reinforcements. About 10:30 p.m. Meade passed on this request to Grant. The general-in-chief had to be wakened to hear this message. After brief consideration he dictated a reply to his military secretary: "General: I am directed by the lieutenant-general commanding to say that you may change the hour of attack to 5 o'clock, as he is afraid that if delayed until 6 o'clock the enemy will take the initiative, which he desires specially to avoid."[15]

As if Meade did not have enough problems, he later received a short report penned by his cavalry commander at 11:10 p.m. Sheridan gave a very brief summary of Wilson's problems and rescue by Gregg, then explained that he had not attacked the Rebel cavalry at Hamilton's Crossing because of his responsibility for guarding the immense wagon train against attack from the rear. He was obviously chafing at this kind of duty and added the quarrelsome query, "Why cannot infantry be sent to guard the trains and let me take the offensive?"[16]

Had Grant seen this note he might have taken pleasure in the fact that at least somebody in the higher command of the Army of the Potomac was eager to attack.

---

1. Steere, *The Wilderness Campaign*, 206.
2. Ibid., 208.
3. Ibid., 214.

4. Earl Schenck Miers, *The Late Campaign: Grant Saves the Union* (New York, 1972), 54.
5. Steere, *The Wilderness Campaign*, 216.
6. Ibid., 225.
7. Trudeau, *Bloody Roads South*, 69.
8. Miers, *The Last Campaign*, 54.
9. Steere, *The Wilderness Campaign*, 255.
10. Ibid., 230.
11. Dowdey, *Lee's Last Campaign*, 123.
12. Ibid., 124.
13. Steere, *The Wilderness Campaign*, 220.
14. Porter, *Campaigning With Grant*, 53–54.
15. Steere, *The Wilderness Campaign*, 280.
16. Ibid., 279.

CHAPTER SEVENTEEN

"We Are Driving Them Most Beautifully"

5–6 May 1864

At 6 p.m., just as Wadsworth's Federal division was starting its move toward Hill's northern flank, Lee had sent off a message to Ewell, up on the turnpike. The Confederate commander still had not been informed of the heavy attacks which his 2nd Corps had beaten off there. Lee had told Ewell that Wilcox had reported seeing the Federals around Wilderness Tavern moving toward the Orange Plank Road. If this was the case, Lee had said, he wanted Ewell to advance and take the high ground around Wilderness Tavern in the morning, thus cutting off Grant's communications with his supposed supply line back to Brandy Station. "But if this cannot be done without too great a sacrifice," the dispatch had continued, "you must be prepared to reenforce our right and make your arrangements accordingly."[1]

At 8 p.m. Ewell finally sent a report to Lee describing the day's action on his front. Then he ordered an attack for 4:30 a.m. He sent Gordon's Brigade from his extreme right flank to rejoin the rest of Early's Division on his extreme left. There it was reinforced by some of the 2nd Corps artillery. Ewell also brought Jones' reorganized Virginians up from reserve to straddle the turnpike again. During the night, Ramseur's Brigade of Rodes' Division reached the front, two days after making its reconnaisance across the Rapidan. It replaced Jones' as the 2nd Corps reserve. Six detached regiments also returned during the night. No effort was made to dampen the noise of these movements, for Ewell wanted the Northerners to think he was being heavily reinforced.

As the Federals had been brought to battle right here in the Wilderness and had given Hill's corps all the fight it could handle, Lee decided that Longstreet's plan to follow the Catharpin Road to Todd's Tavern—which was five miles to the southeast of where Hill was fighting Hancock—would have to be abandoned. With Yankees moving from Wilderness Tavern toward Hill's position and no Southern forces protecting Hill's left, and especially in view of the unusual aggressiveness Grant seemed to have instilled in "those people," Lee needed his 1st Corps closer to his other two. The bold turning movement would have to be postponed for now unless Ewell could get around the Union right. So Colonel Venable had been sent with instructions for Longstreet to alter his line of march and come up to the Orange Plank Road at Parker's Store. Later, as Hill's situation became more desperate, Lee had sent Major H. B. McClellan of Jeb Stuart's staff to find Major General Charles Field, whose division was leading Longstreet's column, and hurry his march.

In the meantime, Wilcox had come to Lee's tent about 9 p.m. with the intention of reporting the broken, irregular nature of his and Heth's formations, and to suggest that the troops be withdrawn under the cover of a skirmish line to reform a little farther back. But before he could make his report, Lee had told him that Anderson's Division and Longstreet's corps had been ordered to hurry forward, and that Heth's and Wilcox's divisions would be relieved before morning. Hearing this, Wilcox had not mentioned reforming the troops.

Major McClellan returned, just as Lee was finally getting a bite of supper, to report that Field, new to division command, had refused to accept a verbal order from a cavalry staff officer and had stated that he was under orders from Longstreet to move at 1 a.m. The 1st Corps had not reached Richards' Shop by noon that day, as Longstreet had written Lee that he would. In fact, it had been 5 p.m. before his column had covered the fifteen miles from its bivouac to that point, and there the 1st Corps commander had stopped to give his troops a six-hour rest. Now it looked like it would be daylight before the exchange of troops could be made. Major McClellan volunteered to ride back to Richards' Shop with written orders, but Lee replied, "No, Major, it is now past 10 o'clock, and by the time you could return to General Field and he could put his division in motion, it would be 1 o'clock; and at that hour he will move."[2]

Hill's men were sleeping on their arms wherever night had found them, some of them not even taking time to eat their meager rations of bacon and hardtack. The Confederate and Federal lines were so close that many men of both sides wandered into enemy camps. The colonel of the 7th North Carolina crept to a small stream for water and was quietly captured by Yankees. Not far away the colonel of the 1st Massachusetts went to the same stream and was silently taken by Rebels.

While Wilcox went to Lee, Heth went to Hill with the same request: to be allowed to regroup his units into some semblance of order. Hill was sick, bundled up by a fire, and he gave Heth the same answer as Lee gave Wilcox: "Longstreet will be up in a few hours. He will form in your front. I don't propose that you shall do any fighting tomorrow; the men have been marching and fighting all day and are tired. I don't wish them disturbed." Heth went away, but he came back, only to hear the answer repeated. Wilcox came, and he too was told the same. Heth came back a third time to argue with Hill, and this time the corps commander lost his temper. "Damn it, Heth," he grumbled, "I don't want to hear any more about it; the men shall not be disturbed."[3] At 3:30 a.m. Wilcox asked that pioneers be sent forward with axes and spades to fell trees and construct defenses, but it was daylight before they arrived and, Wilcox wrote, "the enemy was found to be too close to permit their use."[4]

The Federals, on the other hand, had made good use of the hours of darkness to regroup and reform their units. Examination of captured Confederates revealed to them that Longstreet was expected to be on hand in the morning to attack the Federal left with 12,000 men, so Hancock withdrew Barlow's division to the breastworks along the Brock Road. He put these troops, plus 69 guns of the 2nd Corps' artillery brigade, under Gibbon's command to defend the left flank of the Union army from any attack up the Brock Road or along the road Wilson had taken to escape Rosser. Mott's, Birney's, and Getty's divisions, plus two of Gibbon's brigades, Owen's and Carroll's, were put under Birney's command to make the attack which Grant had ordered for 5 a.m. Webb's brigade of Gibbon's division was put in reserve between these two provisional commands. In anticipation of Wadsworth's division coming in on his right, Birney formed his brigades for an attack *en echelon*—that is, with his left flank units farther advanced than his center, and that farther advanced than his right. He had nine brigades, totalling at least 20,000 men, massed before dawn and waiting for the signal to advance. A half-mile to the northwest, Wadsworth had perhaps another 7,000 in his four brigades.

Grant's determination to launch an all-out assault on Lee's army is indicated by a circular directed by Meade's headquarters to all his corps commanders: "For the present the trains must be protected by the cavalry, and every man who can shoulder a musket must be in the ranks. You will at once send a staff officer to the chief quartermaster at these headquarters to learn the location of your trains and conduct the train guard to the front."[5]

Up on the turnpike, Griffin's 5th Corps division, reinforced by over a thousand engineers from the pontoon trains, was quietly moved forward to the edge of Sander's field again, this time with Crawford's Pennsylvania Reserves on his left. Two brigades of Robinson's division were formed in reserve, reinforced by a brigade of heavy artillerymen from the army's artillery reserve, serving as infantry. To Griffin's right, Sedgwick reformed Wright's three brigades together with Neill's and Seymour's, and brought Brigadier General William H. Morris' 1st Brigade of Ricketts' division up to form in close support of Wright's left flank. Brigadier General Alexander Shaler's small 4th Brigade of Wright's division was brought up from where it had been serving as train guard to a reserve position behind the center of the 6th Corps line.

The pickets of both sides were nervous, and there was sporadic firing all night. The burning woods sent an orange glow flickering through the gloom, and thick smoke choked the air. Wounded men still lay between the lines where no one could safely get to them, some calling for help, others too weak to do anything but endure. Sometimes insane cries of pain or terror would ring out as one of the numerous fires reached a man unable to move out of its path. "I saw one man," a Union artilleryman remembered, "both of whose legs were broken, lying on the ground with his cocked rifle by his side and his ramrod in his hand, and his eyes set on the front. I know he meant to kill himself in case of fire—knew it as surely as though I could read his thoughts."[6] One Confederate picket wrote of "the terrible groans of the wounded, the mournful sound of the owl and the awful shrill shrieks of the whippoorwill," adding that "these birds seemed to mock at our grief and laugh at the groans of the dying."[7]

Around 1 a.m., three of Burnside's divisions began marching southward behind Sedgwick's troops. Two of these were aiming for the critical mile-wide gap between the troops on the turnpike and those on the Orange Plank Road, while the third would constitute Grant's general reserve. Burnside's Provisional Brigade of two cannon-less heavy artillery regiments and one horse-less cavalry regiment, was left to picket the area between Sedgwick's right flank and the Rapidan River. The 4th Division of Burnside's 9th Corps, composed entirely of regiments of U.S. Colored Troops, was still on a forced march from Manassas Junction to Germanna Ford. Its commander, Brigadier General Edward Ferrero, was under orders to cross to the south side of the river "and hold the bridge and situation at all hazard."[8]

At 4 a.m. on the 6th of May Grant and his staff were awakened by the sound of Burnside's men marching along the Germanna Plank Road. The general had a light breakfast. According to Horace Porter: "He took a cucumber, sliced it, poured some vinegar over it, and partook of nothing else except a cup of strong coffee. The first thing he did after rising from the table was to call for a fresh supply of cigars. His colored servant 'Bill' brought him two dozen. After lighting one of them, he filled his pockets with the rest. He then went over to the knoll, and began to walk back and forth slowly upon the cleared portion of the ridge."[9]

Promptly at 4:30 a.m.—the hour at which Grant had planned to launch his own attack before he had allowed Meade a half-hour's grace—Dick Ewell's artillery broke whatever calm had managed to settle on the Wilderness, and Jubal Early's three brigades of infantry on the Rebels' extreme left advanced over swampy ground covered by thorn bushes, driving in the Union skirmishers protecting Seymour's and Neill's brigades as they formed up for their own planned attack from the Union far right. These troops met the Confederates with point-blank volleys and then pushed them back across the marsh and through the thorns until they came upon the Rebel breastworks. There the Southerners had all the advantages, and the Federals in their turn, after taking heavy losses, retreated back across the thorny, marshy ground to their own lines. To the south of Neill's brigade, Wright's division advanced at the appointed hour of 5 a.m. and thrice fought its way to the parapets of Allegheny Johnson's breastworks, being driven back each time by the murderous fire of the Confederates.

Farther south, Warren's skirmishers pressed the Rebel positions to their front, but Griffin and Crawford were not ordered to send in their main lines. At 5:30 a.m. Warren notified army headquarters that his troops were in position but that "the head of Burnside's column is just going on to the (Lacy) field, and in consequence of their not being in position, I have sent the heavy artillery, under Colonel Kitching, 2,400, to support General Wadsworth."[10] Back came urgings that he close with the enemy, so at 6 a.m. Griffin's division again crossed Sanders' field in two lines and drove in the Confederate skirmishers, with Crawford's two brigades struggling through the woods to the south, keeping pace as best they could. Warren also sent some light artillery forward and reported his progress to Meade, along with unsolicited advice not to order the final attack until Burnside, who had a reputation for slowness, was in position.

A young staff lieutenant sent to guide the 9th Corps to the appointed place waited an hour and a half beyond the time at which Burnside should have appeared. "When he came, accompanied by a large staff," the lieutenant remembered, "I rode up to him and told him my instructions . . . Like a sphinx, he made no reply, halted and began to look with a most leaden countenance in the direction he was to go . . . After a while he started off calmly toward the Lacy house, not indicating that my services were needed—he probably was thinking of something that was of vastly more importance. I concluded that I wasn't wanted, and was about to go my own way, when I caught sight of Babcock of Grant's staff coming at great speed down the hill just the other side of the run. He had been out with Hancock, and as he approached, I called, 'What's the news, Babcock?' Without halting he replied, 'Hancock has driven them a mile and we are going to have a great victory!' "[11]

Hancock had also attacked promptly at 5 a.m. Just as the sun was rising above the trees, the North Carolinians of Scales' Brigade on the right center of Hill's front line suddenly found the woods all around them filled with advancing Federal infantry. In a brief struggle the colors of the 13th North Carolina were captured by the 141st Pennsylvania, and the entire Rebel brigade stampeded for the rear. That exposed the right flank of McGowan's South Carolinians, just north of the Orange Plank Road. Their skirmishers gave them enough warning to prevent a rout, but they had to retire in haste. "There was no panic," their brigade historian insisted. "The men fell back from deliberate conviction that it was impossible to hold the ground."[12] Davis' Brigade, on the left end of Hill's front line, was overwhelmed while attempting to form line, and the rout was so sudden that the 55th North Carolina had still not unstacked its rifles.

Thomas' Georgians, on the right of Hill's front line, were scattered and driven back past Lane's North Carolinians of the second line, who in turn were struck simultaneously in front and flank. They joined in the general retreat, many of them without ever having had a chance to fire a shot. Kirkland's Brigade was hit on the left flank by Wadsworth's division while trying to form line, and was "rolled up as a sheet of paper would be rolled without power of resistance," the colonel of the 11th North Carolina remembered.[13] Walker's Brigade was also driven back. Only Cooke's

Brigade, in reserve in the rear of Hill's position, supported by a battery of light guns and the only unit properly entrenched, was able to put up a prolonged and determined defense. Kirkland's and Davis' troops rallied on Cooke's left, but Scales' and Thomas' brigades continued their retreat westward through the thickets, while Lane's and McGowan's streamed back along the Orange Plank Road.

Baxter's and Cutler's Union brigades of Wadsworth's force had swept southward across the Orange Plank Road in pursuit of the Confederates, so that they blocked the right flank units of Birney's westward-moving assault formation. Officers of both forces worked frantically to sort out the traffic jam while Getty's division edged to its left to get around the obstruction. Then it inclined back toward the road and ran up against Cooke's entrenched Southerners. Meanwhile, Wadsworth managed to get his troops realigned facing west on the north side of the Orange Plank Road with Cutler's Iron Brigade in front and the other three following, one behind the other. Cooke, Kirkland, Davis, and the one battery staggered these and Getty's Federals, but could not stop them completely. With his front and both his flanks threatened, Cooke abandoned his prepared position and withdrew toward Widow Tapp's farm. Lee's Army of Northern Virginia was facing its greatest crisis since the battle of Sharpsburg (its name for Antietam) twenty months before.

Lieutenant Colonel Lyman of Meade's staff returned to Hancock's headquarters with a group of mounted orderlies to again keep his commander posted on developments along the Orange Plank Road. He found the 2nd Corps commander in great spirits. "We are driving them beautifully, sir," Hancock called out. "Tell Meade we are driving them most beautifully. Birney has gone in and he is clearing them out be-au-ti-fully."

"I am ordered to tell you, sir," Lyman replied, "that only one division of Burnside's is up but that he will go into action as soon as he can be put into position."

"I knew it," Hancock cried, "just what I expected. If he could attack now we would smash A. P. Hill to pieces."[14]

About 6 a.m. Lee and Hill were conferring in the Widow Tapp's fields behind a line of sixteen guns belonging to Lieutenant Colonel William T. Poague's battalion of 3rd Corps artillery. The smoke and noise of battle had been swelling and rolling their way for an hour, and now small groups of retreating Confederate infantrymen began to emerge from the east edge of the woods. The Rebel artillerymen sprang to their guns to prepare to greet any Yankees who might be following, while readying their teams and limbers in case they needed to join the flight. Lee sent orders for the supply wagons parked at Parker's Store to get ready to fall back, then sent Colonel Venable to find Longstreet and hasten his troops to the front.

The roar of musketry grew ever louder and ever closer to the Tapp clearing, and soon the Orange Plank Road was jammed with fleeing Rebels while entire regiments came running out of the woods into the open ground around Poague's guns, parts of the various brigades intermixed. Lee hurried out into the road to help rally his troops and recognized a brigade commander being swept along in the rout. "My God, General McGowan," he exclaimed, "is this splendid brigade of yours running like a flock of geese?" "General," McGowan replied heatedly, "these men are not whipped. They only want a place to form and they will fight as well as they ever did,"[15] General Wilcox rode up and reported that his men could not hold. He too was sent by the anxious Lee to hurry Longstreet's 1st Corps. Wilcox rode west on the Orange Plank Road and soon came upon Brigadier General Joseph B. Kershaw riding at the head of his division of Longstreet's 1st Corps. Wilcox passed on Lee's instructions for these troops to hasten forward and form line of battle on the right of the road. Then he went in search of Longstreet, to direct him to Lee's headquarters.

Kershaw meanwhile rode ahead with one of Wilcox's aides to find the best spot to deploy his men. Kershaw had only recently taken over what had been Major General Lafayette McLaw's Division of the 1st Corps. He had previously commanded one of its brigades which, under its senior colonel, John W. Henegan, marched at the head of Kershaw's column. Kershaw met Henegan and ordered the colonel to form the brigade in line of battle on the right of the road. Then he personally led the 2nd North Carolina to the left side of the road to protect Poague's guns. Henegan was followed to the right by Brigadier General Benjamin Humphrey's Brigade, which formed just south of the road, and by Brigadier General Goode Bryan's Brigade, which passed beyond Henegan to form on the division's right. However, Kershaw's deployment was delayed by the last of Hill's retreating men. "Do you belong to Lee's army?" Longstreet's veterans asked these refugees derisively. "You don't look like the men we left here. You're worse than Bragg's men," they jeered.[15] But the 1st Corps troops calmly opened ranks to let the fugitives through, then closed ranks again to face the pursuing enemy.

The Federals on the left of Birney's massive formation, meeting no resistance, pushed progressively farther ahead of those near the road. They were tired and disorganized by their advance through the thickets south of the road, but they came on nevertheless, exploiting a gap between two of Henegan's regiments, and shot down the colonel of the 3rd South Carolina. "Men rolled and writhed in their last death struggle;" a member of that regiment remembered, "wounded men groped their way to the rear, being blinded by the stifling smoke. All commands were drowned in this terrible din of battle—the earth and elements shook and trembled with the deadly shock of combat."[17] The 2nd South Carolina's right gave way, and the rest of that regiment was reduced to a huddled mass of men. Then its colonel also fell as he tried to rally his troops, and his lieutenant colonel was carried to the rear with a severe wound, leaving a captain in command.

But Poague's guns, finding their line of fire at last cleared of fugitives, fired cannisters of lead balls obliquely into the Federals like giant shotguns while Kershaw led Humphrey's Brigade into the gap. Then, after Bryan's Brigade had formed on the Confederate right, Kershaw led his division forward. He soon found that he could not drive the Yankees, but they could not budge him either. A member of the 3rd South Carolina saw another member of his regiment, who had been shot in the thigh, struggle to find cover behind a sapling. "Bracing himself against it, he undertook deliberative measures for saving his life. Tying a handkerchief about the wound, and placing a small stone underneath and just over the artery, and putting a stick between the handkerchief and his leg, he began to tighten by twisting the stick around. But too late; life had fled, leaving both hands clasping the stick, his eyes glassy and fixed."[18]

Because it had started farther back and then had been delayed by running into Wadsworth and into Cooke, the right of Birney's formation took longer to reach the Widow Tapp's field than the left had taken to encounter Kershaw. This gave time for Longstreet's other division, Field's, to form up. His leading brigade, under Brigadier General G. T. Anderson, was sent to the south side of the road. Evidently, the entire division was originally intended to form there, but then Field received orders to hurry to the left of the road. Field remembered "throwing the Texas brigade, which was second (in column), on the left of the road and in line perpendicular to it, Benning rear of that, and Law in rear of that, the Texas brigade, led by its gallant General Gregg, dashed forward as soon as it was formed, without waiting for those in its rear to get ready."[19]

"Here they come!" Poague's gunners cried out, and greeted the 1st Corps veterans with a high-pitched Rebel yell.[20] "Who are you, my boys?" Lee asked these troops as they came on the field. "Texas boys," they yelled. They were considered the best troops in the army and they knew it. "Hurrah for Texas," Lee cried, momentarily losing his dignity and waving his hat. "Hurrah for Texas."[21] When the Federals appeared on this front, Poague had turned the fire of his artillery against them. Gregg's Texans formed right behind the guns. Longstreet rode down the line at a walk, telling each company, "Keep cool, men. We will straighten this out in a short time—keep cool."[22] "When you go in there," Lee told Gregg, "I wish you to give those men the cold steel. They will stand and fire all day, and never move unless you charge them," he said of the Federals. "That is my experience," Gregg agreed. Then the brigadier called his men to attention, informed them that General Lee was watching them, and gave the order to advance. "Texans always move them!" Lee proclaimed. The men began to cheer as Lee's words were passed down the line. "I would charge hell itself for that old man," one Texan was heard to say.[23]

The Texas Brigade advanced through Poague's guns with General Lee riding on their left flank. He would lead them in personally. This alarmed the lanky private who was marching at that end of the line. He knew his brigade was going into harm's way, and he did not want anything to happen to Marse Robert. He lifted his hat in respect and asked General Lee to go back. This was taken up by the rest of the regiment and then the brigade. "Go back, General Lee, go back! We won't go on unless you go back!"[24] General Gregg tried to head him off, and a sergeant grabbed his horse's rein. Then Colonel Venable rode up and shouted in his ear that Longstreet was waiting for orders. Lee finally lifted his own hat in salute to the men and rode slowly to the rear. The Texans advanced about 400 yards against stiff resistance, while the rest of Field's Division was coming up. But then their left was enfiladed by heavy Union rifle fire, and a large force of Federals was seen advancing down the road past their right, so Gregg pulled back to about 200 yards in front of Poague's guns. In that brief advance and retreat two thirds of the brigade had become casualties. One Texas company was reduced to a single man, a young lieutenant who for months thereafter paraded alone at roll call each morning.

The fate of Brigadier General Henry L. Benning's Georgia brigade was much the same as Gregg's Texans. They went in hard and returned minus a good many men. Benning himself was carried back on a litter with a serious wound. However, Brigadier General E. McIver Law's Alabama brigade, now under its senior colonel, W. F. Perry, moved to the far left of Field's Division and struck an advancing Union force in the flank as it was crossing swampy ground. The Yankees fired ineffectively and fell back in confusion. Then Perry found a Northern force on his own left and sent his largest regiment, the 15th Alabama, to meet it. He was surprised to learn that the larger Federal force scattered before a single regiment of

Confederates. Questioning prisoners soon revealed the reason. These Yankees belonged to the 15th New York Heavy Artillery, one of the two giant regiments sent down by Warren to reinforce Wadsworth. They knew all about garrison service in the defenses of Washington but next to nothing about marching and fighting in the open field, let alone in thickets where no one could see a hundred yards. They were no match for Perry's veterans.

But in crossing the swampy area, Perry's other four regiments became separated, two regiments to the left and two to the right of the worst of the marsh. Just then they blundered into Wadsworth's force, four brigades, one behind the other, closed up in one mass formation. These were the Federals who had chewed up Gregg's Texans and Benning's Georgians, and they met the Alabamans with volleys fired rank by rank in rapid succession. That staggered Perry's two closest regiments and raked the other two. But when the 15th Alabama came up it overlapped the Union right flank. Its colonel wheeled his men to face this mass of Yankees and ordered deliberate, well-aimed volleys that could not miss such an immense target. The Federals stopped firing and milled in confusion, and when the Alabamans charged, the mass formation, unable to turn to face them, began to fall back, any last order distintegrating. Some Federals retreated north, the way they had originally come, eventually to be rallied by Brigadier General Lysander Cutler of the Iron Brigade. Others fell back to the east, where they were later rallied by Wadsworth. But they all retreated.

Lieutenant Colonel Lyman of Meade's staff, still back at the Brock Road, had noted that after receding to the west as Birney and Wadsworth had advanced, the sound of firing "seemed to wake again with renewed fury." Soon a soldier came up to him with a captured Rebel. "I was ordered to report that this prisoner here belongs to Longstreet's Corps," the soldier said. "Do you belong to Longstreet?" Lyman asked the Confederate. "Ya-as, sir," was the reply. "It was too true!" Lyman remembered thinking. "Longstreet, coming in all haste from Orange Court House, had fallen desperately on our advance."[25]

Meanwhile, Wilcox's men were hastily reorganized and sent down the road they had taken the previous afternoon toward the Chewning plateau, to protect the Confederate left. Heth's men were placed in support of Poague's guns, and in very little time both divisions were ready to resume the contest. Also, after Longstreet's men had cleared the road, Major General Richard H. Anderson was able to bring his 3rd Corps division forward to rejoin Hill from its detached service of guarding the rear. Lee told Anderson to report to Longstreet, who had been his commander before his division had been transferred to the new 3rd Corps the year before.

While battle briefly flared along and north of the turnpike and exploded in expanding violence along both sides of the Orange Plank Road, Burnside's column had pushed up the lane which Crawford had taken the day before from Wilderness Tavern toward the Chewning house and Parker's Store. Brigadier General Robert B. Potter's 2nd Division of the 9th Corps had the lead, followed by Brigadier General Orlando B. Willcox's 3rd Division. When the head of the column reached an open field belonging to the Jones farm, it encountered Confederate skirmishers. The 6th New Hampshire was sent out to drive them back to their supports while other units spread out to protect the left and right. Then, under brisk infantry and artillery fire, three of the column's four brigades were formed in line facing west, while the 1st Michigan Sharpshooters connected the right of the line with Crawford's Pennsylvania Reserves of Warren's force.

Perceiving this as a threat aimed at his own right, Ewell sent his only reserve, Ramseur's newly arrived brigade, to that flank at the double quick. Ramseur's skirmishers were pushed out to the south, and they found A. P. Hill's left flank a half-mile away. Thus by about 8 a.m. the Confederates had at last made a connection, although tenuous, across the gap between the turnpike and the Orange Plank Road. Meanwhile, the Federals were diverted elsewhere. "I was preparing to charge the enemy." General Potter reported, "when I received an order to withdraw my command, move to the left, and attack on the right of General Hancock, near the Plank Road."[26] But it would be hours before the attack went in.

The Federals were striving, with mixed results, to keep the initiative. Hancock called on his reserve, Webb's brigade of Gibbon's division, to reinforce Birney about 7 a.m., and at the same time Gibbon was ordered to send Barlow's entire division against the enemy's right. Gibbon, however, knowing Lee's propensity for flank attacks and fearing that Rebels were lurking to the southwest—neither Anderson's nor Pickett's division had yet been located by the Federals—decided to keep Barlow's men in the breastworks where they were guarding the Brock Road and the left flank of the army. At 7:15 a.m., Meade advised Warren that Longstreet had appeared in Hancock's front and urged the 5th Corps' commander to press his own attack with the utmost vigor, using the bayonet in order to save ammunition. But still Warren did not attack. About 8 a.m. Stevenson's 1st Division of the 9th Corps left its reserve position at Wilderness Tavern to reinforce Hancock. At around the same time Sheridan was ordered by army headquarters to attack the phantom force that was

keeping Gibbon pinned on the Brock Road. This order quickly perco-
lated down through Cavalry Corps and 1st Cavalry Division headquarters
to Brigadier General George Armstrong Custer.

---

1. Dowdey and Manarin, eds., *Wartime Papers of R.E. Lee*, 721.
2. Freeman, *R. E. Lee*, 3:284.
3. Freeman, *Lee's Lieutenants*, 3:354.
4. Steere, *The Wilderness Campaign*, 312.
5. Ibid., 287.
6. Trudeau, *Bloody Roads South*. 79.
7. Ibid., 76.
8. Steere, *The Wilderness Campaign*, 297.
9. Porter, *Campaigning With Grant*, 56.
10. Steere, *The Wilderness Campaign*. 320.
11. Ibid., 326.
12. Ibid., 329–330.
13. Ibid., 330.
14. Ibid., 326.
15. Freeman, *R. E. Lee*, 3:286.
16. Ibid., 3:358.
17. Trudeau, *Bloody Roads South*, 92.
18. Ibid.
19. Steere, *The Wilderness Campaign*, 344.
20. Freeman, *Lee's Lieutenants*, 3:356.
21. Freeman, *R. E. Lee*, 3:287.
22. Steere, *The Wilderness Campaign*, 345.
23. Freeman, *Lee's Lieutenants*, 3:357.
24. Freeman, *R. E. Lee*, 3:287.
25. Trudeau, *Bloody Roads South*, 93.
26. Freeman, *R. E. Lee*, 3:327.

CHAPTER EIGHTEEN

"Then the Minutes Seem Like Hours"

6 May 1864

George Custer, best known in our time for his death at the hands of Indians eleven years after the end of the Civil War, was only 24 years of age in the spring of 1864, one of a handful of "boy generals" who had brought vigor and confidence to the Union cavalry. He had been a cadet at West Point when the war began, graduating at the bottom of the class of 1861, and had risen to general in two years. "We swear by him," Major James H. Kidd of the 6th Michigan Cavalry told his father. "His name is our battle cry. He can get twice the fight out of this brigade than any man can possibly do."[1]

Custer was ordered to take his Michigan Brigade, the 1st of the 1st Division, and Colonel Thomas C. Devin's 2nd Brigade and harrass the Rebel force that was supposedly approaching Hancock's left. However, before he could comply he was himself attacked. Custer's four Michigan regiments were positioned in the woods to the east of the junction of the Brock and Catherine Furnace roads to fill the line between Gibbon's provisional force to his north and Gregg's cavalry to the southeast at Todd's Tavern. To the west was a clearing about 350 yards wide and 600 or 700 yards long, with a deep ravine running diagonally across it. Custer's pickets were strung out in a long line inside the woods on the west edge of that field and the young general was speaking with their captain when a ripple of fire spread down the line and a Rebel yell rang out.

From the woods on the east side of the field, Major Kidd saw Custer burst into the clearing and ride furiously toward his regiment, which was already mounted. At Custer's command the brigade band struck up "Yankee Doodle," and the 1st and 6th Michigan charged with a yell through the thick underbrush and into the open field just as the Confederate cavalry brigade of Tom Rosser, Custer's friend in their West Point days, emerged from the woods on the west side of the clearing. The two forces charged down on each other, but most men of both sides were stopped by the ravine in the middle of the field. However, a few crossed sabers in the middle of the ravine, while some Rebels charged on past, only to charge back again. The Southerners ran a battery of horse artillery out into the field, but the Spencer carbines of Custer's outnumbered men stopped every attempt of the Confederates to break the Federal line.

Custer brought up his other two regiments, and Rosser was reinforced by a couple of regiments from Fitzhugh Lee's division, the rest of which was annoying Gregg down around Todd's Tavern. Custer pulled his right flank back, using the ditch as a defensive work and, as he brought up his own battery of horse artillery to a small elevation, he told Kidd to dismount his troopers and flank the Rebel guns. The Federals had just started through the woods when they ran into three times as many Confederates trying to get into the Union rear. Kidd was saved by the timely appearance of Devin's Federal brigade and two more cannon. Three of the Southern guns were soon smashed by direct hits and the rest were silenced. Custer placed most of the new troops on his left but sent the 17th Pennsylvania and his own 5th Michigan to rescue Kidd. At about 9:45 a.m. they charged the Rebels dismounted, Spencers blazing, driving them through the trees, and when the 1st and 7th Michigan charged their front the Confederates gave way, leaving their wounded and dead scattered over the field. Custer was denied permission to pursue, and the attack he had originally planned was cancelled.

Over on the Rebels' left flank, Brigadier General John Gordon had been making a personal reconnaissance of the Federal right. What he found was, he believed, very interesting. He discovered that the Confederate line extended farther north than the Union line. What was more, the Yankees seemed preoccupied with making repeated attacks against

Johnson's division farther south. Gordon sent out scouting parties to examine the rear of the Federal line, and these returned to report that no Yankee support could be found within two miles of their right flank. Gordon hurried off to inform his division commander, Jubal Early, but when he learned that Early was away conferring with Brigadier General R. D. Johnston, whose brigade had just completed its long march from Hanover Junction, he reported the situation to Ewell and requested permission to attack the dangling Union flank. Ewell was impressed but reluctant to act without consulting Early, who was not only Gordon's immediate superior but Ewell's chief advisor as well.

When Early returned, he was decidedly against the idea. He knew that at least part of Burnside's corps was off there somewhere between Sedgwick and the river—where in fact Ferrero's division of Colored Troops had just relieved the Provisional Brigade, which moved down to form a reserve for Sedgwick—and he did not want to expose his own flank to it, as he would have to do to make the attack. Further, he knew that Ewell's corps had no reserve except for R. D. Johnston's exhausted troops. Ewell decided that the only way he could resolve the differing opinions of his division and brigade commanders was to go have a look for himself, which he intended to do just as soon as he could find time.

At 8:40 a.m. Hancock ordered a renewal of the attack along both sides of the Orange Plank Road, and about 9 a.m. after regrouping and replenishing its ammunition, Birney's dense formation pressed forward again, but little came of this effort. Stevenson led one of his 9th Corps brigades, Carruth's, forward to reinforce Wadsworth, who commanded all the Union forces on the north side of the Orange Plank Road, including Getty's. The Federals could make little progress against Longstreet's troops, who were deployed in heavy skirmish lines to avoid the disruption that the woods had caused all previous close-order formations.

Webb's Union brigade, advancing under orders to join Getty, had failed to send out skirmishers and, losing its way in the thickets, unexpectedly ran into Southern defenses. "The enemy," Webb reported, "finding that my line was but a few hundred yards in length and entirely without support, forced me to change front to rear at a double-quick."[2] Fortunately for Webb, Carruth led his 9th Corps brigade to the rescue. The incident had caused Webb's men to lose all confidence in their leaders, however, and thereafter they fought without belief in victory. Elsewhere the Rebels gave ground when there was no other choice, but the advance cost the Union forces dearly in casualties, organization and time. "The enemy hold a line of earthworks on the Orange Road in my front," Hancock reported. "The skirmishers are pushing the enemy's thin line rapidly before it. The line they abandoned was a finished one, 300 yards behind the rough one from which we drove them yesterday."[3]

About 10 a.m. colonels Comstock and Porter of Grant's staff reported that Burnside had advanced about a mile and a half with Potter's division and one brigade of Willcox's, after leaving the other to picket Jones' field. He would now advance toward the sound of Hancock's firing, which he judged to be about a mile away. Unfortunately for Burnside, volley firing on Birney's front ceased about then. "The only time I ever feel impatient," Grant told Porter, "is when I give an order for an important movement of troops in the presence of the enemy, and am waiting for them to reach their destination. Then the minutes seem like hours."[4] In the case of Burnside's advance, the minutes were hours.

Porter had returned to headquarters in time to see some stragglers of Warren's command come streaming into the clearing around headquarters, and artillery shells start falling on the knoll where Grant was seated on the stump of a tree. The general's only response was to rise slowly to watch the scene. "An officer ventured to remark to him," Porter recorded, "'General, wouldn't it be prudent to move headquarters to the other side of the Germanna road till the result of the present attack is known?' The general replied very quietly, between the puffs of his cigar, 'It strikes me it would be better to order up some artillery and defend the present location.'"[5] A battery was ordered forward, but before it reached the knoll the Rebel attack was turned back.

Around the same time, Colonel John R. Brooke's 4th Brigade of Barlow's 1st Division of Gibbon's provisional command returned from a reconnaissance down the Brock Road and reported finding no enemy units in that direction, only some Federal convalescents, who had mistakenly taken the wrong road, returning to the army. Until Brooke's report, at least, the Federals had continued to worry about their far left, feeding more units into Gibbon's breastworks along and across the Brock Road and ordering Warren and Sedgwick to suspend their operations, entrench their positions, and release from their fronts units that could be sent to reinforce Hancock. This fear for the army's left, Hancock complained, "paralyzed a large number of my best troops, who would otherwise have gone into action at a decisive point."[6]

However, Longstreet was not yet thinking in terms of the Federal army's far left along the Brock Road, but of the tactical left flank of Birney's attacking force much closer to hand. Shortly after taking charge of the Confederate right, Longstreet had sent Lee's chief engineer, Major General Martin L. Smith, to reconnoiter through the woods south of the Orange Plank Road, toward and along an unfinished railroad cut that ran east-west beyond the southern flank of the two armies. Smith returned at 10 a.m. to report. The route cleared through the woods provided a concealed avenue quite acceptable for moving large bodies of infantry around the right of Birney's force. There was no evidence that the Yankees were guarding or even watching the cut. What was more, the cleared path turned to the southeast not far beyond Birney's left and led past, but out of view of, Gibbon's defenses on the Brock Road.

When he sent Smith to check out the railroad cut, Longstreet also ordered Lieutenant Colonel G. Moxley Sorrel of his own staff to assemble three brigades for a special mission. By the time Smith returned, Sorrel had assembled G. T. Anderson's Brigade, which Field had left on the right of the Orange Plank Road before sending the Texans and his other two brigades to the left; Brigadier General William T. Wofford's Brigade of Kershaw's Division, which had been left at Parker's Store to guard wagons but was later called to the front; and Brigadier General William Mahone's Brigade of R. H. Anderson's Division of Hill's corps. The three Mississippi regiments of Davis' Brigade, under Colonel Stone, had also attached themselves to Sorrel's force as a chance to get back into the action. Mahone was the senior officer of the assembled force, but Sorrel was told by Longstreet to lead it in an attack on Birney's flank while Smith was sent back to explore the possibility of a later attack on Gibbon's far left. Longstreet's advice to his young staff officer, commanding troops for the first time, summed up his own philosophy quite well: "Hit hard when you start, but don't start until you have everything ready."[7]

In the relative quiet that had descended upon the field, many of the Northerners felt an ominous sense of foreboding. Colonel McAllister, commanding the 1st Brigade of Mott's division, took an orderly and went exploring beyond the picket line. He reported that "by crawling along from tree to tree in front I discovered a ravine; parallel with it lay a number of very large trees; behind these trees and in a ravine were the enemy's pickets; a short distance in rear of the enemy's pickets was a railroad cut, and on the left across a ravine was an embankment; there was the position of the enemy. After taking a careful survey of it, I came back and sent an aide to report the fact to General Mott, commanding the division."[8]

He was too late. The Rebels surged forward in line of brigades, the sunlight filtering through the trees and flashing on their bayonets. McAllister put his second-line units through a complex maneuver to face them toward the enemy flanking force, but a violent attack struck the Federal troops holding along his original front. With rifle fire pouring in from front, flank, and rear, McAllister's men gave way. The lieutenant colonel of the 124th New York recorded that "the terrific tempest of disaster swept on down the Union Line, beating back brigade after brigade, and tearing to pieces regiment after regiment, until upward of 20,000 veterans were fleeing, every man for himself, through the disorganizing and already bloodstained woods, toward the Union rear."[9]

However, when the Rebel troops of Kershaw and R. H. Anderson attempted to extend the rout to Wadsworth's mixed command north of the Orange Plank Road they were met by a violent counterattack that brought them up short, and the two sides stood and blazed away at each other, face to face in a murderous fire fight. Aware that Birney's force was collapsing, Wadsworth galloped down to the Orange Plank Road to order Webb to mount a holding attack. When he could not find Webb, he ordered Lieutenant Colonel Macy, commanding the 20th Massachusetts, to charge straight up the Orange Plank Road and hold on as long as he could. Then he sent orders to Webb to gather any four regiments to support the attack. Macy protested the useless sacrifice that this would entail, but Wadsworth angrily replied that if the colonel was hesitant, he'd show him how and, waving his sword, he galloped to the front.

Macy ordered his men to follow despite a volley that swept his line. Macy himself was among the wounded, and command of the regiment devolved on Major Abbot, considered by both Gibbon and Hancock as one of the most promising young officers in the army. Abbott led his regiment through a storm of rifle fire until a point-blank volley brought them to a halt. The Major went down, shot through the head. General Wadsworth, meanwhile, lost control of his fear-crazed horse, which bolted and carried him straight toward the Rebel lines. His aide managed to turn the runaway but too late, for the general was shot through the back of the head and fell to the ground, mortally wounded.

The 19th Maine of Webb's brigade was just returning to the front after replenishing its ammunition supply when its colonel, a future governor of Maine, heard firing to the left that indicated the collapse of Birney's force. He sent a staff officer to warn Webb; then he formed his regiment on the north side of the road and parallel with it, facing south, in order to cover the left of the brigade. In a few minutes Colonel L. A. Grant's Vermont Brigade broke out of the woods to the south in a confused mob and streamed down the road. As soon as they were out of the way, the Maine regiment opened fire. Soon after that its colonel was shot in the thigh and carried off the field.

Brigadier General James C. Rice succeeded to the command of Wadsworth's force. His own brigade was at the front of that Federal formation, and he pivoted it through ninety degrees to face the Rebel flanking force. But as it made the move it presented its right flank to

Field's Confederates, who raked it with a terrible enfilade fire, including that of a battery of artillery. Rice's right broke, and the left was hit by a volley from Mahone's men on the south side of the Orange Plank Road. Then, just as flames from burning leaves and twigs blew across the road, the 12th Virginia struck the left of Rice's line, and Union resistance collapsed.

As Longstreet's flank attack ended thus in success, M. L. Smith returned from his second look at the Federals' far left. He reported that it was indeed feasible to turn Gibbon's position on the Brock Road. Longstreet instructed the engineer to take the four brigades that had made the flank attack, turn them around, take them back to the railroad cut and make the move around Hancock's far left. Longstreet would lead the divisions of Field and Kershaw forward to strike Birney's confused, disheartened troops again at the same time. Smith departed to turn his brigades, while Longstreet and his staff, together with Kershaw, Field, and Jenkins and their staffs, led the way down the Orange Plank Road, discussing as they rode how to arrange the troops for the next phase of the attack. Jenkins congratulated the 1st Corps commander on his attack and said, "I have felt despair for the cause for some months, but am relieved, and feel assured that we will put the enemy back across the Rapidan before night."[10] As if he had tempted fate, a few minutes later a volley rang out from the edge of the road. Jenkins fell, mortally wounded, a captain and an orderly on his staff were killed, and Longstreet reeled in the saddle.

The 12th Virginia had started back to the south side of the road when some of Mahone's other men mistook them for a Federal countercharge and fired the volley that caught the Rebel generals on the road. Jenkins' troops, following the high-ranking cavalcade, prepared to return the fire, but the quick-thinking Kershaw saw what was happening. He turned to them and called out, "Friends!" Jenkins' men held their fire but threw themselves to the ground just in case Mahone's did not. Longstreet tried to ride on at first, but soon realized he was bleeding too much. A bullet had struck his throat and passed through his right shoulder. He turned to ride back, but when he started to sway in the saddle some of his staff carried him to the roadside and propped him against a tree. Word was sent to bring up a stretcher and to inform General Lee that Longstreet was wounded.

Through the bloody foam on his lips, the wounded commander explained to Field, the next-ranking general present, what he had planned to do. Then he was carried to the rear, his hat placed over his face to protect it from the midday sun and his massive frame covered in blood. In the six hours since he had arrived at the front he had saved Hill's two divisions, stopped the Federal drive, turned Birney's flank and driven his and Wadsworth's forces back in confusion, and prepared a further attack that might yet sweep the field. It was just a year and four days since Stonewall Jackson had also been wounded by his own men in these same woods, after making an equally devastating flank attack on the Yankees to decide the battle of Chancellorsville. Everybody present knew that Jackson had died six days later.

Lee soon came to the front. Seeing the confusion of Longstreet's units moving in various directions, and doubting the ability of Field, who was new even to division command, to direct the entire critical flank of the army, he cancelled the complex turning movement. In so doing he may well have lost his last, best chance of winning the battle—and the war.

Colonel W. F. Perry's Alabamans who had broken up Wadsworth's attack earlier in the day were still holding the left flank of Field's Division. They suddenly found themselves attacked on the left again at about 2 p.m., forcing them to pull back quite a distance before the brigades of two commanders with similar names came to their support. These were the three Florida regiments of Brigadier General E. A. Perry and the Alabamans of Brigadier General Abner Perrin, both of R. H. Anderson's Division of Hill's 3rd Corps.

The Union force that struck them was the remnant of Burnside's 9th Corps. Of his nine infantry brigades, Burnside had left Ferrero's two to guard Germanna Ford and his Provisional Brigade in reserve to Sedgwick. The two brigades of Stevenson's 1st Division had been sent to reinforce Hancock, and one from Willcox's 3rd Division had been left to hold the position at Jones' field. That left only the other brigade of Willcox's division and the two of Potter's 2nd Division to make the attack for which Grant had been impatiently waiting for five hours while they struggled through two miles of woods. Most of these troops were new recruits getting their first taste of combat. Their first line recoiled from the Confederate breastworks, but the second line came on, and the third brigade carried the works on the right. The Federals' success was short-lived, however. A hard-driving Rebel countercharge drove them back. Burnside then withdrew across some swampy ground and entrenched. Thus ended the long-awaited attack.

When Colonel Lyman heard the sound of Burnside's attack he urged Hancock to try again, but the 2nd Corps commander just shook his head, saying that "it would be to hazard too much."[11] Hancock's troops were busily sorting themselves out and strengthening their defenses along the Brock Road. In the meantime, army headquarters advised Sheridan of what had befallen Hancock and ordered him to draw in his cavalry to protect the wagon trains. Consequently Todd's Tavern was abandoned, and some of the wagons were started back toward Ely's Ford, just in case. At 2 p.m., just as Burnside was making his abortive attack, Hancock was reinforced by one brigade of Robinson's 5th Corps division and the two heavy artillery regiments of the Provisional Brigade of the 9th Corps. Robinson's other brigade was on the way. At 2:15 p.m., after hearing from Burnside, Meade sent orders to Hancock: "Should Burnside not require any assistance and the enemy leave you undisturbed, I would let the men rest till 6 p.m., at which time a vigorous attack made by you, in conjunction with Burnside, will, I think, overthrow the enemy. I wish this done."[12] Hancock replied at 3 p.m. that it would be difficult to assemble enough reliable troops in time to make a really powerful attack, but he would do his best. At 4 p.m. Hancock reported that the woods on his left front were on fire, making it impossible to attack in that direction.

Lee took over direct command of the forces on his right flank, Longstreet's two divisions plus Hill's three. Part of these troops were facing Burnside and extending through the woods to connect with Ewell's right. The rest he intended to hurl against Hancock's center along the Brock Road. At 4:15 p.m., the Rebels advanced to the outer edge of the Union defenses, where the Federals had positioned felled trees facing outward with sharpened branches—what was known as an abatis—to break up and slow any attacking force. The Northerners met the Rebels with a steady, accurate fire that threw back every attempt to cross the abatis. But then the forest fire in front of Mott's division, fanned by a rising wind, suddenly swept across the felled trees. When their log breastworks caught fire, Mott's troops were forced to back off, which they did in good order, maintaining their alignment. However, G. T. Anderson's Georgia brigade took advantage of the fire and smoke to get through the abatis and then charged over the burning logs. Mott's front line wavered and then broke for the third time in 24 hours. Many of the supporting units also gave way, and part of Birney's division was driven back as well. Jenkins' South Carolinians, now under Colonel Bratton, briefly penetrated Owen's Union defenses a bit farther north, "advancing," as a Pennsylvanian remembered, "like so many devils through the flames."[13] Terrified Federals streamed back through the thickets to the Chancellorsville clearing, causing the teamsters there with the parked wagons to panic and lash their teams down the road toward Ely's Ford.

The rest of the front-line Union forces held their positions, however, and the 6th Maine Battery checked the Confederate advance with a crossfire of double-shot cannister. Flames crept into the battery's position and set off the powder in some of the ammunition stacked near the guns.

Five gunners suffered horrible burns, but the cannon continued to fire. They could not have held the Confederate advance much longer, but Birney sent Carroll's brigade to restore the situation. These well-drilled troops double-quicked into position and then faced the enemy with fixed bayonets, answering the shrill Rebel yell with a shout. The cannon fell silent as Carroll's men charged forward to cross steel with the Confederates. The Southern lines wavered, then crumbled, and the Federals broke into a tremendous cheer as Carroll's troops chased the Rebels back over the burning logs, through what was left of the abatis, and into the woods. Then the victorious regiments were pulled back to the burned-out breastworks and put to work restoring the defenses. Many of Mott's men returned to resume their original position.

At 5:25 p.m. Hancock reported to Meade, declaring that "the attack and the repulse was of the handsomest kind."[14] A few minutes later he reported that his best troops were low on ammunition and recommended against going ahead with the attack planned for 6 p.m. Meade concurred, and Grant notified Burnside to stay on the defensive unless the enemy attacked Hancock again, and to give his men all the rest they could get. Burnside had, however, already attacked again at about 5:30 p.m. in an attempt to relieve the pressure on Hancock. The brigades of the two Perrys were driven back in disorder and General Perry of the Florida brigade was seriously wounded. However, Wofford and Heth counterattacked and reestablished the Confederate position. Burnside then fell back and connected his left with Hancock's right.

Having done all that he felt he could do for the time being on the Orange Plank Road front, Lee rode over to the turnpike and pulled up at Ewell's headquarters about 5:30 p.m., as the sun was going down. He wanted to know if there was something more that could be done to the enemy over here. The Federals could not be strong everywhere. Gordon happened to be at corps headquarters when Lee broached the subject. He listened while Lee, Ewell, and Early talked over the situation, and when he got his chance he told the army commander about the open Union flank he had scouted that morning and how he thought it could be rolled up. Early again raised the objections of Federals hovering off in the woods, and the lack of Confederate reserves to meet any countermove or recover any disaster. But Lee needed something, some leverage, something better than another frontal assault. He was always ready to take a high risk if the potential rewards were equally high. He ordered the flank attack to be made immediately, and Gordon admitted that after Lee took the reponsibility, Ewell and Early "did all in their power to help forward the movement when once begun."[15]

Gordon was right. The Federal flank was indeed unprotected and even more so than it had been. Shaler's three New York regiments had been brought forward that morning from 6th Corps reserve and placed in support of Seymour's brigade on Sedgwick's far right. Later the 5th and 6th corps lines had been shortened in order to provide forces for possible forwarding to Hancock or Burnside. Seymour's troops had then been shifted to the left and Shaler's men had been put in Seymour's place. There were so few of them that they all had to be put in a single elongated line, leaving no reserve. The Union troops were entrenching, but the picks and shovels had been given first to the men on the left of the corps, then passed along to the right as each brigade finished with them. The tools were being used by Seymour's men but had not yet reached Shaler's, when the attack hit them.

Gordon took his own and R. D. Johnston's brigades around to an open field to the north of Shaler's position and just out of sight, and formed the men in a line facing south. About 6 p.m. the Confederates moved forward, and an advance of 200 yards brought them to the Federal skirmishers. A volley sent these running for their main line, and the Southerners let out a Rebel yell. Gordon's Alabamans struck the Federal flank while Johnston's North Carolinians passed around it to the rear of Shaler's line. Then the five Virginia regiments of Brigadier General John Pegram's brigade attacked Seymour's front. Seymour's men were known to the rest of the corps as Milroy's Weary Boys because they had spent a lot of time being chased up and down the Shenandoah as part of General Milroy's command, before being transferred to the Army of the Potomac. They dropped their tools, some to run for their rifles, others to run empty-handed for the rear. Shaler's men had no choice but to give way also. But the next Union brigade to the south, Neill's, was formed in two lines, and its second-line units, commanded by Colonel Daniel Bidwell, faced to the rear and formed along a wagon track that gave them a view of what had been Seymour's defenses. There they held fast while some of Seymour's men joined them and some of Shaler's formed on their right. Both Seymour and Shaler were captured, however, as they tried to rally more of their men.

Pegram's Brigade moved to the attack again but struck too far to the right and ran into Wright's well-entrenched division. Meanwhile, the right of Gordon's line recoiled from the new makeshift Federal line, while the rest of Gordon's Brigade and all of Johnston's passed beyond it into the Union rear. Newspaper correspondents who were captured and then released spread panic among Federals far and wide, and a frightened 6th Corps staff officer showed up at army headquarters with exaggerated tales of the disaster he claimed was befalling the army's right, including the death of General Sedgwick. Grant studied the hysterical officer, calmly removed his cigar from his mouth and said, "I don't believe it."[16] Meade ordered the man arrested for spreading false rumors. Two 6th Corps brigades that had been scheduled for transfer to Hancock were sent instead to restore the situation, and Warren was called on to send Crawford's Pennsylvania Reserves.

Brigadier General William H. Morris with three regiments of his 1st Brigade of Ricketts' 3rd Division of the 6th Corps, advanced toward the sound of scattered firing on the corps' right rear. He came on the scene too far east to connect with Bidwell's reversed second line but he put his troops in a position so that any attempt of the Rebels to continue to the south would expose their flank to his fire. Meanwhile he sent an aide to find Sedgwick, report his position and request instructions. The request brought Sedgwick himself. Uncle John busied himself with rallying his troops until a Confederate officer rode up, pointed a revolver at him and shouted, "Surrender, you Yankee Son of a Bitch!"[17] Somebody shot the Rebel, but Sedgwick's horse was wounded and carried him away toward the Union rear.

Colonel Emory Upton sent Lieutenant Colonel Duffy to the right with two regiments, intending to follow personally as soon as he had made arrangements for the rest of his brigade. The two regiments veered even farther to the east than Morris. "The dense undergrowth necessarily lengthened out the column," Upton wrote, "and at the same time masses of men breaking through their ranks threw both regiments into unavoidable confusion."[18] Duffy formed his men in some rifle pits that had been constructed for the defense of Sedgwick's headquarters, but his force was too small to stand off a brigade and a half of Rebels, and soon he had to fall back through the woods. As Upton came searching for his two regiments he came upon stragglers, whom he reformed and brought along with him. Once he had caught up with the main force of his two regiments, he found Morris' line and fell in on its right.

By then darkness was bringing an end to the fighting. Gordon broke off the attack and returned his two brigades to their trenches, taking along about 600 prisoners. Afterwards, Gordon claimed that only night and the failure of supporting attacks against the Union front had saved the Federal 6th Corps, if not Grant's entire army, from a decisive defeat. General Early, on the other hand, contended rather that darkness had saved the Confederate left from a grave disaster. Daylight would have allowed the Federals to discover the confused condition of the attacking Rebels, their limited numbers, and their vulnerability to counterattack. Probably both men exaggerated. The attack had pretty well run its course and there were plenty of Northern troops on hand to stop it even if darkness had not.

Whether these could have turned the tables on the Southerners is arguable, although within the realm of possibility.

About the time that the orders had been given to straighten out the situation on the Federal right, Grant received a visit from an unidentified general who was, Horace Porter said, "speaking rapidly and laboring under considerable excitement: 'General Grant, this is a crisis that cannot be looked upon too seriously. I know Lee's methods well by past experience; he will throw his whole army between us and the Rapidan, and cut us off completely from our communications.' The general rose to his feet, took his cigar out of his mouth, turned to the officer, and replied, with a degree of animation which he seldom manifested: 'Oh, I am heartily tired of hearing about what Lee is going to do. Some of you always seem to think he is suddenly going to turn a double somersault, and land in our rear and on both flanks at the same time. Go back to your command, and try to think what we are going to do ourselves, instead of what Lee is going to do.' The officer retired rather crestfallen, and without saying a word in reply."[19]

Around 8 p.m. Hancock came to army headquarters to report in person, looking like he had been through hell. Grant offered him a cigar but discovered that he was down to his last one. Then "when all proper measures had been taken," Rawlins said, "Grant went into his tent, threw himself face downward on his cot, and gave way to the greatest emotion." Charles Francis Adams, Jr., grandson and great-grandson of presidents and a captain on Meade's staff said, "I never saw a man so agitated in my life." But with the tension thus relieved, Grant was soon his normal, outwardly calm self. When Wilson dropped by about 9 p.m. to see his old boss he found the lieutenant general "surrounded by his staff in a state of perfect composure."[20] When Porter came to Grant's tent later to deliver another alarm from the right flank, "I looked in his tent, and found him sleeping as soundly and as peacefully as an infant." Porter woke him up and gave him the report, but Grant decided it was another false alarm and he "turned over in his bed, and immediately went to sleep again."[21]

A new and better defensive line for the 6th Corps was laid out by the engineers behind the positions then being held, and the troops moved to it during the night. The new line pulled the right flank back across the Germanna Plank Road where the Confederates could not easily get at it again, but the road to the ford was no longer protected. At 9:30 p.m. Grant had ordered Ferrero's division of Colored Troops to abandon the Germanna Ford crossing and move to the turnpike intersection near headquarters. At 11 p.m. Meade ordered the pontoon bridge there dismantled and moved downriver, to be relayed at Ely's Ford. Most of the men of both armies spent much of the night building or strengthening their defensive positions. They had no way of knowing that the battle of the Wilderness was over.

"It was a battle fought with the ear, and not with the eye," Porter said. "All circumstances seemed to combine to make the scene one of unutterable horror. At times the wind howled through the tree-tops, mingling its moans with the groans of the dying, and heavy branches were cut off by the fire of the artillery, and fell crashing upon the heads of the men, adding a new terror to battle. Forest fires raged; ammunition-trains exploded; the dead were roasted in the conflagration; the wounded, roused by its hot breath, dragged themselves along, with their torn and mangled limbs, in the mad energy of despair, to escape the ravages of the flames; and every bush seemed hung with shreds of blood-stained clothing. It was as though Christian men had turned to fiends, and hell itself had usurped the place of earth."[22]

---

1. Gregory J. W. Urwin, *Custer Victorious* (East Brunswick, 1983), 134.
2. Steere, *The Wilderness Campaign*, 365.
3. Ibid., 370.
4. Porter, *Campaigning With Grant*, 63.
5. Ibid., 59.
6. Trudeau, *Bloody Roads South*, 100.
7. Ibid., 99.
8. Steere, *The Wilderness Campaign*, 394.
9. Ibid., 398.
10. Freeman, *Lee's Lieutenants*, 3:363.
11. Steere, *The Wilderness Campaign*, 416.
12. Ibid., 420.
13. Trudeau, *Bloody Roads South*, 109.
14. Steere, *The Wilderness Campaign*, 428.
15. Freeman, *Lee's Lieutenants*, 3:371.
16. Steere, *The Wilderness Campaign*, 443.
17. Catton, *Grant Takes Command*, 200.
18. Steere, *The Wilderness Campaign*, 445.
19. Porter, *Campaigning With Grant*, 69–70.
20. Foote, *The Civil War*, 3:186.
21. Porter, *Campaigning With Grant*, 71.
22. Ibid., 72–73.

CHAPTER NINETEEN

"How To Advance Without Going Ahead"

6–7 May 1864

Down in northern Mississippi on that sixth day of May 1864—the second day of the battle of the Wilderness—General Sam Sturgis reached the town of Ripley in his pursuit of Forrest's raiders, only to discover that their rear guard had passed through there two days ahead of him. With no hope remaining of catching the elusive Rebel and unable to find forage for his horses in the area, Sturgis finally gave up the chase and turned back for Tennessee. "Though we could not catch the scoundrel," he told General Washburn back in Memphis, "we are at least rid of him, and that is something."[1] The question was, for how long?

Another Federal expedition to chase Rebel raiders was just getting under way in the Shenandoah Valley, where Sigel was sending out Colo-

nel Jacob Higgins with 500 cavalry and orders to catch the partisans who
had raided the Baltimore & Ohio Railroad. Southwest of there,
Breckinridge's two infantry brigades were starting on their long march to
try to beat Sigel to Staunton.

Early that morning at Bermuda Hundred, Virginia, Baldy Smith's 18th
Corps took to the road, even while some of Gillmore's 10th Corps troops
were still disembarking. They advanced without opposition, except for a
solitary horseman who stayed just beyond range and occasionally waved
them on as if daring them to come a little farther. As the sun rose higher so
did the temperature, and their path was soon strewn with discarded
blankets, extra shoes, and other impediments. Local citizens gathered up
everything of use to themselves or to the Confederate army. Smith's
troops turned left at a crossroads and headed southwest. At about 8:30
a.m. the vanguard reached Cobb's Hill, where there was a large plantation
house overlooking a sweeping bend of the Appomattox River, by then
holding the Union army's gunboats. The troops took over a Rebel signal
station found atop one of the outbuildings, and engineers soon began
staking out positions for earthworks that would form the southern end of
Butler's defensive line. The Cobb house turned out to be sitting right
where an earthen fort had been planned, so a regiment was detailed to tear
it down.

Gillmore's divisions, following Smith's, continued straight ahead at the
crossroads, after taking the precaution of sending out a skirmish line,
although there was still no opposition. The 10th Corps troops were even
less accustomed to marching than Smith's were and they, too, soon
littered the roadside with valuable clothing and equipment. About 10
a.m. the head of the column reached the planned position and, as the
skirmishers advanced to a building in the woods known as Ware Bottom
Church, the main force began to entrench Gillmore's portion of the
defensive line. At 2:30 p.m., Butler sent a message to Grant proudly
reporting that all his men were ashore and "that we have taken the
positions which were indicated to the commanding general at our last
conference and are carrying out that plan."[2]

Not long afterwards, while most of the men worked on the defenses
and the tail of Gillmore's column toiled along the road, Butler decided to
send one of Smith's brigades a couple of miles ahead to the Richmond &
Petersburg Railroad, directing Gillmore to send a detachment forward to
protect the brigade's right. Smith chose Brigadier General Charles
Heckman's 1st Brigade of Brigadier General Godfrey Weitzel's 2nd Division of the 18th Corps to make the advance, which began at 4 p.m.
Gillmore, however, declined to advance any of his troops, informing

Butler that, "the project of striking the railroad tonight with a detachment from this command has been abandoned for what I deem to be good and sufficient reasons."[3] Butler then decided to make a personal reconnaissance. With his staff and orderlies he rode through the 10th Corps position, without acknowledging the men's cheers, and on beyond the picket line near Ware Bottom Church. When they reached a creek a little further on, a sudden burst of gunfire rang out and Confederate horsemen charged the general and his party. The Federals raced for the safety of their lines, where the troops cheered their escape, but the close call definitely had a damping effect on Butler's optimism.

Up the James River from Bermuda Hundred Landing three wooden gunboats of the Union navy were searching for Rebel torpedoes when one of them, the USS *Commodore Jones,* suddenly exploded. Sixty-nine crewmen were killed.

At 5 that morning Beauregard had wired Confederate adjutant general Cooper, asking permission to take control of the troops passing through his command on their way to Richmond. Cooper's answer was vague, but Beauregard interpreted it to mean that at least Brigadier General Johnson Hagood's South Carolina brigade could be used for the defense of Petersburg. At 10 a.m. he informed Pickett that several hundred of Hagood's men had just passed through Weldon by rail on their way to Petersburg, but Pickett replied that he was not sure that he could wait and suggested that he might have to burn the bridges over the Appomattox. Beauregard advised him not to take that drastic step until absolutely necessary. Such an act would cut all but one of Richmond's rail connections with the country farther south.

Pickett continued to report the Federal advance to Cooper and continued to receive no answer, so finally he addressed himself to the nominal general-in-chief, Braxton Bragg: "Do you intend holding the railroad between this place and Richmond? I sent General Cooper eight or ten telegrams on yesterday, but received no reply. The enemy will try to cut the railroad today, advancing from Bermuda Hundred, I think."[4] In answer, Bragg told Pickett to send Hagood's troops, as they arrived, to a spot about five miles north of Petersburg called Port Walthall Junction. There the railroad to Richmond was met by a spur coming in from a landing on the Appomattox near Cobb's Hill called Port Walthall. Confederate troops posted at the junction would be in a good place to protect Petersburg from the Federals at Cobb's Hill, and to threaten any Union force striking the railroad farther north.

However, except for 300 men of the 21st South Carolina who had already gone on through toward Richmond when Pickett received authority to stop them, Hagood's troops had not yet arrived. Pickett sent the 51st North Carolina and one battery of the Washington Artillery to an earthwork called Fort Clifton on the north bank of the Appomattox. Meanwhile he also had to worry about Hinck's brigade of Colored Troops at City Point, who might advance on Petersburg from the south side of the river. All Pickett had for the defense of the city from that direction was the 31st North Carolina, the rest of the Washington Artillery Battalion, and the local reserves, with a makeshift command of mounted civilians scouting the nearby countryside. As a bluff, locomotives were run noisily in and out of town to give the impression that he was being reinforced.

To the north of Butler's landing Richmond's commander, Major General Robert Ransom, at least had a few more forces to work with. At 3 a.m. he sent Brigadier General Bushrod Johnson's Tennessee brigade south of the James River to the fortifications at Drewry's Bluff to protect the heavy artillery guarding the river approaches to the capital there. Two hours later they were joined by those first 300 men of Hagood's brigade, but Ransom decided to send these men back down to Port Walthall Junction. Since no train was available, they had to march. At 11 a.m. Ransom ordered Johnson to take his brigade there, too. Johnson's van was within two miles of the place when he got word that the Federals were advancing near Ware Bottom Church, almost due east of him, so he decided to halt there to protect the railroad. Johnson's Brigade was one of two that had comprised Major General Simon Bolivar Buckner's division in the Department of East Tennessee. When Longstreet had left that area these two brigades had been sent to Richmond, although Buckner had been left to command what little was left of the department. Now the other brigade of the pair, Brigadier General Archibald Gracie's Alabamans, took Johnson's place at Drewry's Bluff.

At 3:30 p.m. Pickett finally received some reinforcements when the second 300 of Hagood's men arrived at Petersburg. In obedience to Bragg's orders, Pickett reluctantly forwarded these troops, three companies each of the 21st and 25th South Carolina, to Port Walthall Junction, despite reports that Kautz's cavalry was threatening the Blackwater River line. At 4 p.m. the 2,700 men of Heckman's four Union regiments advanced from Cobb's Hill accompanied by two guns of Battery L, 4th U.S. Artillery. Heckman was under orders to advance to the railroad and ascertain the position and strength of the Rebels, but to avoid a general engagement. The road Heckman followed wound toward Port Walthall Junction through a ravine where he encountered Confederate pickets. These retired before the Federal skirmish line past an old mill to another plateau holding the cleared fields of another plantation. At the western end of the field a row of bushes and a fence concealed the Richmond & Petersburg Railroad and the 300 men of the 21st South Carolina sent down by Ransom.

Just as Heckman's troops appeared, the train bearing the second 300 of Hagood's men arrived from the south with Colonel Robert Graham of the 21st South Carolina. He formed all 600 men in line of battle and then advanced them 300 yards to a sunken country road running perpendicular to the road which Heckman was following. This gave the Rebels an instant earthwork with their northern flank covered by the wooded banks of Ashton Creek and their southern flank protected by dense forest.

Heckman saw the Confederates take position but could not determine their strength without a closer look. He deployed three Massachussetts regiments in line, with the right one slightly advanced and the left one deployed inside the woods to the south of the clearing. His other regiment, the 9th New Jersey, he kept in column on the road as a reserve. The two guns unlimbered in the gap between the center and right regiments and opened fire on the Rebel position.

Just after 5 p.m., with the setting sun in their eyes, the Federal line advanced. The Northern skirmishers fired a volley that was answered by Graham's entire force, and soon an all-out fire-fight was in progress, the Confederates badly outnumbered but under cover. Heckman then led the 9th New Jersey forward through his center and ordered a charge. Thirteen bullets struck the general's horse and another hit him in the hand, but he mounted a new horse and rode on. The Jerseymen reached a slight swale about halfway to the sunken road but could advance no farther. Satisfied that he faced a large Confederate force and that he could not reach the railroad, Heckman ordered a withdrawal.

Baldy Smith concluded that the mission's failure was due to Gillmore's refusal to participate, and at 8:30 p.m. he suggested to Butler that a larger force be sent the next day. He recommended sending one brigade from each of the expedition's five divisions, leaving the rest to complete and defend the entrenchments. While he thought that some troops should be sent as a threat along the same route Heckman had taken, the main advance should be made farther to the north. Butler agreed to consider this advice but first he needed to deal with Gillmore. That officer had been late to arrive from South Carolina, slow in embarking his men, slow in disembarking them, and now, without explanation, had refused to cooperate with Smith in a move that might have severed one of the South's most important supply lines. Rather than getting embroiled in a messy court-martial of the West Pointer, Butler typically chose a political solution. He fired off a letter to his friend Senator Henry Wilson requesting that the Senate refuse to confirm Gillmore's promotion to major general.

Not long after Heckman withdrew, Confederate reinforcements arrived at Port Walthall Junction: first a battery of artillery from Richmond and Bushrod Johnson's Tennessee brigade; then from the south, the rest of the 25th South Carolina and all of the 27th with Hagood himself in command. Down in Petersburg, however, George Pickett was still in the dark about what was happening between there and Richmond, and spent another sleepless night worrying about what the Yankees might be up to and what he could do about it.

To the southeast of Petersburg, August Kautz's Cavalry Division of Butler's command had ridden northwest parallel with the Blackwater River until dawn on 6 May when the column reached the village called Isle of Wight Court House. There it turned west as if making for Broadwater Bridge. Kautz called a halt about noon at Fernville to rest the men and horses while detachments probed ahead toward the bridge. At 2 p.m. he put his men in motion again but not westward toward the bridge. Instead he led his men to the north for ten miles where the river turned westward, then he followed it several more miles to Birch Island Bridge. Arriving there in the late afternoon, he found two of the bridge's three spans damaged and some Confederates hard at work breaking up the third. He chased the Rebels off, patched up the bridge and had his entire command across shortly after dark—about the time that the battle of the Wilderness was sputtering to an end some 100 miles to the north. His 2500 troopers were now between the Blackwater defenses and Petersburg, but instead of moving northwest toward the city he advanced to the southwest, to the town of Wakefield on the Norfolk & Petersburg Railroad. His column arrived there about 6:30 p.m., burned the station, several cars, and some Rebel supplies, tore down the telegraph line, and dismantled a short stretch of track. Then Kautz let his men rest. They had covered fifty miles during the day.

At 2 a.m. on the seventh they were back in the saddle. Ten miles to the southwest at the aptly named village of Littleton, the advance surprised a Confederate commissary detachment transporting wagonloads of hams, corn, and crackers to Petersburg. The Federals, who had already eaten up all of their own rations, promptly appropriated this find before continuing to the southwest. By now about forty of their mounts had given out and, as they said in the cavalry, a man without a horse is afoot. A brief halt was called while detachments were sent to seize any horses that could be found. A sufficient quantity was soon rounded up and the march was resumed. Kautz turned south and crossed the Nottoway River, a tributary of the Blackwater, at Peter's Bridge, then moved northward to the town of Sussex Court House, due west of Littleton.

Farther west he came to the Nottoway again, as it makes a large loop around Sussex Court House, and at 3 p.m. he brushed aside a few Rebels trying to destroy Bolling's Bridge. Colonel Spear was sent southward with the 11th Pennsylvania toward Nottoway Bridge, at which point the Petersburg & Weldon Railroad crossed the river. Kautz proceeded a short distance farther west, where he found the 100-foot railroad bridge over Stony Creek defended by sixty men of the Holcombe Legion. Most of the 3rd New York and the two guns confronted the Confederates while two companies of the same regiment crossed the creek and circled to come in on their rear. The Rebel commander, Major M. G. Ziegler, surrendered his men and the bridge, and Kautz put his troopers to work burning the trestle, the station, two water tanks, two wood-storage racks, three freight cars filled with lumber and a pile of spare bridging material. They also destroyed a turntable and a culvert before bivouacking for the night. From his prisoners and from civilians, Kautz learned that three trainloads of Confederate troops had passed through heading north four hours earlier and that at least five more were expected at any time.

Meanwhile, when Colonel Spear reached Nottoway Bridge he discovered that its small garrison had been reinforced. Beauregard had received reports of the Yankee cavalry's advance and had ordered the 59th Virginia of Wise's Brigade, coming up from South Carolina, to proceed to Stony Creek Bridge to protect the railroad. It had only gone as far as Nottoway Bridge by sunset, when its commander learned that Stony Creek Bridge had already been captured. On the heels of this news came Spear and his Pennsylvania troopers, but Spear decided that there were too many Rebels on hand for his one regiment, so he withdrew and joined the rest of the Union force at Stony Creek around 9 p.m. Kautz decided he would take his entire division the next morning, 8 May, to capture Nottoway Bridge. It was his job to cause as much damage as possible to the vital railroad over which reinforcements for Richmond and Petersburg would have to come.

Early that morning, 7 May, Butler decided to take Baldy Smith's suggestions for another, larger, advance on the Petersburg & Richmond Railroad with the intention of making the Rebels think his objective was Petersburg while destroying as much as possible of the railroad. He ordered Gillmore to loan three of his brigades to Smith, who added one of his own plus a battery and the 1st New York Mounted Rifles and put them all under Brigadier General William Brooks, commander of the 1st Division of the 18th Corps. As a diversion, Heckman would return to the same field as the day before.

At 7:30 a.m. Beauregard wired Pickett that he was still too ill to come to Petersburg, but he continued to direct the forwarding of units. The two regiments of cavalry on the Blackwater line were called in to help deal with Kautz, and Hoke was ordered to forward his cavalry as soon as possible. But all the Confederate reinforcements were still south of Weldon at that time. To the north of Butler's expedition, Brigadier General Seth Barton's Virginia brigade, from Pickett's old division, joined Gracie at Drewry's Bluff, while in Richmond the secretaries of war and of the navy were arguing over who was responsible for the obstructions in the James River that were both keeping the Yankee gunboats out and the Confederate ironclads in. Down between Richmond and Petersburg, Bushrod Johnson and Hagood had received only four reinforcements: two batteries of artillery; former Brigadier General Roger Pryor, serving as a scout without rank; and Beauregard's volunteer aide, Major General D. H. Hill.

At 10 a.m. Hagood led his three regiments up the Old Stage Road northeastward from Port Walthall Junction and soon ran into eight companies of the 1st New York Mounted Rifles leading Brooks' column south. The Federal cavalry charged, but was driven back by the fire of the Rebel infantry. However, Brigadier General Hiram Burnham's 2nd Brigade of Brooks' own Federal division advanced to take their place, and Johnson, fearful that Hagood would be outflanked, ordered him to fall back behind the railroad. Just as this move was successfully executed, Heckman's brigade approached along the same road as the day before. To meet this threat, Johnson sent two of his Tennessee regiments and two guns into the woods south of the road. Heckman's regiments deployed into line of battle and advanced cautiously while a shell from his accompanying artillery blew up an ammunition chest of one of the Rebel guns. Johnson pulled the detachment back to keep it from being overwhelmed.

Meanwhile Burnham's brigade gradually edged to the west, and Brooks brought up Colonel Jeremiah Drake's 2nd Brigade of the 3rd Division of the 10th Corps and two guns. While these troops kept the Confederates busy, Brooks sent Colonel Harris Plaisted's 3rd Brigade of the 1st Division of the 10th Corps through the woods to the west, toward the Richmond Turnpike and the railroad. Hagood saw them emerge from the woods to his north and tried to move the 21st South Carolina to meet them, but several volleys from Plaisted's men caused that regiment to break and run for the rear. With considerable difficulty, Hagood and D. H. Hill managed to rally most of them and realign the rest of the brigade with them. They called on Johnson for help, but since his hands were full with Heckman all the Tennessean could spare were two pieces of artillery. These soon ran out of ammunition and withdrew from the field.

Brooks brought up his last brigade, Colonel William Barton's 2nd of the 2nd Division, 10th Corps, to fill the gap between Plaisted and Burn-ham, although the rough terrain delayed his deployment and advance for a while. In the meantime, part of the 24th Massachussetts of Plaisted's brigade had been trying to damage the railroad, although with little success because it lacked tools. The Federals managed to uproot only 100 feet of track, while a detachment of the 100th New York managed to destroy a small trestle, and others cut the telegraph lines.

Then, Plaisted claimed, he received an order from Brooks to withdraw. Brooks denied giving any such order. Nevertheless, Plaisted did pull his men back the way they had come, exposing Barton's right flank so that he too had to fall back. Brooks decided to call off the attack and return to the Union defenses. A young officer in Burnham's brigade called the day's experience, "Possibly the nearest answer ever made to the question: 'How to fight without winning?' 'How to advance without going ahead?' "5

Down in Petersburg, George Pickett was feeling more and more alone. Early that afternoon the wire between himself and Beauregard had gone dead and now the direct line to Richmond was also down, although he could still get through on a more westerly connection. At 5 p.m. he sent a message to Bushrod Johnson suggesting that he fall back to Swift Creek, a west-to-east-running tributary which joined the Appomattox three-and-a-half miles north of Petersburg. But by then the Federals had retreated and the rest of Hagood's Brigade, a regiment and a smaller battalion, had arrived. So had another battery of the Washington Artillery, and Johnson was feeling fairly secure where he was. Pickett was still worrying about an advance against Petersburg from City Point, and at 7 p.m. he again suggested that Johnson fall back to Swift Creek in case Pickett needed to call on him at short notice for help. As suggestions did not seem to work, Pickett issued a direct order to Johnson at 10 p.m. Technically, Johnson belonged to Ransom's Department of Richmond, but since the Federals were between him and Richmond, he decided to obey Pickett.

About 1 p.m. Butler had sent a report to Union Secretary of War Stanton of the moves he was making against the railroad, but added that he was "intrenching for fear of accident to the Army of the Potomac."6 He knew that any failure by Grant to occupy Lee's complete attention would bring all or part of that legendary general's army down on his neck. Butler also asked for 10,000 reinforcements, just in case. During the day, while Brooks moved against Port Walthall Junction, the rest of the Army of the James worked to improve its defenses. At Bermuda Hundred Landing more batteries of artillery were brought ashore, along with supplies and veteran troops returning from furlough. As Butler advanced his headquarters from the landing to Cobb's Hill, another Federal gun-boat was lost, this time to an ambush by Rebel artillery. The morale of the Army of the James was demonstrated by a pertinent question that was making the rounds of the camps: "How long will it take to get to Richmond if you advance two miles every day and come back to your starting point every night?"[7]

---

1. Starr, *Union Cavalry*, 3:413.
2. Robertson, *Back Door To Richmond*, 71.
3. Ibid., 72.
4. Ibid., 77.
5. Ibid., 89.
6. Ibid., 90.
7. Ibid., 89.

PART THREE

SPOTSYLVANIA

*". . . and purpose to fight it out on this line
if it take all summer."*

Ulysses S. Grant

CHAPTER TWENTY

"There Will Be No Turning Back"

7 May 1864

Confederate general Joseph Eggleston Johnston, commander of the Army of Tennessee, had his two infantry corps thoroughly entrenched along north-south Rocky Face Ridge, covering the town of Dalton, Georgia where the railroad from Chattanooga joined the one from Knoxville. His prestige as one of the South's greatest officers and his concern for the men's welfare, shown in improved rations and more leaves of absence, combined with several months' respite from molestation by the Yankees, a wave of religious revival that had swept through the ranks, and improving weather, served to restore his army's morale, shattered by Bragg's hollow victories and outright defeats.

Johnston's army was divided into two infantry corps and one of cavalry. His 1st Army Corps, containing about 27,000 infantry, consisted of four divisions commanded by Lieutenant General William J. Hardee, known as Old Reliable. Before the war Hardee had written an instruction manual on infantry tactics which had been the primer of almost every new officer on both sides when hostilities began. He was a native of Georgia who had graduated from West Point in the class of 1838, along with Beauregard. He had commanded a corps, or its equivalent, in this army since before Shiloh. He had been offered command of the army as Bragg's successor but had declined, feeling that Johnston was the best choice for the job. His corps contained some tough fighting units, including the crack division of Major General Patrick Cleburne. Hardee was never spectacular but, as his nickname implied, always reliable.

Johnston's 2nd Army Corps, with about 24,000 riflemen in three divisions, was commanded by Lieutenant General John Bell Hood, who was new to corps command and relatively new to this western army. A Kentuckian who graduated from West Point in 1853, along with Sheridan, he had been the original commander of the elite Texas Brigade in Lee's army, leading it from the Seven Days before Richmond until promoted to divisional command in time for Antietam. After Gettysburg, where he had been wounded in the arm, he had come west as part of Longstreet's 1st Corps and temporarily commanded the corps when Longstreet was given a multi-corps command for the battle of Chickamauga. Hood had been wounded again in that battle, losing a leg as a result. But he had been promoted to lieutenant general to date from that battle and had returned to the Army of Tennessee. He was known as one of the most aggressive, hard-hitting brigade and division commanders in the Confederate service. How he would handle a corps remained to be seen.

Johnston's cavalry was gathered in a corps of three divisions under Major General Joseph Wheeler, a 27-year-old Alabaman who graduated from West Point in 1859. He had led a regiment at Shiloh, a brigade at Stone's River, and this corps since July 1863. He would live to be a hero of the Spanish-American War 35 years later. He was known for dogged aggressiveness, but like many cavalry leaders of both sides, was overly fond of raiding undefended rear areas, which often took him too far away from the army whose eyes and ears he was supposed to be.

Johnston had wanted to rearrange his infantry into three corps, like Lee's, which would be a more flexible organization. He had asked for Major General W. H. Chase Whiting, one of Lee's cast-offs then serving at Wilmington, North Carolina, to command the third corps. When he was refused Whiting, Johnston had asked for Major General Mansfield Lovell. Typically, Johnston had chosen two men that President Davis disliked. Lovell had been in command of New Orleans when it was captured by Union Admiral Farragut and, after a questionable performance in the Confederate attempt to retake Corinth from Grant and Rosecrans, had been relieved of command. Even though a court of inquiry had cleared him of charges of incompetence at New Orleans, he had never been returned to duty. Johnston had finally been informed by Bragg, in his new position as nominal general-in-chief, that Davis would not allow the formation of the third corps on the grounds that the Army of Tennessee was too small to justify it. The whole affair had served only to widen the gulf between Johnston and Davis.

However, Johnston was to get his third corps after all, not by reorganization, but by reinforcement. On the way to Georgia by rail, from Mississippi and Alabama, were two infantry divisions from the force known as the Army of Mississippi. This also included a division of cavalry, which was marching across, and a third infantry division would soon be formed out of brigades from the Mobile and Savannah garrisons. The commander of this corps-sized force was Lieutenant General Leonidas Polk, who had graduated from West Point back in 1827, the year before Jefferson Davis and two years before Joe Johnston. He had soon left the army to enter the Virginia Theological Seminary, and at the outbreak of the war he had been the Episcopal bishop of Louisiana, but he had lain aside his vestments to again become a soldier. Like Hardee, he had been a corps commander, or its equivalent, in the western army since before Shiloh. But even he had run afoul of the famous temper of Braxton Bragg, and after Chickamauga he had been transferred to Mississippi. Now Bragg was gone from the Army of Tennessee and Polk was returning, bringing his Mississippi troops with him. Although well-loved by the troops, it was generally recognized that his military ability did not measure up to his high rank.

Joe Johnston was a Virginian who had graduated from West Point in 1829 along with Robert E. Lee. In 1861 he had led his army from the Shenandoah to reinforce Beauregard and turn the tide at the first battle of Bull Run. Taking command of the combined force, he had let McClellan get within view of the spires of Richmond before attacking. For his trouble he had picked up a wound that had lost him command of the army to Lee. After he had recovered, Davis had sent him to supervise the West, with the primary purpose of coordinating the armies of Bragg in Tennessee and Pemberton in Mississippi. It had been an assignment ill suited to his temperament. He had declined to take direct charge of either force, yet had seen few ways for the two to help each other. When Grant had beseiged Pemberton at Vicksburg, Johnston had taken personal charge of a relief force, but Grant's reinforcments had arrived faster than his, and he had never attacked. When Bragg had been relieved of command of the Army of Tennessee, Johnston has been the logical choice. Jefferson Davis had bowed to that logic despite his personal dislike for Johnston, who had argued with him over his rank among Confederate generals since early in the war. Grant professed to fear Johnston more

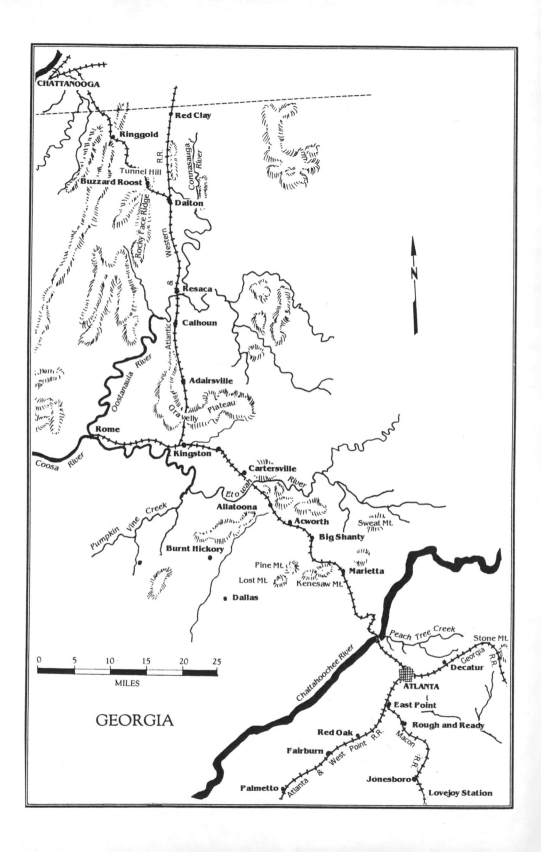

CHATTANOOGA

Red Clay

Ringgold

Tunnel Hill

Buzzard Roost

Rocky Face Ridge

Dalton

R.R.

Connasauga River

Western

& Atlantic

Resaca

Calhoun

Oostanaula River

Adairsville

Gravelly Plateau

Rome

Coosa River

Kingston

Cartersville

Etowah River

Allatoona

Pumpkin Vine Creek

Acworth

Sweat Mt.

Big Shanty

Burnt Hickory

Pine Mt.

Lost Mt.

Kenesaw Mt.

Marietta

Dallas

Peach Tree Creek

Stone Mt.

Georgia

R.R.

Decatur

Chattahoochee River

ATLANTA

East Point

Red Oak

Rough and Ready

Macon

Atlanta & West Point R.R.

R.R.

Fairburn

Jonesboro

Palmetto

Lovejoy Station

0   5   10   15   20   25

MILES

GEORGIA

than Lee, but Johnston had so far demonstrated more talent at retreating than at fighting, perhaps because of a perfectionist streak which almost never judged conditions to be quite right for making an attack.

Sherman also had high regard for Joe Johnston's ability, and knew his renowned opponent would have the 25-mile-long Rocky Face Ridge, rising some 800 feet above its surroundings, built into a position impregnable against frontal attack. Sherman's top-ranking subordinate and West Point classmate, Major General George H. Thomas, commander of the Army of the Cumberland, had suggested a plan for outflanking that position. His scouts had discovered an unguarded pass where the southern end of Rocky Face Ridge met Horn Mountain. It led to Johnston's supply line, the Western & Atlantic Railroad, at the village of Resaca, where it crossed the Oostanaula River. Thomas suggested that Schofield's Army of the Ohio and McPherson's Army of the Tennessee take his place between Johnston and Chattanooga to keep the Rebels' attention focused in that direction. He would then take his 53,000 infantry down to, and through, this unguarded pass, called Snake Creek Gap, and place them squarely across Johnston's supply line. At the very least, such a move would force the Confederates to abandon their well-prepared position, and it might bag the lot of them.

Sherman thought it over and came up with a variation that sounded more practical. Thomas' force was too big, and too close to the Rebels, to make such a move undetected, and Thomas was too slow and methodical on the offensive. Joe Johnston would out maneuver him and get away. On the other hand McPherson's Army of the Tennessee, Sherman's old command and before that, Grant's, was just being brought over to Chattanooga from northern Alabama and was still out of sight of the Rebels.

McPherson, born the year before Johnston graduated from West Point, had been top man in the academy class of 1853 that had included Schofield, Sheridan, and Hood. He had been an aide to Halleck and then Grant's chief engineer, and both generals had sponsored his rapid promotion. He had commanded the 17th Corps in Grant's Vicksburg campaign and had succeeded Sherman to command of the Army of the Tennessee when Sherman took over the Military Division of the Mississippi. McPherson had a charming personality, a noble character, and a brilliant mind, and Sherman suspected that he might eventually prove the man to lead the Union cause to ultimate victory, should Grant and himself fall victims to Rebel armies or Northern politics. However, if he handled his new command as successfully as Sherman expected him to, McPherson might pretty well end the war here and now. He and his 24,000 infantry were being sent to Snake Creek Gap along roads that were hidden from Rebel view, while Thomas closed up on Johnston's front, and Schofield threatened the Confederate right at the northern end of Rocky Face Ridge. If all went smoothly, Johnston would be in big trouble.

Thomas' Army of the Cumberland had been reorganized somewhat, in preparation for the spring campaign. The greatest change had come from the absorption of two small corps that Joe Hooker had brought west from the Army of the Potomac after Rosecrans' defeat at Chickamauga in September. The two corps, the 11th and 12th, had always been something like stepchildren in the Army of the Potomac. They had originally been the forces led by Fremont and Banks respectively when Stonewall Jackson had made them, and others, look foolish in his famous Shenandoah Valley campaign of 1862. Both corps had then served in John Pope's ill-starred Army of Virginia, which Lee had routed at the second battle of Bull Run. The 12th had fought, and fought well, at Antietam but neither corps had been on hand at Fredericksburg. Both had joined the Army of the Potomac in time for Chancellorsville, where the 11th had again fallen victim to Jackson when the latter's attack had come storming through the underbrush of the Wilderness to roll up its flank. The 11th, notable for its high percentage of German-American regiments, had been outflanked and routed again at the first day of Gettysburg, and the rest of the Army of the Potomac had considered it a pariah. The 12th Corps had been reliable enough, simply too small. Anyway, when ordered to send two corps west, Meade had naturally chosen his weakest two.

Hooker, on the shelf since being replaced by Meade just before Gettysburg, but still enjoying the backing of powerful Republican politicians, including Treasury Secretary Salmon Chase, had been given command of the two corps for their western venture. He upheld his nom de guerre of Fighting Joe at Chattanooga in the celebrated Battle Above the Clouds, when he drove the Confederates from formidable Lookout Mountain. He had graduated from West Point in 1837, two years ahead of Halleck, one ahead of Beauregard, and had commanded a division in the 3rd Corps through the Peninsula and Second Bull Run campaigns before being given the 1st Corps in time for Antietam. At Fredericksburg he had commanded a grand division of two corps and had then succeeded Burnside in command of the Army of the Potomac. He had restored that force's morale and had planned a brilliant maneuver against Lee's flank and rear, only to lose his nerve and allow himself to be driven back across the Rappahannock.

As a division and corps commander, he had shown tactical skill and leadership of the highest order, but he was too ambitious to get along well with his superiors. Perhaps to curb Hooker's independent ways, Sherman consolidated his two small corps into one, called the 20th. The fact that its number came from one of the corps which had been eliminated by the recent consolidations in Thomas' army might have been intended as a reminder to Hooker that he was just one of Thomas' three corps commanders, not an army commander within Sherman's force, like Thomas, McPherson, and Schofield. Unfortunately for Sherman's peace of mind, Hooker outranked McPherson and Schofield and everybody else in the assembled force except Thomas, and Sherman himself. Major General Oliver O. Howard, who had commanded the 11th Corps, became the new commander of the 4th Corps in Thomas' army, replacing Gordon Granger, whose performance had not pleased Grant or Sherman. Major General Henry W. Slocum, who had commanded the 12th Corps, and who could not stand Hooker, was sent to command the Federal garrisons in and around Vicksburg.

On 7 May 1864, with McPherson well on his way toward Snake Creek Gap and Schofield maneuvering as if to slip in behind Rocky Face Ridge from the north, Thomas sent Major General John M. Palmer's 14th Corps to fix Johnston's attention by storming a Confederate cavalry outpost on Tunnel Hill, overlooking a gap in the ridge known as Buzzard's Roost. After the Rebels had been driven off, a Federal private, perhaps contemplating the chances of surviving the spring and summer campaigns, watched one of the great scavenger birds for which the pass was named making lazy circles over the heads of the Union forces. "He's counting us," the soldier told his comrades.[1]

Morning fog joined the smoke of campfires and brushfires as dawn struggled through the foliage of the Wilderness on the seventh day of May. Skirmishers from Ewell's corps probed through the murky woods to see what the Yankees were up to. "Several times I put my hand up to see if my cap was on my head," one of them remembered years later. "I think my hair must have been standing straight up."[2] But no burst of musketry met them. Instead, they discovered that the Federal 6th Corps had abandoned its old line and left the road to Germanna Ford unguarded. While the Rebels gathered up the abundance of tents, blankets, canteens and rifles left strewn around the Federals' former camp, Ewell's skirmishers soon discovered their opponents' new position. In the meantime Union skirmishers found that Lee had pulled back his own lines on the Orange Plank Road front to about a mile from the Northern positions along the Brock Road.

Both Federals and Confederates seemed to be fought to a standstill, "each behind its breastworks," Theodore Lyman of Meade's staff wrote, "panting and exhausted, and scowling at each other."[3] The infantrymen of both armies, except for a lot of skirmishing to make sure the other side had not moved, were allowed to stay behind their breastworks and await the enemy's initiative. However, Hancock was ordered to return all the units that he had been sent as reinforcements over the past two days to their respective corps.

Neither Grant nor Lee considered himself defeated, but each seemed to hope that the other would be so foolish as to leave his own entrenchments and come attack him in his. "We cannot call the engagement a positive victory," Grant told his staff that morning as he sat on a stool in front of his tent, "but the enemy have only twice actually reached our lines in their many attacks, and have not gained a single advantage. This will enable me to carry out my intention of moving to the left, and compelling the enemy to fight in a more open country and outside of their breastworks."[4]

At 6:30 a.m. Grant ordered Meade to "make all preparations during the day for a night march, to take position at Spotsylvania Court House with one army corps, at Todds Tavern with one, and another near the intersection of Piney Branch and Spotsylvania road with the road from Alsop's to Old Court House."[5] This order points up a severe handicap which beset the Federals: lack of detailed knowledge of the terrain south of Chancellorsville. Not only was there no such intersection, but neither of the roads existed as described. Major Nathaniel Michler of the engineers reported, in rather cumbersome terms, that the Federals' maps furnished "but little of that detailed information so necessary in selecting and ordering the different routes of marching columns, and were too decidedly deficient in accuracy and detail to enable a general to maneuver with certainty his troops in the face of a brave and everwatchful enemy."[6]

The main point, however, was that Grant was not ordering the army to retreat back across the Rapidan to rest and reorganize and perhaps to change commanders, as most of the men expected, but to advance. Meade put Humphreys to work figuring out the exact movement orders for each corps. At 7:30 a.m. Ferrero's 9th Corps division of U.S. Colored Troops was sent to help Sheridan guard the vast wagon park and the latter was told that he was now free to take the offensive.

Many of the Union soldiers got their first look at black men in uniform that day as Ferrero's division marched by. The latter responded to the presence of the watching white veterans by closing ranks, shifting their rifles to their right shoulders and breaking into song. "Will you, will you, Fight for de Union?" the lead singer asked. "Ah-ha! ah-ha!" the rest responded, "We'll fight for Uncle Sam!" But Theodore Lyman of Meade's staff explained why these troops would do no fighting unless the Rebels attacked the wagons under their care. "We do not dare trust them in the line of battle," he wrote. "Ah, you may make speeches at home, but here, where it is life or death, we dare not risk it."[7]

It was obvious that the Federals could not move to the southeast, as Grant wanted, until the Brock Road was cleared. But when the Union cavalry had abandoned Todd's Tavern the evening before, Stuart had moved in with two of his Confederate divisions. As the fog began to lift, Sheridan ordered his troopers forward in his first large-scale operation against Stuart. Wilson's division, still recuperating, was left around Chancellorsville to guard the wagons, while Sheridan led the other two against Todd's Tavern. The 1st Division, now led by Brigadier General Wesley Merritt, another of the cavalry's boy generals and an 1860 graduate of West Point, would make the first attack. Torbert, suffering from a spinal abscess, was on his way to a hospital in Washington.

Merritt sent Custer back over the ground that he had won the day before, supported again by Devin's brigade. They delivered a powerful mounted attack along the open area adjacent to the Brock Road, scattering Confederate pickets in all directions. Around noon, one of Gregg's brigades moved down the Brock Road to Todd's Tavern, where it found some of Major General Wade Hampton's Rebel troopers behind breastworks at the Catharpin Road intersection. Gregg's leading units dismounted and advanced on foot, pushed Hampton's men out of their works into the woods and then went in after them.

At about the same time, on the other flank, Gregg's other brigade, under Brigadier General Henry E. Davies, Jr., advanced against Fitzhugh Lee. The Rebels charged first in a series of dismounted attacks, but the Federals counterattacked and drove the Southerners all the way to the tavern. "It is almost impossible to conceive of anything finer than the style in which these troopers first received the enemy's charge and then advanced against them, sweeping them back before the fierceness of their fire," wrote one of Davies' regimental chaplains.[8]

Around 3 p.m. Hampton's Confederates managed to drive Gregg's men, many of them out of ammunition, back to the works they had captured earlier. Then, "out of the woods the enemy came," a Maine cavalryman remembered, "yelling as only they could yell, and they had but fairly got into the open field when cannon and carbines opened a terrible fire, and the rebel yell turned into a whine as they quickly disappeared in the woods. The sight was enough to make the boys laugh, so suddenly did the enemy turn."[9] At about the same hour, the Reserve Brigade of Merritt's division, now under Colonel Alfred Gibbs, attacked Fitz Lee. Mostly regulars, these Federals came on, dismounted, at a slow walk, firing as they came, and yard by yard they forced the Rebels back from one defense line to another, pressing on relentlessly until lack of ammunition brought them to a halt near sundown. Then Devin's fresh brigade took over, and at about 7 p.m., after twelve long hours of heavy fighting, Fitz Lee's line broke and fell back. But the Federals were pulled back nearer to Todd's Tavern after dark.

During the day Lee had been mulling over two questions: Who to put in temporary command of Longstreet's corps, and what would be Grant's next move? Early that morning Lee had consulted Longstreet's staff officer, Moxley Sorrel, about who should fill in for his fallen chief. None of the officers now with the 1st Corps had sufficient rank and experience for the job. Three other possibilities were suggested: either Jubal Early or Allegheny Johnson of the 2nd Corps, or Richard Anderson of the 3rd Corps. Sorrel thanked the general for consulting him and opined that Early was probably the most capable of the three, but because of his ascerbic tongue he had the most enemies and would stir up the most resentments. "And now, Colonel, for my friend Ed. Johnson," Lee encouraged, "he is a splendid fellow."

"All say so, General," was Sorrel's reply, "but he is quite unknown to the Corps. His reputation is so high that perhaps he would prove all that could be wished, but I think someone personally known to the Corps would be preferred."[10] He meant Anderson.

Sorrel was left with the impression that Lee's choice would be Early anyway, so he was pleasantly surprised to learn later in the day that it would be Anderson, after all. Dick Anderson and his division had been part of the 1st Corps before the creation of the 3rd Corps the previous spring. Before that he had commanded the brigade which Jenkins had led until he fell the day before to the same volley that wounded Longstreet. Anderson was not aggressive, perhaps a bit slow, but he was brave, prudent, and intelligent. The men of his old brigade started to cheer when he came riding down the line in his new capacity, but were silenced because of the proximity of the enemy. So they silently threw their hats in the air. "My friends," Anderson told them, "your silent expression makes me grateful for your kind remembrance. I thank you sincerely."[11] Tears choked off any more he might have said, and the men wept too, to see how their new general was moved by their greeting.

As for the question of Grant's intentions, it became increasingly obvious as the day wore on that the Federals would not attack the Confederate infantry in their entrenchments again. Therefore it seemed likely that "those people" were going to move. Since the bridge at Germanna Ford had been taken up, their route obviously was not going to lead back that way. That left two logical possibilities. Either they would move eastward toward Fredericksburg—the Yankee wagons had been seen moving off in that direction—or they would go southeastward toward

Spotsylvania Court House. Whichever the case, it would be prudent to move some of his own force toward Spotsylvania, where it would either head the Yankees off or be on their flank. The 1st Corps would have the shortest distance to travel, so it was chosen for the move. Anderson was told to withdraw his men from the lines as soon as possible after dark, to give them some rest, and then to move off by 3 a.m. Throughout the day Brigadier General William M. Pendleton, Lee's chief of artillery, had been directing the clearing of a rough road from the Confederate right southeast to the Catharpin Road. Anderson was to follow that track and then take the Catharpin Road southwest over Corbin's Bridge to Shady Grove Church, then almost due east to the little county seat of Spotsylvania County.

As darkness began to settle over the thickets of the Wilderness, the Federal infantry, screened by its pickets, began withdrawing from its entrenchments. The wagons and the artillery were already on the move. Warren's 5th Corps was to assemble on the Orange Turnpike, turn south down the Germanna Plank Road to where it met the Brock Road, then follow the latter down behind Hancock's entrenched troops and on beyond Todd's Tavern to Spotsylvania Court House. Sedgwick's 6th Corps was to follow the turnpike to Chancellorsville, turn southeast to an intersection near a farmhouse of the Alrich or Aldrich family, then take the Catharpin Road southwest to Piney Branch Church, and there turn due south to that intersection that existed only on Federal maps. Hancock's 2nd Corps would fall in behind Warren's column and follow it to Todd's Tavern. Burnside's 9th Corps, less its 4th Division still guarding the wagons, would follow Sedgwick.

Robinson's 2nd Division led the 5th Corps column. His men heard cheering in the Rebel camps about the time they reached Wilderness Tavern and for some reason, instead of turning right onto the Germanna Plank Road, they marched on to the east. Both the Confederate cheers and their own route tended to confirm the men's suspicions that they were retreating after receiving another thrashing by Bobby Lee. But they soon came to the Brock Road intersection with the turnpike, and they did turn right this time. At about the same time, 9 p.m., Grant, Meade, and their staffs rode past, and the men suddenly realized that they were not retreating at all. They were moving south, toward Richmond. They were advancing. This was something new for the Army of the Potomac, and the men began to cheer the passing generals.

The headquarters party rode on down to the Brock Road-Orange Plank Road intersection, where Grant and Meade stopped to talk with Hancock. Behind them, Warren's exhausted infantry continued their march. Some of them were bowled over by a runaway team of artillery horses and loaded pack mules. Then about 10:30 p.m. the head of Robinson's column, marching in rear of the works of the 2nd Corps' sleeping troops, reached the Orange Plank Road, and found Meade's mounted escort blocking the way. The infantry halted and many of the men promptly fell asleep. When the generals realized that their contigent was holding up the march, they rode ahead again. As they passed behind Birney's division, some of the 2nd Corps troops who were still awake recognized their commanders. Then they saw the long column of Warren's men trudging along behind them, heading south. They, too, suddenly realized the significance of this movement.

"Soldiers weary and sleepy after their long battle, with stiffened limbs and smarting wounds, now sprang to their feet, forgetful of their pains, and rushed forward to the roadside," Horace Porter recorded. "Wild cheers echoed through the forest, and glad shouts of triumph rent the air. Men swung their hats, tossed up their arms, and pressed forward to within touch of their chief, clapping their hands, and speaking to him with the familiarity of comrades. Pine-knots and leaves were set on fire, and lighted the scene with their wierd, flickering glare. The night march had become a triumphal procession for the new commander. The demonstration was the emphatic verdict pronounced by the troops upon his first battle in the East." Instead of being flattered by the troops' show of approval, Grant was worried that it would alert the enemy. "By his direction," Porter said, "staff-officers rode forward and urged the men to keep quiet so as not to attract the enemy's attention; but the demonstration did not really cease until the general was out of sight."[12]

That was not the only cheering for Grant that day.

Business had been nearly at a standstill in New York and Washington as everyone waited for word from Virginia. One anxious caller had asked the president what he knew. "Well, I can't tell much about it," replied Lincoln, who had heavy circles of fatigue under his eyes. "You see, Grant has gone to the Wilderness, crawled in, drawn up the ladder, and pulled in the hole after him, and I guess we'll have to wait until he comes out before we know just what he is up to."[11] A general at the War Department noticed that Secretary Stanton's hand now suffered a nervous tremor.

That night, the sixth, the telegraph key at the War Department chattered out a message from a young reporter named Henry Wing addressed to Assistant Secretary Charles A. Dana, a former newspaperman. Wing said he had left Grant that morning and he was asking permission to use the military telegraph to send a message to the *New York Tribune*. Dana was away at a party, but Stanton was present and he demanded that the reporter tell him what he knew about Grant. Wing asked to be allowed to send a hundred words to the *Tribune* first, then he would tell all. Stanton demanded an answer to his questions first. Wing replied that his news belonged to his employer.

After a five-minute lull, a message came back addressed to the commander of the Federal outpost where the reporter had found protection and a telegraph line, after twice escaping from Confederate partisans. The Secretary of War ordered that the newspaperman be arrested as a spy until he answered all his questions. "Of course that settled it," Wing later wrote. "I would not have told him one little word to save my life."[12] After another pause, the telegraph key on the Virginia end clattered again. The operator turned to Wing with a smile and said, "Mr. Lincoln wants to know if you will tell HIM where Grant is,"[13] Wing repeated his proposition, and the president readily accepted "only suggesting," Wing remembered, "that my statement to my paper be so full as to disclose to the public the general situation,"[14] and with the provision that the Associated Press be given a summary. Wing agreed and proceeded to dictate his story and answer the president's questions.

Lincoln was determined, however, that he must have more information. He sent for Dana, who had served as the War Department's eyes and ears during Grant's Vicksburg campaign the year before. Now Lincoln decided to send him into Virginia to perform a similar service. The train that took him down was to bring young Henry Wing to the White House, where he arrived at 2 a.m. on the seventh. The president and several cabinet members were waiting to hear, first-hand, what he could tell them about the battle. With the help of a big wall map, the young reporter told them all he knew, and when the others had left he told Lincoln that he had a special message for him from General Grant. The president looked at him in surprise. "Something from Grant to me?"[15]

Then the young newspaperman related how, after volunteering to his boss to try to get through to Washington with news of the battle, he had gone to Grant's headquarters and asked if there was any message that he wanted to send the country by way of the *Tribune.* "You may tell the people that things are going swimingly down here," was the general's bland reply. Wing dutifully jotted that down, turned and walked away, but Grant followed him until they were out of hearing of his staff and then stopped him. "You expect to get through to Washington?" he asked. "Well, if you see the President, tell him for me that, whatever happens, there will be no turning back."[16] When Wing repeated these words at the White House, Lincoln's worry-seamed face broke into a broad smile. Then the president of the United States bent down and kissed the young reporter on the cheek.

Wing's story appeared in the papers that day, and that afternoon, Saturday the seventh, the Marine Corps band played on the south lawn of the White House. It was the first such concert since 1861. A huge crowd gathered, and loud cries greeted the president when he appeared on the portico. He proposed, in lieu of a speech, three cheers for General Grant and all the armies under his command, and the crowd responded with roar after roar in a mass release of pent-up emotion.

---

1. McDonough and Jones, *War So Terrible*, 98.
2. William D. Matter, *If It Takes All Summer* (Chapel Hill, 1988), 14.
3. Trudeau, *Bloody Roads South*, 119.
4. Porter, *Campaigning With Grant*, 76.
5. Matter, *If It Takes All Summer*, 22.
6. Ibid., p. 23.
7. Trudeau, *Bloody Roads South*, 118.
8. Edward G. Longacre,"Cavalry Clash at Todd's Tavern," *Civil War Times Illustrated*, 16 (6, October 1977): 19.
9. Ibid., 18.
10. Freeman, *Lee's Lieutenants*, 3:374.
11. Ibid., 3:375.
12. Porter, *Campaigning With Grant*, 79.
13. Louis M. Starr, *Bohemian Brigade* (New York, 1954), 300.
14. Ibid., 301.
15. Ibid.
16. Ibid., 301–302.
17. Ibid., 302.
18. Ibid., 299.

CHAPTER TWENTY-ONE

"Such An Opportunity Does Not Occur Twice"

8 May 1864

At 3 a.m. on the eighth of May, Kautz roused his troopers from their bivouac at Stony Creek Bridge. He sent Colonel Spear and his 2nd Brigade on a circuit that would bring them to Nottoway Bridge from the south. Then, giving orders for Colonel Mix to take most of his 1st Brigade straight down the railroad for the same objective, Kautz set off to the north with two companies of the 1st D.C. Cavalry to reconnoiter the railroad bridge over Rowanty Creek. He found the garrison there too large to attack, however, so he led his small force back to Stony Creek, only to find that Mix and his brigade were still in camp. Deciding that it was too late to carry out his original plan, he ordered Mix to follow Spear.

However, Spear had also disobeyed Kautz's orders. He had bypassed Nottoway Bridge and gone on farther south to Jarratt's Station. Arriving there around dawn, he sent the 11th Pennsylvania Cavalry, dismounted, against the local detachment of the Holcombe Legion, but it was twice repulsed. Spear then retreated up the railroad, destroying it as he went. But when his other regiment, the 5th Pennsylvania, arrived, he sent it in with the support of four light howitzers. The troopers went forward at a rush, captured 37 Rebels, and drove the others off for the loss of two dead and eight wounded. The Federals destroyed all railroad structures in the town, several public buildings, and large amounts of Confederate supplies. The fire also spread to several private homes.

Up at Nottoway Bridge the commander of the Confederate 59th Virginia, Colonel William Tabb, now had his own regiment plus two companies of the 26th Virginia and another company of the Holcombe Legion for a total of 600 men. Seeing what he took to be a Union wagon train bound for Jarratt's Station, he advanced against it with 200 of his men, but could not catch it. He did pick up a straggler, though, who revealed that Kautz was about to attack Nottoway Bridge. Tabb returned just in time to help repel an assault. However, Spear soon arrived to join Kautz, and when the Rebels started to give ground, Tabb ordered a fighting withdrawal across the bridge to an old earthwork on the north side. But as the Confederates ran through the covered bridge the Federal troopers started in after them and set the bridge on fire. Twenty minutes later the 210-foot structure collapsed into the Nottoway River with a roar and a hiss.

Kautz then called a truce, and the two sides worked out an on-the-spot exchange of prisoners. After resting his men, Kautz considered whether it would be worthwhile to invest a little more time and part of his dwindling ammunition supply in what would be the almost-certain capture of Tabb's smaller force. He reluctantly decided against it, as he was already burdened by 130 prisoners and 30 wounded Federals, so at about 5 p.m. his division pulled out and headed toward City Point. By dark it had reached Sussex Court House, where all stopped for the night except two companies of the 11th Pennsylvania which rode ahead and captured Allen's Bridge. At 3 a.m. on the ninth, the division moved out again, followed by several hundred slaves who took advantage of the Federals' passing to run away from their masters.

Butler's infantry spent that Sunday, 8 May, in camp, working on their entrenchments, attending worship services, and swimming in the Appomattox. On the north side of the James, the two regiments of U.S. Colored Cavalry that had marched up the Peninsula arrived opposite the Bermuda Hundred position. All Butler knew then about the Army of the Potomac was that a great battle was taking place in the Wilderness. Still worried about Grant's ability to hold his own against Lee, Butler decided to put off any move against Richmond until he could be more sure of how things were going to the north. In the meantime he needed to do something constructive, so he decided to make another, even bigger, strike at the critical Richmond & Petersburg Railroad. "The enemy are in our front with scarcely 5,000 men," he wrote to Gillmore, "and it is a disgrace that we are cooped up here."[1] Butler ordered that all but three of his twelve brigades make this advance the next day. He would demonstrate against the northern defenses of Petersburg to keep the Rebels busy while he wrecked as much of the railroad as possible.

Around midnight of 7–8 May, Grant and Meade, still preceding Warren's column down the Brock Road, came to Todd's Tavern, where they unexpectedly discovered Gregg's 2nd Cavalry Division encamped. They also found out that two brigades of Merritt's 1st Division were camped about a mile further down the road, and that neither commander had received any orders about covering the movement of the infantry, or even knew that it was taking place. Meade therefore wrote out orders for them, sending Merritt down the Brock Road to clear the way for the infantry, and Gregg southwest to Corbin's Bridge to protect the flank of the moving column. Meade also wrote a note at 1 a.m. to Sheridan, explaining what he had done. As it happened, Sheridan, at his headquarters at Alrich's, was just then writing out his own orders for his three divisions to move out at 5 a.m. Why it took him until 1 a.m. to write orders for his divisions, and especially why those orders did not require any movement for the next four hours, has never been explained. He obviously did not understand the timetable for the southward movement of the army.

Warren, riding at the head of his column, arrived at Todd's Tavern just as Meade was giving directions to the cavalry, and found the road blocked again by the headquarters contingent. He conferred with Meade and was informed that the cavalry would precede his advance. Merritt's headquarters was a mere mile and a half down the road, but when Warren arrived there at 3 a.m. he found the troopers were only then mounting up to move out. Warren ordered his men to get some rest. Merritt's troopers did not get very far before they came across felled trees in the road, and they were fired on by Fitzhugh Lee's pickets as they tried to remove them. This developed into a firefight in the dark woods along the road, both sides firing at the muzzle flashes of the enemy's carbines, and the advance was slowed to a crawl until dawn. Finally, at 6 a.m. Merritt suggested to Warren that the latter's infantry should take over the job of pushing the stubborn Rebels.

The Federal infantry, exhausted after marching through the night on top of all that it had endured in the past few days, slowly drove Fitz Lee's dismounted troopers, reinforced by a four-gun battery, from one position to another. When they came to the clearings of a farmer named Alsop, the fire of two Rebel cannon forced the entire leading brigade of Robinson's division to deploy into line of battle, for a column on the road presented much too compact a target. The Federals followed a wooded fork in the road, and sometime around 8 a.m. they came to another open space extending about 400 yards to a low ridge known as Laurel Hill, a couple of miles northwest of Spotsylvania Court House. Fitz Lee's troopers could be seen hard at work there building breastworks.

Warren urged Robinson to keep going, but the latter pleaded for time to bring up his other two brigades, and the corps commander reluctantly agreed. It was going to be a scorcher of a day, and many of the Federals had already fallen out of ranks from fatigue and sunstroke. The men of the leading brigade, under Colonel Peter Lyle, were allowed to take off their knapsacks and rest. But after five or ten minutes Warren grew impatient of the delay and ordered Robinson to go on. Lyle sent his men across the open field, which was broken by gullies and rail fences, but as they were nearing a fence on a slight rise of ground an unexpectedly heavy volley of rifle fire struck them, followed almost immediately by another. Some of the Federals climbed the fence and advanced to the foot of Laurel Hill, where they lay down in exhaustion, partially protected by the slope and by the pines which the Rebels had felled for an abatis. But most of the brigade fell back in disorder to the shelter of the woods. They did not know it, but their few minutes of rest had just lost them the race for Spotsylvania Court House—a race they had not even known they were in.

Around 11 p.m. the night before, Dick Anderson had pulled his two divisions of the Confederate 1st Corps out of their defenses in accordance with Lee's directions, and they had begun to move down the trail which Pendleton's artillerymen had hacked out of the Wilderness. After marching the troops a mile or so, Anderson began watching for a good place to stop and let the men sleep a few hours, but the woods were burning all around and he found no suitable site. Even beyond the burning area, there seemed to be no sites large enough to accommodate two divisions, so Anderson kept the men moving, although progress was slow amid the stumps and felled trees of the new track.

The head of the column passed Corbin's bridge at about 1 a.m., just as Meade was writing orders for Gregg's cavalry to seize that very crossing, and while Warren's infantry was waiting for the Union cavalry to take the lead. At Shady Grove Corner the Southerners turned to the east. Finally, as the light of dawn was beginning to appear over the tree tops, Anderson ordered a halt, and Kershaw's men fell out on both sides of the road just west of the Block House Bridge over the Po, three miles from Spotsylvania. While the men searched for firewood and soft places to rest they could hear firing to the north. About an hour later Anderson had Kershaw's troops forming up again when a young courier brought a note from Jeb Stuart saying that his troopers were facing Union infantry on the Brock Road and asking for support. Anderson put his infantry in motion again.

As they reached a road junction east of the bridge over the Po another courier brought word from the Brock Road to the north, saying that Union infantry was forming up to charge the Confederate cavalry and help was needed immediately. Anderson, conscious that he still had to fulfill Lee's order to occupy Spotsylvania Court House, ordered Kershaw to send two of his brigades to Stuart's support. Kershaw forwarded his own old brigade, under Colonel Henegan, plus Humphreys' Mississipians. No sooner had these troops departed than another cavalry courier appeared, from the east. Fitzhugh Lee had sent him to say that a large force of Federal cavalry was approaching Spotsylvania from the northeast, along the road from Fredericksburg. One cavalry regiment, the 3rd Virginia, had been sent to delay them, but it could not be expected to do so for long all by itself. Anderson told Kershaw to take his other two brigades on to Spotsylvania to meet this force, then he sent word for Fields to hurry his division forward.

Henegan's and Humphreys' brigades had marched northward about three quarters of a mile when they met a cavalryman who urged them forward: "Run for our rail piles! The Federal infantry will reach them first if you don't run!"[2] Hurrying up a slight rise the footsore infantrymen found Stuart, who placed them in position behind his cavalry's hastily constructed breastworks. They had just settled in and felled a few trees for an abatis when Lyle's Federals advanced, and it was Henegan's South Carolinians whose sudden volleys had sent most of them reeling back again.

Warren, meanwhile, had gone to hurry forward the other two brigades of Robinson's division. When Colonel Andrew Denison's Maryland Brigade came up Warren told them, "Never mind cannon! Never mind bullets! Press on and clear this road. It's the only way to get your rations."[3] There was some truth in that, for the supply wagons had gone by another route and were to meet the troops at Spotsylvania. Robinson formed the Marylanders and Colonel Richard Coulter's 2nd Brigade on each side of the road, supported by two batteries of artillery, and they went forward. They were soon struck by Confederate rifle and cannon fire, and the front regiment of Marylanders stopped to fire back. This caused a pile-up when the other regiments tried to advance through that first regiment as it was reloading. But the Marylanders got to within about fifty yards of the Rebel works before both Robinson and Denison were unhorsed with wounds that would cost them each a limb. Colonel Phelps of the 7th Maryland assumed command of Denison's brigade and called for the men to cease firing and charge. He led the way on horseback until he and his horse were also felled. A captain in his regiment tried to drag the colonel from beneath his dying horse, but had to give up. Then he too was struck down, and the Marylanders broke and ran back across the field.

Coulter's brigade was also repulsed. The Federals still sheltering at the foot of the hill had just risen, with the purpose of charging on up the slope, when they heard a shout behind them and turned to see Confederates emerging from the woods. Realizing they were in danger of being surrounded, they retreated as fast as they could. A private slung their wounded colonel over his shoulder and carried him off the field. More of Warren's troops were coming up, and just as the Marylanders advanced Bartlett's brigade of Griffin's division, minus three regiments left behind on picket duty, went forward a few hundred yards to the right, still thinking that nothing but dismounted cavalry opposed them. They received scattered fire from Rebel skirmishers in the woods to their right, and as they chased other skirmishers over a slight rise they suddenly realized that they were approaching Confederate infantry in crude defensive works. Some Pennsylvanians crossed the works and drove the Rebels back at bayonet point, but the Southerners who had been pursuing the retreating Marylanders came in on Bartlett's left flank and suddenly his two front regiments dissolved and ran back across the field, carrying the second line with them. The Confederates pursued but were momentarily checked by more of Griffin's units. More Rebels struck these in flank, however, and the Federal's were driven back as far as the Alsop house.

By 10:15 a.m. Crawford's Pennsylvania Reserve Division arrived along with the 4th Division—which had been Wadsworth's and was now commanded by Cutler—as well as the bulk of the 5th Corps' artillery. Some of Griffin's men and the Pennsylvanians counterattacked against light resistance and reestablished a line opposite the Confederate position on Laurel Hill. Cutler's division was allowed to fall out and prepare coffee, and one of its bands began to play "Hail Columbia," but an artillery shell exploded just above the musicians, scattering them and their instruments, and the tune was never finished. The division was ordered into line and

"Such An Opportunity Does Not Occur Twice"　　　257

advanced toward Laurel Hill, but it too was outflanked on the right and fell back. By then Field's division had reinforced the Confederate line.

The Federal cavalry that had been seen approaching Spotsylvania from the northeast was Wilson's 3rd Division, which Sheridan had sent by way of the Fredericksburg-Spotsylvania road. The Union horsemen easily outflanked the 3rd Virginia Cavalry and routed it, capturing 41 Rebels. Wilson was then about a mile to the right rear of Henegan's infantry, and he had learned of Anderson's arrival, and Warren's, from his prisoners. He was preparing to send his 1st Brigade, now under Colonel John B. McIntosh, against the rear of the Confederate infantry when he got word of a large Rebel force coming up from the south. This was Kershaw with two of his brigades. Wilson fell back to the village and prepared to hold it, but he received orders from Sheridan to withdraw, and he fell back the way he had come. A lull descended upon the field around noon.

By then Grant and Meade had been at their new headquarters at Piney Branch Church, northeast of Todd's Tavern, for four hours. It was Sunday, but no congregation had come to make use of the country meeting house. Assistant Secretary of War Dana did show up, however, and the troops of the 6th Corps were passing by before turning off to the south. Among them was a drum and bugle corps, and when the musicians caught sight of the generals they struck up a popular negro spiritual. The staff officers all began to laugh, and Rawlins cried out, "Good for the drummers!" The tone-deaf Grant asked what the joke was. "Why," he was told, "they're playing 'Ain't I glad to get out ob de wilderness!'"[4]

Around noon Sheridan reported to Meade just as the army commander was having lunch with his staff. Meade "had worked himself into a towering passion regarding the delays encountered in the forward movement," Horace Porter remembered, "and when Sheridan appeared went at him hammer and tongs, accusing him of blunders, and charging him with not making a proper disposition of his troops, and letting the cavalry block the advance of the infantry. Sheridan was equally fiery, and, smarting under the belief that he was unjustly treated, all the hotspur in his nature was aroused. He insisted that Meade had created the trouble by countermanding his (Sheridan's) orders, and that it was this act which had resulted in mixing up his troops with the infantry, exposing to great danger Wilson's division, which had advanced as far as Spottsylvania Court-house, and rendering ineffectual all his combinations regarding the movements of the cavalry corps. Sheridan declared with great warmth that he would not command the cavalry any longer under such conditions, and said if he could have matters his own way he would concentrate all the cavalry, move out in force against Stuart's command, and whip it. His language throughout was highly spiced and conspicuously italicized with expletives. General Meade came over to General Grant's tent immediately after, and related the interview to him. The excitement of the one was in singular contrast with the calmness of the other. When Meade repeated the remarks made by Sheridan, that he could move out with his cavalry and whip Stuart, General Grant quietly observed, 'Did Sheridan say that? Well, he generally knows what he is talking about. Let him start right out and do it.' "[5] It surely was not the answer that Meade had been hoping for, but he had the order written up by 1 p.m., and Sheridan started concentrating his divisions for departure the next morning.

Lee, preceding Ewell's 2nd Corps, was by then at Shady Grove Church. He had found it necessary to make further command changes, for A. P. Hill was too sick to remain in command of the 3rd Corps. Lee named Early as his temporary replacement, perhaps at least partly because it allowed him to promote Gordon, who had designed and led the attack on Sedgwick's flank. To clear the road for Gordon to take over Early's division, Lee transferred Brigadier General Harry Hays' Brigade from that division to Allegheny Johnson's, where it was combined with the other Louisiana brigade, which was without a general since Leroy Stafford had been killed in the Wilderness fighting. R. D. Johnson's brigade, which had made the long march from Hanover Junction, was assigned to Gordon's Division to bring it back up to a reasonable size.

At 9 a.m. Lee sent a message to Confederate secretary of war James A. Seddon saying, "The enemy has abandoned his position and is moving towards Fredericksburg. This army is in motion on his right flank, and our advance is now at Spottsylvania Court House."[6] Much has been made of Lee's prescience in divining Grant's intention to move toward Spotsylvania and in sending Anderson to head him off. But Anderson had moved much earlier than Lee had ordered him to, and this message shows that, even when Anderson and Warren were in combat, Lee did not yet realize that Grant was trying to get between him and Richmond. Also, Early had been ordered to take the 3rd Corps down the Brock Road to Spotsylvania. This indicates that Lee did not expect the Federals to be using the same route to reach the same place.

Gregg's Union cavalry and Hampton's Confederate troopers had been pushing each other back and forth along the Catharpin Road between Todd's Tavern and Corbin's Bridge all morning, and after Hancock's 2nd Corps arrived at Todd's Tavern, that general sent Colonel Nelson A. Miles' 1st Brigade of Barlow's 1st Division down the road to help out. Around 12:45 p.m. they arrived, under artillery fire, at a ridge overlooking the Po River and the road past Shady Grove Church, which was filled with the ambulances and wagons in the tail of Anderson's column. While the artillery accompanying the Federals dueled with Rebel guns on the far side of the river, the head of Ewell's corps came into view and continued on down the road, suffering heavily from the heat.

After they were gone, Miles left two regiments to picket the road and the nearby woods and pulled the other three back about half a mile. Around 3 p.m. he got word that Gregg's troopers were being withdrawn, and more pickets had been sent to replace them. Just then a volley rang out north of the road, about where the new pickets had been sent. Miles turned his three rear regiments to face north, called in the two advanced regiments, and beat off an attack by what proved to be Wade Hampton's cavalry and Mahone's—formerly Anderson's—Division of Early's 3rd Corps. Barlow ordered Miles to withdraw to the earthworks around Todd's Tavern, and when Early found out that these were stoutly held he decided to abandon any attempt to use that route and to go on to Spotsylvania by way of Shady Grove instead.

At 12:30 p.m. Warren sent Meade a report of his situation. He was facing two divisions of Longstreet's corps, and his own infantry was running out of ammunition. He could not reach Spotsylvania Court House without reinforcements. Meade replied that Sedgwick's corps was on the way and that the two corps should cooperate in a massive assault as soon as it arrived. Warren snapped back that Meade could "give your orders and I will obey them, or you can put Sedgwick in command and he can give the orders and I will obey them; or you can put me in command and I will give the orders . . . but I'll be God d—d if I'll cooperate with General Sedgwick or anybody else."[7] Warren had a good point about the necessity for unity of command at the front, but Meade did not seem to hear him. At 1:45 p.m. Grant and Meade moved their headquarters to the intersection of the road past Piney Branch Church with the Brock Road, where they intercepted Gibbon's division on its way from Hancock at Todd's Tavern to reinforce Warren. Meade explained to Warren that the latter could call on the division in case of great emergency but that it was expected—correctly as we have seen—that Hill or Ewell would be showing up at Todd's Tavern soon. Gibbon might be needed to help hold it. Meanwhile Grant prepared orders for the next day's intended march toward the North Anna River.

The combined attack of the 5th and 6th Corps, for which Grant and Meade waited all afternoon, did not go in until after 6 p.m. And due to confusion and exhaustion among the troops, less than half of those available seem to have advanced. They went forward to the east of the

Brock Road and ran straight into Major General Robert E. Rodes' division at the head of Ewell's Confederate 2nd Corps just going into position on Anderson's right. The Pennsylvania Reserves unexpectedly ran into Ramseur's North Carolina Brigade. Both sides started firing, but the Reserves, their enlistments almost up, soon broke for the rear, leaving about 400 to be captured.

In support behind the Reserves were three regiments and parts of two others that had been on picket duty when the 5th Corps pulled out of its entrenchments in the Wilderness the night before. They had caught up with the rest of the corps too late to be sent back to their own brigades before the attack and they went forward together as an ad hoc brigade. When the firing started they peered ahead through the gathering gloom and saw the Pennsylvanians streaming back. Behind them came a confused mass of Confederates, yelling and firing as they advanced. The Federals met them with point-blank fire. The Rebels, Battle's Brigade, fell back a short way and them came on again, and soon the fight degenerated into a hand-to-hand brawl in the growing darkness. Officers used their swords and revolvers, men swung their rifles like clubs and forgot "all the noble and refined elements of manhood," as one member of the 20th Maine put it, "and for that hour on Laurel Hill they were brutes, made wild with passion and blood, engaged in a conflict as deadly and fierce as ever raged upon the continent."[8]

During a lull the Northerners fell back about 100 yards. The Southerners, encouraged by this, came after them, but a close-range volley put an end to that. Two Confederate regiments tried to use a ravine to get into the rear of the Federals, but they ran into the 16th Michigan and finally gave up. They withdrew, leaving behind over sixty prisoners and the colors of the 6th Alabama. The Federals could hear the Rebel officers exhorting their men to try another advance, but the Confederates were exhausted. Finally, Rodes ordered his men to fall back and entrench. The Northerners waited until 3 a.m. and then quietly withdrew to the main Union position. Other Federal units to the left had also engaged in confused hand-to-hand combat in the dark. When all had died down the two Union corps and the two Confederate corps faced each other from behind parallel lines of improvised earthworks about five or six hundred yards apart.

Up in the Shenandoah Valley that day, 8 May, Sigel was issuing orders for an advance to begin the next morning. That same evening, Breckinridge himself finally arrived at Staunton, although his troops were still on the way. There he learned that Sigel was still at Winchester and that

McNeill had successfully raided the Baltimore & Ohio Railroad. Imboden wanted to hit it again with his entire brigade, but when Breckinridge heard that Sigel had sent a force, erroneously reported as 1,300 strong, after McNeill he ordered Imboden to intercept it. Word also came, however, that Crook's Federal column was only ten miles from the Virginia & Tennessee Railroad at Dublin. Jenkins' and McCausland's Rebel brigades were moving to meet him. With local reserves and militia, Brigadier General Albert Jenkins, the senior Confederate officer on the spot, had about 3,000 men arranged in defenses along a spur of Cloyd's Mountain, blocking Crook's path. "They may whip us," the laconic Crook said after examining the Rebel position through binoculars, "but I guess not."[9]

The 5,000 Federal infantry had slithered across the Allegheny Mountains for ten days in drenching rain and snowstorms along roads turned to mush. Now on the morning of 9 May Crook led the brigades of Colonels Horatio G. Sickel and Rutherford B. Hayes (the future president) to threaten the Southerners' front, while Colonel Carr B. White's 2nd Brigade was sent to turn the Confederate right flank. After a vicious firefight and hand-to-hand combat, the Rebels were driven back to a second ridge where the Federals hit them again, and the Confederate line collapsed, leaving two cannon in Union hands. Jenkins was mortally wounded and captured, while Crook fainted from exhaustion as soon as he saw that he had won. He soon recovered, however, and ordered an immediate advance to Dublin. His forces arrived there before dark and destroyed the railway installations and a large stock of Rebel supplies. Among Confederate messages captured at the telegraph office was one from Richmond stating that Grant had been repulsed in the Wilderness and was retreating, which caused Crook to worry about the safety of his command.

Also on the eighth, Averell and his Union cavalry had reached Tazewell, 45 miles west of Dublin, where he learned that Saltville was being defended by the famous Rebel cavalryman John Hunt Morgan, with a force reportedly twice the size of Averell's own. Averell feinted in that direction on the ninth, but made up his mind to swing east again and go for the lead works at Wytheville instead.

Down in Georgia on 8 May one brigade of Thomas' Army of the Cumberland climbed the northern end of Rocky Face Ridge and struck the right flank of Johnston's imposing position, but could not dislodge the Rebels. Meanwhile other units threatened Buzzard's Roost, and Brigadier General John W. Geary, former mayor of gold-rush San Francisco and territorial governor of Bleeding Kansas, led his 2nd Division of Hooker's

20th Corps against Dug Gap, near the southern end of the Confederate position. The Federals clambered up the difficult pass and ran into a small force of Kentucky cavalry and Arkansas infantry that held them off with point-blank volleys and hand-to-hand combat until nightfall, when troops of Cleburne's division of Hardee's corps took over. One of the Kentucky troopers remembered that as they filed back through Cleburne's ranks many veterans of that crack division who, like most Civil War infantrymen, had previously shown little regard for the fighting abilities of cavalry, removed their hats in respect. "Boys, you covered yourselves with glory," he heard them say. "We will never call you 'Butter-milk Rangers' any more."[10]

While Johnston's attention was thus diverted, McPherson's Army of the Tennessee reached Snake Creek Gap and found it defended by nothing more than a brigade of cavalry, which the Federals easily drove before them. Sherman banged the supper table so hard that he made the dishes jump when he heard of this, and exclaimed, "I've got Joe Johnston dead!"[11] But later that night he got another dispatch from McPherson. When the latter had approached Resaca he had discovered that it was defended by a sizable body of Rebel infantry behind well prepared earthworks. These men were only the first 4,000 of Polk's Army of Mississippi on their way to join Johnston, but McPherson did not know that. Feeling that the position was too strong to assault, he pulled his two corps back to the eastern end of Snake Creek Gap where his own flanks were covered, and began to entrench his front. Johnston learned that night of the sudden appearance of Yankees in the rear of his main line and ordered Hood with one of his own divisions and two of Hardee's to reinforce Resaca.

"McPherson had startled Johnston in his fancied security, but had not done the full measure of his work," Sherman wrote in his memoirs. "He had in hand twenty-three thousand of the best men of the army, and could have walked into Resaca (then held only by a small brigade), or he could have placed his whole force astride the railroad above Resaca, and there have easily withstood the attack of all of Johnston's army, with the knowledge that Thomas and Schofield were on his heels. Had he done so, I am certain that Johnston would not have ventured to attack him in position, but would have retreated eastward by Spring Place, and we should have captured half his army and all his artillery and wagons at the very beginning of the campaign. Such an opportunitiy does not occur twice in a single life, but at the critical moment McPherson seems to have been a little cautious."[12]

1. Robertson, *Back Door to Richmond*, 109.
2. Foote, *The Civil War*, 3:196.
3. Matter, *If It Takes All Summer*, 60–61.
4. Porter, *Campaigning With Grant*, 83.
5. Ibid., 84.
6. Dowdey and Manarin, eds., *Wartime Papers of R. E. Lee*, 724–725.
7. Trudeau, *Bloody Roads South*, 140.
8. Pullen, *The 20th Maine*, 206.
9. Foote, *The Civil War*, 3:244.
10. McDonough and Jones, *War So Terrible*, 103.
11. Foote, *The Civil War*, 3:325.
12. Sherman, *Memoirs*, 2:34.

CHAPTER TWENTY-TWO

"How Near We Have Been To This Thing Before"

9 May 1864

Charles Owen was a 17-year-old who, only forty days before, had been an innocent boy on his father's farm in Monroe County, Michigan. Just one day before, he had been a private in the 1st Michigan Volunteers, but on 9 May 1864 he was a prisoner of war. He had lived through desperate fighting in the Wilderness only to be captured at Laurel Hill on the eighth. All through that day, as he was held in the rear of the Confederate lines, he could hear heavy volleys of musketry every hour or two, each marking a Federal charge, and then another crop of Union prisoners would join him. By the end of the day there were 378 of them, counting Owen, two colonels, a major, and several other officers. After a sleepless night without food or blankets, they were all marched south under guard.

Owen had plenty of time to wish that he had listened to his father about staying out of the army, and to contemplate his bleak future in a Confederate prison camp.

By 5 p.m. on the ninth, the prisoners were fifteen or sixteen miles south of Spotsylvania, and within a half-mile of Beaver Dam Station on the Virginia Central Railroad, marching along in the fading light, exhausted, hungry, and depressed. They could hear the whistle of a train waiting to take them to Richmond or points south. Suddenly, one of the mounted guards came galloping from the rear of the column shouting, "The Yanks are coming! The Yanks are coming!" There followed the sound of a shot, and Owen turned in time to see a solid line of Union cavalry emerge from the woods half a mile back, "coming as fast as their horses could go." The Rebel guards ordered their prisoners to run, but instead they edged into the woods on one side of the road and against a rail fence on the other. Out in front of the charging horsemen was a "gallant officer" whom Owen described as "the very picture of the dare devil fighter." He was dressed all in black velvet and gold braid, with a scarlet tie, and he was waving his huge black hat in his left hand and his sword in his right, while holding the reins in his teeth. Even without seeing his long golden curls flying in the breeze, Owen would easily have recognized the pride of Monroe, Michigan: General George Armstrong Custer. "I shall always remember him," Owen wrote 46 years later, adding that the "rebel guard flew for their lives, leaving us prisoners to fend for ourselves."[1]

Custer's Michigan Brigade was the vanguard of Sheridan's entire Cavalry Corps, 10,000 men and 10,000 horses plus six batteries of horse artillery. They had been on the road since 6 a.m., passing to the east of Spotsylvania and heading almost due south, straight for Richmond. Riding four abreast, their column was thirteen miles long and took four hours to pass any given point. Sheridan set the pace at a slow walk to preserve the horses. Besides, he was in no hurry. He wanted Stuart to find him. By mid-afternoon, he had. Pickets at Massaponax Church brought Stuart the word, and he sent Brigadier General William Wickham's brigade of Fitzhugh Lee's Division to overtake and harass Sheridan's rear guard. Later Wickham was joined by Fitz Lee and his other brigade, under Brigadier General Lunsford Lomax, and by Stuart himself with one of Rooney Lee's brigades, commanded by Brigadier General James B. Gordon—about 5,000 troopers in all.

After tossing hardtack crackers and other rations to the newly liberated prisoners, Custer's men rode on into Beaver Dam Station and captured a hundred freight cars carrying a million and a half rations meant for Lee's army, along with medical supplies, and a few hundred rifles. The weapons were distributed to the former prisoners, while they and the troopers took all they wanted of the food. Then, in the middle of a drenching thunderstorm, the remaining rations, along with the trains and the depot, were put to the torch. The artillery blew holes in the locomotives, some track was torn up, and ten miles of telegraph line were cut. After this the troopers were allowed to get what rest they could. Before hitting the road again in the morning Merritt's entire division was turned loose on the railroad and tore up about ten miles of track.

Out on the Red River, Colonel Bailey's dams were now ready for use. The water level in the channel had been raised five and a half feet to a total depth of eight feet, eight and a half inches. However, the navy had been slow to take the army's work seriously, and only three light-draft vessels were ready to take advantage of it. At 5 a.m. on 9 May the pressure of the current drove out of position two of the four coal barges that formed part of the dams, and opened a 66-foot gap. Porter, seeing his unexpected opportunity for escape slipping through his fingers, ordered the old wooden gunboat *Lexington* to run the falls. "She entered the gap with a full head of steam on," an onlooker remembered, "pitched down the roaring torrent, made two or three spasmodic rolls, hung for a moment on the rocks below, and was then swept into deep water by the current, and rounded safely into the bank."[2] The crowd of 30,000 onlooking soldiers burst into a deafening cheer. The three light-drafts then followed, suffering only minor damage, and the spectators roared again. But the water had soon dropped too far for the remaining six gunboats and two tugs to make it. "The jaws of danger, for an instant relaxed, had once more shut tightly on the prey," as one soldier put it.[3] Bailey was annoyed at the navy's failure to more fully exploit the fruits of his labor, but he set to work to build more dams.

In Virginia, early on the morning of 9 May, a courier brought an order to Jubal Early at Shady Grove. He was to take the 3rd Corps along the Shady Grove Church Road to join the rest of the army at Spotsylvania, and his men were on the march by 6 a.m. On the Federal side, Burnside had originally been ordered to move his corps southeast from Aldrich's to the Fredericksburg-Spotsylvania road, then down to Spotsylvania and on another dozen miles or so to a town called Chilesburg just north of the North Anna River, behind which Grant expected Lee to make his next stand. When it was found that Lee was defending Spotsylvania instead, Burnside was told to halt at a place called "Gate" on the Federal maps, about four miles northeast of Spotsylvania. His lead division, Willcox's 3rd, only got about 200 yards from Aldrich's, however, before it found its path blocked by Sheridan's cavalry as it began its own march south. It was an hour before Willcox's men were able to resume their advance. Once they got onto the Fredericksburg Road, a colonel remembered, "the road was now broad and good, and we marched with ease. We were out of the unbroken wilderness."[4] Without knowing it, they marched right past the place called "Gate." Nobody knew just what it was anyway, perhaps only a gate in a fence. Finally, Willcox ordered some skirmishers sent out in advance, and these soon ran into Rebel cavalry vedettes, who fell back toward Spotsylvania.

Willcox called a halt to rest the men and rode forward with the commander of his leading brigade, Colonel Benjamin C. Christ, across the grounds of a house belonging to the Gayle family to have a look at what lay ahead. They found that the ground sloped down about a third of a mile to the Ni River. This is one of four streams, the others being the Mat, the Ta, and the Po, that combine to form the Matta and the Poni, which then further merge to form the Mattaponi. "While these streams are not wide," Horace Porter related, "their banks are steep in some places and lined by marshes in other. The country is undulating, and was at that time broken by alternations of cleared spaces and dense forests. In the woods there was a thick tangled undergrowth of hazel, dwarf pine, and scrub-oak."[5] Farther to the southeast the Mattaponi combines with the Pamunkey to form the York.

On the high ground on the south side of the Ni were some buildings and a few mounted troopers from Fitz Lee's division who had been sent to investigate this Union advance. General R. E. Lee was notified of the Federal approach by 8 a.m. Around 9 a.m., Willcox ordered Christ to take his brigade across the river and occupy the high ground on the other side. Willcox also sent across his other brigade, under Colonel John F. Hartranft, in support. No opposition was encountered until Christ's skirmishers entered some woods beyond the crest of the rise on the far side of the river. There they were assaulted by a brigade of dismounted Rebel cavalry, and driven in. But the main line of Union infantry held along the crest, aided by the division's two batteries of light artillery, and the Confederates backed off. The Federals had no idea, because their maps were so bad, that they were only a mile and quarter northeast of Spotsylvania.

Stevenson's 1st Division of the 9th Corps arrived about noon. Fifteen minutes earlier Grant had ordered Burnside to search for roads running between his position and that of the Army of the Potomac, over on the Brock Road. Meanwhile, Potter's 2nd Division of the 9th Corps was to proceed to Piney Branch Church, where it could serve as a support for any one of the other three corps. Ferrero's 4th Division would remain at Chancellorsville to guard the wagons.

The Union 5th and 6th corps spent the day shuffling units, strengthening their entrenchments, and extending them somewhat farther to the northeast. Meade, evidently dissatisfied with Warren's handling of the joint attack the evening before, told Sedgwick to take command of any future combined action in Meade's absence. Sedgwick, however, generously told Warren to go right on commanding the 5th Corps since he had perfect confidence in the younger man. Not long afterwards Warren wrote a confidential letter to Meade. First he reported that a long Confederate wagon train was moving toward Shady Grove on the road from Parker's Store. This, he opined, should relieve any apprehension about the Federal right, since it indicated that the Rebels were moving toward their own right. Typically, he also offered some unsolicited advice, some of it good. Among other things he suggested that whenever the army made a general movement such as the one of the seventh and eighth, Meade should accompany the column moving to the critical objective, so that an overall commander would be present if it became necessary to combine the operations of two or more corps. He then added that whether or not Meade had confidence in him, he personally had doubts about the abilities of both Sedgwick and Hancock. The letter was never delivered, however, probably because bad news arrived before it could be sent.

About 9 a.m. Sedgwick had been overseeing the redeployment of some of his units and, observing that some of the infantry were overlapping a battery, he interrupted the joke which he was telling his chief of staff, Lieutenant Colonel Martin L. McMahon, to explain what he wanted. "I started out to execute the order," McMahon later recorded, "and he rose at the same moment, and we sauntered out slowly to the gun on the right. About an hour before, I had remarked to the general, pointing to the two pieces in a half-jesting manner, which he well understood, 'General, do you see that section of artillery? Well, you are not to go near it today.' He answered good-naturedly, 'McMahon, I would like to know who commands this corps, you or I?' I said playfully, 'Well, General, sometimes I am in doubt myself'; but added, 'Seriously, General, I beg of you not to go to that angle; every officer who has shown himself there has been hit, both yesterday and today.' He answered quietly, 'Well, I don't know that there is any reason for my going there.' When afterward we walked out to the position indicated, this conversation had entirely escaped the memory of both.

"I gave the necessary order to move the troops to the right," McMahon continued, "and as they rose to execute the movement the enemy opened sprinkling fire, partly from sharp-shooters. As the bullets whistled by, some of the men dodged. The general said laughingly, 'What! what! men, dodging this way for single bullets! What will you do when they open fire along the whole line? I am ashamed of you. They couldn't hit an elephant at this distance.' A few seconds after, a man who had been separated from his regiment passed directly in front of the general, and at the same moment a sharp-shooter's bullet passed with a long shrill whistle very close, and the soldier, who was then just in front of the general, dodged to the ground. The general touched him gently with his foot, and said, 'Why, my man, I am ashamed of you, dodging that way,' and repeated the remark, 'They couldn't hit an elephant at this distance.' The man rose and saluted, and said good-naturedly, 'General, I dodged a shell once, and if I hadn't, it would have taken my head off. I believe in dodging.' The general laughed and replied, 'All right, my man; go to your place.'

"For a third time the same shrill whistle, closing with a dull, heavy stroke, interrupted our talk, when, as I was about to resume, the general's face turned slowly to me, the blood spurting from his left cheek under the eye in a steady stream. He fell in my direction; I was so close to him that my effort to support him failed, and I fell with him."[6] Uncle John Sedgwick was dead. Brigadier General James B. Ricketts was the senior surviving officer in the 6th Corps, but he and his 3rd Division had just recently been transferred from the defunct 3rd Corps, and he refused to take command because he knew that Sedgwick would have preferred Wright to succeed him. By the time McMahon found Meade to report all this, the latter had already heard the sad news and had issued the order placing Wright in command. Sedgwick's body was taken to army headquarters, where a bower of evergreens was built for it in which it lay until nightfall, mourned by all. Grant, who had been talking with Sedgwick not very long before he was shot, could scarcely believe the news Horace Porter brought him. "His loss to the army is greater than the loss of a whole division of troops," Grant said.[7]

At about 10 a.m. Grant received word that Willcox had run into Confederates at a point that was, on his maps, about three and a half miles east of Spotsylvania Court House. Soon thereafter he got a report from Hancock indicating that the Rebels were gone from around Todd's Tavern, and he began to suspect that Lee might try to get around him to the east, to cut him off from Fredericksburg. At any rate, Burnside's two divisions on the Fredericksburg Road might be in danger. He ordered Meade to send out scouts to check the gap between the 6th Corps' left flank and Burnside's force. With almost all of his cavalry off with Sheridan, Grant was at a disadvantage when it came to keeping track of the enemy's movements. He did have a small, ad hoc brigade of cavalry but it was patroling the roads between Todd's Tavern and the Rapidan. Colonel Hammond of the 5th New York commanded this force, made up of two regiments from Burnside's corps plus Hammond's regiment, still detached from Wilson's division. Burnside had been left with the 13th Pennsylvania Cavalry, but did not seem to be making much use of it.

Early that morning Grant had sent a message to Halleck: "The enemy hold our front in very strong force, and evince a strong determination to interpose between us and Richmond to the last. I shall take no backward steps."[8] At noon Grant received a package of dispatches from Washington. They informed the general-in-chief that Sherman was advancing in Georgia, threatening Resaca; that Butler had landed at City Point and Bermuda Hundred and wanted reinforcements; and that Sigel had so far met no opposition. "Grant did not express any particular gratification regarding these reports," Porter remembered, "except the one from Sherman."[9] He did authorize the reinforcements for Butler.

Meanwhile, if any large body of the enemy was moving east, Meade would have to recall the train of wagons, which was then moving southeast from Chancellorsville. He would also need to put strong pressure on Lee's western flank to draw his attention and forces back in that direction. At 12:45 p.m. Grant received a report that Willcox was heavily engaged with what he (mistakenly) thought was a superior force of enemy infantry. Burnside was told to have Willcox hold to the last extremity, and Meade was told to be ready to follow the Confederates and attack them vigorously. Hancock received an order from Meade about noon to leave one division at Todd's Tavern and to bring the other three down the Brock Road. "All information here leads to the belief that they are passing to our left and you will be needed here," it said.[10] Barlow's 1st Division was immediately withdrawn from its works and started down the Brock Road. Birney's 3rd Division followed it about an hour later. Mott's 4th Division and the foot-slogging heavy artillerymen of the Artillery Reserve were left to hold Todd's Tavern. Gibbon's 2nd Division had already been sent from near army headquarters southeast toward the Po River, about halfway between Todd's Tavern and the Alsop house. Barlow and Birney joined it there.

About 3 p.m. Grant and Meade visited Gibbon's position. From there they could see all the way across the Po to the Shady Grove Church Road, where a Confederate wagon train was moving toward Spotsylvania. A staff officer suggested that artillery could easily hit the wagons, but Meade answered that it would only scare a few mules and teamsters. Some guns were brought forward anyway, and their fire did put a bit more speed into the Rebel train. Part of Young's Brigade of Wade Hampton's Rebel cavalry division and a couple of guns of horse artillery were pushed back across the Po, and at about 4:30 p.m. it was decided to force a crossing. Half an hour later Barlow ordered Colonel John R. Brooke to lead his 4th Brigade across the Po and take possession of the nearest part of the road. At 6 p.m. Brooke reported his mission completed against only light opposition. The river was just two and a half feet deep. Hancock then ordered the rest of Barlow's division and all of Birney's to cross, then Gibbon's.

Barlow's division assembled on the Shady Grove Road, with Colonel Nelson Miles' brigade leading in battle formation and the others following in column, and marched forward to the Block House Bridge. They arrived about dark and found the river too deep there to ford, yet crossing the bridge might make them easy targets. At 10 p.m. Hancock reported the situation to Meade and was told to continue the movement first thing the next day. The nearest Confederates were those occupying the left end of Anderson's line about a half-mile to the northeast. And at that moment they had no idea that the Federals were at the Block House Bridge. But Hampton had notified Lee, and things would be different in the morning.

A little after noon, Willcox had reported that from the top of the Gayle house he could see Rebel cavalry, infantry, and wagons moving both towards and away from him. The cavalry moving away would have been Stuart taking off after Sheridan. The infantry coming his way was the division of Cadmus Wilcox in the van of Early's 3rd Corps. Wilcox was facing Willcox. The Federal general had two L's, the Confederate only one. The Rebels formed a defensive line a few hundred yards east of Spotsylvania, and were eventually joined by Early's other two divisions. Grant, hearing artillery fire coming from that direction, ordered Burnside, still back at Aldrich's, to go forward and take personal command. But at 4:20 p.m. the 9th Corps commander was still back at the Orange Plank Road, and by 10:30 p.m. he had gone no more than half way to the front, to the home of another member of the Alsop family, and there he stopped for the night. He was joined there by his Provisional Brigade, and later by Potter's 2nd Division. At least he was able to clarify, in a message to Grant, that Willcox's position was at the Gayle house, only a mile and a half from Spotsylvania. There did not seem to be any such place as "Gate."

Sometime during the night Lee ordered Early to send a division back to cover the Block House Bridge from the threat reported by Hampton. Early sent Mahone's, formerly Anderson's, Division. Lee also ordered Early to send another division to drive the Federals back across the Po, probably not realizing that it would face three Union divisions. Early selected Heth for that job. That left only the Confederate Wilcox to face Burnside's two divisions. It also left a mile-wide gap between Wilcox's left and Ewell's right, but the Yankees were unaware of it because of their bad maps and lack of cavalry for reconnaisance. However, at 1:30 a.m. on the tenth Grant notified Burnside that one division of Hancock's corps, namely Mott's, had been ordered to take position between the 6th Corps on Meade's left and Burnside's divisions over on the Fredericksburg Road. Burnside was authorized to call on it if necessary.

The first wagon train of Federals wounded in the Wilderness arrived at Fredericksburg around noon on 9 May, and division hospitals were rapidly set up in the city on the Rappahannock. Preparations were also under way to establish a supply base just north of there, at Belle Plain on the Potomac. Grant's experiences in the West had taught him the value of naval cooperation and the relative security of riverine lines of supply. With a base at Belle Plain, Grant had a shorter supply line than did Lee. And Sheridan was already tearing up portions of the latter.

Down on the Bermuda Hundred peninsula that day, Butler made his planned advance against the Richmond & Petersburg Railroad. Baldy Smith was sent with both of his divisions toward Port Walthall Junction to keep the Rebels to the south busy. Gillmore was sent due west to strike the railroad, but each of his three divisions left a brigade behind to improve the defensive works with spades and shovels, or what they called "Gillmore's rifles." Smith met no opposition but advanced cautiously, taking four hours to make three miles. Near the junction Smith's men found the blackened, bloated bodies left from the fight of the seventh. They had been stripped of all clothing and equipment that could be of use to the Confederates. The body of one Federal, who had been pinned to the ground by a bayonet through the mouth while still alive, enraged the Union troops. Two badly wounded survivors of that previous fight were found and rushed back to Bermuda Hundred for medical treatment. Smith paused only long enough to do minor damage to the railroad, then proceeded south toward Petersburg.

Meanwhile, the van of Gillmore's corps reached the railroad just south of Chester Station. This time he came prepared. Engineers were along to direct the infantry in the destruction of the railroad. The latter picked up whole sections of track and turned them over, knocked the ties loose, stacked them, and burned them on top of the rails, which were thus warped by the heat. Around midmorning Smith suggested that the Rebels in his front could be trapped if Gillmore would swing his forces around in a big arc and come in on their left and rear. Butler approved this plan and ordered Gillmore to carry it out. It was a good idea except for the fact that there were no Confederates in Smith's front. It was not until noon, as the men advanced through heavy woods in 102-degree heat, that Rebel opposition was encountered in the form of an elusive line of skirmishers and the exploding shells of unseen artillery. But the heat caused more casualties than did the Confederates. The Federals pushed on to the south, and by midafternoon they came in sight of Swift Creek. Beyond it was a sizable body of Southern infantry and seven guns. The Yankees paused to consider what to do next.

Bushrod Johnson was in charge of the Rebels, but he was under orders not to bring on a general engagement. Unaware that the Federals were again between Richmond and Petersburg, Bragg wired Pickett at 11:10 a.m. to "push forward all the troops as fast as they arrive to recover the position lost and reopen the road telegraph to this point." So at 2 p.m. Pickett ordered Johnson to "move forward at once and see what the enemy are doing."[11] Johnson realized this was ridiculous, for he could see that the Yankees greatly outnumbered him, but he ordered Hagood to cross the creek and advance on the enemy. However, at 3:45 p.m., just as Hagood's Brigade was approaching the bridge over the turnpike, another message from Pickett ordered a halt until reinforcements came up. Then another message cancelled the attack completely.

It was too late. Just as Hagood was getting the word, his men ran into Heckman's brigade, the same Federals whom they had fought three days before at Port Walthall Junction, now mad and eager for revenge. Heckman ordered his two front-line regiments to hold their fire and let the wildly yelling Rebels approach to within fifty yards. That was murderously short range for rifles firing at men in the open. When the Union volley finally came, "that line of grey melted away like snow," one Union soldier wrote.[12] Momentum carried some of the Confederates on into the Federal formation, where they were captured. The other survivors milled in confusion while their officer tried to move them forward and the Northerners poured volley after volley into their midst. Then Heckman brought up his two rear regiments and told them to charge, but Hagood had already ordered a withdrawal, and what was left of his men ran for all they were worth down the slope to the bridge and back across the creek. The Federals were content to occupy the high ground on the north side as darkness came on. Butler had achieved what he had set out to do: threaten Petersburg from the north while tearing up more of the railroad. He reported to Secretary Stanton that, "Beauregard, with a large portion of his command, was left south by the cutting of the railroad by Kautz. That portion which reached Petersburg under Hill I have whipped to-day . . . General Grant will not be troubled with any further re-enforcements to Lee from Beauregard's force."[13]

One brigade of Brooks' Union division had spent the afternoon near the mouth of Swift Creek dueling with Fort Clifton at long range. The army's three gunboats, and one of the navy's, also engaged Fort Clifton, but one of the army gunboats was sunk and another had grounded on a sandbar, the other two vessels withdrew. The fort also put a stop to an advance by 1800 of the Colored Troops from City Point along the south bank of the Appomattox. Colonel Hincks, their commander, tried to find an inland route but his path was repeatedly blocked by Major John Scott's civilian volunteer cavalry. Finally he gave up and marched his men back to City Point. Meanwhile, Kautz led his cavalry northward that day to within nine miles of Petersburg. Assuming that it was too well defended for him to tackle, he swung to the northeast. As the troopers crossed the Norfolk & Petersburg Railroad again they paused to destroy a small bridge, then moved on, stopping for the night at Mount Sinai Church, just ten miles from City Point. At 10 the next morning they reached Hincks' lines.

At nightfall on 9 May George Pickett was feeling better. Not only had Hagood held off Butler and Fort Clifton fought off three threats, but Beauregard had sent word that he was on his way to take personal command. Even better, as dark was falling Colonel William G. Lewis marched in with the North Carolina infantry brigade that had been Hoke's before his promotion. The people of Petersburg swarmed into the streets to welcome these reinforcements. More were said to be on the way.

There was still very little real news in Washington and the North that day, only rumors of continued hard fighting. Around 4 p.m. Secretary of War Stanton released an official dispatch stating that Lee was in retreat and Grant was on his heels. Lincoln told his secretary, John Hay, "How near we have been to this thing before and failed. I believe if any other general had been at the head of that army it would have been now on this side of the Rapidan. It is the dogged pertinacity of Grant that wins."[14] That evening another crowd gathered at the White House. The band of the 27th Ohio, a regiment on its way to the front, serenaded and the president made a brief speech. He had slept very little since Grant crossed the Rapidan, and it showed in his face. He said that he was "exceedingly gratified to know that General Grant had not been jostled from his plans" but reminded his listeners that much remained to be done.[15] They paid scant heed to such reservations.

That night, the first boatload of wounded men reached the city.

---

1. Urwin, *Custer Victorious*, 25–26.
2. Edward G. Longacre, "Rescue on the Red River," *Civil War Times Illustrated* 14 (6, October 1975): 40.
3. Ibid., p. 41.

4. Matter, *If It Takes All Summer,* 99.

5. Porter, *Campaigning With Grant,* 88.

6. Martin T. McMahon, "The Death of General John Sedgwick," in *Battles and Leaders of the Civil War,* 4:175.

7. Porter, *Campaigning With Grant,* 90.

8. Trudeau, *Bloody Roads South,* 145–146.

9. Porter, *Campaigning With Grant,* 91.

10. Matter, *If It Takes All Summer,* 110.

11. Robertson, *Back Door To Richmond,* 112.

12. Ibid.

13. Ibid., 116.

14. Williams, *Lincoln and His Generals,* 317.

15. Leech, *Reveille In Washington,* 321.

CHAPTER TWENTY-THREE

"One of the Classic Infantry Attacks of Military History"

10 May 1864

By the morning of 10 May, Imboden was approaching Lost River, West Virginia, having slipped away from his camp in the Shenandoah the afternoon before. He had left one regiment and a few smaller units to keep watch on Sigel and had told civilians that he was only going to look for better grazing for his horses. Actually he and the 800 men of two cavalry regiments were in pursuit of the Federals who were pursuing McNeill's partisans. The latter, under Colonel Jacob Higgins, had chased McNeill out of Moorefield, West Virginia on the eighth, and that seemed to be about as far as they intended to go. Then, on hearing a rumor that Imboden was after his 500 men with 4,500 Rebels, Higgins had started out on the evening of the ninth to return to Winchester—by way of Lost River.

Shortly before dawn on the tenth the Federal advance guard ran into Imboden's pickets. The Federals drove them back at first, but soon Confederate resistance stiffened, and Higgins decided he had to take a different road, quickly. He led his force northward toward Romney on what one of his men called "a ride for life." Imboden and his troopers "run them all day," as a sergeant put it. A Southern war correspondent who was along for the ride called it "the hardest, longest race during this war, nip and tuck, head up and tail up."[1] The Rebels struck at the Union rear guard and then backed off a bit, and the Federal column, which was slowed by its supply wagons, stopped at noon to feed and water its horses. Then Imboden struck again. The Union horsemen mounted and fled, leaving the road behind them strewn with pistols, sabers, and other impedimenta, but the wagon teams had been unhitched and the wagons had to be either burned or abandoned. McNeill soon joined Imboden, and they caught up with Higgins' column again at Romney that afternoon. They attacked the town and took it in minutes, driving the Federals another nine miles and over the South Branch of the Potomac to Springfield, where Higgins abandoned his men and rode off to Maryland and safety. What was left of his command eventually rejoined him there after a total flight of nearly sixty miles.

Near Spotsylvania, during the night of 9–10 May Mahone's Division of the Confederate 3rd Corps was busy entrenching a new defensive line on high ground just east of, and overlooking, the Block House Bridge to protect the Rebel army's left flank. At the same time, not far to the west, Hancock was having three bridges constructed across the Po where it ran west to east, to allow rapid movement of his troops. He was also abandoning Todd's Tavern. Mott's division left at 3 a.m. to try to fill the gap between the 6th Corps and the 9th Corps, and the gunless heavy artillery regiments were moved into reserve at Piney Branch Church.

At dawn Hancock told Miles to reconnoiter the Block House Bridge, and when Miles reported that the Rebels were in strong force there, he was ordered to send a regiment farther south in search of a safer crossing point. He sent the 61st New York, which proceeded about a mile and discovered a log lying across the stream. Twenty men were sent across the log but they were soon fired on, and returned with five wounded. Lieutenant Robertson of Miles' staff inquired at a nearby house and learned that the river could be forded farther south, but that the Federals would first have to cross a tributary called Gladys Run at a mill dam. The lieutenant took twenty men south to the mill and was told by another local that a lot of Confederates were on the other side of Gladys Run, moving west. Robertson did not believe this and rode on to have a look. He soon found out that it was true. Early himself had led Heth's Division back through Spotsylvania that morning and marched west to Block House Bridge. There he had turned south past the old courthouse and crossed the Po.

Meanwhile, reports of the strength of Mahone's position at the bridge led Grant to cancel Hancock's flanking movement. He reasoned that Lee must have weakened the position around Laurel Hill in order to man these new defenses, so he ordered Hancock to send two of his divisions back to the north side of the Po. These would combine with the 5th Corps for an attack on Anderson's position at 5 p.m., with Hancock in command of both corps. Wright, with Mott's division attached, would simultaneously attack Ewell. Gibbon's division was immediately sent back across the Po, followed by Birney's. Barlow's 1st Division remained south of the river, threatening Mahone.

About noon Heth's Confederates pushed across Gladys Run. Barlow had to realign most of his division to face south, and his troops began to build crude fieldworks. When Meade was informed of the approach of a large body of Rebels from the south, he ordered Hancock to return to the south side of the Po and personally supervise the withdrawal of Barlow's division. At about 2 p.m. it began to pull back to high ground 200 yards south of the Po. Not long afterward Heth's men attacked but were driven back. They returned twice more but with similar result. The woods in the area caught fire, confronting the men of both sides with an additional hazard.

Meanwhile, most of the artillery of the Union 2nd Corps plus Birney's 3rd Division were positioned on high ground north of the Po to cover Barlow's withdrawal, and a large-scale artillery duel broke out across the river. Barlow's division finally crossed in considerable confusion, some units failing to get timely word of the withdrawal, and one regiment even breaking up into small groups to make its way to the other side. A gun from a retreating battery of light artillery became wedged between two trees by its terrified team of horses and had to be abandoned, despite heroic efforts of the battery commander and some of his men. According to Hancock, that was the first gun ever lost in action by the 2nd Corps. Once Heth's Division had cleared the south bank of the Po, Mahone's Division crossed the Block House Bridge to join it. Hancock returned to Warren's front at 5:30 p.m. to discover that the Federal attack there had begun without him.

Griffin's and Cutler's divisions of Warren's 5th Corps spent most of the day fighting to retake picket positions they had lost to the Confederates during the night, and trying to get as close as possible to the Rebel defenses. The advanced units were pinned down by a continual storm of bullets, as one participant put it. "Major General Warren soon came running up the hill to have a look at the rebel works, when I seized his yellow sash and pulled him violently back," wrote the commander of the 6th Wisconsin. "To have exposed himself above the hill was certain death. I accompanied General Warren to another point where we secured a good view of the rebel works."[2]

Wright's 6th Corps skirmishers spent the morning finding the exact location of the main Confederate works opposite them. They discovered that these gradually bent to the east, so that Allegheny Johnson's division faced more to the north than Rodes' Division on its left. A company of the 15th New York Heavy Artillery took charge of two 24-pounder Coehorn mortars that were positioned near the spot where Sedgwick had been killed. Mortars had previously been so heavy and cumbersome that they had been used only in permanent fortifications and seige trains. But these were small, bronze weapons set in wooden blocks and light enough to be carried short distances by four men each. Like all mortars, they were designed to throw shells high into the air so they would come down behind the enemy breastworks and, if the fuses were timed correctly, explode over the heads of the enemy troops, sending fragments of the iron shells flying in all directions. This was the first known use of these weapons in the field.

Around 8 a.m. Mott's small division of the Union 2nd Corps arrived near the house of a Captain Brown, well to the northeast of the main 6th Corps position. There Mott found the 1st and 15th New Jersey of the 6th Corps that had been sent out the day before to reconnoiter the area. He took temporary charge of these two regiments, while he in turn was temporarily attached to the 6th Corps. Not long afterwards, Colonel Lyman of Meade's staff came to brief the general on his mission. Mott was to send skirmishers to the south to find out what the Rebels had in that area as well as to find Burnside's front line, which he was to support if called upon. Lyman felt that Mott was dull and listless, and reported that the general refused to do anything until his men had their coffee. After about an hour he sent a New York regiment out to relieve the New Jersey skirmishers, but just as the exchange of troops had begun in their rifle pits, Johnson's Confederate pickets opened fire and began to advance against them. The New Yorkers turned and ran, but the Jerseymen got back down in their holes and repulsed the Rebels. At 10 a.m. Mott sent a reconnaisance in force to the south. It got just far enough to see the northernmost tip of the Confederate position, but at the first Southern volley these Federals retreated all the way to the Brown house, taking the skirmish line with them. At 11 a.m. young Oliver Wendell Holmes, Jr., an aide on Wright's staff, came to urge Mott to push the Rebels to his right, toward the 6th Corps position. Holmes found Mott to be stupid and flustered.

Over on the 9th Corps front that morning Brigadier General Thomas G. Stevenson, commander of the 1st Division, was lying in the shade of a tree talking with his staff when firing broke out between his pickets and those of the Rebels. A stray bullet struck Stevenson in the back of the head and wounded him fatally. Colonel Daniel Leasure, commander of its 2nd Brigade, took over the division. Around noon Horace Porter of Grant's staff arrived at Burnside's headquarters, still back at the J. Alsop house, about halfway between Chancellorsville and his front-line divisions across the Ni. "I explained to him," Porter wrote, "that a general attack was to be made in the afternoon on the enemy's center by Warren's and Hancock's troops, and that he was to move forward for the purpose of reconnoitering Lee's extreme right, and keeping him from detaching troops from his flanks to reinforce his center. If Burnside could see a chance to attack, he was to do so with all vigor, and in a general way make the best cooperative effort that was possible." There was a problem, however. "Burnside was in great doubt," Porter said, "as to whether he should concentrate his three divisions and attack the enemy's right vigorously, or demonstrate with two divisions, and place the third in rear of Mott, who was on his right. I felt sure that General Grant would prefer the former, and urged it strenuously; but Burnside was so anxious to have General Grant make a decision in the matter himself that he sent him a note at 2:15 p.m." It took two hours for the note to reach Grant and an answer to come back. "The general said in his reply that it was then too late to bring up the third division, and he thought that Burnside would be secure in attacking as he was."[3] But Burnside ordered his other division, Potter's, forward anyway and finally went to the front himself to take personal command. The three divisions went forward around 6 p.m. in what Burnside termed a reconnaissance in force, advanced about half a mile, driving in some Confederate skirmishers, and began to entrench.

Early that afternoon Warren notified Meade that he thought he could break the Rebel line opposite his position. At 3:30 p.m. Meade informed Hancock, still south of the Po, that the opportunity for a successful assault looked so good that he had told Warren to attack at once, using Gibbon's 2nd Corps division for support. He had also ordered Wright to be prepared to attack immediately or to send help to Warren if needed.

Hancock was told to send Birney's division to support Warren as soon as Barlow's was safely back across the Po. Warren's attack began around 4:15 p.m. Griffin's division did not participate beyond sending a skirmish line forward, but Cutler's and Crawford's did, as well as Gibbon's 2nd Corps division. Robinson's 2nd Division of the 5th Corps had been disbanded the day before, after its commander was wounded and no suitable replacement was available. Lyle's brigade had been transferred to Cutler's 4th Division and Bates's brigade to Crawford's 3rd Division. The Maryland Brigade had become an independent formation directly under Warren's control and was not involved in the attack.

Cutler's division was the closest to the Confederate line, which bulged into some woods at that point and was manned by Law's Alabamans of Field's Division. The latter had picked up extra muskets from dead and wounded Yankees in their front and they used these to put up an extra-heavy fire that forced the Federals, already disorganized by advancing through the thick woods, to fall back. Law's men then went out and gathered up even more muskets and ammunition from a fresh crop of Union casualties. Gibbon went in just to the west of Cutler, with no better luck. His men had had plenty of time to study the terrain ahead of them and had already decided that the Rebel position could not be carried. To Gibbon's right, Crawford advanced against Gregg's Texas Brigade. The ground was more open here, giving the Confederates a clear field of fire and the help of artillery support. Crawford's men also fell back, although Federal artillery provided accurate covering fire.

Hancock returned from south of the Po about the time that Warren's attack was breaking up, and assumed command of the combined force. Meade ordered him to attack the same area again at 6:30 p.m., but later postponed that while directing Hancock to send a strong force to counter a Confederate thrust that had reportedly crossed to the north side of the Po and was threatening the army's right flank. This turned out to be a false alarm, probably prompted by some Rebel scouts reconnoitering the area. At 7 p.m. Hancock's attack on Laurel Hill stepped off. It consisted of two brigades of Cutler's division, two brigades of Gibbon's, two brigades of Crawford's, and Ward's brigade of Birney's. The results were pretty much the same as before except that Ward's men caught Gregg's Texans napping—literally. Some of the latter, after beating off the first attack, had decided that the fighting was over for the day and went to sleep. Others were busy fixing supper from rations taken off the Federal casualties to their front. Their artillerymen were busy watching some movement of Mahone's Division in the distance, across the Po. One of them turned just in time to see the front rank of Ward's formation only about 100 yards from them running across the field in the gathering dusk toward the Confederate works.

Southern artillery fire stopped some of the Yankees and drove others back, but the 86th New York and the 3rd Maine came on over the breastworks and applied their bayonets to the 1st Texas and the 3rd Arkansas. The Rebels broke and ran despite the efforts of Colonel Robert S. Taylor of the 3rd Arkansas, who was seen shouting and excitedly swinging a frying pan over his head in lieu of a sword, spraying hot grease in all directions. The disorganized Federals came after them but were slowed, then stopped by double- and triple-shotted rounds of cannister from a pair of Rebel guns. The Texans and Arkansans counterattacked with the help of the troops on each side of the breakthrough, and finally the Yankees were forced back over the breastworks and across the field to the safety of the woods. Fewer than half of the New Yorkers returned. Until that day the Texans had always refused to carry bayonets, looking upon them as useless dead weight. But they carried them after that.

When Wright had succeeded Sedgwick as commander of the 6th Corps his place at the head of its 1st Division was taken by the commander of its 3rd Brigade, Brigadier General David A. Russell. Early that afternoon Russell reported that a position had been found in his front from which an assault could be successfully launched. It was a wooded area that came within 200 yards of the enemy's works and from which the Federal skirmishers had driven Confederate pickets. Lieutenant Ranald S. Mackenzie of the engineers had led Russell forward down a secluded path and from the edge of the trees the two examined the Rebel works. These were formidable. They had a light abatis out front, and the earthworks had logs running along the top to protect the Southern infantryman's heads as they fired from slits below the logs. They also had traverses, small breastworks at right angles to the main line, to protect against flank attack. But with the woods to hide it and no pickets to raise an alarm, a large Union force could be formed along that path and should be able to cross the 200 yards to the works before enough fire could be brought to bear to stop it.

Wright approved the plan and chose twelve regiments from Russell's and Neill's divisions, totalling nearly 5,000 men, with Colonel Emory Upton of Russell's 2nd Brigade in command. Upton was 25 years old and only three years out of West Point. But he had led his brigade since Gettysburg and had proven himself a brilliant fighter the previous November at Rappahannock Station. Upton took the twelve regimental commanders through the woods to the end of the path to study the Rebel position and the approaches to it, then gave them the details of his plan. The men were to be brought forward along the path and formed on both sides of it in a dense formation, three regiments wide and four deep with only ten feet separating the four lines. After crossing the Confederate works, the front-line regiments were to turn to their left and right to take other Rebel units in flank. The second line was to halt at the works and fire to the front. The third was to lie down behind the second and wait for orders, and the fourth was to go only as far as the edge of the trees, lie down, and be ready for anything, including oblique movement to the left or right to protect the flanks of the other lines. The regiments were duly moved down the path and silently placed in their proper positions, then ordered to lie down and remain quiet. Some of them were told that they would be supported on their left by Mott's division.

Mott had extended pickets to his left until they finally connected with Burnside's force on the Fredericksburg Road, and he was under orders to support the 9th Corps if it was attacked. Then he was told, instead, that if the 9th Corps was attacked he should attack the Confederates in his own front. Then, at 2 p.m., he was told to attack in any case, as part of the general assault planned for 5 p.m. He informed Wright that so many of his men were tied up in the picket line connecting with Burnside that he would only have 1,200 to 1,500 men to attack with and he could not get the pickets back in time. He was told to attack anyway and have the pickets advance simultaneously from where they were. Mott's route of advance was to be due south through a large wood and then another 500 or 600 yards across open ground where his men would strike the Confederate field works 400 or 500 yards to the left of Upton's formation.

Thus Wright, brand new to corps command, had the almost impossible problem of coordinating two widely separated forces from different commands over unmapped terrain, one of which had to travel at least five times as far as the other. Meade made the difficult impossible when he let Warren attack early. At 3:45 p.m. he also ordered Wright to attack with his own troops and Mott's, but Upton's force was not yet ready. Then, when Warren's attack failed, the combined assault was rescheduled for 6 p.m. Evidently this word did reach Upton but did not reach Mott in time, and the latter started forward at 5 p.m. as originally planned. He had his 1st Brigade, under Colonel Robert McAllister, in the front line and his 2nd Brigade, under Colonel William Blaisdell, in a second line. Actually, most of the 2nd Brigade was in the picket line extending to the 9th Corps, and McAllister's was short the 6th New Jersey, which was sent ahead as skirmishers. However, the two regiments from the 6th Corps formed on McAllister's right.

Rebel pickets in the southern part of the woods fired on Mott's advancing skirmishers and then fell back into their works. The Confederate artillery waited until the Federals had reached a slight crest along which ran a lane to the Landrum house, and at a range of about a quarter-mile blasted them with cannister fire. Mott's entire force broke and ran in confusion for the cover of the trees. Most of the men did not stop until they reached their starting position, which Mott himself had never left. The 11th New Jersey, however, stayed to form a picket line in the southern edge of the woods.

One Union battery had also failed to get the word on the change of time and started firing on the Confederate works opposite Upton at 5 p.m. At six, two others, who had received the word, added their weight. Ten minutes later all three ceased fire, and Upton's massed infantry advanced. "I felt my gorge rise, and my stomach and intestines shrink together in a knot," one Federal recalled, "and a thousand things rushed through my mind."[4] When they emerged from the trees and saw the Rebel works, the men of the front line raised a cheer and rushed forward to open what a later British writer termed "one of the classic infantry attacks of military history."[5] In less than two minutes the first three regiments crossed the open ground without firing, as the Georgians of Dole's Brigade of Rodes' Division, caught by surprise, fired on them individually instead of by controlled volleys. Fire from the adjoining Stonewall Brigade was more effective and caused the Federals to crowd to their right. The first Yankees to climb up onto the breastworks were shot down, but others held their rifles over the works and fired downward into the defenders, while still others hurled over rifles with fixed bayonets like spears. Then they made a concerted rush and overpowered Dole's troops in brief, but bloody, hand-to-hand combat.

A large group of captured Georgians was sent back across the field and other Confederates farther up the line, thinking they were retreating Federals, fired into them. The men of Captain B. H. Smith's Virginia battery thought at first that they were counterattacking Rebels and cheered them on, but finally realized their mistake. In the heat of battle some of the Union regiments seem to have forgotten their special roles. Some of them continued straight ahead and captured a lightly defended second line of works about 75 yards beyond the first. Others turned to their right and began to fire into Smith's battery from the flank and rear. The four guns were captured by another advance, along with Smith and about 26 of his men. Also captured were six officers and 225 men of the 32nd North Carolina, the right-flank regiment of Daniel's Brigade, on Dole's left. Other Federals from the first and succeeding waves proceeded beyond the second defense line and turned left. They came in on the rear of the Stonewall Brigade's left flank, and their fire caused the 2nd Virginia to flee in confusion into some trees on its right, carrying the 33rd Virginia with it. Brigadier General James A. Walker, the brigade commander, rallied these men in the woods and brought the rest of his regiments to join them in firing on the Union breakthrough. The Federals stood their ground and fired back, but they had advanced as far as they could. Either through poor planning or poor execution, the rest of the 6th Corps, except the 65th New York of Russell's division, stayed in its own defenses and made no attempt to exploit Upton's success.

As soon as Lee learned of the Union breakthrough, he rode forward to rally those fugitives who were fleeing to the south, but his staff officers prevailed upon him not to go where he would be in danger. "Then you must see to it that the ground is recovered," he told them.[6] Colonel Taylor galloped into the heart of the fight while Lee found a nearby battery and ordered its commander to take his men forward to man the guns that he was sure would be recaptured soon. Another staff officer hurried away to what had been J. M. Jones' Brigade, now commanded by Colonel William Wichter. He ordered it to face left, move down the line abandoned by the Stonewall Brigade, and engage Upton's left flank. Maryland Steuart's Brigade, to the northeast, was ordered to face to the rear and move toward the threatened area but was stopped by Federal fire and lay down, ready to dispute any further Union advance. While Ewell was rallying Daniel's Brigade, south of the breakthrough, Battle's Brigade hurried past, formed line of battle and opened fire on Upton's force. Then Daniel's men began to advance toward Smith's guns.

The Federals had turned three of the guns around and were trying to fire them or spike them, either one, when Gordon's Rebel division, which had been in reserve, came up. Brigade commander R. D. Johnston found Ewell excitedly pulling on his moustache with both hands. "Charge them, General," Ewell told him. "Damn 'em, charge 'em!"[7] He did just that, and Upton's men began to give ground. When Smith's guns were recaptured, some of his gunners sprang up from their hiding place behind a traverse and swung them around again. They were joined by Lee's artillerymen, and two of the guns were soon firing cannister again. Upton's men clung to Dole's two lines of breastworks, however, and refused to budge. Upton rode back to bring up the three Vermont regiments in his fourth line but discovered they had already advanced. Without reinforcements, all he could do was hang on. This he did for another hour as darkness gathered. Finally he received orders to withdraw, and the men were brought out, although some of them had to be ordered twice. Lee told Ewell to prepare his men and his position for a possible renewal of the contest in the morning or even a night attack, and the 33rd Virginia spent most of the night cutting down small pine trees in front of the works, with which they built an abatis.

Upton had shown what could be done if the attackers got in close to the defenders' works in concentrated force and advanced quickly, not pausing to return fire until inside the defenses. He had lost about 1,000 men, but the Rebels had lost that many as prisoners alone. The men of the Army of the Potomac were beginning to appreciate Grant. They did not love him, but, although he marched them hard and fought them harder, they could see the man was not intimidated by Bobbie Lee. Some wounded men of the 5th Wisconsin were being carried past Grant, sitting on a fallen tree to write a dispatch, when an artillery shell exploded right in front of the general. He looked up for an instant, then, without the slightest change of expression, went on writing. One of the wounded men observed, "Ulysses don't scare worth a d—n."[8]

Grant had two reactions to the attack. One was to confer field promotions to brigadier general on Upton and on Colonel Sam Carroll. The other was a comment overheard by an orderly at headquarters: "A brigade today—we'll try a corps tomorrow."[9] Wright's reaction was to tell Meade, "General, I don't *want* Mott's troops on my left; they are not a support; I would rather have no troops there."[10]

That evening a Confederate band serenaded both armies with the hymn "Nearer, My God, to Thee." A Federal band answered with the "Dead March." The Rebel band then rendered "The Bonnie Blue Flag," which elicited a Rebel yell from the Southerners, and the Union musicians countered with "The Star Spangled Banner," after which it seemed to one listener that every man in the Army of the Potomac joined the following cheer. The Confederates brought the evening's performance to a close with "Home, Sweet Home," and this time both armies cheered together.

In southwestern Virginia that tenth of May Crook's column of Federal infantry left Dublin at first light for the railroad bridge over New River, eight miles to the east. By noon the 400-foot structure was ablaze and shortly thereafter it collapsed into the river in a great hiss of steam. Crook was supposed to join up with Averell's cavalry and move northeast through Lexington to meet Sigel at Staunton. But a Confederate dispatch that he had seen at the telegraph office in Dublin led him to change his plans. If Grant was retreating, as the message had indicated, the Rebels could divert forces from Lee's army to overwhelm all the subsidiary Federal columns in Virginia, including his own. Crook developed a strong desire to get back to the west side of the Allegheny Mountains "as rapidly as possible."[11] Not even word from Averell that he had found Saltville too well defended but was headed for Wytheville, after which he would catch up with Crook, could keep the latter from starting out right away. Meanwhile he sent word for Averell to proceed to the rendezvous with Sigel alone. Approaching Wytheville on the afternoon of 10 May, Averell found Confederates waiting in defensive formation at Crockett's Cove.

Brigadier General John Hunt Morgan was one of the South's most famous cavalrymen. He was a Kentuckian who was known for his daring behind-the-lines raids in Tennessee, and particularly from there into his native state. In the summer of 1863 he had gone even farther and crossed the Ohio River into southern Indiana and Ohio. That had caused a great commotion in the lower Midwest, but he and many of his men had eventually been captured and thrown into the Ohio Penitentiary. Morgan had escaped that November and had made his way to Confederate lines. He had been sent to the east Tennessee-southwestern Virginia area, where he had found about 1,000 men of his old command plus about 2,000 more in two other brigades of Kentucky cavalry. When word had reached him on 8 May of the approach of Crook and Averell he had been preparing for another foray into the Bluegrass state. Instead, he had sent his dismounted men, about 400, to reinforce Jenkins at Dublin and had taken the rest to confront Averell.

Not deceived by the latter's feint, he pressed on past Saltville and beat him to Wytheville, where he found Colonel George B. Crittenden with a detachment from Brigadier General W. E. "Grumble" Jones' Virginia cavalry brigade that had arrived the day before. Crittenden, a former major general who had been demoted for drunkenness in 1862, had taken an excellent defensive position and had beaten off one attack, but Morgan was not one to sit quietly and await his opponent's initiative. Morgan charged and charged, and eventually drove the Federals off to the east. "Averell fought his men elegantly," Morgan wrote to his wife, "tried time and time again to get them to charge, but our boys gave them no time to form."[12] While Averell rode on toward Dublin, Morgan turned back toward his headquarters at Abingdon to complete his plans for his raid.

On the night of 9 May, Butler, Gillmore, and Smith had met to make their plans for the next day. They had still not heard from Grant, so Butler was not yet ready to move on Richmond. Instead, he had decided to make another threat to Petersburg, this time with the hope of pushing the Rebels away from Swift Creek and destroying the railroad bridge there—maybe even getting at the bridge over the Appomattox. Moreover, orders had been sent to Hincks to again move on Petersburg from the south. If all went well, the Confederates might be so busy with the attack from the north that Hincks could walk right in, unopposed. After asking

Smith and Gillmore for further comments and receiving none, Butler had departed for Cobb's Hill.

As soon as Butler had gone, Gillmore had suggested an alternate plan to Smith. He had proposed that the Army of the James return to its base that night, tearing up more railroad on the way; build a pontoon bridge across the Appomattox at Cobb's Hill; and cross over the south bank. From there it could operate against the supply lines into Petersburg or against the city itself. Smith had agreed that Gillmore's plan was better than Butler's, and the two had written it out and sent it to headquarters. Meanwhile, at Cobb's Hill Butler had found messages from Secretary Stanton indicating, incorrectly, that Lee was retreating and that Grant was pursuing him to Richmond. At 9:30 p.m. Butler wrote to Hincks that good news from Grant made it necessary to change his plans. Then he received his subordinates' proposal. He replied, "Military affairs cannot be carried on, in my judgment, with this sort of vacillation."[13] He concluded with orders to withdraw the army from Swift Creek and to move toward Richmond, where he expected to meet the Army of the Potomac. Smith and Gillmore spent the early hours of the morning arguing about which corps should form the rear guard until Butler finally ruled that it would have to be the 10th Corps.

Down in Petersburg, just before 9 a.m., Beauregard stepped off his special train and finally took personal command of the situation. Right behind him came Wise's Virginia brigade, followed by Matt Ransom's. Terry's and Corse's were on the way. Robert Hoke arrived at 1:30 p.m. and Beauregard telegraphed Bragg to clarify the previous night's order for Hoke to move north against the Yankees with his whole force. As he knew it would take hours for an answer to arrive, he proceeded with his own plans in the meantime. He arranged for the forwarding of plenty of food and ammunition from Weldon, and directed Colonel James Dearing to assemble all available cavalry on the railroad to protect it and the supplies. While this was going on, Bushrod Johnson, up at Swift Creek, tried to find out what the Federals were up to.

The day began normally enough. Around 7 a.m. Union artillery shelled the railroad bridge in a futile attempt to destroy it. But as the day wore on, it became quiet. Several times the Confederate artillery fired on the Federal positions without drawing any return fire. Finally, Johnson sent a skirmish line forward and discovered Yankee pickets, but there were no signs of large enemy units. When Hagood sent over a flag of truce in an effort to recover his wounded and bury his dead, his emissaries were detained until the Federal withdrawal was completed, around 4 p.m.

The Union move had been hastened by alarming news from the 10th Corps units sent toward Chester Station the day before. Colonel Joshua

Howell had taken a blocking position with three regiments near Ware Bottom Church and had placed the 67th Ohio a mile away at the junction of the Richmond–Petersburg turnpike and the Bermuda Hundred–Chester Station road, supported by two guns. Troopers of the black cavalry units had screened to the north, toward Richmond. Late on the ninth the cavalry had been chased off and the Ohio regiment forced to fall back to avoid being outflanked by two Confederate regiments sent down by Robert Ransom.

At 5:15 a.m. on the tenth the Rebels advanced again, and soon the two regiments had grown to two brigades, Gracie's Alabamans and Barton's Virginians. Ransom was in a bad mood and picked several quarrels with Barton over the latter's handling of his forces. The Rebels pushed southward through heavily wooded terrain, extending from a loop of the James River on the east to the Bermuda Hundred–Chester Station road on the west. Then they began to meet stiffening resistance.

The 67th Ohio had been joined at dawn by two more Federal regiments and another pair of guns. Colonel Alvin Voris of the 67th Ohio was the senior officer in this ad hoc force. The other three regiments of Howell's brigade were still over a mile to the southeast, at Ware Bottom Church. Around 11 a.m. two of Barton's regiments moved down the Richmond–Petersburg turnpike and drove off several companies of the 169th New York, and captured one of the two guns of the 4th New Jersey battery. However, the colonel of the 38th Virginia was mortally wounded and his regiment lost its organization rushing through the trees. Then the advance stalled as rifle fire came in from Voris' other regiments and cannon fire from Howell's guns at Ware Bottom Church. To make matters worse, the woods caught on fire.

The right of Barton's Brigade was checked by cannister fire from two guns of the 1st Connecticut Light Battery. Just as these guns were running low on ammunition, they were reinforced by the other four guns of the battery, which had arrived with Brigadier General Alfred Terry. The latter had also brought Colonel Joseph Abbott with three more regiments of infantry. He dropped off the 7th New Hampshire to back up the gunners and sent the 6th and 7th Connecticut regiments up the turnpike, where they drove Barton's men back and recaptured the lost gun. After that the two sides pushed each other back and forth for a while through the burning woods. A Confederate effort to get around the Federal right was foiled by dismounted troopers of the 2nd U.S. Colored Cavalry supported by Battery D, 1st U.S. Artillery, and the mountain howitzers of the 1st New York Mounted Rifles. Thus Barton found his own flank threatened. When he got no reply to a message reporting this to Ransom, he went to find his commander in person. Ransom started another argument and sent him back to his command, but he ordered Gracie to extend to his right to protect Barton's left. Then he decided to withdraw both brigades. It was a fortunate decision, because more Union brigades soon arrived from Swift Creek, although their ranks were badly depleted by the 100-degree heat. A truce was called to allow attempts to rescue wounded men from the burning woods around the crossroads. Then at about 4:20 p.m. Gillmore ordered the Federals to fall back toward the Bermuda Hundred defenses.

At 3:30 p.m. Bragg, aware that Sheridan's cavalry was heading toward Richmond from the north, telegraphed Beauregard that Ransom had advanced but had found the Yankees too strong for his forces alone. "Let us know when you will be ready, that Ransom may co-operate. Every hour is now very important," he said. Later he added, "We are seriously threatened here from above. You should make a heavy demonstration and change to attack, if practicable, at an early hour in the morning."[14] Beauregard was not so easily rushed, however. At 7:15 p.m. he informed Bragg that he would be ready to advance by the evening of the 11th. He had put Wise, with his brigade, in charge of the city and the district. Terry's Brigade had arrived at Petersburg but two more were still on the way. Beauregard had organized his forces into two divisions, under Pickett and Hoke, but that evening Pickett collapsed from exhaustion.

----

1. Davis, *The Battle of New Market*, 57.
2. Trudeau, *Bloody Roads South*, 153.
3. Porter, *Campaigning With Grant*, 94.
4. Trudeau, *Bloody Roads South*, 159.
5. Matter, *If It Takes All Summer*, 162.
6. Freeman, *R. E. Lee*, 3:313.
7. Matter, *If It Takes All Summer*, 165.
8. Porter, *Campaigning With Grant*, 97.
9. Catton, *A Stillness At Appomattox*, 116.
10. Ibid.
11. Foote, *The Civil War*, 3:244.
12. Ibid., 246.
13. Robertson, *Back Door to Richmond*, 120–121.
14. Ibid., 128.

CHAPTER TWENTY-FOUR

"I Had Rather Die Than Be Whipped"

11–12 May 1864

On the morning of 11 May Grant ordered Meade and Burnside to send all available wagons back to the new base at Belle Plain for supplies, under escort of Ferrero's division of U.S. Colored Troops and Hammond's ad hoc cavalry brigade. Congressman Washburne was accompanying this force on his way back to Washington, and as he was about to ride off he asked Grant if he could carry any "encouragement" to Lincoln and Stanton. The general replied that he thought he was making fair progress, "but the campaign promises to be a long one, and I am particularly anxious not to say anything just now that might hold out false hopes to the people." After a pause he added, "I will write a letter to Halleck, as I generally communicate through him, giving the general situation, and you can take it with you."[1] He went into his tent, sat down, and wrote one of his most famous dispatches:

"We have now ended the sixth day of very heavy fighting. The result to this time is much in our favor. But our losses have been heavy, as well as those of the enemy. We have lost to this time eleven general officers killed, wounded and missing, and probably twenty thousand men. I think the loss of the enemy must be greater, we having taken over four thousand prisoners, whilst he has taken from us but few except a few stragglers. I am now sending back to Belle Plain all my wagons for a fresh supply of provisions and ammunition, and purpose to fight it out on this line if it takes all summer.

"The arrival of reinforcements here will be very encouraging to the men, and I hope they will be sent as fast as possible, and in as great numbers. My object in having them sent to Belle Plain was to use them as an escort to our supply trains. If it is more convenient to send them out by train to march from the railroad to Belle Plain or Fredericksburg, send them so.

"I am satisfied that the enemy are very shaky, and are only kept up to the mark by the greatest exertions on the part of their officers, and by keeping them entrenched in every position they take.

"Up to this time there is no indication of any portion of Lee's army being detached for the defense of Richmond."[2]

Much has been made of this message ever since it was first received in Washington. The phrase "fight it out on this line if it takes all summer" was picked up by the press as another example of Grant's tenacity, and became as popular as "unconditional surrender" had been after Fort Donelson. Some historians have held that Lee forced Grant to give up "this line" before the summer was half gone. That of course depends on what he meant by "this line." If he meant Lee's defensive lines around Spotsylvania, they were right. If he meant the line of advance from Culpeper to the James, they were wrong. In either case, Grant was over-optimistic about the casualties Lee had suffered and the state of Confederate morale. But then Lee was equally so about the damage he had done to the Federals, and before the day was out the latter's miscalculation would lead to an error that almost proved fatal to his army and his cause.

Washburne was gone, but Assistant Secretary Dana was still at Grant's headquarters. His reports became the basis of frequent War Department bulletins issued in the form of brief telegrams from Stanton to General John A. Dix in New York, who then released them to the Associated Press. The public was hungry for any word from the front, and the papers were eager to supply whatever they could find. That very day, 11 May, the *Washington Star* published a telegram sent home by Brigadier General Rufus Ingalls, quartermaster general of the Army of the Potomac and a West Point classmate of Grant. There had been heavy losses, he said, with constant fighting—a whole new tempo of warfare: "The world never heard of war before."[3] And yet the struggle was about to become even more intense.

Grant also received more dispatches from other fronts that day. "The general, after glancing over the reports hurriedly, stepped to the front of his tent, and read them aloud to the staff-officers, who had gathered about him, eager to learn the news from the cooperating armies," Horace Porter remembered. One of the dispatches was the one from Butler about entrenching, cutting the railroad, and whipping the forces under Hill. Evidently Butler had assumed that D. H. Hill was in command of the forces opposed to his. Another report was from Sheridan, describing the damage he had done to the Virginia Central Railroad. "The general-in-chief expressed himself as particularly pleased with destruction of the railroad in rear of Lee," Porter wrote, "as it would increase the difficulty of moving troops suddenly between Richmond and Spottsylvania for the purpose of reinforcing either of those points."[4]

Just before noon, Hancock was ordered to reconnoiter the army's right as far back as Todd's Tavern and across the Po, to make sure the Rebels were not up to anything in those areas. Hancock gave the assignment to Miles' brigade. Lee, meanwhile, had Heth's division moved back across the Block House Bridge to the vicinity of Spotsylvania Court House, where it formed on Wilcox's right, facing east. Mahone's division remained west of the bridge to protect the Confederate left. When word reached Lee of Miles' reconnaisance he at first assumed that Grant was trying to get around his left and ordered Early to move Mahone's Division, reinforced by two of Wilcox's brigades, to Shady Grove Church. Later Lee decided that Miles' moves were just a feint and cancelled Mahone's move. That afternoon, rain began to fall.

At 3 p.m. Grant ordered Meade to wait until dark and then to move Hancock's three divisions from the army's right flank behind Warren's and Wright's corps, to join Mott's division in the area around the Brown house. Hancock and Burnside would attack the next morning. Burnside received the order about 4 p.m. but evidently misunderstood what was wanted of him. He withdrew his troops to the northeast side of the Ni River and destroyed the bridge behind him. When Lieutenant Colonel Comstock of Grant's staff arrived late that afternoon to guide (and perhaps prod) Burnside to where Grant wanted him, Burnside's men had to cross back to the southwest side in a heavy thunderstorm. It took them until 10 p.m., but they met no opposition.

Union major general Thomas L. Crittenden arrived that evening to assume command of the 1st Division of Burnside's 9th Corps, which had been Stevenson's before he had been shot. This Crittenden was the younger brother of the Confederate colonel George B. Crittenden who had helped defeat Averell at Wytheville the day before. Their father had been Senator John J. Crittenden of Kentucky, leader of pre-war efforts to compromise the political differences between the North and South. It was typical of the divided loyalties of his home state that his two sons had chosen opposite sides when his efforts at compromise failed. The Federal Crittenden had been commander of the 21st Corps in Rosecrans' Army of the Cumberland, but he and his command had been among the forces routed at the battle of Chickamauga. Rosecrans had removed him from command before he too was removed, by Grant. After being exonerated by a court of inquiry, Crittenden was returned to duty, but in the meantime his corps had been consolidated with the old 20th to form the new 4th. He had been sent east for a second chance in a new setting.

"The result of the day's work on our front," Porter wrote of the Federals' activity, "was to discover more definitely the character of the salient in Lee's defenses on the right of his center. It was in the shape of a V with a flattened apex. The ground in front sloped down toward our position, and was in most places thickly wooded. There was a clearing, however, about four hundred yards in width immediately in front of the apex."[5]

At Spotsylvania Lee brought the art of field fortifications to a new peak. "With such intrenchments as these," wrote Humphreys, "having artillery throughout, with flank fire along their lines wherever practicable, and with the rifled muskets then in use, which were as effective at three hundred yards as the smooth-bore muskets at sixty yards, the strength of an army sustaining attack was more than quadrupled, provided they had force enough to man the intrenchments well. In fact there is scarcely any measure by which to gauge the increased strength thereby gained."[6] Lee, the engineer, had an outstanding eye for the natural advantages of ground, and his works blended into the land as if they were a part of nature. The V shape of his lines at Spotsylvania allowed him to move reinforcements from one flank to the other along a much shorter line than could the Federals on the outside of the V. The point, "the apex," due south of Mott's position at the Brown house, was the weak spot, and Lee knew it. But it covered some high ground that Ewell thought essential to keep out of Yankee hands, for Union artillery placed there might dominate the Confederate position. As a precaution, however, a reserve line was dug across the base of this salient, known to the Confederate troops, because of its shape, as "the mule shoe."

Between 4 and 5 p.m. Lee received two messages from the commander of one of his three cavalry divisions, W. H. F. Lee. This was his son, better known as Rooney and described as "too big to be a man and not big enough to be a horse." Rooney reported that a large train of Federal wagons was moving to Fredericksburg and that Burnside's forces had pulled back across the Ni. "There is evidently a general move going on," he concluded.[7] Putting this together with vague reports of Union withdrawals at various places and what he had taken as a feint by the Federals toward their own right, Lee came to the wrong conclusion. That evening he was at Harry Heth's headquarters, where he heard some of his officers disparaging Grant's generalship. "Gentlemen," Lee said, "I think that General Grant has managed his affairs remarkably well up to the present time." But then he turned to Heth and said, "My opinion is the enemy are preparing to retreat tonight to Fredericksburg. I wish you to have everything in readiness to pull out at a moment's notice, but do not disturb your artillery, until you commence moving. We must attack these people if they retreat." A. P. Hill was present, although still too sick to command his corps. He urged Lee to remain on the defensive: "Let them continue to attack our breastworks; we can stand that very well." Lee, however, did not agree. "This army cannot stand a siege," he said as he rose to leave. "We must end this business on the battlefield, not in a fortified position."[8]

Lee next went to Dick Ewell's headquarters, where he received further reports that the Federals were moving guns and wagons away from the front. He told his 2nd Corps commander to withdraw from his defenses, but Ewell suggested that the men would rest better in their trenches where they had some shelter against the rain, and Lee agreed. He wanted the artillery withdrawn that night, however, because it would take longer to move it.

The eleventh of May was another hot day in southeastern Virginia, with temperatures reaching the high nineties. Butler gave his men a day of rest in the entrenchments. He wanted to "put the lines in the best possible order to be held with a small force," and they needed more work. He also wanted to give Kautz a chance to rest his horses and troopers before sending them out on another raid. "We shall demonstrate toward Richmond tomorrow," Butler told his wife. "I have now done all I agreed to do with Grant," he added.[9] At 9:30 p.m. he issued his orders for the next day's advance. Smith would take his own two divisions and one of Gillmore's north along the turnpike and attempt to outflank the Confederates, while Gillmore and his other two would protect the rear against interference from Petersburg and form a reserve. Kautz was to take his cavalry westward to raid the Richmond & Danville Railroad, the only supply line to the Confederate capital from the south which did not pass through Petersburg. Hincks, meanwhile, was to establish another fortified toehold on the south side of the Appomattox, this time just across from Cobb's Hill.

Down in Petersburg around 3 a.m. that day Beauregard received a telegram from Bragg ordering him to send Hoke northward with all available units for a junction with Robert Ransom's forces at Drewry's Bluff as soon as possible. At 7 a.m. Beauregard wired Bragg that they were on the way, although it would actually be another three hours before the troops began to move. He had put Brigadier General Matt Ransom, Robert Ransom's older brother, in charge of the ad hoc division which he had originally intended for Pickett. The older Ransom and Hoke each had three infantry brigades, four batteries of light artillery, and one company of cavalry. Hoke was due to receive a fourth brigade, Clingman's, as soon as it could be relieved in the Petersburg defenses by some of Wise's regiments. Colquitt's Brigade, just in from Charleston, would also be held at Petersburg as a reserve. One more brigade was still to come. Beauregard wired his old friend Major General Chase Whiting at Wilmington, North Carolina to come up to Petersburg as well, and Dearing was also to bring the cavalry brigade to that point.

At 10 a.m. Hoke's Division stepped off with orders to make a forced reconnaissance toward Bermuda Hundred on its way to Drewry's Bluff. If the Yankees were found to be returning to their boats, he was to attack; but when informed of this, the War Department objected. At 1 p.m. another wire from Secretary of War Seddon showed that Richmond was getting nervous, what with Sheridan pounding down from the north and Butler stirring around to the south: "This city is in hot danger. It should be defended with all our resources to the sacrifice of minor considerations. You are relied on to use every effort to unite all your forces at the earliest practicable time with the troops in our defenses, and then together either fight the enemy in the field or defend the intrenchments."[10] But not long afterwards he received a message from Bragg authorizing Hoke's reconnaissance after all. To Seddon, Beauregard replied, "If my course be not approved by the War Department I wish to be relieved at once." To Bragg he said, "I must insist on receiving orders only from one source, and that from the general commanding."[11] Seddon was conciliatory, but Beauregard was not easily mollified. At 5:15 p.m. he wired Jefferson Davis a report on the entire affair, saying that he would not leave Petersburg until his last two brigades arrived and asking if this course was approved by the president.

The nervousness in Richmond was due more to the approach of Sheridan than that of Butler. Robert Ransom spent the day worrying about whether he should stay at Drewry's Bluff or return to the defenses on the north side of the James. He sent Hunton's Brigade north early that morning. When he heard that Hoke was marching to join him he requested Hunton's return, but his request was refused.

A violent thunderstorm was building up on the western horizon as Hoke arrived at Drewry's Bluff about 5 p.m., but his men were strung out along the road behind him. He reported that Federals had moved in behind him and that Beauregard and his other troops might find it difficult to follow. Just before dark the storm broke over the area, and during the night Gracie's Alabamans marched through the rain and lightning for Richmond while Ransom's and Hoke's men tried to get some sleep on the wet ground.

As Sheridan's cavalry proceeded at an unhurried pace toward Richmond, Jeb Stuart moved to intercept it. On the tenth he had split his pursuing force, leaving Gordon's Brigade of North Carolina cavalry to follow the Yankees and harass them while he took Fitzhugh Lee's Division by a different route to try to head them off. He pushed his men, his horses, and himself hard in order to be the first to arrive at a crossroads six miles north of Richmond, known for a nearby hostelry as Yellow Tavern, where his route and Sheridan's would meet. And he won the race, arriving at about 10 a.m. on the eleventh. Stuart was tired and uncertain of what his best move would be. He sent a staff officer to Richmond to confer with Bragg. Meanwhile he arrayed his ten guns and Fitz Lee's two brigades, dismounted, along a ridge in a position to threaten the flank of the Federals if they tried to push past him.

However, when the head of Sheridan's column, Colonel Gibbs' Reserve Brigade of Merritt's 1st Division, arrived at about 11 a.m., Stuart remained strangely passive. Perhaps he felt his men were too tired to do more than defend their position, or perhaps he himself was too tired to take the initiative. At any rate, while Gibbs' troopers felt out the Confederate position, the next brigade, Devin's, was ordered to explore to the south. One of his regiments, the 6th New York, got onto the road to Richmond, drove off a small group of Rebels, and pursued them all the way to the capital's defenses. Another of Devin's regiments, the 17th Pennsylvania, found the left flank of Stuart's line and attacked it, while the 5th and 6th Michigan of Custer's brigade attacked the 15th Virginia at the center of the Southern position. As a result, Lomax's Brigade was pushed back, and the road to Richmond was left wide open. Sheridan did not take it. He was more interested in defeating Stuart.

About 2 p.m. Stuart's staff officer returned from Richmond with word that Bragg had about 4,000 local defense troops and convalescents there, and had ordered up three brigades of veteran infantry from south of the James. With those troops and the garrison artillery, he thought he could hold the defenses of the city. Stuart felt relieved, and told his staff that he would hang on Sheridan's flank. If the Yankees attacked Richmond, or were attacked by Bragg, he would take the offensive.

As more Federals arrived, Custer was moved to the right of the Union line, with Chapman's brigade of Wilson's division to his left. Dismounted Rebels and a battery of guns began firing at Custer's men, and he ordered the 5th and 6th Michigan to dismount and drive the Confederates back. The colonel of the 5th, perhaps a little overeager to impress Sheridan, who was nearby, did not wait for the 6th to dismount before leading his men forward. When the 5th had advanced about 100 yards, a large number of Rebels appeared in the woods on its left and rear, catching the Federals in a killing crossfire. Custer spurred forward to rally the regiment, ordering the men to lie down while he conspicuously remained mounted. His dramatic courage inspired them to stay put. Soon the 6th Michigan caught up, and Custer put it on the 5th's left to deal with the flanking fire from among the trees. Then he led the two regiments forward and pressed the Confederates back to their main line on the ridge, halting his men in the edge of the woods while he went off to reconnoiter.

Those Rebel guns were doing considerable damage to Custer's other two regiments, the 1st and 7th Michigan, mounted and in reserve. Nineteen-year-old Lieutenant Asa B. Isham of the 7th felt sure that every shot those guns fired was aimed directly at him, and when a fragment from a near miss nicked his lower leg, he began to pray "that the relations of myself and the battery should be changed in some manner." Custer was already working on the problem. The guns were on a hill and well screened by surrounding trees but, Custer later reported, "from a personal examination of the ground I discovered that a successful charge might be made upon the battery of the enemy by keeping well to the right." He rode up to Merritt and announced, "I am going to charge that battery." Wesley Merritt, in temporary command of the 1st Division, was five years older than Custer but had been only one year ahead of him at West Point. He knew Custer had an uncanny eye for terrain. "Go in, General," he told him, "I will give you all the support in my power." Shortly after Custer rode back to his brigade, Sheridan joined Merritt and was told the plan. "Bully for Custer! I'll wait and see it," he replied.[12]

Custer picked his favorite saber regiment, the 1st Michigan, to make the charge. During the winter it had been recruited back up to about 1,000 men. Custer formed it in a column of squadrons covered by the woods on his right. Then he rode over to Chapman's brigade and searched out the 1st Vermont Cavalry, which had in the past been part of his own command. He told its colonel that he was going to charge those guns and asked if he wanted to come along. The colonel did, but Chapman objected. Custer appealed directly to Sheridan, however, and was told he could take any regiment that was willing to go, so he formed the Vermonters on his left, also in column of squadrons. Just before 4 p.m., the 5th and 6th Michigan pushed ahead on foot to draw the Rebels' attention, and the two mounted regiments on the flanks started forward at a walk.

Lieutenant Isham saw the 1st Michigan wheel into position "with beautiful precision," a 600-ton, "magnificent engine of warfare," and his fear of the Confederate guns suddenly turned to contempt. Custer placed himself at the regiment's head, with his colorful headquarters guidon flying and the brigade band blaring "Yankee Doodle." The column changed to a trot, and when it broke out of the cover of the trees the Southern guns swung to face it, firing exploding shells and cannisters of iron balls. Five times the Wolverines had to stop to clear fences out of the way, and then they had to file, three at a time, across a beat-up old bridge over a deep ditch and reform on the other side. This the Michiganders did as coolly as if on parade while the guns continued to fire—mostly too high. Finally, having come within 200 yards of the cannon, the Federals broke into a gallop with a terrifying yell and overran the battery, sabering the gunners and their supports. They were soon joined by the 5th and 6th Michigan, the 1st Vermont, and the rest of Chapman's brigade, while the remainder of the 1st Division cheered them on. Sheridan told Merritt to send a staff officer to Custer with his personal compliments.

The Confederates fell back about 400 yards, chased by the Northerners, led by the 7th Michigan. The pursuit ran right by Jeb Stuart, who had come forward to rally his men. The 1st Virginia countercharged and drove the Federals back past Stuart again, and the general emptied his revolver at the Yankees as they went by. Some of the Federals returned the favor, firing at the Rebel officer in his conspicuous red-lined cape and yellow sash, and Stuart swayed in the saddle. He was led to the rear by a staff officer, in pain and in shock. It was found that he had been shot through the liver, and he was placed in an ambulance wagon. As it was driving away he saw some of his men streaming to the rear and he called out weakly, "Go back, go back! I had rather die than be whipped."[13] But he was whipped, and he would soon be dead as well, for his wound was fatal. While Custer and Chapman were driving Lomax back, Gibbs and Devin had charged Wickham, so Fitz Lee's entire division was driven from the field and retired across the north fork of the Chickahominy River four miles away. Meanwhile, Gregg's 2nd Division had repulsed an attack on the Union rear by Brigadier General James Gordon's North Carolinians, killing Gordon in the process.

The battle of Yellow Tavern was the first time the Union cavalry had

ever won a clear-cut, overwhelming victory over Jeb Stuart and a sizable
portion of his command. "The men were jubilant and enthusiastic over
what had been accomplished," wrote the historian of the 17th Pennsylvania. "It was the first opportunity the cavalry of the Army of the
Potomac had had to show what they could do under an efficient leader.
The praises of General Sheridan were on every lip."[14] The Federal troopers buried the dead, tended the wounded, cooked their supper, and rested
themselves while Sheridan contemplated his next move.

"I could capture Richmond, if I wanted, but I can't hold it," the Union
commander told one of his officers. "It isn't worth the men it would
cost."[15] Instead, he decided to march his command to Haxall's Landing
on the James River, across from the Bermuda Hundred peninsula, where
Butler could provide supplies. Wilson's 3rd Division took the lead at 11
p.m. in extreme darkness, amid pelting rain and howling thunder. During
the march a number of men and horses were wounded by what they
called "subterran torpedoes." These were land mines in the form of
buried cannon shells set to be exploded by trip wires stretched across the
road. Sheridan ordered captured Rebels to the front to find and remove
them, "their timid groping and shrinking being a curious and rather
entertaining sight," wrote the historian of the 1st New Jersey Cavalry. "A
lady . . . bewailed bitterly our barbarity in placing the torpedoes in her
cellar instead of leaving them to blow us up in the road; but her expostula-
tions had no effect upon our hardened natures."[16]

The rain ended before sunrise on the twelfth, but at daybreak the
Union column ran into artillery fire from heavy guns in the Richmond
defenses only 200 yards in its front. Wilson's guide had led him into a trap.
Sheridan realized that it would not be possible to pass safely between the
Chickahominy and the Rebel battery, so he ordered Custer to capture the
Meadow Bridge near Mechanicsville for a crossing to the north side of the
river. But the bridge was found to be destroyed and the far side of the river
to be held by Fitz Lee's dismounted cavalry and a couple of guns in a very
strong position. Meanwhile, Gordon's Rebel cavalry resumed its attacks
on Gregg's rear guard and barred any move to the west. Many of his men
and officers felt they were trapped, but not Sheridan, or so he later said.
Anyway, he sent Merritt's division to repair the bridge with orders to
make the crossing at all hazards.

Actually, although the main bridge was wrecked, there was a railroad
trestle nearby that was still standing. Horses could not cross it, but men
could. Without waiting for the rest of Merritt's division to arrive, Custer
sent the 5th and 6th Michigan to cross, dismounted. Under fire from the
Confederate guns, the 5th went across in small squads, scrambling for
handholds, while the 6th covered them with their Spencers. When the 5th

was across it began to skirmish with the Rebels while the 6th crossed. Custer stood watching from the south bank, his conversation with an officer of the 6th uninterrupted by a cannon shell that exploded in a nearby ditch, throwing mud over both. While the two regiments kept the Confederates busy, Merritt sent men forward to lay a floor across the trestle, using fence rails and boards torn from nearby houses. It took two hours, but when it was done Custer led the 7th Michigan, two of Devin's regiments, and two of Gibbs' across. The Southerners put up a good fight until the 5th Michigan got around on their left flank and enfiladed their line. Then the Rebels mounted up and took off so fast that the dismounted Federals could not catch them; but the 1st Michigan and two more of Gibbs' regiments were brought over, mounted, and pursued them for two miles. Sheridan told the colonel of the 5th Michigan, "Custer is the ablest man in the Cavalry Corps."[17]

While Custer and Merritt were securing the crossing, Wilson and Gregg beat off an attack by Confederate infantry and dismounted cavalry. It was not yet noon when the fighting ended. The Federals gathered in the wounded, buried the dead, grazed their horses, and caught a little rest. Some of them bought that day's issue of the *Richmond Inquirer* from a pair of enterprising newsboys who appeared on the scene. They were amused to read that they were surrounded and not a man should escape, and that General Bragg and President Davis themselves were leading the attack against them. Late that afternoon Sheridan took Wilson's and Gregg's divisions across the river and resumed his march for Haxall's Landing, destroying the bridge behind him.

Around 4 a.m. on 12 May, just as Wilson's column was running into the northern defenses of Richmond, Butler's advance got under way against its southern defenses. His purpose was not to capture the Confederate capital, he later said, but merely to keep the Rebels busy so that Kautz could slip away for a raid on the Richmond & Danville Railroad. Baldy Smith's leading division, Weitzel's, moved out westwards at dawn and immediately ran into Southern skirmishers, forcing the Northerners to deploy into battle formation. The rain continued to fall as they pushed ahead slowly. By 9 a.m. they had reached the Richmond–Petersburg turnpike and began to turn north toward Drewry's Bluff. At about that hour Kautz's troopers passed through the Union entrenchments, and as Smith formed Turner's division, borrowed from Gillmore, on Weitzel's right, facing north, the cavalry headed west toward Chester Station.

Smith's line was a mile and a half wide as it pressed forward through the dense underbrush in the pouring rain. Confederate skirmishers disputed every yard, but soon the Federals came to the battlefield of the tenth.

Charred corpses still lay where the forest fires had found them. Along the turnpike they saw signs that a large force of infantry had recently passed that way, headed north. In fact, although they could not know it, the tail of Hoke's column had passed only two hours before. Before long the Federals came to a small branch of Redwater Creek, about a mile from where they had turned north. There the Rebel skirmishers were joined by artillery that brought Smith's men to a halt. Weitzel sent to the rear for his own guns, but soon the Confederate battery withdrew, and the Northerners moved on. However, Smith now discovered that his eastern flank was uncovered, for the James River swung farther east from there on. He moved Turner and Weitzel to the right and brought two brigades of Brooks' division up on Weitzel's left, leaving only one brigade in reserve.

After advancing another mile through the wet woods, Smith's force came to a high ridge overlooking the swampy course of Proctor's Creek. On the other side of the valley were the skirmishers of Corse's Brigade and a couple of guns from the Washington Artillery. Half a mile farther north were more of Hoke's brigades. Matt Ransom's and Terry's were prepared to assist Corse, while Clingman's Brigade continued to march toward Drewry's Bluff, where Hagood's, Johnson's, and Lewis' had already gone. Smith took the time to make a personal reconnaissance and came to the conclusion that he needed more men, for the only way he could see to get across Proctor's Creek was to outflank the Rebels to the west. He asked for Kautz's cavalry but found that it was already out of reach. He then asked for more of the 10th Corps. Butler ordered Gillmore to bring up all the force he could spare.

Gillmore had already brought two brigades of Terry's division to the turnpike, in accordance with Butler's plan, although he had not thought to have them bring sufficient ammunition and rations to be able to do much marching or fighting. Now he was called on to march them north to join Smith. Brigadier General Adelbert Ames was left at Port Walthall Junction with a brigade and a half of his division to guard the army's rear and destroy more railroad. After a difficult march along the muddy turnpike, already turned into a quagmire by Hoke's and Smith's men, Gillmore's force got just beyond the Redwater before bivouacking for the night. Since Gillmore did not arrive in time for an attack to be made that day, Smith withdrew his men behind the crest of the ridge overlooking Proctor's Creek until morning. There they tried to improvise shelter from the unceasing rain. Many of them were denied permission to build fires, for their officers feared to give away their position.

Kautz's troopers had passed beyond Weitzel's left and proceeded to Chester Station. They found little there worth destroying and moved on another four miles to Chesterfield Court House. This time they found

and burned a few Confederate supplies and released some Union sympathizers from jail, then rode on another thirteen miles to the Richmond
& Danville Railroad at Coalfield Station, only ten miles southwest of
Richmond. The Federals arrived there at 11 p.m. and wrecked the telegraph office, the train station, wood-storage facilities, a water tank, six
railroad cars loaded with munitions, a tannery, and some of the track.
They could see the lights of Richmond in the distance. Kautz and his
officers considered the idea of continuing on to the Bellona Arsenal, only
four miles away on the south bank of the James, but from what they could
gather it was too well guarded for a quick raid. Colonel Spear suggested
setting the nearby coal pits on fire, but when told that such a fire would
be impossible to put out, Kautz decided against it and even ordered the
pits to be guarded until his column was gone.

Down in Petersburg on the twelfth, Beauregard finally received President Davis' approval of his course of action the day before. Around noon
the general had to deploy some of his remaining regiments at Swift Creek
to defend against a cavalry probe sent down by Ames, but it soon turned
back. Then Beauregard returned to his preparations for joining Hoke.
Robert Ransom had been ordered to return to Richmond on the morning
of the twelfth with two brigades so Gracie's Alabamans had marched
north during the night, and Barton's Virginians were sent by boat up the
James that morning. These were the troops who had skirmished with
Sheridan that day. Hoke was left in command at Drewry's Bluff, and he
spent most of the day deploying his forces in the fortifications there. That
afternoon he was ordered to send two more brigades to Richmond, so he
sent Terry's by land and his own former brigade, under Lewis, by water.
As word of Kautz's movements came in, he feared that the Federal cavalry
was trying to get behind him, but he told Bragg, "I shall fight them if met
from all sides."[18]

---

1. Porter, *Campaigning With Grant*, 98.
2. Catton, *Grant Takes Command*, 223.
3. Porter, *Campaigning With Grant*, 99.
4. Leech, *Reveille In Washington*, 321.
5. Ibid.
6. Andrew A. Humphreys, *The Virginia Campaign of '64* (New York, 1883),
   75–76.
7. Dowdey, *Lee's Last Campaign*, 199.
8. Trudeau, *Bloody Roads South*, 166.

9. Robertson, *Back Door To Richmond,* 139.

10. Ibid, 141.

11. Ibid.

12. All quotes in this paragraph from Urwin, *Custer Victorious,* 140.

13. Freeman, *Lee's Lieutenants,* 426.

14. Starr, *The Union Cavalry in the Civil War,* 107.

15. Ibid., 110.

16. Henry R. Pyne, *Ride To War* (New Brunswick, 1961), 201.

17. Urwin, *Custer Victorious,* 147.

18. Robertson, *Back Door To Richmond,* 146.

CHAPTER TWENTY-FIVE

"Push The Enemy With All Your Might"

12 May 1864

In the midnight darkness of 11–12 May Confederate pickets, posted in the drizzling rain beyond the apex of Lee's salient, reported that they could hear a steady rumbling in the distance. Two of Maryland Steuart's aides went out to listen for themselves and heard what they said sounded like the subdued roar of a distant waterfall. They concluded that the noise was caused by moving masses of troops. Either the Federals were making a flanking movement or massing for an attack. They woke up Steuart to report what they had heard, and he sent word to his division commander, Allegheny Johnson, that he expected to be attacked at daylight and requested the return of the artillery that had been withdrawn from the salient the previous afternoon. Johnson sent a staff officer to repeat all this to Ewell about 1 a.m. Ewell replied that the guns would be returned by 2 a.m., but it took until 3:30 a.m. for his courier even to find General Long, Ewell's chief of artillery. The battery horses were all unhitched and unharnessed and the men were asleep. It was unlikely that the guns could return to their position before dawn broke in less than an hour, but the Rebels worked desperately in the attempt.

Steuart's aides were right. The Federals were not retreating, as Lee had surmised to Heth. Through the rainy darkness and mud of the night of 11–12 May, while bands played to try to cover the noise, three tired divisions of Hancock's 2nd Corps moved from the right of the Union position to join Mott's 4th Division near the Brown house. However, nobody involved seemed to know exactly what was expected of them. It was vaguely understood that a general assault on the Confederate entrenchments was desired, but no one seemed to know much about those defenses, exactly where they were, or what lay between them and the Brown house. Barlow, whose 1st Division would head the assault, told the staff officers leading his column to the jump-off point that he hoped they would at least face his troops in the right direction so that they would not have to circle the earth to reach the Confederate works. Mott was no help, although he had been in the area for two days, but Barlow finally found a colonel in Mott's division who was able to give him a generalized description of the ground, and the information that the distance to the Rebel position was something less than a mile.

Barlow formed his division for the attack facing southeast behind a small tributary of the Ni River. He placed his four brigades in an almost-solid mass, about 300 men wide and twenty deep, with the 2nd Delaware positioned to protect the left flank. To Barlow's right, Birney formed his two brigades, one behind the other, in normal line formation. Mott's two brigades were formed behind Birney's, and Gibbon's division brought up the rear as a reserve. Birney's troops faced the swampy woods that Mott's men had traversed on the tenth, but Barlow's had a corridor of open ground to their front. Meanwhile, Wright had ordered Neill's and Russell's divisions withdrawn from the front line while Ricketts' smaller division took over all of the 6th Corps' defenses. Warren was told to extend his 5th Corps to fill Hancock's former entrenchments as well as his own.

As the air temperature dropped during the night and the rain continued to fall intermittently on the relatively warm earth, a ground fog began to form, and visibility soon decreased to less than fifty feet. The attack was scheduled for 4 a.m., but because of the poor visibility, Hancock waited. At 4:30 a.m. he ordered the advance to begin in five minutes. The men stepped off exactly on schedule with their bayonets fixed and their rifles on their right shoulders. Pioneers with axes accompanied the front line, and the 66th New York, deployed as skirmishers, preceded the main force by about thirty yards. The Federals crossed the small stream and ascended the hill on the south side, where they overwhelmed an advanced line of Rebel pickets before they could either fire or run. The attack continued on over the hill and encountered fire from more pickets to the east. Hancock ordered Gibbon to support Barlow's left, so he sent Owen's and Carroll's brigades, keeping Webb's in reserve. What was left of those pickets retreated to the southeast.

The Federal advance continued down the rear slope of the first hill and began to climb the next. The lane to the Landrum house ran along the crest of this hill, and the main line of Rebel pickets was stationed there. They managed to get off a few shots when the Federals appeared out of the fog, then they ran. The Northerners, thinking that the crest was the site of the main enemy line, raised a cheer and ran for the top of the hill, only to discover another open field on the downward slope stretching as far as they could see, which was then about 200 yards. The run had destroyed the small intervals between the units in Barlow's division so that it now constituted one great mass of men. Birney's troops had managed to keep pace on the right despite the marshy woods. One Confederate picket remembered seeing flocks of small birds and owls flying from the trees as if fleeing from a forest fire. Then the Federals in the front rank could see, at the limit of their visibility, a change in the color of the ground—turned earth—entrenchments! They were still about 200 yards out.

After he had been warned by Steuart, Allegheny Johnson alerted his other brigades and ordered them to be ready to resist an attack at dawn. Johnson also told John Gordon about his apprehensions. The latter, commanding Early's former division, was in corps reserve. He loaned Johnson what had been Pegram's Virginia brigade, now commanded by Colonel John S. Hoffman, and Johnson placed it in the second line of works, behind the Stonewall Brigade. This put it to the right of Gordon's old brigade, now commanded by Colonel Clement A. Evans. Gordon's other brigade, R. D. Johnston's, remained behind the reserve line at the base of the salient. In the main line, one half of the consolidated Louisiana brigade was stationed to each side of the Stonewall Brigade, and what had been Jones' Brigade, now under Colonel Witcher, was next on the right, beyond the apex of the salient, facing northeast. Then came Steuart's Brigade. Two of Witcher's regiments were in the process of exchanging places on the picket line when they heard the Federals' cheer. It sounded like the Yankees were nearby, but they could not see anything for the fog. So these two regiments also moved to the southeast, as had their advanced pickets, leaving only two regiments to man the brigade's sector of the main line. Altogether, there were still about 4,000 Confederates in the mule-shoe salient when Hancock's 20,000 or so struck it.

When Barlow's division came in sight of the Confederate works, its alignment was adjusted slightly to the left so that it would strike the Rebel line squarely. This meant that Brooke's 4th Brigade, on the left, would overlap the apex. It also opened a space between Barlow's right and Birney's left, and McAllister's brigade of Mott's division advanced into the gap. About 100 or 150 yards from the Confederate entrenchments the Northerners entered a slight depression at the foot of the slope up to the enemy works, just as a volley of cannon fire aimed at the ridge behind them passed over their heads. There the Federals encountered an abatis of small pine trees. The rear ranks pressed forward into those in the front while the pioneers used their axes, and the infantry their bare hands to clear the trees away. York's Louisianans, startled by a sound "like the roaring of a tempetuous sea," took aim at this mass of Yankees, but most of them found that their powder was too damp to fire.[1] By then the leading Federals had penetrated the abatis, and they charged up the slope, yelling in their excitement and enthusiasm. After a brief melee most of the Louisianans were captured. Union colonel Nelson A. Miles said he saw bayonet wounds there for the first time in three years of war.

Confederate captain William Carter's battery was the first of Ewell's artillery to return to the salient. His men managed to get one gun unlimbered at the very apex, and got off one round. Carter was helping his gunners reload when he heard an authoritative voice behind him order the firing to stop. He turned around and was astonished to see a large number of Yankees only a few yards away with rifles pointed in his direction. He surrendered his men and guns. By then thousands of Federals were pouring over the breastworks, and hundreds of Rebel prisoners were being herded to the rear. Northerners moved in force behind the Confederate lines in both directions while others continued straight down the salient. One Federal, probably a former millhand, jumped down between a couple of traverses and was heard to shout, "Look out, throw down your arms, we run this machine now."[2]

Brooke's brigade, and the two brigades Gibbon had sent to protect the Federal left, approached the front of the Rebel lines east of the apex at an angle, and were stopped by the fire of Steuart's and Witcher's men, but these defenders were also taken in rear by those who had broken through on York's front. "Come on, boys," yelled a Pennsylvania captain from the top of the Confederate defenses, "the last day of the Rebellion is here!" Major Robert Hunter of Allegheny Johnson's staff wrote: "I could see General Johnson with his cane striking at the enemy as they leaped over the works, and a sputtering fire swept up and down our line, many guns being damp. I found myself . . . in the midst of . . . a general melee in full blast . . . I came upon an artillery horse of Carter's battery, jumped on him, and sinking in my spurs, galloped to the rear, with bullets buzzing around me."[3] Steuart managed to turn the southern portion of his command to his left and rear to face this new menace, only to be overwhelmed by Yankees clambering over his works from the outside. More Southern guns were captured after firing only a few rounds each.

The three Federal brigades continued to follow the rear of the Rebel works down the eastern side of the salient. The regiments intermingled in a disorganized mass of men, eager to follow up their initial successes but steadily losing strength as some men escorted prisoners to the rear and others dropped out to loot the Confederate camps. They got behind the two regiments on the left of Brigadier General James H. Lane's North Carolina brigade of Wilcox's 3rd Corps division and captured many more prisoners before Lane could extricate the rest of his men. However, a charge by some fifty or sixty Rebels brought the disorganized Yankees up short, and Lane got five regiments in line behind some old works facing north to put an end to further Union advances on that face of the salient.

Birney's and McAllister's men and Webb's brigade of Gibbon's division had crossed the Confederate works just to the right of Barlow's division and captured almost all of York's Louisianans, and eight cannon. Most of these Federals then proceeded southwest down the western flank of the salient, gobbling up the Stonewall Brigade in bitter hand-to-hand combat. The other half of the combined Louisiana Brigade was next in line, and some of its members were also captured, but many got away by moving down the line and mingling with the next brigade, Brigadier General Junius Daniel's North Carolinians of Rodes' Division. Daniel had time to swing his two right-flank regiments back at a right angle to face the Federals. They had to stay low, however, because two Rebel batteries, on a low hill about fifty yards behind them, were firing cannister over their heads at the Yankees.

In less than an hour Hancock's corps had overrun most of Ewell's salient and captured the majority of Johnson's Division and twenty guns. Horace Porter recorded that at 5:30 a.m. an officer came galloping through the woods to bring Grant and Meade Hancock's first report, saying that he had captured the first line of works. He was followed closely by another, reporting that many prisoners had been taken. "That's the kind of news I like to hear," Grant said. "I had hoped that a bold dash at daylight would secure a large number of prisoners. Hancock is doing well."[4] Fifteen minutes later another officer reported that two Rebel generals had been captured. Grant passed this news to Burnside, telling him to "push on with all vigor."[5]

Gordon's standing orders had been to support either Rodes' or Johnson's division as required, and when he had heard the gunfire from the direction of the apex he had sent R. D. Johnston's brigade toward the sound. The four North Carolina regiments advanced rapidly over the empty reserve line, into the woods in the eastern half of the salient. Visibility there was only about ten or twenty yards, and the Confederates suddenly came across a mass of Yankees moving south. The Federals fired first, and the outnumbered Rebels fell back with heavy losses. The colonel of one of the regiments was killed, and General Johnston was wounded.

Gordon could tell by the sound of the firing that the Northerners were advancing down the east face of the salient. He sent an order to Evans to hurry his brigade from its position on the left side of the mule shoe to the McCoull house, near its center. He also sent an officer to find Hoffman's Brigade and send it, if possible, to the same place. When Evans reached the McCoull house he was told to send three of his regiments into the woods to the east, find the head of the Yankee advance, and delay it as long as he could to give Gordon time to form a line. The men of these three Georgia regiments fought desperately until almost surrounded, then those who were not forced to surrender broke for the rear. Meanwhile, as Federals approached the McCoull house from the northeast, Gordon had Evans withdraw his other three regiments.

Hoffman's Brigade had just arrived at the second-line position behind the Stonewall Brigade when the first shots of the Federal attack were heard. As the Virginians were getting used to their new surroundings, those near the left end of their line noticed a battery to their left swing its guns around and start firing obliquely to the rear of their brigade. The infantrymen yelled to them that they were firing into their own men, but the artillerymen ignored them and kept firing. Soon Gordon's staff officer came and led the brigade to the east, but when the Virginians saw the huge mass of Yankees that had taken Johnson's works, they turned around and moved back to the McCoull house. From there the guide pointed to the Harrison house, 600 yards to the south, beyond the reserve line, and they made their way to it as quickly as they could. There they found those three regiments of Evans' brigade forming behind a small stream, and also General R. E. Lee.

Lee had just finished breakfast and ridden forward to visit the front lines when he heard the first shots of Hancock's attack. He hurried on and soon came upon some of Johnson's infantry running from the salient. He removed his hat so that they would recognize him and shouted for them to stop and reform. Some of them did, but many of them had kept on going. Lee was near the reserve line across the base of the salient when Major Hunter of Johnson's staff came galloping out of the woods on his borrowed artillery horse and shouted to him, "General, the line is broken at the angle in General Johnson's front!"[6] Lee's expression changed and he told the major to ride with him to see General Gordon, who was in charge of the reserve. They arrived near the Harrison house just as Hoffman's brigade took position to the left of Evans' three regiments, and a few minutes later Gordon returned from the woods on the eastern side of the salient, where he had been trying to rally what was left of the other half of Evans' brigade. He spotted Lee and rode forward to report, saying that he intended to attack up the salient with Hoffman's and Evans' brigades.

Lee approved, and when Gordon turned away, Lee took position in front of the junction between the two brigades, with his hat still in his hand and staring impassively forward. Bullets were beginning to find this Confederate position now. In fact, one grazed Gordon's coat just inches from his spine. No doubt Gordon had heard of Lee's attempts to lead counterattacks in the Wilderness and against Upton two days before. The younger general rode out and tried to dissuade his commander from risking himself, but Lee ignored him. So Gordon called on his troops to help him, and the men began to shout, "General Lee to the rear; Lee to the rear! Go back, General Lee, we can't charge until you go back!" Gordon and some of his officers placed their horses between Lee and the enemy, and finally a sergeant came forward, took hold of Lee's reins, and led his horse to the rear. Then Gordon's voice rang out, "Forward! Guide right!"[7] Lee turned to Major Hunter and told him to collect the men of Johnson's division and report to General Gordon.

Gordon's two brigades moved to the northeast across the small stream and through a pine wood and approached the reserve works. Here they found a large number of Yankees, who opened fire upon them. Hoffman's Virginians, on the left, fired a return volley and charged forward with a Rebel yell. The Federals stood their ground and the two forces engaged in a bitter melee for about a minute before Hancock's men broke and ran. The Virginians chased them and came to the works on the east side of the mule shoe, originally manned by Steuart's Brigade. Two of Hoffman's regiments pursued the Federals across these works but quickly returned to occupy the defenses. The other two regiments came to Steuart's works about 350 yards south of the apex. There some Yankees put up a brief resistance before retreating to the north. The 13th Virginia followed them, flushing more Federals out of the traverses along the way until they were within 150 yards of the apex. There they were stopped by enemy fire. Hoffman's men recaptured four guns and two Confederate battle flags, and Union colonel Hiram L. Brown, commander of Barlow's 3rd Brigade, was taken prisoner.

Evans' three regiments had advanced on Hoffman's right, but once in the woods they lost their connection with Hoffman. The 61st Georgia, on the left of Evans' line, was overpowered by a large group of Federals near the reserve line, and 65 men and the unit's colors were captured. The rest fled to the west and were rallied by Lee near the west end of the reserve line. Evans' other two regiments took position to the south of Hoffman in the original works.

Ewell's staff officer and new son-in-law, Major Campbell Brown, out of touch with Ewell and Rodes, took it upon himself to send what was left of Doles' Brigade of Rodes' Division eastward across the salient. He then asked General Kershaw of the 1st Corps if he would also send some troops to the right. The general refused but offered to slide Wofford's and Humphreys' brigades northward to take over the sectors occupied by Battle and Ramseur along the southwest end of the mule shoe, so that the latter two could be moved. Ramseur, in fact, was already engaged. Rodes had sent him to help Daniel about 5:30 a.m. and to regain the western leg of the salient. Ramseur formed his men in a line facing north, extending out into the fields of the McCoull family. From there they fired on Hancock's men along the north side of the second line of the Confederate works which Hoffman had abandoned. Daniel's men on their left, however, were beginning to waver, so Ramseur ordered his brigade to charge. The Carolinians took many casualties from the fire of Birney's and Mott's troops sheltering behind the inner line of Rebel works, but they came on with a dash and a yell. The Federals fired one more volley and then fell back to the outside of the outer line of works. Ramseur was wounded in the arm, but Colonel Bryan Grimes took command and ordered the brigade forward again. The Northerners held their ground, and a bitter hand-to-hand struggle ensued. Eventually the Federals broke, ran back across the clearing, and disappeared into the woods to the north. Ramseur's regiments reoccupied the entrenchments along the northwest face of the salient. There they were reinforced by Battle.

Most of the men Mahone's Division of Anderson's corps had spent the night near Shady Grove Church until they were recalled, but they reached Spotsylvania just a few minutes after the Federals had penetrated Ewell's salient. Brigadier General Abner Perrin's Alabama brigade was sent northward, and near the reserve line across the base of the mule shoe Perrin stopped and told his men to lie down while he conferred with Ewell, Rodes, and Gordon. One of Perrin's soldiers, Alfred Scott, watched this conference of generals and noted that Perrin was turning to each in turn as if begging for instructions. Ewell looked down and seemed to notice the Alabamans lying under his horse's hooves for the first time. He reminded them that it did not look good for them to lie down in the presence of the enemy. Scott jumped up and informed the general that the men had been ordered to do so. In that case, Ewell allowed, it was permissible. About then Gordon told Perrin that he would take the responsibility for ordering the latter's brigade into the salient. Perrin called his men to attention, rode to the front, and ordered the advance. His men moved forward with a yell just about a half-hour after Ramseur's counterattack. Almost immediately Perrin was shot out of the saddle with a mortal wound, but at least some of his troops went on as far as the inner line of works.

Just before 6 a.m. Hancock asked Meade to send the 6th Corps in on his right. Back came word that headquarters was pleased with his success and that Wright had been ordered to attack immediately. Hancock was urged to hold what he had and to press on if possible, and was informed that Burnside had attacked on schedule. Grant and Meade were discussing the situation at about 6:30 a.m., when "a horseman rode up wearing the uniform of a Confederate general," Horace Porter recorded. "Halting near the campfire, he dismounted and walked forward, saluting the group of Union officers as he approached. His clothing was covered with mud, and a hole had been torn in the crown of his felt hat, through which a tuft of hair protruded, looking like a Sioux chief's warlock. Meade looked at him attentively for a moment, and then stepped up to him, grasped him cordially by the hand, and cried, 'Why, how do you do, general?' and then turned to the general-in-chief and said, 'General Grant, this is General Johnson—Edward Johnson.'"[8]

Like most of his men, Allegheny Johnson had been taken prisoner. Hancock had provided him with a horse on which to make his way to the rear. "General Grant shook hands warmly with the distinguished prisoner," Porter continued, "and exclaimed, 'How do you do? It is a long time since we last met.' 'Yes,' replied Johnson; 'it is a great many years, and I had not expected to meet you under such circumstances.' 'It is one of the many sad fortunes of war,' answered General Grant, who offered the captured officer a cigar, and then picked up a camp-chair, placed it with his own hands near the fire, and added, 'Be seated, and we will do all in our power to make you as comfortable as possible.' Johnson sat down, and said in a voice and with a manner which showed that he was deeply touched by these manifestations of courtesy, 'Thank you, general, thank you; you are very kind.' He had been in the corps of cadets with General Meade, and had served in the Mexican war with General Grant, but they probably would not have recognized him if they had not already heard that he had been made a prisoner."[9]

Porter had also known Johnson before the war, and he introduced him to the rest of the staff. "After some pleasant conversation with Grant and Meade about old times and the strange chances of war, he bade us good-by, and started under escort for our base of supplies," Porter recalled. "General George H. Steuart was also captured, but was not sent in to general headquarters on account of a scene which had been brought about by an unseemly exhibition of temper on his part. Hancock had known him in the old army, and in his usual frank way went up to him, greeted him kindly, and offered his hand. Steuart drew back, rejected the offer, and said rather haughtily, 'Under the present circumstances, I must decline to take your hand.' Hancock, who was somewhat nettled by this remark, replied, 'Under any other circumstances, general, I should not have offered it.' No further attempt was made to extend any courtesies to his prisoner, who was left to make his way to the rear on foot with the others who had been captured."[10]

While Meade and Grant were talking with Johnson, a dispatch arrived from Hancock: "I have finished up Johnson, and am now going into Early [Gordon]." Porter related that, "General Grant passed this despatch around, but did not read it aloud, as usual, out of consideration for Johnson's feelings. Soon after came another report that Hancock had taken three thousand prisoners; then another that he had turned his captured guns upon the enemy and made a whole division prisoners, including the famous Stonewall Brigade. Burnside now reported that his right had lost its connection with Hancock's corps. General Grant sent him a brief, characteristic note in reply, saying, 'Push the enemy with all your might; that's the way to connect.' "[11]

At first Burnside thought he was supposed to attack down the Fredericksburg Road toward the courthouse, but Colonel Comstock of Grant's staff convinced him that he was supposed to go in farther to his right, against the east side of the mule shoe. There he was to connect with Hancock's left. At 4 a.m. Potter's division led the advance, with Crittenden's following, and Willcox's in reserve. The Provisional Brigade composed of two gunless heavy artillery regiments and one dismounted cavalry regiment, reinforced by the 60th Ohio from Willcox's division, was left to hold the works on the Fredericksburg Road. Potter reported that his two brigades captured two lines of detached rifle pits and a few prisoners. These were probably picket positions. Then the Federals advanced against the main Confederate line and captured part of it, and two guns.

On the right of Potter's line was the 9th New Hampshire, which was cheered on by some of Hancock's hard-pressed men. A 2nd Corps officer rode over and asked the 9th Corps regiment to face to its left and fire on some advancing Rebels. The officer was shot off his horse just after delivering his request, but the New Hampshiremen complied. Unfortunately for them, their powder was damp, and many of their rifles misfired. When a Southern force suddenly appeared out of the fog, a mere fifty yards to their front, a wicked firefight ensued. Then as Confederates began working around their flank the Federals withdrew to some woods to the east, where they found the rest of their brigade. The regiment had lost over 200 of its 500 men in that brief fight. Meanwhile the 2nd Corps troops with whom they had connected had retreated to the north. At 7 a.m. Comstock used a portable field telegraph to notify Grant that the connection between Burnside and Hancock had been broken.

Near the center of Potter's line, the 17th Vermont took position on a knoll. From there they looked down on some Rebels in a swampy ravine about 150 yards away. For more than two hours they fired on these Southerners, whose only retreat led through open terrain. Just as the Vermonters fired off the last of their ammunition they were replaced by the 48th Pennsylvania. While the two regiments were changing places about fifty Confederates ran forward and surrendered. They were from Evans' Brigade. The 48th's commander, Lieutenant Colonel Henry Pleasants, advanced his men to within 75 yards of the ravine, from where they opened fire. Another 200 Rebels threw down their muskets and surrendered. On the left of Potter's line as the 36th Massachusetts advanced it received a volley from some Confederates in woods up ahead, who then retired to the south, threatening the Union left. Three companies of the 36th were turned to face in that direction, and the Rebels withdrew farther south.

Potter's Federals were about to assault the main enemy position to the west when word of Hancock's success came down the line. As this information was being digested, a large number of Rebels were seen marching south between the Northerners and the salient. Potter's skirmishers fired on these Confederates, but they kept on marching. Someone said that they were Hancock's prisoners moving to the rear, but then word came from those three companies on the left flank that the Southerners were forming line facing north and threatening the Federals' left. The Massachusetts captain in charge of the three companies on the left flank went toward the Confederates, waving his sword and advising them to surrender. He was very close to their front rank when they suddenly raised their rifles and fired. Miraculously unscathed, the captain returned to his three companies and ordered them to return the fire. Thereupon the Confederates charged, but were, with some difficulty, beaten off. The 21st Massachusetts of Crittenden's division came up and joined the 36th in a charge, and the Rebels were driven into their entrenchments at about the time that Gordon's counterattack cleared Hancock's men out of the eastern face of the salient. Potter's men fell back and started digging rifle pits.

Comstock continued to telegraph reports to Grant and to urge and advise Burnside. The latter finally snapped back that he would command his own divisions but apologized ten minutes later. Comstock concluded that the general was unfit for corps command. At one point Grant admonished Burnside to "see that your orders are executed."[12] This caused Burnside to accuse Comstock of complaining to Grant, which the colonel denied.

Just after 6 a.m. Wright had been ordered to advance Neill's and Ricketts' divisions on Hancock's right. Neill's 2nd Division had been in a field to the northwest of the Brown house since about the time that Hancock's attack had stepped off. Wright's staff officer found Colonel Oliver Edwards' 4th Brigade of Neill's division ready to advance and ordered it forward. The brigade, which was down to 900 men in three regiments because one had been left on picket duty in the division's old entrenchments, moved south through the trees and across the Landrum lane ridge, and at about 6:30 a.m. arrived at a segment of the Confederate works that would soon be known as the Bloody Angle. This was not the actual apex of the salient but an area about 300 yards west of it, where there were two bends in the line: the eastern one, of about ten degrees, marked by an oak tree just inside the entrenchments and the other one, of about twenty degrees, about 55 yards farther west. North of the breastworks was a small valley in the Landrums' field that ran at an angle with the works. It was only thirty yards from the entrenchments opposite the oak tree but ran nearly 100 yards to the northeast before curving south almost to the works, about seventy yards east of the oak.

When Edwards' brigade deployed along the outside of the Confederate works, Brewster's Excelsior Brigade of Mott's division was on its right,

but there were no Rebels closer than Ramseur's men, who were farther
down the works. That condition soon changed as some of Perrin's men
came charging out of the woods to the south. However, their attack was
beaten off with the help of oblique fire from Mott's men. Soon Bidwell's
3rd Brigade came up to support Edwards from 100 yards back, and
Wheaton's 1st Brigade came up on Bidwell's right. The remaining brigade
of Neill's division, Colonel L. A. Grant's 2nd, was sent to the left to
relieve Barlow's division in the front line. As these Vermonters advanced
they were struck by Southern artillery fire from the reserve line. Wright
was wounded by a shell from the same source, but he did not relinquish
command. Colonel Grant's men formed in two lines on the north side of
the Rebel works, with skirmishers on the south side. To their right some
of Birney's and Gibbon's men were fighting off an attack, probably from
some of Perrin's men. About 7:30 a.m. the Excelsior Brigade saw a force
of Rebels marching toward them in column through a hail of artillery fire
from guns that Hancock had positioned along the Landrum lane ridge.
The Federal infantry stopped firing on Ramseur's men down the west
flank of the entrenchments and prepared to meet this new threat. Wright
sent off a request for help to Meade, who ordered Warren both to attack
on his own front and to send help to Wright.

These new Confederates were the 800 Mississippians of Brigadier General Nate Harris' brigade of Mahone's Division. Colonel Venable of Lee's
staff had found them taking a short break near the Block House Bridge on
their way back from their sojourn west of the Po, and had sent them
northward. Near the Harrison house, south of the reserve line, Harris
and Venable were joined by Lee. The commanding general's gray horse,
Traveller, was excited by the firing. Once it reared just as a bouncing, 12-
pound solid shot from a Union cannon passed under it, barely missing
Lee's foot. "Go back, General," the Mississippians pleaded, "Go back!
For God's sake, go back!" Lee answered, "If you will promise me to drive
those people from our works, I will go back."[13] The men promised with
loud shouts, and Lee directed Venable to guide the brigade to General
Rodes, who had been calling for help. Venable found Rodes just northeast
of the McCoull house, and as the two were talking a courier brought
word from Ramseur that he could not hold on much longer. Rodes
immediately ordered Harris' brigade forward to connect with Ramseur's
right.

The Federals fired a volley that stopped Harris' column when it was
around sixty yards south of the second line of works. Harris had not been
briefed on the lay of the land, and the staff officer provided by Rodes had
bolted for the rear at the first volley. Harris learned the location of

Ramseur's right, and of the Federals, from a private from Perrin's Brigade. He decided to file his regiments off to the right and to face them to the north in line for an advance on the outer works. But as they began this move the Excelsior Brigade and Edwards' troops poured a killing fire into them, which broke up the deployment. Harris therefore ordered two of his regiments to face left and charge the works. They did so with heavy losses, including both colonels, but two or three hundred Yankees were captured behind the second line and in the traverses of the first. Harris' Brigade then came to grips with Mott's two brigades and drove them back in hand-to-hand combat. Edwards' troops still held on to the area around the two angles, but some of Ramseur's men crossed the entrenchments taken from Mott's division and entered the trees 100 yards north. From there they opened an enfilading fire on Edwards' right regiment, the 10th Massachusetts, which was running out of ammunition, and drove it too from the works. It fell back to a slight knoll to the rear of Edwards' 2nd Rhode Island, which swung back its right to connect with it.

This action caused Wright to ask Hancock for help. The latter sent Brooke, who had been able to reassemble about 1,000 men of his brigade near the Landrum house and replenish their ammunition after they and the rest of Barlow's division had been replaced at the Confederate works by Colonel Grant's brigade. With orders from Hancock not to become engaged except as a last resort, Brooke led his men west along the Landrum house lane, then south to arrive in rear of Wheaton's brigade about 9 a.m. They lay down behind Wheaton's two lines, which were lying prone behind their own skirmish line.

Also about 9 a.m. the Confederate general Wilcox ordered McGowan's South Carolina brigade, located on the east leg of the V of works, just north of the Fredericksburg Road, to move north to help Ewell. Near the McCoull house McGowan formed his regiments into line, then they advanced to within fifty yards of the inner line of works. There McGowan received a serious arm wound and his senior colonel was mortally wounded. Colonel Joseph N. Brown was now the senior officer but did not know it. Lieutenant Colonel Isaac F. Hunt, commander of one of the regiments, uncertain whether or not Brown was alive, ordered all four regiments to advance against the Yankees in the main line. The brigade ran forward through the smoke, rain, and mud and came up behind Harris' Mississippians, who were desperately trying to fight off a Union attack on their position. The Carolinians moved in on Harris' right and occupied the trench behind the main breastworks, which was ankle-deep in water. There were no other Confederates east of them as far as they could see, but there were plenty of Yankees on the north side of the breastworks over there.

Pretty soon some of those Federals crossed to the south side of the works, but Hunt positioned some of his men in an empty artillery emplacement to his right rear, and their fire checked that enemy movement. Eventually Hunt got word to Colonel Brown that he should assume command of the brigade. Brown joined Hunt near the west angle and realized that his line from that point east had to be held at all hazards. Only his brigade's presence on their flank was keeping the Federals from moving on to the south, past his right. Brown stationed Hunt near the left of the brigade to shift troops periodically to the right as replacements for casualties, which were bound to be heaviest at the end of the line. Brown would stay near the right where he could keep an eye on the Yankees. He did not know it then, but he would be there for seventeen hours. The two-acre area that included the west angle in the Confederate fortifications and the ground to its north and northeast was to become the site of the most prolonged, intense, close-range fighting that had ever been seen in American history.

1. Trudeau, *Bloody Roads South*, 172.
2. Matter, *If It Takes All Summer*, 195.
3. Trudeau, *Bloody Roads South*, 173.
4. Porter, *Campaigning With Grant*, 103.
5. Ibid., 102.
6. Freeman, *R. E. Lee*, 3:317.
7. Ibid., 3:318.
8. Porter, *Campaigning With Grant*, 103–104.
9. Ibid., 104.
10. Ibid., 104–105.
11. Ibid., 105.
12. Matter, *If It Takes All Summer*, 226.
13. Freeman, *R. E. Lee*, 3:321.

CHAPTER TWENTY-SIX

The Bloody Angle

12 May 1864

Not long after Colonel L. A. Grant had arrived near the east angle to replace Barlow's disorganized division, Hancock ordered him to take his second line of regiments to reinforce the right of the 6th Corps, and promised to send the rest of his troops after him as soon as they could be replaced with some of his own men. Colonel Grant moved to the right and found Wheaton's brigade trying to advance through thick brush and small trees, under heavy rifle fire. But Wheaton's attack was soon called off. Colonel Grant left his 4th Vermont under Wheaton's command and moved the other two regiments to the area near the west angle, where he was joined by the rest of his units.

Russell's 1st Division of the 6th Corps arrived in the area between 9 and 9:30 a.m., and Upton's brigade moved forward to support the right flank of the 2nd Corps. Upton rode ahead to the slight crest just north of the west angle. From there he could see Union troops occupying the outside of the Confederate works as far to the southwest as the point at which his attack had penetrated two days before. He went back to bring up his lead regiment, but when he got it to the top of the crest he saw that all of the Federals southwest of the west angle had been driven back from the entrenchments. This was the result of the advance of Harris' and

McGowan's brigades. In the pouring rain Upton placed his men along the crest overlooking the small valley on the outside of the works and just to the right of Edwards' brigade and the west angle.

About 10 a.m., when his own right flank was bent back by Rebels in the woods beyond the works, General Wheaton ordered Colonel Brooke to advance his reformed 2nd Corps brigade to the front. Brooke pointed out that Hancock had specified that his men should only be used as a last resort, but Wheaton insisted. "I obeyed," Brooke reported, "passing over two lines of the Sixth Corps, which were lying on their bellies in my front, and reaching the front line relieved it."[1] In an hour of heavy firing, Brooke's men shot off all of their ammunition. Some of his sergeants crawled back to get more from the 6th Corps units behind them, but Brooke put a stop to that. Instead, he went to Wheaton and reported that his ammunition was used up and that someone else would have to take the front line. Wheaton sent some of his own units to the front, and Brooke withdrew his men to the left rear and went to report to Hancock.

Two regiments of Bidwell's brigade of Niell's division went forward to the northern edge of the works at the west angle but were soon driven back to the crest across the little valley. The rest of Bidwell's units were put on the right, in support of Upton. Brown's New Jersey Brigade of Russell's division arrived near the west angle at about 10 a.m. and stopped just in front of the part of the entrenchments held by the left of Harris' Mississippians and the right of Ramseur's North Carolinians. When the Federals came out of the woods north of the Rebel defenses they were struck by a volley and turned to their left, toward the west angle. As they ran across the open ground toward the entrenchments, Ramseur's men hit them with an enfilading fire that seemed to blow away the entire right wing of the 15th New Jersey. The brigade lost almost 200 men crossing that clearing but it pressed on, and many of the Federals, including what was left of the 15th, got into the works and captured a battle flag and some prisoners before being pushed out again, leaving another 150 casualties. They fell back to their starting place, through for the day.

The 6th Corps artillery had been left near the corps' original defensive works, firing at long range into the Confederate position. So when two of its infantry divisions moved up to support the 2nd Corps attack, the 6th Corps' chief of artillery borrowed a battery of six smoothbore 12-pounder Napoleons from Hancock. This was Battery C of the 5th U.S. Artillery. It was placed where it could fire solid iron balls into the salient at 1,000 yards range, but without being able to observe the effect of its fire it was probably only wasting ammunition. At Upton's repeated request this battery sent a two-gun section forward to a position on the crest to his right, a mere 300 yards from the Southern works. On the way forward several of the horses in the gun teams were shot and were dragged along by the others, while the wheels crushed the bodies of dead and wounded Federals.

The two cannon arrived just in time to help Upton beat off an attack by Harris' Mississippians with double charges of cannister. But Confederate rifle fire began to pick off the gunners, and so many horses were hit that the guns could not be limbered up. The crews had to abandon their pieces, and later the infantry helped drag the guns to safety by hand. The sponge bucket under one of the Napoleons was found to have 39 bullet holes in it. Each side tried to prevent the other from making any further advances with this murderous fire, the Northerners aiming at the top of the Confederate breastworks and the Rebels at the crest on the other side of the little valley.

At 7:30 a.m., in response to Wright's call for help, Warren sent Kitching's two oversized heavy artillery regiments and Bartlett's brigade of Griffin's division, minus a couple of regiments left on the skirmish line, toward the right of the 6th Corps. At 8 a.m. Grant and Meade told Warren to attack Anderson's entrenchments with as much force as possible, to keep the Confederate 1st Corps from sending help to Ewell. Warren answered that he had given the order, but complained that Meade had not given him a chance to first take out a couple of troublesome positions in the Rebel line. Warren had picked a bad time to complain. His reply reached Meade about the same time as word that Mott's troops had been driven away from the northern face of the entrenchments.

At 8:15 a.m. some of Griffin's men drove in the Confederate pickets on their front, and got to within fifty yards of the main line before the Rebels there opened fire. Most of the surviving Federals hit the ground, then broke for the rear a regiment at a time. Cutler's and Crawford's divisions edged forward but did not make contact with the main enemy line until later in the day. At 9:10 a.m. Warren asked to have Bartlett's brigade returned, but was refused. He also told the army commander, "My left cannot advance without a most destructive enfilade fire until the Sixth Corps has cleared its front. My right is close up to the enemy's works, and ordered to assault. The enemy's line here appears to be strongly held."[2] Meade's temper boiled over. Warren had already said that he was attacking an hour before. This message indicated that he still had not done so. Meade had Humphreys inform Warren that he was peremptorily ordered to attack immediately at all hazards. Humphreys softened the message with word that Bartlett's brigade would be returned to Griffin, and that since both Hancock and Wright said they were hard pressed Meade believed the Rebels could not be very strong in Warren's front.

"Don't hesitate to attack with the bayonet," the chief of staff told him. "Meade has assumed the responsibility and will take the consequences."[3]

Warren passed Meade's latest order on to his division commanders at 9:30 a.m. Colonel John Bratton, commanding a South Carolina brigade in Field's Division, saw Sweitzer's men of Griffin's division advance across the clearing toward his works in two lines. Confederate infantry and artillery fire soon drove them back, however. Some Federals took refuge behind irregularities of ground in the field but were later driven off by skirmishers sent out by Bratton. To Sweitzer's right, Ayres' regulars were driven back with heavy losses by DuBose's Georgia brigade. To Ayres' right, Cutler's division went forward in three double lines, with the Iron Brigade in front. These black-hatted Westerners advanced through a wooded area down one slope and started up another, where they soon ran into a belt of abatis. Before the Federals could do anything about that, General McIver Law's Alabamans opened a deadly fire on them, supported by Rebel artillery. The Iron Brigade did not break and run like the other Northerners had. Instead the Westerners stood their ground and returned the fire despite their disadvantage of being in the open while the Southerners were in elaborate entrenchments. Bragg's brigade of Pennsylvanians caught up, intermingled with the Iron Brigade, and added its fire, but officers of the two commands could not make their men stop firing and advance. Cutler sent word of this development to Warren at 10:40 a.m. Warren asked Cutler to put it in writing, for he was having more trouble with Meade. To Cutler's right, Crawford's Pennsylvania Reserves, with only days left in their enlistments, made no concerted effort to advance.

At 10:40 a.m. Grant told Meade, "If Warren fails to attack promptly, send Humphreys to command his corps, and relieve him."[4] Meade did not go that far, but he told Humphreys to supervise the shortening of the 5th Corps line and the forwarding of reinforcements from it to the other two corps. Around 11:25 a.m. Meade arrived at Hancock's headquarters, which were now at the Landrum house. From there the army commander could see the heavy fighting in progress a half-mile to the south, near the west angle. At midday Warren reported that Cutler's division was beginning to march to the left, and an hour later he asked if he should bring the rest of his corps also. A half-hour later Meade told Warren and Humphreys that Cutler should report to Wright, and Griffin to Hancock. Humphreys was to deploy Crawford's division, the Maryland Brigade, and the 5th Corps artillery in defense but be prepared to send even these to the left, if called for.

The Federal Willcox's division was the 9th Corps' reserve and had followed Potter's and Crittenden's divisions to the corps' right, meanwhile serving to protect their left flank. One of Willcox's regiments, the 79th New York, had not reenlisted and had been withdrawn from the line to get ready to return home. It was the first of many such losses to Grant's strength that spring and summer. At 10:20 a.m. Grant directed Burnside to send one division to help Hancock, and Willcox's started to make the move, but then the order was cancelled. Around 2 p.m. Willcox was ordered to attack to the left of Crittenden's position. Willcox replied that he expected to be attacked on his own left flank, but the order was repeated. So Willcox had his artillery positioned to the left and rear of his infantry, and when all was ready he ordered Colonel Hartranft's brigade to lead the advance.

Backed up by 33 pieces of artillery, Wilcox's and Heth's divisions of the Confederate 3rd Corps were holding the Confederate line from the southeast corner of the mule shoe south to Spotsylvania. Scales' and Thomas' brigades of Wilcox's Division were just returning from west of the Po River when the sound of Hancock's attack was heard to the north. Unsure of exactly where the battle was taking place, Wilcox sent the two brigades north to form in support of Lane's Brigade, which had been faced to the north behind an old line of works. The Yankees were just falling back from Lane's front. The Rebels chased them northward for 300 to 400 yards before being recalled by Wilcox. Then Lane's men were withdrawn to the rear to rest and the other two brigades were put in the trenches facing east. Just south of them was a bulge in the line known as Heth's salient.

After a rest, Lane's brigade was moved to the southeast face of this smaller salient to replace McGowan's Brigade, which had been withdrawn at about 9 a.m. The brigade's battalion of sharpshooters was sent out to reconnoiter the area to the east and found Union troops in line facing Heth's salient. The southeastern end of the Yankee line seemed to lie in some woods about four or five hundred yards east of the eastern face of the bulge. That, of course, was Willcox's division. Lane sent two regiments into the woods to the southeast of the visible enemy line to see whether it continued into these trees. It did not, so Lane brought his other three regiments into the woods also and formed for an attack. Just after 2 p.m. his men stepped off. Weisiger's brigade of Mahone's Division was supposed to follow them in support.

The Confederates drove a few skirmishers from the northern part of the woods, and when they came out into the open they found a dozen guns of the Union 9th Corps to their right front, only about 100 yards away. The Rebels faced slightly toward their right and advanced on these cannon, their rifle fire disabling all the gunners of the nearest two-gun section. The battery commander ordered his drivers forward to man those guns, and some infantry from the supporting 2nd Michigan, including Captain James Farrand, the acting regimental commander, also advanced to help. The rest of the Federal artillery opened on the Southerners with cannister, and other Union guns almost a half-mile to the east added their fire. Some of the Carolinians advanced to within twenty or thirty yards of the two nearest guns when the rest of the 2nd Michigan charged out of a ravine where it had been concealed, and the Confederates fell back into some trees to the west.

Lane's men then moved northwest in a disorganized mass through the wet, dark woods until they unexpectedly collided with the left of Hartranft's brigade, which was leading the Union Willcox's advance upon Heth's salient. Wild hand-to-hand combat broke out. The Rebels, despite their disarray, reacted more quickly than the Federals and surrounded and captured most of the 17th Michigan on Hartranft's left, although the colonel and 47 men managed to escape, bringing along a similar number of Confederate prisoners, including the colonel of the 37th North Carolina. Next the 51st Pennsylvania was routed with the loss of both of its flags. About 100 men of the 50th Pennsylvania of Willcox's other brigade, following Hartranft, were also captured. The 20th Michigan, also of the supporting brigade, made two left turns, charged back through Lane's disorganized men, and fought its way out to the east, taking and losing prisoners in the process. The 1st Michigan Sharpshooters and the 27th Michigan were pinned down behind a light breastwork of fence rails that had belonged to Southern skirmishers about fifty yards from the main line of Heth's salient. With both ends of their line enfiladed by Confederate fire and their ammunition running low, the two units finally received permission to withdraw, after repeated requests and the loss of over 300 men between them.

Lane claimed that Weisiger's brigade never advanced and that it fired on his from the rear. He sent a request to Weisiger that the latter bring his brigade up on his right so that together they could swing back toward their entrenchments, netting all the Federals in between on the way. Receiving no reply, and spotting what he said were two lines of Federals moving down from Ewell's position, Lane withdrew his troops into the Confederate defenses.

To Willcox's right, part of Crittenden's division advanced at about the same time. A couple of his regiments got to within fifty yards of the Rebel defenses in their front. From there they lay on the ground and fired at any Confederate that showed himself. But when they heard what happened to Willcox, they withdrew.

Lee wanted to try outflanking Burnside's corps from a bit farther south, using Weisinger's brigade plus Cooke's Brigade of Heth's Division, and possibly other units of the 3rd Corps. Lane's sharpshooter battalion was sent up the Fredericksburg Road and it found the terrain on both sides of the road to be very rugged. It also discovered at least one entrenched line of Yankees across the road, maybe more. This caused Lee to give up the idea but, at Early's urging, Weisinger and Cooke were sent up both sides of the road anyway. They crossed two unoccupied lines of entrenchments before encountering a third, stronger, line farther on, well manned by Burnside's Provisional Brigade. After taking a few casualties from artillery fire, the Rebels fell back. Later that afternoon the Provisional Brigade was permanently assigned to Crittenden's 1st Division, probably in an effort to make that officer's command measure up to his two-star rank.

Sometime that morning Lee had realized that his men could not drive the Yankees away from the northern end of the salient. But any attempt to withdraw his troops from the mule shoe before dark would be to invite disaster. He also needed to have a new line of entrenchments across its base. Part of one was already in existence: the reserve line which had been started by the engineers the day before. All that day, in the rain and with occasional artillery fire coming in, the engineers, the survivors of Allegheny Johnson's division, and perhaps also some artillerymen labored to complete the new defenses.

Meanwhile, near the east angle, Miles' and Brooke's brigades of Barlow's Federal 2nd Corps division were also busy constructing defenses. Unsure of what Burnside was doing, they were extending the line of the north face of the salient about 200 yards east of the apex, in order to protect Hancock's left flank. About noon, just as the rain finally began to ease a little, the 100 men still with the colors of the 26th Michigan of Miles' brigade were withdrawn from the construction work and, with some men of the 61st New York, they crawled along between Gibbon's, Birney's, and Edwards' men on the one side and the Confederate works on the other, unobserved by any Rebels. They stopped just before they were opposite the oak tree at the west angle, suddenly jumped to their feet, and fired a volley over the top of the works into Brown's men. Then some of the Federals climbed over the breastworks and fell among the Southerners with bayonets and clubbed muskets. More of Brown's men charged down the line from farther to the Confederate left and drove the Union troops back across the works, but that was not the end of the fight, only the beginning. The two forces then engaged a deadly firefight at point-blank range with only the breastworks to separate them by about twenty yards. To add to the carnage and the frenzy, a Federal battery near the Landrum house was firing shells with fuses cut so that they exploded just over the works, making them equally dangerous to both sides.

Around 2 p.m. Captain Nathan Church, acting commander of the 26th Michigan, saw a handkerchief being held aloft on a ramrod from within a traverse near the east end of the Rebel position. Then he saw other tokens of surrender a bit farther along the line. With considerable difficulty he got his men to stop firing, and some of them stood up, holding their rifles pointed down. When Colonel Brown saw that, he called on them to surrender, but a Union officer replied that he was waiting for the Rebels to surrender. They had raised a white flag, so his men had stopped firing. Brown said that he was in command and that if any white flag had been raised it had been without authority and that, if the Yankee officer did not come over to the Confederate side and surrender, his men would resume firing immediately. The Northern officer asked Brown for a conference, which was granted. While this rather heated parley was going on, another Federal officer climbed atop the works manned by the 12th South Carolina and, with sword in hand, announced that they had been surrendered by some unnamed Mississippi colonel. In reply, Colonel Thomas F. Clayton began to shout, "Shoot, men, shoot!" However, each cry was countered by Captain Cadwallader Jones, standing at his side, who shouted "Don't shoot! Don't shoot!"[5] Another Union officer approached Brown carrying a flag of truce and informed him that a white flag was being shown on the right of the Carolinian's position. Brown lost his temper and told this Yankee that if his commander did not surrender, firing would be resumed. The Federal officer started back to his own line but evidently failed to hold his flag of truce high enough, and was shot. Both sides immediately opened fire again. Similar incidents happened all up and down the line between Brown's and Church's men. Two or three other Northern officers were shot trying to convince the Confederates to surrender. Church's small force maintained its position until around 2:30 or 3 p.m., when it rejoined its brigade on the Union left.

A little to the west of the area where Church was fighting, four Federal brigades, Edwards', Upton's, Grant's, and McAllister's, were lying in the mud along the slight crest opposite the Rebel works. Both sides kept up a continuous fire to keep the other from charging. Some of the men of the 37th Massachusetts of Edwards' brigade were clinging to the north face of the entrenchments, firing under the head logs while Brown's South Carolinians were firing from the other side, and both parties thrust bayonets through these openings. Men on both sides would hold their rifles over the top of the works and fire blindly down on their enemies, sometimes having their weapons pulled from their hands, sometimes finding them-

selves pulled over and made prisoner or killed. Many of the Federals' rifle
barrels became so hot that they burst, others became so fouled with
burned gunpowder that they would no longer function. Edwards was
afraid to withdraw his men or even to have them replaced by some of the
2nd Corps units behind them because they would have to cross open
ground to their rear and be further exposed to the Confederate fire.
Instead he had one of the 2nd Corps regiments crawl forward under cover
of his own men's fire and exchange rifles with them. The 2nd Corps unit
then cleaned the fouled weapons and exchanged them back as needed.

To Edwards' right Bidwell's and Eustis' brigades moved forward and
became intermingled with Upton's. Edwards asked Eustis, the senior
officer, to bring them all forward from the crest to the outer face of the
Rebel works. But in the confusion and the intense firing a concerted
advance could not be organized. Groups would surge forward and be
driven back. Sometimes individual Federals, driven by desperation, or
madness, or frustration, would leap on top of the works and fire down
into Brown's and Harris' Confederates with their own muskets and those
passed up to them by comrades, until they were shot down themselves.
Many of the Union regiments fired off three or four hundred rounds per
man that day, five to ten times the normal load carried by infantrymen of
that era. Boxes of ammunition were brought up by pack mules to the rear
of the mass of troops and passed forward to the front line.

Hancock's artillery fired from positions along the Landrum house lane
all day. A few guns were sent forward to pour cannister into the area
between the two angles, and when they ran out of cannister they fired
solid shot and exploding shells—whatever they had—until finally pulled
back to the Landrum lane again. Some of the Rebel guns were turned
against their former owners by Federal infantrymen and by gunners sent
forward, until their ammunition was also fired off.

Around noon, Humphreys asked Wright if he knew of a point in the
Confederate line which might be attacked with success if the entire 5th
Corps were used. Wright replied that a large force might be able to break
through at the west angle, but it would require more troops than he had
available. Several times he told army headquarters that his men were hard
pressed to maintain their position. Between 2 and 2:30 p.m., Cutler's
division reached Wright, who used it not to spearhead another assault but
to relieve some of his units in the line. He was then given discretion to use
the other two 5th Corps divisions for an assault, but when he learned that
together they would only total about 5,000 men he told Humphreys that
he doubted this would be enough to ensure success, and that he feared a
Rebel counterattack. At 5:15 p.m., he finally informed headquarters that

he had decided against making the attack, "not that it might not succeed, but in view of the disaster which would possibly follow a failure."[6] An hour later Meade approved the decision. Griffin's division arrived north of the Landrum house after dark, and the Maryland Brigade was placed in reserve behind the 6th Corps.

About 4 p.m. the Rebel fire against Edwards' brigade slacked off a bit and he successfully withdrew his men about 25 or 30 yards, replacing them with some of the 2nd Corps troops nearby. He asked his division commander, Neill, for his exhausted men to be relieved, but instead he was told that they must not only hold their part of the line but also take over Upton's, so that the latter could be withdrawn as soon as it was dark. General Russell, commander of another division, sympathized with Edwards and told him that he would send him his own 10th New Jersey as a reinforcement and that, if Edwards had not been relieved by daylight, he would bring part of his division and relieve him personally.

Edwards sent Colonel Parsons of the 10th Massachusetts to lead the 10th New Jersey into position. Parsons led it forward after 5 p.m., beyond Upton's position on the crest and right to the outside of the Rebel works themselves. Edwards then ordered these newcomers to fire obliquely to their left to take some of the pressure off of his own sector. About 6 p.m. the 2nd Corps units in his front line had used up all their ammunition, so Edwards brought his own men to the front again. Just after that the regiment to Edwards' left fell back, saying they too were out of ammunition, so Edwards had to fill their position as well, even though he could only send men with empty muskets. When the commander of the 2nd Corps brigade to his rear also attempted to withdraw his men for lack of ammunition and rations, Edwards had had enough. While some of his men leveled their rifles at the officer, Edwards informed him that neither he nor any of his men were going anywhere until so ordered by higher authority.

The Confederate infantry of Harris' and Brown's brigades had the advantage of the cover of their entrenchments, whereas the Northerners were more exposed when firing, and especially when advancing. But the Rebels were badly outnumbered. And while they were protected by head logs over the firing slits when firing to their front, they lacked this cover when firing to the flank at Yankees to the east. They were pinned to their muddy trenches, and no one came to relieve them or to help them. Only ammunition was passed forward. The situation was in the hands of these 1,900 men—or what was left of them. Brown's right flank, where the Southern position ended, was the most critical point and where the highest casualties were being taken. As Brown called for replacements,

Hunt sent them from the left to take their places in the defenses to the right of the landmark oak tree. Hunt also called on Harris to sidle to his right to take up the slack in Brown's formation, and by late afternoon Hunt was sending Mississippians to the right to fight alongside the South Carolinians.

Whenever fifty or a hundred Federals would clamber over the breast-works, Rebels on each side would attack over the adjacent traverses while others moved along behind the trenches to come in from the rear, and in vicious, bloody, hand-to-hand combat would overpower the locally out-numbered Yankees until all had been killed, wounded, captured, or driven back over the works. Wounded men and the bodies of the dead lay in the muddy water at the bottom of the trenches and were often stepped on by those of both sides fighting around them. During the rare lulls, the Confederates would drag out the bodies of the dead to make room for the living. There was no time to provide care for the wounded.

Because Warren had not attacked since late morning, Lee decided he could afford to weaken his left to support the salient. Shortly before sunset he ordered R. H. Anderson to send two of his 1st Corps brigades as a reserve for the fighting in the area of the west angle. Anderson sent Humphreys' and Bratton's brigades, and they filed into position behind the reserve works and lay there, listening to the roar of musketry 600 yards to their front.

As darkness descended, Colonel Edwards had his men reduce their fire to see what the Confederates would do, but the Rebels maintained their heavy firing, so he ordered his men to resume. Both sides had been shooting at the same areas all day and, with the muzzle flashes of the other side's rifles to mark their positions, they continued to do so after dark. Men of the Iron Brigade, relative newcomers to the position on the crest opposite the Southern works, were standing in mud halfway up to their knees with bodies all around them, shooting at the top of the Confederate works until they were numb with fatigue. Their officers moved along the line to shake and shout at those who slumped to the ground, sound asleep amid the firing. Many of the officers were so tired themselves that they failed to notice that in many cases they were talking to dead men.

Lee's reputation as a devastating counterpuncher was his best defense that day. After approving of Wright's decision not to attack—itself brought on mostly by fear of counterattack—Grant and Meade sent out orders for the positions gained to be consolidated. Hancock was told to strengthen his defenses as much as possible and to maintain a reserve for use against any Confederate attack. Hancock had already notified Burnside that the connection between their two corps had been broken and expressed a fear that the Rebels might break through at that point. After dark, Wright asked for Warren's troops to relieve his own men at the west angle but was curtly informed that Warren's men had also been under fire all day and that Griffin's and Cutler's divisions had been sent to make an attack, not to replace Wright's forces. At any rate, the 5th Corps troops were needed to protect the 6th Corps' right flank. In fact, Meade wanted to know if Wright could shorten his own line. The 6th Corps commander replied that he could not because Hancock could not extend to his right. Wright claimed that he was unable to maintain his connection with the 2nd Corps without Cutler's men, and asked that he be allowed to keep them until he could readjust his lines in the night. Meade returned Griffin's division to Warren with orders to extend Wright's line of defense across the Brock Road at Alsop's. All three of Meade's corps commanders were told that no offensive actions were planned for the thirteenth and that they should be alert for possible Southern counterattacks. Grant told Burnside to strengthen his position, rest his men, and prepare to harass the Rebel position with artillery fire the next day. He must be sure his men were awake and ready to fight by 3:30 a.m. as it was expected that Lee would try to seize the initiative at dawn, and the 9th Corps was considered the most likely target.

Altogether, the Federals lost about 7,000 men that day, killed, wounded, and missing. Brigadier Generals Webb and Carroll were seriously wounded. An estimated 5,000 to 6,000 Confederates were lost, including 3,000 captured from Johnson's Division. Lee also lost 18 or 20 cannon, one major general, and seven brigadiers. Moreover, sometime during the battle word reached him that Jeb Stuart had died of the wound which he had received at Yellow Tavern.

On the Southern side, when darkness brought no relief from the pressure on his position, Colonel Brown sent Hunt to find some help for his exhausted men. First he went to the left, to Ramseur's Brigade, where he was told that the troops, although only under light fire from their right front, were required to hold their present position. After reporting this to Brown, Hunt wandered in the darkness down through the fields of the McCoull farm until he came upon Bratton's Brigade in the reserve line of defenses, but once again he was told that orders forbade these men from leaving their position. Hunt went back and reported this to Brown, who turned command of the brigade over to him and personally went in search of Harris. When he finally found him and the two conferred it was raining again. Harris sent a courier to the rear with a request for instructions, and

at last they received an order from Rodes for the two brigades to withdraw at 4 a.m., by which time the new line should be completed.

Between midnight and 2 a.m. the prominent oak tree near the west
angle fell crashing to the ground. Its trunk, with a diameter of approximately twenty inches, had been cut in half by Union bullets that overshot
the Confederate line. And still the firing continued, although it had
gradually decreased after midnight. Ramseur's Brigade fell back about 3
a.m. and at the appointed hour of 4 a.m., just before dawn, the dead-tired
men of Brown's and Harris' brigades slogged through the mud and
reassembled in a field a half-mile northwest of Spotsylvania Court House.
One half of Harris' men were dead or wounded, including the commanders of two of his regiments. Most of these casualties had been taken in
their advance and recapture of the works. In what had been McGowan's
Brigade the previous morning—now Brown's—451 men had been killed
or wounded out of the original 1,000 or 1,100. Brown's men had fought
for over eighteen hours, Harris' for almost twenty, without any food.
Their only water, beyond what little they had brought with them, had to
be scooped from the muddy puddles in their trenches. All the other
Confederate troops in the mule shoe salient were also withdrawn before
dawn to, or beyond, the new line which lay along a slight crest, well
south of the reserve line and three to five hundred yards northeast of the
Brock Road, which it roughly paralleled.

The Federals made no attempt to interfere with the withdrawing Rebels. Some of them crawled forward after daylight to have a look at the
abandoned trenches. In the area northeast of Brown's former positon lay
the bodies of Union soldiers who had been hit so many times in life and
death that they were literally shot to pieces. Most of them were impossible to identify. Captain Fred Sanburn of Upton's brigade found the body
of another captain from his regiment near the works. There was no space
wider than four inches on the body that had not been hit by a bullet, and
there were eleven bullet holes in the soles of his friend's shoes. A soldier
from the 20th Indiana wrote that the horses from one of the Union
batteries "were so shot that each was not over ten or twelve inches
thick."[7] There were many similar stories told by survivors of the battle.
But what was found outside the entrenchments was nothing to what was
seen inside. Dead bodies lay piled on each other, three and four deep in
places. Some had been trampled completely out of sight in the mud, and
wounded Rebels were found pinned under two or three dead men.
Veteran soldiers of the New Jersey Brigade, no strangers to the war's
carnage, became ill at the sight, but they recovered enough to drag
wounded Rebels from the bloody mud to drier ground. Colonel Edwards
saw a hand moving in the middle of a pile of dead Confederates, and when

the bodies were removed the hand was found to belong to a still-breathing Southern colonel with a broken leg.

A sergeant in the 149th Pennsylvania wrote home, "I cannot describe to you what I have seen so I will not try. If it should be my luck to come home, I can tell it you but I cannot write it . . . Kiss the boys, tell them that I think of them often and hope they may never see what I have."[8]

---

1. Matter, *If It Takes All Summer*, 219.
2. Ibid., 229.
3. Ibid., 230.
4. Ibid., 232.
5. Ibid., 247.
6. Ibid., 252.
7. Ibid., 266.
8. Ibid., 267.

CHAPTER TWENTY-SEVEN

"For The Next Fight"

12–15 May 1864

Out on the Red River in Louisiana that twelfth day of May, Colonel Bailey's newest wing dams were completed after three days of extremely hard work. They had narrowed the shallow but raging stream to a single channel and raised the water level fourteen inches. Admiral Porter had removed all the cargo from his remaining gunboats and had it transported by wagons to a spot below the rapids. The weight in the boats had been further reduced by throwing a dozen old 32-pounder guns overboard, as well as some armor. On the evening of the twelfth and the morning of the thirteenth, as army bands played in accompaniment from the shore, the gunboats ran the rapids without serious incident. For what Porter called "the best engineering feat ever performed,"[1] Bailey was eventually to receive a $700 sword from Porter, a $1600 silver vase from the navy, a vote of thanks from Congress, and promotion to brigadier general. Banks put his men back on the road on the thirteenth with Emory's 19th Corps in the lead and A. J. Smith's Gorillas bringing up the rear. Behind them was a wind-blown column of greasy smoke where Alexandria had once stood.

Down in Georgia on the twelfth day of May, Joe Johnston finally realized that Sherman was moving his main force to outflank him. A report from Pat Cleburne's division indicated that Federals were arriving at Snake Creek Gap in ever-increasing numbers, while cavalryman Joe Wheeler informed him that only two of Sherman's divisions still threatened Rocky Face Ridge. Still, Johnston waited until the morning of the thirteenth to order his two corps to give up their strong, well-prepared position and fall back to Resaca, where they would meet Polk's reinforcements coming from Alabama. The Confederates arrived at Resaca near midday, just in time to take up defensive positions before Sherman could attack. The Confederates deployed along a three-mile-long entrenched line, shaped like an upside-down L. Those of Polk's forces who had arrived manned the southern end of Johnston's line, with their left flank touching the Oostanaula River and their front covered by a tributary called Camp Creek. To Polk's right, also facing west, were Hardee's corps and one of Hood's divisions. Hood's other two divisions manned the short leg of the L, facing north, with their right flank anchored on another tributary of the Oostanaula, the Connasauga River. Wheeler's cavalry patrolled beyond both rivers. Sherman's men spent the afternoon reconnoitering the Rebel position, and one Southern bullet put Federal general Kilpatrick, commanding one of Thomas' cavalry divisions, out of action for some weeks.

In Virginia on the thirteenth, General Russell kept his promise and personally brought one of his brigades to relieve Colonel Edwards' three regiments at the angle in the former Confederate works at 6:30 a.m. Edwards' New Englanders moved back to the vicinity of the Landrum house. There they stacked their arms, lay down in the mud and rain, and immediately fell asleep, without thought of food or shelter. In the afternoon they awakened a few at a time, gathered in small groups to boil and drink coffee, then lay down in the mud again and went back to sleep. It was not until just before dark that they bothered to pitch their little "dog house" tents for protection from the rain. Then they crawled inside them and slept once more.

Even in times and places as grim and uncomfortable as the army camps around Spotsylvania, however, soldiers still have a sense of humor. A story was soon making the rounds of the army about a staff officer who was very fond of reading novels and seemed always to assume that everyone else was too. Lately he had been absorbed in an English translation of Victor Hugo's *Les Miserables*. As he was passing a house near the now-famous angle this officer spotted a young lady seated on the porch and, such opportunities being rare, naturally stopped to chat. Inevitably he brought up the subject of his latest literary acquisition, asking if she had seen "Lees Miserables," as he anglicized the title. The Rebel miss tartly replied, "Don't you talk to me that way; they're a good deal better than Grant's miserables anyhow!"[2]

At 5:30 a.m. on the thirteenth, Wright informed army headquarters that the Rebels had apparently abandoned their lines around the mule shoe. Hancock reported that his skirmishers had advanced a half-mile into the salient and had found no Confederates. At 8:40 a.m. Grant told Meade that he thought Lee was retreating and that any Confederates encountered would be merely a covering force, but Warren and Burnside reported that the enemy remained in place on their fronts. At 10:15 a.m. Hancock sent word that his skirmishers had found that, although the Southerners had completely abandoned the salient, they had built a new line of works that was essentially an eastward extention of their entrenchments opposite Warren's corps. That afternoon Grant expressed his opinion that it was necessary to "get by the right flank of the enemy for the next fight."[3] Meade gave instructions to Warren and Wright to prepare their two corps for movement after dark and to report to army headquarters for instructions. The plan was for the 5th and 6th corps to march that night behind the 2nd and 9th. Warren would attack at 4 a.m. down the Fredericksburg Road, while Wright, on his left, advanced along the Massaponax Church Road, both aiming toward Spotsylvania Court House. Grant believed, correctly, that Lee's far right flank was weak.

Grant summed up his estimate of the situation that day in a letter to his wife, Julia. "The world has never seen so bloody or so protracted a battle as the one being fought and I hope never will again," he said. "The enemy were really whipped yesterday but their situation is desperate beyond anything heretofore known. To lose this battle they lose their cause. As bad as it is they have fought for it with a gallantry worthy of a better."[4]

Meanwhile, Hancock requested, and was given, permission to consolidate the two divisions which he had received from the old 3rd Corps, Birney's and Mott's. Hancock said that, if it remained separate, Mott's 4th Division would soon be useless, as its commander seemed to be unable to control his troops. Mott therefore resumed command of his old brigade, until then under McAllister, and it and Brewster's became the 3rd and 4th brigades of Birney's 3rd Division.

Grant wrote to Secretary of War Stanton that day to recommend a number of promotions. Confirmation was requested for the field promotions of Carroll, from the 2nd Corps, and Upton, from the 6th. And, in order to give the 5th Corps a new brigadier too, Colonel McCandless, one of the brigade commanders in the Pennsylvania Reserves, was recommended also. Wright and Gibbon were recommended to be made major generals of volunteers, Meade and Sherman to be made major generals in the regular army, and Hancock a brigadier general in the regulars. "General Meade has more than met my most sanguine expectations," Grant wrote. "He and Sherman are the fittest officers for large commands I have come in contact with."

Horace Porter recorded that "an animated discussion took place at headquarters that day regarding General Meade's somewhat anomalous position, and the embarrassments which were at times caused on the field by the necessity of issuing orders through him instead of direct to the corps commanders." Among other problems, it was pointed out that Meade "had an irascible temper, and often irritated officers who came in contact with him, while General Grant was even-tempered, and succeeded in securing a more hearty cooperation of his generals when he dealt with them direct. The discussion became heated at times." Grant, as usual, waited for everybody to have their say, then gave his opinion.

"I am commanding all the armies," he said, "and I cannot neglect others by giving my time exclusively to the Army of the Potomac, which would involve performing all the detailed duties of an army commander, directing its administration, enforcing discipline, reviewing its court-martial proceedings, etc. I have Burnside's, Butler's, and Sigel's armies to look after in Virginia, to say nothing of our Western armies, and I may make Sheridan's cavalry a separate command. Besides, Meade has served a long time with the Army of the Potomac, knows its subordinate officers thoroughly, and led it to a memorable victory at Gettysburg. I have just come from the West, and if I removed a deserving Eastern man from the position of army commander, my motives might be misunderstood, and the effect be bad upon the spirits of the troops. General Meade and I are in close contact on the field; he is capable and perfectly subordinate, and by attending to the details he relieves me of much unnecessary work, and gives me more time to think and to mature my general plans." But Porter noted that "after that day he gave a closer personal direction in battle to the movements of subdivisions of the armies."[5]

That thirteenth day of May 1864, Private William Christman of Company G, 67th Pennsylvania Infantry, became the first of thousands of battle casualties of this and many subsequent wars to be buried on the grounds of the Arlington mansion on the south side of the Potomac, opposite Washington. The 1100-acre estate had been the well-known home of George Washington Parke Custis, the adopted son of the first president and a grandson of Martha Washington's first marriage. Custis had had only one child, Mary, and she had become Mrs. Robert Edward Lee. Upon her father's death in 1857 she had inherited a life interest in Arlington, which after her own death was to pass to her eldest son, George Washington Custis Lee. In May of 1861 Union forces had occupied the mansion and the grounds, and in January 1864 the property had been confiscated by the federal government on charges of non-payment of taxes. By then the army was running out of places to bury soldiers who died in the numerous hospitals in and around Washington, including one that had been established at Arlington. Stanton convinced Lincoln that the grounds of the mansion were ideally suited for a cemetery.

The sleepy Shenandoah Valley village of New Market, in the 99th year since its founding, was about to be illuminated by the spotlight of history. That spring it consisted of about 700 inhabitants who lived in a row of houses on each side of the macadamized Valley Turnpike. A youngster named Elon Henkel, playing behind his family's house that thirteenth of May, heard an unusual noise in the road and ran to see what was happening. Two regiments of Imboden's troopers were pounding down the road from the north, "neck and neck, the horses' hoofs hammering the pike, the scabbards of the sabers rattling, and the cavalrymen giving the Rebel yell." The big men on the big horses galloped past Brock's Ham Store and turned east at the crossroads, but the terrified young Elon ran and hid behind his house, "about the worst scared kid in all Rebeldom."[6]

Since returning from his recent chase after Higgins' cavalry, Imboden had chosen New Market as a handy place from which to keep an eye on Sigel's slowly advancing Yankees. It was the site of the junction of the Valley Pike with the only road that crossed Massanutten Mountain, a ridge that for a while divides the valley into two unequal parts. The main valley, including the turnpike and New Market, is northwest of this ridge, while the lesser Luray Valley lies to the southeast of it. The men and horses that had scared little Elon were being sent to meet some Federal cavalry that had been seen coming down Massanutten Mountain. This was a force of 300 troopers which had found and destroyed a good-sized quantity of Confederate supplies in the town of Luray that morning and had come up the mountain to see what it could see.

What the Northerners saw, besides the little village, was the camp of several hundred men north of town, a column of troops heading south, a grazing herd of cattle, and a train of white-topped wagons. The Union commander, Colonel William Boyd, conferred with his officers, and all agreed that the distant troops were Rebels—all except Boyd, that is. Despite the fact that the wagons were farther south than the troops, Boyd was convinced that the soldiers below were the van of Sigel's column and ordered his men down the mountain to meet them. His advance guard soon saw a body of cavalry with two cannon coming rapidly toward the base of the mountain and called him forward for a look, but Boyd remained convinced that they must be Federals and ordered his men to push on. Near the bridge over Smith's Creek they saw some pickets apparently dressed in blue, but these fell back when approached. Boyd's men had just reached the other side of the creek when it erupted in smoke, flame, flying bullets, and yelling Rebels. "Now we've got the d—d Yankees!" they heard someone shout, "Give 'em h—l!"[7] Imboden had spotted the Federals coming down the mountain and sent his 23rd Virginia Cavalry to stop them at the creek while the 18th Virginia worked around to their rear, but the Union troopers broke out that way nevertheless, mostly on foot, and headed for the cover of the trees on the mountain. The two Confederate guns helped turn the retreat into a rout. Only the dark of a rain-filled night saved many of the Federals from capture. Nevertheless, 300 more Union cavalry had been subtracted from Sigel's little force just a couple of days before it was due to meet Breckinridge's small army at the same sleepy hamlet of New Market.

By dawn of the thirteenth, in southeastern Virginia, Kautz's Union cavalry division was back on the road, four miles west of Coalfield and following the Richmond & Danville Railroad to the southwest. At 8:30 a.m. the advance reached Powhatan Station, where the telegraph instrument was removed and the wires cut. Large stocks of bacon and corn found there were used to replenish the men's supplies, and forage was captured for the horses. What could not be consumed or carried was burned, including fifteen freight cars of hay, along with the station, freight house, and water tank. As much track was ripped up as the limited supply of tools allowed. Continuing down the track, the Federal troopers next stopped at Mattoax Bridge over the Appomattox River. This, however, could not be burned because it was found to be made of iron. Furthermore, it was protected by a Rebel garrison, including artillery, entrenched on the south bank. Kautz ordered the 5th Pennsylvania to keep the Confederates' attention while he led the division several miles downstream to cross at Goode's Bridge.

He found this structure already damaged, and it was 8 p.m. before the troopers were on the south side of the Appomattox, riding through the rainy night toward Chula Station, three miles away on the railroad. That point was reached at 10 p.m., where Spear's brigade bivouacked for the night, while the 1st Brigade, now under Major Ferris Jacobs, stopped a half-mile short of the station. Kautz learned from locals that three trainloads of Confederates had passed Chula Station that afternoon, headed toward Mattoax Bridge, and that two of the trains had come back empty while the third had not yet returned. He had the switch set to derail any southbound train and awaited results. Soon a locomotive could be heard, and then its headlight was seen. When it struck the switch, the engine ran off the track. The engineer and two important passengers, the superintendents of the railroad and of the telegraph who had been using the locomotive to inspect the damage done by the Yankees, all escaped. But the Federals happily destroyed the engine.

Responding to an urgent request from Bragg, at 6 a.m. on the morning of the thirteenth Beauregard sent two regiments of Corse's Virginia brigade westward by freight train to protect the Richmond & Danville Railroad. Later that morning a train arrived at Petersburg from North Carolina, carrying Major General Chase Whiting. He was unwell and, expecting only a brief conference with Beauregard, had brought only a single aide with him, but Beauregard wanted him to take temporary command of the entire department, with headquarters at Petersburg, while he took the field north of the Appomattox himself. After briefing his replacement for less than an hour, Beauregard and his staff set out, escorted by the 3rd North Carolina Cavalry and three infantry regiments of Colquitt's Brigade. In order to avoid Butler's forces blocking the turnpike, the Confederates swung westward toward Chesterfield Court House.

Gillmore was also heading for the same village that day. Butler had sent him westward in an attempt to outflank the Rebel line guarding Drewry's Bluff. He had with him eleven regiments of infantry, a battery of artillery, and a detachment of the 1st New York Mounted Rifles. In the continuing rain, the column set off along the Chester Station road at about 6:30 a.m. Colonel Richard White was dropped off at the station with two regiments and instructions to wait for the rest of the column to get into position and then to make a diversionary attack up the railroad. The rest of the Federals followed a road that gradually curved to the north, routing a small Rebel cavalry detachment about a mile from Chesterfield Court House. Dropping off two more regiments to protect the rear of his main force, Gillmore turned the column to the east, heading for a Confederate fort that local slaves said was just ahead.

Baldy Smith, meanwhile, had found a hill that commanded the Rebel position on the north side of Proctor's Creek. After spending some hours getting troops up on this hill he sent skirmishers splashing across the creek, only to find that the Confederates had slipped away during the night. At 9 a.m. he ordered his three divisions to advance into the thick woods north of the creek. Worrying about his left flank and hearing nothing from Gillmore, Smith ordered Turner's division to move from the right flank to the left. It was noon before the switch could be completed, by which time Brooks' and Weitzel's skirmishers were engaged with Rebels in the woods. The early afternoon was spent gradually pressing

NO TURNING BACK

forward against stiffening opposition until the Federals finally emerged from the northern edge of the woods to find a clearing about 700 yards wide, with fortifications on the other side. Smith crept forward and studied the Rebel defenses carefully. The earthworks had a ditch in front and many embrasures for artillery to fire through. He sent word to Butler "that if the line was held in force by the enemy, it could not be carried by assault, and that I should not attempt it unless I received orders to do so."[8] Butler, still relying on Smith's professional judgment, allowed the advance to grind to a halt again.

Gillmore's column, however, had reached swampy Crooked Branch, a tributary of Proctor's Creek, and just beyond it was a steep hill that constituted the western end of the outer Confederate works. These defenses faced to the east except for a few yards on the hill that faced to the south, but none faced to the west, from which direction the Federals were now approaching. Two regiments were deployed along the road, and the 3rd New Hampshire was sent to the extreme Union left, where a log bridge crossed the stream. The 5th New Jersey Battery unlimbered its guns to support the advance up the hill, which began at 4 p.m.

The swamp soon stopped the two regiments moving along the road and they also had to be sent to the left to cross the bridge. Meanwhile, the 3rd New Hampshire went ahead alone. Reaching the edge of the woods near the crest of the hill, it found itself facing over a thousand of Matt Ransom's North Carolinians. Both sides were a bit surprised, but the Yankees deployed into line and drove the Rebels beyond their defenses. The Confederates recovered quickly, however, and began to dig in on the reverse side of their works while pouring a heavy fire into the lone New Hampshire regiment. Then they began to work around its left flank. The Federal commander withdrew his regiment to the edge of the woods, intending to stop there, but the men went on down the hill and back across the branch. However, the other Union regiments held the line, and the troops sent up the railroad as a diversion finally took the hill when the Rebels pulled back to the east after Matt Ransom had taken a disabling wound in his arm. Gillmore then brought up his whole force and occupied the vacated works. Word of Gillmore's success came too late for Butler and Smith to take advantage of it that day, and the Northerners had to spend another wet night without fires. Smith raised his men's spirits, however, by riding among them with news of a great victory won by Grant near Spotsylvania Court House.

With his right flank turned, Hoke had withdrawn to an intermediate line of defenses. Throughout the night he sent telegrams to Bragg asking for reinforcements from Richmond and for news of Beauregard. He received no reply. Beauregard was, in fact, marching through the stormy night around Gillmore's left flank, and at 3 a.m. on the fourteenth he rode up to the Drewry mansion near Fort Darling and took command of the Confederate forces defending the southern approaches to Richmond. Conferring with Colonel Walter Stevens, engineer of the Richmond defenses, he learned of Hoke's retreat and that Robert Ransom had about 5,000 mobile troops in the Department of Richmond. He also was given a description of Lee's position at Spotsylvania. Typically, he at once came up with a daring plan that went far beyond his immediate command and called for winning the war with bold, sweeping movements and combinations. There was much strategic soundness in his plan, but also much risk. Since both his and Lee's forces were between Grant's and Butler's, he logically concluded that they should concentrate both Confederate forces against first one opponent and then the other, as Kirby Smith and Dick Taylor had recently done to Banks and Steele out in the Trans-Mississippi Department. He sent Colonel Stevens to Richmond with the proposal that Lee withdraw into the powerful defenses of the capital so that he could send Beauregard 15,000 men, with which reinforcement he would attack Butler in front while Whiting took him in the rear with Wise's and Martin's brigades. Butler would be cut off and destroyed, after which Beauregard would reinforce Lee for an attack on Grant.

At 4:30 a.m. on the fourteenth, Smith's skirmishers moved cautiously forward in the cold, rainy dawn and began to slowly force the Confederate pickets to give ground, but it was 8 a.m. before these were driven into the works abandoned by the main Rebel force the night before. Shortly thereafter skirmishers from the 13th New Hampshire rushed the fortifications west of the turnpike and scattered the Rebels on both sides, and by 9 a.m. Smith's forces were in possession of the entire line. However, a second and even more formidable line could be seen in the distance at the far side of a plateau that was covered with stumps, brush, and a cluster of abandoned barracks. This line extended westward beyond the railroad and then turned to the north. Its eastern anchor was a redoubt known as Fort Stevens, on a high hill a few yards east of the turnpike. From that fort lines ran north to the inner lines around Fort Darling and south to the outer line now held by the Federals. Gillmore made sure his right connected with Smith's left and went forward until he too was confronted by the second Confederate line.

Around 9 a.m. General Braxton Bragg arrived at Drewry's Bluff to confer with Beauregard, his former commander. Stevens had been unable to see President Davis and so had presented Beauregard's plan to Bragg, who had come to discuss it in person. Beauregard launched into an impassioned description of his grand design and a plea for its adoption, but Bragg refused to do more than lay the proposal before the president.

Beauregard later claimed that Bragg wholeheartedly approved of his plan, but from his later analysis of it, Bragg apparently had grave doubts. It would take too much time to implement, he wrote, and would cause the loss of Petersburg, the Shenandoah Valley, and other important areas. In any case, Beauregard sent orders for Dearing's cavalry and the last mobile unit in North Carolina, Walker's brigade of South Carolinians, to move north to Petersburg. Meanwhile Butler's men advanced on the new Confederate position, some of the Union skirmishers reaching the abatis outside Fort Stevens.

Just then Confederate president Jefferson Davis himself showed up to confer with Beauregard. The conversation soon came around to the general's grandiose scheme, but he could not get Davis to approve the idea of ordering Lee to fall back to the capital's defenses. The president did, however, authorize the use of Robert Ransom's 5,000 men from Richmond for an attack on Butler. Davis also disagreed with Beauregard's plan for Whiting to strike the Yankee rear. Aware of the difficulties in coordinating converging columns, Davis insisted that Whiting should march his two brigades around Butler, as Beauregard had done, so that all the available Confederate forces could attack together. Beauregard finally gave in, mumbling something about preparing new orders for Whiting when he found time. After the president departed, the general gave orders for Whiting to leave Petersburg at dawn on the sixteenth with Wise's, Martin's, and the remainder of Colquitt's brigades, and to march to Drewry's Bluff by an even more indirect route than the one Beauregard had taken, to arrive by that afternoon. Petersburg would then be defended by Walker's Brigade and Dearing's cavalry, both then still on their way there.

Petersburg was already having the same effect on Chase Whiting, however, as it had had on George Pickett. He was completely unfamiliar with the town and felt himself threatened from every direction. His telegraphic connection with Richmond via Burkeville had been cut by Kautz's cavalry, which was now threatening the wire to Weldon. His pickets at Swift Creek were in contact with Union forces of unknown size, and it was reported that three brigades of Federals were advancing from City Point. Meanwhile, Bragg kept telling him to abandon the city and move to Drewry's Bluff. But, like Pickett, he realized that Petersburg was too important to be abandoned, and he believed the Federals could not help but realize that importance also, and would come marching in his direction any minute now.

Meanwhile, Baldy Smith's skirmishers had captured the empty barracks between the outer and intermediate Rebel lines but had been driven out again by Southern artillery which blasted the buildings into a shower of flying splinters. Gillmore's men captured a house and garden and a rail fence between the two lines, but had all they could do to hold on to what they had gained, let alone advance any farther. As the day came to a close and the fire slackened, fresh Northern units came forward and began to dig defenses, using whatever tools were available, mostly their bayonets and tin cups. Where the Union line ran through some woods in Smith's sector, logs were available to pile on top of the mounds of dirt. For their part, the Rebels worked all night at filling sand bags with which to repair the damage to Fort Stevens. Also that night the brigades of Gracie, Lewis, and Terry returned from Richmond, which Sheridan was no longer threatening.

That evening Smith sent a Lieutenant Michie to report to Butler on the results of the day's activities. Instead, the lieutenant told Butler that he knew a place where the Rebel defenses could be carried by assault. Believing this to be a proposal from Smith, Butler approved it and promised to bring up four more regiments from Port Walthall Junction for support. In reply, Smith denied proposing any such thing, but said he would try it if Butler wished. Butler let his approval stand, so Smith reluctantly began to issue the necessary orders. Butler had also received word that Phil Sheridan's cavalry had arrived at Haxall's Landing across the James River from Bermuda Hundred, and he asked the cavalryman to join him for a conference. At 11 p.m. Sheridan replied that he would call upon Butler the next day.

At dawn on 14 May, Kautz sent Colonel Spear back up the tracks toward the Appomattox River to a wooden railroad bridge over a tributary called Flat Creek. Meanwhile the rest of the division was put to work destroying all railroad property at Chula. Spear found the bridge defended by one of the two regiments of Corse's Brigade which Beauregard had just sent down the line. The Rebels retreated across the creek, but a Union dash toward a nearby highway bridge was repulsed and a dismounted charge toward the railway bridge was also beaten off. Disregarding Kautz's instructions not to become heavily engaged if the bridge was strongly defended, Spears showed, as Kautz later wrote, "that his judgment was not on a par with his bravery."[9] Despite the fact that he lacked the means to burn the rain-soaked bridge even if he took it, he sent his men forward again. The sound of heavy firing caused Kautz to send a courier to check on Spear. When he learned that the latter had already lost more men than the bridge was worth, he ordered the detachment to return to Chula. Spear obeyed promptly, leaving his dead and wounded on the field.

Considering that the Richmond & Danville Railroad was sufficiently damaged, Kautz turned his column to the southeast, heading for the

Southside Railroad, about twenty miles away. Feinting at Goode's and Bevill's bridges, the Federals passed a number of large, prosperous plantations and, despite Kautz's orders to the contrary, many of the men plundered these establishments. Crowds of escaping slaves followed the Union troopers. As he approached the Southside Railroad, Kautz split his force. Jacob's 1st Brigade was sent to Wellville and Spear's 2nd, two miles east to Wilson's Station. Jacob's men burned the freight station at Wellville and an empty railroad car and tore up about a mile of track. Spear also found slim pickings at Wilson's, burning the depot and a stock of locomotive fuel and pulling up some rails. Both brigades then moved westward to another station called Black's and White's, after a pair of local taverns. The Federals arrived about 8 p.m. and found the station full of forage and many other provisions. The troopers took what they could consume or carry and burned the rest, along with the depot, warehouses, woodshed, water tanks, and thirteen freight cars. More track and telegraph wire were also torn up. Then the Northerners resumed the march southward, not stopping until 2 a.m.

At 10 p.m. on the rainy night of the thirteenth the Union 5th Corps began the movement toward the Federal left ordered by Grant and at 11:45 p.m. Warren notified Meade that the last of his units had just taken up the march. He apologized for the lateness of his start but explained that, due to the short notice he had been given, there had not been time to bring his supply wagons forward from Salem Church, unload them and issue supplies to the troops before it came time to march. Many of these wagons were now stuck in the muddy road. Warren promised to do his best, but added that "very difficult things are being attempted on these night movements over such roads."[10]

The exhausted troops straggled badly as the rain continued to fall intermittently. Around 3 a.m. on the fourteenth Wright reported to Meade that the rear of Warren's column had just passed his 6th Corps headquarters, and thus it would be impossible for his own men to be in position for the planned 4 a.m. attack. In fact, at the appointed hour only about a thousand of Warren's men were in position, and he reported to Meade that even these were too tired to be of any immediate use. At 7:30 p.m. he reported that about 3,800 men of Griffin's and Cutler's divisions were on hand. The corps artillery had arrived, but Crawford's division and Kitching's gunless heavy artillerymen had not. However, he said that Griffin was sending out a detachment to occupy a hill southwest of the Ni River, where there appeared to be a small force of Rebels with artillery.

This hill was part of the Myers farm, and the Confederates who occupied it were pickets of Rooney Lee's cavalry with a battery of horse artillery. Griffin sent the 140th New York and 91st Pennsylvania of Ayres' brigade to take the hill, and twelve Federal guns started a long-range duel with the Rebel battery. The Confederates sent a galloper to bring up the rest of their brigade, which immediately moved to reinforce its pickets, but by the time it arrived the two union regiments held the Myers buildings in force and, with the help of those twelve guns, beat off an attempt to retake them. The Northerners now had an excellent view of the Confederate position near, and south of, the village of Spotsylvania, and Meade ordered Wright, whose men began to arrive around 9 a.m., to occupy the hill. The job was given to Upton, whose four regiments were down to fewer than 800 men. He asked for a second brigade to help, but was given only two more regiments. His men began to construct breastworks from fence rails while a lookout posted on the roof of the Myers house kept watch with field glasses on the Rebel cavalry still lurking nearby. At 9 a.m. Meade notified Warren that the main attack was cancelled for the day. He was to keep his 5th Corps hidden as far as possible while sending out skirmishers to learn all they could about the Southern position.

Around 4 p.m. Upton's lookout reported that Rebel infantry skirmishers were advancing toward the hill. Upton sent one of his own regiments and two companies of one of the borrowed regiments forward to occupy some woods in advance of the position. The commander of this force, Lieutenant Colonel William H. Lessig, entered the woods and found two Confederate infantry brigades forming up for an advance on the Myers hill. He quickly withdrew his troops and reported his findings to Upton. These Rebels were Ambrose Wright's brigade of Georgians and Nate Harris' Mississippians from Mahone's Division, sent out by Early to see what the Yankees were up to. The Georgians advanced about thirty yards from the edge of the woods, stopped, and opened fire. When Harris' troops joined them, both brigades let out a yell and charged. At the same time the Rebel cavalry and horse battery opened fire on Upton's flank. The Federals got off a volley or two and then ran down the hill and crossed the Ni River.

Meade, who had been near the left end of the picket line, was temporarily cut off and in danger of being captured, but he found a ford and recrossed the Ni himself. He then ordered the Federal Wright to retake the Myers farm, and ordered Warren to assist. Wright formed Russell's and Rickett's divisions in line with Neill's in reserve, and Warren had Ayres' brigade prepare to retrace its earlier steps, while twelve Union guns began to bombard the hill. It was eventually discovered, however, that the Rebels had withdrawn, and after the guns stopped firing, the infantry advanced and reoccupied the hill. Wright still worried about his flank and requested permission to pull back across the Ni again. Instead, Meade ordered him to stay and dig in. Then, passing on Warren's concern that the Confederates seemed to be threatening the army's southern flank, and desirous of reuniting his forces, he convinced Grant to let him bring Hancock's 2nd Corps around behind Burnside's 9th Corps, to the army's left. Grant's only stipulation was that one of Hancock's divisions be left as a support for Burnside's right until that flank could be realigned and secured. Birney's division, now including Mott's, was chosen for that task.

That day, what was left of Allegheny Johnson's division had been broken up and parcelled out. The remnants of the Stonewall Brigade, Witcher's (formerly J. M. Jones') Brigade and the three Virginia regiments of Maryland Steuart's brigade were all consolidated into one brigade and assigned to Gordon's Division. What was left of the consolidated Louisiana Brigade was also assigned to Gordon, who was recommended for promotion to major general. The two North Carolina regiments of Steuart's Brigade were temporarily transferred to Ramseur's Brigade in Rodes' Division.

Command of the Cavalry Corps, now that Jeb Stuart was dead, also had to be settled. Rooney Lee had just recently been promoted to divisional command, but both Fitzhugh Lee and Wade Hampton might expect to be named Stuart's successor. In fact, that was the problem. To name either one of them was to offend the other and his supporters. The ever-tactful army commander therefore took yet another burden upon his own shoulders and ordered that the three division commanders would thereafter report directly to him. For the time being, at least, he would be his own chief of cavalry.

It had been after 3 p.m. that day, the fourteenth, when Lee learned that the Union 5th and 6th corps had left their positions on his left, their right, and it was dark before his forces started moving to counter the threat to his own right, of which he had been informed by his son Rooney. Field's Division of Anderson's 1st Corps set off through the night along the muddy Brock Road, heading for a church about a mile south of Spotsylvania.

---

1. Foote, *The Civil War,* 3:84.
2. Porter, *Campaigning With Grant,* 117.
3. Matter, *If It Takes All Summer,* 274.
4. Catton, *Grant Takes Command,* 239.

5. All quotes regarding Grant's opinion of Meade are from Porter, *Campaigning With Grant*, 114.

6. Davis, *The Battle of New Market*, 66.

7. Ibid., 65.

8. Matter, *If It Takes All Summer*, 148.

9. Robertson, *Back Door To Richmond*, 165.

10. Matter, *If It Takes All Summer*, 279.

CHAPTER TWENTY-EIGHT

"We Can Attack and Whip Them Here"

14–15 May 1864

Since all reports indicated that the only Confederates in his front were the members of Imboden's cavalry brigade, Franz Sigel made up his mind to take New Market. Instead of marching his entire army forward to that point, however, he decided to split his force, even though he knew that Breckinridge had been as near as Staunton four days before. Sigel called Colonel August Moor to his headquarters on the morning of 14 May and ordered him "to feel the position and strength of the rebels under Imboden, reported to be on Rude's Hill."[1] The height in question was the location of Imboden's camp, about four miles north of New Market. Moor was the commander of the 1st Brigade of Brigadier General Jeremiah Sullivan's 1st Infantry Division of Sigel's Army of West Virginia.

Sigel compounded the error of splitting his force by sending Moor, not with his own brigade, but with units completely unknown to him. At 11 that morning Moor marched out of Woodstock with the 1st West Virginia and 34th Massachussetts, four guns of Battery B, Maryland Light Artillery, two guns of Battery G, 1st West Virginia Light Artillery, and detachments, totaling 300 troopers, from the 20th Pennsylvania Cavalry and the 15th New York Cavalry. When he reached the village of Edinburg he was joined by the 123rd Ohio Infantry, the 1st New York (Veteran) Cavalry, the 21st New York Cavalry, and 600 men of the 1st New York (Lincoln) Cavalry. Moor's combined force then totalled 2,350 men, or about one third of the army under Sigel's immediate command. Sigel's aide-de-camp lamented that, in sending these men a good twenty miles in advance of the rest of the column, his commander seemed "to court destruction."[2] The rest of Sigel's men at Woodstock remained in their tents that day to stay out of the persistent rain. They could hear firing to the south that began about 3 P.M. and continued until 9 P.M. or later. The sound worried Sigel enough for him to send the 18th Connecticut forward to Edinburg, where it encountered Rebel pickets.

Moor had pushed his men hard in the falling rain and they had soon encountered the bedraggled, dismounted survivors of Boyd's cavalry heading north, including Boyd himself. He related the story of his debacle the day before and then continued toward Woodstock. To the south, Major Timothy Quinn, with the 600 troopers of the Lincoln Cavalry, seized the bridge over the North Fork of the Shenandoah from which Imboden's men had removed the flooring planks. Quinn's men repaired the bridge while an advance guard was sent up Rude's Hill, driving away about 100 Rebel pickets. Pushing on about a half-mile, Quinn found the Confederates forming up for a charge, but beat them off and chased them nearly two miles until he came upon Imboden's main line, just north of New Market.

The Southern cavalry commander was not there in person. He had left at 10 that morning to meet Breckinridge at Lacey's Springs, which the latter had reached on his march north from Staunton. The two were having dinner when a courier brought word of Quinn's advance, and about an hour later they heard the boom of distant artillery. Breckinridge ordered Imboden to return and hold New Market until dark, if he could, and then to fall back three or four miles, where the infantry would join him.

About 5P.M. the Union artillery joined Quinn's cavalry and began a duel with the six guns of Captain John H. McClanahan's Staunton Horse Artillery. By 6 P.M. Moor's entire force was in line, with skirmishers out, and began pushing toward New Market, but night fell before the town was taken. Imboden twice led harassing attacks against Moor's emcampment on a slight eminence called Bushong's Hill, just to see whether the Federals were really settling in for the night. Then he ordered his men out of town to the south, leaving only skirmishers in the outskirts of the village.

It was a miserable night for the Federals, who made camp in the rain and the mud, without fires or dinner. The artillery horses were kept in harness for fear of a surprise attack. The people of New Market, those who had not already fled, also found it hard to sleep. Breckinridge's infantry had it even worse. The Rebels were on the march. They had slogged through the rain on the fourteenth to reach Lacey's Springs, then stopped to cook two days' rations. At 1 A.M. on the fifteenth they took to the road again.

Down in Georgia that fourteenth day of May, McPherson's Army of the Tennessee formed on the Federal right near the Oostanaula River while most of Thomas' larger force connected on his left. To Thomas' left was Schofield's small Army of the Ohio, and on the Union far left was the 4th Corps of Thomas' army, which had followed Joe Johnston's Confederates down from Dalton. Skirmishing had begun at dawn, and by 6 A.M. heavy firing had broken out all up and down the line. The men of the 4th Corps were hot, scratched, bruised, and tired after spending most of the day "creeping up among the bushes, rocks and ravines" as they closed in on the Rebel defenses around Resaca. They were a bit disgusted to see the rumpled, unshaven General Sherman sitting on a log with his back against a tree, apparently sound asleep. "A pretty way we are commanded!" one of the men grumbled.

"Stop, my man," Sherman called out, evidently more awake than he had looked. "While you were sleeping last night, I was planning for you."[3]

Sherman's plan took advantage of the fact that Johnston's army had its back to the Connasauga and Oostanaula rivers. If any Federals crossed the stream south of Resaca they would be a threat to the Confederate line of supply, the railroad to Atlanta, while Johnston would have trouble retreating his men across the river in the face of the superior Union force. Sherman decided to send Brigadier General Thomas Sweeny's 2nd Division of the 16th Corps from McPherson's army to cross the Oostanaula at Lay's Ferry, southwest of Johnston's position. He also ordered one of Thomas' cavalry divisions, under Brigadier General Kenner Garrard, southwest to Rome, Georgia where there were factories and iron works on a branch line of the railroad. Meanwhile the Union commander would probe for weaknesses in the Rebels' position and keep Johnston's attention away from Sweeny.

The main Union attack was aimed at the angle in Johnston's L-shaped line. Major General John M. Palmer's 14th Corps of Thomas' army and two divisions of Schofield's 23rd Corps had to cross a deep, muddy fork of Camp Creek, the tangled brush along its banks, and then a flat valley floor, several hundred yards wide, that gave the Southerners a clear field of fire. One of these divisions of the 23rd Corps was commanded by Brigadier General Henry P. Judah, a West Point classmate of Grant who was already in trouble with Schofield for poor performance. Without properly reconnoitering the terrain to his front, he led his men into the swampy ground around the creek, and as they struggled through the mud, one brigade at a time, they were hit by a heavy fire from both front and flank. The right of Judah's division became entangled with the left-most brigade of the 14th Corps, destroying what was left of the formation of both units. Judah refused to stop and reform his men, but the creek brought them to a halt, with the men trying to fire and load their rifles while standing in waist-deep mud and water. "Under these circumstances we were forced back," the commander of Judah's first brigade wrote, "leaving fully one-third of the attacking party killed and wounded on the field." Only then did Judah's other brigade arrive, to confront the Rebels alone. "The result was what might have been expected," this second brigade commander wrote, "a most disastrous defeat."[4]

The other division Schofield advanced was commanded by the highly competent Brigadier General Jacob D. Cox. He had been a Republican senator from Ohio before the war, but he showed more military ability than most of the political generals. His division took the first line, "driving the enemy back upon a second line some 250 yards from the first," he wrote. "The enemy immediately opened with both artillery and musketry from their second line, which extended far beyond both flanks of the division, and no troops being as yet in position on either our right or left, the division was halted."[5] Cox's men fell back to the outside edge of the first line of entrenchments and held on. To Cox's left came one-armed Major General Oliver O. Howard's 4th Corps, but it was struck about 4 P.M. by a counterattack by John Bell Hood at the head of two Confederate divisions and four additional brigades. Hood took the Federal flank division, Major General David S. Stanley's 1st of the 4th Corps, by surprise. Stanley reported that his men "got out of the way with such order as troops can hurrying through a thick brush."[6] The Confederates were stopped in turn by the 5th Indiana Battery firing double-shotted cannister at the point-blank range of fifty yards. The Rebels were beginning to edge around the flanks of the Union gunners when a division of Joe Hooker's 20th Corps came to their rescue. Thomas had pulled this formation out of the center of the Federal line when he saw the danger to Howard and Schofield. Hooker's leading brigade came down a steep wooded ridge, surprised the Confederates with a staggering volley, and then followed it up with a charge that drove the Rebels "clear over the hill out of sight in great confusion," as the Federal brigade commander described it.[7] The Southern officers tried to reform their men for another attack, but darkness brought an end to the struggle first.

While Johnston's attention had thus been drawn to his right, troops of the 15th Corps of McPherson's army, at the opposite end of the line, forced their way across Camp Creek and captured a hill from which Union artillery could reach the Confederate bridges over the Oostanaula, and from which the additional units brought up by McPherson threatened Polk's troops on the Rebel left. Polk realized the danger that the Federal gains represented and launched several counterattacks, but managed only to lengthen the casualty list. Meanwhile, at Lay's Ferry, Sweeny got his division across the river in pontoon boats and drove off some of Wheeler's Southern cavalry. When he received a report that a large Rebel force had interposed between him and the rest of Sherman's army, however, Sweeny pulled back. Too late, it was found that the report was false. When Johnston heard about Sweeny's incursion he sent a division to repulse it, but it turned back when it was discovered that the Yankees had recrossed the river. In any case, Johnston cancelled his plan to renew the attack on the Union right the next morning, and had pontoon bridges laid upstream, out of range of McPherson's guns.

Instead, it was the Federals who attacked again on the morning of the fifteenth, this time with Hooker's 20th Corps, composed primarily of the men brought west from the Army of the Potomac the previous autumn. The main Rebel line stopped the advance of most of the Federals with little difficulty, but on a spur of land about eighty yards in front of the main works on the Confederate right the men of a Georgia battery were still busily throwing up earthworks around their four guns. These cannon were in position to enfilade the Union attack, so Major General Daniel Butterfield's division of Hooker's 20th Corps was sent to take them.

Butterfield, son of the stage-line magnate, was an interesting character. He had been chief of staff of the Army of the Potomac when Hooker had been its commander. He had designed the corps badges for that army, forerunners of modern unit emblems, and had composed the haunting bugle call known as "taps" that replaced the old day's-end drum roll. He had been wounded at Gettysburg, after which Meade had replaced him with A. A. Humphreys, and he had come west with Hooker after the Federal defeat at Chickamauga. Now Butterfield's men rushed through the fire of the Georgia guns and took shelter on the outside of the battery's works. Colonel Benjamin Harrison of the 70th Indiana, grandson of a president of the United States and later to become one himself, saw the infantry supports of the Rebel battery falling back and led his men over the parapet into the Confederate works. All but five of the Georgia gunners were killed, wounded, or captured in the melee that ensued. That was the end of the Union success on that flank, however, as the main Rebel line was not taken, and its fire soon forced Butterfield's men out of the captured battery. "The men laid on their faces on the hillside, and when those in front were killed, wounded or out of ammunition, those in rear crawled forward and took their places," a captain from the 149th New York remembered. "The enemy was not more than fifty yards away," he added. "One poor fellow, against the remonstrances of his comrades, crawled up where he could get a better view, and almost instantly was killed in his place. In falling his head was exposed and, during the afternoon, the enemy literally filled it with bullets."[8] Harrison's Hoosiers were not to be denied, however, and that night, under the cover of darkness, they crept forward and tore down enough of the Southern earthworks to haul the four guns away.

Once more the fighting on this flank served to distract Confederate attention from the other, where Sweeny was again sent across the river. This time he stayed, and Sherman reinforced him with a division of cavalry. The Confederate division of Major General W. H. T. Walker arrived too late to prevent the Federals from establishing a bridgehead and was unable to drive the Yankees back. That night, Johnston had his bridges covered with cornstalks to muffle the sound, and quietly pulled his army out of its works and across the river. The pontoons were then taken up for future use and the railroad bridge was burned, but in their haste the Rebels failed to destroy the turnpike bridge, leaving Sherman an easy crossing. Both sides had lost between 3,000 and 5,000 men. Johnston had avoided another of Sherman's traps, but he had been manuevered out of another strong defensive position.

In Virginia, where the rain continued to fall, the artillery and two divisions of Hancock's 2nd Corps began moving from the Federal right to the left at 4 a.m., while Birney's division edged to its left along the Union defenses, followed in turn by Kershaw's Division of Anderson's Confederate 1st Corps which was keeping an eye on these Yankees. At 12:45 p.m. Birney informed Hancock that he had established a solid line behind breastworks from Burnside's right to the Landrum house, and pickets from there to the Brown house and to the Ni River. He had also placed two brigades to the right rear of Burnside's position, as a tactical reserve. The rest of Hancock's 2nd Corps was put in temporary general reserve farther behind Burnside's 9th Corps. The new supply base at Belle Plain on the Potomac northeast of Fredericksburg was now operational, and the Fredericksburg-Spotsylvania road had become the Federal army's main supply line. The Union army now faced west, with Birney and Burnside on its right, Warren's 5th Corps in the center, and Wright's 6th Corps on the left. The trenches were becoming so soaked that the troops had taken to referring to their earthworks as waterworks.

Both Grant and Lee sent out cavalry to probe the other's new positions. Rosser's Confederate brigade moved up the Catharpin Road, pushing the 2nd Ohio Cavalry from the 9th Corps back to a field near Aldrich's, where it was repulsed by the 23rd U.S. Colored Troops infantry regiment from Ferrero's 4th Division of the 9th Corps, which was still guarding the area around Chancellorsville. But Rosser was able to report to Lee that the right of the Union line now lay near the Brown house, and that the enemy supply wagons had moved toward Fredericksburg. Meanwhile the 5th New York Cavalry, left behind by Wilson, and the 13th Pennsylvania Cavalry of Burnside's corps, were reconnoitering to the south down the Telegraph Road past Massaponax Church, driving Rebel vedettes over the Po River at Stanard's Mill.

When Rooney Lee reported this fact to his father, Lee decided to stretch his line to the south. Anderson received orders to move his corps headquarters and Kershaw's Division to extend the right of the Confederate line. The troops began to move at 11 p m , and three hours later arrived two miles south of Spotsylvania on the road to Snell's Bridge over the Po. Meanwhile Wright's Georgia brigade of the Rebel 3rd Corps was sent forward to secure a hill that would be needed for the extended line. Wright mishandled this assignment and Nate Harris' Mississippians had to be sent to complete the task. Lee and A. P. Hill, who was still too sick to resume command, watched from a nearby church. Hill fumed at Wright's incompetence, vowing to call him before a court of inquiry. But Lee would not agree and gave Hill a lesson in his style of command: "These men are not an army, they are citizens defending their country. General Wright is not a soldier; he's a lawyer. I cannot do many things that I could do with a trained army," he added. "The soldiers know their duties better than the general officers do, and they have fought magnificently. Sometimes I would like to mask troops and then deploy them, but if I were to give the proper order, the general officers would not understand it; so I have to make the best of what I have and lose much time in making dispositions. You understand all this," he told Hill, "but if you humiliated General Wright, the people of Georgia would not understand. Besides, whom would you put in his place? You'll have to do what I do:

When a man makes a mistake, I call him to my tent, talk to him, and use the authority of my position to make him do the right thing the next time."[9]

The survivors of Johnson's Division, about 600 men, were returned to the line that night. The hardened veterans of the 21st Virginia made the move reluctantly for they had to leave behind a nest of four little orphaned bunnies which they had found in the field where they had been camped.

In southeastern Virginia, Kautz's raiding troopers spent that fifteenth day of May moving southward over 25 miles of muddy road to the town of Lawrenceville, which they reached at 8 p.m. There they found Confederate stockpiles of corn, bacon, and salt. After consuming what they needed, they destroyed the rest while detachments of the 5th and 7th South Carolina Cavalry regiments were fanning out from Black's and White's in search of these Union raiders.

Another Federal cavalry division, that under Averell, finally overtook the infantry of General George Crook at Union, West Virginia that day, but both forces continued to retreat toward Meadow Bluff. Their department commander, Sigel, was having his own problems.

Breckinridge appeared at Imboden's headquarters south of New Market sometime after 3 a.m. on the fifteenth with word that his infantry would arrive before dawn. His men had marched all through the rainy night and just after dawn were eating their breakfasts in hasty camps along the roadside when they heard firing break out up ahead. Among the Rebel infantry was the battalion of cadets from the Virginia Military Institute (VMI), called out to help strengthen the small force available in the Valley. When they saw their commander ride by, one cadet called out, "Boys! three cheers for Gen. Breckenridge." But the general stopped and cautioned the cadets that they were near the enemy and should be as quiet as possible. "We have more serious work to do," he said.[10]

The Confederate general rode on and surveyed the fields around New Market. He selected high ground two miles south of the town, called Williamson's Hill, as the site for his infantry to defend. While the men built breastworks out of fence rails and dirt, Breckinridge decided to prod the Yankees to get them to attack his strong position. He ordered Imboden to attack Moor and then feign retreat, in order to lure the Federals into counterattacking. But Moor saw through this stratagem and stayed put. The Southerner then sent his guns forward to try to stir up a fight. He managed to bring on a two-hour artillery duel, but that was all.

With Imboden's help, Breckinridge then studied the terrain and decided that this area, bounded on the west by the North Fork of the Shenandoah River and on the east by Smith's Creek, was ideal for the deployment of his small army. Most of the ground between the Valley Turnpike and the creek was marshy, so any advance that he made between the pike and the river would have both flanks protected, one by the river, the other by the swampy ground. The area in question consisted of a series of fairly gentle hills, almost all of which were cleared and cultivated. Soon a message arrived informing him that Morgan had successfully defended Wytheville from Averell, and that Crook was on his way back over the mountains into West Virginia. Then Rebel signalmen up on Massanutten Mountain informed him of Moor's position and numbers, clearly indicating that he faced only part of Sigel's force. All this, coupled with his feeling that Yankees probably did not yet know that he had joined Imboden, led him to a change of plan. At 10 a.m. he looked at his watch and said to one of his battalion commanders, "Well, I have offered him battle and he declines to advance on us, I shall advance on him." Turning to Imboden, he said, "We can attack and whip them here, and I'll do it."[11]

---

1. Davis, *The Battle of New Market*, 68.
2. Ibid., 69.
3. Earl Schenck Miers, *The General Who Marched To Hell* (New York, 1951), 94.
4. McDonough and Jones, *War So Terrible*, 112–113.
5. Ibid., 111.
6. Michael J. Klinger, "Botched Union Attack," *America's Civil War* September 1989, 24.
7. McDonough and Jones, *War So Terrible*, 114.
8. Ibid., 116.
9. Freeman, *R. E. Lee*, 3:331.
10. Davis, *The Battle of New Market*, 79.
11. Ibid., 83.

CHAPTER TWENTY-NINE

"Well Done, Virginians!"

15 May 1864

At 7 a.m. on 15 May, Colonel Moor received reports from citizens of the area that Breckenridge had joined Imboden, and before 8 a.m. the Union general had seen the Rebel infantry take position on Williamson's Hill. Early that morning a Major Lang had arrived with a squad of couriers to keep Sigel advised of the situation at the front, and one of these messengers was sent back almost immediately with the news of Breckinridge's arrival. A little after 10 a.m. another was sent with a more urgent message, "The enemy advances."[1] Just after the courier left, Stahel arrived with the rest of the Federal cavalry and assumed overall command.

Major General Julius Stahel-Szamvald, commander of the 1st Cavalry Division of Sigel's Department of West Virginia, was born in Hungary and had been a lieutenant in the Austrian army before joining the unsuccessful Hungarian revolt of 1848. He had then fled to London and Berlin, and immigrated to the United States in 1859. He had been a lieutenant colonel of infantry at the first battle of Bull Run, had commanded a brigade under Fremont during Stonewall Jackson's Shenandoah Valley campaign of 1862, a division in Sigel's corps at Second Bull Run, the cavalry of the defenses of Washington, and Lincoln's guard of honor for the Gettysburg address. Sigel was very fond of him and asked for him when taking over the Department of West Virginia. One of Sigel's staff officers, however, described him as "a little fellow, rather insignificant, looking for all the world like a traveling clerk. Stahel is a very good fancy cavalry officer," he added, "who has never done anything in the field and never will do anything."[2] Now Stahel decided to pull the Union forces back in order to shorten the distance between them and the rest of the Federal column coming forward under Sigel.

By 11 a.m. Breckinridge had Wharton's Brigade, reinforced by the dismounted 23rd Virginia Cavalry, 62nd Virginia Mounted Infantry, and an independent company of Missouri cavalry, all from Imboden's Brigade, deployed as the main Confederate line on Shirley's Hill, west of the turnpike. The 26th Virginia Battalion of Echol's command and the battalion of VMI cadets formed a reserve behind the center of this line, and the rest of Echol's small brigade formed to the right of, and about 200 yards behind, Wharton's, with its right flank just east of the pike.

Then the Kentuckian began to move his units about and change formations. The commander of the 26th Virginia recognized that the former vice-president "was playing the old strategic trick of countermarching his men with the view of multiplying their numbers in the eyes of the enemy. It impressed me most favorably as to his strategy."[3] Eventually the infantry units were back in their original arrangement, and fourteen guns were in position to support them. Imboden was ordered to take what was left of his cavalry and four guns of horse artillery, move north between Smith's Creek and Massanutten Mountain, get behind the Yankees, and destroy the bridge over the Shenandoah. An order was also sent over the mountain to the forty-man 2nd Maryland Cavalry Battalion in the Luray Valley, directing it toward the same bridge. If either cavalry force could destroy that span and Breckinridge could defeat Sigel, he would, as he wrote to the commander of the Marylanders, "capture his whole army, trains and all."[4]

Wharton, while he was waiting for Echols to get his brigade into position, crept forward for a personal reconnaissance. The Federal forces occupied Manor's Hill, the next high ground north of the Confederate position on Shirley's Hill. In between was low ground known as New Market Valley. The Union infantry was behind a low stone wall bordering a road that ran down the hill to St. Matthew's Church, on the turnpike at the northern end of the town. A battery of artillery was in the church's cemetery near the eastern end of the Federal line, and another was in a clump of cedars on the western end of the line. It was not a bad position, but not strongly held, and Wharton believed his own brigade could take it alone. He knew the Northern artillery, always well handled, would have his men in sight as soon as they started forward, but he calculated that once the Southerners reached the low ground between the two hills they would be safe, because the Union guns sat too far back on Manor's Hill to fire into the valley. So Wharton returned to his brigade and gave instructions that when the order came to advance his men should rush down the hill, without worrying about their formations until they reached a rail fence in the low ground. There they could reform for the move up Manor's Hill.

A little after 11 a.m., through a light rain, the Confederate skirmishers moved forward, driving Moor's pickets out of New Market Valley and back to their main line. As the Rebel skirmishers formed along the fence at the bottom of the hill Southern guns began shelling them by mistake, but word was quickly sent back uphill, and the fire stopped. Then the main line of Wharton's infantry started down the hill "like a swarm of bees," wrote a Northern gunner. "A cold chill runs down our backs." One Federal, knowing that Sigel's force was spread out over twenty miles of road said, "It was easy to comprehend what the outcome was going to be." Major Lang immediately sent off another courier to Sigel, and soon after, when Echol's Brigade was seen, yet another was sent. The Union guns opened on Wharton's men as they raced down Shirley's Hill, but not one was hit. Echol's men also rushed forward, but the reserve line, including the VMI cadets, came down the hill in perfect order with fifes and drums playing, and the Union gunners began to find the range. "The ball opens," muttered one of Wharton's men looking back from the valley.[5]

A shell exploded in the midst of the cadets, fracturing the skull of one and wounding several others less seriously, but they closed ranks and continued on down to the fence in the valley. There the Rebel infantry rested a half-hour while the artillery was brought up to the southern outskirts of New Market. One cadet found it "a half hour of intense suspense—the artillery on either side firing—the shot and shell flying and bursting high over our heads—knowing that in a short time we must charge the Infantry, whose dark line we saw drawn up in the woods. What resolutions and vows were made then." Wharton brought the 26th Virginia forward to extend his front line, and Breckinridge gave the order to advance. Wharton's men put their rifle butts against the railings of the fence, knocked it to the ground, and started up Manor's Hill. Then Echol's Brigade started forward, and finally the cadets, now alone in the reserve line. "Nothing could have been finer than their advance," wrote a Union colonel. "The air filled with bullets and bursting shells, and my men began to fall."[6]

Stahel, considering the Rebels "far superior to us in strength," ordered the Federals to withdraw, and a few minutes later Sigel arrived and took personal command. The day had gotten off to a bad start for the Union commander. He had arisen at 5 a.m. to find that his brandy flask had been stolen. After further diminishing his main force by detaching 500 men to guard a wagon train headed back to Martinsburg, he and his staff had left Woodstock for New Market. As he advanced, reports from Major Lang began to reach him. The Rebels had 10,000 men, one said. Another said 15,000. He doubted that, but he ordered his units to concentrate at a good defensive position back at Mount Jackson. Then he had changed his mind. "We may as well fight them today as any day," he announced. "We will advance." And so he rode on to the front. Unfortunately for him, two infantry regiments, a battery of artillery, and General Sullivan, the infantry division commander, guarding the baggage trains in the rear, were not informed of the change of plan. Sigel arrived about noon, just as the Federals began to fall back to Bushong's Hill, and he confirmed Stahel's decision, ordering the latter to cover the move with his cavalry. Major Lang asked his commander about the rest of his army and was told it was on the way. "Yes, General," the major replied, "but too late."[7] Sigel and his staff began laying out a new defensive line and brought up recently arrived units. Finally he thought to send orders to Sullivan to bring all but one regiment forward.

Breckinridge climbed onto the chimney of the Henkel house in New Market to study the new Federal line, but almost immediately Union fire forced him back down again. He then rode forward to St. Matthew's Church to survey the enemy position from there. A projectile from a Northern cannon struck a gatepost about five feet from the general. The shell's failure to explode saved his life, although he and his staff were showered with splinters. The Southern commander considered the Union position a strong one, and he spent an hour or more adjusting his units. A 37-man company of engineers was sent to extend the extreme left end of Wharton's line, and the 23rd Virginia Battalion of Echols' Brigade was spread out in a skirmish line east of the turnpike, although it and Echol's other unit, the 22nd Virginia under Colonel George S. Patton (grandfather of the World War II general) remained echeloned three or four hundred yards to Wharton's right rear. Ten of the Confederate guns were positioned east of the turnpike so that they could fire obliquely into the Federals without getting in the way of the Rebel infantry.

Imboden was preparing his men for their move across Smith's Creek when he discovered that Stahel's Union cavalry was massed in very close order in a field behind some woods, between the pike and the creek. Imboden sent word to Breckinridge that he thought he could enfilade the Federal horse from a position east of the creek. The commander told the courier to "tell General Imboden, as he knows this ground, and I don't, to make any movement he thinks advantageous, and I will take all the responsibility and consequences."[8] Imboden took his 18th Virginia Cavalry and four guns off at a trot. After crossing to the east side of the creek they turned onto a road running along its bank where the artillery was placed on a slight rise, in rear of Stahel's line. The cavalry proceeded on down the creek toward the bridge over the Shenandoah behind the Federals. The first shot from the Rebel guns threw the Union troopers into confusion, but Stahel pulled them back, which was what Sigel now wanted him to do anyway.

Sigel had nullified his slight numerical superiority by splitting his forces again. Moor had been put in charge of an advanced line on a spur of high ground called Rice's Hill, and it was this that the Confederates were about to attack. Moor had the 350 men of the 18th Connecticut on his right, the 700 men of the 123rd Ohio in the center, some behind a stone fence, and six 12-pounder smoothbore cannon across the pike. Stahel's cavalry had been east of the road and farther north until forced to retire by Imboden's guns. Even farther north, and west of the pike, was Sigel's main line on Bushong's Hill.

The rain began to fall harder around 2 P.M., just as Stahel's cavalry fell back, and the Southern infantry finally advanced again, scaring a flock of sparrows who started up in fright and flew away. The Union artillery opened fire, but the shells passed harmlessly over the Rebels' heads. The Confederate guns east of the pike, soon joined by the horse artillery beyond the creek, then fired on the Federals and "seemed to strike them with consternation," in the opinion of an officer on Breckinridge's staff. One Southern shell knocked a wheel off a Union gun, and then the Rebel infantry charged with a cheer. "They came down on our . . . line like an avalanche," one Federal remembered.[9] The men of Moor's front line, seeing themselves outnumbered and their line overlapped on both flanks, fired one volley at the charging Rebels and fell back without waiting for orders. They disrupted Sigel's main line as they passed through it, and while most of the Connecticut regiment reformed behind this cover, the Ohioans kept right on going, all the way back to Mount Jackson.

Nevertheless, Sigel had chosen a strong defensive position where the distance between the Shenandoah and Smith's Creek was shorter than anywhere else on the field, giving protection to his flanks. Bushong's Hill was good high ground on his right, sloping down to level ground east of the pike, where the Confederate approach would be across rocky, muddy ground with little cover. On his right, Sigel had placed the twelve 3-inch rifles of a pair of batteries. Then came the infantry of the 34th Massachussetts, part of it behind a stone wall, the 1st West Virginia, and the 54th Pennsylvania, the latter extending to the turnpike with some cover

from a fence and a grove of cedars. East of the road was Stahel's cavalry in
three lines, overlooking a wooded ravine that any attackers on this side of
the pike would have to cross. In front of the cavalry, near the pike, was a
battery of four 3-inch rifles. The five smoothbore guns that had been in
Moor's advanced line were placed on a slight rise in front of the 34th
Massachussetts. The infantry of the 12th West Virginia, a hard-luck unit,
were in column formation behind the New Englanders, as a reserve. Later
Sigel wanted to ride to his left to check on his cavalry but to his surprise
he found that, when he moved, the 12th West Virginia, like a scared
puppy, insisted on going with him. The only way he could keep it in place
behind his main line was to stay there himself.

Breckinridge kept his units advancing, and soon Wharton's line reached
the crest of a small rise near the Bushong house, in front of the Union
position. Here the 26th Virginia was squeezed out of the line by an
eastward loop of the Shenandoah, and fell back as a reserve again. The
Federal guns, which had been dueling with the Rebel artillery, swivelled
to bear on the infantry with double loads of cannister while the Northern
infantry lay down to stay out of the way. The effect on the Confederates
was deadly, but they kept coming, yelling like demons. Then, company
by company, the men of the 51st Virginia ground to a halt. "Their first
line was almost annihilated," one Federal witness wrote. Then they began
to fall back, and the Yankees gave them a taunting cheer. Part of the 30th
Virginia was also driven back, and then so was the 62nd. Over on the east
side of the turnpike Echols' men reached the crest of a slight ridge
overlooking the wooded ravine in front of Stahel's cavalry and were
brought to a halt by the fire of these troopers. Breckinridge faced a critical
situation with his center falling back and the rest of his men pinned by
Federal fire. A staff officer urged him to use his only reserve, the VMI
cadets, to fill the gap in his line. He had tried his best to keep these
youngsters out of the fight, but now necessity forced his hand. "Put the
boys in," he said, "and may God forgive me for the order."[10]

The cadets advanced to the rise of ground near the Bushong house and
were met by the fire of the Union guns. The battalion's colors were soon
riddled with holes, and another shell exploded in their midst, but the
boys closed ranks and came on. As two companies went around the left
side of the house, and the other two around the right, they could hear
Federal bullets thudding against the clapboards. The two halves of the
little battalion rejoined as they pushed on into an orchard under a withering fire, and casualties mounted rapidly. The boys faltered when their
commandant was knocked down by a spent shell fragment, but another
officer assumed command, and they ran another thirty yards and took

cover behind a fence along the north edge of the orchard, closing the gap. From this slight cover they rose to one knee and delivered a disciplined volley. Then many of the cadets discovered that the rain had so swollen their old-fashioned, wooden ramrods that they could not be drawn from their clasps to reload the rifles. Fire from the Union guns was tearing over their heads and into the orchard behind them like a gale. To their left, the 26th Virginia advanced to help fill the gap in the Confederate line, mingling with remnants of the 51st.

Over on his right, Breckinridge could see Stahel's 2,000 troopers massing in a column of squadrons for an advance against Echols, and at about 2:45 P.M., just as the sky darkened, the rain quickened, and lightning split the sky, they came on. Directly in their path was the main body of the 23rd Virginia Infantry Battalion, whose men grouped together in clumps of three or four to form miniature versions of the hollow square that was infantry's traditional defense against a mounted charge. Breckinridge brought up most of his artillery to a low stone wall near the road, and a volley of cannister slowed the Yankee mass. Then two companies of the 23rd that were strung out in skirmish formation on the far right flank of Echol's line wheeled to their left to fire into one Federal flank, and Patton's 22nd Virginia turned to its right to fire into the other. When Imboden's horse artillery added its fire from east of the creek, the Union charge broke down into a confused mass of horsemen, some still trying to go forward, some trying to go back, and some going down under the crossfire. Patton's infantry started forward, and soon the disordered Northern troopers broke for the rear. Stahel was just riding up to report to Sigel when he looked back to see his command disintegrating like a wet lump of sugar. "Mein Gott, General Sigel!" he cried in bewilderment. "Vare ish mein cavalrie?"[11]

Sigel now, one staff officer recorded, "rode here and there with Stahel and Moor, all jabbering in German. In his excitement he seemed to forget his English entirely, and the purely American portion of his staff were totally useless to him."[12] With his cavalry on his left routed and Rebel skirmishers working their way through the woods on his right to harass his artillerymen there, Sigel decided he must do something to keep the momentum of the battle from swinging back to the Confederates. He ordered Colonel Joseph Thoburn, a good officer commanding the infantry of the main Union line, to advance. By now the noise of battle was so great that when Thoburn rode past Colonel Wells of the 34th Massachusetts and yelled something to him, Wells could not understand him. It was only when he saw the 1st West Virginia advance that Wells realized that Thoburn had ordered him to charge. The colonel of the 54th Pennsylvania got the word the same way. A few minutes before, the Federal advance would have struck the gap in Wharton's line. Now that gap was filled by the 26th Virginia and the VMI cadets.

Because it was in the center and had moved out first, both of the 1st West Virginia's flanks were exposed, and it advanced only about 100 yards before rifle fire in its front, and artillery fire from the pike, stopped it and caused it to fall back. The Pennsylvanians, on the Union left, were enfiladed by Echols' men across the turnpike and, after a gallant attempt to stand, also pulled back. On the right, the 34th Massachusetts kept going because the men could not hear Colonel Wells' order to halt, thereby losing nearly half its men in just a few minutes. Finally Wells himself took hold of the color-bearer and turned him to the rear, and the rest of the men finally got the idea. Like the Pennsylvanians, they withdrew in good order. However, the 1st West Virginia had continued on to the rear. Then the Federal guns began to limber up to pull out.

Color Sergeant Frank Lindamood of the 51st Virginia strode out in front of Wharton's line, waved his banner, and called for his regiment to rally on him and charge the Yankees. A few men did, only to be shot down by the 34th Massachusetts, but Lindamood kept trying, and soon he was joined by the color-bearer of the 26th. By 3 P.M., Wharton's entire line was moving up the hill. The cadets' path took them through about fifty yards of mud that pulled the shoes right off the feet of some of them, but they made it across. Over on the far right, Echols' line also joined the new advance, and the Confederate guns fired round after round in support. Everyone, on both sides, knew that the decisive moment had come. With Stahel's cavalry out of the way, there were no Yankees in Echols' front, so his men threatened the flank of the 54th Pennsylvania, which had to withdraw after losing almost half its men that afternoon. In the center, the 1st West Virginia put up almost no resistance, and another of the Federal smoothbore cannons was lost when it could not be withdrawn before the VMI battalion overran the battery's position. "A wild yell went up," Imboden recorded, "when a cadet mounted a caisson and waved the Institute flag in triumph over it."[13] Part of the cadets and the captured gun were then turned to enfilade the 34th Massachusetts.

This regiment was also faced with the 26th Virginia in its front, and the 51st on its front and right. It too had to withdraw, and once again Colonel Wells had to lead his color-bearer to the rear to make his men understand, because the noise was still too great for them to hear his orders. Sigel might not have been brilliant, but he was no coward. He stayed with the 34th, riding back and forth behind the line. "How he escaped is a mystery to me," Colonel Wells would later say.[14] The 12th West Virginia was ordered to cover the withdrawal of the guns on the Federal right, but refused to obey, joining the retreat instead. Two more guns had to be abandoned, and in the confusion one man was run down by a cannon wheel. His life was saved by the cushioning effect of the mud beneath him as the heavy carriage rolled over his body. Another gun became stuck in the mire, and Sigel personally helped try to free it but finally had to order it abandoned also. Except for the 34th Massachusetts and the 54th Pennsylvania, which formed the rear guard, most of the Union army was fleeing down the turnpike in disorder. One company of the 34th, detached to the woods by the bluffs of the Shenandoah, was cut off and forced to surrender.

About 3:30 p.m. one more Union reinforcement arrived on the field: a battery of six 3-inch rifles commanded by Captain Henry A. du Pont, scion of the wealthy Delaware du Ponts and a very able artillerist. He placed his 2-gun sections about 500 yards behind each other so that one could fire until almost overrun by the Confederates, then retire under the cover of the other two and take up a position from which to help cover each of the others in turn. These leap-frogging guns did much to slow the Rebel pursuit and save the disorganized army. Another of the luckless smoothbore guns, meanwhile, became stuck in the road and had to be abandoned.

Breckinridge rode up to the battalion of VMI cadets and called them to a halt. "Young gentlemen," he told them, "I have to thank you for the result of today's operations." They had lost 57 killed and wounded, or better than one out of every five. He would not further expose to danger what Jefferson Davis referred to as the seed corn of the nation. The boys were ordered to fall out and rest on the north slope of Bushong's Hill. With a final, "Well done, Virginians! Well done, men!" the general rode on.[15] The rest of the Confederate force was also given a rest while ammunition was brought up to replenish their cartridge boxes. The former vice president expected Sigel to make another stand on Rude's Hill, especially if the Southern cavalry had succeeded in cutting off the Federal retreat by downing the bridge over the Shenandoah between that eminence and Mount Jackson. But Imboden soon returned to announce that he had found Smith's Creek to be so swollen by the rain that he was unable to get his horsemen across it behind the Yankees. Thus it was evident that the vital bridge still stood for Sigel's use, as the 2nd Maryland Cavalry Battalion could not possibly reach it in time from the Luray Valley. Breckinridge ordered Imboden to bring his 18th Virginia Cavalry back across the bridge at New Market to join in the pursuit.

When the retreating Federals got to Rude's Hill they found there the 28th and 116th Ohio infantry regiments in line of battle, lying on the ground. General Sullivan had, after much hesitation and apparent fear of taking responsibility, finally caught up with the main force. Sigel later

NO TURNING BACK

blamed Sullivan for most of his problems. The two Ohio regiments and
what was left of the Union artillery formed Sigel's right, west of the pike,
and what could be salvaged of Stahel's cavalry again held the left, east of
the road, somewhat farther back than the infantry. Then Sigel conferred
with Sullivan, whose men were exhausted from their forced march to
reach the battlefield. Losses had been heavy, ammunition was low, and
the supply wagons were north of the Shenandoah bridge. The Union
commander decided that he could not risk another fight. He ordered a
withdrawal across the bridge to Mount Jackson, from where the army
would go on to Cedar Creek, near Strasburg, to reform. Stahel was put in
charge of the retreat, and Sullivan of the rear guard.

The Rebel artillery advanced to the foot of the hill and dueled with the
Union guns, while the Southern infantry came on again. Most of the
Federal shells were too high, but one struck a Confederate ammunition
chest and blew it to smithereens, killing a Rebel captain and badly
burning three other gunners. Wharton's skirmish line came within a half-
mile of Sullivan's line when the latter suddenly pulled back out of sight.
When the Southerners got to the top of Rude's Hill they looked down to
see the Federal army streaming across a piece of low ground known as
Meem's Bottom. The Rebel guns lashed at the fleeing column, but the
Confederate infantry could not catch the Yankees before they got across
the Shenandoah bridge. Du Pont's artillery was the last unit across, at
about 7 p.m., and the gunners burned the span behind them to prevent
further pursuit. The Rebels were heard six or seven miles away, cheering
their victory. "I never saw troops in better spirits," one Confederate
officer declared. "It is the first time that many of them have ever won a
victory, having served under slow coach generals in a slow coach department till Breckinridge handled them."[16]

The Federals stopped to rest a mile north of the bridge, but at 9 p.m.
they were on the road again. During their halt and night march the men
talked over their defeat, most taking it manfully. "All I have to say," one
artilleryman decided, "is they whipped us in a fair stand up fight and the
only reason that I can give for our defeat is that they fought better than
our men."[17]

"We are doing a good business in this department," Colonel David H.
Strother of Sigel's staff quipped. "Averell is tearing up the Virginia and
Tennessee Railroad while Sigel is tearing down the Valley turnpike."[18]

---

1. Davis, *The Battle of New Market*, 84.
2. Ibid., 13.

3. Ibid., 87.

4. Ibid., 88.

5. All quotes in this paragraph from Ibid., 90–92.

6. Ibid., 93–95.

7. Ibid., 96–99.

8. Ibid., 103.

9. Ibid., 103–105.

10. Ibid., 119.

11. Ibid., 126.

12. Ibid., 127–128.

13. Foote, *The Civil War,* 3:249.

14. Davis, *The Battle of New Market,* 138.

15. Ibid., 143.

16. Ibid., 153.

17. Ibid., 152.

18. Ibid., 162.

CHAPTER THIRTY

"Will Try My Best"

15–16 May 1864

In southern Virginia on 15 May, Baldy Smith had his forces preparing for the attack that Butler had ordered. Because he had no reserve, Smith wanted Turner's division to cover the flank of his attacking column but was informed that Gillmore, now that he was on the field, commanded Turner's division again. Then Smith sought to have Marston's brigade returned from the army's extreme left flank, but it could not be brought back in time. This gave Smith an excuse, and in a conference with Butler, he persuaded the latter to abandon the attack. Therefore the Federal troops did little that day but work at improving their own defenses and try to dry themselves between the intermittent showers into which the previous days' rain had degenerated. It being Sunday, some of the Federal units held religious services.

The troops manning the right end of Smith's line discovered that, not only was there about a mile of open ground between them and the James River, but there was a road, the Old Stage Road, not far beyond the last regiment, and it led straight to Burmuda Hundred. All this was defended solely by scattered pickets of the 2nd U.S. Colored Cavalry. To fill this gap, Butler gave Smith the 21st Connecticut, a recently arrived reinforcement, and one regiment of Ames' division of the 10th Corps. Near dark,

work parties collected telegraph wire from the turnpike and used it to
create entanglements in front of much of the Federal line. This was
suggested by Smith, who possibly had heard of the use of wire obstacles
in Burnside's defense of Knoxville the previous autumn. That had been
the first, and so far only, use of wire entanglements in military history.
Richmond papers would later call them "a devilish contrivance none but a
Yankee could devise."[1]

Butler entertained Phil Sheridan and several of his officers later that day.
Sheridan described for Butler the battle of the Wilderness and all that had
transpired prior to his departure on his current raid. Butler asked how
long it would take to get the Cavalry Corps back in fighting trim, and
Sheridan said seven or eight days. Butler then suggested that, since Grant
would have reached Richmond by that time, the cavalry might just as well
cross the James and join his forces. Sheridan declined, however.

While Butler and Sheridan were conferring, Wilson visited his old
friend Baldy Smith, receiving confidential information from the latter on
the internal politics of the Army of the James. Sheridan also talked with
Smith, who asked the former to tell Grant of the situation south of the
James, including the relationships of the three commanders, and recommended the cancellation of the campaign.

Two miles north of Butler's headquarters, at the Drewry mansion,
Beauregard was working on plans for an attack of his own. In a telegram
to Bragg he mentioned that it was to take place on Wednesday, the
eighteenth. Secretary of War Seddon objected to the delay, and President
Davis agreed. Bragg sent off orders to Whiting to move north immediately, as the defense of Richmond was more important than that of
Petersburg. Then Bragg informed Beauregard of these orders and suggested that the latter's attack begin the next day, the sixteenth. Beauregard
contemplated this latest interference from Richmond but did not protest
it, probably because it gave him an excuse to revert to his plan for a
converging attack. The only way Whiting could join in an attack the next
day was for his forces to aim for Butler's rear, while the rest of the
Confederates attacked the Yankee front. Orders were written for Whiting
to this effect and given to a young officer to carry around the Federal flank
to Petersburg, while another officer carried an explanation and justifica-
tion of the plan to Davis.

Beauregard spent the afternoon writing orders and preparing for the
coming battle. His hope was to separate Butler's army from its base at
Bermuda Hundred so that he could capture, or destroy, most of it. He
would do this by getting around the Union right flank by way of the Old

Stage Road while pinning the Yankees in place with frontal attacks. Robert Ransom was given the key assignment of turning the Federal right with 6,400 infantry in the brigades of Gracie, Barton, Lewis, and Terry, supported by Lieutenant Colonel C. E. Lightfoot's artillery battalion and part of the 5th South Carolina Cavalry. Hoke would make the attacks on the Union center and left with the 7,100 infantry of the brigades of Hagood, Johnson, Clingman, and Corse, supported by the Washington Artillery Battalion and the 3rd North Carolina Cavalry. Alfred Colquitt would hold the 4,000 infantry of his own and Matt Ransom's brigades in reserve, 500 yards behind Hoke's Division, with Captain S. T. Martin's artillery battalion and part of the 7th South Carolina Cavalry. Ransom was to move his men to the Confederate left after dark, form them into two lines, and advance at dawn, roll up the Union flank and seize the crossing of the Old Stage Road over Proctor's Creek. Hoke was to send a strong skirmish line forward at daylight to drive in the Federal pickets, then follow with two assault waves, 400 yards apart.

Beauregard met with his division commanders at 6 p.m. to go over the plan, and after dark the troops were quietly and efficiently moved to their assigned positions. Twelve miles away, in Petersburg, Chase Whiting was in a quandary. He had been working all day, preparing to advance the next morning on the circuitous route around Butler's flank to join Beauregard in time for a battle on the eighteenth. Then came belated orders from Bragg to abandon Petersburg and advance to the relief of Richmond. Whiting still believed Petersburg was itself vital to the safety of the capital, since most of the railroads to the latter passed through the former, and he was agonizing over whether to disobey this order when he received further orders from Beauregard, which he decided to implement, even though they would also leave Petersburg practically defenseless. Finally, at 11 p.m., he received the order which Beauregard had sent out at 10:45 a.m. for Whiting to advance directly against the rear of Butler's force. This was more to his liking. "All right," he wired Bragg. "Got the orders I want now. Will try my best."[2]

By 10 o'clock that night, fog was rolling up from the James River to blanket the opposing armies near Drewry's Bluff. The stillness was interrupted by numerous clashes between the pickets of the two sides all through the night. At 4:45 a.m. on the sixteenth, Robert Ransom gave the order for his troops to advance. Gracie's Alabamans formed the left of the front line and Lewis' North Carolinians the right, while the two Virginia brigades formed the second line. Skirmishers probed ahead through the fifteen-yard visibility. Those on the left almost immediately came to the

Willis house, garrisoned by Company H of the 9th New Jersey as an advanced outpost. These Federals quickly decided that it was time to get out.

The Union right was held by Brigadier General Charles A. Heckman's 1st Brigade of the 2nd Division of Smith's 18th Corps. This unit's four regiments had been reinforced by three others. These attached regiments occupied the defenses originally constructed by the brigade, while the original four had been moved to extend the line farther to the right. Even so, only seven companies of the right-most regiment, the 9th New Jersey, were east of the Old Stage Road, and almost no defenses had been constructed for the four regiments. The New Jersey troops were partially protected by a pond and a small stream in their front, and near the center of the brigade was a slightly sunken road that offered some shelter. Otherwise the only cover for these troops was the forest.

As soon as Heckman's pickets were out of the way, his seven regiments fired a booming volley into the fog, then reloaded and fired individually as fast as they could. Ransom's men gave a cheer and came on, but their advance soon began to stall. In the fog, Lewis' brigade, on the right of Ransom's front line, became divided. The left half was stalled by the deadly fire of the three regiments attached to Heckman, while the other half edged off to the right and became entangled in the telegraph wire stretched a foot above the ground in front of Wistar's 2nd Brigade, 2nd Division, 18th Corps. There these troops stayed, firing blindly into the fog, and within a half-hour they had shot off all their ammunition. Barton's Brigade from the second line blundered into the gap in the middle of Lewis' formation and into deadly volleys from the 8th Maine and 21st Connecticut on the left of Heckman's long line. These Virginians took heavy casualties, fell back, and joined Lewis' men in blindly firing off their ammunition into the fog. Ransom's entire attack would have failed except that Gracie's left regiment, the 41st Alabama, eventually discovered that the 9th New Jersey's flank could be turned.

This regiment had already lost its 23-year-old colonel, and its lieutenant colonel twice pulled back his three right companies to protect against the new threat. When Heckman arrived to check on this flank he was told that the Jerseymen had taken heavy losses and were almost out of ammunition, so he ordered the regiment to retreat. The men fell back through the mist and the gunsmoke in small groups, the color-bearers ripping the national and state flags from their staffs and stuffing them into their jackets to hide them from capture. Two companies did not receive the order to retreat but, after refusing a "rude and ill-mannered request" to surrender, fled to the rear, only to run into, and be captured by, more Rebels.[3]

The Old Stage Road was now unprotected, but Gracie did not realize it. He saw only that his own troops had taken heavy losses without gaining ground, and he let them lie down to fire blindly into the fog while he rode back in search of Terry's Brigade in the Confederate second line. Riding up to Terry, "cursing and swearing like a sailor, apparently oblivious of the danger from the balls that were flying through the air, calling his men 'd----d cowards,' and using much strong language," he asked for the loan of a regiment or two. Terry's Brigade had been part of Pickett's Division at Gettysburg, where it had taken tremendous losses, and it still numbered fewer than 900 men. Rather than send it in piecemeal, Terry decided to take the entire brigade forward. The Virginians plunged into the fog with a wild scream and soon passed over Gracie's Alabamans, still lying in the mud. "Hurry up, boys," one of these called out, "they are tearing us all to pieces."[4]

Terry's right two regiments, the 11th and 24th Virginia, ran into a hail of fire from Heckman's three Massachusetts regiments and soon ground to a halt, but the other two, the 1st and 7th, met no opposition and continued south about 100 yards beyond the original Federal position before swinging to their right into the woods. Before long they came upon several untended fires and coffee pots, a sure sign that they were behind the Union line. While some stopped to sample the coffee, a rare item in the blockaded South, others captured General Heckman, who almost succeeded in bluffing his way out by claiming to be an officer of Hoke's staff. After a friendly chat with Gracie he was marched to Fort Darling, and he was in Libby Prison in Richmond by 9 a.m.

With the 9th New Jersey gone, the 23rd Massachusetts now held the Union right flank. It too had lost its commander. The senior captain discovered the Virginians moving west behind his line and ordered the regiment to fix bayonets, face to the rear, and fall back. Fifty-one men, including the bearer of the state colors, were captured, and forty others were left behind dead or wounded, out of 220 in the unit. That left the 27th Massachusetts, which met a Rebel demand for surrender with a point-blank volley that took out nine Virginians, but it was soon cut off, and 249 Federals were captured. That, in turn, exposed the flank of the 25th Massachusetts. Its lieutenant colonel ordered his men to face about and charge. The regiment lost 140 men and all organization, but the move checked the Confederate advance long enough for the next Union regiment, the 98th New York, to change its facing from north to east and temporarily stabilize the Federal flank. About an hour had passed since the Southern advance had begun. Due to the fog, inexperienced commanders, and stubborn Union resistance, Ransom's four brigades were badly disorganized and running low on ammunition. He called a halt.

Baldy Smith had been asleep at the Friend house when he was awakened by the first volleys of the engagement. He moved to the turnpike, established his headquarters in a central spot, reported the attack to Butler, and asked for reinforcements. Butler relayed his request to General Adelbert Ames, commanding the reserve at the Half-Way House. Ames sent the 112th New York toward the Union right, but the regiment encountered Confederates sooner than had been expected, lost its commander, and was driven back in confusion. Meanwhile, Smith ordered the corps artillery and supply trains to the rear to prevent their capture, and sent an officer to Ames to ask for even more help. The 9th Maine was quickly dispatched, and before long it ran into the retreating 112th New York. Both units belonged to the brigade of Colonel J. C. Drake, who was with the 9th Maine at the time, and he deployed the two regiments to control the junction of the road on which they had advanced with the Old Stage Road. Here they were soon joined by Brigadier General Godfrey Weitzel, commander of the division that included Heckman's and Wistar's brigades. He gathered up retreating remnants of Heckman's brigade and placed them under the command of Colonel Josiah Pickett of the 25th Massachusetts. Pickett collected about 400 men, who joined Drake's line. Weitzel sent off a message to Smith that the far right was still in danger, then rode off to see to the rest of his line.

At 6 a.m. Butler wrote to Gillmore: "The enemy has advanced from his works on our right and made a vigorous demonstration there; a rapid movement on the left would, I think, carry his lines in your front. Make it at once."[5] But before Butler could transfer the fight from one flank to the other, Hoke's Confederates attacked the center. Because of the length of front he had to cover, Hoke was only supposed to make a demonstration, keeping the Federals in his front too busy to cause trouble until Ransom had disposed of the Union right. When he had heard Ransom's attack begin, Hoke had sent skirmishers forward and opened with his artillery, but the fog prevented him from seeing how Ransom was doing. About 6 a.m. he advanced Hagood's and Johnson's brigades on each side of the turnpike in expectation of connecting with Ransom's right, but soon both were heavily engaged with the Federals, who obviously were not beaten.

East of the turnpike, Hagood reached the protection of an old line of entrenchments, but just ahead he could see another line of defenses occupied by the Yankees. Hoke came along and, expecting to see Ransom's division sweeping westward at any moment, ordered Hagood to face his men in the same direction. As soon as Hoke had gone on, the movement came to grief, running into the wire entanglements in front of Wistar's brigade, which poured a heavy fire into the South Carolinians

from three directions. Hagood pulled his men back to the old entrenchments. West of the pike, Johnson's small brigade ran into more wire
entanglements in front of Brigadier General Hiram Burnham's 2nd Brigade of the 1st Division of the 18th Corps. These Federals hit the Rebels
with a heavy fire, but Johnson's left struck the 8th Connecticut at an angle
in the old entrenchments which the Yankees were occupying and drove it
back, capturing two 12-pounder smoothbore cannon and three 20-
pounder rifles. But the Rebels who took over this stretch of trenches were
almost surrounded, and eventually about fifty of the Tennesseans surrendered.

Johnson called for help, and two regiments from Matt Ransom's Brigade were sent forward by Beauregard, but they went in too far to the
right, striking Barton's 2nd Brigade of the 2nd Division of the 10th
Corps. They were then flanked and they made a disorganized retreat back
to their starting point. So Hoke sent forward two regiments from
Clingman's Brigade, but these also became lost in the fog. Finally Beauregard ordered Hoke to send in the rest of Clingman's Brigade and
Corse's also. Their attack was spirited but uncoordinated, and soon they
too were driven back almost to their starting places. It was only midmorning, but Hoke's attack had also ground to a halt.

However, although the Confederates had not defeated the Union
troops, they had beaten Baldly Smith. Unable to see the true state of
affairs, his imagination too readily filled the fog with potential disasters. A
small probe down the Old Stage Road by Rebel cavalry became in Smith's
mind an imminent, all-out attack against his already-weakened right. At
7:45 a.m. he ordered his two divisions to fall back slowly. Most of the
troops were unhappy with this order, as they believed they had been
winning, but they obeyed.

After the movement was under way, the fog finally lifted, and Smith
saw his error. He countermanded the order, but that was easier said than
done. Most of the units could not quickly be turned about. Wistar did
manage to get the 11th Connecticut and the 2nd New Hampshire back to
his brigade's original position, where they were able to spike several
abandoned cannon with horseshoe nails before rejoining the rest of
Weitzel's division along a new line covering the Half-Way House and the
intersection of the road from there with the Old Stage Road. The three
regiments that had been attached to Heckman's brigade, along with any of
Heckman's men that could be found, all under the command of Colonel
Wead of the 98th New York, formed the right of this line and Wistar's
brigade, the left.

It was 8 a.m. by the time the order to withdraw reached the two
remaining regiments of Burnham's brigade, west of the turnpike. Their

commanders were reluctant to leave the safety of their earthworks to retreat across an open field in full view of the Rebels. The officer who brought the order sympathized with their reasoning, noting the thousands of Confederates in the open to their front, who would have been perfect targets for Federal guns had Smith not ordered them withdrawn that morning. He volunteered to ride back and try to get this latest withdrawal order changed, but all he got for his trouble was a chewing out from Brooks, the division commander. So around 9 a.m. the two regiments fell back to form on Wistar's left.

As Smith's corps fell back, Beauregard tried to get his attack moving again. He had already sent Colquitt's Brigade to reinforce Ransom's division. Now he asked for its return so that it could be sent to stiffen Hoke's thin line. Colquitt's men were already in contact with the enemy, however, so Ransom sent Barton's Brigade instead. Beauregard then ordered Ransom to continue the flank attack down the Old Stage Road, but the latter took until 10 a.m. to get his units straightened out, by which time Beauregard had decided to hold off. He was concerned about Hoke's lack of progress and possible need for more reinforcements, and the fact that his general reserve was down to only three small regiments. More than anything, perhaps, he was hoping to see or hear Whiting's two brigades attack Butler's rear. Already, at about 8 a.m., some sounds of firing had been heard to the south, but only briefly. At 9 a.m. and again at 9:30 a.m. he sent off messages saying, "Press on and press over everything in your front, and the day will be complete."[6] But there was no sign or sound of any response.

Baldy Smith's men were also looking fruitlessly for help. No sign had been seen of the attack which Butler had ordered Gillmore to make at 6 a.m. Gillmore had received the order at 6:20 a.m., considered it briefly, and then told his division commanders, Terry on the left and Turner on the right, to prepare to advance. Just then, however, some of Hoke's skirmishers probed Terry's front, and Gillmore reported to Butler that his men were under attack. Then in the middle of preparing for his own advance Turner learned that, due to a rearrangement of 18th Corps units on his right, he would have to extend his own line in that direction, and Terry was ordered to send two regiments to reinforce Smith. More relatively weak Confederate probes were reported to Butler as attacks in force in a message sent by Gillmore at 7:01 a.m. The message ended: "If I move to the assault and meet a repulse, our loss would be fearful." At 7:25 a.m. Gillmore sent Butler a report from Turner claiming that Brooks' right flank had been turned and some artillery lost. This time he closed with the statement: "I am ready to assault, but shall wait until I hear from you, as I may have to support Smith. Please answer soon." This note soon came back with an endorsement denying that Brooks was flanked but giving Gillmore permission to "use discretion as to assault."[7] Considering that he had already balked for an hour and a half while under orders, there could be little doubt that now that he had official permission to use his own judgement he would not attack. It did not seem to occur to him that the best way for him to help Smith was to assault the Rebels.

Meanwhile, as the fight progressed on Smith's front, Turner kept getting messages from Brooks, in command of Smith's left, that he was moving farther to the right. Turner had to take two regiments from his left and move them to extend his own right. They arrived just in time to eject some Confederates who had penetrated the new gap between the two corps. Then Turner sent another regiment to join them. Meanwhile their brigade commander, Colonel Alford, was somewhere in the rear, suffering from what one of his men called a "severe attack of discretion."[8] At 8:34 a.m., Gillmore received word from Butler that Smith was moving to the right to protect his flank. Gillmore reasoned that if the Rebels were concentrating against Smith's right, an advance by his own forces would take them in the flank, so he finally decided to make his long-delayed assault. He ordered Terry to leave his skirmishers in place so as to fool the Confederates facing them, and to move the rest of his men to the right to join Turner in an attack to the northeast.

However, just as Gillmore was finally deciding to make an attack, the Rebels launched a real one of their own. One of Turner's regiments retreated before a heavy assault, and the pursuing Southerners were only driven out of the Federal entrenchments with considerable difficulty. One of Terry's brigades became disorganized while withdrawing and required some time to get straightened out again. Another brigade never got the order, found itself alone, ran into the Confederates, and was flanked and driven back. When at last the head of Terry's division could be seen approaching Turner's position, the latter found that yet another withdrawal by Brooks on his right had allowed the Rebels to get around on that flank, so that instead of attacking he was lucky to be able to hold his ground. Then Gillmore received a message from Butler's chief of staff that Smith's two divisions were falling back and that the 10th Corps commander must govern his actions accordingly. Worried about keeping an escape route open down the turnpike, Gillmore sent two regiments of Marston's brigade from his left to cover the road. The 39th Illinois was left to hold the brigade's old position on the army's left.

At 9:30 a.m., Gillmore ambiguously reported that he was "forming line of battle in the brush in rear of my old position." A string of even more confusing replies from headquarters seemed to justify his own decision to withdraw, and just as his men began to move he received an order to hurry because Ames was being attacked at Port Walthall Junction. Turner received Gillmore's order to retreat just as he was being hit on the right flank by the Rebels, who had again penetrated the gap between the two Union corps. The 117th New York covered the withdrawal of Turner's division, which fell back behind Proctor's Creek to the east of the turnpike. The retreat did not go so well for Terry's division. Some regiments wandered all around, getting separated from their brigades, and the 100th New York was attacked in the flank and shattered. Nobody thought to tell the 39th Illinois about the retreat. It too was soon flanked by advancing Confederates and overrun, and a detachment of Rebel cavalry captured most of what was left of both regiments.

Beauregard's troops took over the Federal defenses and five abandoned cannon, but they were too fought-out to do much more. Besides, the Southern commander was afraid that if he pushed the Federals too hard they would just retreat into the Bermuda Hundred defenses before Whiting arrived to block their way. Yet, try as he might, he could get no word of the troops from Petersburg. The quiet became embarrassing when President Davis, who had opposed the converging attack, showed up to see the battle with other government big-wigs from Richmond. Except for light skirmishing, there was no fighting to see. Just after 1 p.m. a message from Bragg arrived, suggesting that Beauregard send part of his force around the Union left, but Beauregard feared that even this move would drive the Yankees back to Bermuda Hundred. At 1:45 p.m. faint sounds of firing were heard to the south, and Davis, standing on a parapet, exclaimed, "At last!"[9] But the firing soon stopped and silence again descended.

Except for a few remnants, the entire Army of the James had established a new line around the Half-Way House by 2 p.m. East of the turnpike were Smith's two 18th Corps divisions, west of it was Terry's division of the 10th Corps, and Turner's division was in reserve south of Proctor's Creek. Then Butler decided to send Smith's corps back to recover the wounded and to scout out the position of the Rebels, and Gillmore was directed to take over part of Smith's new line and to protect his flank as he advanced. Between 2 and 3 p.m. the Federals advanced cautiously into the woods but ran into Confederate fire before they could reach most of the casualties from the morning's fight. After collecting those they could reach, Smith ordered his men to fall back again without making any serious effort to dislodge the Confederates.

Meanwhile, Butler received a message from Gillmore saying "that the intrenchments which I was ordered to fall back upon this morning have been reoccupied by the enemy."[10] Butler responded angrily that he had not ordered Gillmore to fall back until the latter had already ordered a withdrawal. Gillmore then rushed to army headquarters, where he engaged in a heated discussion with Butler about who had initiated the retreat. Finally, influenced by Smith's caution, Butler ordered a general retirement to the Bermuda Hundred defenses. He later claimed that he retreated because Grant had not lived up to his part of their bargain to meet near Richmond within ten days, thus revealing that he was still thinking as a politician who makes bargains, not a general who gives and takes orders. He feared just the sort of move Beauregard had proposed: a combination of Lee's and Beauregard's forces to overwhelm his own. But by withdrawing behind the Bermuda Hundred lines, he reasoned, he would be holding a secure base for the Army of the Potomac when it did arrive.

About 4 p.m. Beauregard finally received word from Whiting. According to the officer reporting, Whiting had stopped at Port Walthall Junction and could not be counted on to advance farther. Chase Whiting was forty years old in 1864. He had compiled the best academic records ever at both Georgetown College and West Point and had served as J. E. Johnston's chief engineer at the first battle of Bull Run. He had commanded an infantry division during the Peninsula campaign, then had been assigned to the District of Wilmington, North Carolina. There he had used his considerable engineering skills to design and build the famous Fort Fisher which protected that important port. But garrisoning coastal defenses was boring work and he longed to return to field duty. Meanwhile, rumor had it, he drank more than was prudent. Since coming to Petersburg constant worry, lack of sleep, and either drinking or suddenly not drinking had rapidly been wearing him down.

That morning he left the Swift Creek defenses, north of Petersburg, with Wise's 2,300 Virginia infantry, Martin's 3,000 North Carolinians, several batteries of artillery, and part of Dearing's cavalry brigade. About a mile north they ran into Federal pickets who slowed the advance. At the divergence of the two highways, Whiting sent Martin, with D. H. Hill along as unofficial adviser, up the Old Stage Road and personally led Wise up the turnpike. One cavalry regiment was sent to guard each flank. Slowly the Confederates pushed the handful of Union pickets northward to Port Walthall Junction, which was reached at about 8:30 a.m. There they were only six miles south of the main battle near Drewry's Bluff. Whiting claimed later that he heard only a few cannon shots from the battle to the north. Fearing an ambush, he brought up his artillery to bombard the wooded ridge north of Ashton Creek, where the elusive Yankee pickets had been seen to disappear into the trees.

In fact, Ames' division defending the Federal rear had been reduced by detachments to only two regiments of infantry, one battery of artillery and a detachment of the 1st U.S. Colored Cavalry. Assuming the Confederate bombardment to be the prelude to an attack, Ames had his men slowly pull back farther north. At 9 a.m. he was reinforced by the 97th Pennsylvania, sent down by Butler from his own headquarters. D. H. Hill witnessed both Ames' withdrawal and the arrival of the 97th, and he urged Whiting to advance, but it was 10:30 a.m. before his infantry reached the top of the ridge north of the creek. Again Whiting halted, worried because his right flank was only two miles west of the Union Bermuda Hundred defenses, where more Yankees might be lurking. He sent another former general, Roger Pryor, who was along as a scout, to reconnoiter. While he waited, his doubts played on his exhausted mind, and he began to worry about his left flank as well, and about the Federals slipping across the Appomattox to hit Petersburg in his absence. So he sent off a message to Beauregard requesting that the latter press on southward to connect with him where he was.

Meanwhile, D. H. Hill had been out observing Ames' Federals and was on his way to Whiting to recommend the resumption of the advance, when he came upon General Wise. Wise was a former governor of Virginia and an outspoken character. He suspected that Whiting was drunk, but then he himself had reported the nonexistent Yankee move around the left. Hill was doubtful whether that could be true, but he pointed out that if it was, Wise's brigade was in a bad position since the creek behind it would block any retreat, and he recommended a temporary withdrawal behind that stream. Wise was not convinced, but then he received direct orders from Whiting to do just that. Reluctantly he ordered the pull-back, which was conducted in a heavy shower. Then he was stunned to discover that his men were not stopping at the high ground south of the creek. Unknown to him, Whiting had ordered the retreat to continue.

Hill rode to Whiting and persuaded him to return the men to the high ground south of the creek while he and Colonel Logan, the staff officer who had brought Beauregard's orders the night before, went to find the Federals. They soon determined that the only enemy troops in the area were the few units which they had been facing all day. Hill sent Logan to inform Beauregard of the state of affairs and fired off a note to Whiting recommending an immediate advance. Whiting ignored this advice and did nothing more than order his artillery to fire at the Federals. Then he went to Martin and ordered him to withdraw his skirmishers. Hill, who was present, said, "General Whiting, you cannot occupy this place if you withdraw your skirmishers." Whiting replied, "You don't think that I intend to remain here?" The frustrated Hill said he did not know what Whiting's intentions were. The exhausted commander then directed Martin to withdraw his entire brigade, commenting that it made no difference in what order they went as "there is no enemy in our front."[11] Whiting had finally given in to his fears for the safety of Petersburg.

Half an hour later, Hill came upon a traffic jam of retreating units, all trying to use the Old Stage Road, and went to report the situation to Whiting. The latter asked Hill's advice. Hill answered that he had sent him his advice two hours earlier: to advance and brush the Yankees aside. Whiting replied that he had never received Hill's note. At that the disgusted Hill gave up and rode off for Swift Creek. Shortly thereafter, a courier brought Whiting Beauregard's note of 9 a.m., which by then was hopelessly obsolete. Nevertheless, this evidence of Beauregard's advance led Whiting to call a halt, and Dearing soon showed up with news of Beauregard's attack. By then Ames had been reinforced by two more regiments, and Whiting did not contemplate advancing again, but decided to wait a while to see if Beauregard showed up.

Guided by Dearing and a detachment of cavalry, Colonel Logan rode toward Beauregard by way of Chester Station, pressing on while his escort paused to round up a number of Federal stragglers. He found the general conversing with President Davis near the captured Union defenses and, as previously mentioned, reported that Whiting could not be relied upon to advance any farther. Beauregard took the news calmly, giving Logan the impression that he had long since given up any hope of good results from that quarter. The Rebel commander then ordered Hoke to send Corse's and Clingman's brigades across Proctor's Creek to Woolridge's Hill, and at 4:15 p.m. he sent Whiting notice of these dispositions and orders to join in the movement. When Whiting still did not appear, Corse and Clingman were ordered to follow the retreating Federals, but even this advance was delayed by a heavy thunderstorm. At 6:45 p.m. Beauregard sent Whiting word that he would attack again at daybreak, and told the latter to meet his forces three miles north of Port Walthall Junction.

Around 7 p.m. Whiting received Beauregard's message of 4:15 p.m. announcing his final advance, but by then the sun had already set and the light was fading. "Too late for action on my part," Whiting murmured. He sent back a note explaining that his inaction was due to the lack of any sound of sustained fighting to the north, and the delay of Beauregard's orders. He promised to do better the next day but still believed his own situation was perilous. "Don't let him press me tonight; position very bad," he said.[12] He sought out Wise and ordered him to let his men rest until 1 a.m. and then to fall back behind Swift Creek. Wise begged to be allowed to stay put. When that failed, he demanded the order be put in writing, and when it was, he reluctantly obeyed.

With no opposition from the Confederates, Terry's and Weitzel's divisions had masked the withdrawal of the rest of the Union army that afternoon and finally, between 8 and 9 p.m., the weary Federals filed back into the Bermuda Hundred defenses, where they were soon joined by Ames' little command. Waiting for them was the newly arrived 1st Connecticut Heavy Artillery, whose clean uniforms contrasted strongly with those of the bedraggled veterans. Union losses, in what became known as the Battle of Drewry's Bluff, had amounted to just over 3,000 killed, wounded, and missing. Confederate losses had been just under 3,000. On both sides officers immediately began to apportion the blame for failure.

1. Foote, *The Civil War,* 3:261
2. Robertson, *Back Door To Richmond,* 178.
3. Ibid., 185.
4. Both quotes from Ibid., 186.
5. Ibid., 189.
6. Freeman, *Lee's Lieutenants,* 3:488.
7. Robertson, *Back Door To Richmond,* 199–200.
8. Ibid., 200.
9. Freeman, *Lee's Lieutenants,* 3:489.
10. Robertson, *Back Door To Richmond,* 206.
11. Freeman, *Lee's Lieutenants,* 3:491.
12. Robertson, *Back Door To Richmond,* 215.

CHAPTER THIRTY-ONE

"All This News Was Very Discouraging"

16–19 May 1864

At 8 a.m. on 16 May Grant sent a message to Halleck that said: "We have had five days' almost constant rain without any prospect yet of its clearing up. The roads have now become so impassable that ambulances with wounded can no longer run between here and Fredericksburg. All offensive operations necessarily cease until we can have twenty-four hours of dry weather. The army is in the best of spirits and feel the greatest confidence in ultimate success. The promptness with which you have forwarded reenforcements will contribute greatly to diminishing our mortality list in insuring a complete victory. You can assure the President and Secretary of War that the elements alone have suspended hostilities and that it is in no manner due to weakness or exhaustion on our part."[1]

The roads were so bad, in fact, that there were 6,000 wounded men at Fredericksburg who could not be moved to Belle Plain for shipment to Washington. Where Grant got his information about the army's spirits he did not say, but probably not from the men in the front lines. Most of their letters home at this time indicated a decided distaste for assaulting prepared defenses and a profound weariness, since few of them had enjoyed more than two hours of uninterrupted sleep since 2 May. However, Walt Whitman's brother George, in the 9th Corps, wrote home that day that "we have had the best of the fighting so far and its my opinion that Genl Grant has got Lee in a pretty tight spot."[2] Most of the reinforcements to which Grant referred were still at Belle Plain and mainly consisted of more heavy artillery regiments sent down from Washington to serve as infantry. Also, on the evening of the sixteenth a brigade of four inexperienced New York infantry regiments, known as the Irish Legion, arrived from the same source.

New men were badly needed. Due to the rain-imposed inactivity, there was time to count noses and add up the losses, and the figures showed that, through 13 May, the 9th Corps and the Army of the Potomac, excluding the Cavalry Corps, had between them lost a bit over 36,872 men killed, wounded, and missing. When Grant expressed regret over such great losses, Assistant Secretary of War Dana remembered, Meade replied, "Well, General, we can't do these little tricks without losses."[3]

There were other subtractions to deal with also. The enlistments of more individuals and whole regiments were expiring, and some had already been sent home. That day, the sixteenth, Meade told Warren that he could muster out and discharge the Pennsylvania Reserves effective 31 May, provided that those individual members whose time was up before the 31st agreed to serve until then. Warren reported back that the 8th regiment, whose time had run out the day before, refused to accept that condition and that General Crawford doubted whether any of the others would either. There were only 75 men left in the 8th regiment anyway, so Warren was told to send them home.

Some losses were intentional. Back on 11 May Grant had suggested that Meade send the reserve artillery back to Belle Plain, as there never seemed to be any opportunity to use all those guns, and they and their ammunition wagons just added to the enormous, vulnerable tail of the army. Meade had not acted on that advice, so on the afternoon of 16 May Grant issued orders to both Meade and Burnside to send all their reserve artillery and its wagons to the supply depot the next day. Meade's chief of artillery was Brigadier General Henry J. Hunt, an excellent organizer and superb gunner who had spent nearly three years in building up the artillery reserve and its special ammunition train. It, and he, had been instrumental in Meade's victory at Gettysburg. When Hunt received word of Grant's order he offered a counterproposal. He recommended that all the batteries in the army be reduced from a norm of six, to four guns each, with the surplus being sent to Belle Plain. Each battery would keep its best horses and its six caissons, however, and the more cumbersome ammunition wagons would be sent back with the worst horses. Some infantrymen who had been detached to serve with the guns could thus be sent back to their regiments. This plan was approved for the Army of the Potomac. Burnside dutifully sent his reserve batteries back as ordered.

Gibbon's division of Hancock's 2nd Corps was sent in the early afternoon, with some 200 ambulances and wagons, back to the area west of the former Confederate salient to retrieve the wounded men of the 5th and 6th Corps who had been left at the home of Mrs. Katherine Couse. The wounded soldiers and their administering doctors were found crammed into all the outbuildings and under fly tents in the yard. They had twice been visited by Rosser's Rebel cavalry, who had stolen their rations and liberated any wounded Confederates who could walk, but they had otherwise been left unmolested.

On the Confederate side, Anderson's two divisions established themselves in new positions on Lee's right, extending all the way down to the Po River, with one battalion of artillery south of that stream in a position to enfilade any Union unit advancing against Anderson's front. In the absence of his late chief of cavalry, Lee was having trouble figuring out what Grant and Meade were up to. "Ah, Major," he remarked to H. B. McClellan, "if my poor friend Stuart were here I should know all about what those people are doing."[4] A little after noon that day Lee sent a telegram to Breckinridge up in the Shenandoah offering him "the thanks of this army for your victory over Genl Sigel. Press him down the Valley, & if practicable follow him into Maryland." He expanded upon that later in the day: "If you [do not deem] it practicable to carry out the suggestion of my dispatch of this morning to drive the enemy from the Valley & pursue him into Maryland, you can be of great service with this army. If you can follow Sigel into Maryland, you will do more good than by joining us. If you cannot, & your command is not otherwise needed in the Valley or in your department, I desire you to prepare to join me. Advise me whether the condition of affairs in your department will admit of this movement safely, & if so, I will notify you of the time and route."[5] With the bridge down over the North Fork of the Shenandoah, Breckinridge decided that pursuit was impractical, and to take the second alternative.

Out in Louisiana that sixteenth day of May, Banks' retreating army found its path blocked by Dick Taylor's Confederates in defensive positions, complete with thirty-plus guns, many of which had belonged to Banks until recently. The Federal commander sent his skirmishers forward and brought up his own guns, posted his cavalry on the flanks, and sent his infantry forward across a level prairie that Taylor described as "smooth as a billiard table."[6] The open terrain gave both sides a rare glimpse of the whole field with all its forces, silken flags flying—a panoply of war that recalls the biblical expression, "terrible as an army with banners."[7] But neither side seemed anxious to close with the enemy. Banks did not know that he had his nemesis outnumberd five to one. Finally, after four hours of long-range dueling, he brought forward A. J. Smith's veterans for an attack on the Rebel left, and Taylor, fuming because Kirby Smith still had not rejoined him with the infantry from Arkansas, drew off to the south and west to avoid the blow, leaving the road open for the resumption of the Union retreat.

In Georgia that day Sherman's armies were crossing the Oostanaula River in pursuit of Joe Johnston's Confederates. The latter, always defensive-minded, made no attempt to take advantage of the fact that the Federals were spread out and crossing the river in three different places, but continued on down the railroad to the town of Calhoun. In his post-war memoirs, Johnston wrote that during the previous winter he had wanted to fall back from Resaca to a better position at Calhoun, and yet a few pages later he related that when he arrived at Calhoun on the sixteenth of May he found that it was not a good defensive position. Maybe it just looked better when it was behind him than it did when he was there. At any rate, he continued south for another dozen miles through open country to Adairsville. Meanwhile, Sherman sent Garrard's cavalry division and an infantry division (under a general with the improbable name, for a Union officer, of Jefferson C. Davis) down a parallel road to the west. They captured without a fight the industrial town of Rome, Georgia, at the western terminus of a branch railroad leading to Alabama.

In southern Virginia, Kautz's Federal troopers were still on the road. They had traveled south all day on the fifteenth without incident and stopped at Lawrenceville that night. Early on the morning of the sixteenth they headed east toward a railroad bridge over the Meherrin River on the line running south from Petersburg to Weldon, North Carolina. But that afternoon, when Kautz approached Belfield, at the north end of the bridge, he found it defended by a sizable garrison behind a pair of earthworks. His own ammunition supply was running low, so he reluctantly turned his column to the north without challenging the defenders.

About 5 p.m. the Federals reached Jarratt's Station, the place they had stormed from the opposite direction eight days before. They were chagrined to find that the tracks they had ripped up had since been relaid and that most of the railroad buildings had been rebuilt. A train could be seen disappearing into the distance to the north, indicating that Nottoway Bridge had also been rebuilt during the past week. The troopers were put to destroying the station a second time, but they worked without spirit after seeing how quickly their previous destruction had been repaired. They merely pulled up a few rails and burned the new water tank, as well as destroying a pontoon train and some baggage left behind by Hoke's division.

Scouts reported that Nottoway Bridge was heavily defended, and considering his command to be in no condition to fight, Kautz bypassed it, following the Nottoway River northeast to Freeman's Bridge, which was reached around midnight. The Federals chased off some Confederates who had just destroyed two of the bridge's three spans. They then proceeded to prove that they too could perform prodigies of repair. Most of the 1st District of Columbia Cavalry had actually been recruited in Maine, and loggers from that regiment reconstructed the forty destroyed feet of bridge in less than three hours. Just before dawn on the seventeenth the column crossed to the north bank. When the Federals reached the Norfolk & Petersburg Railroad they found a crew hard at work repairing the damage they had done the week before. They scattered the workers and tore up the track again before moving on. Near 6 p.m. the advance guard reached City Point, and two hours later the tail of the column was safely inside the defenses. After what they had seen on their way back, the troopers had to wonder just what all their hard riding, hard work, and occasional combat had accomplished.

Sheridan's cavalry left the James River on the seventeenth, headed north to rejoin Grant, while Butler's troops spent the seventeenth settling back into their Bermuda Hundred defenses. The Confederates slowly pushed forward to reestablish contact with the Yankees. When the units from Petersburg finally linked up with Beauregard's main army, they were no longer under Whiting's command. Wise and Martin had refused to serve under him anymore, so he had turned the command over to D. H. Hill. Whiting had come along, however, and he asked Beauregard to officially relieve him and send him back to Wilmington. This was agreed to, and Hill's position was made more official, pending approval from the President, for Hill was still in Davis' bad graces. Robert Ransom also had to be replaced because he had been recalled to his Department of Richmond. Beauregard appointed Bushrod Johnson to take over his division.

At Adairsville, Georgia on 17 May, Joe Johnston was still not satisfied that he had found a good defensive position, so he called a council of war with his principal subordinates that night. His senior corps commander, the dependable Hardee, recommended that the army make a stand there. The cavalry division of Polk's Army of Mississippi had arrived and another infantry division was nearby, and word had arrived from General Stephen Dill Lee, left in command in Mississippi and Alabama by Polk, that Forrest would soon attack Sherman's railroad supply lines in middle Tennessee. But Johnston decided to fall back again. He had a plan.

At 5 a.m. in the Shenandoah Valley that seventeenth of May, Breckinridge had his two little brigades of infantry on the road south of New Market, headed for Staunton, and soon another wire from Lee arrived saying: "It is reported that Averell & Crook have retired. If you can organize a guard for Valley and be spared from it, proceed with infantry to Hanover Junction by railroad. Cavalry, if available, can march."[8] With the enemy driven from his own distant Department of Southwestern Virginia, Breckinridge returned the care of the Shenandoah to Imboden, and late that afternoon he boarded a buggy with his adjutant and started for Staunton himself. That same day Lee read the results of Beauregard's attack on Butler in the newspaper. The two victories, in the Valley and south of Richmond, relieved him of any immediate anxiety about those fronts and presented the possibility of help arriving from both directions for his own army.

The rain began to slack off around Spotsylvania that morning and the sun broke through with increasing confidence until by afternoon it was shining brightly. At 8 a.m. Meade sent orders for Hancock to prepare his corps for a move beyond the left of the 6th Corps, and an attack by the two corps at dawn on the eighteenth, pending the arrival of a division of heavy artillery regiments from Belle Plain that night. Burnside was told by Grant's headquarters to have his corps ready to move around behind Warren's troops to support the attack. Since these moves would make his 5th Corps the right of the Union army, Warren sent scouts and staff officers out to reconnoiter the area over which the planned assault would advance the next morning, and that afternoon they reported that the area was entirely unsuited for the passage of troops. The attack was cancelled.

However, Wright and Humphreys had been discussing the likelihood that Lee had weakened his left—the new line in rear of the captured salient—to strengthen his right against the Union shift in that direction. Wright believed that an attack on the left of the Confederate line at dawn would succeed, and Humphreys agreed. They took the plan to Meade and Grant, who decided to try it, using both the 6th and the 2nd Corps. Hancock was to return to the area around the Landrum house and Wright was to form on his right for an attack at 4 a.m. Burnside was ordered to be ready to follow the attack if it should succeed in breaking into the Rebel defenses. He was also to be ready to go to Warren's assistance if the 5th Corps should be attacked east of the Fredericksburg Road. As soon as it was dark the 2nd Corps began its movement over now-familiar and somewhat drier roads. Gibbon's 2nd Division was joined by the Irish Legion. Tyler's division of five over-large heavy artillery regiments also began to arrive, and the two new units added about 8,000 men to Hancock's corps.

That morning Grant, not yet aware of recent events in the Valley, had sent a message to Halleck saying that he wanted Sigel to advance from Woodstock to Staunton. Near midnight the reply came back: "I have sent the substance of your dispatch to General Sigel. Instead of advancing on Staunton he is already in full retreat on Strasburg. If you expect anything from him you will be mistaken. He will do nothing but run. He never did anything else. The Secretary of War proposes to put General Hunter in his place."[9] Grant replied, "By all means I would say appoint General Hunter, or anyone else, to the command of West Virginia."[10] Halleck had also sent word that Butler had been driven back into his Bermuda Hundred defenses. "All this news was very discouraging," Grant wrote in his memoirs, adding Banks' defeat in Louisiana to his list of troubles. "All of it must have been known by the enemy before it was by me," he noted. "In fact, the good news (for the enemy) must have been known to him at the moment I thought he was in despair, and his anguish had been already relieved when we were enjoying his supposed discomfiture."[11]

During the pre-dawn hours of 18 May Hancock's and Wright's troops moved into position. At 4:05 a.m., Hancock reported that two of Wright's divisions were not yet in place, so the attack would have to be delayed. One of Wright's divisions was still not ready at 4:35 a.m. but Hancock ordered the advance to begin anyway. Barlow's division formed the left of the attacking force with Gibbon's on his right, the two starting from just north of the breastworks of the old Confederate salient. To Gibbon's right was Neill's division of the 6th Corps. Ricketts' division was supposed to go in to the right of Neill, but was not ready yet, and Russell's formed in support behind the old Union works west of the salient. Tyler's new troops, forming a new 4th Division, 2nd Corps, were placed in the Union rifle pits that ran from the east angle to the Landrum house, where Birney's division and the 2nd Corps artillery were in reserve. To the left of these, Burnside had Crittenden's and Potter's divisions ready.

Ewell's Confederate 2nd Corps still manned the lines at which the attack was aimed. The evening before, his troops had received warning of a possible Union attack early in the morning. Their line ran along a rise of ground and had traverses every fifteen or twenty feet, with an abatis out in front to slow up the attackers. Rodes' Division manned the Rebel left and Gordon's, the right, and there were 29 cannon supporting the infantry.

The four brigades in Barlow's and Gibbon's front lines climbed over the old works in the area between the oak tree that had been shot down on the twelfth and the east angle, and moved into the woods to the south. The second line of each division stopped at the works to await developments. As the front line advanced, Gibbon's right brigade emerged from the trees into the fields around the McCoull house, in the center of the old salient, and was spotted by Confederate artillerymen, who opened fire. When the attacking Federals reached the old Confederate reserve line, Gibbon ordered his two second-line brigades forward. Meanwhile, the front-line brigades of both divisions advanced to the abatis in front of the Confederate defenses, which Barlow informed Hancock was the thickest he had ever seen, over 100 yards deep. He said he did not think his men could get through it. The front-line troops lay down to avoid the worst of the Rebel fire and returned it as best they could from that position. It was now 5:30 a.m. and Gibbon reported that he had lost connection with the 6th Corps to his right.

Neill's three brigades had moved forward, one behind the other, straddling the empty entrenchments that had been the west face of the old Confederate salient, but the difficulty of moving through its pits, traverses, and abatis soon caused them to veer to the west and lose connection with Gibbon. They then crossed the old works and advanced through the woods that Upton had penetrated on the tenth until they came to the old reserve line, about 220 yards out from the current Rebel position. That was as far as they could get. At 6:50 a.m. Hancock reported that Gibbon's right and Neill's left had pulled back under severe cannister fire. One of the second-line brigades that Gibbon had ordered forward was driven back to the safety of the trees north of the McCoull house, and the other got only as far as the old reserve line. At 8 a.m. one brigade of Ricketts' 6th Corps division came forward on Neill's right, where it too hugged the ground without accomplishing anything.

Parts of Crittenden's and Potter's divisions had advanced through patches of fog on Burnside's front and overrun the Rebel picket line, but were soon driven back by infantry and artillery fire from the main Confederate position, manned by Wilcox's division of the 3rd Corps. After firing a few volleys, these Yankees withdrew. At 8:30 a.m. Hancock reported that Barlow, after a close personal examination, thought it impossible to carry the lines to his front because of the abatis and the Rebel artillery. Hancock recommended withdrawing Barlow's men from their advanced position. Upon receipt of this and a similar report from Wright, Grant called off the attack. The infantry of Ewell's corps, who had had little to do but watch their artillery at work, later gathered around the gunners to congratulate them, shake their hands and affectionately pat the slowly cooling barrels of their guns. All the Federals had to show for the morning's losses was the knowledge that Lee had not weakened his left in order to strengthen his right after all.

Lee made little mention of the attack to the authorities at Richmond, other than that it was easily repulsed, but he began to angle for some of Beauregard's troops. "If the changed circumstances as around Richmond will permit," he wired the president, "I recommend that such troops as can be spared be sent to me at once. Reports from our scouts unite in stating that reinforcements to Genl Grant are arriving." Later he added that "the question is whether we shall fight the battle here or around Richmond. If the troops are obliged to be retained at Richmond I may be forced back."[12]

At the same time, Beauregard was suggesting just that—Lee should retreat to Richmond, after which Beauregard would march with 15,000 men to attack Grant's flank. Then, after Grant's "certain and decisive" defeat, he would return to the south side of the James with his own and some of Lee's troops, to drive Butler into the river.[13] "Without such concentration nothing decisive can be effected, and the picture presented is one of ultimate starvation," he said.[14] Butler, meanwhile, believed that part of Lee's army was already in his front, probably Longstreet's corps. (This belief might have arisen from the presence of brigades that had originally been in Pickett's Division.) At any rate, he believed that he was outnumbered and asked the secretary of war for reinforcements. That same day, Sheridan and Wilson were sending off letters to Comstock and Rawlins, on Grant's staff, with informal recommendations that Butler should be replaced by Baldy Smith, and that the Army of the James should be used to attack Petersburg and its railroads. Both Butler's and Beauregard's troops spent the day improving their defenses, the latter putting special effort into the construction of an earthwork on a bluff from which heavy guns could command a long stretch of the James River known as Trent's Reach.

Also on the eighteenth, General Torbert, who had turned over command of the 1st Cavalry Division to Merritt just before Sheridan started on his raid, returned from sick leave. He was put in charge of all the cavalry still with Grant's immediate forces, and that afternoon he led some of it southeast to Guinea Station on the Richmond, Fredericksburg & Potomac Railroad. There the troopers burned the depot, the post office and a small bridge.

That afternoon Tyler's new division and the 6th Corps moved back to the area around the Anderson house, east of the Fredericksburg Road. Grant also had Ferrero move his division of Colored Troops from near Chancellorsville eastward to Salem Church, the better to protect Fredericksburg from Rebel probes. Grant told Meade that after dark he intended to move Burnside's corps back to the army's left and he wanted Hancock's corps put in reserve as if in support of the 6th and 9th Corps. It was his plan, however, that on the following night the 2nd Corps should move as far down the railroad toward Richmond as possible, fighting any enemy it encountered. Torbert and some cavalry would go with it. Grant's hope was to lure the Confederates out from behind their entrenchments so that he could get at them by dangling the bait of a single corps alone on the road. He had confidence in Hancock's ability to hold off all comers until the rest of the army could catch the Rebels in the open and attack them. Warren was advised that he would again constitute the right flank of the army, and it was suggested that he send a brigade back to the vicinity of the Harris house to watch any Confederates who might follow the Union withdrawal from the right. Warren sent Colonel Kitching's two large heavy artillery regiments which had been transferred to him from the artillery reserve.

In Georgia on the eighteenth, Johnston's plan was working to perfection. South of Adairsville the main roads and the railroads split into two branches. One ran southeast to Cassville, Atlanta, and points south and east from there. The other continued due south to Kingston, where it dead-ended against the rail line and road from Rome, which themselves went on east to join the main line south of Cassville. Johnston had sent Hardee's corps with the army's wagon trains down the western branch to Kingston, in hopes that Sherman would follow him with all, or most of, his army. Meanwhile, Hood and Polk had proceeded down the other branch to Cassville. When Sherman ran into Hardee, the latter would hold his attention while the other two corps would fall on and overwhelm whatever part of the Federal army had followed toward Cassville, and proceed to flank the main Union forces facing Hardee.

And Sherman was following Johnston's script exactly. "All signs continue of Johnston's having retreated to Kingston," he wrote to Schofield on the eighteenth, although he wondered why.[15] He sent McPherson's army and most of Thomas' in that direction, with only Hooker's 20th Corps of the latter going directly toward Cassville. Schofield's small army was sent along roads east of Hooker, with Cassville as his objective also. That afternoon the Rebels moved into position and waited.

Out in Louisiana that day Richard Taylor thought he saw a way to inflict some more damage on Banks' retreating Federals. Backwater from the Mississippi had swollen the Atchafalaya to such an extent that they could not ford it. The troops could be ferried across by steamers, but that would be a slow process, and as the army crossed its diminishing tail on the west bank would become increasingly vulnerable to an attack by the Confederates. Taylor advanced his infantry on the morning of the 18th with the intention of establishing a semi-circle of entrenchments in which to await the best moment to attack. When Banks heard of this around midmorning, he sent A. J. Smith back to drive the Rebels away. Smith's Gorillas drove in the Southern skirmishers and then advanced against the main line, which counterattacked and drove the Federals back. Back and forth it went for a couple of hours, each side having about 5,000 men on hand, until the underbrush caught fire and forced the two sides to separate.

Actually, Taylor was the least of Banks' problems just then. When he reached Simsport, on the west bank of the Atchafalaya, he found waiting for him there Major General Edward R. S. Canby, recently appointed to command a newly created Military Division of West Mississippi. This was a multi-departmental command such as the one Sherman had inherited from Grant, and it consisted of Steele's Department of Arkansas and Banks' Department of the Gulf. It was the War Department's way of insuring cooperation between the two forces and keeping Banks from further foul-ups, without actually removing the politically influential general and losing his undoubted administrative abilities. Canby was Halleck's choice for the job, but Grant had concurred. Back in 1862 he has thwarted a Confederate invasion of New Mexico Territory from Texas, and in 1863 he had put down anti-draft riots in New York City.

While Smith kept Taylor busy, Banks turned over the river-crossing problem to Colonel Bailey, who had built the dams that had saved the fleet. Bailey had all the available transports moored side-by-side across the river, bolted them together with timbers, and covered these with planks to provide an instant bridge across the half-mile-wide stream. The wagons crossed on the nineteenth, followed that night by the ambulances and artillery.

It was on the nineteenth that Crook's Union infantry and Averell's cavalry reached Meadow Bluff, West Virginia after their raid on the Virginia & Tennessee Railroad, and went into camp to rest. The infantry had been marching for seventeen days, the last eight without a regular issue of rations, over seventeen mountain ranges.

That day the Federal War Department officially appointed Hunter to command of the Department of West Virginia. Sigel would remain, but in a subordinate position. Major General David Hunter was one of the oldest generals on either side. He was born five years before R. E. Lee and graduated from West Point seven years ahead of him, in 1822. He had commanded a division at the first battle of Bull Run and then had served under Fremont in Missouri, temporarily replacing him until Halleck showed up. In 1862 and '63 he had commanded the Department of the South, comprised of Federal holdings in South Carolina, Georgia, and Florida, where he had been the first to raise a regiment from escaped slaves. For almost a year he had been serving on various boards and commissions, which is how he came to be available when a replacement for Sigel was needed.

At Staunton that day, Breckinridge was putting his troops on flatcars for the trip to Hanover Junction, where the Virginia Central and the Richmond, Fredericksburg & Potomac Railroads crossed each other, about 25 miles north of Richmond. From there they could easily reinforce Lee or return to the Valley if needed. In the meantime they would guard this important junction.

Other reinforcements were soon on the way to Lee. That morning President Davis received Beauregard's proposal to strike Grant's flank, if Lee would only fall back to Richmond to put him within range. The president ignored the idea but endorsed on the proposal that "if 15,000 men can be spared for the flank movement proposed, certainly 10,000 may be sent to re-inforce General Lee."[16] He then told Bragg to order the return to Lee of Hoke's old brigade, now under Lewis, which had been taken from Early's Division of the 2nd Corps some months back; plus Barton's, Terry's, and Corses' brigades, which would reconstitute Pickett's Division of the 1st Corps. Lee would also be sent Lightfoot's artillery battalion and the 3rd North Carolina Cavalry. Beauregard received the order at 3:15 p.m. and argued against it, asking that it at least be suspended until he could shorten his defensive lines. Finally, at 7:30 p.m., Bragg replied, "The troops cannot be delayed. Transportation is now at Drewry's Bluff awaiting them. The emergency is most pressing."[17] Two of the brigades went up the river by boat and the other two marched for Richmond. As partial compensation, Beauregard ordered Walker's Brigade up from Petersburg, leaving that town defended by only two regiments of infantry, some militia, and part of Dearing's cavalry.

1. Matter, *If It Takes All Summer*, 296.
2. Trudeau, *Bloody Roads South*, 192.
3. Charles A. Dana, *Recollections of the Civil War* (New York, 1963) 179.
4. Freeman, *R. E. Lee*, 3: 334.
5. Dowdey & Manarin, eds., *Wartime Papers of R. E. Lee*, 731–732.
6. Foote, *The Civil War*, 3: 86.
7. *Song of Solomon*, 6: 10.
8. Dowdey & Manarin, eds., *Wartime Papers of R. E. Lee*, 732–733.
9. Catton, *Grant Takes Command*, 248.
10. Davis, *The Battle of New Market*, 164.
11. Grant, *Memoirs*, 2: 238.
12. Dowdey & Manarin, eds., *Wartime Papers of R. E. Lee*, 733.
13. Robertson, *Back Door To Richmond*, 219.
14. J. F. C. Fuller, *Grant and Lee* (Bloomington, 1957), 219.
15. McDonough and Jones, *War So Terrible*, 132.
16. Robertson, *Back Door To Richmond*, 220.
17. Ibid.

PART FOUR

THE ROAD SOUTH

*"We must destroy this army of Grant's be-
fore he gets to the James River. If he gets there
it will become a siege, and then it will be a
mere question of time."*

—Robert E. Lee

CHAPTER THIRTY-TWO

"The Yanks Did Not Shoot At Us Today"

19–22 May 1864

Grant informed Halleck on the nineteenth of May of his plan to advance Hancock and to follow with the entire army. He urged Old Brains to secure the cooperation of the navy to open a supply line up the Rappahannock River and suggested Port Royal, southeast of Fredericksburg, as a new supply base for his forces, now that they were about to move farther south. At 1:30 p.m. Hancock received orders to begin his move at 2 a.m. on the twentieth and to proceed by way of Guinea Station to the south side of the Mattaponi River, if possible. He answered that there was a Rebel signal station that would detect his move as soon as it was light, so he requested, and received, permission to start earlier in order to get as far as possible before dawn.

Lee, meanwhile, had become aware of the strengthening of the Federal left and, like Grant the day before, he wondered if that indicated a weakening of the other flank. So he ordered Ewell to advance and locate the right of the main Union line. For some reason, Ewell had not detected the withdrawal of the Federals from the works along the old Confederate salient and he did not want to attack them head on, so he obtained permission to take his infantry, now reduced to 6,000 men, on a detour to the west before moving to the northeast. While the corps artillery stayed behind to hold the defenses, the infantry of Rodes' Division started off between 2 and 3 p.m., followed by Gordon's. The Rebels, as weary as their Federal counterparts, marched up the Brock Road, past rotting corpses that the recent rains had uncovered around the Spindle house. "It was an awful sight," one Southerner recorded, "and the stench was horrible."[1] They continued on to Alsop's, then turned to the northeast up the Gordon Road toward the Armstrong house. Kershaw's Division of the 1st Corps was brought from its reserve position behind the Confederate right to man Ewell's trenches while the 2nd Corps was gone.

Wade Hampton, with Rosser's cavalry brigade, accompanied the 2nd Corps, but when the troopers got to the Armstrong house they continued on to the northeast, while Ewell's men turned there to the southeast. At the clearing around the Stevens house, Rodes' Division stopped and let Gordon's troops go past to the east. Neither Rodes nor Ewell was near the head of the column when Ramseur's Brigade ran into pickets of the 4th New York Heavy Artillery of Kitching's Union brigade around 4:30 or 5 p.m. Ramseur drove these Federals back and then stopped to await further orders. He could see a brigade-sized mass of Union infantry standing in the clearing around the Harris house near the Fredericksburg Road, perhaps a half-mile away. He sent back a request for permission to attack, which was quickly granted.

The Federal infantry which Ramseur had spotted was the oversized 1st Massachusetts Heavy Artillery of Tyler's new division. When firing had broken out between Ramseur's men and the pickets of the 4th New York these Bay-Staters had been sent forward as a reinforcement. Each as large as a veteran infantry regiment, the regiment's three battalions deployed and nervously awaited the beginning of their first combat. The 1st Battalion was sent forward to discover the size of the Rebel force and was shattered by a volley from Ramseur's Brigade. Its commander was killed, and all those who did not run were killed, wounded, or captured. But the pursuing Confederates were soon stopped by the fire of the 2nd Battalion and of two 3-inch rifles from a battery of light artillery, and they fell back into some trees. Two or three more times the Rebels came on, but each time they were driven back, and then Ramseur realized his flanks were being threatened. He withdrew his men about 200 yards, where he was joined by Grimes' Brigade on his left and Battle's on his right. The Federals who had threatened his flanks were the 2nd New York and 1st

Maine heavy artillery regiments, the latter, along with the 7th New York Heavy Artillery, having first chased Gordon's troops away from some supply wagons on the road to Fredericksburg. Now the two sides faced each other across a small tributary of the Ni in the falling rain. There the Federals were joined by the 1st Maryland Infantry, which had been passing on its way from Fredericksburg to rejoin the army after its veterans' furlough.

When the firing had been heard at Meade's headquarters he had ordered Hancock to send a division on the run, and to follow with the rest of his corps. Birney's division was the closest and was sent immediately. Warren was also ordered to send help, and he dispatched his independent Maryland Brigade followed by the Pennsylvania Reserve Division. In addition Hunt, the artillery commander, was told to send two batteries each from the 2nd and 5th corps. However the Maryland Brigade and one battery were all that arrived at the threatened area in time to get in on the fighting before dark. Until then the firing between the two sides had been heavy. There was considerable confusion among the inexperienced Federal former gunners, who sometimes fired into each other as well as the Rebels, but they stood up in the open and volleyed gamely, taking their losses without panic. One of their bullets shot a horse out from under Ewell, who suffered a severe jolt when he fell from the wounded animal.

When Lee realized that his 2nd Corps was heavily engaged outside the entrenchments and without artillery support, he ordered Early to advance some of his 3rd Corps troops against Warren's defenses, as a diversion. Early sent part of Wilcox's Division forward and drove in some of Cutler's pickets, but pulled his men back when they came under artillery fire. Ewell's Confederates determined to hold their position along the small stream until night and then return to their defenses, but shortly after dark some of the Union heavy artillery units advanced against them. These Yankees were repulsed, although they kept the Rebels from withdrawing. Around 8 p.m. Hampton returned to the area after having gone as far as the Orange Plank Road, where he had run into the 2nd Ohio Cavalry backed up by Ferrero's Colored Troops. Now he placed two guns from his horse artillery to enfilade any further Federal advances. The infantry firing stopped at about 9 p.m. At 10 p.m. Grant notified Halleck of Ewell's reconnaissance and explained that, because of the danger to his supply route to Fredericksburg, he was delaying Hancock's move south until Ewell's movements and intentions were better known. At about the same hour Ewell's troops began slipping away to the south, past the Landrum and McCoull houses, back to their defenses. Like the Northerners the day before, all the Confederates had to show for their losses was the knowledge that their enemies were still in place and full of fight. "After Spotsylvania," one Federal recalled, "I never heard a word spoken against the heavy-artillerymen."[2]

Down in Georgia on the morning of the nineteenth each regiment in Joe Johnston's army was read an order, full of inspiring phrases such as the following: "Fully confiding in the conduct of the officers, the courage of the soldiers, I lead you to battle. We may confidently trust that the Almighty Father will still reward the patriots' toils and the patriots' banners. Cheered by the success of our brothers in Virginia and beyond the Mississippi, our efforts will equal theirs. Strengthened by His support, these efforts will be crowned with the like glories."[3] The men were encouraged, and after retreating forty miles without being defeated they were ready to fight.

Everything seemed to be going according to Johnston's plan. At 10 a.m. he heard from Hardee that Thomas' Army of the Cumberland was moving on Kingston in force and would be kept too busy to interfere with the ambush being laid farther east. By 10:30 a.m. Polk's troops were skirmishing with Hooker's men advancing down the Adairsville-Cassville road, and Hood's corps was moving into position to hit the flank of the unsuspecting Federals. Then a problem developed. Hood discovered that there was another column of Yankees coming in on a road to his right. If he attacked Hooker's flank, this enemy column could attack his own flank or rear. Angry that the Confederate cavalry had not warned him of this situation, Hood felt it necessary to cancel his attack and pull his corps back to join Polk's. Johnston later alleged to President Davis that Hood had been deceived by a false report, thus touching off a never-resolved argument between the two generals as to whether or not there really were Yankees on Hood's flank. The dispute has since been taken up by historians, but the evidence seems to support Hood's contention. Ironically, this Federal column seems to have been a part of Butterfield's division that had taken a wrong road, plus, perhaps, some Union cavalry. Whether or not their presence justified calling off the entire attack is another question.

Anyway, Johnston had lost the advantage of surprise, so he pulled his army back a short distance and had it dig in along a wooded, north-south ridge just southeast of Cassville, still on the north side of the Etowah River, in hopes that Sherman would attack him there. Johnston later called this position "the best that I saw occupied during the war . . . with a broad, open, elevated valley in front of it completely commanded by the fire of troops occupying its crest."[4] Hood's corps occupied the Confederate right, Polk's the center, and Hardee's the left. Johnston's chief of artillery pointed out to him a weak spot in his defenses where Polk's corps joined Hood's. There were no trees there and the line could be enfiladed by Union artillery. But Johnston was not worried. Sherman's new position was over a mile away, and besides, if Union artillery fire did become too hot, the men could fall back behind the ridge until the bombardment ceased and still return to their position before any attacking infantry could reach it. Hood and Polk, however, both thought the line would be untenable. And fears of the Union guns soon proved well-founded. A Confederate brigade commander recorded that when the Southern artillery opened fire the Northern guns "came into action in beautiful style, and selecting their positions with great skill, opened fire on ours, and soon showed an almost overwhelming superiority."5 Two batteries in French's Division of Polk's Corps were badly shot up. The Federals did not attack, though, and the firing gradually died down.

The Rebels continued to work on their defenses, and that night Johnston met with his generals for another council of war. Afterwards no one could agree on much of what was said, nor even on why they had met. It was pretty clear that, as at the previous council, Hardee was for standing and fighting. Hood and Polk seem to have concurred that they could not hold their position against the kind of artillery fire that the Federals could bring to bear. The real argument was over what they proposed to do instead. Hood later contended that he and Polk had urged Johnston to attack. Johnston said they had both urged him to retreat across the Etowah on the grounds that "the confidence of the commanders of two of the three corps of the army, of their inability to resist the enemy, would inevitably be communicated to their troops, and produce that inability."6 Hood countered that he and Polk had advised Johnston to retreat only "if he did not intend to force a pitched battle."7 Either way, shortly after the council broke up Johnston did order a retreat. The seeds of contention between Johnston and Hood had thus been sown, and the chronic discontent of the Army of Tennessee, which had already led to Bragg's downfall, raised its ugly head again. When the Confederate army that night began yet another retreat without a battle many of its officers and men were disgusted.

Among the Federal troops, who had gone to sleep expecting a hard battle the next day only to find the Rebels gone in the morning, morale soared to a new high. "It was sufficient for us," Sherman recounted, "that the rebel army did retreat that night, leaving us masters of all the country above the Etowah River."8 However, the Union commander also pointed out that "it was to my interest to bring [Johnston] to battle as soon as possible, when our numerical superiority was at the greatest; for he was picking up his detachments as he fell back, whereas I was compelled to make similar and stronger detachments to repair the railroads as we advanced, and to guard them."[9]

Sherman sent his cavalry to follow and watch the Rebels, but he held the rest of the army in camp with orders to prepare rations for twenty days, while the railroad bridge at Resaca was repaired and supplies were brought forward. For the Confederate soldiers on the road south that twentieth of May there was one consolation. As a member of Cleburne's Division recorded in his diary: "For the first time since we left Resaca the Yanks did not shoot at us today."[10]

Out in Louisiana that day Banks' retreating Federals completed their crossing of the swollen Atchafalaya. And Bailey's improvised bridge, which Banks declared was "as important to the army as the dam at Alexandria was to the navy," was dismantled behind them, leaving the frustrated Dick Taylor to fume about Kirby Smith's lack of killer instinct.[11] The same day, Washburn, up at Memphis, was writing to Banks' new boss, Canby, asking that A. J. Smith's force be sent to him. He had reason to believe that Forrest was about to cross the Tennessee River and break up Sherman's supply lines, and he needed reinforcements for an offensive to forestall such a move. "Without some help," he said, "I will not be responsible for any disaster that may arise."[12]

In southeastern Virginia that day, while Colonel William R. Terry's brigade paraded its captured battle flags through Richmond on its way to join Lee's army, and the last of the dead were buried around Drewry's Bluff, Beauregard sent his remaining troops forward to attack Butler's defenses. The front of Baldy Smith's 18th Corps on the Union left was covered by a deep ravine, but Gillmore's 10th Corps defenses were on more level ground, and it was there that the Confederates struck. D. H. Hill, with Wise's and Martin's brigades, overran the Federal picket positions and advanced nearly three-quarters of a mile. That afternoon Gillmore counterattacked but could drive the Rebels from only a part of their newly won gains.

Brigadier General Alfred H. Terry's Federal division did succeed in retaking part of the old line, but just then Brigadier General William Walker's South Carolina brigade arrived from Petersburg. The Confederate was ordered to attack and drive the Yankees out again, but he was unfamiliar with the terrain and the situation. His advance was disjointed and his regiments were repeatedly flanked by Terry's Northerners. As one of Walker's men put it: "It was just such a place that this child never wants to be caught in again."[13] Walker rode in search of help, but in the wrong direction. He headed right for the Union lines and was shot down by the 67th Ohio, and his men fell back in disorder. Walker was eventually brought into the Federal lines, where that night a Yankee surgeon saved his life by amputating his wounded leg. Meanwhile, Beauregard reported to Bragg that the ground needed for the shortest possible defense line across the Bermuda Hundred peninsula had been acquired. It was none too soon, for the War Department had already ordered him to send Gracie's Brigade to the Department of Richmond, and Jefferson Davis was promising to send more of Beauregard's troops to Lee if Butler should, as expected, be sent to reinforce Grant.

Dissension was now rife in the Federal ranks. The Rebel attack had shown that the Union defenses were weak at the boundary of the two corps, and Butler appointed his old friend Godfrey Weitzel to oversee all engineering operations, such as the improvement of the entrenchments. This arrangement was so bitterly resisted by Gillmore and his own engineer, Colonel Edward Serrell, that Butler had to reprimand the colonel. Also, that afternoon, when Butler had ordered Smith to send a division to help Gillmore retake his lost picket line, Smith was alleged to have said, "Damn Gillmore! He has got himself into a scrape; let him get out of it the best way he can."[14] Smith denied having made the remark, but he sent no help. Then that night Butler managed to get into a fight with the navy. The USS Commodore Perry had opened fire at the army's request but without getting prior approval from Butler's army gunboat commander, Brigadier General Charles Graham, who demanded an explanation from the Perry's captain. The captain, however, was forbidden by Admiral Lee to comply with such a demand.

At dawn on the twentieth, near Spotsylvania, Union skirmishers advanced by Harris' farm and found that Ewell's Confederates were gone, except for a few hundred stragglers many of them still asleep, whom the Federals captured. Birney's and Tyler's divisions were then withdrawn and returned to Hancock, who was told to use the same plan as had been developed for the previous night and to proceed south, along with Torbert's cavalry, any time after dark. Warren was told to be ready to follow Hancock at any moment during the night, if the latter was attacked. Otherwise he was to follow at 10 a.m. on the 21st. Wright was advised to be ready to protect what would become the army's rear as it advanced.

As the forces under his own eyes were preparing for a new phase of the campaign, Grant's mind was also on the Shenandoah. "In regard to the operations it is better for General Hunter to engage in, with the disposable forces at his command," he wrote to Halleck, "I am a little in doubt. It is evident that he can move South, covering the road he has to guard, with a larger force than he can spare to be removed to reinforce armies elsewhere. Then, too, under the instructions of General Sigel, Crook was to get through to the Virginia and Tennessee Railroad, at New River Bridge, and move eastward to Lynchburg, if he could; if not, to Fincastle, Staunton, and down the Shenandoah Valley. Sigel was to collect what force he could spare from the railroad, and move up the Valley with a supply-train, to meet him. The enemy are evidently relying for supplies greatly on such as are brought over the branch road running through Staunton. On the whole, therefore, I think it would be better for General Hunter to move in that direction, and reach Staunton and Gordonsville or Charlottesville, if he does not meet with too much opposition. If he can hold at bay a force equal to his own, he will be doing good service."[15]

Lee received word from President Davis that day that Pickett's Division and Hoke's Brigade, under Colonel Terry, were being returned to him. Late that morning, with Ewell's 2nd Corps back in its defenses, Lee sent Kershaw's 1st Corps division back to its reserve position on his right. He was watching for some indication of Grant's intentions but received few clues. When Rooney Lee's pickets were driven in at Smith's Mill on the lower Ni River by a reconnoitering force sent out by Burnside, Lee asked Ewell if he could see any enemy movement in his front—showing that he suspected another Federal switch from the Union army's right to its left. At 8:30 p.m. he advised Ewell that Grant appeared to be extending his lines southward, and ordered the 2nd Corps to move at dawn to a new position south of the Po and to the right of the 1st Corps as long as no threat to his present position prevented such a move. Before daylight Gregg's Texas Brigade was also moved south of the Po. Lee knew that something was up, he just did not know what.

At 11 p.m. Hancock's corps began moving south. When the column arrived at Massoponax Church, Hancock found that Torbert's cavalry was still being issued rations and that many of his horses were not yet saddled. The infantry was allowed to rest beside the road and wait for the troopers to finish their preparations, and finally the horsemen took the lead around 1:30 a.m. on the 21st. About a half-mile farther south the column turned onto a side road leading southeast, and around dawn Torbert's horsemen reached Guinea Station on the Richmond, Fredericksburg & Potomac Railroad. They were fired on by about a half-dozen Rebel cavalrymen who immediately withdrew. At 4:30 a.m. Hancock reported that the head of his infantry column was one and a half miles southeast of Guinea Station. By noon the lead division had crossed the Mattaponi opposite the town of Milford and, as planned, was establishing a defensive position on the south side of that river.

At 7:30 a.m. Warren was told that, if he was not attacked by 10 a.m., he was to move at that hour to the Telegraph Road and on due south, past

Massaponax Church to Stanard's Mill on the Po River, where he was to cross and establish a bridgehead on the south side. Wright was ordered to fall back to his newly prepared covering line when Warren's troops departed, and was informed that his corps would probably be sent that night to follow Hancock's route. Grant told Burnside to be ready to follow Warren's route that night. But at 9:45 a.m., fifteen minutes before he was to begin moving, Warren was told instead to follow Hancock's route to Guinea Station, then turn southwest to Guinea Bridge over the Po. Burnside was told that he was still to proceed due south to Stanard's Mill and that Wright would follow him.

"The enemy is apparently again changing his base," Lee wired to the Secretary of War at 8:40 a.m. "Three gunboats came up to Port Royal two days since. This morning an infantry force appeared at Guiney's. His cavalry advanced at Downer's Bridge, on Bowling Green Road. He is apparently placing the Mattapony between us, and will probably open communication with Port Royal. I am extending on the Telegraph Road, andd will regulate my movements by the information [received. The character] of his route I fear will secure him from attack till he crosses Pamunkey."[16] In short, Lee did not attempt to attack Hancock because the latter was too far east and behind the Ni-Poni-Mattaponi stream.

Warren's corps was a half-hour late in getting away, but as the rear of the 5th Corps passed, the 6th Corps retired to its new positions a half-mile back. By 1 p.m. Lee had ordered Ewell to move his corps south on the Telegraph Road to Hanover Junction, to protect the two railroads which crossed there and the direct road to Richmond. If Warren's route had not been changed, the two forces would have collided near an intersection called Mud Tavern that afternoon and brought on the fight in the open that Grant was hoping for. But in the event, Warren marched east while Ewell went south.

Early that afternoon Anderson was told to prepare his troops for movement at a moment's notice. Meanwhile, Lee told Jubal Early to find out if the Yankees were still in front of his 3rd Corps defenses. "I wish they were all dead," the crusty Early remarked of the Federals. "How can you say so, General?" Lee asked, taken aback by his subordinate's vehemence. "Now, I wish they were all at home, attending to their own business, leaving us to do the same." Early did not reply, but when Lee had moved away he turned to an aide and said, "I would not say so before General Lee, but I wish they were not only all dead, but in hell."[17] By midafternoon Early had reported that there were only skirmishers in his front. Late in the afternoon Anderson was told to march the 1st Corps south over Snell's Bridge, east to Mud Tavern, and then to follow Ewell's corps south. The men were to march until 3 a.m. before stopping to rest.

Around noon Grant ordered Burnside to begin his march as soon as possible, straight down the Telegraph Road to Mud Tavern, unless the enemy strongly contested the crossing of the Po at Stanard's Mill, in which case he was to move down the Po to Guinea Bridge. Burnside sent one of his brigades and a battery ahead to secure the crossing at Stanard's Mill, but it reported finding the Rebels strongly entrenched across the river with artillery support. So Burnside sent the rest of his corps downriver, as ordered.

Late in the afternoon Early decided to make a more thorough check of the Federal withdrawal and sent two brigades forward about 6 p.m. Eighty yards from the Union entrenchments a Rebel lieutenant turned to a friend and said, "I'll bet five dollars there isn't a Yankee in those works."[18] Immediately two lines of Federal skirmishers rose up and fired—rather high, fortunately for the lieutenant—then fell back. The Rebels continued to advance despite a thundershower which suddenly drenched them. Then four Union batteries opened fire from the 6th Corps' new defenses, their shells bursting with brilliant flashes in the gathering darkness, and the Confederates retired in haste. It was the final action of the battle of Spotsylvania. About that time Lee ordered Early to return command of the 3rd Corps to A. P. Hill, who had reported himself fit for duty again. Hill was ordered to withdraw his divisions at 9 p.m. and proceed south by a more westerly route than that taken by the other two corps. Between 8 and 9 p.m. the Federal 6th Corps also began to move south.

Those letters from Sheridan and Wilson to members of Grant's staff must have reached them that day, because it was on the 21st that Grant wired Halleck: "I fear there is some difficulty with the forces at City Point which prevents their effective use. The fault may be with the commander, and it may be with his subordinates. General Smith, whilst a very able officer, is obstinate, and is likely to condemn whatever is not suggested by himself. Either those forces should be so occupied as to detain a force nearly equal to their own, or the garrison in the entrenchments at City Point should be reduced to a minimum and the remainder ordered here. I wish you would send a competent officer there to inspect and report by telegraph what is being done and what in his judgment it is advisable to do."[19] Early that afternoon, Halleck wired back that he was sending not one but two competent officers, Quartermaster General Montgomery Meigs and Chief Engineer John Barnard. Before they sailed from Washington at 4 p.m., these two conferred with Halleck, who told them, "General Grant wishes particularly to know what is being done there, and what, in your judgment, it is advisable to do. This of course involves an estimate of the enemy's force and defenses, the condition of our army, whether active operations on our part are advisable, or whether it should limit itself to its defensive position, and, if so, what troops can be spared from that department to reenforce the Army of the Potomac."[20]

That evening Grant's headquarters tent was pitched in the yard of the very house at Guinea's Station in which Stonewall Jackson had died the year before. The lieutenant general exchanged remembrances of the late Confederate with the lady of the house. Grant had known Jackson at West Point and in Mexico. "He was a gallant soldier and a Christian gentleman," he told her, "and I can understand fully the admiration your people have for him."[21]

At sunset on the 21st, General Hunter reached the Union camp at Cedar Creek. Sigel was away from his headquarters, but the new commander was greeted by Colonel Strother, who happened to be Hunter's cousin. "I have come to relieve General Sigel," he told Strother. "You know it is customary with a general who has been unfortunate, to relieve him whether he has committed a fault or not." Strother had no doubts about whether Sigel had committed any faults. "We can afford to lose such a battle as New Market to get rid of such a mistake as Major General Sigel," he had once said. And Hunter soon recorded that he found his new army "utterly demoralized and stampeded and the three generals with it, Sigel, Stahel, and Sullivan, not worth one cent, in fact, very much in my way."[22] Sigel was offered his choice of commands under Hunter: the cavalry division, the infantry division, or the reserve division protecting the Baltimore & Ohio Railroad. He chose the reserve force.

"We were now to operate in a different country from any we had before seen in Virginia," Grant remembered. "The roads were wide and good, and the country well cultivated." The major armies had not fought over this region before, so it still had crops, and fences, and livestock. It was also unmapped territory to the Federals, so engineers and staff officers were sent out to locate the roads and landmarks. "Our course was south, and we took all roads leading in that direction which would not separate the army too widely," Grant wrote.[23] The next river south of the Mattaponi and its monosyllabic tributaries is the Pamunkey, which joins the Mattaponi at West Point to form the York. The Pamunkey is formed by the confluence of the North Anna and the South Anna just east of Hanover Junction. On 21 May Sheridan's Cavalry Corps reached White House plantation—which belonged to Rooney Lee—on the north bank of the Pamunkey, where it was crossed by the Richmond & York River Railroad. Lee took note of the Federal horsemen's presence. In a letter to

President Davis on the 22nd he said that it appeared to him that Grant "was endeavoring to place the Mattapony River between him & our army, which secured his flank, & by rapid movements to join his cavalry under Sheridan to attack Richmond. I therefore thought it safest to move to the Annas to intercept his march, and to be within easy reach of Richmond."[24] Moving south with Ewell's troops, Lee rode with the topographical engineer of the 2nd Corps, Jed Hotchkiss, discussing the fighting around Spotsylvania. "We wish no more salients," the general said.[25]

Ewell's 2nd Corps crossed the North Anna at the Chesterfield Bridge about 8 a.m. on the 22nd and fanned out to cover it and the railroad span a half-mile downstream, both of which were left standing with bridgeheads covering their north ends. Breckinridge's two brigades from the Valley, already on hand, were placed on Ewell's left, reporting directly to Lee, and Anderson's 1st Corps, which arrived about noon, extended the line a mile and a half upstream to Ox Ford, the only spot where the south bank was higher than the north. The men were not required to dig in but were allowed to rest on their first day out of contact with the Federals since the opening of the battle of the Wilderness seventeen days before. Pickett's Division had also arrived, although without its commander, and it was put in line to the left of Anderson, but temporarily attached to A. P. Hill's 3rd Corps, which was still on the road. The return of Hill to duty meant that Early returned to his division in the 2nd Corps, and that in turn meant that a command had to be found for the newly promoted Gordon. Lee therefore recreated Allegheny Johnson's division, now reduced to one combined Virginia brigade and the consolidated Louisiana brigade. To this he added Gordon's old brigade, under Evans, and gave command of the division to Gordon. Hoke's old brigade, under Lewis, just arrived, was added to Early's Division as a replacement for Evans'.

Hancock's Union 2nd Corps was allowed to rest in its bridgehead at Milford, and Wright's 6th Corps at Guinea Station, through the 22nd. Warren's 5th Corps advanced to Harris' Store, due west of Milford, with Burnside's 9th Corps in between. Grant and his headquarters also moved south that day. They stopped for a while and rested on the porch of a plantation house. The lady of the place remarked that she had come from Richmond not long before, where she had seen thousands and thousands of Union prisoners. Just then General Burnside rode up. In an attempt to make polite conversation with the Rebel lady he indicated his soldiers marching by and said, "I don't suppose, madam, that you ever saw so many Yankee soldiers before." Grant and his staff officers got a good laugh when the reply shot back, "Not at liberty, sir."[26]

Meanwhile, Beauregard had reorganized his remaining forces into two divisions, commanded by Hoke and Bushrod Johnson. President Davis had disapproved of the appointment of D. H. Hill to division command, so the latter was made superintendent of the defenses. Chase Whiting left Petersburg to return to Wilmington that day, the 22nd. Over on the Federal side of the Bermuda Hundred peninsula Meigs and Barnard, the two generals sent by Halleck, steamed past City Point at dusk and continued on to Trent's Reach, where they spent the night with Admiral Lee. Grant, however, had already reached a decision without waiting for their report. At 8 p.m. he wired Halleck: "The force under General Butler is not detaining 10,000 men in Richmond, and is not even keeping the roads south of the city cut. Under these circumstances I think it advisable to have all of it here except enough to keep a foothold at City Point . . . Send Smith in command."[27]

Out in Louisiana, A. J. Smith's Gorillas embarked on transports that 22nd of May and headed back up the Mississippi toward Vicksburg, a full month behind their scheduled return to Sherman. The Red River campaign had finally ended. "Franklin quitted the department in disgust," recalled an officer on Banks' staff; "Stone was replaced by Dwight as chief of staff, and Lee as chief of cavalry by Arnold; A. J. Smith departed more in anger than in sorrow; while between the admiral and the general commanding, recriminations were exchanged in language well up to the limits of 'parliamentary privilege.' "[28]

1. Trudeau, *Bloody Roads South,* 201.
2. Ibid., 208.
3. McDonough and Jones, *War So Terrible,* 133–134.
4. Ibid., 136.
5. Ibid., 137.
6. Ibid., 138.
7. Ibid., 139.
8. Sherman, *Memoirs,* 2:41.
9. Ibid., 2:39.
10. McDonough and Jones, *War So Terrible,* 144.
11. Foote, *The Civil War,* 3:88.
12. Edwin C. Bearss, *Forrest at Brice's Cross Roads* (Dayton, Ohio, 1979), 38.
13. Robertson, *Back Door To Richmond,* 221.
14. Ibid., 222.

15. George E. Pond, *The Shenandoah Valley in 1864* (New York, 1883), 23–24.

16. Dowdey and Manarin, *Wartime Papers of R. E. Lee*, 744–745.

17. Trudeau, *Bloody Roads South*, 212.

18. Matter, *If It Takes All Summer*, 341.

19. Catton, *Grant Takes Command*, 249–250.

20. Robertson, *Back Door To Richmond*, 224.

21. Porter, *Campaigning With Grant*, 133.

22. Davis, *The Battle of New Market*, 165.

23. Grant, *Memoirs*, 2:243.

24. Dowdey and Manarin, *Wartime Papers of R. E. Lee*, 746.

25. Freeman, *R. E. Lee*, 3:350.

26. Porter, *Campaigning With Grant*, 139.

27. Robertson, *Back Door To Richmond*, 225.

28. Irwin, "The Red River Campaign," 361.

CHAPTER THIRTY-THREE

"I Begrudge Every Step He Makes"

23–27 May 1864

"The Etowah is the Rubicon of Georgia," Sherman wrote.[1] And he had given his men three days of rest before crossing it. Joe Johnston's Confederates, during that time, had retreated several miles, to the area where the railroad passed through the Allatoona Mountains. Sherman was personally familiar with the part of Georgia he was entering because as a young lieutenant, back in 1844, he had been sent on army business to Marietta, had courted a young lady there, and had ridden over much of the surrounding countryside. He knew, for instance, that Joe Johnston's new position at Allatoona Pass "was very strong, would be hard to force, and resolved not even to attempt it, but to turn the position, by moving from Kingston to Marietta via Dallas."[2] The railroad ran southeast from Cassville, through Cartersville and Allatoona, to Marietta and on to Atlanta, but Sherman planned to leave the railroad, head due south to the town of Dallas, and then turn east to Marietta, thus bypassing the mountains. If Johnston stayed in place, Sherman would be behind him. If he fell back, at least the Federals would not have to attack the Rebels in those highly defensible mountains. Either way, Sherman's men would be out of contact with the railroad for a while, which accounted for the 20 days' rations he had prepared. "It seems that we are turning the enemy's left," one Union soldier wrote. "Allatoona Mountains held by Joe Johnston's army are not the thing to run squarely against."[3]

On 23 May, the same day as Sigel left Cedar Creek to take up his new duties at Harpers Ferry, Sherman's forces set out. "As the country was very obscure, mostly in a state of nature, densely wooded, and with few roads," Sherman explained, "our movements were necessarily slow. We crossed the Etowah by several bridges and fords, and took as many roads as possible, keeping up communication by cross-roads, or by couriers through the woods."[4] Confederate scouts soon discovered the movement and reported it to Johnston. Late that same day he started Hardee's corps toward Dallas to intercept it, with Polk to follow, then Hood.

Early on the morning of the 23rd, unaware that Grant had already decided to withdraw most of Butler's troops, Generals Meigs and Barnard landed at Bermuda Hundred. They met with Butler and toured the Federal defenses on the peninsula, then crossed over to City Point to inspect Hincks' bridgehead there. Then, at the end of the day, they returned to Bermuda Hundred and composed an interim report. Butler demurred, but they thought it possible "that very recently, and since our force has been entirely on the defensive, rebel troops have gone to Lee." At any rate the defenses could be held by as few as 10,000 men, thus freeing 20,000 for offensive uses. They found that the relationships between the commanders were better than expected, the morale of the troops was good, and therefore they concluded that "this force should not be diminished, and that a skillful use of it will aid General Grant more than the numbers which might be drawn from here."[5] Of course, "skillful" was the operative word in that sentence.

Lee sent off a letter to President Davis on the morning of the 23rd. Word had been brought to him that the Federals were repairing the railroad south from Belle Plain. This was old news, but from it he mistakenly concluded that Grant would continue to use that as his supply base, not Port Royal after all. "During its reconstruction, General Grant will have time to recruit and reorganize his army, which as far as I am able to judge, has been very much shaken. I think it is on that account that he interposed the Mattapony between us," Lee wrote. Like Grant, he underestimated the morale of his opponent's troops. And, like Grant, he still hoped to defeat his enemy in the open field, if only he could somehow get at him. "Whatever route he pursues I am in a position to move against him, and shall endeavor to engage him while in motion," he added. Then he went on to recommend the same sort of concentration as Beauregard had been urging. "I shall also be near enough Richmond I think, to combine the operations of this army with that under General Beauregard and shall be as ready to reinforce him if occasion requires, as to receive his assistance. As far as I can understand, General Butler is in a position from which he can only be driven by assault, and which I have no doubt, has been made as strong as possible. Whether it would be proper or advantageous to attack it, General Beauregard can determine, but if not, no more troops are necessary there than to retain the enemy in his entrenchments. On the contrary General Grant's army will be in the field, strengthened by all available troops from the north, and it seems to me our best policy to unite upon it and endeavor to crush it. I should be very glad to have the aid of General Beauregard in such a blow, and if it is possible to combine, I think it will succeed." Unlike Beauregard, however, he did not believe it was necessary, nor the best course for him to fall back to Richmond first. "I do not think it would be well to permit the enemy to approach the Chickahominy, if it can be prevented, and do not see why we could not combine against him after he has crossed the Pamunkey as on the Chickahominy. His difficulties will be increased as he advances, and ours diminished, and I think it would be a great disadvantage to us to uncover our railroads to the west, and injurious to open to him more country than we can avoid." In a letter to his wife written the same day he put it this way: "We have the advantage of being nearer our supplies & less liable to have our communication, trains, &c., cut by his cavalry & he is getting farther from his base. Still I begrudge every step he makes toward Richmond."[6]

About noon on the 23rd, shortly after A. P. Hill's Confederate 3rd Corps arrived to extend Lee's line even farther to the northwest, the Federals began to appear on the north bank of the North Anna. Hancock's 2nd Corps approached opposite Ewell's Confederate 2nd Corps around the railroad and Chesterfield bridges. Burnside's 9th Corps came up opposite Anderson's 1st Corps at Ox Ford, and Warren's 5th and Sedgwick's 6th corps appeared farther upstream at Jericho and Quarle's fords. The weather was good and morale was high. "When we reached the North Anna," wrote an officer in Hancock's corps, "I think the general feeling was that we should roll on, like a wave, up to the very gates of Richmond."[7]

Lee watched the Yankees' approach from the front yard of the Fox home until Mr. Fox insisted that he take a seat on the porch and have some refreshments. The general was in the act of drinking some buttermilk when a Union battery on the other side of the river, evidently spotting uniforms around the Fox house, fired a solid shot that passed within a few feet of Lee and embedded itself in the doorframe. To Fox's amazement, the general finished his drink, thanked his host, and rode away as if nothing had happened. Lee was not feeling well that afternoon, however, and he switched to a carriage before proceeding further upstream to investigate the sound of artillery fire. He found some Confederate cavalry and horse artillery firing from behind a light fortification of fence rails. He studied the Federals across the river through his field glasses for a while and then turned to a courier. "Go back and tell General A. P. Hill to leave his men in camp," he said, "this is nothing but a feint; the enemy is preparing to cross below."[6] In this he was both right and wrong.

He was wrong in that the enemy did cross west of Hill's position, and soon. Hill sent Wilcox's Division northwestward along the road that paralleled the Virginia Central Railroad to examine the ground, and about 3 p.m. it discovered that the Yankees had crossed the river at Jericho Mills, about three miles upstream from Ox Ford, and were moving south through dense woods. Hill ordered Wilcox to attack, and the latter formed a line near Noel's Station, blocking the road coming in from Jericho Mills. Lane's Brigade was on his right, McGowan's under Brown, in the center, and Thomas' on the left, with Scales' Brigade behind Thomas' scheduled to swing around the Union flank. When the line was formed, the division advanced into the woods. It soon encountered the newly arrived and unformed Federals of Cutler's division, on the right end of Warren's 5th Corps line, and drove them back toward the river. A herd of cattle, caught between the contending forces "ran back and forth between the lines, bellowing madly, adding to the noise and din of battle."[9]

But, when the Confederates ran into Griffin's division and the 5th Corps artillery, Thomas' troops gave way, leaving Brown's left flank exposed. Scales found the Union flank but when Thomas' Georgians fell back Scales' men edged to the right to fill the gap. One of Lane's best regiments, the 37th North Carolina, broke and ran, and then Griffin's reserve brigade, Bartlett's, fell on Lane's flank and brought the Rebel advance to a halt. Lane sent his men forward again, telling them, "Once more and we will drive them into the river."[10] But the 37th broke again, and Lane gave up and pulled the rest of his men back with a Federal cheer ringing in their ears. After accomplishing nothing, Wilcox's Division was glad to be withdrawn that evening, under cover of the woods and a sudden rainstorm. As it fell back it met Heth's Division coming to its support but too late to be of use. Colonel Joseph N. Brown, who had so gallantly defended the angle at Spotsylvania eleven days before, was among the Confederates captured that day.

Soon Warren had his entire 5th Corps across the river, and it began to entrench across the tracks of the Virginia Central, which was Lee's, and Richmond's, connection to supplies from the lower Shenandoah Valley. The colonel of the 6th Wisconsin in the Iron Brigade, Cutler's division, wrote that day that "the enemy has lost vigor in attack. Their men are getting so they will not fight except in rifle pits. My conclusion is that Gen. Hill's corps could be defeated on an open field by half their number of resolute men."[11] Lee, who was suffering increasingly from an intestinal illness that made him cranky, demanded of Hill the next morning, "Why did you not do as Jackson would have done—thrown your whole force upon those people and driven them back?"[12]

Lee, however, had been correct in thinking that Grant would cross downriver. At about 7:15 p.m., under cover of the same rainstorm that had hidden Wilcox's withdrawal, Hancock sent two brigades of Birney's division forward to attack the Confederate bridgehead at Chesterfield Bridge. The Rebel artillery on the south bank lashed out at them, but the Northern guns struck back, and the blue infantry rushed forward to capture a couple of hundred defenders and the bridge. That night, initially fearing that Grant would move on again, Lee ordered Anderson to pack his wagons and be ready to move the next morning. But it seemed more likely that the Federal general meant to cross over his captured bridge. The land on the north side of the river was higher than the south bank—giving the Union artillery the advantage—everywhere except at Ox Ford. So, hinging on that point, Lee swung both flanks back from the river to form a V-shaped position as at Spotsylvania, and his troops spent the day of the 24th digging defenses. Hill's 3rd Corps constituted the shorter, left leg of the V, running southwest from the North Anna to a tributary called Little River. The right leg, running southeast to some swampy ground beyond Hanover Junction, was held by Anderson's 1st and Ewell's 2nd corps. This time the apex, and Anderson's left, was covered by the North Anna River. There would be no more salients.

On the morning of the 24th the Union 2nd Corps crossed the North Anna at Chesterfield Bridge, meeting only light opposition. At the other end of the Federal line, Wright's 6th Corps crossed at Jericho Mills and formed on Warren's right. Burnside, in the center, could not force a crossing at Ox Ford, where his men were vulnerable to Anderson's artillery and sharpshooters on the higher south bank. Thus Lee's entire army was solidly entrenched between the two wings of the Federal army and was theoretically free to fall on either one without fear of much interference from the other. The Yankees would have to cross the river twice to march from one flank to the other, while the Rebels had only to cross the four-mile wide base of their V-shaped defenses. Hancock's corps was the most vulnerable part of the Union army, since it was all alone as it pushed across the river to feel out the Confederate position, but the Rebels did not attack. Lee was feeling even worse by then, and yet he had no one to whom he could turn over command of such an attack. Hill had not completely recuperated and had just demonstrated his inability to coordinate a large-scale attack. Now Ewell was also ill, and Anderson was new and uninspiring as a corps commander.

Historians ever since have generally agreed that only Lee's increasingly severe illness kept him from pulling off a great victory by overwhelming Hancock on that occasion. But just a few days before, Grant had dangled Hancock's corps in front of Lee in the vain hope of bringing on a stand-up fight, and the rest of the Union army was closer to Hancock at the North Anna than it had been upon leaving Spotsylvania. An attack on Hancock certainly would not have been a sure thing, and with each passing minute it became less promising. When it was found that Burnside could not cross at Ox Ford, Potter's division of the 9th Corps was sent to follow Hancock, while Crittenden's division joined Warren and Wright, leaving only Willcox's division to hold the north bank. Then the Federals began to entrench. "Hancock's force, including Potter's division, did not probably exceed 24,000 officers and enlisted men of infantry," Humphreys later wrote. "Leaving 7,000 to hold the west face of his entrenchments and the apex on the river, Lee might have attacked Hancock with about 36,000 officers and enlisted men of infantry; but intrenchments make up for greater differences than that in numbers."[13] So, once Hancock entrenched, whatever opportunity had existed was gone.

That day Sheridan returned to the Army of the Potomac from his raid toward Richmond and was greeted warmly by Grant, who listened to the animated account of his bronzed lieutenant's adventures. Sheridan's return did not help Meade's temper any, and when a message arrived from Sherman in which the western commander recounted his own progress and expressed the hope that Grant would inspire the Army of the Potomac to similar deeds, Meade exploded. His eyes stood out about an inch from his head, Colonel Lyman of his staff remembered, and in a voice like a hacksaw cutting iron he said, "Sir! I consider that despatch an insult to the army I command and to me personally. The Army of the Potomac does not require General Grant's inspiration or anybody's else inspiration to make it fight!" According to Lyman, Meade "did not get over it all day."[14]

That evening, perhaps at least partially to improve Meade's disposition,

Grant issued an order assigning Burnside's 9th Corps to the Army of the Potomac, despite the fact that Burnside outranked Meade. This move simplified Grant's life, and Meade's as well, by putting all the corps present under one command. The next morning, as Grant was riding past Burnside's headquarters, the latter came up to him, shook his hand and said, "That order is excellent; it is a military necessity, and I am glad it has been issued." Horace Porter wrote that "this conduct of Burnside gave the greatest satisfaction to the general-in-chief, and he commented very favorably upon it afterward."[15]

Fitz Lee's Confederate cavalry division was still down on the James, and that afternoon it approached the Union garrison which Butler had dropped off at Wilson's Wharf on his way up the river. When Brigadier General Edward Wild refused to surrender, the Rebels attempted to storm the defenses, but the 1,100 U.S. Colored Troops, knowing their fate if they should lose, fought them off with the help of the gunboat USS Dawn and a number of men—replacements and soldiers returning from furlough—who were landed from passing transports. Reinforcements were also sent downriver from City Point, being replaced in turn by troops sent from Bermuda Hundred, but the Southerners fell back before this help arrived.

Although the fragility of Butler's supply line was thus emphasized, Halleck, who had never cared for the James River expedition anyway, had already prepared orders that would detach Baldy Smith and 20,000 men. To Grant he said, "I wish everything was away from the south side of the James and with you."[16] But now Grant told Halleck to hold off, for he would soon be moving south again, and if Lee fell back to Richmond it would be better to have Smith remain where he was. So Butler was told to have Smith's contingent ready to go, but to await further orders. Meanwhile, after another tour of the Bermuda Hundred defenses, Meigs and Barnard drafted their final report, which they sent by telegraph from Jamestown on their way back to Washington. It listed the campaign's accomplishments as the occupation and fortification of a base, the diversion of large numbers of Rebels from other fronts, the temporary disruption of Confederate supply lines, and the collection of large stocks of supplies. They proposed two possible futures for the Army of the James. Either take the offensive to cut the railroads, seize Petersburg, and draw troops away from Lee, or go on the defensive, give up the river garrisons, and send 20,000 men to Grant.

As for the three principal commanders, they said: "General Butler is a man of rare and great ability, but he has not experience and training to enable him to direct and control movements in battle. A corps gives its commander full occupation on the battle-field, and leaves him no time to make suggestions to the commander-in-chief as to the movements of two corps. General Butler is satisfied with the ability and aid of General William F. Smith. He does not appear to be satisfied with General Gillmore. General Butler evidently desires to retain command in the field. If his desires must be gratified, withdraw Gillmore, place Smith in command of both corps under the supreme command of Butler . . . You will thus have a command which will be a unit, and General Butler will probably be guided by Smith, and leave to him the suggestion and practical execution of army movements ordered. Success would be more certain were Smith in command untrammeled, and General Butler remanded to the administrative duties of the department in which he has shown such rare and great ability."[17]

However, since it now looked unlikely that Lee would fall back to Richmond after all, Grant told Halleck on the 25th, before even receiving this report, to go ahead and order Smith and the 20,000 men to join him. As for the rest of Butler's army, "the James River should be held to City Point," he said, "but leave nothing more than is absolutely necessary to hold it, acting purely on the defensive."[18]

Lee's illness was worse on the 25th. He continued to receive reports and send dispatches, but he could not leave his tent. He wrote to President Davis again, enclosing a dispatch from Grant to Burnside which had been captured and which disclosed information about Federal reinforcements. "I understand that all the forts and posts have been stripped of their garrisons. Norfolk, Fort Monroe, Washington, &c., are left with but small guards, and every available man has been brought to the front. This makes it necessary for us to do likewise, and I have no doubt that Your Excellency will do all in your power to meet the present emergency. If Genl Beauregard is in condition to unite with me in any operation against Genl Grant, I should like to know it, and at what point a combination of the troops could be made most advantageously to him."[19]

His illness made him irritable and he quarreled with Colonel Venable of his staff. Venable blurted out to another staff officer, "I have just told the old man that he is not fit to command this army, and that he had better send for Beauregard." Instead, Lee rolled on his cot and ranted, "We must strike them a blow—we must never let them pass us again—we must strike them a blow!" He was visited by a doctor and even talked to him about Grant. "If I can get one more pull at him, I will defeat him," he said.[20] But no blows were struck that day by either side, as each eyed the other's defenses.

Grant was telling his staff that day that he would have to make another flank march to his left, but wanted to destroy as much as possible of the Virginia Central Railroad first. Horace Porter accompanied some of Wright's men and watched their technique. "A brigade was extended along one side of the road in single rank, and at a given signal the men took hold of the rails, lifted up the road, and turned it upside down," he recorded. "Then, breaking the rails loose, they used them as levers in prying off the cross-ties, which they piled up at different points, laid the rails across them, and set fire to the ties. As soon as the rails became sufficiently hot they bent in the middle by their own weight; efforts were then made to twist them so as to render them still more unserviceable. Several miles of railway were thus destroyed."[21] Meanwhile, Wilson's 3rd Division of the Cavalry Corps was sent across the North Anna farther upstream, and proceeded to the Little River to make a demonstration there in hopes of drawing Lee's attention away from his other flank. That night Russell's division of the 6th Corps and the Union army's wagons and artillery were quietly moved back to the north bank of the North Anna.

Down in Georgia that 25th of May, Sherman's armies were still marching south. In the lead was the 2nd Division of Hooker's 20th Corps, commanded by six-foot-four, 300-pound Major General John W. Geary, and accompanied by Hooker himself. Not long after starting the day's march they came to a bridge over a tributary of the Etowah called Pumpkinvine Creek. They found the bridge burning. While putting out the flames the Federals were fired on, and Hooker had his small cavalry escort ford the creek to drive off some Confederate horsemen. Then, after repairing the bridge, the infantry crossed. They followed the retreating Rebels, and a few miles farther on they ran into a couple of regiments of Hood's infantry. Geary had to deploy his three brigades to force these Southerners back upon their main line, which was at a crossroads called New Hope Church. It would soon be renamed the Hell Hole. Their prisoners told them that Hood's entire corps was on hand and that Hardee's was not far to the southwest, around Dallas. Geary and Hooker were worried, because his division was a good five miles away from any support. Hooker notified Thomas and told Geary to dig in on a ridge. Skirmishers were sent out farther than usual with orders to act aggressively so as to fool the Confederates into thinking that the Federals were more numerous than they really were.

Thomas approved of these arrangements, but Sherman did not. Doubting the size of the Confederate forces, believing that he had found Johnston's flank, and recognizing the importance of the New Hope Church crossroads, he ordered Hooker to take it. Thomas and Hooker both protested, and Sherman reluctantly agreed to wait until Hooker's other two divisions came up, griping that he did not "see what they are waiting for in front now. There haven't been twenty rebels there today."[22] Williams' 1st Division of the 20th Corps got to within about a mile of Dallas before receiving orders to go to the support of Geary.

At about 4 p.m. Hooker sent his three divisions, about 20,000 men, most of them veterans from the Army of the Potomac who had come west after Chickamauga, to attack Hood's defenses. They had to struggle through dense woods and tangled undergrowth, as bad as anything in the Wilderness of Virginia, to the accompaniment of thunder and lightning from an approaching storm. Geary was in the center, Williams on the right, and Butterfield on the left, each division deployed with its brigades lined up one behind the other. This meant that the entire corps struck the division of 42-year-old Major General Alexander P. Stewart, known since his days as a mathematics instructor at West Point as Old Straight. It was a determined, fierce attack, but the dense Union formation meant that the Confederates' sixteen cannon could hardly miss. "As the advancing line would break," a Southern officer remembered, "we could only greet their departure with a yell before another line would come." The commander of the 123rd New York, in William's division, wrote that his regiment got so close to the enemy guns before lying down that nearly all their shots passed harmlessly overhead. But another regiment, coming to his support, was hit so hard that its men "rushed in disorder to the rear, all attempts to stop them and force them back to their place, even with a line of bayonets, proving useless."[23]

For about three hours the killing went on, with the Federals hugging whatever cover they could find, unable to bring up their own artillery because of the dense woods. In the midst of the battle, with the crash of the guns and thousands of muskets, a thunderstorm struck. Cold rain pelted down harder and harder, and a chilling wind added to the discomfort of both sides. Hooker's men fell back at last, under cover of the intense darkness of the storm. "When the enemy finally withdrew, many of my men had their last cartridges in their guns," wrote one of Stewart's brigade commanders. "No more persistent attack or determined resistance was anywhere made," Stewart reported. Union general Howard, who had lost an arm earlier in the war, said that "the nearest house to the field was filled with the wounded. Torch-lights and candles lighted up dimly the incoming stretchers and the surgeon's tables and instruments. The very woods seemed to moan and groan with the sufferers not yet brought in." A Confederate officer wrote that dawn revealed a "seething mass of quivering flesh, the dead piled upon each other and the groans of the dying."[24]

Sherman blamed the repulse on the delay, believing it had given the

Rebels time to bring up reinforcements. Hooker insisted that the Confederates were already there in strength when he ran into them. Sherman did not care much for Hooker, and the feeling was mutual. The two had served together at Chattanooga, after which Hooker told his political sponsor, Treasury Secretary Salmon Chase, that Sherman was "as infirm as Burnside" and that he "will never be successful."[25] Meanwhile, the rest of Thomas' Army of the Cumberland arrived during the night. McPherson's Army of the Tennessee came slanting in from the west, to be blocked short of Dallas by Hardee's defenses, and Schofield's small Army of the Ohio came in on Thomas' left. Schofield himself was knocked off his horse by a low-hanging limb and was hurt in the fall, so Cox took over his command for a while. Sherman spent the day of the 26th probing the Confederate position, where Hardee held the left, Polk the center, and Hood the right. Hood shifted Hindman's Division to his right flank, and Johnston sent Cleburne's Division from Hardee's Corps to reinforce Hood. The latter put these crack troops in on Hindman's right, near a tiny community a couple of miles northeast of New Hope Church called Pickett's Mill.

Union major general Frank Blair reached Decatur, Alabama on 26 May with the two divisions of the 17th Corps that had been on veterans' furlough. They were on their way to reinforce McPherson's Army of the Tennessee. At Decatur they met up with Colonel Eli Long's brigade of cavalry from Thomas' Army of the Cumberland, which had been left in that area when Sherman moved south.

In the Shenandoah that 26th of May the Union army, under its new commander, General Hunter, reinforced to a total of about 8,500 men, broke camp at Cedar Creek and started back up the Valley.

In southeastern Virginia, Baldy Smith sent a couple of brigades to probe Beauregard's defenses, but recalled them when he received a War Department order to get ready to join the Army of the Potomac. Butler figured he could spare 17,000 men if a number of drastic measures were taken. Terry's 1st Division would take over the entire 10th Corps sector of the defenses, Kautz's cavalry would replace Brooks' division of the 18th Corps in the trenches, Martindale's (formerly Weitzel's) division would be replaced by the 2nd Colored Cavalry and two infantry regiments, and Hincks would form a provisional brigade to serve as a reserve. Gillmore would command the entire line of Bermuda Hundred defenses, and Smith would take with him most of Turner's and Ames' divisions of the 10th Corps as well as Brooks' and Martindale's divisions of his own 18th

Corps. The two 10th Corps divisions would soon be consolidated into one, under Brigadier General Charles Devens, Jr., just returning to duty after being wounded the year before at Chancellorsville and designated the 3rd Division of the 18th Corps.

Butler looked upon this withdrawal of men from his army as a violation of his "agreement" with Grant. "This is a sign of weakness I did not look for," he wrote his wife, "and to my mind augurs worse for our cause than anything I have seen."[26] He began to cast about for some way to avoid losing Smith and all those men. Since they could not leave until enough shipping had been collected, he would, perhaps, still have a little time to use them himself. Maybe they could be sent across the Appomattox for an attack on Petersburg. He conferred with Smith and sent for Hincks to get his view.

Early on the morning of the 26th, Grant issued orders to pull the Army of the Potomac back across the North Anna and move it downstream. He explained his reasoning in a message to Halleck: "To make a direct attack from either wing would cause a slaughter of our men that even success would not justify. To turn the enemy by his right, between the two Annas, is impossible on account of the swamp upon which his right rests. To turn him by the left leaves Little River, New Found River and South Anna River, all of them streams presenting considerable obstacles to the movement of our army, to be crossed. I have determined therefore to turn the enemy's right by crossing at or near Hanover Town. [There were several villages in Hanover County that had the county's name as part of their own. Hanover Town was southeast of Hanover Junction, well beyond the point where the two Annas joined to form the Pamunkey.] This crosses all three streams at once and leaves us still where we can draw supplies." Unaware of Lee's illness, Grant attributed the Confederates' passivity to poor morale. "Lee's army is really whipped," he said. "The prisoners we now take show it, and the action of his army shows it unmistakably. A battle with them outside of intrenchments cannot be had. Our men feel that they have gained the morale over the enemy, and attack him with confidence. I may be mistaken, but I feel that our success over Lee's army is already assured."[27] He closed with orders to move the army's supply base again, from Port Royal to White House plantation on the Pamunkey, to which point Baldy Smith and his reinforcements were to be sent.

On the afternoon of the 26th, Sheridan took Gregg's and Torbert's cavalry divisions to Taylor's and Littlepage's fords over the Pamunkey River between Lee's army and Hanover Town. Russell's division of the 6th Corps, which had recrossed the North Anna the night before, followed the cavalry down the north bank. As soon as it was dark, both cavalry divisions stealthily moved on down to Hanover Ferry, leaving small detachments behind to maintain the impression that the Federals would try to cross at the first two places the next morning. Meanwhile, the rest of the Union infantry quietly pulled out of their lines after dark and, under cover of a thunderstorm, recrossed the North Anna, leaving pickets in place until the last minute to deceive the Rebels. Wright and Warren pulled out first, passing behind Burnside and Hancock. Then those two followed. Wilson's cavalry brought up the rear, and by morning the entire army was across the river and the pontoon bridges were removed. The withdrawal was so well planned and executed that the Confederates did not detect it until daylight on the 27th. By then Sheridan's cavalry was crossing the Pamunkey at Hanover Ferry, followed by Russell's division. The latter stopped on the south bank to form a bridgehead while Sheridan pushed on to Hanover Town, brushing aside what had been Gordon's, now Barringer's, Rebel cavalry brigade.

Barringer sent word of the crossing to the Confederate commander, who started Ewell's Corps south, followed by Anderson's and then Hill's. Still sick and still riding in his borrowed carriage, Lee led the way. Ewell, who was suffering from the same illness, had to travel by ambulance, and by that evening he was so incapacitated that he turned over temporary command of the 2nd Corps to Early. Lee called a halt for the night at Atlee's Station, a point on the Virginia Central Railroad between the headwaters of the Chickahominy River, a tributary of the James, and Totopotomoy Creek, a tributary of the Pamunkey. The Federal advanced units rested during the day of the 27th, while the four corps of Union infantry marched down the north bank of the North Anna and the Pamunkey to reach the newly seized crossing point, a mere fifteen miles northeast of Richmond. "Rely upon it," Assistant Secretary of War Dana wrote to Secretary Stanton, "the end is near as well as sure."[28]

1. McDonough and Jones, *War So Terrible*, 141.
2. Sherman, *Memoirs*, 2: 42.
3. McDonough and Jones, *War So Terrible*, 144.
4. Sherman, *Memoirs*, 2: 43.
5. Robertson, *Back Door To Richmond*, 231.
6. Dowdey and Manarin, *Wartime Papers of R. E. Lee*, 747–748.
7. Catton, *Grant Takes Command*, 251.
8. Freeman, *R. E. Lee*, 3: 353.

9. Trudeau, *Bloody Roads South*, 232.

10. Ibid., 234.

11. Catton, *Grant Takes Command*, 254.

12. Freeman, *R. E. Lee*, 3: 357.

13. Humphreys, *The Virginia Campaign*, 132.

14. Trudeau, *Bloody Roads South*, 238.

15. Both quotes from Porter, *Campaigning With Grant*, 145.

16. Robertson, *Back Door To Richmond*, 231.

17. Ibid., 232.

18. Ibid.

19. Dowdey and Manarin, *Wartime Papers of R. E. Lee*, 750.

20. Freeman, *R. E. Lee*, 3: 359.

21. Porter, *Campaigning With Grant*, 146.

22. McDonough and Jones, *War So Terrible*, 150.

23. Ibid., 151–152.

24. Ibid., 152–153.

25. Ibid., 154.

26. Robertson, *Back Door To Richmond*, 234.

27. Grant, *Memoirs*, 2: 253–254.

28. Dana, *Recollections*, 183.

CHAPTER THIRTY-FOUR

"It Will Be a Mere Question of Time"

27 May–1 June 1864

After spending 26 May scouting and probing Johnston's defenses around Dallas and New Hope Church, Sherman decided to try to turn the Confederate right, and Major General O. O. Howard was chosen to command the move. Leading the way was the 4th Corps division of Brigadier General Thomas J. Wood, a Kentuckian who had roomed with Grant at West Point but who was better known for obeying an unfortunate order from Rosecrans that had opened a hole in the Union line at Chickamauga through which Longstreet had driven an entire corps. Wood was to be supported by Brigadier General Richard W. Johnson's division of the 14th Corps and one brigade from Schofield's Army of the Ohio. The artillery of Hooker's, Howard's, and Schofield's corps bombarded the Rebel lines from dawn until 9 a.m., while Hooker and McPherson made threatening moves to keep the attention of the Confederates focused on them.

Howard said that his march "was over rough and poor roads, when we had any roads at all. The way at times was almost impassable for the 'mud forests' closed us in on either side, and the underbrush shut off all distant objects." Consequently, it was 4:35 p.m. when Howard hesitantly reported to Thomas, "I am now turning the enemy's right flank, I think." Wood formed his three brigades one behind the other, with Brigadier General William B. Hazen's 2nd Brigade in front. "We will put in Hazen and see what success he has," Wood cavalierly told Howard.[1] Hazen's brigade was, in turn, formed in column of battalions, so that the attack of a corps-sized force had dwindled down to a front one regiment wide.

About 5 p.m. the attack stepped off with battle flags flying in the stiff breeze. Hazen's men, followed by the brigades of Colonels Gibson and Knefler, advanced across rough ground, through dense brush, and over ravines, while taking harassing fire from dismounted Rebel cavalry posted in the woods to their left front. As they stumbled through a steep ravine they were hit by heavy musketry from a solid line of Confederate infantry, whose position on a low ridge to their right front was marked by the distinctive blue battle flags of Pat Cleburne's crack division. Cleburne, seeing that the Yankees were about to flank his front line, held by Govan's Brigade, sent Granbury's Brigade from a supporting line to extend Govan's right. "So sudden and vigorous was the rush of the Federals that Granbury was barely in time to prevent Govan's flank from being turned, his men firing by file as they came into line," wrote a Rebel captain. The Northerners came on, some shouting, according to Cleburne, "Ah! damn you, we have caught you without your logs now!" But the Southerners "slaughtered them with deliberate aim," Cleburne said, taunting the Yankees with cries of, "Come on, we are demoralized!"[2]

The Federals shifted farther to their left, and some of Hazen's units charged across a cornfield, again threatening the Rebel flank. In response, Cleburne shifted two Arkansas regiments from Govan's Brigade, freed because the brigade from the 23rd Corps had not supported Hazen's right. These Confederates were soon joined by Brigadier General Mark Lowery's brigade brought up from the rear, and together they forced the Yankees back across the cornfield, where they in turn were repulsed by the reformed Federals. Hazen's other support, Johnson's division, also failed to show up because its lead brigade could not force its way across Pickett's Mill Creek in the face of Kelly's Rebel cavalrymen. In less than an hour Hazen's unsupported brigade suffered over 500 casualties and had to fall back from within fifteen paces of the Confederate lines. Bad as it was, that was only the beginning.

Now it was Gibson's turn. His brigade charged past Hazen's right into the ravine and up the steep slope of the ridge, under musket fire from the left and front and deadly enfilading artillery fire from the right. The Federals were soon pinned down on the slope, and Cleburne's only regret was that he did not have more guns. "This fire did little damage to the men closest to the enemy's line," one member of Gibson's brigade remembered, "but was killing the wounded who were lying in the ravine and on its slope to our rear." According to another survivor, nearly "every regiment seemed to have lost all formation in the mad and futile charge into the angle of the enemy's works."[3] It was as deadly to withdraw as to advance, so all the Northerners could do was hug the earth and wait for dark. By then Gibson's casualties exceeded 700 men.

Meanwhile, Howard and Wood began to cast blame upon the other units for not coming to their support. Then Wood was overcome by the death of one of his aides killed near his side, and Howard was disoriented by a spent shell fragment that struck his foot. At first the one-armed general thought that he had lost part of his leg, but when he worked up enough nerve to have a look he discovered that he was only bruised. About 6 p.m. he received a dispatch from Thomas telling him to connect with Schofield on his right and take a defensive position. By then Hazen's and Gibson's men were running out of ammunition and the division's supply wagons had not yet reached the battle area, so Knefler's brigade was sent forward to protect the other two. "The first line was completely enfiladed by the enemy's artillery, suffering severely," Kefler wrote. "The advance was made rapidly and in good order. After sustaining a murderous fire, I regret to say, it was thrown into disorder."[4] About then Johnson's lead brigade finally pushed back Kelly's Rebel cavalry and joined Knefler's left flank at the edge of the cornfield to fight off repeated attacks by Lowrey's and Quarles' Confederate brigades. Johnson's Federals held firm and were the last to withdraw. Near 10 p.m. Cleburne approved Granbury's request for permission to clear his front, and with demonic yells his men advanced under a rising moon, startling the Federals and capturing many. The next morning the Confederates surveyed their handiwork. "Such piles of dead men were seldom or never seen before on such a small space of ground," one Alabaman recorded.[5]

In northern Alabama that day two Union columns marched out of Decatur. The 8,000 infantry, 400 wagons and 2,300 beef cattle of Blair's 17th Corps moved southeastward into the mountains, while Long's cavalry brigade and a brigade of infantry from the Decatur garrison moved westward down the valley of the Tennessee River as a diversion. Some twenty miles out, near Courtland, Long encountered Brigadier General

Philip Roddey's undersized Rebel cavalry division and drove it through town.

In southeastern Virginia, Beauregard's troops had detected unusual activity in Butler's camp and prepared to receive an attack at dawn on the 27th, but none came. Soon it was noticed that at least some of the Federals were striking their tents, and increased wagon traffic was observed behind the Yankee lines. Yet signal stations downriver reported that pontoons and transports were moving up the James. At 9 p.m. Beauregard wired Bragg that a Union move was imminent but admitted that he did not know whether it would be a retreat or an attack. However, rumors were rife in Richmond and in Beauregard's defenses that Grant was about to move the Army of the Potomac to the south bank of the James.

The truth was that Butler was perfecting his plan to seize Petersburg before Smith's forces left him. Smith would secretly move 11,000 men across the Appomattox River on a new pontoon bridge and concentrate behind a cavalry screen which Hincks would stretch from Spring Hill to City Point. At dawn on the 29th Hinck's men would surprise the Confederate pickets, and Smith's force would dash into Petersburg before the Rebels knew they were there. Smith received his orders in writing at 2:30 p.m. on the 28th, but just a few hours later Butler cancelled the operation. Enough transportation had arrived to start loading Smith's troops in accordance with Grant's order, and Butler could no longer put off the move. He sent off messages to Grant and to Stanton reporting that Smith was embarking, but to the latter he added, "I regret exceedingly the loss of this opportunity upon Petersburg."[6]

The next day, 28 May, as Maximilian of Hapsburg landed at Vera Cruz to begin his reign as French-sponsored emperor of Mexico, the Federals and Confederates in Georgia reversed their rolls. This time it was the Rebels' turn to make a futile and bloody attack. Early that day Sherman ordered McPherson to withdraw his Army of the Tennessee from its position on the Union right, around Dallas, and move toward New Hope Church. But the Southern skirmishers were active and made it risky to try to move McPherson's forces. Joe Johnston, suspecting that Sherman would make such a move, had ordered Hardee to make a reconnaissance in force to determine whether the Yankees were in fact pulling out. Hardee selected Bate's Division, his smallest, for this task, and Bate sent his three brigades forward to approach the Federal positions at different points. The cavalry brigade of Brigadier General Frank C. Armstrong formed on Bate's left and advanced first. As a signal, it was arranged that if the Yankees were gone the cavalrymen were to fire their guns and then the infantry would advance and catch the Northerners outside their hastily constructed defenses. "Nobody seems to have asked," one Confederate observed, "what would happen if the Federals were still in their trenches!"[7]

Around 3:30 p.m. the Southern troopers advanced and ran into McPherson's men, still in place. The Federals opened fire, and, naturally, Bate's infantry took the sound of firing to be the signal to advance. The unfortunate Rebels ran straight into the defenses of Major General John Logan's 15th Corps. However, the first blow happened to hit a weak spot, where Brigadier General William Harrow's 4th Division was positioned in an area that was difficult to entrench. The Union skirmishers were driven in and three guns from an Iowa battery were overrun, but fire from the main Federal infantry line kept the graycoats from turning the guns against their former owners, while a Northern brigade commander "stood on the parapet amid the storm of bullets, ruling the fight."[8]

Meanwhile, the attacks on the other two divisions of the 15th Corps had no success, and Logan—a pre-war politician but a hard fighter known to his men as Black Jack—galloped to Harrow's sector. Soldiers from disorganized units gathered about their commander asking for directions to their regiments and their officers. "Damn your regiments! Damn your officers!" Logan stormed. "Forward and yell like hell!"[9] Still mounted, he led Harrow's troops in an attack that recaptured the Iowa guns and drove the Rebels back, taking a slight wound in the forearm in the process. Several times Bate's Confederates returned to the attack, but Logan, his arm in a hastily rigged sling, rode along the front urging his men to hold, and they repulsed every assault.

McPherson was gradually able to disengage his men and shift them to the east as directed, by sending details to the rear to prepare new defenses, where he deployed a heavy skirmish line. Then he had the main force fall back behind this new protection. Thus began the slow movement of both sides back toward the railroad to the east. All this time a continual battle was in progress by strong skirmish-lines," Sherman wrote, "taking advantage of every species of cover, and both parties fortifying each night by rifle-trenches, with head logs, many of which grew to be as formidable as first-class works of defense. Occasionally one party or the other would make a dash in the nature of a sally, but usually it sustained a repulse with great loss of life."[10]

In Virginia that day, the 28th, while the main forces of the Army of the Potomac crossed the Pamunkey at Hanover Ferry, Sheridan was ordered to find Lee's army. Gregg's 2nd Division of cavalry was sent out toward Richmond, and three miles southwest of Hanover Town it came to a crossroads called Haw's Shop. About three-quarters of a mile farther on Gregg ran into the dismounted Rebel cavalry divisions of Wade Hampton and Fitzhugh Lee, strongly posted in dense woods and in light defensive works of logs and rails, with their horse artillery also strongly posted, and protected by swamps. Gregg was unable to make any progress against the determined resistance of the Confederates. In fact, part of a new brigade of South Carolinians in Hampton's Division made such good use of their imported short Enfield rifles that they were mistaken for infantry. Finally Sheridan ordered Custer's Michigan Brigade of Torbert's division to reinforce Gregg. It arrived near nightfall and Custer and Gregg sent their men forward, dismounted, through the thick woods and dense underbrush. With a tremendous yell, as Custer reported it, they drove "the enemy from his position in great confusion."[11] In Gregg's words: "We went right over the rebels, who resisted with courage and desperation unsurpassed."[12] Custer and one aide were reportedly the only mounted men on the field, making them conspicuous targets. The young general's horse was shot from under him, but he was unhurt.

The location of Lee's infantry, however, was still unknown to Grant, whereas the Confederate horsemen had discovered the presence of the Union 5th and 6th Corps behind Sheridan's troopers. Lee's illness had now grown so bad that, for the first time during the war, he was forced to accept a room in a private house. His 2nd Corps, now under Early, was three miles southwest of Haw's Shop, behind the swampy headwaters of Totopotomoy Creek. To its left was Breckinridge's small division and then Hill's 3rd Corps, which was still within five miles of the railroad and Telegraph Road, just in case the Federals doubled back to strike at the Virginia Central Railroad again. Behind and between the other two was Anderson's 1st Corps in reserve, now completed by the return of Pickett's Division.

Despite its proximity to Richmond, Lee's army suffered as usual from short supplies. Pickett sent an urgent message to Anderson's chief of staff that day saying, "The men are calling loudly for bread . . . We must get something or the division will be worse than useless."[13] Some units went two days without any rations. Then, after receiving three hard biscuits and a slice of fat pork, they went two more days with nothing. Then they got a single cracker each. "Hunger to starving men is wholly unrelated to the desire for food as that is commonly understood and felt," one Rebel explained. "It is a great agony of the whole body and of the soul as well. It is unimaginable, all-pervading pain inflicted when the strength to endure pain is utterly gone. It is a great despairing cry of a wasting body—a cry of flesh and blood, marrow, nerves, bones, and faculties for strength with which to exist and to endure existence."[14]

In northern Alabama that day, the 28th, Blair's 17th Corps continued toward Rome, Georgia as it marched to join Sherman. That morning the infantry brigade from the Union garrison marched back to Decatur, while Long's cavalry turned to the south toward Moulton. Roddey's Confederate horsemen followed them and attacked at dawn on the 29th, but were driven off after a three-hour fight. The Rebels fell back to Moulton, while the Federals turned to the east and headed for Somerville.

On the 29th, Sheridan's cavalry, less Wilson's division still north of the Pamunkey guarding the wagon trains, crossed Totopotomoy Creek, watching the roads leading south and west. A reconnaissance in force by the infantry was ordered. As one of Sheridan's officers later put it, "We could easily find his cavalry—too easily sometimes—but the main Army of Northern Virginia seemed to have hidden itself, and Grant's infantry moved cautiously to the left and front."[15] The 2nd, 5th and 6th corps each advanced along a different road north of the creek. Wright's 6th Corps moved northwest along the south bank of the Pamunkey to Hanover Court House without opposition. Hancock's 2nd Corps pushed forward along the main road to Atlee's and Richmond up to the crossing of the creek, where it was stopped by the Confederate defenses. Warren's 5th Corps crossed the Totopotomoy and moved along the Shady Grove Church Road. Burnside's 9th Corps was held in reserve at Haw's Shop.

Lee, who was feeling somewhat better, watched these movements carefully and alerted Anderson to be ready to support the 2nd Corps, but he also had other things to worry about. Ewell's condition had become worse and he was given leave of absence, with Early officially replacing him in command of the 2nd Corps. That afternoon, President Davis appeared at Atlee's to discuss the strategic situation with Lee, and after he left, Beauregard arrived. The latter maintained that not more than 4,000 of Butler's Yankees had gone to join Grant and that he could not spare any of his own 12,000 men. Lee wired this information to Davis and added, "If Genl Grant advances tomorrow I will engage him with my present force."[16] That day the last of Baldy Smith's men left Bermuda Hundred and steamed down the James. On the morning of the thirtieth the head of Smith's force, having rounded the Virginia Peninsula and come up the York and Pamunkey, began to land at White House plantation.

On the thirtieth Grant, thinking ahead, wrote to Halleck ordering all the pontoons in Washington to be sent to City Point. Meanwhile, he sent Wilson's cavalry division back up the Pamunkey toward the railroads. Sheridan, with the other two divisions, ran into Fitz Lee's Confederate troopers east of Cold Harbor. Again it was Custer's brigade that drove the Rebels from their position. His Wolverines pursued the Southerners to within a mile and a half of Cold Harbor. Meade's infantry closed up along Totopotomoy Creek opposite Anderson's 1st Corps, which was now manning Lee's center, and overlapping Early's 2nd Corps on the right. That made it clear that the Federal infantry did not plan to slip past Lee's left to regain the direct road between Fredericksburg and Richmond, or make another strike at the Virginia Central. Meanwhile Lee's most reliable scout reported that the Federals seemed to be marching for Old Cold Harbor. That made it easier for Lee to surmise what they were really up to. "After fortifying this line they will probably make another move by their left over towards the Chickahominy," Lee told Anderson. "This is just a repetition of their former movements. It can only be arrested by striking at once at that part of their force which has crossed the Totopotomoi in Genl Early's front."[17]

Early was ordered to make such an attack and Anderson to support it. To Early Lee said, "We must destroy this army of Grant's before he gets to James River. If he gets there it will become a siege, and then it will be a mere question of time."[18] However, Early neither waited for Anderson's support nor used his entire corps, but repeated the mistake recently made by Hill at the North Anna and by Howard and Hardee in Georgia, of sending in only one division. He assigned the job to Rodes, who moved forward, driving away some Union cavalry, and passed into a broad field near Bethesda Church. There an infantry brigade sent out by Crawford was driven back. Rodes paused while Early brought up Ramseur's Division, and Early's own old brigade, recently Pegram's and now under Colonel Edward Willis, led the renewed attack, taking most of the casualties, which included Willis. But their advance brought the Southerners under very heavy fire from a battery of artillery that had found the exact range. They got to within twenty feet of the guns, where the color-bearer of the 49th Virginia was torn to pieces by cannister, but they could go no farther. Crawford had sent in another brigade, and soon Cutler's division came to his support. The Rebels were badly cut up and forced to withdraw. Many Confederates blamed the young Ramseur for being too impetuous in his first attack as division commander.

It was the final battle for the Pennsylvania Reserves. The next day they started their journey home after three years of valuable service. All the soldiers who had joined the division as reinforcements, or who had individually reenlisted, were consolidated as two new regiments, the 190th and 191st Pennsylvania Volunteers. Wholesale reshuffling of units within the 5th Corps followed.

Lee did not upbraid Early as he had Hill at the North Anna. He had other problems. The signal officer on the lower James reported that afternoon that seventeen Union transports had passed down the river, carrying at least 7,000 men. Robert Ransom, commanding at Richmond, reported to Bragg that a Northern newspaper correspondent had been captured bearing a letter indicating that he believed that Smith's 18th Corps was at White House plantation. This was confirmed by a spy who had heard Custer and his junior officers discussing the arrival of reinforcements from Butler. Lee feared that a Federal corps so located would advance due west, past his right flank. To meet this threat he sent Fitzhugh Lee's cavalry division to a crossroads called Cold Harbor, to block such an advance until he could find something stronger to send.

That something would have to come from south of the James. He had been trying to tell President Davis, as tactfully as he could, that he needed more of Beauregard's troops. Now there was no time left for tact, or for Davis either. He sent a wire straight to Beauregard asking for help. It did him no good. That officer replied that the "War Dept. must determine when & what troops to order from here."[19] At 7:30 p.m. Lee wired Davis: "General Beauregard says the department must determine what troops to send for him. He gives it all necessary information. The result of this delay will be disaster. Butler's troops (Smith's corps) will be with Grant tomorrow. Hoke's Division, at least, should be with me by light tomorrow."[20] Lee did not use words like disaster lightly or often, and Davis knew it. He told Bragg to send a preemptory order detaching Hoke's Division from Beauregard for immediate transport to Lee by rail. But Bragg's message crossed with one to Bragg from Beauregard saying that he had decided to send Hoke's Division to Lee anyway. Before midnight Davis was assuring Lee that every effort was being made to have Hoke with him the next day. The division contained 7,000 men in the brigades of Martin, Clingman, Hagood, and Colquitt.

In response to Washburn's appeal to Canby, T. Kilby Smith's 1,900 men landed at Memphis that day. They were the vanguard of A. J. Smith's force, returning from the Red River expedition.

That same day, the thirtieth of May, Crook's Federals left Meadow Bluff, West Virginia after a brief rest, on their way to meet Hunter at Staunton in the Shenandoah Valley. Many of his men, Crook said, were barefoot, and all were "scantily supplied with rations."[21]

Somewhat to the southwest of Crook a column of Confederate horsemen was riding in the opposite direction. Brigadier General John Hunt Morgan was once again heading back to his native Kentucky. After defending southwestern Virginia from Averell, the famous raider had asked the War Department in Richmond for permission to make another strike into the Bluegrass State, but he had been told that he was needed more where he was. He was not inclined to take "no" for an answer, however, and started out on the thirtieth anyway. The next day he wrote to Adjutant General Samuel Cooper that he had learned that the Union commanders in Kentucky were gathering forces for a raid into south-western Virginia. "This information has determined me to move at once into Kentucky, and thus distract the plans of the enemy by initiating a movement within his lines. My force will be about 2000 men."[22]

If the government in Richmond was troubled with pending disasters and insubordinate generals, that in Washington was plagued by dis-gruntled politicians. The more radical Republicans—New England aboli-tionists and German-American former revolutionaries—seemed to be about to bolt the party. They felt that Lincoln paid lip service to their views but always sided with the more conservative wing of the party. It was an election year, and the radicals wanted to dump Lincoln. They realized, however, that they lacked the political strength to dominate the upcoming national convention, so they called one of their own, which convened in Cleveland on 31 May. There they nominated John C. Fre-mont as their candidate for president by acclamation. Fremont, an army officer who had played a controversial part in acquiring California for the United States, had been the Republican party's first presidential candidate back in 1856—the one whom Grant had known well enough to not vote for. On the shelf since he refused to serve under John Pope in 1862, Fremont accepted the nomination for the expressed purpose of preventing the reelection of Lincoln, an eventuality which he thought "would be fatal to the country." Fremont's most influential backers, however, could not afford to support him openly, for to do so would be to commit political suicide. As a result, the convention failed to attract the thousands of attendees expected. When informed that only about 400 had actually shown up at Cleveland, Lincoln thumbed through the Bible that he kept on his desk until he found the passage he wanted in 1 Samuel and read it aloud: "And every one that was in distress, and every one that was in debt, and every one that was discontented, gathered themselves unto him; and he became a captain over them; and there were with him about four hundred men."[23]

At 5:15 a.m. on 31 May Clingman's Brigade of Hoke's Division pulled out of Chester Station on a train heading north. Baldy Smith spent most of that day getting his troops unloaded at White House, while Sheridan spent the morning making arrangements to oust Fitzhugh Lee's cavalry from Cold Harbor. Early that afternoon Fitz received word that Clingman's Brigade had arrived but had halted a few miles to the west of him. Then his outposts warned that Union cavalry was approaching. He reported this to his uncle and asked for Clingman's support.

In accordance with a plan suggested by Torbert and Custer, Sheridan sent Merritt's and Custer's brigades to drive in Fitz Lee's pickets and skirmishers, and then make a holding frontal attack, while Devin took two of his regiments on a wider circuit to turn the Confederates' left and get at their horses. The plan broke down as soon as Devin reported that he could not make the turning movement, although Torbert later reported that it did not appear that Devin had tried very hard.

By dusk Clingman's infantry had arrived to bolster Lee's defenses, but Merritt saw an opportunity to turn the Rebels' other flank. He sent the 1st and 2nd United States regiments on a wide swing "under a galling fire from infantry and cavalry" which turned the Confederate's flank and forced them to fall back in order to avoid being surrounded. The moment the Southerners left the shelter of their breastworks Custer sent forward a battalion of the 1st Michigan in a saber-swinging mounted charge, which, as he reported, "had the desired effect. The enemy, without waiting to receive it, threw down their arms and fled, leaving their dead and wounded on the field."[23] The Union troopers drove Fitz Lee and Clingman three-quarters of a mile, but Sheridan knew that Lee's entire army was nearby and had learned from prisoners that Hoke's other three brigades were on their way. Despite the arrival of Gregg's cavalry division, therefore, he decided to fall back to where he had started the morning. The last of his men were just filing out of Cold Harbor when he received orders to hold the place at all hazards, so the men were turned around and put to work at rearranging its defenses.

Grant had decided to make another shift to his left, and as soon as it was dark he sent Wright's corps back around through Haw's Shop and then southeast, behind the rest of the army and across Totopotomoy Creek. Cold Harbor, at the intersection of the road which Wright was taking with the one from White House, along which Smith was expected to advance, would be crucial. Smith finally got his troops moving around 3:30 p.m., but on the wrong road, leaving Ames' brigade behind to guard the new base at White House. Unfortunately for him, the orders he was acting on were out of date, and somebody had forgotten to tell him that the army was moving. At 10 p.m. he put his men in camp and sent an aide to report his location to Grant and get further orders.

Lee, meanwhile, had decided to forestall the Federal shift that was evidently under way, by retaking Cold Harbor. Anderson was told to move around behind Early that night and connect with, and take command of, Hoke's Division, the rest of which would be in place by daylight the next morning. Anderson attacked early in the morning, the 1st of

June, but his offensive was as disjointed as Early's and Hill's recent ones had been. It was his plan to assault with his lead division, Kershaw's, and with Hoke's Division at dawn, and follow them up with Field's and Pickett's divisions as these completed their night march, but for some reason Hoke did not move. Kershaw did, but he gave the lead to his own old brigade, under Colonel Lawrence Keitt, who, when his inexperienced regiment had recently been added to the brigade, had become its senior officer. Keitt was going into his first attack. He led it in the old style, mounted on his spirited steed, and was shot dead by the first blast from the Northern carbines. Seeing him fall, his own green regiment broke and ran for the rear in what a Rebel artilleryman called "the most abject rout ever committed by men in Confederate uniform."[25]

The rest of the brigade also fell back, and then so did the rest of the division. Kershaw managed to stop the retreat and start another attack, but it fared little better, and by midmorning, when Pickett's and Field's divisions arrived, Wright's Union 6th Corps had also come up, taking over the breastworks from Sheridan's troopers. The Union infantrymen, after marching all night, set to work with picks and shovels to improve the defenses, and they were soon joined by Baldy Smith's weary men, on the right road at last, who connected Wright's position with Warren's. Burnside held the Federal right, extending to the Totopotomoy. Wilson's cavalry division returned that day after striking the Virginia Central Railroad again, and joined Hancock, who was still on the north bank of the creek, with orders to cross after dark and proceed to extend the left flank, where Sheridan's other two divisions were now patrolling the space between Wright's line and the Chickahominy River. When Hancock arrived next morning, all five corps would attack.

Meade, however, suggested a preliminary attack for that evening by Wright and Smith alone in order for them to secure better jump-off positions for the main attack the next day. Grant approved, and the six Federal divisions went forward shortly after 5 p.m. to strike Anderson's four. They not only put an end to any thoughts Anderson might have had of renewing his own attack, but came close to driving the Confederate 1st Corps from its own unfinished works. In Smith's corps the green 188th Pennsylvania mistakenly fired into the rear of the 21st Connecticut, but a captain in the latter regiment remembered seeing his young brigade commander, Colonel Guy V. Henry, "with a smile of cool defiance," spur his horse over the Rebel breastworks. "As the dying steed lay struggling on the parapet," the captain wrote, "its rider coolly standing in his stirrups empties his revolver into the very faces of the awe-struck foe."[26] Field's and Pickett's divisions held fast but a brigade panicked on Hoke's left, where it joined Kershaw's right. Anderson sent a brigade from Pickett's Division to plug the hole, but Meade had the jump-off positions he wanted. However, during the night the Confederates built new defenses that reestablished a continuous line.

The day thus ended was the second anniversary of Lee's first day in command of the Army of Northern Virginia. And he found himself back on almost the same ground as he had occupied then, once more trying desperately to drive off a larger Federal force despite the ineptitude of his subordinate generals.

That day Meade wrote to his wife: "The papers are giving Grant all the credit for what they call successes; I hope they will remember this if anything goes wrong."[27]

---

1. Both quotes from McDonough and Jones, *War So Terrible*, 157.
2. Ibid., 159–161.
3. Ibid., 162.
4. Ibid., 163.
5. Ibid, 166.
6. Robertson, *Back Door To Richmond*, 235.
7. McDonough and Jones, *War So Terrible*, 167.
8. Ibid.
9. Ibid.
10. Sherman, *Memoirs*, 2:45.
11. Starr, *Union Cavalry*, 2:118.
12. Theo. F. Rodenbough, "Sheridan's Richmond Raid," in *Battles and Leaders*, 4:193.
13. Dowdey, *Lee's Last Campaign*, 275.
14. Ibid., 276.
15. Rodenbough, "Sheridan's Richmond Raid," 193.
16. Dowdey and Manarin, *Wartime Papers of R. E. Lee*, 756.
17. Ibid., 757–758.
18. Foote, *The Civil War*, 3:279.
19. Robertson, *Back Door To Richmond*, 236.
20. Dowdey and Manarin, *Wartime Papers of R. E. Lee*, 758–759.
21. Pond, *The Shenandoah Valley*, 28.
22. Basil W. Duke, "John Morgan in 1864," in *Battles and Leaders*, 4:424.
23. Both quotes from Foote, *The Civil War*, 3:377.

24. Starr, *Union Cavalry*, 121.

25. Foote, *The Civil War*, 3:185.

26. Brian C. Pohanka, "Not War But Murder," *America's Civil War*, January 1989, 36.

27. Trudeau, *Bloody Roads South*, 274–275.

CHAPTER THIRTY-FIVE

"Where The Tiger Lies In Wait"

1–4 June 1864

Down in Georgia on the first day of June, Union forces continued to sidle eastward "until," Sherman wrote, "our strong infantry-lines had reached and secured possession of all the wagon-roads between New Hope, Allatoona, and Acworth, when I dispatched Generals Garrard's and Stoneman's divisions of cavalry into Allatoona, the first around by the west end of the pass, and the latter by the direct road. Both reached their destination without opposition, and orders were at once given to repair the railroad forward from Kingston to Allatoona, embracing the bridge across the Etowah River." The formidable position at Allatoona Pass was now in Union hands. Then heavy rains began to fall, "making the roads infamous."[1]

After two weeks of careful preparation, a force of 8,300 Federals left Memphis on 1 June headed for northern Mississippi, looking for Nathan Bedford Forrest. Knowing that the wily Confederate cavalryman would soon be raiding his supply lines if left alone, Sherman was determined to keep him too busy defending his own territory. The commander of this expedition was the same Brigadier General Samuel Sturgis who had failed to catch Forrest a month before. This time he had with him three brigades of infantry under Colonel William L. McMillen, two brigades of cavalry under Brigadier General Benjamin Grierson, 22 pieces of artillery, and 250 wagons loaded with twenty days' supply of food and ammunition. One of the brigades of infantry consisted entirely of U.S. Colored Troops eager to wreak vengeance for the massacre at Fort Pillow. One of the other two brigades included two regiments—800 men—from T. Kilby Smith's Provisional Division of the 17th Corps. Sherman had been right. Forrest was riding out of Tupelo, Mississippi that same day with 2600 men and six guns, heading for middle Tennessee.

In the Shenandoah Valley, Hunter continued to push south with the forces that had been Sigel's, and chased Imboden's cavalry out of Harrisonburg that day.

In the Bermuda Hundred defenses that first day of June, Benjamin Butler was still looking for some way to take the offensive against Petersburg using his new pontoon bridge over the Appomattox from Point of Rocks to Spring Hill. With Smith and the bulk of his infantry gone, Butler toyed with the idea of using Kautz's cavalry, supported by Hincks' City Point garrison, to make a dash at the vulnerable city. Hincks proposed a similar plan. Kautz was unenthusiastic but expressed himself willing to try it if so ordered, and the raid was scheduled for the next day.

Meanwhile, Beauregard's attention was focused in the other direction. Early that afternoon he received a wire from Lee: "It would be disadvantageous to abandon the line between Richmond and Petersburg, but as two-thirds of Butler's force has joined Grant can you not leave sufficient guard to move with the balance of your command to north side of James River and take command of right wing of army?"[2] Beauregard replied at 7 p.m. that he could not leave his Bermuda Hundred lines as long as he still faced the 8,000 or so Federals there, unless the "government shall have determined to abandon line of communication from Petersburg to Richmond."[3] A half-hour later he ordered Bushrod Johnson, commanding his sole remaining division, to make a strong reconnaissance at dawn, because President Davis had decided to detach Matt Ransom's Brigade and send it north unless Beauregard could show that the Yankees were still present in force. At 6 a.m. on 2 June heavy skirmish lines from Ransom's, Wise's, and Walker's brigades advanced and captured the Union picket line but, except that it roughed up a couple of Federal regiments, that was about all the attack accomplished. However, Butler assumed it to be the prelude to an attack on his main defenses and called off his planned raid on Petersburg. Once again the nearly defenseless city had received a temporary reprieve.

It was raining in Georgia on 2 June, and 300 miles to the northwest the rains also fell on Sam Sturgis and his Forrest-hunting expedition, so that its wagons were soon hub-deep in mud. In Virginia it was hot and dry most of the day. Grant called off the attack that had been scheduled for dawn because Hancock's 2nd Corps had taken a wrong road during its night march and had not arrived on the Union left until 6:30 a.m. "We became entangled in the woods," one of Hancock's men remembered; "the artillery and infantry got mixed up in unutterable confusion; the heat was oppressive; the sand was shoe-mouth deep; the air was thick with choking dust, and we did not reach Cold Harbor until late on the morning of June 2. We were in a condition of utter physical exhaustion."[4] The attack was rescheduled for 5 o'clock that afternoon.

Lee, however, did not wait so long. He felt well enough to mount his horse that day, and he was in fighting spirit, even though his troops also took a wrong road and were late in arriving where he wanted them. He finally got Breckinridge's two brigades to his right flank, and they were followed by A. P. Hill, with Mahone's and Wilcox's divisions. About 3 p.m. Breckinridge went forward, with the assistance of two of Wilcox's brigades, and captured Turkey Hill on the north bank of the Chickahominy. From there artillery could dominate the river bottoms to secure the Confederate right flank. That afternoon Lee called Major McClellan to his tent. It had been that young cavalry officer, working without a map, who had led Breckinridge's troops astray and caused them to be late. Lee traced a line with his finger on a map and calmly informed him that this was the road to Cold Harbor. The major remembered that the "quiet reproof sunk deeper and cut more keenly than words of violent vituperation would have done."[5]

At the same time, on the Confederate left, Early's 2nd Corps and Heth's division of the 3rd attacked north of Bethesda Church. They hit just as Burnside's 9th Corps was pulling back to a new position behind Warren's 5th. Burnside's skirmishers were still occupying his original position and were driven back by Rodes' division. This put the Rebels behind Warren's skirmish line and a large number of prisoners were taken from both corps. Griffin's division of the 5th Corps was massed at Bethesda Church and it counterattacked, killing Brigadier General Doles, one of Rodes' brigade commanders, and driving the latter's division back. Meanwhile, Crittenden's 9th Corps division held off Heth until Willcox and Potter got into position. The Confederates ground to a complete halt and began digging in. Grant did not learn of Early's attack until it was all over, and "his chagrin was extreme," as one of his staff officers put it, when he learned that no advantage was taken of this chance to hit the Southerners while they were outside of their entrenchments.[6] About 5 p.m. it started to rain, finally laying the dust and cooling the air.

The infantry of the two armies now stretched from Totopotomoy Creek, southeast to the Chickahominy, with cavalry covering the flanks beyond those two streams. Meade was unhappy about spreading his army over so much space. "I do not like extending too much," he told General Wright. "It is the trouble we have had all along of occupying too long lines and not massing enough."[7] However, Horace Porter wrote that "General Grant had manoeuvered skillfully, with a view to compelling Lee to stretch out his line and make it as thin and weak as possible, and it was at present over six miles long." Short of retracing his steps, Grant now had two choices, as he saw it. He could cross the shallow, swampy Chickahominy and the broad, tidal James for an attack on Petersburg and Richmond's lines of supply, completing the job that Butler had begun, or he could attack Lee's army here between the Totopotomoy and the Chickahominy. "The general considered the question not only from a military standpoint," Porter wrote, "but he took a still broader view of the situation. The expenses of the war had reached nearly four million dollars a day. Many of the people in the North were becoming discouraged at the prolongation of the contest. If the army were transferred south of the James without fighting a battle on the north side, people would be impatient at the prospect of an apparently indefinite continuation of operations; and as the sickly season of summer was approaching, the deaths from disease among the troops meanwhile would be greater than any possible loss encountered in the contemplated attack."[8] The possible rewards of victory were great. "The breaking of Lee's lines meant his destruction and the collapse of the rebellion," Assistant Secretary Dana wrote.[9]

So Grant decided that he must assault Lee where he was. Meade reasoned that, since Lee was strong enough to attack with his left, he must be weak on his right. The main effort would therefore be made on the Union left, where the preliminary attack of the day before had brought the Federals closest to the Confederate works, by Hancock's 2nd, Wright's 6th, and Smith's 18th Corps—from left to right. Warren's 5th Corps was beyond a gap to Smith's right, and Burnside's 9th was on the far right flank. That afternoon the attack was rescheduled again, this time for 4:30 the next morning. There was no detailed plan. The order postponing the attack merely said that "corps commanders will employ the interim in making examinations of the ground in their front and perfecting the arrangements for the assault." Baldy Smith sent a note to Wright asking to know his plan "that I might conform to it, and thus have two corps acting in unison." Wright replied that he was "going to pitch in."[10] This seemed to represent the extent of planning all along the line.

The prolonged campaign was wearing down the Union commanders just as much as it was the Confederates. Meade in particular seemed to be having his problems, and his famous temper was passing them along to his staff and subordinates. In the past day or two he had denounced Warren for moving without orders, and Wright for moving too slowly. Then Hancock and Baldy Smith had taken the wrong roads, and Smith reported that he had brought little ammunition with him, provoking Meade to ask, "Then why in hell did he come at all?"[11] It mattered not a whit that Smith had merely followed the road he had been told to take, and that he had moved without waiting for his ammunition because he did not know but that his men might be urgently needed and thought he should not wait for the wagons to disembark. He was just another target for Meade's frustrations. Meade was the man in the middle, and he was feeling squeezed between the immovable Lee to his front, and the relentless Grant looking over his shoulder.

Meanwhile, the Confederates spent the day improving their defenses with all the skill and expertise learned in the past thirty days of continuous combat. The works were built along a chain of hills and ridges just low enough not to look formidable, but high enough to give the Rebels a clear view of the ground over which the attackers would have to advance. A newspaper correspondent wrote: "They are intricate, zig-zagged lines within lines, lines protecting flanks of lines, lines built to enfilade an opposing line, lines within which lies a battery . . . a maze and labyrinth of works within works and works without works, each laid out with some definite design either of defense or offense."[12] The men who would have to attack those defenses were not fooled. Horace Porter recorded that, "as I came near one of the regiments which was making preparations for the next morning's assault, I noticed that many of the soldiers had taken off their coats, and seemed to be engaged in sewing up rents in them. This exhibition of tailoring seemed rather peculiar at such a moment, but upon closer examination it was found that the men were calmly writing their names and home addresses on slips of paper, and pinning them on the backs of their coats, so that their dead bodies might be recognized upon the field, and their fate made known to their families at home."[13]

Just before light on 3 June the rain stopped and the dawn came in cool and damp. In the Northern units the men fixed bayonets. "And now there

is a metallic rustle and a faint gleam of steel among the waiting host," one
wrote. "The officers are drawing their swords, the symbol of command.
Then, amid a profound hush, the heavy tramp begins, forward into the
lair where the tiger lies in wait."[14] The corps commanders had syn-
chronized their watches, and precisely at 4:30 a.m. dozens of Union
cannon roared, and 40,000 Federal infantrymen advanced to attack Lee's
defenses across a half-mile of fields and groves. The skirmishers out front
added the crackle of their rifle fire, and then thousands of hats and musket
barrels appeared briefly over the rim of the Confederate trenches before
they were blotted out by a huge cloud of gunsmoke, and a volley of
musketry split the air with a sound like ripping canvas. A gunner in
Hancock's corp watching the attack go forward, wrote that the noise of
battle "had the fury of the Wilderness musketry with the thunders of the
Gettysburg artillery superadded. It was simply terrific."[15]

On the Union left Hancock had Barlow's and Gibbon's divisions in the
front line—the same troops who had cracked the mule shoe salient at
Spotsylvania—with Birney's in support. But the two leading divisions
quickly became separated. Barlow's two lead brigades swept across Confederate skirmishers holding a sunken road, and into the main line of
works along Breckinridge's front on Turkey Hill. Two or three hundred
prisoners were sent to the rear and three guns were captured, but the
Federal support troops were broken and driven back by a crossfire from
Rebels to both sides of the breakthrough. Meanwhile Confederate artillery began plastering Barlow's front line from three sides, and when a
Florida brigade counterattacked, the Yankees were driven out of the
works. They did not go far, but ran back to a low swell of ground 30 to 75
yards out and frantically began to dig with their bayonets and tin cups.
Two Union colonels were killed, and one severely wounded, in Barlow's
attack.

To Barlow's right, Gibbon's division advanced about 200 yards before
running into swampy ground of which the Federals had not been aware.
A brigade went around each side of the morass. One was led by the 164th
New York, an Irish outfit clad in zouave fashion, which got into the main
Rebel line for a brief moment but was then pushed out again, leaving its
young colonel lying in the mud with seven fatal wounds. The other
brigade was shot to pieces before it got within fifty yards of the Confederate lines. "Our artillery fired double-shotted cannister at a distance
of a hundred yards," one Rebel remembered. "At every discharge of our
guns, heads, arms, legs, guns, were seen flying high in the air. They
closed the gaps in their line as fast as we made them, and on they came,
their lines swaying like great waves of the sea."[15] In the space of twenty
minutes Gibbon lost 1,000 men, including three brigade commanders,

with nothing to show for the loss. Like Barlow's men, Gibbon's fell back only far enough to find a bit of shelter, and began to dig in.

Wright's 6th Corps suffered a similar fate, except that it only took about ten minutes for those men who were not hit to begin to dig for protection. Guns a mile away were throwing shells that burst over the Federals' heads or among their ranks, while "all the time," one remembered, "there was poured from the rebel lines, which we could not see, those volleys of hurtling death."[17] Baldy Smith, after using one division to connect with the 6th Corps on his left, and another to connect with Warren on his right, had only Martindale's division with which to make the assault. This he formed in a column of regiments in order to take advantage of the cover provided by a shallow ravine near the center of his position. The 12th New Hampshire was in front, the men bending forward as if walking into a stiff wind. A captain in that regiment wrote that "to those exposed to the full force and fury of that dreadful storm of lead and iron that met the charging column, it seemed more like a volcanic blast than a battle, and was just about as destructive."[18] The front line reached the foot of the Confederate works but then fell back to the edge of some woods still within short rifle range. Warren's 5th Corps was spread too thin to make any assault at all, but Burnside's 9th, reinforced by Griffin's division of the 5th, captured the rifle pits of Early's skirmishers and took up a position close to the main enemy line. Early counterattacked, but was repulsed. North of Totopotomoy Creek, Wilson's Union cavalry drove Rooney Lee's Confederate troopers from their rifle pits near Haw's Shop and then attacked the left rear of Heth's infantry, capturing some of their defenses. But when Wilson was unable to connect with Burnside's right, he withdrew to Haw's Shop.

The Army of the Potomac lost 7,000 men that day, most of them in the first ten or twenty minutes of the attack. But the Federal artillery continued to hammer away, and the infantrymen stubbornly continued to dig in where they were, rather than fall back to where they had started, in some places piling up their own dead to form a breastwork. Meade, as he wrote his wife next day, "had immediate and entire command on the field all day, the Lieutenant General honoring the field with his presence only about one hour in the middle of the day." Meade had taken position at dawn at Wright's headquarters to be closer to the front, and was in contact with the other corps headquarters by field telegraph. But the battlefield was too large for one man to see and control. All he could know was what he was told, and the first reports he received were fairly optimistic. He sent off a report to Grant and added, "I should be glad to have your views as to the continuance of these attacks, if successful."[19] Grant replied, "The moment it becomes certain that an assault cannot succeed, suspend the offensive, but when one does succeed push it vigorously, and if necessary pile in troops at the successful point wherever they can be taken."[20]

Meade sent orders forward to renew the attack, but each corps commander protested that he could not advance unless the others did something to protect his flank against being enfiladed by the enemy troops and guns in their fronts. Meade's answer was an exasperated directive for each corps to go forward on its own without regard to its flanks. Orders to advance reached the front lines periodically—brought by officers who had to crawl forward because of the deadly fire that continued to whip just over the heads of the Federals—the men would step up the return fire for a while, but it was impossible for anyone to get up and charge, and nobody tried. At 12:30 p.m., after talking to the corps commanders, Grant told Meade that he could stop the attack but should hold the advanced positions gained. Then he added, "To aid the expedition under General Hunter, it is necessary that we should detain all the army now with Lee until the former gets well on his way to Lynchburg. To do this effectively, it will be better to keep the enemy out of the intrenchments of Richmond than to have them go back there." To his staff, Grant said, "I am still of the opinion I have held since leaving the North Anna, that Lee will not come out and take the offensive against us; but I want to prepare for every contingency, and I am particularly anxious to be able to turn the tables upon the enemy in case they should, after their success this morning in acting on the defensive, be tempted to make a counter-attack upon our lines." That evening, after he had learned more details of the course of the attack, he told them, "I regret this assault more than any one I have ever ordered."[21] Even darkness did not bring an end to the fighting. "The lines were now so close," wrote Humphreys, Meade's chief of staff, "that an attempt to establish a picket line brought on a sharp contest, in which each side thought the other the attacking party."[22]

For the Rebels it was, as Colonel Venable called it, "perhaps the easiest victory ever granted to Confederate arms by the folly of Federal commanders." Southern casualties were light, perhaps twelve or fifteen hundred men. Among the leaders a brigade commander in Anderson's corps was hit in the head by a stray bullet, and Breckinridge was hurt by a fall when his horse was struck by a solid shot from a Union cannon. Citizens of Richmond were awakened that day by the loudest firing they had ever heard, and soon Lee started to receive visitors, including Postmaster General John H. Reagan and a couple of friends. When they opined that the artillery was particularly active that day Lee agreed, but gestured toward the infantry lines where the fire of thousands of rifles was blending together into a continuous roar. "It is that that kills men," he said.

They asked him what reserves he had in case Grant broke through. "Not a regiment," was the answer, "and that has been my condition ever since the fighting commenced on the Rappahannock. If I shorten my lines to provide a reserve, he will turn me. If I weaken my lines to provide a reserve, he will break them."²³ He went on to ask his visitors to urge the commissary general in Richmond to send potatoes and onions to his army, for some of his men were coming down with scurvy.

That day was Jefferson Davis' 56th birthday, and the president had spent the morning with his wife and children for a change. But after lunch he could no longer resist the urge to ride out and visit Lee too. The general presented him with evidence that Smith's 18th Corps was among the attackers in his front, and asked for more reinforcements from Beauregard's department. A little after 9 p.m. an order reached Beauregard for Matt Ransom's Brigade to be sent north of the James. It marched away at dawn of 4 June, being replaced in the trenches by the 4th North Carolina Cavalry from Dearing's Brigade. There were then only about 3,200 men in the Bermuda Hundred defenses and 2,200 around Petersburg, counting reserves and militia.

The attack near Cold Harbor had increased the dissension among the officers of the Army of the Potomac. "For thirty days it has been one funeral procession past me, and it has been too much!" Warren told a friend. "I think Grant has had his eyes opened," Meade wrote to his wife, "and is willing to admit now that Virginia and Lee's army is not Tennessee and Bragg's army." Recently promoted Brigadier General Emory Upton wrote that, "some of our corps commanders are not fit to be corporals. Lazy and indolent, they will not even ride along their lines; yet, without hesitancy, they will order us to attack the enemy, no matter what their position or numbers. Twenty thousand of our killed and wounded should today be in our ranks."²⁴

Yet morale in the ranks remained high enough. The men seemed to be grim but determined. "If there is ever again any rejoicing in this world," one cannonless heavy artilleryman wrote after experiencing his first battle, "it will be when this war is over. One who has never been under fire has no idea of war."²⁵ But Porter told his wife that the old veterans were comparing Grant with McClellan, who had brought them this close to the Confederate capital once before. "They all say if he had not retreated with them, himself leading the way, but stood and let them fight it out as Grant is doing, they would have been in Richmond two years sooner." One of Baldy Smith's men wrote that "we have the gray backs in a pretty close corner at present and intend to keep them so. There is no fall back with U. S. Grant."²⁶ One Union soldier, upon reading a newspaper account of a public meeting up North to protest against the continuing bloodshed asked, "Who's shedding this blood, anyhow? They better wait till we fellows down here at the front hollo, 'Enough!' "[27]

---

1. Sherman, *Memoirs,* 2:46, 50.
2. Dowdey and Manarin, *Wartime Papers of R. E. Lee,* 761.
3. Robertson, *Back Door to Richmond,* 237.
4. Pohanka, "Not War But Murder," *America's Civil War,* January 1989, 37.
5. Freeman, *R. E. Lee,* 3:383.
6. Foote, *The Civil War,* 3:261.
7. Trudeau, *Bloody Roads South,* 274.
8. Porter, *Campaigning With Grant,* 172.
9. Dana, *Recollections of the Civil War,* 187.
10. William Farrar Smith, "The Eighteenth Corps At Cold Harbor," in *Battles and Leaders,* 4:225.
11. Catton, *A Stillness At Appomattox,* 156.
12. Ibid., 159.
13. Porter, *Campaigning With Grant,* 174–175.
14. Pohanka, "Not War But Murder," 37.
15. Catton, *A Stillness at Appomattox,* 160.
16. Pohanka, "Not War But Murder," 38.
17. Catton, *A Stillness At Appomattox,* 162.
18. Ibid.
19. Catton, *Grant Takes Command,* 265.
20. Porter, *Campaigning With Grant,* 176–177.
21. Ibid., 177–179.
22. Humphreys, *The Virginia Campaign,* 190.
23. Freeman, *R. E. Lee,* 3:389–391.
24. Foote, *The Civil War,* 3:294–295.
25. Pohanka, "Not War But Murder," 40.
26. Catton, *Grant Takes Command,* 268.
27. Porter, *Campaigning With Grant,* 180.

CHAPTER THIRTY-SIX

"The Disease He Would Like To Die Of"

4–8 June 1864

Down in Georgia on the night of 4 June, Joe Johnston moved his army under the cover of the continuing rain, until it again covered the northern approaches to Marietta and the railroad to Atlanta. Hood's 2nd Corps held the right of the new position, along a 300-foot-high ridge called Brush Mountain and across the railroad itself. The Army of Mississippi, coming to be known now as Polk's Corps, occupied another 300-foot height called Pine Mountain, and Hardee's 1st Corps held the left on 500-foot-tall Lost Mountain. Joe Wheeler's Cavalry Corps protected the right flank, and Red Jackson's cavalry division from the Army of Mississippi extended the left. The entire area was covered by what General Howard called "interminable wilderness."[1] A brigade of Federal reinforcements reached the front that day from Kentucky and became the 3rd Brigade of Cox's 3rd Division of Schofield's 23rd Corps.

In the Shenandoah Valley on 4 June, Hunter, with Sigel's old command,

arrived at the North River, a tributary of the Shenandoah, across from
Mt. Crawford, fifteen miles north of Staunton. Rather than attack Confederate defenses on the other side, Hunter bypassed them by marching
east and crossed at the village of Port Republic. The Rebels thus outflanked consisted not only of Imboden's Brigade, but two others that had
arrived to reinforce him: John C. Vaughn's and W. E. Jones'. The total
force, about 5,600 men, was now under the command of Jones. Like the
Smiths, the Joneses had nicknames to identify them. This one was known
as Grumble Jones and very aptly so. The cantankerous Virginian was a
skilled combat leader but could not get along with his fellow officers. He
had once commanded the famous Laurel Brigade, formed in the early
days of the war by the late, legendary Turner Ashby. Jones was one of
Stonewall Jackson's favorites, but he had given Jeb Stuart such a hard time
that the latter had court-martialed him. While Tom Rosser took over the
Laurel Brigade, Jones was transferred to western Virginia, where he had
recently helped to turn back Averell's raid. With that job accomplished he
had moved down the Valley to help oppose Hunter, marching 175 miles in
ten days.

He had promptly irritated Vaughn, who had also moved down the
Valley, and Imboden as well, but since he outranked them both, he was
now in charge. When they learned that Hunter had crossed at Port
Republic the three evidently did agree that the place to stop him was
Mowry's Hill, south of the little town of Piedmont, between Port Republic and Staunton. However, when he arrived at that town Jones, over
Vaughn's and Imboden's objections, deployed his own brigade north of
Piedmont, in some woods west of the road to Staunton with his left
protected by a bluff overlooking the Middle River, another tributary of
the Shenandoah. A battery of six 3-inch rifles covered his right. Imboden's and Vaughn's brigades and another four guns were placed on the
north slope of Mowry's Hill, about 500 yards southeast of the village.

On the morning of 5 June, Julius Stahel, with Colonel William B.
Tibbits' 1st Brigade of his cavalry division, arrived at Piedmont at the
head of Hunter's column, pushed back the 18th Virginia Cavalry, and
discovered Jones' position. Stahel himself was wounded in the arm by a
shell fragment but continued to lead his horsemen. Sullivan's infantry
division soon came up and took position opposite Jones' Confederates.
Hunter arrived about noon and gave the field a hasty look but failed to
notice the Rebels on Mowry's Hill. About 1:30 p.m. Moor's Union
infantry brigade attacked the Confederate left and drove in Jones' skirmishers, but could not take his main position and so fell back. Jones
counterattacked and was also repulsed. Meanwhile, Hunter ordered a

double envelopment. While Federal artillery pinned the Southerners down, Moor and Tibbits attacked the Confederate left, and Colonel Joseph Thoburn's infantry and Colonel John Wynkoop's cavalry enveloped their right. Imboden and Vaughn, both rankled by Jones' treatment of them, stayed put on Mowry's Hill while Hunter's entire command fell on Jones' lone brigade and captured three guns and over 1,000 men, driving others down the bluff into the river. Grumble was found dead on the field with a bullet in the head. He would never irritate anyone again. Vaughn led what was left of the Rebel force to Waynesboro, at a gap in the Blue Ridge Mountains.

Two brigades of Forrest's Confederate cavalry had been moved to Alabama to oppose any attempt by Blair's 17th Corps to further penetrate that state. However, Blair's force marched into Rome, Georgia on 5 June, en route to join Sherman. In northern Mississippi that day, Sam Sturgis' Federals, after slogging through the mud for five days at seven miles per day, reached the hamlet of Salem, whose only distinction lay in being the boyhood home of Nathan Bedford Forrest. As he had done on his last expedition, Sturgis sent a detachment ahead. Four hundred cavalrymen were directed toward Rienzi, on the Mobile & Ohio Railroad, in hopes of breaking up any Confederate efforts to concentrate troops against the main Union column. The splitting of the Northern force had the fortuitous result of confusing Forrest as to Sturgis' objective. The Southern cavalryman had been about to cross the Tennessee River in northern Alabama two days before, when he had received orders to turn back and head Sturgis off. He returned to Tupelo on the fifth and was ordered by Major General S. D. Lee, the acting department commander, to place his force, now augmented to about 4,300 men, between Tupelo and Corinth until it became evident which way Sturgis would move. Lee, meanwhile, would try to find reinforcements to send to his aid.

In Virginia "on the morning of June 5th," Baldy Smith wrote, "General Meade came to my headquarters to say that he was going to fill the gap on my right." This was done with Burnside's 9th Corps brought down from the right flank. "And during his visit," Smith continued, "I asked him how he came to give such an order for battle as that of the 2d. He replied that he had worked out every plan for every move from the crossing of the Rapidan onward, that the papers were full of the doings of Grant's army, and that he was tired of it, and was determined to let General Grant plan his own battles. I have no knowledge of the facts," Smith added, "but have always supposed that General Grant's order was to attack the enemy at 4:30 a.m. of the 3d, leaving the details to his subordinate."[2] As we have already seen, Meade wrote to his wife that he had complete control of the battle on the third. But Smith's comment show's that Meade was certainly feeling the strain of being in Grant's shadow.

That same day Hancock asked Meade if some arrangement could not be made for rescuing the wounded men still lying between the lines. Meade passed the request on to Grant, pointing out that Confederate sharp-shooters made it impossible to reach the wounded, and suggested a flag of truce to arrange a short armistice. He added, revealingly, that such a flag would have to be sent by Grant since "the enemy do not recognize me as in command whilst you are present."[3] The lieutenant general wrote a letter to Lee proposing that, when no actual fighting was going on, either side should feel free to send out unarmed litter-bearers to bring in the wounded. But he added that "any other method equally fair to both parties you may propose for meeting the end desired will be accepted by me."[4] An officer with a white flag carried this message to the Rebel outposts at 3 p.m.

Warren's 5th Corps was withdrawn to a reserve position at Cold Harbor that day. Wright was directed to send two divisions of his 6th Corps to the army's left to extend it along the north bank of the Chick-ahominy to the crossing at Bottom's Bridge, while the cavalry extended the flank downriver to Jones' Bridge.

Meanwhile, Grant made up his mind about what to do next. Dana recorded that "Grant was disappointed" over the failure of the attack at Cold Harbor "and talked to me a good deal about the failure to get at Lee in an open battle which would wind up the Confederacy." After saying that he thought the officers of the Army of the Potomac were beginning to lose their fear of Lee, Dana added, "I think Grant respected Lee's military ability and character, yet the boldness with which he maneuvered in Lee's presence is proof that he was not overawed by Lee's prestige as a strategist and tactician. He thought Lee's great forte was as a defensive fighter."[5]

"Lee's position was now so near Richmond, and the intervening swamps of the Chickahominy so great an obstacle to the movement of troops in the face of an enemy," Grant later wrote, "that I determined to make my next left flank move carry the Army of the Potomac south of the James River."[6] Horace Porter wrote that "Halleck, who was rather fertile in suggestions, although few of them were ever practicable, had written Grant about the advisability of throwing his army round by the right flank, taking up a line northeast of Richmond, controlling the railroads leading north of Richmond, and using them to supply the Union army. This view," Porter added, "may have been favored in Washington for the reason that it was thought it would better protect the capital." But Grant told his staff, "We can defend Washington best by keeping Lee so occupied that he cannot detach enough troops to capture it." He added that "If the safety of the city should really become imperiled, we have water communication, and can transport a sufficient number of troops to Washington at any time to hold it against attack."[7] Besides, he said, Halleck's plan would leave Lee between Meade's Army of the Potomac and Butler's Army of the James.

Grant replied to his former boss that day to explain his reasoning. "A full survey of all the ground satisfies me that it would be impracticable to hold a line north-east of Richmond that would protect the Fredericksburg Railroad to enable us to use that road for supplying the army," he wrote. "To do so would give us a long vulnerable line of road to protect, exhausting much of our strength to guard it, and would leave open to the enemy all of his lines of communication on the south side of the James. My idea from the start has been to beat Lee's army if possible north of Richmond; then after destroying his lines of communication on the north side of the James River to transfer the army to the south side and besiege Lee in Richmond, or follow him south if he should retreat.

"I now find, after over thirty days of trial, the enemy deems it of the first importance to run no risks with the armies they now have. They act purely on the defensive behind breastworks, or feebly on the offensive immediately in front of them, and where in case of repulse they can instantly retire behind them. Without a greater sacrifice of human life than I am willing to make all cannot be accomplished that I had designed outside of the city. I have therefore resolved upon the following plan:

"I will continue to hold substantially the ground now occupied by the Army of the Potomac, taking advantage of any favorable circumstance that may present itself until the cavalry can be sent west to destroy the Virginia Central Railroad from about Beaver Dam for some twenty-five or thirty miles west. When this is effected I will move the army to the south side of the James River, either by crossing the Chickahominy and marching near to City Point, or by going to the mouth of the Chickahominy on north side and crossing there. To provide for this last and most possible contingency, several ferry-boats of the largest class ought to be immediately provided." On the south side of the James River, he said, he could cut off all other lines of supply to Richmond and Lee's army except the James River canal to Lynchburg. "If Hunter succeeds in reaching Lynchburg," Grant added, "that will be lost to him also. Should Hunter not succeed, I will still make the effort to destroy the canal by sending cavalry up the south side of the river with a pontoon train to cross wherever they can."[8]

Grant learned that evening that Hunter had made a good start by defeating Grumble Jones at Piedmont the day before, and he immediately set in motion the first part of his plan: the destruction of the Virginia Central Railroad so that supplies could not be brought to Lee and Richmond from the Shenandoah Valley. He called for Sheridan and gave him instructions to leave at dawn of 7 June on a trip northwestward, around Lee's left flank, to strike the railroad. He had, since writing to Halleck earlier in the day, decided to send the cavalry even farther west than originally planned. Instead of Beaver Dam Station a bit west of Hanover Junction, Sheridan's objective would be Gordonsville, where the Virginia Central was joined by the Orange & Alexandria Railroad; or even Charlottesville, where the two separated again, one going west to Waynesboro, where Vaughn had retreated, and on to Staunton in the Valley, the other going southwest to Lynchburg and on to Tennessee.

To Meade he wrote: "The object of the cavalry expedition to Charlottesville and Gordonsville is to effectually break up the railroad connection between Richmond and the Shenandoah Valley and Lynchburg. To secure this end they should go as far as Charlottesville and work upon the Lynchburg branch and main line to Staunton for several miles beyond the junction. This done, they could work back this way to where the road is already destroyed, or until driven off by a superior force."[9]

Instructions were sent by way of Washington and the Shenandoah for Hunter to connect with Sheridan, and the cavalryman would carry further instructions to that officer. In these, after explaining that Sheridan was to destroy the Virginia Central, Grant said: "The complete destruction of this road and of the canal on James River is of great importance to us. According to the instructions I sent to General Halleck for your guidance, you were to proceed to Lynchburg and commence there. It would be of great value to us to get possession of Lynchburg for a single day. But that point is of so much importance to the enemy, that in attempting to get it such resistance may be met as to defeat your getting onto the road or canal at all. I see, in looking over the letter to General Halleck on the subject of your instructions, that it rather indicates that your route should be from Staunton via Charlottesville. If you have so understood it, you will be doing just what I want. The direction I would now give is, that if this letter reaches you in the valley between Staunton and Lynchburg, you immediately turn east by the most practicable road until you strike the Lynchburg branch of the Va. Central road. From thence move eastward along the line of the road, destroying it completely and thoroughly, until you join General Sheridan. After the work laid out for General Sheridan and yourself is thoroughly done, proceed to join the Army of the Potomac by the route laid out in General Sheridan's instructions.

"If any portion of your force, especially your cavalry, is needed back in your Department," Grant added, "you are authorized to send it back.

"If on receipt of this you should be near to Lynchburg and deem it practicable to reach that point, you will exercise your judgment about going on.

"If you should be on the railroad between Charlottesville and Lynchburg, it may be practicable to detach a cavalry force to destroy the canal. Lose no opportunity to destroy the canal," he emphasized.[10]

At midnight, Lee's reply to Grant's note about bringing in the wounded was brought to the front, but it did not reach Grant until the next morning, the sixth. "I fear," Lee said, "that such an arrangement will lead to misunderstanding and difficulty. I propose, therefore, instead, that when either party desires to remove their dead or wounded a flag of truce be sent, as is customary. It will always afford me pleasure to comply with such a request as far as circumstances will permit."[11] In answer Grant wrote, "I will send immediately, as you propose, to collect the dead and wounded between the lines of the two armies, and will also instruct that you be allowed to do the same. I propose that the time for doing this be between the hours of 12 p.m. and 3 p.m. to-day. I will direct all parties going out to bear a white flag, and not to attempt to go beyond where we have dead or wounded, and not beyond or on ground occupied by your troops."[12]

Lee refused to go along with that, however, replying that he regretted "to find that I did not make myself understood in my communication," but that if what Grant wanted was a cease-fire he should ask for one "by a flag of truce in the usual way."[13] Until Lee received "a proposition from you on the subject to which I can accede with propriety, I have directed any parties you may send out under white flags as mentioned in your letter to be turned back."[14] An obscure point of military procedure was the stumbling block here—that and human pride. As a Federal staff officer explained, "An impression prevails in the popular mind, and with some reason perhaps, that a commander who sends a flag of truce asking permission to bury his dead and bring in his wounded has lost the field of battle. Hence the resistance upon our part to ask a flag of truce."[15]

Whether or not Grant was trying to avoid such an admission, Lee was obviously insisting that he make one, with the wounded men, most but by no means all Federals, as his hostages. Grant readily conceded, replying that afternoon that "the knowledge that wounded men are now suffering from want of attention, between the two armies, compels me to ask a suspension of hostilities for sufficient time to collect them in, say two hours. Permit me to say that the hours you may fix upon for this will be agreeable to me, and the same privilege will be extended to such parties as you may wish to send out on the same duty without further application."[16] At 7 p.m. Lee replied that he was sorry that it had not been possible to set a truce during the day but that the period between 8 and 10 that night would be satisfactory. It was, however, already past 10 by the time this message was delivered to the Union outposts, and it did not reach Grant until near midnight. Meanwhile, those wounded men who had survived the sharpshooters' bullets and the heat of the day spent another night lying between the lines without food, water or medical attention. And the unburied dead were now a great burden on the living. One of Baldy Smith's men wrote that "the air was laden with insufferable putrescence. We breathed it in every breath, tasted it in the food we ate and water we drank."[17]

Cavalry division commander James Wilson, a former member of Grant's staff, visited headquarters that day. As he passed Meade, who was nervously pacing in front of his tent and flicking his boots with a riding crop, the army commander called out, "Wilson, when is Grant going to take Richmond?" Wilson talked with Rawlins and Dana that day and the next, and found them both concerned about the influence of aide Cyrus Comstock on the lieutenant general. With "blanched lips, glittering teeth and flashing eyes," as Wilson remembered it, Rawlins told him that "that officer, having gained Grant's confidence, was now leading him and his army to ruin by senselessly advocating the direct attack, and driving it home by the deadly reiteration of 'Smash 'em up! Smash 'em up.' "[18]

That afternoon Grant called in Comstock and Horace Porter and told them "with more impressiveness of manner than he usually manifested," according to Porter, that he had an important mission for them. He wanted them to go to Bermuda Hundred to explain the planned movement to Butler in detail, including the fact that Baldy Smith's 18th Corps would soon be returned to him by transports up the James so that he would be strong enough to defend himself from Lee's army until Meade's forces linked up with his. The two staff officers were then to select the best point on the river for the Army of the Potomac to cross. "Comstock and I had served on General McClellan's staff when his army occupied the north bank of the James two years before," Porter explained, "and the country for many miles along the river was quite familiar to us."[19] Rawlins and Dana must have been relieved to see Comstock go. "Certain it is," Wilson recorded, "that the 'smash-'em-up' policy was abandoned about that time and was never again favored at headquarters."[20]

Lee's mind was also diverted to other fields. He learned that day that Hunter had occupied Staunton—the first Federal to do so during the war—and that Grumble Jones had been defeated and killed at Piedmont the day before. Lee had hoped to be able to dispose of Grant before Hunter became too great a problem, but he could afford to ignore the situation in the Valley no longer. Staunton was at the Shenandoah end of the Virginia Central Railroad, and Yankees there would cut off his supplies from the Valley. If they got to the great supply depot at Lynchburg they could cause irreparable damage. Reluctantly, Lee sent for Breckinridge and told him that he and his two small brigades were to leave the next morning for that city, where they were to combine with the survivors from Piedmont.

In Georgia that day, 6 June, Sherman personally rode into Allatoona and gave orders for it to be fortified and prepared as his forward supply base. He also did a bit of reorganizing. Brigadier General A. P. Hovey, commander of the 1st Division of Schofield's 23rd Corps, had chosen to go home on leave to Indiana in the midst of the campaign, so Sherman broke up his division of two brigades and assigned one to each of Schofield's other divisions.

Forrest, at Tupelo, Mississippi, learned that day of Sturgis' advance to Salem. That afternoon S. D. Lee, in temporary command in Alabama, Mississippi and east Louisiana in the absence of Polk, arrived at Forrest's headquarters. He looked over the scouts' reports, which said that the Federals were commanded by A. J. Smith, and concluded that, the low level of the rivers had compelled these Yankees to march eastward in order to join Sherman. But just in case they were heading for the rich croplands of east-central Mississippi, he ordered Forrest to concentrate his forces at or near Okolona.

Colonel Kargé, with the 400-man detachment sent out by Sturgis, pounded into Rienzi that day, scattering a few Rebels. They listened in on the telegraph while several miles of railroad were being torn up. Then they cut the wires and rode north. Sturgis' infantry met their first opposition that day, when a few Rebel patrols opened fire and then faded away. Early on the morning of the seventh, a messenger from Kargé reached Grierson with word that the Confederates had abandoned Corinth and gone south. He forwarded this report to Sturgis and sent word that the countryside around Ruckersville lacked forage for the horses and mules. He recommended a turn to the south toward Ripley. Sturgis took this advice, and that afternoon Grierson's cavalry ran into part of Rucker's Brigade of Forrest's corps. The infantry marched only as far as Ripley.

The next morning, 7 June, Breckinridge and his Confederate infantry set out by train for Lexington, while at the same time Sheridan and his time troopers started out by horseback for Charlottesville.

Also that morning Grant sent one last note to Lee about the wounded. After explaining that Lee's note setting the time for the truce had arrived too late to be acted upon, he added: "As a consequence, it was not understood by the troops of this army that there was a cessation of hostilities for the purpose of collecting the dead and wounded, and none were collected. Two officers and six men of the 8th and 25th North Carolina Regts., who were out in search of the bodies of officers of their respective regiments, were captured and brought into our lines, owing to this want of understanding. I regret this, but will state that as soon as I learned the fact, I directed that they should not be held as prisoners, but must be returned to their commands." After discussing how this was to be accomplished, he added, in a phrase that sounded more like Rawlins, his ex-lawyer chief of staff, that he regretted "that all my efforts for alleviating the sufferings of wounded men left upon the battlefield have been rendered nugatory."[21]

That afternoon Lee answered that he was sorry about the mix-up and suggested the hours from 6 to 8 p.m. for parties with white flags to bring in the wounded, which was pretty much what Grant had suggested two days before. At the designated time the stretcher-bearers finally went out. They came back with only two living men. Any others who had survived the original attack had either made it back to safety on their own, been killed by subsequent firing, bled to death from their wounds, or died of thirst, starvation and exposure during the four hot days they had lain unreachable between the lines while their commanders corresponded.

Although the wounded were thus put out of their misery, one way or the other, Meade was not. Looking through a five-day-old copy of the *Philadelphia Inquirer* he found an implication that he had wanted to retreat back across the Rapidan after the second day of the battle of the Wilderness and that only "Grant's presence saved the army, and the nation too . . . Grant assumed the responsibility and we are still on to Richmond." Meade had the *Inquirer*'s correspondent, Edward Crapsey, brought to his tent. The reporter admitted writing the piece and as authority for his story could cite only "the talk of the camp." Enraged by this "base and wicked lie," Meade put Crapsey under arrest and had an order drawn up directing that he "be put without the lines and not permitted to return."[22]

That day, 7 June, Grant ordered Brigadier General John Abercrombie, in command of the new supply base at White House, to take up the rails from the York River Railroad, which ran through that area, and put them on boats, ready to be shipped to City Point. Grant was notified that same day that Halleck was running out of reinforcements for him and that, beyond a few more regiments soon to be sent, "all resources will be exhausted till another draft is made."[23]

It was, however, a bad time to expect President Lincoln to order another draft. Delegates were gathering that very day at the Front Street Theatre in Baltimore to open the National Union political convention. This was the name adopted by the Republicans that year to encompass a large contingent of pro-war Democrats who would join with them to nominate a candidate for president. At noon the convention was called to order and turned over to the temporary chairman, the Reverend Doctor Robert J. Breckinridge of Kentucky, uncle of Confederate major general John C. Breckinridge and father of two other Rebel officers. The Old War Horse, as he was called, was applauded when he told the assembled delegates, "As a Union party, I will follow you to the ends of the earth, and to the gates of death. But as an Abolition party—as a Republican party—as a Whig party—as a Democratic party—as an American party, I will not follow you one foot." Although from a slave state, he conceded that slavery was dead, telling the delegates, "I join myself with those who say, away with it forever; and I fervently pray God that the day may come when throughout the whole land every man may be free as you are, and as capable of enjoying regulated liberty."[24]

When he was through and had been followed by a prayer, the convention got down to wrangling over whether or not to seat delegates from the seceded states. The next morning, 8 June, the convention voted to seat a radical delegation from Missouri, a faction that was not friendly to Lincoln. A delegation from South Carolina was not admitted. Virginia and Florida got seats but no votes. Arkansas, Louisiana and Tennessee, all states which were mostly in the grip of the Federal army, received full voting rights. Next came the adoption of the platform. There were no surprises. The party came down solidly behind the Constitution, the Union, and the war, and against slavery and rebellion. It promised aid for disabled veterans, and it favored immigration, a transcontinental railroad, and full redemption of the public debt.

Then it was time for nominations. Simon Cameron of Pennsylvania sent up a written resolution calling for the unanimous renomination of President Abraham Lincoln of Illinois and Vice President Hannibal Hamlin of Maine, and when it was read out, pandemonium reigned. The decision was finally made to poll the state delegations. One by one, they announced undivided votes for Lincoln, except for the Missouri radicals, who cast 22 votes for Ulysses S. Grant. "Growls of disapproval arose from all parts of the convention," one reporter recorded.[25] However, after the total was read—484 to 22—Missouri changed its vote to make the nomination of Lincoln unanimous after all. "Men hurrahed, embraced one another, threw up their hats, danced in the aisles or on the platform, jumped on the benches, waved flags, yelled, and committed every possible extravagance," the reporter wrote.

The convention finally settled down and proceeded to the business of nominating a vice president. Cameron put forward Hamlin's name for renomination, but a New York delegate proposed Daniel S. Dickinson of his own state. Then Indiana offered the name of Andrew Johnson, a pro-Union east Tennessean, formerly senator and then military governor of his home state. As the roll call progressed, Johnson began to pick up support, and after the votes were counted they added up to 200 for the Tennessean, 150 for Hamlin, 108 for Dickinson, 21 for Major General Lovell Rousseau of Kentucky, 20 for Ben Butler—those from the Missouri radicals—and 1 for David Tod of Ohio. Kentucky then changed its votes for Rousseau and Tod to 21 more for Johnson. This started a gathering avalanche of vote-switching until the Tennessean wound up with 494 votes, against 17 for Dickinson and 9 for Hamlin.

Johnson was a shrewd choice, and many later came to believe that Lincoln had engineered his nomination. He was a War Democrat, perhaps the ablest of them, and thus the nature of the National Union as a coalition was properly emphasized. He was a Southerner, and thus confounded the sectional nature of the Republican party. "There is no man in the country, unless it be Mr. Lincoln himself," it was written in *Harper's Weekly*, "whom the rebels more cordially hate. He fought them in the Senate, when they counted upon his aid, and he has fought them steadily ever since." Horace Greeley of the *New York Tribune* was happy with Johnson as "a man who would be hanged at noon on the day the Confederates captured him."[26]

Lincoln had now cleared the first hurdle, renomination, but the tougher job of getting reelected remained. If he pulled it off, he would be the first president elected to a second term since Andrew Jackson, 32 years before. If the war went badly, a wave of defeatism might prevent his election. But if it went well, there could be problems too. That spring someone had told him that nothing could prevent his reelection unless Grant captured Richmond, in which case the Democrats would nominate the general, who would ride to victory on a wave of hero-worship. "Well," Lincoln was reported to have answered, "I feel very much like the man who said he didn't want to die particularly, but if he had got to die that was precisely the disease he would like to die of."[27]

---

1. McDonough and Jones, *War So Terrible*, 170.
2. Smith, "The Eighteenth Corps At Cold Harbor," 228.
3. Catton, *Grant Takes Command*, 270.
4. Grant, *Memoirs*, 2:274.
5. Dana, *Recollections of the Civil War*, 192.
6. Grant, *Memoirs*, 2:279.
7. Porter, *Campaigning With Grant*, 182.
8. Grant, *Memoirs*, 2:279–281.
9. Catton, *Grant Takes Command*, 278.
10. Grant, *Memoirs*, 2:282–283.
11. Foote, *The Civil War*, 3:295–296.
12. Grant, *Memoirs*, 2:274.
13. Foote, *The Civil War*, 3:296.
14. Catton, *Grant Takes Command*, 271.
15. Foote, *The Civil War*, 3:295.
16. Grant, *Memoirs*, 2:275.
17. Trudeau, *Bloody Roads South*, 304.
18. Ibid., 304–305.
19. Porter, *Campaigning With Grant*, 187–188.
20. Foote, *The Civil War*, 3:295.
21. Grant, *Memoirs*, 2:276.
22. Foote, *The Civil War*, 3:298.
23. Ibid., 3:299.
24. Carl Sandburg, *Abraham Lincoln: The War Years*, 1864–1865 (New York, 1926), 535.
25. Ibid., 538.
26. Ibid., 540.
27. Ibid., 526.

CHAPTER THIRTY-SEVEN

"With a Sad Foreboding of the Consequences"

8–10 June 1864

Rain continued to fall as the 17th Corps arrived at Sherman's railhead at Ackworth, Georgia on 8 June. The corps consisted of two divisions and was commanded by Major General Francis Preston ("Frank") Blair, Jr. An interesting character, he was the son of a powerful Maryland politician who had been advisor to presidents as far back as Andrew Jackson and was now a supporter of Lincoln. The general's brother, Montgomery, was postmaster general in Lincoln's cabinet, and he, himself, was a Congressman from Missouri as well as a major general of volunteers. After leaving 1,500 men to garrison Allatoona, Blair led 9,000 veterans to join McPherson's Army of the Tennessee. He also brought with him wagons of iced champagne to throw a party for McPherson and Schofield.

Sherman was not the only Union commander who received reinforcements on 8 June. In the Shenandoah Valley that day Crook's infantry division and Averell's cavalry division marched into Staunton to join Hunter's main column after tearing up the railroad on the west side of town. They found that Hunter had already destroyed all the Virginia Central's facilities in the town as well as a woolens factory, steam mill, wagon shops, and warehouses full of saddles, harness, uniforms and shoes, a thousand small arms, and four cannon. The addition of Crook and Averell brought Hunter's force up to about 18,000 horse and foot, with thirty pieces of artillery—much stronger than all the Confederates in the Valley. Shoes were provided for Crook's and Averell's barefoot men, and 800 troops whose enlistments were expiring were sent north under Colonel Moor as escorts for a convoy of prisoners, runaway slaves, and refugees.

Also on that eighth day of June, after seven days of marching, Sturgis' expedition into Mississippi gathered at Ripley, eighty miles southeast of Memphis, and the point from which he had turned back on his previous attempt to catch Forrest's raiders. Colonel William L. McMillen, commander of Sturgis' ad hoc infantry division, wrote that "the line of march was through a country devastated by the war, and containing little or no forage, rendering it extremely difficult, and for the greater portion of the time impossible, to maintain the animals in a serviceable condition. The roads were narrow, leading through dense forests, and over streams rendered almost impassable by the heavy rains which fell daily." At Ripley, Sturgis held an informal council of war with McMillen, Brigadier General Benjamin Grierson, his cavalry commander, and Colonel George B. Hoge, commander of one of McMillen's infantry brigades. Grierson, famous for his raid across the length of Mississippi a year before, warned that a further advance of the present expedition would "lead to disaster." But McMillen said that he "would rather go on and meet the enemy, even if we should be whipped, than to return to Memphis without having met them," as Sturgis had done the previous month. Sturgis lamented the delay caused by the rain and the poor roads, and pointed out that Forrest was probably making good use of the "time thus afforded him to concentrate an overwhelming force against us." He was also worried about "the utter hopelessness of saving our train or artillery in case of defeat, on account of the narrowness and general bad condition of the roads and the impossibility of procuring supplies of forage for the animals." However, with "a sad foreboding of the consequences," he decided to go on.[1]

The force which Forrest was concentrating was far from overwhelming in terms of numbers, but he was making good use of the time that Sturgis' slow advance had given him. He had sent Colonel Tyree Bell's brigade of 2,800 men to Rienzi, and with two smaller brigades, totaling about 1,500 men and eight cannon, had moved to Booneville. It was there that he learned on 8 June that Sturgis had reached Ripley, twenty miles away.

Far to the north, John Hunt Morgan's 2,700 Confederate raiders came down out of the mountains of Kentucky that eighth of June, 150 miles from their starting point in Virginia. Due to a shortage of horses and losses on the rough trip, nearly a third of the Rebels were on foot. That morning they surrounded the town of Mount Sterling, thirty miles from Lexington, Kentucky, and captured 380 Federals guarding supplies, which included some badly needed boots. While the Yankees were being paroled, some of the Confederates—the kind who had joined the cavalry to avoid more serious duty—broke into shops and plundered private homes. Some even held up citizens at gunpoint, and a group of indignant townspeople called on Morgan to show him an order signed by one of his brigade commanders, who had demanded all the money in the bank on threat of burning down every house in town. The sum of $72,000 had been delivered, but now the citizens wanted to know if Morgan had authorized this action. Morgan demanded an explanation from the colonel who had signed the order, only to find that it was a forgery. Witnesses' descriptions of the officer who had presented the order matched Surgeon R. R. Goode, who had disappeared. Neither he nor the money was ever seen again. Anyway, Morgan left part of his command, including all the dismounted men, to distribute and destroy the captured horses and supplies, and he rode off with the rest toward Lexington, his home town.

Morgan had been right when he told the Southern War Department that the Federals were preparing a raid of their own from Kentucky into Virginia. Brigadier General Stephen G. Burbridge was the commander of the District of Kentucky, part of Schofield's Department of the Ohio. He had been leading a force of mounted units across the mountains when he received word that Morgan had beat him to the punch and crossed to the south of him, going in the opposite direction. Burbridge turned around and marched his men ninety miles in 24 hours and they arrived just outside of Mount Sterling on the night of 8 June.

Still other cavalry was on the move that day. In Virginia, Wade Hampton reported to Lee that Sheridan's troopers had recrossed the Pamunkey the day before and were moving northwest. Lee ordered Hampton to take his own and Fitzhugh Lee's divisions and head the Yankees off. Since Jeb Stuart's death, the cavalry divisions had been separate commands, but now it was necessary that two of them act together, and Hampton received the first chance to prove himself capable of handling the combined force. The men of the two Rebel divisions were issued bacon and hardtack crackers. They would move out at dawn.

Across the lines, in the Army of the Potomac, the reporter who had made Meade angry with his "base and wicked lie" was ridden out of camp on the morning of the eighth, facing backwards on the worst-looking mule that could be found and wearing a big placard that said "Libeler of the Press." He was paraded thus all through the camp, to the tune of the "Rogue's March," then taken to White House plantation, put on a steamer for Washington, and told to never return. Provost Marshal General Marsena Patrick, the army's chief of military police, gladly presided over the proceedings with the hope that "it will be a warning to his tribe." The soldiers found the whole thing funny enough. Newspapermen, who often stretched the truth and sometimes revealed important information to the enemy—for which the troops had to pay in blood—were not popular with the men. But Meade had hurt himself as much as he had the reporter. By common consent, none of the correspondents who remained with the army would ever mention Meade in their stories again. From that day on it was "Grant's army," in the papers, and therefore in the popular mind.

Grant, meanwhile, gave orders that day for Meade "to fortify a line down the bank of the Chickahominy, under cover of which the army could move."[2] The next day, 9 June, Grant told Abercrombie, in command at the White House supply base, to send on to Butler all organized reinforcements arriving there, without letting them debark from their transports. Halleck was told to send any further replacements directly to City Point.

A man in the Confederate 1st Corps recorded that "a negro soldier was captured on the picket line, and brought to the rear. The men were very much inflamed at seeing a negro in arms. It was the first I had ever seen, and I must confess I was considerably stirred. The poor creature was almost frightened to death as he looked around on the scowling faces of the curious crowd. He was ashly pale. I do not remember now how the guard happened to give him up," the soldier wrote, "but some non-combatant officer . . . who did not belong to our division, took charge of him and . . . carried him off. I soon after heard the report of a gun, and was told that the negro had been shot in the woods."[3]

A letter which Lee wrote to President Davis on the ninth showed that he understood Sheridan's move: "I have received no definite information as to his purpose, but conjecture that his object is to cooperate with Genl Hunter, and endeavor to reach the James, breaking the railroads &c., as he passes, and probably to descend on the south side of that river. The pause in the operations of Genl Grant induces me to believe that he is awaiting the effect of movements in some other quarter to make us change our position, and renders the suggestion I make with reference to the intention and destination of Genl Sheridan more probable."⁴

In the Shenandoah, Hunter, who of course had not yet received the letter Grant was sending him by way of Sheridan's cavalry, had decided to march toward Richmond by way of Lynchburg instead of taking the more direct route through Charlottesville as Grant was hoping that he would. On the ninth he assigned one of Averell's brigade commanders to take over the wounded Stahel's 1st Cavalry Division. The Hungarian was replaced by a Frenchman, Brigadier General Alfred N. Duffié, who had graduated from the French military academy at St. Cyr and had fought as a lieutenant in the French cavalry before coming to America at the outbreak of the Civil War.

Hunter then asked Averell to prepare a plan for the capture of Lynchburg. Averell proposed that Duffié's division be sent east of the Blue Ridge Mountains, as a diversion and to destroy track on the Southside Railroad, while Hunter's main force would move up the Valley, cross the Blue Ridge farther south, and proceed to Lynchburg.

In southeastern Virginia, Butler was astir again on the ninth of June. He had revived his plan for a sudden dash into Petersburg, and Gillmore had insisted on taking personal charge of the move, as his rank and position entitled him to do. Butler relented, although he doubted Gillmore's capacity. Hincks thought even less of Gillmore, Kautz had his reservations about the whole plan, and Hawley, a brigade commander in the operation, thought it "almost insane."⁵ Kautz's cavalry had farther to go than was expected and did not reach its position until that afternoon. Gillmore, with Hawley's infantry, had meanwhile approached the outer defenses of Petersburg. Overly impressed with the apparent strength of the defenses and with the terrain that his men would have to cross, Gillmore ordered Hawley to fake an attack and then retire. Without Hawley's support, Hincks had no choice but to fall back also. As the infantry withdrew, Kautz's troopers pushed aside some old men and boys south of the town, but just before getting into the city they ran into some of Dearing's Rebel cavalry backed up by artillery and a patchwork of convalescents and convicts, and, having heard nothing from Gillmore, Kautz also decided to retreat. Once more Petersburg had survived impending doom.

Beauregard had already sent a request to Bragg for the return of Hoke's Division to protect Petersburg, but even this latest demonstration of the city's vulnerability failed to impress Lee enough to convince him to let go of the reinforcements which he had worked so hard to obtain. "I know no necessity for the removal of these troops," he told Bragg, "but if directed will send them. No troops have left Genl Grant's army to my knowledge, and none could have crossed James River without being discovered. I think it very improbable that he would weaken himself under existing circumstances."[6] Lee did move Early's corps to his right just in case he had to pull Hoke out of the trenches. Bragg had been about to send Gracie's Brigade back to Beauregard from the Richmond defenses, but when it was learned that Gillmore had retreated, the order was suspended.

In Kentucky at dawn that ninth day of June, Burbridge attacked the 800 or so Rebel troopers whom Morgan had left behind at Mount Sterling, catching many of them asleep. Only a little over half of the Confederates managed to retreat out the west end of town. The Federals, however, were still too tired from their recent forced march to pursue them. Morgan was already halfway to Lexington when he learned what had happened. At first he wanted to turn about and counterattack, but considering that Burbridge outnumbered him two to one, and had artillery while he had none, he thought better of it. He continued on to Lexington and camped just outside the town that night.

Lincoln was officially notified of his nomination for reelection that day. Although it had been anticipated, the nomination was drawing plenty of comment in the press, both favorable and unfavorable. The *New York World* of 9 June spoke for most respectable, wealthy Democrats when it said of Lincoln and Johnson: "In a crisis of the most appalling magnitude, requiring statesmanship of the highest order, the country is asked to consider the claims of two ignorant, boorish, third-rate backwoods lawyers, for the highest stations in the government."[7] To a delegation from the National Union League, come to present resolutions endorsing his nomination, Lincoln noted that, "I have not permitted myself, gentlemen, to conclude that I am the best man in the country; but I am reminded, in this connection, of a story of an old Dutch farmer, who remarked to a companion once that 'it was not best to swap horses when crossing streams.'"

In his official reply to this committee notifying him of his nomination, the president stated that he approved of the convention's declaration in favor of a constitutional amendment to prohibit slavery throughout the nation. He had given the south fair notice in his Emancipation Proclamation, which had allowed the Rebels 100 days to resume their allegiance to the Federal government or suffer the consequences. Now the proposed amendment "became a fitting, and necessary conclusion to the final success of the Union cause. Such alone can meet and cover all cavils. Now, the unconditional Union men, North and South, perceive its importance, and embrace it. In the joint names of Liberty and Union, let us labor to give it legal form, and practical effect." In response to a delegation from Ohio, which serenaded him with a brass band, he said that "what we want, still more than Baltimore conventions or presidential elections, is success under Gen. Grant." He then proposed "three rousing cheers for Gen. Grant and the officers and soldiers under his command."[8]

Down in Georgia on the ninth of June Brigadier General Kenner Garrard's division of Union cavalry drove Wheeler's Rebel troopers back to Big Shanty on the Atlantic & Western Railroad. Both sides fought dismounted, and the Confederate horsemen made use of the cover of barricades and telegraph wire strung close to the ground, just as Baldy Smith had used it near Drewry's Bluff. "If it afforded the rebels any amusement to see the boys in blue tumbling over the wires," one of the Federal troopers remarked, "they were welcome to it, as the harmless thing did us no damage."[9] Sherman wrote that day to his brother John, the senator: "My long and single line of railroad to my rear, of limited capacity, is the delicate point of my game, as also the fact that all of Georgia, except the cleared bottoms, is densely wooded, with few roads, and at many points an enterprising enemy can, in a few hours with axes and spades, make across our path formidable works . . . It is a big Indian war, still thus far I have won four strong positions, advanced a hundred miles . . . Johnston's army is still in my front and can fight or fall back, as he pleases. The future is uncertain, but I will do all that is possible."[10]

Sherman's long, single line of railroad was somewhat safer just then because Forrest had been induced to turn back from raiding it in order to defend Mississippi. Reports reached S. D. Lee and Forrest that day that Sturgis' column was moving southeast from Ripley on a road that would bring it to the Mobile & Ohio Railroad at Guntown, ten miles north of Tupelo. This satisfied Lee that the Federals were not moving to reinforce Sherman but striking for the fertile Black Prairie region of eastern Mississippi. He therefore sent orders for part of the division of Forrest's corps that had been sent to Alabama to return, and for Forrest to concentrate his forces farther south, at Okolona, where reinforcements would be sent to him from central Mississippi and from Mobile. Before boarding a train for Okolona, however, Lee told Forrest to use his own judgment as to where and when to fight the Yankees. After Lee departed, Forrest met with his principal subordinates and advised them of the situation and

Lee's plan. He added, however, that battle might ensue before they could reach Okolona.

Forrest received 500 troopers under Colonel William A. Johnson from northern Alabama that day. He ordered them to rest near Baldwyn, about five miles north of Guntown. And before going to bed, Forrest gave orders for the rest of his forces to take a road toward Okolona that would intersect Sturgis' route to Guntown the next morning. This would almost certainly bring on a fight on the low, wooded plateau where the road which the Yankees were taking crossed the one that Forrest would follow southwest from Booneville. The spot was six miles northwest of Guntown, and it was called Brice's Cross Roads.

Sherman's three armies advanced six miles the next day, the tenth, despite muddy roads and swollen streams, to close up to the Confederate positions around Big Shanty. Johnston had pulled his right back from Brush Mountain to Kenesaw Mountain, a mile or so to the south, although his center and left were still on Pine and Lost mountains. "On each of these hills the enemy had signal-stations and fresh lines of parapets," Sherman wrote. "Heavy masses of infantry could be distinctly seen with the naked eye, and it was manifest that Johnston had chosen his ground well, and with deliberation had prepared for battle; but his line was at least ten miles in extent—too long, in my judgment, to be held successfully by his force, then estimated at sixty thousand. As his position, however, gave him a perfect view over our field, we had to proceed with due caution."[11] McPherson's newly strengthened Army of the Tennessee held Sherman's left, near the railroad, which curved around the north base of Kenesaw. Thomas' Army of the Cumberland had the center, deployed below Kenesaw and facing Pine Mountain, and Schofield's small Army of the Ohio was on the right, facing south, toward Lost Mountain. Garrard's cavalry division extended the left and Stoneman's, the right, while McCook's guarded the rear.

John Hunt Morgan's raiders, including those who had escaped from Mount Sterling the day before, entered Lexington, Kentucky 10 June and captured, among other things, enough horses in its government stables to mount any of his men who still needed a ride. "Though the stay of Morgan's command in Lexington was brief, embracing but a few hours," the local newspaper said the next day, "he made good use of his time—as many empty shelves and pockets will testify."[12] Once again the more unsavory element among his troopers began looting, and this time his veterans joined in. They put a pistol to a cashier's head at the local bank, forced him to open the vault, and made off with $10,000. Several buildings were burned, and so much whiskey was stolen, and drunk, that many of the men had to be loaded onto wagons for the trip thirty miles northeast to Cynthiana, where Morgan had heard that there were more Federal supplies, guarded by a mere 500 men.

Also on 10 June, Wade Hampton's and Fitz Lee's Confederate cavalry divisions were on the march. It was hot and dry in Virginia that day, and the column of men and horses stirred the roads into clouds of choking dust. "The only water obtainable for man or beast," one Rebel remembered, "was from small streams crossed, and this, churned up by thousands of hoofs, was almost undrinkable."[13] By nightfall Hampton's Division had reached Green Spring Valley in Louisa County. This was a lovely area, untouched by the war so far, and the tired troopers threw themselves down to rest on the thick grass while their horses feasted on the wide pastures. Fitz Lee's Division went into camp about eight miles back at Louisa Court House. That night Hampton learned that his shorter route had brought him to the threatened stretch of the Virginia Central Railroad ahead of Sheridan, who had crossed the North Anna at Carpenter's Ford. From there the road led to Clayton's Store, from which two roads proceeded south. One led due south to Louisa Court House; the other went southwest to Trevilian Station. Both towns were on the railroad. Hampton decided that the certain way to head off the Federals, whichever way they marched next day, would be for Fitz Lee to move north from Louisa Court House and his own division to take the road from Trevilian Station. The two columns would converge on Clayton's Store until they ran into Sheridan's troopers, whom he hoped to drive into the North Anna.

In Richmond that day the Confederate Congress, to ease its manpower problems, extended the age of compulsory military service to include men from 45 to 50, and from 17 to 18.

---

1. Starr, *Union Cavalry,* 3:426–427.
2. Grant, *Memoirs,* 2:284.
3. Trudeau, *Bloody Roads South,* 311–312.
4. Dowdey and Manarin, eds., *Wartime Papers of R. E. Lee,* 771.
5. Robertson, *Back Door To Richmond,* 240.
6. Dowdey and Manarin, eds., *Wartime Papers of R. E. Lee,* 770.
7. Sandburg, *The War Years,* 542.
8. Basler, ed., *Collected Works of Abraham Lincoln,* 7:380–384.

9. Phil Noblitt, "Heedless Frontal Assault," *America's Civil War,* January 1990, 36.

10. McDonough and Jones, *War So Terrible,* 171.

11. Sherman, *Memoirs,* 2:51.

12. Foote, *The Civil War,* 3:360.

13. Freeman, *Lee's Lieutenants,* 3:518.

CHAPTER THIRTY-EIGHT

"Order Gave Way To Confusion"

10–11 June 1864

Down in Mississippi on 10 June Forrest had evidently decided to fight Sturgis without waiting to reach Okolona. On the road south toward Brice's Cross Roads, Forrest spoke of the Federals to Colonel Rucker, one of his brigade commanders: "I know they greatly outnumber the troops I have at hand, but the road along which they will march is narrow and muddy; they will make slow progress. The country is densely wooded and the undergrowth so heavy that when we strike them they will not know how few men we have." The rain had finally let up and the day promised to be hot and humid. "Their cavalry will move out ahead of their infantry," Forrest explained, "and should reach the crossroads three hours in advance. We can whip their cavalry in that time. As soon as the fight opens they will send back to have the infantry hurried in. It is going to be hot as hell, and coming on the run for five or six miles, their infantry will be so tired out we will ride right over them."[1]

The battle worked out pretty much as Forrest had predicted. Grierson's

Union cavalry moved out at 5:30 that morning, but Sturgis let the infantry stay in camp until past 7 a.m. to dry themselves and get ready for another hard day of marching. About 9:30 a.m. Waring's Federal cavalry brigade approached Brice's Cross Roads from the northwest, along an elevated road through a swampy area bordering Tishomingo Creek. They had driven off a Rebel patrol trying to damage the bridge spanning the stream. At the crossroads, where there was a house, a store, and a church, Grierson halted the column and had Waring's troopers dismount. The area around the junction was wooded for about a mile in every direction. Beyond that were open fields to the east and south. From tracks in the road and the questioning of civilians, it was learned that the Rebels were massing somewhere to the northeast, toward Baldwyn. Patrols were sent out that way and also toward Guntown, to the southeast. The patrol on the Baldwyn road soon ran into Confederates, and Waring rode to its support with two regiments and two little mountain howitzers. His other three regiments and two howitzers were deployed in a thicket commanding a field to the northeast of the crossroads.

Forrest sent Lyon's 750-man brigade of mounted infantry forward. Dismounting, these Kentuckians drove the reinforced Union patrol across the field, where it joined the rest of Waring's brigade. Meanwhile, orders were sent for Johnson's and Rucker's brigades to rest and draw ammunition and for General Buford, who had the farthest to go, to push forward as rapidly as possible with Bell's Brigade and the artillery. He was also to send one regiment to follow a farm road westward to gain the Federal rear near the Tishimingo Creek bridge.

About 10 a.m. Grierson sent a courier to Sturgis with word that he was engaged with a force of about 600 Rebels. He held what he considered an important position and suggested that an infantry brigade be rushed to his support. It took about an hour for this message to reach Sturgis, who was supervising some pioneers corduroying a particularly muddy stretch of the road. He ordered McMillen to make a forced march with his lead brigade, Hoge's, to join Grierson. He also sent word to Grierson to leave 600 or 700 troopers on the Guntown road and to deploy the rest of his division to the northeast to protect McMillen's infantry and the wagons while they and the few hundred cavalry continued on to Guntown. Then Sturgis rode to the front. Meanwhile, Grierson had called forward his other brigade, Winslow's, to block a Confederate force—actually a squadron from Lyon's Brigade—reportedly headed around his right flank toward the Guntown road. Winslow's troops formed a dismounted line connecting with Waring's right and facing southeast, except for a mounted detachment which was sent to watch the road running southwest, toward Pontotoc. Winslow's four cannon were left at Brice's Cross Roads.

To keep Grierson on the defensive, Forrest had Lyon make a reconnaissance in force, reinforced by Forrest's large escort company and an independent company of Georgians. This kept the Federals occupied for about an hour, by which time Rucker's Brigade had arrived. One regiment was sent to watch the Guntown road and the rest of the brigade was ordered forward, dismounted, across a muddy cornfield to Lyon's left to keep the Yankees busy. Carried away with their role, however, they advanced too far and were hit by a deadly crossfire that drove them in confusion back to their starting place. But by then Johnson's Alabamans were on hand. They were dismounted and put in position on Lyon's right. This time Forrest sent all three brigades forward in a real attack. The bugles sounded the charge, and they advanced with a Rebel yell.

Two guns which Waring had brought up near the Baldwyn road, and the four mountain howitzers to the northwest of it, opened fire on Lyon's and Rucker's men as they emerged from the woods. Then the Federal troopers began to bang away with their carbines. But the Confederates came on and pulled apart an abatis of felled trees in front of the 210 men of the 7th Indiana Cavalry. Then began a deadly fight for possession of the Union defenses. "So close was this struggle that guns once fired were not reloaded, but used as clubs, and pistols were brought into play, while the two lines struggled with the ferocity of wild beasts," one Southerner wrote. "Never did men fight more gallantly for their position than did the determined men of the North for this black-jack thicket on that hot June day."[2]

Rucker went down with a bullet in his belly and five in his horse, but he stayed on the field. The Confederates broke through on the 7th Indiana's right, from where the 2nd New Jersey had been removed to support Waring's left, and the Hoosiers were forced to retreat. On the other side of the breakthrough was a battalion of the 3rd Iowa Cavalry of Winslow's brigade. With their flank and rear threatened, these Hawkeyes also pulled out. That exposed the left of the 4th Iowa, but it managed to bend back at an angle, reestablish contact with the 3rd, and hold on. On the other side of the breakthrough, Waring's men also fell back, followed by Lyon's and Johnson's Confederates. But the 2nd New Jersey, armed with Spencer repeating carbines, was brought back, and the Southern attack ground to a halt. The two sides lay in the woods just far enough apart to be out of each other's sight.

When he reached Brice's Cross Roads around noon, Sturgis found Grierson's troopers hard pressed and somewhat confused. Both brigade commanders were ready to give way. Grierson said that his men had beaten off three "desperate charges," were exhausted, and nearly out of ammunition, but he was still willing to hold on if the infantry would hurry. Sturgis sent word to McMillen to "make all haste," followed by another message to "lose no time in coming up."[3] The crossroads was in chaos. Bullets were kicking up dirt and zipping through the trees where Sturgis was conferring with Grierson, while the roads were jammed with led horses, ambulances, and stragglers.

Sturgis ordered the commanders of the four artillery pieces parked nearby to unlimber their guns on both sides of the Baldwyn road and to be prepared to fire as soon as they saw any Rebels. When one of the artillery officers asked, "Who is going to support my guns?" Sturgis replied, "The cavalry to your front and the infantry which will soon be coming up." But the officer said there was no cavalry to his front. Waring's brigade had pulled out. Sturgis was sure he was mistaken, but just then a frightened cavalry officer rode up and confirmed the bad news, adding that he had been the last to leave. "By whose order did you withdraw?" Sturgis demanded. But the cavalryman replied, "I don't know."[4] Sturgis sent his own escort, 100 men from the 19th Pennsylvania Cavalry, up the Baldwyn road to establish a roadblock.

About 1 p.m. General Buford arrived at the Confederate front with Forrest's artillery, followed closely by Colonel Bell with the last, and by far the largest, of the Rebel cavalry brigades. Buford reported that the 2nd Tennessee had been sent westward along the farm road north of the Union position, as ordered. Leaving Buford in command of Lyon's and Johnson's brigades and the artillery, Forrest led Bell's troops beyond Rucker's line to the Guntown road. There he found the 8th Mississippi of Rucker's Brigade and a squadron of Lyon's Kentuckians, both of which he placed on Bell's left to extend his line to within 200 yards of the Pontotoc road.

By then the Confederate artillery was in place and was bursting shells over the crossroads and among Winslow's troopers. Winslow knew the Rebels were massing in his front and sent repeated requests for permission to withdraw. Back came orders to hold his ground until the infantry arrived. Meanwhile, McMillen had received several orders to get his infantry to the front as fast as possible and spurred his men on at a killing pace. Several of them were overcome with sunstroke. When the vanguard of Hoge's brigade finally reached the crossroads the 113th Illinois was allowed to stop long enough to load muskets and was then hastened out the Baldwyn road to replace Sturgis' escort. The 120th and 108th Illinois regiments soon followed, the three of them forming line between the Baldwyn road and Winslow's brigade. Then the 81st and 95th Illinois, the two regiments from T. Kilby Smith's Red River division, were sent to replace most of Winslow's troopers. While skirmishers were sent out to engage the Rebels, Battery B of the 2nd Illinois Artillery unlimbered its four guns in the yard of the Brice house and began firing over the infantry's heads at the woods beyond.

Soon Wilkin's infantry brigade came pounding up, just as exhausted as Hoge's. McMillen led its first two regiments, the 114th Illinois and 93rd Indiana, down the Guntown road to replace the rest of Winslow's cavalry, some of which Sturgis then sent to guard the army's southern flank. The 72nd Ohio and the two guns of the 6th Indiana Battery were sent a half-mile back the way they had come, to occupy a knoll north of the road and protect the army's rear and the bridge over Tishomingo Creek. About 75 dismounted cavalrymen were sent to reinforce this detachment. The rest of Wilkin's brigade—the 9th Minnesota and Battery E of the 1st Illinois Artillery—was held in reserve at the crossroads. Bouton's brigade of U.S. Colored Troops was marching with the wagon train, still hastening to the front.

Fighting had all but ceased between 1:30 and 2 p.m. while McMillen's infantry took position and Forrest prepared Bell's brigade for another attack. He sent word for Buford to advance Johnson's, Lyon's, and Rucker's men as soon as Bell attacked. Guiding on the Guntown road, Bell's Tennesseans worked their way through the thickets. Some of them were evidently wearing blue uniforms, which misled some of the Federals and helped the Rebels to get into close range before being fired on. They outflanked the 93rd Indiana, which held the end of Wilkin's line, and forced it back toward the Pontotoc road. There the Hoosiers were reinforced by the 9th Minnesota, which was rushed down from the crossroads, as well as two small regiments of Winslow's cavalry.

Such confusion reigned among the Union commanders that Winslow's two Iowa regiments were ordered to cross to the west side of Tishomingo Creek just when they were needed at the front. Winslow and Grierson also moved to the west side of the stream, followed shortly by Sturgis, who announced that McMillen was driving the enemy before he rode away again. The Federal infantry did briefly gain the initiative. Bell's men were repulsed several times and then the 93rd Indiana and 9th Minnesota counterattacked. The 8th Mississippi broke and ran, and its panic quickly spread to the 19th Tennessee. The Yankees pushed the Rebels back in such disarray that Forrest led his escort company forward to threaten them with drawn revolvers to stop their retreat. According to one of his men, Forrest "would curse, then praise, then threaten to shoot us himself, if we were so afraid the Yankees might hit us."[5] When the Mississippians were reformed he ordered their colonel to attack again, sending his escort company and the Georgians in beside them. Rucker's men had also been pushed back, but the colonel shouted that they should kneel on the ground, "draw your six-shooters, and don't run."[6] The attacking 95th

Illinois lost its commander and his first three successors in rapid order and then began to run out of ammunition.

Seeing that Bell was advancing again and that Rucker was holding his own, Forrest rode to the right to see how Buford was doing. When he reached the Baldwyn road he was disappointed to find that only two of his cannon were firing. He sent an officer to get the rest of them into action and ordered Buford to send Lyon's and Johnson's brigades forward. These Confederates advanced and drove in Hoge's Union skirmishers and then assaulted his main line.

On the Federals' far left, the 72nd Ohio was still deployed on the knoll protecting the bridge over Tishomingo Creek. But when the cavalry was withdrawn across the stream, the regiment's main battle line was moved to the south of the Ripley-Guntown road, leaving only four companies in skirmish line on the north side. These were soon attacked by the 2nd Tennessee, which had followed the farm road around the Union north flank. Its commander, Colonel Barteau, deployed his men as skirmishers and advanced, but the main body of the Ohio regiment came in on their flank and drove them back. However, Buford heard the firing behind the Federal lines and informed Forrest that Barteau must be attacking the Union rear.

Forrest rode along behind his lines on his big sorrel horse, with his coat off, and his sleeves rolled up, shouting encouragement to his men. Captain Morton, his chief of artillery, saw that the general was exhausted and urged him to get some rest. To his surprise, his advice was heeded. The two rode a short way to the rear and dismounted. Forrest stretched out in the shade of a big oak and told the captain that he thought the enemy was beaten and that he would order a charge within ten minutes. He told him to have four of his guns loaded with double cannister and limbered up. When the charge was sounded they were to gallop forward as close to the Yankees as possible, wheel into battery, and open fire.

Then Forrest went and explained the plan to Buford and rode back to the left, where he saw Captain Tyler, commanding the Kentucky squadron on the far flank. Supported by the escort company and the Georgians, Tyler was to sweep around the Union right and engage at pistol range any Federals encountered between the Pontotoc road and Tishomingo Creek. When all was ready, Forrest told his bugler to sound the charge. Morton's four guns thundered down the Baldwyn road to within sixty yards of the enemy, unlimbered, and blasted away like huge shotguns. Lyon's and Johnson's troops surged forward on their left and right. The Kentuckians broke through the Federal line and Hoge's brigade began to fall apart. This uncovered Wilkin's left flank, and his units were forced to retreat as well. McMillen, who had been with Wilkin when the attack struck, rode back to the crossroads and found that the troops were streaming back, dispirited and exhausted. There was considerable confusion as they converged on each other from several directions. Nevertheless, McMillen managed to paste together a new line, but he sent word to Sturgis that he was "hard-pressed and that unless relieved soon" he would have to give up the crossroads.[7] Back came the answer that he would have to hold his ground until Bouton's black troops could be deployed to cover a retreat.

Judging more by sound than sight in the dense woods, Forrest sent word to Captain Tyler on the left flank that it was time to "hit 'em on the ee-end."[8] With the company of Georgians, Forrest's escort, and his Kentucky squadron, Tyler charged across the Pontotoc road and outflanked the detachment of Waring's brigade guarding that approach. With both of his flanks threatened, McMillen decided it was time to withdraw. He ordered the artillery to stand fast and to continue to plaster the roads and thickets with shell and cannister while the infantry fell back. Meanwhile, he scraped up a few regiments for a second line that would shield the retreat of the artillery. The last guns pulled out when the Rebels were closing to within 25 yards on their left and rear.

Colonel Bouton, riding at the head of his brigade, had reached the Ames house, about a half-mile west of Tishomingo Creek, about 2:30 p.m., when an order arrived from Sturgis to corral the wagons. So aides were sent to gather up the train guards, reform the companies, and hurry forward, while Bouton rode to the bridge. There he saw the cavalry reforming in the fields nearby, and stragglers from Hoge's and Wilkin's brigades moving west. Then he sent two companies of the 55th U.S. Colored Troops across to the east side of the creek, where they checked the advance of Barteau's 2nd Tennessee around the flank of the 72nd Ohio. In doing so they lost all their officers in ten minutes of fighting. Bouton brought up seven more companies of the 55th and deployed them north of the road near the bridge to cover the retreat. And as he was riding back to bring up more troops he was overtaken by McMillen, who asked what he was going to do. Bouton explained briefly what he had done so far and said that he was going to place his two cannon on the ridge by Ames' house, supported by his remaining infantry, "and fight the enemy as long as I . . . have a man left."[9]

The commander of the 4th Iowa Cavalry found that he could not obey his orders to cross to the west side of the creek because the bridge was blocked by broken down wagons. So he had his men dismount and told the horseholders to get the animals across the creek any way they could. Meanwhile he led his troops to the knoll near the bridge, where they helped the 72nd Ohio and the blacks fight off attacks by Barteau's and Johnson's Confederates long enough for all the units east of the creek to make it across. Then, just as Buford was leading a full-scale attack on them, the Iowans forded the creek, while pioneers obstructed the bridge with a barricade of wagons.

All the retreating Federals, "crowding in like an avalanche from the battlefield," as Sturgis put it, had to funnel across the causeway through the swampy ground around Tishomingo Creek, and Confederate artillery, including four newly captured guns, soon found the range.[10] A wagon overturned, causing a log-jam that a retreating colonel called "one indiscriminate mass of artillery, caissons, ambulances, and broken, disordered troops."[11] As Sturgis put it: "Everywhere the army now drifted toward the rear, and was soon altogether beyond control. Order gave way to confusion and confusion to panic."[12]

The pursuing Confederates were delayed by the creek and the obstructed bridge, but Forrest ordered the horses brought to the front while the bridge and roadway were cleared. The sun was setting by then, and most of the Rebels had been riding and fighting for over 12 hours. But the men who had been holding the horses—one-fifth of Forrest's strength—were fresh, so Forrest and Buford led them and the artillery across first to press the pursuit. Not far down the road they came upon nine companies of the 55th U.S. Colored Troops posted in some trees. These men held off the Southerners for a half-hour until both their flanks were threatened. Then they fell back about a quarter of a mile to the high ground around the Ames house, where they found McMillen with Bouton and the rest of his brigade, namely the 59th U.S. Colored Troops and the two guns of Battery F, 2nd U.S. Colored Artillery. McMillen told Bouton to hold the Confederates as long as possible, while he rode ahead to set up another line to cover the blacks' withdrawal.

About a mile farther west McMillen came to the home of Dr. Samuel A. Agnew, commonly referred to as the White House. It stood on high ground separating two streams known as Dry Creek and Little Dry Creek. There he found Generals Sturgis and Grierson. With the help of several other officers they had rallied 1,200 to 1,500 men. Sturgis told McMillen that the retreat would continue to Stubbs' plantation, where they had camped the night before, and Grierson was ordered to send Winslow's troopers to establish a straggler line there to stop the disorganized infantry. Waring's brigade would go all the way back to Ripley to hold the retreat route open. McMillen was to put a good officer in charge of the rear guard and then go on to Stubbs' to reorganize and resupply his infantry as it arrived. Colonel Wilkin, commander of his 1st Brigade, was put in charge of the rear guard.

As Forrest's Rebels approached, Bouton's black artillerymen fired exploding shells at them over the heads of a fleeing mob of retreating Federals. Then, when the stragglers were out of the way, they switched to cannister fire. A Confederate battery returned fire, and a column of Rebels surged up the road. The black infantry let them get to within 100 yards before opening fire. When they did, the head of the column melted away. But the Southerners came on. Soon they were threatening the right flank of the 59th U.S. Colored Troops, which had to fall back. The whole brigade then withdrew across Dry Creek, occasionally stopping to send several volleys towards the pursuing Rebels. They found the road blocked with abandoned wagons, and the two regiments became separated, but both made it back to the White House ridge about dark. There they found some badly needed ammunition and reformed behind Wilkin's white rear guard, composed of the 114th Illinois and 9th Minnesota.

Forrest sent a battery of his artillery charging forward, and it unlimbered within sixty yards of the Union line and opened fire while his dismounted cavalrymen charged across the field. The Federals opened fire at close range, and then the 59th U.S. Colored Troops charged and drove the Confederates back with clubbed muskets and bayonets. Under cover of the vicious melee that ensued, Wilkin withdrew the two white regiments. When Buford threw Lyon's Kentuckians into the fight, the 59th also fell back and got away in the gathering darkness.

It was after 8 p.m. when, "it being dark and my men and horses requiring rest," Forrest reported, "I threw out an advance to follow slowly and cautiously after the enemy, and ordered the command to halt, feed, and rest."[13] Wilkin marched his men a short way up the Ripley road, but when he realized the Confederates were not pursuing he allowed his men to rest. Just then a cavalry officer rode up and informed him that his squadron had built camp fires a short distance to the west to fool the Rebels into thinking the Federals had stopped for the night, although in reality they had marched on. And he said that the cavalry would take over the job of guarding the column's rear.

When the infantry resumed their march, they found the going very slow. They passed numerous wagons that had been abandoned and set on fire by teamsters and soldiers who had ridden off on the mules. Wilkins had his men torch any wagons that were not already burning. Then they came to Hatchie Bottom, a swampy tributary of the Hatchie River, where they sank up to their knees in the mud. There they found ambulances mired in the road, and they were not empty. "As the retreating column passed along," one infantryman remembered, "the wounded begged piteously for water or to be taken with us, but nothing could be done for them."[14]

Colonel Bouton caught up with the column as it was crossing Hatchie

Bottom, and there he found Sturgis. "General, for God's sake don't let us give it up so," he implored. "What can we do?" Sturgis asked. Bouton said that if the general would reinforce him with one regiment and give his blacks the ammunition that the whites were throwing in the mud they would hold back the Rebels until the ambulances, wagons and artillery could get across Hatchie Bottom. He said he would stake his life on it. But Sturgis replied, "For God's sake, if Mr. Forrest will let me alone I will let him alone. You have done all you could and more than was expected of you, and now all you can do is to save yourselves."[15]

The mud of Hatchie Bottom was even more of a problem for the Union artillery than for the infantry. The guns became bogged in the mire. About 11 p.m. Sturgis reached Stubbs' plantation, where he found Colonel Winslow with the 3rd and 4th Iowa Cavalry regiments blocking the retreat as ordered. Sturgis now told him to lift the roadblock, for the retreat would continue to Ripley, fourteen miles farther on, and Winslow was to take over as rear guard. Winslow pointed out that such a retreat would lose them the wagons and artillery then stuck in the mud at Hatchie Bottom. But Sturgis said that "the artillery and train had already gone to hell, and that if they got through the swamp, they could not eventually be saved, because there was no forage for the animals."[16] Fourteen cannon had to be abandoned, along with numerous limbers and caissons. Most of them were spiked by the gunners and many of the spokes were cut to make them harder for the Rebels to haul away. McMillen was ordered to leave a staff officer to help Winslow reform the infantry units as they caught up. Winslow stayed at Stubbs' farm until 2:50 a.m. on the eleventh waiting for the tail of the column to pass, and then put his troopers on the road. Colonel Wilkin, with the 114th Illinois and the 9th Minnesota, took a different route up from the swamp and by-passed Stubbs' before returning to the Ripley road. When Winslow learned that this infantry was still behind him he called a halt. Dawn was breaking as they filed past him, and Winslow waited until they were out of sight on the road ahead before he started his troopers moving again.

Forrest had put his men back on the road in pursuit of Sturgis by 1 a.m. In addition to badly needed rest, his men had filled their stomachs and their haversacks from Union supplies with ham, bacon, coffee, sugar, cheese, and other items that had become all too rare in their own diets. Even the Confederate horses were treated, with shelled corn, dry oats, and hay. The 7th Tennessee of Rucker's Brigade took the lead and Forrest rode not far behind with Captain Morton of his artillery. Morton later recalled how the general summed up his style of fighting. "Get 'em skeered," Forrest had said, "and then keep the skeer on 'em."[17] By 3 a.m.

the Rebels had reached the Hatchie Bottom. There was more than abandoned wagons and guns stuck in the swamp, a Rebel lieutenant remembered: "This slough was near knee-deep in mud and water, with logs lying here and there. On top of every log were Yanks perched as thick as possible, for there were more Yanks than logs."[18] A few men were detailed to take these Federals prisoner while the main column pressed on. As the Confederates approached Stubbs, Forrest was joined by Barteau's 2nd Tennessee, which had followed a different route. The general deployed it to the right of the road and the 7th Tennessee on the left to round up Union stragglers, and personally led Bell's brigade at the head of the main column.

Forrest caught up with Winslow's rear guard shortly after the latter had stopped to let Wilkin's infantry go by. The Federal cavalryman deployed a battalion of the 3rd Iowa to delay the Rebels and replaced it a few hours later with the 4th Iowa, whose commander kept one company at a time facing the Confederates, continually leapfrogging each other. Forrest also employed his units successively, sending one regiment to charge down the road in column of fours until the Yankees gave ground, and then letting them rest and reform while the next regiment took the lead. Four miles southeast of Ripley the Southerners came to another swamp, Little Hatchie Bottom, crossed by a causeway some 300 yards long. They found the 4th Iowa posted on high ground on the other side. Forrest took his escort company and two regiments upstream, where they forded and threatened the Iowans' right, forcing them to abandon their roadblock in haste. At Ripley the 3rd Iowa rejoined the fray, as did Bouton's black infantry, who fought off the Confederates long enough for the 4th Iowa to escape. But in its haste it broke into two parts, and so did Bouton's brigade. Half of each of these units, as well as Wilkin's two regiments, then followed a different road than that taken by the main column.

"From this place," Forrest later reported, "the enemy offered no organized resistance, but retreated in the most complete disorder, throwing away guns, clothing, and everything calculated to impede his flight."[19] This was an exaggeration, for Colonel Winslow and his troopers continued to take advantage of any favorable terrain to face about and defy their pursuers as long as possible. Forrest was not on hand to witness this, however. Buford was put in charge of the pursuit beyond Ripley, while Forrest led part of his force by another route to try to intercept the Northerners at Salem.

However, at the crossing of yet another stream, Little Tippah Creek, Winslow's cavalry overtook the infantry, and the 4th Missouri Cavalry of Waring's brigade assumed rear-guard duties. Just ahead of them was the 72nd Ohio Infantry. Colonel Barteau's 2nd Tennessee had taken shortcuts through woods and along farm roads and suddenly attacked the Ohioans, their adversaries of the previous afternoon at the approaches to the Tishomingo bridge. The four lead companies of the 72nd hurried on up the road to escape, but the other six companies deployed to face this threat, and Barteau backed off. However, Lyon's Kentuckians had meanwhile charged and routed the 4th Missouri and went on to scatter the 72nd Ohio and several other Federal infantry regiments. Again the 3rd and 4th Iowa formed a roadblock and repulsed the Kentuckians, then resumed their former role as rear guards. Late that afternoon the 2nd New Jersey Cavalry, with its Spencer repeating carbines, was sent to take their place.

The Federals had already passed Salem by the time Forrest arrived by way of his short-cut, about sundown on the eleventh, so he called off the chase and turned back to gather up prisoners and loot. These eventually added up to 18 guns—all that Sturgis had brought with him except the four little mountain howitzers—176 wagons, 1500 rifles, 300,000 rounds of ammunition, and 1600 prisoners.

That evening a Confederate captain and one of his men saw Forrest's horse trotting down the center of the road with the exhausted general sound asleep in the saddle. "Go wake him up, Mack," the officer told the private. "No, sir," the man replied, imagining the general's reaction, "you wake him."[20] But before the question could be settled, the horse ran head-on into a tree and woke the general himself by throwing him unceremoniously to the ground.

1. Foote, *The Civil War*, 3:366–367.
2. Ibid., 370.
3. Ibid., 368.
4. Bearss, *Forrest at Brice's Cross Roads*, 83.
5. Samuel Carter III, *The Last Cavaliers* (New York, 1979), 233.
6. Bearss, *Forrest at Brice's Cross Roads*, 91.
7. Ibid., 96.
8. Ibid., 97.
9. Ibid., 101.
10. Ibid., 103.
11. Foote, *The Civil War*, 3:370.
12. Carter, *The Last Cavaliers*, 233.
13. Foote, *The Civil War*, 3:372.

14. Bearss, *Forrest at Brice's Cross Roads*, 114.
15. Ibid.
16. Ibid., 116.
17. Ibid., 118.
18. Ibid.
19. Foote, *The Civil War*, 3:372.
20. Carter, *The Last Cavaliers*, 244.

CHAPTER THIRTY-NINE

"Where In Hell Is The Rear?"

11–12 June 1864

On the same day that Forrest was chasing Sturgis' demoralized troops back toward Memphis, *Harper's Weekly* published portraits of Lincoln and Grant, commenting on the former that "in this earnest care-worn face, saddened by a solemn sense of the great responsibility which in God's providence has devolved upon him, we see the man who said to his neighbors, as he left his home three years ago, that he was called to a graver task than any chief magistrate since Washington. Through an infinite perplexity of events the faith of the President has never faltered . . . Look thoughtfully at this rugged face. In its candor, its sagacity, its calmness, its steadiness and strength, there is especially conspicuous the distinctive American. Turn then to the portrait of General Grant . . . and there you see another purely American face, the same homely honesty, capacity and tenacity. Children of the people both of them . . . these two men illustrate at once the character of American civilization. There is but one prayer in the great multitude of American hearts today, God bless President Lincoln and General Grant."[1]

Down in Georgia that day, 11 June, newspapers brought the Northern troops "the cheering news of Uncle Abe's nomination," as one of them put it, adding, "Three cheers for that. It did heeps of good. I want to cast one more vote for him next fall."[2] In spite of the rain, which had been falling for nine straight days, Sherman's engineers and track crews had bridged the Etowah River and had the railroad running all the way to Big Shanty. When the first supply train pulled in that day the engineer detached his cars at a safe distance from the Rebels and then ran his locomotive up to the water tank within their view and within the range of their artillery. In a matter of seconds the Confederate guns opened on him but, to the cheers of the onlooking Federals, the engineer answered their fire with defiant screams from his steam-powered whistle, took on his water, and then backed out of range to rejoin his train.

Morgan's Confederate raiders reached Cynthiana, Kentucky that day and demanded the town's surrender. This was refused, prompting a house-to-house fight during which, Morgan later reported, "I was forced to burn a large portion of the town." The Federal garrison finally surrendered, but then a column of about 1200 Yankee cavalry was seen approaching from the east. This was the smaller of the two Union columns which had turned back from a proposed invasion of southwest Virginia upon hearing of Morgan's raid into the Bluegrass State. It was commanded by Brigadier General Edward Henry Hobson, the man who had led the pursuit and eventual capture of Morgan the previous summer when the latter had crossed the broad Ohio River and briefly carried the war into the North.

Morgan sent two of his Rebel brigades forward in a frontal attack and led the other around to get behind the Federals and attack their rear. Tired and surprised, the slightly smaller Union force was soon compelled to surrender, and Morgan's pleasure at thus turning the tables on Hobson led him into overconfidence. When scouts brought him word that Burbridge was heading his way with almost 5,000 Yankees, he decided to stand and fight even though his own force was down to about 1400 men, due to losses, desertions, and detachments sent out to scour the area. Moreover, his ammunition was low. Plenty of captured Federal rifles and ammunition were available, but his men refused to give up their British-made Enfields. His troops were exhausted, and Morgan was determined to allow them a good night's rest where they were, rather than spend another night on the move. He told his brigade commanders that he would meet Burbridge the next morning, on ground that he had selected two miles south of town. "It is my order that you hold your position at all hazard," he told a colonel who protested this stand. "We can whip him with empty guns."[3]

In southeastern Virginia that Saturday, 11 June, Gracie's Brigade arrived at Bermuda Hundred from Richmond to provide Beauregard with the only reinforcements available, short of Lee's army. Gracie's Alabamans replaced Wise's Virginians, who were sent to strengthen the garrison of Petersburg at last.

Grant's mind was impatiently turned in that very direction, even as he waited for preparations to be completed. He wrote to Butler that day: "Colonel Comstock has not yet returned, so that I cannot make instructions as definite as I would wish, but the time between this and Sunday night being so short in which to get word to you, I must do the best I can." He was, he said, sending Lieutenant Colonel Fred Dent of his staff (who was his brother-in-law and former West Point roommate) to arrange for transports and escorting gunboats to pick up Baldy Smith's 18th Corps. This force, minus its artillery and wagons, would be shipped back to Butler to arrive "as soon as the enemy could, going by the way of Richmond," so that Lee could not overwhelm the Army of the James while the Army of the Potomac was making its crossing of the James River. Meade's army "will not be more than one day behind, unless detained by the whole of Lee's army, in which case you will be strong enough," he explained. Meanwhile, Butler was to get ready to cross the river himself. "Expecting the arrival of the 18th corps by Monday night, if you deem it practicable from the force you have to seize and hold Petersburg, you may prepare to start, on the arrival of troops to hold your present lines. I do not want Petersburg visited, however, unless it is held, nor an attempt to take it, unless you feel a reasonable degree of confidence of success."[4]

Lee's attention, on the other hand, was directed in the opposite direction. Jefferson Davis was pressing him to do something about Hunter. "There is a calm in military matters," a clerk in the Confederate War Department recorded in his diary that day, "but a storm is gathering in the Valley of Virginia."[5] "I acknowledge the advantage of expelling enemy from the Valley," Lee wrote the president that day. "The only difficulty with me is the means. It would [take] one corps of this army. If it is deemed prudent to hazard the defense of Richmond, the interests involved by thus diminishing the force here, I will do so." He added, however, that, "I think this is what the enemy would desire." Almost wistfully he went on, "A victory over General Grant would also relieve our difficulties." But he could offer no immediate prospects for such an eventuality. "I see no indications of his attacking me in his present position. Think he is strengthening his defenses to withdraw a portion of his force, and with the other move to the James River." Thus there was little hope of a defensive victory. As for an offensive, he said, "To attack him here I must assault a very strong line of intrenchments and run great risk to the safety of the army."[6]

Hunter approached Lexington, Virginia around noon that day, sending Averell's cavalry and one brigade of infantry to flank it. McCausland, who had come north with the brigade of Confederate horsemen that he had inherited from Jenkins, burned the bridge over the North River to slow up the Yankees, then withdrew from the town. Imboden's troopers were meanwhile trying to deal with Hunter's other cavalry division under Duffié. The latter had demonstrated against Breckinridge, who, with the help of Vaughn's cavalry, was holding the direct route to Charlottesville by way of Waynesboro. Then Duffié had crossed the Blue Ridge farther south, to raid the railroad between Charlottesville and Lynchburg. Hunter decided to wait at Lexington for Duffié to rejoin him, and for a train of 200 supply wagons to catch up with him.

At dawn that Sunday, 11 June, Wade Hampton had his Confederate troopers already in the saddle. He had seen to it that they were awakened quietly, without bugles or other noise, so as not to alert Sheridan's nearby camp. Hampton was determined to make a good showing in his first battle in overall command of Lee's cavalry. He was 46 years old, tall, wearing a great spade of a beard, and he was a rarity among Lee's senior generals for being neither a West Pointer nor a Virginian. He had been a South Carolina planter and reputedly the wealthiest man in the South. And when the war had come he had raised and equipped a regiment-sized unit at his own expense, known as Hampton's Legion. Since the summer of 1862 he had been one of Jeb Stuart's most trusted subordinates, a natural leader and fast learner, commanding first a brigade of cavalry, then a division. Where Stuart had been flamboyant of dress and a seeker of glory, Hampton was sober and business-like. Despite his wealth and rank he dressed very plainly. And while Stuart, one Rebel trooper recorded, "sometimes seemed to have a delight in trying to discharge his mission with the smallest possible number of men, Hampton believed in superiority of force and exerted himself to concentrate all the men he could at the point of contact."[7]

That was just what he had planned for that morning of 11 June. While Fitzhugh Lee's two brigades moved due north from Louisa Court House, Hampton sent two of his own brigades, Pierce Young's Georgians and Calbraith Butler's South Carolinians, northeastward up the road from

Trevilian Station. All these forces were to converge on Sheridan's camp at Clayton's Store. The Laurel Brigade—Virginians under Tom Rosser—was to act as a reserve, and to cover a side road to make sure that the Yankees did not slip past his left flank and reach the railroad farther west. Altogether he had about 4,700 troopers to Sheridan's 6,000. His plan was a good one, but it failed to consider one fact: that Sheridan was not at all the kind of man to stand around waiting to be attacked. The Union cavalry leader knew Hampton and Fitz Lee had been sent to head him off, and his troopers were also put in motion at daylight. Torbert, back in command of the 1st Division, led the way down the road toward Trevilian Station with Merritt's Reserve Brigade, followed by Devin's 2nd Brigade. Custer's 1st Brigade took a narrow road through the woods, about a mile farther east, that also led to Trevilian Station.

There was another flaw in Hampton's plan. Fitz Lee's division had farther to travel than did his own, so when a detachment from Matt Butler's relatively inexperienced brigade ran into Merritt's advance guard, Lee was still a long way off. Butler's and Young's Confederates collided with Merritt's and Devin's Federals, and both sides later claimed to have driven the other back in dismounted fighting through dense woods, which, as Torbert reported, "it was with the greatest difficulty that a man could get through even if there had been no enemy in front."[8] Eventually, Gregg's Union division collided with Fitz Lee's Confederates and drove them back. Then Hampton received word that an enemy force had appeared in his rear.

That was Custer. Screened by the woods, the Michigan Brigade had followed its side road, which was so narrow that the men could not be kept in their normal, four-man-wide column of march. About 8 a.m. Custer's advance guard, the 3rd Battalion of the 5th Michigan, came out into some open fields to find not only Trevilian Station and the railroad, but Hampton's entire supply train of wagons, pack mules, and artillery caissons.

Custer was hardly the man to hesitate with such a prize in sight. He ordered the 5th Michigan to charge. The regiment routed the Confederate baggage guard and, despite Custer's orders not to go beyond the station, proceeded after the led horses of Butler's and Young's dismounted troopers. The regiment captured 1,500 horses and 800 men, six caissons, forty ambulances and fifty wagons. But almost as soon as the 5th Michigan had passed the station, one of Fitz Lee's regiments, which had ridden to the sound of firing, recaptured the lot of them, along with the Yankees who had been left behind to guard the Rebel prisoners and loot. Custer was thus cut off from his leading regiment. He and his staff and orderlies

fought off the advancing Rebels while word was sent for his next regiment, the 6th Michigan, to bypass the battery of horse artillery which had
been next in the line of march, and hasten to the front at the gallop.

Major Kidd, commander of the 6th, had only one of his three battalions
clear of the woods when he received this order, but he brought it forward
at once. Custer pointed toward the Rebels and told him to "Charge
them!"[9] Kidd ordered his men, still in a column of fours, to draw sabers,
and they pounded down on the enemy, who just faded back to left and
right and let the small column gallop past. Kidd tried to call a halt, but his
horse had other ideas, carrying him, and his following troopers, on until
they came to the edge of the woods beyond. There Kidd was captured by
a Confederate officer and a squad of troopers, but the other two battalions of the 6th Michigan soon came along and set him free again. With a
more manageable horse, Kidd led his regiment back to Custer. There he
found the 5th Michigan fighting for its life against Rosser's Laurel Brigade, which had been sent back by Hampton to clear the Yankees out of
his rear.

Tom Rosser was a stocky, swarthy, six-foot-two Texan who had been
Custer's best friend at West Point, although he was a class ahead of the
blond, freckle-faced Federal. Both were better remembered at the academy for their demerits, their high-jinks, and their horsemanship than for
their scholarship. Now Rosser could see his old friend across the battlefield. "He made a gallant and manly effort to resist me," Rosser wrote.
"Sitting on his horse in the midst of the advancing platoons, and near
enough to be easily recognized by me, he encouraged and inspired his
men by appeal as well as example."[10] Custer had lost half the 5th Michigan, but his third regiment, the 7th Michigan, was in action now, and he
brought up two guns from his battery of horse artillery. One of these he
put in position behind a board fence where it could enfilade a Confederate
battery. The gunners were just about to knock a hole in the fence to shoot
through, when a line of dismounted Rebel cavalry was seen clambering
over a rail fence about 100 yards to their right. "Custer ordered everyone
'to get out of there,'" the battery commander remembered, "and we lost
no time."[11]

Custer's final regiment, the 1st Michigan, was just coming up when
suddenly a storm of rifle fire and the high-pitched Rebel yell announced
the arrival of the rest of Fitz Lee's division from the east. The 1st Michigan
turned to face this new, and even larger, menace but was driven rapidly
back. The officer in charge of Custer's own baggage train asked the young
general if it would not be best to start moving the wagons to the rear for
safety. "Yes, by all means," the distracted Custer replied. But a few

seconds after the officer had ridden away the general looked around, as Rosser's men moved in from the west, Fitz Lee's from the east, and some of Butler's from the north, and called out, "Where in hell is the rear?"[12] Custer drew his dismounted men up in a circle to face all these attackers with their carbines. The Confederates mounted a continuous series of charges, dashing up to point-blank range, where they would empty their revolvers into the Federals before falling back to reload and come on again. The officer in charge of the wagons tried to make a dash for it but the Confederates captured the wagons along with their loads of ammunition and supplies, as well as Custer's headquarters wagon and a carriage carrying his black cook, Eliza.

Then the commander of his horse artillery told him, almost tearfully, "General, they have taken one of my guns!" Custer replied, "I'll be damned if they have! Come on!"[13] He quickly rounded up thirty men and hurried to the spot where a large number of Confederates were dragging one of his guns away. But the Rebels picked up their weapons and beat off the Federal attack. Custer rushed to a nearby group of his horse-holders, detached every other one, and added them to his flying column, along with Company F of the 7th Michigan. Then he raced back to the place where the Confederates were still hauling away his cannon. The commander of F Company called it "one of the sharpest hand-to-hand contests I ever witnessed." The Rebels were driven off and the Federals used the recovered gun to increase the pace of their retreat. Custer's elation was short-lived, however, because the sergeant who carried his personal guidon was mortally wounded by an officer of Rosser's staff. "General, they have killed me," the man gasped. "Take the flag!"[14] Rosser recorded that "Custer grabbed the staff to save the flag, but the death grip of the sergeant would not release it; so with a quick jerk, Custer tore the flag from its staff."[15] The young general's well-deserved reputation for profanity reached new heights that day, and the object of his wrath was not the Confederates but the rest of his own 1st Division, which had failed, so far, to come to his aid.

Torbert and his other two brigade commanders, however, were having their own problems. They had expected Hampton's troopers to break and run when the Michigan Brigade appeared in their rear, but the Rebels had instead made the Federals pay for every yard gained. Finally, not long after Custer's guidon went down, Sheridan sent one brigade of Gregg's 2nd Division in on Merritt's left. The combined attack pushed some of the Rebels into Custer's hands, and he gathered up about 500 prisoners. Hampton's Division was then driven to the west beyond Trevilian Station. The other brigade of Gregg's 2nd Division attacked Fitz Lee's right and drove his division back toward Louisa Court House. Thus the two Federal divisions were firmly planted between the two Confederate divisions as darkness put an end to the fighting.

That night a shower laid the stiffling dust of the day's fight, and under cover of the rain Fitz Lee led his troopers around the Federals on the south, to join Hampton about two miles to the west of Trevilian Station. There the Rebels began to dig in, blocking the Yankees' way to Gordonsville and Charlottesville. Before dawn Eliza, Custer's cook, appeared in the Union camp with a big grin and the general's personal valise, which she had brought out with her when she slipped away from her Rebel captors.

The next morning the Union troopers were put to work tearing up the railroad track as far east as Louisa Court House while Sheridan decided what to do next. From Confederate prisoners he learned that Hunter was not marching eastward toward Charlottesville as Grant had hoped, but southward toward Lynchburg. Further, he learned that Breckinridge's infantry was between him and Hunter, putting a junction with the latter beyond "all reasonable probability." So he decided "to abandon that part of the scheme, and to return by leisurely marches, which would keep Hampton's cavalry away from Lee while Grant was crossing the James River." His decision was influenced by the presence of his 500 wounded men and 500 Confederate prisoners, all of whom he would have to abandon if he went on, and by the fact that he had only enough ammunition left "for one more respectable engagement."[16]

Sheridan decided to move northwest to Mallory's Ford and cross the North Anna, then follow the Catharpin Road to Spotsylvania before riding southeast to White House. In midafternoon Torbert's division reached Mallory's Cross Roads just beyond the divergence of the roads to Gordonsville and Charlottesville. There the Federals discovered the Rebel troopers blocking the way. Butler's Brigade faced north, using a railroad embankment for cover, while the rest of Hampton's Division and all of Fitz Lee's faced eastward, sheltering behind breastworks built up of fence rails. Seven times the Northerners charged the angle of this L-shaped line, but they were driven back every time. Finally they gave up and went back the way they had come to recross the river at Carpenter's Ford that night, 12 June.

Far to the west, Sturgis' retreating Federals reached the railroad at Collierville at 10:30 a.m. on 12 June, where they found reinforcements, supplies, and rest. They had covered, in the two nights and the intervening day of their retreat, all the distance they had taken nine days to cover on their advance. A train was sent out to take them the final seventeen miles into Memphis. One Union infantry officer reported that during their wait for the train his men "became so stiffened as to require assistance to enable them to walk. Some of them, too foot-sore to stand upon their feet, crawled upon their hands and knees to the cars." A Federal cavalry officer reflected that "it is the fate of war that one or the other side should suffer defeat, but here there was more. The men were cowed, and there pressed upon them a sense of bitter humiliation, which rankles after nearly a quarter of a century has passed."[17] Sturgis insisted that he had been outnumbered, reporting Forrest's 5,000 men as 15,000 to 20,000. But he spent the rest of the war on the shelf, waiting for a new assignment that never came.

At dawn on 12 June General Burbridge's 5,200 Federal troopers attacked Morgan's 1,400 Confederates at Cynthiana, Kentucky. The disparity in numbers prevented Morgan from using his favorite tactic of sending part of his force to circle around behind the enemy. He needed every man in the front line. But the Confederates were holding off the superior enemy force until the cry "Out of ammunition!" was sounded all up and down the Rebel line. "Our whole command was soon forced back into the streets of the town, routed and demoralized," one Southerner remembered. "The confusion was indescribable . . . There was much shooting, swearing and yelling—some from sheer mortification were crying." Morgan's force was soon split into two parts and then the parts began to disintegrate. At least half of the Rebels were killed or captured and the rest scattered. Morgan, on what one of his men called a "step-trotting roan horse," got away to the northeast. His raid was over, and all he could do was make his way as best he could back to Virginia with what force he could round up.[18]

At Lexington, Virginia, Hunter had found what he called "a violent and inflammatory proclamation from John Letcher, lately governor of Virginia, inciting the population of the country to rise and wage a guerrilla warfare on my troops; and ascertaining," he continued, "that after having advised his fellow-citizens to this cause the ex-governor had himself ignominiously taken to flight, I ordered his property to be burned, under my Orders, published May 24th, against persons practising or abetting such unlawful and uncivilized warfare." The Virginia Military Institute, whose cadets had fought at New Market, was also burned on the twelfth, along with several iron mills. And the statue of George Washington was taken from the hall of Washington College for shipment to Wheeling, West Virginia, "to rescue it," a Union colonel said, "from the degenerate sons of worthy sires."[19] Some of Hunter's men engaged in stealing from other civilians as well. Captures of a more military nature included a few Rebel soldiers, some small arms and cartridges, and six canal barges loaded with commissary stores and about half a dozen cannon with their ammunition. Meanwhile, Hunter continued to wait for Duffié's raiding cavalry to rejoin his main force and for a wagon train bringing him vital supplies, including much-needed ammunition.

It was obvious to Lee and to Jefferson Davis that Hunter's next objective would be Lynchburg, in the eastern foothills of the Blue Ridge. It was an important town because of its railroads, and because of some small manufacturing plants and large depots of military supplies. That day, the twelfth, Lee summoned Jubal Early for a long discussion of prospects and strategy which concluded with orders for Early to prepare his 2nd Corps to leave the army the next morning and proceed to Lynchburg. Something had to be done about Hunter, and the 2nd Corps was the obvious choice to do it. As Lee had told Davis, the job would require an entire corps of his army. The 2nd Corps, after its losses in the mule shoe salient at Spotsylvania, was the smallest of Lee's three, and it was already in reserve behind his right. Besides, most of the corps had originally been in Stonewall Jackson's old Army of the Valley, before it was brought to Richmond to help drive McClellan away from the capital two years back. And many of the men of the 2nd Corps were originally from the Shenandoah area. Moreover, Early had been a brigade commander under Jackson, and had served a stint the previous winter as commander in the Valley, so he was familiar with the area.

By combining with Breckinridge's small division, which had already been sent ahead, and with the various cavalry commands in the area, Early would command a force of approximately 15,000 men, almost equal to Hunter's own. With a force that size Early was expected not only to defend Lynchburg but to take the offensive in the Shenandoah, recover the Valley, and perhaps even threaten Washington, D.C. and the North. Stonewall Jackson had tied up large Union forces for weeks in 1862 with a drive down the Shenandoah, until he slipped away to join Lee at Richmond. Now it was hoped that Early could again play on Lincoln's fears for the safety of his capital and for the cities and farms of the North, and cause him to draw forces away from Grant's threat to Richmond.

One obstacle to Lee's plans for Early was Richard Ewell. Several days before, Ewell had reported to Lee that he was sufficiently recovered from his illness to resume command of the 2nd Corps. Lee had taken no action at first. Now he sent a letter filled with his famous tact to General Samuel Cooper, adjutant general of the Confederate army, whose duties included

personnel assignments. Lee reported that although Ewell was "now restored to his usual health, I think the labor and exposure to which he
would be inevitably exposed would at this time again incapacitate him for
field service. The general, who has all the feelings of a good soldier, differs
from me in this opinion, and is not only willing but anxious to resume his
command. I, however, think in the present emergency it would jeopar-
dize his life, and should his strength fail, it would prove disadvantageous
to the service. I therefore propose that he be placed on some duty
attended with less labor and exposure. It has occurred to me that the
command of the defenses of Richmond would be more in accordance with
his state of health, and give him a position where he could perform
valuable service."[20] Lee went on to say that the arrangement was intended
to be temporary. His wishes were promptly complied with, and Robert
Ransom was removed from the Department of Richmond and sent off to
take command, under Early, of the various cavalry brigades operating in
the Shenandoah.

While Lee's attention was diverted to the Valley, Grant's continued to
be focused on crossing the James. In the wee hours of the morning of the
twelfth, Lieutenant Colonels Comstock and Porter finally returned to the
general-in-chief from their trip up the river. "On our arrival we went at
once to his tent," Porter remembered, "and were closeted with him for
nearly an hour discussing the contemplated operation. While listening to
our verbal report and preparing the orders for the movement which was
to take place, the general showed the only anxiety and nervousness of
manner he had ever manifested on any occasion." Grant even let his
perennial cigar go out. "In giving him the information he desired," Porter
continued, "we could hardly get the words out of our mouths fast enough
to suit him. He kept repeating, 'Yes, yes,' in a manner which was
equivalent to saying, 'Go on, go on,'; and the numerous questions he
asked were uttered with much greater rapidity than usual."[21]

At 7 p.m., as a Union soldier noted, "the music from the brass bands
resounded along the whole line of eight miles."[22] As at Spotsylvania,
tone-deaf Grant was putting the army's musicians to good use: drowning
out the noise of a quiet, careful withdrawal of his forces from close
proximity to the enemy. But this time it would be his entire force that
would break contact with Lee's army, which was nowhere more than a
few hundred yards away along a front of several miles. Such a move is one
of the most difficult in the art of war. Once contact was broken, the
Federal infantry would still have to cross the swampy Chickahominy
stream, march fifty miles, then cross a tidal river that was half a mile wide

and ninety feet deep. Moreover, Grant needed enough of a lead to get his whole army across the James, or Lee could attack part of it after the rest had already crossed.

The moves of each corps were expertly timed and intricately choreographed with all this in mind. Hancock's 2nd and Wright's 6th Corps fell back to a new line of trenches that had been constructed to cover the move. Smith's 18th Corps, meanwhile, marched to White House to embark for its return to Bermuda Hundred. Burnside's 9th Corps followed in Smith's wake but turned south a few miles short of the plantation. There was a bright moon to light the march, but the night was hot and the roads were dusty and led through scenes of recent fighting. The dust combined with sweat to coat the marching infantrymen in grime, while the smell of dead horses and mules along the route added to their discomfort. Wilson's 3rd Cavalry Division, left behind by Sheridan when he rode off to raid the Virginia Central, led the army over the Chickahominy as it had at the Rapidan, more than a month before. The troopers splashed across the shallow stream while a pontoon bridge was being laid for the infantry and guns, then, again as at the Rapidan, Warren's 5th Corps followed.

----

1. Sandburg, *The War Years*, 544.
2. McDonough and Jones, *War So Terrible*, 173.
3. Foote, *The Civil War*, 3:361.
4. Grant, *Memoirs*, 2:287.
5. Jones, *A Rebel War Clerk's Diary* (New York, 1958), 390.
6. Dowdey and Manarin, *Wartime Papers of R. E. Lee*, 774–775.
7. Freeman, *The Civil War*, 3:522.
8. Starr, *The Union Cavalry*, 2:138.
9. Urwin, *Custer Victorious*,157.
10. Thomas A. Lewis, *The Guns of Cedar Creek* (New York, 1988), 94.
11. Theo. F. Rodenbough, "Sheridan's Trevillian Raid," in *Battles and Leaders*, 4:233.
12. Urwin, *Custer Victorious*, 159.
13. Ibid., 160.
14. both quotes from ibid., 161.
15. Lewis, *The Guns of Cedar Creek*, 94.
16. Starr, *The Union Cavalry*, 2:142–143.
17. Foote, *The Civil War*, 3:373–374.

18. Carter, *The Last Cavaliers*, 283.
19. Pond, *The Shenandoah Valley*, 30.
20. Dowdey and Manarin, *Wartime Papers of R. E. Lee*, 776.
21. Porter, *Campaigning With Grant*, 189–190.
22. Trudeau, *Bloody Roads South*, 315.

CHAPTER FORTY

"I Begin To See It"

13–15 June 1864

On the morning of 13 June, Hunter—whose men were calling him Black Davy now because of all the burning he had ordered—sent Averell ahead with his cavalry division to Buchanan, on the upper reaches of the James River. Averell in turn sent a picked force of 200 troopers toward Lynchburg, to cut its communications, and to gather news of the enemy. The expected train of supply wagons finally caught up with Hunter, and Duffié's cavalry division finally rejoined the main force that afternoon. Meanwhile, Hunter heard rumors that "a formidable rebel force was hastening toward the Valley from Richmond, and that Sheridan had met with a reverse near Louisa Court House."[1] He also received word that Lynchburg was weakly defended, so he decided to set out the next day to take it before it could be reinforced.

At 2 a.m. on that thirteenth of June, Early's 2nd Corps, numbering a little over 8,000 rifles plus two battalions of artillery, set out for Lynchburg. With the railroad broken by Sheridan's raid, these remnants of Stonewall Jackson's old "foot cavalry" had to march as far as Charlottesville. They covered a routine 23 miles that first day. But they were barely on their way when Lee's skirmishers brought him word that the

Union trenches around Cold Harbor were empty. Grant's entire army had marched away so quietly that the Rebel pickets had not realized that it was moving. The Confederates' skirmishers proceeded a mile or two beyond the old Federal position and still there was no sign of the enemy. "It was said," reported a brigade commander in Pickett's Division, "that General Lee was in a furious passion—one of the few times during the war. When he did get mad he was mad all over."[2] However, there could be little doubt about the direction in which the Yankees were heading. As always, they must be moving south, trying to get around Lee's right flank. Immediately he ordered his entire army to cross the Chickahominy and head them off.

Eventually, outposts from Lee's one remaining cavalry division, that of his son, Rooney, were met coming in from Riddell's Shop, south of the Chickahominy, and they reported that Federals had come down the Long Bridge Road from the direction of that swampy stream. Late in the afternoon Hill's corps ran into some of Wilson's Union cavalry and pushed them slowly eastward. Anderson's corps and Hoke's Division extended the Confederate line to the south, and Rooney Lee's cavalry protected its right from the height of Malvern Hill, so that all the ground between the Chickahominy and the James was covered. President Davis suggested that it might be wise to recall Early, but Lee, having just reluctantly decided to send his 2nd Corps to Lynchburg at Davis' own suggestion, now intended to stick by that decision. He replied somewhat testily, "I do not know that the necessity for his presence today is greater than it was yesterday," adding that "his troops would make us more secure here, but success in the Valley would relieve our difficulties that at present press heavily upon us."[3]

After crossing the Chickahominy early that morning, Wilson's Federal cavalry and Warren's 5th Corps had moved west until they ran into Hill's Rebels, and then took up position to protect the rest of the Union army as it continued to march southward behind them. It was a hot day, but the men did not mind. They were glad to be out of their trenches and out of range of the Rebels. Two years before, they had marched these same roads, but then they had been retreating. Now they felt that they were on their way to victory, and they marched with a spring in their step. The move had surprised them as much as it had the enemy, and one veteran noted that "it was not now the custom to inform the rank and file, and the newspapers and the enemy, of intended movements."[4]

By that evening Smith's 18th Corps was on transports heading around the Virginia Peninsula and back to Bermuda Hundred. Burnside's 9th Corps and Wright's 6th were on the lower Chickahominy, which they crossed that night. Hancock's 2nd Corps had already crossed behind Warren and was at Charles City Court House and at the plantation of the late president John Tyler on the James River. Near the river they saw sailors from the fleet, as well as members of Brigadier General Henry W. Benham's Engineer Brigade who were beginning to marshal their pontoons for the bridge which they would build at the point chosen by Comstock and Porter. A staff officer studied the sailors and engineers for a while, trying to pinpoint what it was about them that looked so strange. Then it came to him. They were clean. Their uniforms were not faded from rain and sun, and they were not covered with the mud and dust of forty days of campaigning from the Rapidan to the James.

The bridge would need protection. "It was known," Grant wrote in his memoirs, "that the enemy had some gunboats at Richmond. These might run down at night and inflict great damage upon us before they could be sunk or captured by our navy. General Butler had, in advance, loaded some vessels with stone ready to be sunk so as to obstruct the channel in an emergency. On the 13th I sent orders to have these sunk as high up the river as we could guard them, and prevent their removal by the enemy."[5]

On the south side of the James that day, Beauregard was also worried about potential enemy moves on the river. Finally, although reluctantly, he agreed to the Confederate Navy's persistant proposal to place naval guns and crews in an earthwork near the Howlett mansion on a bluff overlooking the James. This work commanded a long stretch of the river known as Trent's Reach, and a battery there would effectively close the James to the Federal fleet upstream from there. Beauregard was reluctant to accept the guns because he doubted his ability to defend them from a determined attack.

The next day, 14 June, Hunter marched his main force the 25 miles to Buchanan. Even though the James was easily fordable that far upstream, McCausland's Rebel cavalry zealously burned the bridge there, and eleven buildings in the little town caught fire too, but were saved with the help of the Federal troops. The same day, Breckinridge put his two small brigades of infantry on trains for Lynchburg, where they joined Imboden's cavalry, a few pieces of artillery, some survivors from the fight at Piedmont, convalescents from the local hospital, local militiamen and the VMI cadets. All these forces plus McCausland's troopers totaled little more than 5,000 men. Early's 2nd Corps, meanwhile, marched another 25 miles that day, bringing it to Gardiner's Cross Roads in Louisa County. Early himself rode on ahead to the telegraph office at Louisa Court House—where Fitz Lee's cavalry had camped four days before. From

there Early sent a message to Breckinridge, to let him know that he was
on the way.

Warren's 5th Corps had withdrawn from its blocking position during
the night and reached the James on the afternoon of the fourteenth, as did
Wright and Burnside. Meanwhile Grant had taken a small steamer up the
James that morning to Bermuda Hundred to have a talk with Butler about
the latter's attack on Petersburg the next day. "Grant knew now that he
had stolen a march on Lee," Horace Porter wrote, "and that Petersburg
was almost undefended; and with his usual fondness for taking the
offensive, he was anxious to hasten the movement which he had had in
contemplation against that place, to be begun before the Army of the
Potomac should arrive. His instructions were that as soon as Smith's
troops reached their destination they should be reinforced by as many
men as could be spared from Butler's troops—about 6,000—and move at
once against Petersburg."6

At 1 p.m. Grant sent a dispatch to Halleck at Washington saying, "Our
forces will commence crossing the James to-day. The enemy show no
signs yet of having brought troops to the south side of Richmond. I will
have Petersburg secured, if possible, before they get there in much force.
Our movement from Cold Harbor to the James River has been made with
great celerity and so far without loss or accident."7 Grant then returned to
Wilcox's Landing, where the pontoon bridge was being built. There he
received reports on Lee's current position.

Grant's move was already having its effects south of the James. At 7:15
a.m. on the fourteenth, a nervous Beauregard sent a telegram to Bragg:
"Movement of Grant's across Chickahominy and increase of Butler's force
render my position here critical. With my present forces I cannot answer
for consequences. Cannot my troops sent to General Lee be returned at
once?"8 He received no answer. The increase in Butler's force to which he
referred was the reinforcements Grant had directed Halleck to send to
Bermuda Hundred. But that afternoon a more substantial increase arrived
in the form of Baldy Smith's 18th Corps. Glad as Smith might have been
to get away from Butler when he had departed a couple of weeks before,
he was even more glad to get away from the trenches of Cold Harbor and
what he considered Meade's bungling. His return must have been made
even happier by the news that Butler had relieved Gillmore of his command that very day.

At 8:10 p.m. Beauregard decided to bypass the War Department and
telegraphed straight to Lee: "A deserter from the enemy reports that
Butler has been reenforced by the Eighteenth and a part of the Tenth

Army Corps."⁹ This drew no reply either, so he dispatched one of his aides to Lee to explain the situation south of the James.

Lee, however, seems to have appreciated, at least to some extent, the danger to Petersburg. At 12:10 p.m. he had sent a letter to President Davis in which he said: "I think the enemy must be preparing to move south of James River. Our scouts and pickets yesterday stated that Genl Grant's whole army was in motion for the fords of the Chickahominy from Long Bridge down, from which I inferred that he was making his way to the James River as his new base. I cannot however learn positively that more than a small part of his army has crossed the Chickahominy. Our contest last evening, as far as I am able to judge was with a heavy force of cavalry and the 5th Corps of his army. They were driven back until dark as I informed you, by a part of Hill's corps. Presuming that this force was either the advance of his army, or the cover behind which it would move to James River, I prepared to attack it again this morning, but it disappeared from before us during the night, and as far as we can judge from the statements of prisoners, it has gone to Harrison's landing." He went on to speculate that Grant might place his army in McClellan's old fortifications there, in which case these defenses and the Union gunboats in the river would make it too costly to attack him. "He could then either refresh it or transfer it to the other side of the river without our being able to molest it, unless our ironclads are stronger than his," he added.

As for the possible dispatch of reinforcements from Grant to Butler, Lee was not so sure. He knew that a portion of Grant's army had embarked at White House, but he thought these were probably discharged men returning to the North. "Still I apprehend that he may be sending troops up the James River with the view of getting possession of Petersburg before we can reinforce it," Lee wrote. "We ought therefore to be extremely watchful & guarded." He was, he said, moving Hoke's Division to the vicinity of the Confederate bridge over the James south of Richmond, so that it could cross over and return to Beauregard if necessary. "The rest of the army can follow should circumstances require it." The sentences that followed summed up his entire philosophy most succinctly: "The victories of Forrest and Hampton are very grateful at this time, and show that we are not forsaken by a gracious Providence. We have only to do our whole duty, and everything will be well."¹⁰

By 11 p.m. the great pontoon bridge across the James was completed and the Army of the Potomac began to cross. The bridge was 2,100 feet in length and contained 101 pontoons. In midstream, where the current was swift, schooners were anchored both above and below the bridge, and the pontoons were fastened to them for support. The bridge, however, was used mostly by the artillery and wagons. River boats were used to ferry the infantry across. All of Hancock's 2nd Corps infantry and four batteries of his artillery were over the river by daylight of the next day, the fifteenth.

As Grant "stood upon the bluff on the north bank of the river on the morning of June 15, watching with unusual interest the busy scene spread out before him," Horace Porter remembered, "it presented a sight which had never been equaled even in his extended experience in all the varied phases of warfare. His cigar had been thrown aside, his hands were clasped behind him, and he seemed lost in the contemplation of the spectacle. The great bridge was the scene of a continuous movement of infantry columns, batteries of artillery, and wagon-trains. The approaches to the river on both banks were covered with masses of troops moving briskly to their positions or waiting patiently their turn to cross. At the two improvised ferries, steamboats were gliding back and forth with the regularity of weavers' shuttles. A fleet of transports covered the surface of the water below the bridge, and gunboats floated lazily upon the stream, guarding the river above. Drums were beating the march, bands were playing stirring quicksteps, the distant booming of cannon on Warren's front showed that he and the enemy were still exchanging compliments; and mingled with these sounds were the cheers of the sailors, the shouting of the troops, the rumbling of wheels, and the shrieks of steam-whistles. The bright sun, shining through a clear sky upon the scene, cast its sheen upon the water, was reflected from the burnished gun-barrels and glittering cannon, and brought out with increased brilliancy the gay colors of the waving banners. The calmly flowing river reflected the blue of the heavens, and mirrored on its surface the beauties of nature that bordered it . . . It was a matchless pageant that could not fail to inspire all beholders with the grandeur of achievement and the majesty of military power. The man whose genius had conceived and whose skill had executed this masterly movement stood watching the spectacle in profound silence. Whether his mind was occupied with the contemplation of its magnitude and success, or was busied with maturing plans for the future, no one can tell. After a time he woke from his reverie, mounted his horse, and gave orders to have headquarters ferried across to the south bank of the river."[11]

A few miles to the west, Baldy Smith had crossed the Appomattox on Butler's pontoon bridge between Port Walthall and City Point and, in conjunction with Hincks' U.S. Colored Troops and Kautz's cavalry, was on his way to Petersburg at last. Hancock's 2nd Corps was across the James with orders to march west and support Smith's attack. Far up the valley of the James River, Hunter's Army of West Virginia was crossing the Blue Ridge Mountains and approaching Lynchburg. Down in

Georgia, the rains that had been holding up Sherman's advance had finally stopped falling.

Sometime that day Grant received a telegram in reply to the report he had sent to Halleck from Bermuda Hundred: "Have just read your despatch of 1 p.m. yesterday. I begin to see it. You will succeed. God bless you all." It was signed, "A. Lincoln."[12]

1. Pond, *The Shenandoah Valley*, 32.
2. Trudeau, *Bloody Roads South*, 316.
3. Dowdey and Manarin, eds. *Wartime Papers of R. E. Lee*, 782–783.
4. Catton, *A Stillness At Appomattox*, 181.
5. Grant, *Memoirs*, 2:288.
6. Porter, *Campaigning With Grant*, 198.
7. Basler, ed., *Collected Works of Abraham Lincoln*, 7:393.
8. G. T. Beauregard, "Four Days of Battle at Petersburg," in *Battles and Leaders*, 4:540.
9. Ibid.
10. Dowdey and Manarin, eds., *Wartime Papers of R. E. Lee*, 777–778.
11. Porter, *Campaigning With Grant*, 199–200.
12. Basler, ed., *Collected Works of Abraham Lincoln*, 7:393.

EPILOGUE

The war entered a new phase when Grant crossed the James, Early departed for Lynchburg, and the rains ended in Georgia.

As Lee had observed, once Grant got to the James it would only be a matter of time. However, two questions remained: How much time would it take to force Lee to either surrender or break loose from Richmond? And, how much time did Grant have? Grant, of course, did not suspect that it would take ten months of seige and battle just to get into Petersburg.

It is easy now, after the fact, to say that the North's victory was inevitable. But nothing is inevitable until it happens. There was no doubt that the Federal government had much greater resources at its command than did the Confederacy. But the South had the ability to inflict terrible losses as it was slowly ground down, and there had to be a limit to how much suffering and death the North would be willing to take before giving up. Lincoln had made it clear that as long as he was president he would fight on. But 1864 was an election year, and if a Democrat was to be elected it would surely be on an anti-war platform. Had the Northern people wearied of the war enough to replace Lincoln with a man of lesser resolve, or had Grant or Sherman made one fatal mistake, then all the Union's resources would have been of no avail. And all the Federal dead would indeed have died in vain.

Tactically, the detachment of Early to the Shenandoah was a success. For a while the Federals were cleared from the Valley, Washington was threatened, and Union forces were diverted from Petersburg. But Grant's grip was not shaken, Early was eventually defeated, and Sherman marched on. Grant's forty-day campaign from the Rapidan to the James had not accomplished all that he had hoped for it. Lee had not been defeated in the field. But, on the other hand, neither had Grant. Despite his losses, Grant moved south, ultimately forcing Lee into the kind of siege that the Southern commander had dreaded from the beginning.

There are some ways—not all original—in which the present account differs from the traditional telling of this period of the war:

1. It has usually been assumed that, on 5 May 1864, Lee caught Grant in the process of moving south and, by attacking him, brought the movement to a halt. In fact, Grant was not trying to pass Lee's front, but to turn his southern flank should he take up his old position along Mine Run. Lee, on the other hand, seems to have believed Longstreet's assumption that Grant was trying to draw him down toward Fredericksburg. Lee intended to avoid a major battle until his forces were united. It was Grant, matching tactics to strategy, who ordered an attack on Lee as soon as his forces were encountered, in order to put him on the defensive and keep him too busy to launch one of his famous flank attacks.

2. It has often been claimed that Lee showed great perspicacity in divining Grant's intention to move to Spotsylvania on 8 May and in sending Anderson's corps to head him off. But Lee did not know that Grant was going there, he only knew that it was a good place to have a corps if Grant was still—in Lee's view—making for Fredericksburg, or if he intended to head south. That Anderson got to Spotsylvania before Warren was an accident brought about by Anderson's inability to find a suitable place for his troops to go into camp, and by the mix-up between Sheridan and Meade over orders for Torbert's and Gregg's cavalry divisions.

3. It has been popular to describe Butler's situation, after his retreat from Drewry's Bluff, as being "in a bottle tightly corked." Grant himself once used the phrase, although he did not originate it and he later changed his mind. In fact, although Beauregard's defenses across the neck of the Bermuda Hundred peninsula did prevent Butler from moving west against the railroad which connected Petersburg and Richmond, he was free to move in any other direction, as his raid on Petersburg and the movement of Smith's corps in and out by river demonstrate.

4. It is conventional to assume that only Lee's illness saved Grant from defeat at the North Anna. But at the very most Lee might have severely mauled one of Grant's four infantry corps. And even that was not a foregone conclusion, considering the advantages of the defense in that era, and the shortcomings that Lee's corps commanders had already evinced. Only days earlier, Grant had sent that same corps a day's march ahead of the rest of his army in hopes that it would draw Lee out of his entrenchments in an attack.

5. Grant is usually blamed for letting his reluctance to lose face prolong the suffering of the wounded between the lines at Cold Harbor, but Lee's insistence on following some strict formality would seem to have played at least as great a role as any evasion of form on Grant's part. It

would take a military lawyer to discern the difference between the arrangement that Grant suggested on 5 June and the one that was finally agreed to on 7 June.

6. Grant has often been depicted as a butcher whose only strategy was to overcome the smaller enemy force by attrition, knowing that he could replace his losses more easily than Lee. There is no evidence, however, that Grant ever thought in those terms. Moreover, it was by no means certain at the time that his losses could be replaced more easily than Lee's. The Confederacy was enforcing total conscription. Every man in the South was not only liable for military service, but was actually in the service, unless conscription agents could not reach him, or his civilian occupation was essential to the economy. In the North, manpower was raised by occasional drafts—lotteries—and by the spur to volunteering that large enlistment bonuses and the threat of the drafts represented.

Moreover, Federal troops served for a limited time, usually three years but sometimes as little, even at this late stage of the war, as 100 days. Many of the Union's best regiments went home in the middle of the campaign. At any rate, as the Army of the Potomac crossed the James its strength stood at 115,000 men, 1,000 fewer than when it had crossed the Rapidan. But the Army of Northern Virginia had around 64,000 men, about 4,000 more than it had started with.

"While we lay at Cold Harbor," Assistant Secretary of War Charles A. Dana wrote, "as when we had been at Spotsylvania, the principal topic of conversation was the losses of the army. The discussion never ceased. There are still many persons who bitterly accuse Grant of butchery in this campaign. As a matter of fact, Grant lost fewer men in his successful effort to take Richmond and end the war than his predecessors lost in making the attempt and failing."[1]

---

1. Dana, *Recollections of the Civil War*, 187.

Appendix A

Cast of Characters

The principal characters mentioned in this book are listed here alphabetically, with a brief description of their place in the scheme of events. Those who have only minor roles in the text, and are not likely to be confused with others, are not listed.

Abbreviations used below:
CSA—Confederate States Army
USA—United States (regular) Army
USMA—United States Military Academy (given with class)
USN—United States Navy
USV—United States Volunteers

AMES, Adelbert—Brigadier General, USV (USMA May 1861). Commander of the 3rd Division of Gillmore's 10th Corps in Butler's Army of the James (Dept. of Va. and N.C.).

ANDERSON, George T.—Brigadier General, CSA. Commander of a brigade of Georgia infantry in Field's Division of the 1st Corps of Lee's Army of Northern Virginia.

ANDERSON, Richard H. ("Dick")—Major General, CSA (USMA 1842). Commander of a division in the 3rd Corps, and successor to Longstreet as commander of the 1st Corps, in Lee's Army of Northern Virginia.

AVERELL, William Woods—Brigadier General, USV (USMA 1855). Commander of the 2nd Cavalry Division of Sigel's (later Hunter's) Department of West Virginia. Sent to raid lead mines and salt works in southwestern Virginia before joining Crook's infantry and Sigel's (Hunter's) army.

AYRES, Romeyne B.—Brigadier General, USV (USMA, 1847). Commander of the 1st Brigade (regulars and zouaves) of Griffin's 1st Division of Warren's 5th Corps in Meade's Army of the Potomac.

BABCOCK, Orville—Lieutenant Colonel, USA (USMA May 1861). Aide on Grant's staff.

BAILEY, Joseph—Lieutenant Colonel, USV. Former logger who designed and built wing dams on the Red River to save Adm. Porter's gunboats, and built a bridge using river boats to get Banks' Army of the Gulf across the swollen Atchafalaya.

BANKS, Nathaniel P.—Major General, USV. Commander of the Department and Army of the Gulf. Prominent Republican politician before the war. Former Union commander in the Shenandoah Valley.

BARLOW, Francis C.—Brigadier General, USV. Commander of the 1st Division of Hancock's 2nd Corps in Meade's Army of the Potomac.

BARNARD, John G.—Brigadier General, USV (USMA 1833). Chief Engineer of the Department of Washington. One of two officers sent by Halleck to report on the situation at Bermuda Hundred.

BARTLETT, Joseph J.—Brigadier General, USV. Commander of the 3rd Brigade of Griffin's 1st Division of Warren's 5th Corps in Meade's Army of the Potomac.

BATTLE, Cullen A.—Brigadier General, CSA. Commander of a brigade of Alabama infantry in Rodes' Division of the 2nd Corps of Lee's Army of Northern Virginia.

BEAUREGARD, P. G. T.—General, CSA (USMA 1838). New commander of the Department of Southern Virginia and North Carolina. The South's first "hero," for commanding the forces that compelled the surrender of Fort Sumter in Charleston Harbor.

BIRNEY, David B.—Major General, USV. Commander of the 3rd Division of Hancock's 2nd Corps in Meade's Army of the Potomac.

BLAIR, Francis P. ("Frank"), Jr.—Major General, USV. Commander of the 17th Corps in McPherson's Army of the Tennessee in Sherman's Military Division of the Mississippi. Simultaneously a member of Congress. Brother of Lincoln's postmaster general.

BRAGG, Braxton—General, CSA (USMA 1837). Nominal general-in-chief of the Confederate army. Former commander of the Army of Tennessee. Famous for his inability to get along with anybody but President Davis.

BRECKINRIDGE, John C.—Major General, CSA. Commander of the Department of Southwestern Virginia. Former vice president of the United States. Presidential candidate of the Southern wing of the Democratic party in 1860.

BRECKINRIDGE, Robert J.—Temporary chairman of the National Union convention which nominated Lincoln for a second term as president. Uncle of Confederate Maj. Gen. John C. Breckinridge.

BROOKE, John R.—Brigadier General, USV. Commander of the 4th Brigade of Barlow's 1st Division of Hancock's 2nd Corps in Meade's Army of the Potomac.

BROOKS, W. T. H.—Brigadier General, USV (USMA 1841). Commander of the 1st Division of W. F. Smith's 18th Corps in Butler's Army of the James (Dept. of Va. and N.C.).

BROWN, Joseph N.—Colonel, CSA. Succeeded to command of McGowan's brigade of South Carolina infantry in Wilcox's Division of the 3rd Corps in Lee's Army of Northern Virginia—one of two brigades that held the "bloody angle" at Spotsylvania for 17 hours.

BUELL, Don Carlos—Major General, USV (USMA 1841). Former commander of the Army of the Ohio (renamed Army of the Cumberland under his successor, Rosecrans).

BURBRIDGE, Stephen G.—Brigadier General, USV. Commander of the District of Kentucky in Schofield's Department of the Ohio of Sherman's Military Division of the Mississippi.

BURNSIDE, Ambrose E.—Major General, USV (USMA 1847). Commander of the 9th Corps, directly subordinate to Grant; later assigned to Meade's Army of the Potomac. Had been McClellan's successor as commander of the Army of the Potomac, then Schofield's predecessor as commander of the Army of the Ohio.

BUTLER, Benjamin Franklin—Major General, USV. Commander of the Department of Virginia and North Carolina and the Army of the James. Prominent Democratic politician before the war. Banks' predecessor in command of the Department of the Gulf.

BUTLER, Matthew Calbraith—Brigadier General, CSA. Commander of a brigade of South Carolina cavalry that joined Hampton's Division of Lee's Army of Northern Virginia from near Richmond in late May 1864.

BUTTERFIELD, Daniel—Major General, USV. Commander of the 3rd

Division of Hooker's 20th Corps in Thomas' Army of the Cumberland of Sherman's Military Division of the Mississippi. Former chief of staff of the Army of the Potomac (under Hooker), designer of corps badges, composer of bugle call "Taps."

CANBY, Edward R. S.—Major General, USV (USMA 1839). Appointed commander of a new Military Division of West Mississippi, consisting of Steele's Department of Arkansas and Banks' Department of the Gulf.

CHALMERS, James R.—Brigadier General, CSA. Division commander in Forrest's cavalry.

CHURCHILL, Thomas J.—Brigadier General, CSA. Commander of the two small infantry divisions sent from Arkansas to reinforce Taylor in Louisiana and then sent back to Arkansas.

CLEBURNE, Patrick R.—Major General, CSA. Commander of a division in Hardee's 1st Corps of J. E. Johnston's Army of Tennessee.

CLINGMAN, Thomas L.—Brigadier General, CSA. Commander of a brigade of North Carolina infantry in Beauregard's Department of Southern Virginia and North Carolina. The brigade became part of Hoke's division, with which it reinforced Lee's Army of Northern Virginia at Cold Harbor.

COMSTOCK, Cyrus—Lieutenant Colonel, USA (USMA 1855). Aide on Grant's staff.

COOPER, Samuel—General, CSA (USMA 1815). The adjutant and inspector general of, and highest ranking officer in, the Confederate army.

CORSE, John M.—Brigadier General, USV (USMA ex-1857). Inspector general on Sherman's staff. Sent to deliver a letter to Banks about A. J. Smith's forces.

CORSE, Montgomery D.—Brigadier General, CSA. Commander of a brigade of Virginia infantry in Beauregard's Department of Southern Virginia and North Carolina. When Pickett's Division was reassembled, the brigade returned with it to Lee's Army of Northern Virginia at the North Anna.

COX, Jacob D.—Major General, USV. Commander of the 3rd Division of the 23rd Corps in Schofield's Army of the Ohio of Sherman's Military Division of the Mississippi.

CRAWFORD, Samuel W.—Brigadier General, USV. Commander of the 3rd Division (The Pennsylvania Reserves) of Warren's 5th Corps in Meade's Army of the Potomac.

CRITTENDEN, George B.—Colonel (former major general), CSA (USMA 1832). Commander of a detachment of Confederate cavalry which defended Wytheville, Virginia from Averell. Brother of Union general Thomas L. Crittenden.

CRITTENDEN, Thomas L.—Major General, USV. Succeeded Stevenson in command of the 1st Division of Burnside's 9th Corps. Former commander of the 21st Corps in the Army of the Cumberland until routed at Chickamauga. Brother of Confederate colonel George B. Crittenden.

CROOK, George—Brigadier General, USV (USMA 1852). Commander of the Kanawha District and the 2nd Infantry Division of Sigel's Department of West Virginia. Sent to raid the Virginia & Tennessee Railroad before combining with Sigel's (later Hunter's) main column.

CUSTER, George Armstrong—Brigadier General, USV (USMA June 1861). Commander of the 1st (Michigan) Brigade of Torbert's 1st Division of Sheridan's Cavalry Corps of Meade's Army of the Potomac.

CUTLER, Lysander—Brigadier General, USV. Commander of the 1st (Iron) Brigade of Wadsworth's 4th Division of Warren's 5th Corps in Meade's Army of the Potomac. Succeeded Wadsworth in command of the division after the latter's death in the Wilderness.

DANA, Charles A.—U.S. Assistant Secretary of War. Sent by Lincoln to accompany Grant and report on the general's progress.

DANA, Richard Henry—Author of *Two Years Before the Mast*, who saw Grant's arrival at Willard's Hotel in Washington.

DAVIS, Jefferson—(USMA 1828). First and only president of the Confederate States of America.

DAVIS, Jefferson C.—Brigadier General, USV. Commander of the 2nd Division of Palmer's 14th Corps of Thomas' Army of the Cumberland in Sherman's Military Division of the Mississippi.

DAVIS, Joseph R.—Brigadier General, CSA. Commander of a brigade of Mississippi and North Carolina infantry in Heth's Division of the 3rd Corps of Lee's Army of Northern Virginia. Nephew of the Confederate president.

DEARING, James—Brigadier General, CSA (USMA ex-1862). Commander of the cavalry brigade in Beauregard's Department of Southern Virginia and North Carolina.

DEVENS, Charles—Brigadier General, USV. Appointed to command a new 3rd Division of W. F. Smith's 18th Corps, formed by consolidating the former 2nd and 3rd divisions of Gillmore's 10th Corps, when the 18th Corps was sent to reinforce Meade's Army of the Potomac at Cold Harbor.

DEVIN, Thomas C.—Colonel, USV. Commander of the 2nd Brigade of Torbert's 1st Division of Sheridan's Cavalry Corps of Meade's Army of the Potomac.

DODGE, Grenville M.—Brigadier General, USV. Commander of the Right Wing of the 16th Corps, part of McPherson's Army of the Tennessee in Sherman's Military Division of the Mississippi.

DOLES, George P.—Brigadier General, CSA. Commander of a Georgia brigade in Rodes' Division of the 2nd Corps in Lee's Army of Northern Virginia. Killed near Cold Harbor, 2 June 1864.

DUFFIÉ, Alfred N.—Brigadier General, USV. Commander of the 1st Brigade of Averell's 2nd Cavalry Division of Sigel's (later Hunter's) Department of West Virginia. Succeeded Stahel in command of the 1st Cavalry Division of the same department.

EARLY, Jubal Anderson—Major General, CSA (USMA 1837). Commander of a division in Ewell's 2nd Corps of Lee's Army of Northern Virginia. Given temporary charge of A. P. Hill's 3rd Corps during the latter's illness at Spotsylvania. Succeeded Ewell in command of the 2nd Corps.

EDWARDS, Oliver—Colonel, USV. Commander of the 37th Massachusetts Volunteer Infantry Regiment. Succeeded Eustis in command of the 4th Brigade of Neill's (formerly Getty's) 2nd Division of Wright's (formerly Sedgwick's) 6th Corps in Meade's Army of the Potomac. Held the "bloody angle" at Spotsylvania for 24 hours.

EVANS, Clement A.—Colonel (Brigadier General from 19 May 1864), CSA. Succeeded to command of John B. Gordon's brigade of Georgia infantry in Gordon's Division of the 2nd Corps of Lee's Army of Northern Virginia.

EWELL, Richard S. ("Dick")—Lieutenant General, CSA (USMA 1840). Stonewall Jackson's successor as commander of the 2nd Corps of Lee's Army of Northern Virginia.

FAGAN, James Fleming—Major General, CSA. Commander of a cavalry division under Price in Arkansas.

FERRERO, Edward—Brigadier General, USV. Commander of the 4th Division (composed entirely of regiments of U.S. Colored Troops) of Burnside's 9th Corps.

FIELD, Charles W.—Major General, CSA (USMA 1849). Commander of a division in the 1st Corps of Lee's Army of Northern Virginia.

FORREST, Nathan Bedford—Major General, CSA. Commander of Confederate forces in northern Mississippi and western Tennessee.

FRANKLIN, William B.—Major General, USV (USMA 1843). Commander of the 19th Corps in Banks' Army of the Gulf. Former commander of the 6th Corps and the Left Grand Division in the Army of the Potomac.

FREMONT, John Charles—Former major general, USV. The Republican party's first candidate for president (1856). Union commander in Missouri early in the war. Later commander in West Virginia but resigned rather than serve under John Pope. Nominated for president in 1864 by a convention of radical Republicans.

GARRARD, Kenner—Brigadier General, USV, (USMA 1851). Commander of the 2nd Cavalry Division of Thomas' Army of the Cumberland in Sherman's Military Division of the Mississippi.

GEARY, John W.—Brigadier General, USV. Commander of the 2nd Division of Hooker's 20th Corps in Thomas' Army of the Cumberland of Sherman's Military Division of the Mississippi.

GETTY, George Washington—Brigadier General, USV (USMA 1840). Commander of the 2nd Division of the 6th Corps in Meade's Army of the Potomac.

GIBBON, John—Brigadier General, USV (USMA 1847). Commander of the 2nd Division of Hancock's 2nd Corps in Meade's Army of the Potomac.

GILLMORE, Quincy Adams—Major General, USV (USMA 1849). Commander of the 10th Corps in Butler's Army of the James. Formerly commander of the Department of the South (Union holdings in South Carolina, Georgia, and Florida).

GORDON, James B.—Brigadier General, CSA. Commander of a brigade of North Carolina cavalry in W. H. F. Lee's Division of Stuart's Cavalry Corps of Lee's Army of Northern Virginia. Killed by Union cavalry near Richmond on 12 May 1864.

GORDON, John B.—Brigadier General (later major general), CSA. Commander of a brigade of Georgia infantry in Early's Division of Ewell's 2nd Corps of Lee's Army of Northern Virginia. Succeeded to command of the division when Early temporarily replaced A. P. Hill in command of the 3rd Corps. Took over Johnson's reorganized division when Early returned to his own command.

GRAHAM, Charles K.—Brigadier General, USV. Commander of the army gunboats attached to Butler's Army of the James (Dept. of Va. and N.C.).

GRANT, Lewis A.—Colonel (later brigadier general), USV. Commander of the 2nd (Vermont) Brigade of Getty's 2nd Division of the 6th Corps in Meade's Army of the Potomac. No kin to the general-in-chief.

GRANT, Ulysses Simpson—Lieutenant General, USA (USMA 1843). General-in-chief of the United States Army.

GREENE, Thomas—Brigadier General, CSA. Commander of a division of Texas cavalry sent to reinforce Taylor in Louisiana.

GREGG, David McMurtrie—Brigadier General, USV (USMA 1855). Commander of the 2nd Division of Sheridan's Cavalry Corps of Meade's Army of the Potomac.

GREGG, John—Brigadier General, CSA. Commander of a brigade of Texas and Arkansas infantry in Field's Division of the 1st Corps of Lee's Army of Northern Virginia.

GRIERSON, Benjamin H.—Brigadier General, USV. Commander of the 1st Cavalry Division of the 16th Corps of McPherson's Department of the Tennessee in Sherman's Military Division of the Mississippi. Stationed in western Tennessee, his division was twice sent with Sturgis to chase Forrest in northern Mississippi. He had led the North's most famous and most successful cavalry raid the summer before during Grant's Vicksburg campaign.

GRIFFIN, Charles—Brigadier General, USV (USMA 1847). Commander of the 1st Division of Warren's 5th Corps in Meade's Army of the Potomac.

HAGOOD, Johnson—Brigadier General, CSA. Commander of a brigade of South Carolina infantry sent from South Carolina to reinforce Beauregard in the Department of Southern Virginia and North Carolina. There the brigade became part of Hoke's division, with which it reinforced Lee's Army of Northern Virginia at Cold Harbor.

HALLECK, Henry Wager—Major General, USA (USMA 1839). Grant's predecessor as general-in-chief and former boss in the trans-Allegheny West. Named by Grant as the chief of staff of the U.S. Army.

HAMMOND, John—Lieutenant Colonel, USV. Commander of the 5th New York Cavalry Regiment in Bryan's 1st Brigade of Wilson's 3rd Division of Sheridan's Cavalry Corps of Meade's Army of the Potomac. Later commanded an ad hoc brigade of cavalry units, temporarily attached to Ferrero's 4th Division of Burnside's 9th Corps.

HAMPTON, Wade—Major General, CSA. Commander of a division in Jeb Stuart's Cavalry Corps in Lee's Army of Northern Virginia.

HANCOCK, Winfield Scott—Major General, USV (USMA 1840). Commander of the 2nd Corps in Meade's Army of the Potomac.

HARDEE, William J.—Lieutenant General, CSA (USMA 1838). Commander of the 1st Corps of J. E. Johnston's Army of Tennessee.

HARRIS, Nathaniel H. ("Nate")—Brigadier General, CSA. Commander of a brigade of Mississippi infantry in Anderson's (later Mahone's) Division of the 3rd Corps of Lee's Army of Northern Virginia—one of two brigades that held the "bloody angle" at Spotsylvania for 17 hours.

HETH (pronounced heath), Henry—Major General, CSA (USMA 1847). Commander of a division in the 3rd Corps of Lee's Army of Northern Virginia.

HIGGINS, Jacob—Colonel, USV. Commander of a detachment of 500 cavalry sent to chase McNeill's partisans who had raided the Baltimore & Ohio Railroad.

HILL, Ambrose Powell—Lieutenant General, CSA (USMA 1847). Commander of the 3rd Corps of Lee's Army of Northern Virginia.

HILL, Daniel Harvey—Major General, CSA (USMA 1842). Without assignment, due to a quarrel with President Davis over the latter's withdrawal of his promotion to lieutenant general. Served as volunteer aide to Beauregard.

HINCKS, Edward W.—Brigadier General, USV. Commander of a division (composed entirely of regiments of U.S. Colored Troops) in W. F. Smith's 18th Corps in Butler's Army of the James (Dept. of Va. and N.C.).

HOKE, Robert F.—Brigadier General, CSA. Led Confederate ground forces in the recapture of Plymouth, N.C., for which he was promoted to major general. Led a division under Beauregard at Drewry's Bluff and was sent with it to reinforce Lee's Army of Northern Virginia at Cold Harbor.

HOOD, John Bell—Lieutenant General, CSA (USMA 1853). Commander of the 2nd Corps of J. E. Johnston's Army of Tennessee. Came west as a division commander in Longstreet's corps in time for the battle of Chickamauga.

HOOKER, Joseph—Major General, USV (USMA 1837). Commander of the 20th Corps under Thomas and Sherman. Had been commander of the Army of the Potomac between Burnside and Meade. Came west with the 11th and 12th corps after Chickamauga.

HOWARD, Oliver O.—Major General, USV (USMA 1854). Commander of the 4th Corps in Thomas' Army of the Cumberland in Sherman's Military Division of the Mississippi. Former commander of the 11th Corps in the Army of the Potomac. Came west with Hooker.

HUMPHREYS, Andrew A.—Major General, USV (USMA 1831). Chief of staff of Meade's Army of the Potomac.

HUMPHREYS, Benjamin G.—Brigadier General, CSA. Commander of a brigade of Mississippi infantry in Kershaw's Division of the 1st Corps of Lee's Army of Northern Virginia.

HUNT, Henry J.—Brigadier General, USV (USMA 1839). Chief of Artillery in Meade's Army of the Potomac.

HUNTER, David—Major General, USV (USMA 1822). Sent by Grant with orders for Banks to cut his Red River campaign short. Later appointed to supercede Sigel in command of the Department of West Virginia.

HURLBUT, Stephan A.—Major General, USV. Former commander of the 16th Corps, Army of the Tennessee, headquartered at Memphis.

IMBODEN, John D.—Brigadier General, CSA. Commander of a brigade of cavalry in the Shenandoah Valley and of the Valley District of Lee's Army of Northern Virginia.

JACKSON, Thomas J. ("Stonewall")—Lieutenant General, CSA (USMA 1846). Late commander of the Army of the Valley, and the 2nd Corps of the Army of Northern Virginia. Mortally wounded at the battle of Chancellorsville in May 1863.

JACKSON, William H. ("Red")—Brigadier General, CSA (USMA 1856). Commander of a division of cavalry that went as part of Polk's Army of Mississippi to reinforce J. E. Johnston's Army of Tennessee.

JENKINS, Albert G.—Brigadier General, CSA. Commander of a brigade of Virginia cavalry in Breckinridge's Department of Southwestern Virginia. Mortally wounded at Cloyd's Mountain.

JENKINS, Micah—Brigadier General, CSA. Commander of a brigade of South Carolina infantry in Kershaw's Division of the 1st Corps of Lee's Army of Northern Virginia. Mortally wounded in the Wilderness by the same volley that wounded Longstreet.

JOHNSON, Andrew—Brigadier General, USV. Military governor of Tennessee. Former governor of, and senator from, Tennessee who remained loyal to the federal government. Nominated by the National Union convention for vice president on the ticket with Lincoln.

JOHNSON, Bushrod R.—Brigadier General, CSA (USMA 1840). Commander of a brigade of Tennessee infantry in Robert Ransom's Department of Richmond.

JOHNSON, William A.—Colonel, CSA. Commander of a small brigade of cavalry in Forrest's command.

JOHNSON, Edward ("Allegheny")—Major General, CSA (USMA 1838). Commander of a division in the 2nd Corps of Lee's Army of Northern Virginia.

JOHNSON, Richard W.—Brigadier General, USV (USMA 1849). Commander of the 1st Division of Palmer's 14th Corps in Thomas' Army of the Cumberland of Sherman's Military Division of the Mississippi.

JOHNSTON, Albert Sidney—General, CSA (USMA 1826). Commander of all Confederate forces west of the Alleghenies, until killed at Shiloh in 1862.

JOHNSTON, Joseph Eggleston—General, CSA (USMA 1829). Commander of the Army of Tennessee, defending Georgia. Had commanded Confederate forces with Beauregard at the first battle of Bull Run. Lee's predecessor in command of the Army of Northern Virginia.

JOHNSTON, Robert D.—Brigadier General, CSA. Commander of a brigade of North Carolina infantry from Rodes' Division of the 2nd Corps of Lee's Army of Northern Virginia which had been detached to guard Hanover Junction. It rejoined the main army the night of 5 May 1864. A few days later it was transferred to the division of the newly promoted John B. Gordon.

JONES, John M.—Brigadier General, CSA (USMA 1841). Commander of a brigade of Virginia infantry in Johnson's Division of the 2nd Corps of Lee's Army of Northern Virginia. Killed in the Wilderness 5 May 1864.

JONES, W. E. ("Grumble")—Brigadier General, CSA (USMA 1848). Commander of a brigade of Virginia cavalry in the Department of East Tennessee sent to reinforce southwestern Virginia and the Shenandoah Valley. Killed at Piedmont, Virginia.

JUDAH, Henry M.—Brigadier General, USV (USMA 1843). Commander of the 2nd Division of the 23rd Corps (Schofield's Army of the Ohio) of Sherman's Military Division of the Mississippi.

KAUTZ, August V.—Brigadier General, USV (USMA 1852). Commander of the Cavalry Division of Butler's Army of the James. Had briefly been Wilson's successor as chief of the Cavalry Bureau.

KERSHAW, Joseph B.—Brigadier General (later major general), CSA. Commander of a division in the 1st Corps of Lee's Army of Northern Virginia.

KILPATRICK, Hugh Judson—Brigadier General, USV (USMA 1861). Commander of the 3rd Cavalry Division of Thomas' Army of the Cumberland in Sherman's Military Division of the Mississippi. Wilson's predecessor as commander of the 3rd Division of the Cavalry Corps of the Army of the Potomac.

KITCHING, John H.—Colonel, USV. Commander of a brigade of heavy artillery regiments serving as infantry. Originally part of the Artillery Reserve of Meade's Army of the Potomac. Later transferred to Warren's 5th Corps.

LEE, Albert L.—Brigadier General, USV. Commander of the Cavalry Division in Banks' Army of the Gulf.

LEE, Fitzhugh ("Fitz")—Major General, CSA (USMA 1856). Commander of a division in Stuart's Cavalry Corps of R. E. Lee's Army of Northern Virginia. Nephew of R. E. Lee.

LEE, Robert Edward—General, CSA (USMA 1829). Commander of the Army of Northern Virginia.

LEE, Samuel P.—Rear Admiral, USN. Commander of the North Atlantic Blockading Squadron, which covered the coasts of Virginia and North Carolina.

LEE, Stephen Dill—Major general, CSA (USMA 1854). Polk's chief of cavalry and successor in the Department of Alabama, Mississippi and Eastern Louisiana. Only very distantly related to the Virginia Lees.

LEE, W. H. F. ("Rooney")—Major General, CSA. Commander of a division in Stuart's Cavalry Corps of R. E. Lee's Army of Northern Virginia. Son of R. E. Lee.

LINCOLN, Abraham—Sixteenth president of the United States.

LOGAN, John A.—Major General, USV. Commander of the 15th Corps in McPherson's Army of the Tennessee in Sherman's Military Division of the Mississippi.

LONGSTREET, James—Lieutenant General, CSA (USMA 1842). Commander of the 1st Corps of Lee's Army of Northern Virginia, just returned from detached service with the Army of Tennessee and in the Department of East Tennessee.

LYMAN, Theodore—Lieutenant Colonel, USV. Aide on Meade's staff. Sent to watch Hancock's progress on the first day of the Wilderness.

MAHONE, William ("Billy")—Brigadier General, CSA. Commander of a brigade of Virginia infantry in Anderson's Division of the 3rd Corps of Lee's Army of Northern Virginia, and successor to command of the division when Anderson replaced Longstreet in command of the 1st Corps.

MARMADUKE, John S.—Major General, CSA (USMA 1857). Commander of a cavalry division under Price in Arkansas.

MARTINDALE, John H.—Brigadier General, USV (USMA 1835). Succeeded Weitzel in command of the 2nd Division of W. F. Smith's 18th Corps in Butler's Army of the James (Dept. of Va. and N.C.).

McCAUSLAND, John—Colonel (later brigadier general), CSA. Commander of a brigade of Virginia infantry in Breckinridge's Department of Southwestern Virginia. Later named to command a brigade of cavalry in the Shenandoah/Lynchburg area.

McCLELLAN, George B.—Former major general, USA (USMA 1846). Founder of the Army of the Potomac. Halleck's predecessor as general-in-chief of the U.S. Army.

McCLELLAN, H. B.—Major, CSA. Officer on the staff of Jeb Stuart.

McCOOK, Edward M.—Brigadier General, USV. Commander of the 1st Cavalry Division of Thomas' Army of the Cumberland in Sherman's Military Division of the Mississippi. One of 17 McCook brothers, sons and cousins who served in the Union army.

McDOWELL, Irvin—Former major general, USV (USMA 1838). Commander of Union forces at the first battle of Bull Run, then commander of the 1st Corps. Relieved after the second battle of Bull Run.

McNEILL, John H.—Captain, CSA. Commander of a company of partisan rangers in the Shenandoah Valley/West Virginia area.

McPHERSON, James B.—Major General, USV (USMA 1853). Commander of the Army of the Tennessee, part of Sherman's Military Division of the Mississippi.

MEADE, George Gordon—Major General, USV (USMA 1835). Commander of the Army of the Potomac.

MEIGS, Montgomery C.—Brigadier General, USA (USMA 1836). Quartermaster General of the U.S. Army. One of two officers sent by Halleck to report on the situation at Bermuda Hundred.

MERRITT, Wesley—Brigadier General, USV (USMA 1860). Commander of the Reserve Brigade in Torbert's 1st Division of Sheridan's Cavalry Corps, and temporary commander of the division while Torbert was on medical leave.

MIX, Simon—Colonel, USV. Commander of the 1st Brigade of Kautz's Cavalry Division of Butler's Army of the James (Dept. of Va. and N.C.).

MOOR, Augustus—Colonel, USV. Commander of the 1st Brigade of Sullivan's 1st Infantry Division of Sigel's (later Hunter's) Department of West Virginia. Sent with an ad hoc advance guard to occupy New Market ahead of Sigel's main column.

MORGAN, John Hunt—Brigadier General, CSA. Commander of a

brigade of Kentucky cavalry in the Department of Southwestern Virginia. Temporarily succeeded Breckinridge in command of the department, before leaving on a raid into Kentucky.

MOSBY, John Singleton—Lieutenant Colonel, CSA. Commander of a battalion of partisan rangers in northern Virginia.

MOTT, Gershom—Brigadier General, USV. Commander of the 4th Division of Hancock's 2nd Corps of Meade's Army of the Potomac until his division was consolidated with the 3rd, after which he commanded the 3rd Brigade of that division.

MOWER, J. A.—Brigadier General, USV. Commander of the Right Wing of the 16th Corps, two divisions that were part of A. J. Smith's Detachment, Army of the Tennessee.

NEILL, Thomas H.—Brigadier General, USV (USMA 1847). Commander of the 3rd Brigade of Getty's 2nd Division of the 6th Corps in Meade's Army of the Potomac. Succeeded to the command of the division when Getty was wounded on 6 May 1864.

ORD, Edward O. C.—Major General, USV (USMA 1839). Briefly assigned to command a force in Sigel's Department of West Virginia.

PALMER, John M.—Major General, USV. Commander of the 14th Corps in Thomas' Army of the Cumberland in Sherman's Military Division of the Mississippi.

PERRIN, Abner M.—Brigadier General, CSA. Commander of a brigade of Alabama infantry in Anderson's (later Mahone's) Division of the 3rd Corps of Lee's Army of Northern Virginia.

PERRY, E. A.—Brigadier General, CSA. Commanded a brigade of Florida infantry in Anderson's (later Mahone's) Division of the 3rd Corps of Lee's Army of Northern Virginia.

PERRY, William F.—Colonel, CSA. Commanded a brigade of Alabama infantry in Field's Division in the 1st Corps of Lee's Army of Northern Virginia.

PHELPS, S. L.—Lieutenant Commander, USN. Captain of the USS Eastport, the largest ironclad in Admiral David Porter's fleet on the Red River.

PICKETT, George E.—Major General, CSA (USMA 1846). Beauregard's predecessor in command of Confederate forces in southern Virginia, including the scattered brigades of his own division, formerly of the 1st Corps of the Army of Northern Virginia. Temporarily retained in command at Petersburg by Beauregard. Sent with his reassembled division to rejoin Lee at the North Anna.

POLK, Leonidas—Lieutenant General, CSA (USMA 1827). Commander of the Department of Alabama, Mississippi and Eastern Louisiana until sent with most of his forces (known as the Army of Mississippi, or Polk's Corps) to reinforce J. E. Johnston's Army of Tennessee in Georgia. Former Episcopal bishop of Louisiana.

POPE, John—Major General, USV (USMA 1842). Commander of the short-lived Army of Virginia, until defeated at the second battle of Bull Run. Before that, one of Halleck's three principal subordinates (with Grant and Buell) in the trans-Allegheny West.

PORTER, David Dixon—Rear Admiral, USN. Commander of the gunboat fleet on the Mississippi and its tributaries, including the Red River.

PORTER, Horace—Captain (later lieutenant colonel), USA (USMA 1860). Witnessed Grant's first meeting with Lincoln. Later became an aide on Grant's staff. His book *Campaigning With Grant* is frequently quoted in these pages.

POTTER, Robert B.—Brigadier General, USV. Commander of the 2nd Division of Burnside's 9th Corps.

PRICE, Sterling—Major General, CSA. Commander of Confederate forces in Arkansas. Former governor of Missouri.

RANSON, Matthew W. ("Matt")—Brigadier General, CSA. Commander of a brigade of North Carolina infantry in Beauregard's Dept. of Southern Virginia and N.C. Brother of Robert Ransom.

RANSOM, Robert, Jr.—Major General, CSA (USMA 1850). Commander of the Department of Richmond, and an ad hoc division under Beauregard at the battle of Drewry's Bluff. Brother of Matt Ransom.

RANSOM, Thomas—Brigadier General, USV. Commander of the 13th Corps in Banks' Army of the Gulf.

RAWLINS, John A.—Brigadier General, USV. Grant's chief of staff and former neighbor in Galena, Illinois.

RICE, James C.—Brigadier General, USV. Commander of the 2nd Brigade of the 4th Division of Warren's 5th Corps in Meade's Army of the Potomac.

RICKETTS, James B.—Brigadier General, USV (USMA 1839). Commander of the 3rd Division of Sedgwick's 6th Corps in Meade's Army of the Potomac.

ROBINSON, John C.—Brigadier General, USV (USMA ex-1839). Commander of the 2nd Division of Warren's 5th Corps in Meade's Army of the Potomac.

RODES, Robert E.—Major General, CSA. Commander of a division in the 2nd Corps of Lee's Army of Northern Virginia.

ROEBLING, Washington A.—Major, USV. Aide on Warren's staff.

ROSECRANS, William S.—Major General, USV (USMA 1842). Thomas' predecessor as commander of the Army of the Cumberland. Removed after his defeat at Chickamauga.

ROSSER, Thomas L.—Brigadier General, CSA (USMA ex-May 1861). Commander of a brigade of Virginia cavalry (known as the Laurel Brigade) in Hampton's Division of Jeb Stuart's Cavalry Corps of Lee's Army of Northern Virginia. Good friend of Union general George A. Custer.

RUSSELL, David A.—Brigadier General, USV (USMA 1845). Commander of the 3rd Brigade of the 1st Division of the 6th Corps in Meade's Army of the Potomac. Succeeded to command of the division when Wright succeeded Sedgwick in command of the corps.

SCHOFIELD, John M.—Major General, USV (USMA 1853). Commander of the Army of the Ohio (also know as the 23rd Corps) in Sherman's Military Division of the Mississippi.

SCOTT, Winfield—Brevet Lieutenant General, USA. Hero of the War of 1812 and the Mexican War. Had been general-in-chief of the U.S. Army when the Civil War began.

SEDDEN, James A.—Confederate Secretary of War.

SEDGWICK, John—Major General, USV (USMA 1837). Commander of the 6th Corps in Meade's Army of the Potomac.

SEWARD, William Henry—Secretary of State in Lincoln's cabinet.

SHERIDAN, Philip Henry—Major General, USV (USMA 1853). New commander of the Cavalry Corps of the Army of the Potomac.

SHERMAN, William Tecumseh—Major General, USV (USMA 1840). Grant's favorite subordinate and his successor in command, first of the Army of the Tennessee, and then of the Military Division of the Mississippi.

SIGEL (rhymes with regal), Franz—Major General, USV. Commander of the Department of West Virginia. Prominent leader of the German-American community, which was very important to the Republican party.

SLOCUM, Henry W.—Major General, USV (USMA 1852). Commander of the District of Vicksburg in McPherson's Department of the Tennessee in Sherman's Military Division of the Mississippi. Former commander of the 12th Corps in the Army of the Potomac. Came west with Hooker after Chickamauga.

SMITH, Andrew Jackson—Brigadier General (later major general), USV (USMA 1838). Commander of the Detachment, Army of the Tennessee lent by Sherman to Banks for the Red River campaign.

SMITH, B. H.—Captain, CSA. Commander of a battery of Virginia artillery in the 2nd Corps of Lee's Army of Northern Virginia.

SMITH, E. Kirby—General, CSA (USMA 1845). Commander of the Trans-Mississippi Department.

SMITH, Martin Luther—Major General, CSA (USMA 1842). Chief engineer of Lee's Army of Northern Virginia.

SMITH, T. Kilby—Brigadier General, USV. Commander of the Provisional Division of the 17th Corps, part of A. J. Smith's Detachment, Army of the Tennessee.

SMITH, William Farrar ("Baldy")—Major General, USV (USMA 1845). Commander of the 18th Corps in Butler's Army of the James (Dept. of Va. and N.C.).

SORREL, G. Moxley—Lieutenant Colonel, CSA. Chief of staff of the 1st Corps of Lee's Army of Northern Virginia.

SPEAR, Samuel P.—Colonel, USV. Commander of the 2nd Brigade of Kautz's Cavalry Division of Butler's Army of the James (Dept. of Va. and N.C.).

STAHEL-SZAMVALD ("STAHEL"), Julius—Major General, USV. Commander of the 1st Cavalry Division of Sigel's (later Hunter's) Department of West Virginia.

STANLEY, David S.—Major General, USV (USMA 1852). Commander of the 1st Division of Howard's 4th Corps in Thomas' Army of the Cumberland of Sherman's Military Division of the Mississippi.

STANTON, Edwin McMasters—Secretary of War in Lincoln's cabinet.

STEELE, Frederick—Major General, USV (USMA 1843). Commander of the Department of Arkansas.

STEUART, George H. ("Maryland")—Brigadier General, CSA (USMA 1848). Commanded a brigade of Virginia and North Carolina infantry in Johnson's Division of the 2nd Corps of Lee's Army of Northern Virginia.

STEVENSON, Thomas G.—Brigadier General, USV. Commander of the 1st Division of Burnside's 9th Corps.

STEWART, Alexander P.—Major General, CSA (USMA 1842). Commander of a division in Hood's 2nd Corps of J. E. Johnston's Army of Tennessee.

STONEMAN, George—Major General, USV (USMA 1846). Commander of the Cavalry Division of Schofield's Army of the Ohio in Sherman's Military Division of the Mississippi. Had been the first commander of the Cavalry Corps in the Army of the Potomac, before Pleasonton and Sheridan.

STUART, James Ewell Brown ("Jeb")—Major General, CSA (USMA 1854). Commander of the Cavalry Corps of Lee's Army of Northern Virginia.

STURGIS, Samuel D.—Brigadier General, USV (USMA 1846). Chief of cavalry of McPherson's Department of the Tennessee in Sherman's Military Division of the Mississippi. Twice sent out from the Memphis area to keep Forrest busy.

SULLIVAN, Jeremiah C.—Brigadier General, USV. Commander of the 1st Infantry Division of Sigel's (later Hunter's) Department of West Virginia.

SWEENY, Thomas W.—Brigadier General, USV. Commander of the 2nd Division in Dodge's Left Wing of the 16th Corps in McPherson's Army of the Tennessee of Sherman's Military Division of the Mississippi.

TAYLOR, Richard ("Dick")—Major General, CSA. Commander of Confederate forces in western Louisiana. Son of former U.S. president Zachary Taylor.

TAYLOR, Walter H.—Lieutenant Colonel, CSA. R. E. Lee's chief of staff.

TERRY, Alfred H.—Brigadier General, USV. Commander of the 1st Division of Gillmore's 10th Corps in Butler's Army of the James (Dept. of Va. and N.C.).

TERRY, William R.—Colonel (brigadier general from 31 May 1864), CSA. Commander of a brigade of Virginia infantry in Beauregard's Department of Southern Virginia and N.C. The brigade was part of Pickett's Division, which was reassembled and sent to reinforce Lee's Army of Northern Virginia at the North Anna.

THAYER, John Milton—Brigadier General, USV. Commander of the Frontier Division of Steele's Department of Arkansas.

THOMAS, George H.—Major General, USV (USMA 1840). Commander of the Department and Army of the Cumberland, the largest force in Sherman's Military Division of the Mississippi.

THOMAS, Edward L.—Brigadier General, CSA. Commander of a brigade of Georgia infantry in Wilcox's Division of the 3rd Corps of Lee's Army of Northern Virginia.

TORBERT, Alfred T. A.—Brigadier General, USV (USMA 1855). Commander of the 1st Division of Sheridan's Cavalry Corps of Meade's Army of the Potomac. After a medical leave he temporarily commanded an ad hoc brigade consisting of most of the cavalry still with Meade's and Burnside's forces, while Sheridan was on his raid to Richmond.

TURNER, John W.—Brigadier General, USV (USMA 1855). Commander of the 2nd Division of Gillmore's 10th Corps in Butler's Army of the James (Dept. of Va. and N.C.)

TYLER, Robert O.—Brigadier General, USV (USMA 1853). Commander of a new 4th Division of Hancock's 2nd Corps in Meade's Army of the Potomac, composed of five heavy artillery regiments (serving as infantry) brought from the defenses of Washington after Mott's old 4th Division had been consolidated with Birney's 3rd.

UPTON, Emory—Colonel (later brigadier general), USV (USMA May 1861). Commander of the 2nd Brigade of the 1st Division of the 6th Corps in Meade's Army of the Potomac.

VENABLE, Charles S.—Colonel, CSA. Officer on the staff of General R. E. Lee.

WADSWORTH, James S.—Brigadier General, USV. Commander of the 4th Division of Warren's 5th Corps in Meade's Army of the Potomac.

WALKER, Henry Harrison—Brigadier General, CSA. Commander of a brigade of Virginia infantry in Heth's Division of the 3rd Corps of Lee's Army of Northern Virginia.

WALKER, James A.—Brigadier General, CSA. Commander of the Stonewall Brigade of Virginia infantry in Johnson's Division of the 2nd Corps of Lee's Army of Northern Virginia.

WALKER, John G.—Major General, CSA. Commander of a division of Texas infantry sent to reinforce Taylor in Louisiana.

WALKER, Tandy—Colonel, CSA. Commander of a brigade of Choctaw Indians in Kirby Smith's Trans-Mississippi Department.

WALKER, William H. T.—Major General, CSA. Commander of a division in Hardee's 1st Corps of J. E. Johnston's Army of Tennessee.

WALKER, William S.—Brigadier General, CSA. Commander of a brigade of South Carolina infantry sent from that state to reinforce Beauregard in the Department of Southern Virginia and N.C. Captured during an attack on Butler's Bermuda Hundred defenses.

WARREN, Gouverneur Kemble—Major General, USV (USMA 1850). Commander of the 5th Corps in Meade's Army of the Potomac.

WASHBURN, Cadwallader Colder—Major General, USV. Commander of the District of West Tennessee in McPherson's Department of the

Tennessee in Sherman's Military Division of the Mississippi. Brother of Elihu Washburne (sic).

WASHBURNE, Elihu—United States Congressman from Galena, Illinois. Grant's political sponsor. Brother of Cadwallader C. Washburn (sic).

WEBB, Alexander S.—Brigadier General, USV (USMA 1855). Commander of the 1st Brigade in Gibbon's 2nd Division of Hancock's 2nd Corps in Meade's Army of the Potomac.

WEITZEL, Godfrey—Brigadier General, USV (USMA 1855). Commander of the 2nd Division of W. F. Smith's 18th Corps in Butler's Army of the James (Dept. of Va. and N.C.). Then named chief engineer of the Army of the James.

WHARTON, Gabriel C.—Brigadier General, CSA. Commander of one of Breckinridge's two infantry brigades sent from the Department of Southwestern Virginia to fight at New Market in the Shenandoah and then to reinforce Lee's Army of Northern Virginia at the North Anna.

WHEATON, Frank—Brigadier General, USV. Commander of the 1st Brigade of Getty's (later Neill's) 2nd Division of the 6th Corps in Meade's Army of the Potomac.

WHEELER, Joseph—Major General, CSA (USMA 1859). Commander of the Cavalry Corps of J. E. Johnston's Army of Tennessee.

WHITING, William Henry Chase—Major General, CSA (USMA 1845). Commander of the District of Wilmington in Beauregard's Department of Southern Virginia and N.C. Put in charge of forces at Petersburg after Beauregard left.

WILCOX, Cadmus Marcellus—Major General, CSA (USMA 1846). Commander of a division in the 3rd Corps of Lee's Army of Northern Virginia.

WILLCOX, Orlando B.—Brigadier General, USV (USMA 1847). Commander of the 3rd Division of Burnside's 9th Corps.

WILSON, James Harrison—Brigadier General, USV (USMA 1860). Commander of the 3rd Division of the Cavalry Corps of the Army of the Potomac. Former chief of the Cavalry Bureau and before that, chief engineer on Grant's staff.

WISE, Henry A.—Brigadier General, CSA. Commander of a brigade of Virginia infantry sent from South Carolina to reinforce Beauregard in the Department of Southern Virginia and N.C. Former governor of Virginia.

WRIGHT, Ambrose R.—Brigadier General, CSA. Commander of a

brigade of Georgia infantry in Anderson's (later Mahone's) Division of the 3rd Corps of Lee's Army of Northern Virginia.

WRIGHT, Horatio G.—Brigadier General (major general from 12 May 1864), USV (USMA 1841). Commander of the 1st Division of Sedgwick's 6th Corps in Meade's Army of the Potomac and Sedgwick's successor in command of the corps.

Appendix B

Military Organizations (early May)

UNITED STATES ARMY:
Commander-in-Chief—President Abraham Lincoln
Secretary of War—Edwin McMasters Stanton
General-in-Chief—Lieutenant General Ulysses S. Grant
Chief of Staff—Major General Henry W. Halleck
Quartermaster General—Brigadier General Montgomery C. Miegs

9th ARMY CORPS: Major General Ambrose E. Burnside

1st Division: Brigadier General Thomas G. Stevenson
1st Brigade: Colonel Sumner Carruth
2nd Brigade: Colonel Daniel Leasure

2nd Division: Brigadier General Robert B. Potter
1st Brigade: Colonel John I. Curtin
2nd Brigade: Colonel Simon G. Griffin

3rd Division: Brigadier General Orlando B. Willcox
1st Brigade: Colonel John F. Hartranft
2nd Brigade: Colonel Benjamin C. Christ

4th (USCT) Division: Brigadier General Edward Ferrero
1st Brigade: Colonel Joshua K. Sigfried
2nd Brigade: Colonel Henry G. Thomas

Provisional Brigade: Colonel Elsha G. Marshall

Artillery Reserve: Colonel John Edwards, Jr.

ARMY OF THE POTOMAC:
Commanding General—Major General George Gordon Meade
Chief of Staff—Major General Andrew Humphreys
Chief of Artillery—Brigadier General Henry J. Hunt
Chief Engineer—Brigadier General Henry W. Benham
Provost Marshal General—Brigadier General Marsena R. Patrick

ARTILLERY RESERVE: Colonel Henry S. Burton
1st Brigade (heavy art. as inf.): Col. J. Howard Kitching
2nd Brigade: Major John A. Tompkins
3rd Brigade: Major Robert H. Fitzhugh

2nd ARMY CORPS: Major General Winfield S. Hancock

1st Division: Brigadier General Francis C. Barlow
1st Brigade: Colonel Nelson A. Miles
2nd ("Irish") Brigade: Colonel Thomas A. Smyth
3rd Brigade: Colonel Paul Frank
4th Brigade: Colonel John R. Brooke

2nd Division: Brigadier General John Gibbon
1st Brigade: Brigadier General Alexander Webb
2nd Brigade: Brigadier General Joshua T. Owen
3rd Brigade: Colonel Samuel S. Carroll

3rd Division: Major General David B. Birney
1st Brigade: Brigadier General J. H. H. Ward
2nd Brigade: Brigadier General Alexander Hays

4th Division: Brigadier General Gershom Mott
1st Brigade: Colonel Robert McAllister
2nd ("Excelsior") Brigade: Colonel William R. Brewster

Artillery Brigade: Colonel John C. Tidball

5th ARMY CORPS: Major General Gouverneur K. Warren

1st Division: Brigadier General Charles Griffin
1st Brigade: Brigadier General Romeyn B. Ayres
2nd Brigade: Colonel Jacob B. Sweitzer
3rd Brigade: Brigadier General Joseph J. Bartlett

2nd Division: Brigadier General John C. Robinson
1st Brigade: Colonel Samuel H. Leonard
2nd Brigade: Brigadier General Henry Baxter
3rd ("Maryland") Brigade: Colonel Andrew W. Denison

3rd ("Pa. Reserve") Division: Brig. Gen. Samuel W. Crawford
1st Brigade: Colonel William McCandless
3rd Brigade: Colonel Joseph W. Fisher

4th Division: Brigadier General James S. Wadsworth
1st ("Iron") Brigade: Brigadier General Lysander Cutler
2nd Brigade: Brigadier General James C. Rice
3rd Brigade: Colonel Roy Stone

Artillery Brigade: Colonel Charles S. Wainwright

6th ARMY CORPS: Major General John Sedgwick

1st Division: Brigadier General Horatio G. Wright
1st ("Jersey") Brigade: Colonel Henry W. Brown
2nd Brigade: Colonel Emory Upton
3rd Brigade: Brigadier General David A. Russell
4th Brigade: Brigadier General Alexander Shaler

2nd Division: Brigadier General George W. Getty
1st Brigade: Brigadier General Frank Wheaton
2nd ("Vermont") Brigade: Colonel Lewis A. Grant
3rd Brigade: Brigadier General Thomas H. Neill
4th Brigade: Brigadier General Henry L. Eustis

3rd Division: Brigadier General James B. Ricketts
1st Brigade: Brigadier General William H. Morris
2nd Brigade: Brigadier General Truman Seymour

Artillery Brigade: Colonel Charles H. Tompkins

CAVALRY CORPS: Major General Philip H. Sheridan

1st Division: Brigadier General Alfred T. A. Torbert
1st ("Michigan") Brigade: Brig. Gen. George A. Custer
2nd Brigade: Colonel Thomas C. Devin
Reserve Brigade: Brigadier General Wesley Merritt

2nd Division: Brigadier General David McMurtrie Gregg
1st Brigade: Brigadier General Henry E. Davies, Jr.
2nd Brigade: Colonel J. Irvin Gregg

3rd Division: Brigadier General James H. Wilson
1st Brigade: Colonel John G. McIntosh
2nd Brigade: Colonel George H. Chapman

1st Brigade, Horse Artillery: Captain James M. Robertson
2nd Brigade, Horse Artillery: Captain Dunbar R. Ransom

DEPT. OF VIRGINIA AND NORTH CAROLINA (ARMY OF THE JAMES):
Commanding General—Major General Benjamin F. Butler

10th ARMY CORPS: Major General Quincy A. Gillmore

1st Division: Brigadier General Alfred H. Terry
1st Brigade: Colonel Joshua B. Howell
2nd Brigade: Colonel Joseph R. Hawley
3rd Brigade: Colonel Harris M. Plaisted

2nd Division: Brigadier General John W. Turner
1st Brigade: Colonel Samuel M. Alford
2nd Brigade: Colonel William B. Barton

3rd Division: Brigadier General Adelbert Ames
1st Brigade: Colonel Richard White
2nd Brigade: Colonel Jeremiah C. Drake

18th ARMY CORPS: Major General William F. ("Baldy") Smith

1st Division: Brigadier General William T. H. Brook
1st Brigade: Brigadier General Gilman Marston
2nd Brigade: Brigadier General Hiram Barnham
3rd Brigade: Colonel Horace T. Sanders

2nd Division: Brigadier General Godfrey Weitzel
1st Brigade: Brigadier General Charles A. Heckman
2nd Brigade: Brigadier General Isaac J. Wistar

USCT Division: Brigadier General Edward W. Hincks
1st Brigade: Brigadier General Edward A. Wild
2nd Brigade: Colonal Samuel A. Duncan

Naval Brigade: Brigadier General Charles K. Graham

Cavalry Division: Brigadier General August V. Kautz
1st Brigade: Colonel Simon H. Mix
2nd Brigade: Colonel Samuel P. Spear

Independent (USCT) Cavalry Brigade: Colonel Robert West

District of St. Mary's: Colonel Alonzo Granville Draper

District of North Carolina: Brigadier General Innis N. Palmer
Subdistrict of the Albemarle: Brig. Gen. Henry W. Wessells
Subdistrict of Beaufort: Colonel James Jourdan
Defenses of New Berne: Colonel Thomas J. C. Armory

District of Eastern Virginia: Brig. Gen. George F. Shepley

DEPARTMENT OF THE SOUTH:
Commanding General—Brigadier General John P. Hatch

Northern District: Brigadier General Alexander Schimmelfennig
Folly Island: Colonel L. von Gilsa
Morris Island: Colonel William Gurney

District of Beaufort, S.C.: Brigadier General Rufus Saxton

District of Hilton Head, S.C.: Colonel William W. H. Davis

District of Florida: Brigadier General William Birney

DEPARTMENT OF WASHINGTON (22nd Army Corps):
Commanding General—Major General Christopher C. Augur
Chief Engineer—Brigadier General John G. Barnard

District of Washington: Colonel Moses N. Wisewell
1st Brigade: Colonel R. H. Rush

Light Artillery Camp: Brigadier General Albion P. Howe

Independent Cavalry Brigade: Col. Charles Russell Lowell, Jr.

Tyler's Division: Brigadier General Robert O. Tyler
1st Brigade: Colonel A. H. Grimshaw
2nd Brigade: Colonel M. Murphy

Cavalry Division, Camp Stoneman: Colonel William Gamble

Defenses North of the Potomac: Lt. Col. J. A. Haskins
1st Brigade: Colonel James M. Warner
2nd Brigade: Colonel L. O. Morris
3rd Brigade: Colonel J. Welling

Defenses South of the Potomac: Brig. Gen. G. A. DeRussy
1st Brigade: Colonel A. A. Gibson
2nd Brigade: Colonel T. R. Tannatt
3rd Brigade: Colonel Alexander Piper

MIDDLE DEPARTMENT (8th ARMY CORPS) (Maryland and Delaware):
Commanding General—Major General Lew Wallace

1st Separate Brigade: Brigadier General Erastus B. Tyler
2nd Separate Brigade: Colonel P. A. Porter
3rd Separate Brigade: Brigadier General Henry H. Lockwood

District of Delaware: Brigadier General John R. Kenly

DEPARTMENT OF WEST VIRGINIA:
Commanding General—Major General Franz Sigel

1st Infantry Division: Brigadier General Jeremiah C. Sullivan
1st Brigade: Colonel Augustus Moor
2nd Brigade: Colonel Joseph Thoburn

1st Cavalry Division: Brigadier General Julius Stahel
1st Brigade: Colonel William B. Tibbets
2nd Brigade: Colonel J. E. Wynkoop

Reserve Division: Brigadier General Benjamin F. Kelley

District of the Kanawha: Brigadier General George Crook

2nd Infantry Division: (Brigadier General George Crook)
1st Brigade: Colonel Rutherford B. Hayes
2nd Brigade: Colonel Carr B. White
3rd Brigade: Colonel Horatio G. Sickel

2nd Cavalry Division: Brigadier General William W. Averell
1st Brigade: Brigadier General Alfred N. Duffie
2nd Brigade: Colonel J. M. Schoonmaker
3rd Brigade: Colonel John H. Oley

NORTHERN DEPARTMENT:
Commanding General—Major General Samuel P. Heintzelman

DEPARTMENT OF THE EAST:
Commanding General—Major General John A. Dix

DEPARTMENT OF MISSOURI:
Commanding General—Major General William S. Rosecrans
District of Southwest Missouri: Brig. Gen. John B. Sanborn
District of St. Louis: Brigadier General Thomas Ewing, Jr.
Districts of Rolla and Northern Missouri: Brig. Gen. O. Guitar
District of Central Missouri: Brig. Gen. Egbert B. Brown

DEPARTMENT OF KANSAS:
Commanding General—Major General Samuel R. Curtis
District of Nebraska: Brigadier General Robert B. Mitchell
District of Colorado: Colonel J. M. Chivington

DEPARTMENT OF THE NORTHWEST:
Commanding General—Major General John Pope

DEPARTMENT OF NEW MEXICO:
Commanding General—Brigadier General James H. Carleton

DEPARTMENT OF THE PACIFIC:
Commanding Officer—Colonel George Wright

DEPARTMENT OF THE GULF:
Commanding General—Major General Nathaniel P. Banks
DETACHMENT, 13th ARMY CORPS: Brig. Gen. T. E. G. Ransom

3rd Division: Brigadier General Robert A. Cameron
1st Brigade: Lieutenant Colonel A. M. Flory
2nd Brigade: Colonel William H. Raynor

4th Division: Colonel William J. Landram
1st Brigade: Colonel F. Emerson
2nd Brigade: Colonel J. W. Vance

DETACHMENT, ARMY OF THE TENNESSEE: Brig. Gen. A. J. Smith

RIGHT WING, 16th CORPS: Brigadier General Joseph A. Mower

2nd Brig., 1st Div.: Colonel Lucius F. Hubbard
3rd Brig., 1st Div.: Colonel Sylvester G. Hill
1st Brig., 3rd Div.: Colonel William F. Lynch
2nd Brig., 3rd Div.: Colonel T. W. Shaw
3rd Brig., 3rd Div.: Colonel R. M. Moore

Provisional Division, 17th Corps: Brig. Gen. T. Kilby Smith
1st Brigade: Colonel Jonathan B. Moore
2nd Brigade: Colonel Lyman M. Ward

19th ARMY CORPS: Major General William B. Franklin

1st Division: Brigadier General William H. Emory
1st Brigade: Brigadier General William Dwight
2nd Brigade: Brigadier General James W. McMillan
3rd Brigade: Colonel Lewis Benedict

2nd Division: Brigadier General Cuvier Grover
1st Brigade: Brigadier General Franklin S. Nickerson
2nd Brigade: Brigadier General Henry W. Birge
3rd Brigade: Colonel Jacob Sharpe

Cavalry Division: Brigadier General A. L. Lee
1st Brigade: Colonel Thomas J. Lucas
2nd Brigade: Colonel John G. Fonda
3rd Brigade: Colonel H. Robinson

4th Brigade: Colonel Nathan A. M. Dudley
5th Brigade: Colonel Oliver P. Gooding

District of Key West and Tortugas: Brig. Gen. D. P. Woodbury

District of Baton Rouge: Brig. Gen. Philip St. George Cooke

District of Port Hudson: Brigadier General George L. Andrews

CORPS DE AFRIQUE: Brigadier General Daniel Ullman

1st Division: (Brigadier General Daniel Ullman)
1st Brigade: Colonel William H. Dickey
2nd Brigade: Colonel Cyrus Hamlin

2nd Division: Colonel Charles W. Drew
2nd Brigade: Colonel L. Goodrich

District of La Fourche: Brigadier General Henry W. Birge

1st Division, 13th Corps: Brigadier General Fitz-Henry Warren
1st Brigade: Colonel Henry D. Washburn
2nd Brigade: Brigadier General Michael K. Lawler

2nd Division, 13th Corps (in Texas): Maj. Gen. F. J. Herron
1st Brigade: Lieutenant Colonel Joseph O. Hudnutt
2nd Brigade: Colonel John McNulta
Provisional (USCT) Brigade: Colonel J. C. Cobb

MILITARY DIVISION OF THE MISSISSIPPI:
Commanding General—Major General William Tecumseh Sherman
Chief of Artillery—Brigadier General William F. Barry

DEPARTMENT OF ARKANSAS (7th ARMY CORPS):
Commanding General—Major General Frederick Steele

1st (Cavalry) Division: Brigadier General Eugene A. Carr
1st Brigade: Colonel J. F. Ritter
2nd Brigade: Colonel W. F. Geiger
3rd Brigade: Colonel Daniel Anderson

2nd Division: Brigadier General Joseph R. West
3rd Brigade: Colonel James M. True

3rd Division: Brigadier General Frederick Salomon
1st Brigade: Colonel Charles E. Salomon
2nd Brigade: Colonel W. F. McLean
3rd Brigade: Colonel Adolph Engleman

Frontier Division: Brigadier General John M. Thayer
1st Brigade: Colonel John Edwards
2nd Brigade: Colonel Charles W. Adams
3rd Brigade: Colonel E. Lynde

Independent Cavalry Brigade: Colonel Powell Clayton
Post of Pine Bluff: Colonel Powell Clayton
District of Eastern Arkansas: Brig. Gen. Napoleon B. Buford
District of Northeast Arkansas: Colonel Robert R. Livingston
District of the Frontier: Colonel William R. Judson
Indian Brigade: Colonel William A. Phillips

DEPARTMENT AND ARMY OF THE CUMBERLAND:
Commanding General—Major General George H. Thomas
Chief of Artillery—Brigadier General John Milton Brannan

Reserve Brigade: Colonel Joseph W. Burke
Engineer Brigade: Colonel W. B. McCreary
Pioneer Brigade: Colonel George P. Buell

4th ARMY CORPS: Major General Oliver O. Howard

1st Division: Major General David S. Stanley
1st Brigade: Brigadier General Charles Cruft
2nd Brigade: Brigadier General W. C. Whitaker
3rd Brigade: Colonel William Grose

2nd Division: Brigadier General John Newton
1st Brigade: Colonel Francis T. Sherman
2nd Brigade: Brigadier General George D. Wagner
3rd Brigade: Colonel Charles G. Harker

3rd Division: Brigadier General Thomas J. Wood
1st Brigade: Brigadier General August Willich
2nd Brigade: Brigadier General William B. Hazen
3rd Brigade: Brigadier General Samuel Beatty

14th ARMY CORPS: Major General John M. Palmer

1st Division: Brigadier General Richard W. Johnson
1st Brigade: Brigadier General William P. Carlin
2nd Brigade: Brigadier General John H. King
3rd Brigade: Colonel Benjamin Franklin Scribner

2nd Division: Brigadier General Jefferson C. Davis
1st Brigade: Brigadier General James D. Morgan
2nd Brigade: Colonel John Grant Mitchell
3rd Brigade: Colonel Daniel McCook

3rd Division: Brigadier General Absalom Baird
1st Brigade: Brigadier General John B. Turchin
2nd Brigade: Colonel Ferdinand Vanderveer
3rd Brigade: Colonel George Peabody Este

20th ARMY CORPS: Major General Joseph Hooker

1st Division: Brigadier General Alpheus S. Williams
1st Brigade: Brigadier General Joseph F. Knipe
2nd Brigade: Brigadier General Thomas H. Ruger
3rd Brigade: Colonel James Sidney Robinson

2nd Division: Brigadier General John W. Geary
1st Brigade: Colonel Charles Candy
2nd Brigade: Colonel A. Buschbeck
3rd Brigade: Colonel D. Ireland

3rd Division: Major General Daniel Butterfield
1st Brigade: Brigadier General William T. Ward
2nd Brigade: Colonel Samuel Ross
3rd Brigade: Colonel James Wood, Jr.

CAVALRY CORPS: Brigadier General W. L. Elliott

1st Division: Brigadier General Edward M. McCook
1st Brigade: Colonel J. B. Dorr
2nd Brigade: Colonel Oscar H. LaGrange
3rd Brigade: Colonel Louis D. Watkins

2nd Division: Brigadier General Kenner Garrard
1st Brigade: Colonel Robert H. G. Minty
2nd Brigade: Colonel Eli Long
3rd ("Lightning") Brigade: Colonel John T. Wilder

3rd Division: Brigadier General Hugh Judson Kilpatrick
1st Brigade: Colonel William W. Lowe
2nd Brigade: Colonel C. C. Smith
3rd Brigade: Colonel Eli H. Murray

Post of Chattanooga: Major General James B. Steedman

District of Nashville (4th Division, 20th Corps):
  Major General Lovell H. Rousseau

Post of Nashville: Brigadier General Robert S. Granger

4th Cavalry Division: Brigadier General Alvan C. Gillem
1st Brigade: Lieutenant Colonel D. G. Thornburg
2nd Brigade: Lieutenant Colonel George Spalding
3rd Brigade: Colonel J. K. Miller

DEPARTMENT AND ARMY OF THE TENNESSEE:
Commanding General—Major General James B. McPherson
Chief of Cavalry—Brigadier General Samuel Sturgis
15th ARMY CORPS: Major General John Logan

1st Division: Brigadier General Peter J. Osterhaus
1st Brigade: Brigadier General Charles R. Woods
2nd Brigade: Colonel James A. Williamson
3rd Brigade: Colonel Hugo Wangelin

2nd Division: Brigadier General Morgan L. Smith
1st Brigade: Brigadier General Giles A. Smith
2nd Brigade: Brigadier General Joseph A. J. Lightburn

3rd Division (Huntsville, Ala.): Brig. Gen. J. E. Smith
1st Brigade: Colonel J. I. Alexander
2nd Brigade: Colonel Green B. Raum
3rd Brigade: Brigadier General Charles L. Matthies

4th Division: Brigadier General William Harrow
1st Brigade: Colonel R. Williams
2nd Brigade: Colonel C. C. Walcutt
3rd Brigade: Colonel J. M. Oliver

LEFT WING, 16th ARMY CORPS: Major General Grenville Dodge

2nd Division: Brigadier General Thomas W. Sweeney
1st Brigade: Brigadier General Elliott W. Rice
2nd Brigade: Colonel P. E. Burke
3rd Brigade: Colonel M. M. Bane

4th Division: Brigadier General James C. Veatch
1st Brigade: Colonel John W. Fuller
2nd Brigade: Colonel John W. Sprague
3rd Brigade: Colonel John H. Howe

17th ARMY CORPS: Major General Francis P. Blair

3rd Division: Brigadier General Mortimer D. Leggett
1st Brigade: Brigadier General Manning F. Force
2nd Brigade: Colonel Robert K. Scott
3rd Brigade: Colonel Adam G. Malloy

4th Division: Brigadier General Marcellus M. Crocker
1st Brigade: Colonel W. L. Sanderson
2nd Brigade: Colonel Benjamin Dornblaser
3rd Brigade: Brigadier General Walter Q. Gresham

District of West Tennessee: Major General C. C. Washburn
1st Brigade, 1st Div., 16th Corps: Col. W. L. McMillan

1st Cavalry Div., 16th Corps: Brig. Gen. Benjamin Grierson
1st Brigade: Colonel George E. Waring, Jr.
2nd Brigade: Colonel Edward F. Winslow
3rd Brigade: Colonel H. B. Burgh

District of Memphis: Brigadier General R. P. Buckland
1st Colored Brigade: Colonel Edward Bouton
2nd Brigade: Colonel George B. Hoge

District of Vicksburg: Major General Henry W. Slocum
Maltby's Brigade: Brigadier General J. A. Maltby

1st Division, 17th Corps: Brigadier General E. S. Dennis
1st Brigade: Colonel Frederick A. Starring
2nd Brigade: Colonel James H. Coates

1st Division, U.S. Colored Troops: Brig. Gen. J. P. Hawkins
1st Brigade: Brigadier General Isaac F. Shepard
2nd Brigade: Colonel Hiram Scofield

Cavalry Brigade: Colonel Embury D. Osband

Post of Natchez, Miss.: Brigadier General James M. Tuttle

District of Columbus (Ky.): Brigadier General Henry Prince

DEPARTMENT AND ARMY OF THE OHIO (23rd ARMY CORPS): Commanding General—Major General John M. Schofield

1st Division: Brigadier General Alvin P. Hovey
1st Brigade: Colonel R. F. Barter
2nd Brigade: Colonel John C. McQuiston

2nd Division: Brigadier General Henry M. Judah
1st Brigade: Brigadier General Nathaniel C. McLean
2nd Brigade: Brigadier General Milo S. Hascall

3rd Division: Brigadier General Jacob D. Cox
1st Brigade: Colonel James W. Reilly
2nd Brigade: Brigadier General Mahlon D. Manson

Cavalry Division: Major General George Stoneman
1st Brigade: Colonel James Biddle

4th Division (E. Tenn.): Brigadier General Jacob Ammen
1st Brigade: Colonel John Mehringer
2nd Brigade: Brigadier General Davis Tillson
3rd Brigade: Colonel Benjamin P. Runkle

District of Kentucky (5th Div.): Brig. Gen. S. G. Burbridge

1st Division: Brigadier General Edward H. Hobson
1st Brigade: Colonel George W. Gallup
2nd Brigade: Colonel C. J. True
3rd Brigade: Colonel C. S. Hanson
4th Brigade: Colonel J. M. Brown

2nd Division: Brigadier General Hugh Ewing
1st Brigade: Lieutenant Colonel T. B. Farleigh
2nd Brigade: Colonel Cicero Maxwell

1st Cavalry Brigade: Colonel Israel Garrard
3rd Cavalry Brigade: Colonel Horace Capron

CONFEDERATE STATES ARMY:
Commander-in-Chief—President Jefferson Davis
Secretary of War—James Alexander Seddon
Commanding General—General Braxton Bragg
Adjutant and Inspector General—General Samuel Cooper

ARMY OF NORTHERN VIRGINIA:
Commanding General—General Robert Edward Lee
Chief Engineer—Major General Martin L.Smith
Chief of Artillery—Brigadier General William N. Pendleton

1st ARMY CORPS: Lieutenant General James Longstreet

Kershaw's Division: Brigadier General Joseph B. Kershaw
Kershaw's Brigade: Colonel John Henagan
Wofford's Brigade: Brigadier General William T. Wofford
Humphrey's Brigade: Brig. Gen. Benjamin G. Humphreys
Bryan's Brigade: Brigadier General Goode Bryan

Field's Division: Major General Charles W. Field
Jenkins' Brigade: Brigadier General Micah Jenkins
Law's Brigade: Colonel William F. Perry
Anderson's Brigade: Brigadier General George T. Anderson
Gregg's Brigade: Brigadier General John Gregg
Benning's Brigade: Brigadier General Henry L. Banning

Artillery: Brigadier General E. Porter Alexander
Huger's Battalion: Lieutenant Colonel Frank Huger
Haskell's Battalion: Major John C. Haskell
Cabell's Battalion: Colonel Henry C. Cabell

2nd ARMY CORPS: Lieutenant General Richard S. Ewell

Early's Division: Major General Jubal A. Early
Hays' Brigade: Brigadier General Harry T. Hays
Pegram's Brigade: Brigadier General John Pegram
Gordon's Brigade: Brigadier General John B. Gordon

Johnson's Division: Maj. Gen. Edward ("Allegheny") Johnson
The Stonewall Brigade: Brigadier General James A. Walker

Jones' Brigade: Brigadier General John M. Jones
Steuart's Brigade: Brig. Gen. George ("Maryland") Steuart
Stafford's Brigade: Brigadier General Leroy A. Stafford

Rodes' Division: Major General Robert E. Rodes
Daniel's Brigade: Brigadier General Junius Daniel
Doles' Brigade: Brigadier General George Doles
Ramseur's Brigade: Brigadier General Stephen D. Ramseur
Battle's Brigade: Brigadier General Cullen A. Battle
Johnston's Brigade: Brigadier General Robert D. Johnston

Artillery: Brigadier General Armistead A. Long
Hardaway's Battalion: Lieutenant Colonel R. A. Hardaway
Nelson's Battalion: Lieutenant Colonel William Nelson
Braxton's Battalion: Lieutenant Colonel Carter M. Braxton
Cutshaw's Battalion: Major W. E. Cutshaw
Page's Battalion: Major R. C. M. Page

3rd ARMY CORPS: Lieutenant General Ambrose Powell Hill

Anderson's Division: Major General Richard H. Anderson
Perrin's Brigade: Brigadier General Abner Perrin
Harris' Brigade: Brigadier General Nathaniel H. Harris
Mahone's Brigade: Brigadier General William Mahone
Wright's Brigade: Brigadier General Ambrose R. Wright
Perry's Brigade: Brigadier General Edward A. Perry

Heth's Division: Major General Henry Heth
Davis' Brigade: Brigadier General Joseph R. Davis
Cooke's Brigade: Brigadier General John R. Cooke
Kirkland's Brigade: Brigadier General William W. Kirkland
Walker's Brigade: Brigadier General Henry H. Walker
Archer's Brigade: Brigadier General James J. Archer

Wilcox's Division: Major General Cadmus M. Wilcox
Lane's Brigade: Brigadier General James H. Lane
Scales' Brigade: Brigadier General Alfred M. Scales
McGowan's Brigade: Brigadier General Samuel McGowan
Thomas' Brigade: Brigadier General Edward L. Thomas

Artillery: Colonel R. Lindsay Walker
Poague's Battalion: Lieutenant Colonel William T. Poague
McIntosh's Battalion: Lieutenant Colonel D. G. McIntosh
Pegram's Battalion: Lieutenant Colonel W. J. Pegram
Cutts' Battalion: Colonel A. S. Cutts
Richardson's Battalion: Lt. Col. Charles Richardson

CAVALRY CORPS: Major General James Ewell Brown ("Jeb") Stuart

Hampton's Division: Major General Wade Hampton
Young's Brigade: Brigadier General Pierce M. B. Young
The Laurel Brigade: Brigadier General Thomas L. Rosser

Fitzhugh Lee's Division: Major General Fitzhugh Lee
Lomax's Brigade: Brigadier General Lunsford Lomax
Wickham's Brigade: Brigadier General Williams Wickham

W. H. F. Lee's Division: Maj. Gen. W. H. F. ("Rooney") Lee
Chambliss' Brigade: Brigadier General John R. Chambliss
Gordon's Brigade: Brigadier General James B. Gordon

Horse Artillery: Major R. P. Chew

Valley District: Brigadier General John D. Imboden
Imboden's (cavalry) Brigade: (Brig. Gen. John D. Imboden)
Valley Reserves: Colonel William Harman

DEPARTMENT OF SOUTHWESTERN VIRGINIA:
Commanding General—Major General John C. Breckinridge
Chief of Artillery—Major William McLaughlin

Echols' Brigade: Brigadier General John Echols
Wharton's Brigade: Brigadier General Gabriel Wharton
McCausland's Brigade: Colonel John McCausland
Jenkins' (cavalry) Brigade: Brig. Gen. Albert Jenkins
Jackson's (cavalry) Brigade: Colonel William Jackson

Morgan's (cavalry) Division: Brig. Gen. John Hunt Morgan
Morgan's (cavalry) Brigade: (Brig. Gen. John Hunt Morgan)
Giltner's (cavalry) Brigade: Colonel Henry L. Giltner
Cosby's (cavalry) Brigade: Colonel George B. Cosby

DEPARTMENT OF EAST TENNESSEE:
Commanding General—Major General Simon Bolivar Buckner

Jones' (cavalry) Brigade: Brig. Gen. W. E. Jones
Vaughn's (cavalry) Brigade: Brig. Gen. John C. Vaughn
Jackson's (cavalry) Brigade: Brig. Gen. Alfred E. Jackson

DEPARTMENT OF RICHMOND:
Commanding General—Major General Robert Ransom

Hunton's Brigade: Brigadier General Eppa Hunton*@
Corse's Brigade: Brigadier General Montgomery D. Corse*@
Johnson's Brigade: Brigadier General Bushrod R. Johnson@

Gracie's Brigade: Brig. Gen. Archibald Gracie, Jr.@
Butler's (cavalry) Brigade: Brig. Gen. Matthew C. Butler+

Richmond Defenses: Colonel W. H. Stevens
1st Division (artillery), Inner Line: Lt. Col. J. W. Atkinson
2nd Division (artillery), Inner Line: Lt. Col. James Howard

Chaffin's Farm (artillery): Major A. W. Stark

Chaffin's Bluff (artillery): Lieutenant Colonel J. M. Maury

Drewry's Bluff (artillery): Major F. S. Smith

Artillery: Colonel H. P. Jones
Moseley's Battalion: Lieutenant Colonel E. F. Moseley
Coit's Battalion: Major J. C. Coit

DEPARTMENT OF SOUTHERN VIRGINIA AND NORTH CAROLINA:

Commanding General—General Pierre Gustave Toutant Beauregard
Volunteer Aide de Camp—Major General Daniel Harvey Hill

District of Southern Virginia: Major General George Pickett
Clingman's Brigade: Brigadier General Thomas L. Clingman
Maryland Line (mixed): Colonel Bradley T. Johnson
Dearing's (cavalry) Brigade: Brig. Gen. James Dearing
Washington Artillery Battalion: Lt. Col. B. F. Eshelman

District of North Carolina: Major General Robert F. Hoke
Hoke's Brigade: Colonel William G. Lewis
Ransom's Brigade: Brigadier General Matthew Ransom
Kemper's Brigade: Colonel William R. Terry*
Barton's Brigade: Colonel Birkett D. Fry*
Artillery Battalion: Lieutenant Colonel C. E. Lightfoot

District of Cape Fear: Major General W. H. Chase Whiting
Garrison of Fort Fisher: (Maj. Gen. W. H. Chase Whiting)
Martin's Brigade: Brigadier General James G. Martin

DEPARTMENT OF SOUTH CAROLINA, GEORGIA AND FLORIDA:

Commanding General—Major General Samuel Jones

Hagood's Brigade: Brigadier General Johnson Hagood@
Wise's Brigade: Brigadier General Henry A. Wise@
Colquitt's Brigade: Brigadier General Alfred H. Colquitt@
Walker's Brigade: Brigadier General W. S. Walker@

1st Military District: Brigadier General Roswell S. Ripley

1st Subdivision: Brigadier General William B. Taliaferro
4th Subdivision: Major Stephen Elliott, Jr.
5th Subdivision: Brigadier General W. G. De Saussure
District of East Florida: Brigadier General Joseph Finegan

DEPARTMENT AND ARMY OF TENNESSEE:
Commanding General—General Joseph Eggleston Johnston
Chief Engineer—Major General Jeremy Francis Gilmer
Chief of Artillery—Brigadier General Francis Asbury Shoup

Engineer Troops: Lieutenant Colonel S. W. Presstman

1st ARMY CORPS: Lieutenant General William J. Hardee

Cheatham's Division: Major General Benjamin F. Cheatham
Maney's Brigade: Brigadier General George E. Maney
Wright's Brigade: Colonel John Carpenter Carter
Strahl's Brigade: Brigadier General Otho French Strahl
Vaughn's Brigade: Brigadier General Alfred J. Vaughn, Jr.

Cleburne's Division: Major General Patrick Cleburne
Polk's Brigade: Brigadier General Lucius E. Polk
Lowrey's Brigade: Brigadier General Mark Perrin Lowrey
Govan's Brigade: Brigadier General Daviel C. Govan
Granbury's Brigade: Brigadier General Hiram B. Granbury

Walker's Division: Major General William H. T. Walker
Jackson's Brigade: Brigadier General John K. Jackson
Gist's Brigade: Brigadier General States Rights Gist
Stevens' Brigade: Brigadier General Clement H. Stevens
Mercer's Brigade: Brigadier General Hugh W. Mercer

Bate's Division: Major General William Brimage Bate
The Orphan Brigade: Brigadier General Joseph H. Lewis
Tyler's Brigade: Colonel Thomas B. Smith
Finley's Brigade: Brigadier General Jesse J. Finley

Artillery: Colonel Melancthon Smith
Hoxton's Battalion: Major L. Hoxton
Hotchkiss's Battalion: Major T. R. Hotchkiss
Martin's Battalion: (unknown)
Cobb's Battalion: Major Robert Cobb
Palmer's Battalion: (unknown)

2nd ARMY CORPS: Lieutenant General John Bell Hood

Hindman's Division: Major General T. C. Hindman
Deas' Brigade: Brigadier General Zachary C. Deas

Manigault's Brigade: Brigadier General A. M. Manigault
Tucker's Brigade: Brigadier General William F. Tucker
Walthall's Brigade: Brigadier General Edward C. Walthall

Stevenson's Division: Major General Carter L. Stevenson
Brown's Brigade: Brigadier General John C. Brown
Cumming's Brigade: Brigadier General Alfred Cumming
Reynolds' Brigade: Brigadier General A. W. Reynolds
Pettus's Brigade: Brigadier General Edmund W. Pettus

Stewart's Division: Major General Alexader P. Stewart
Stovall's Brigade: Brigadier General Marcellus A. Stovall
Clayton's Brigade: Brigadier General Henry D. Clayton
Baker's Brigade: Brigadier General Alphael Baker
Gibson's Brigade: Brigadier General Randall L. Gibson

Artillery: Colonel Robert F. Beckham
Courtney's Battalion: Major A. R. Courtney
Eldridge's Battalion: Major J. W. Eldridge
Johnston's Battalion: Major J. W. Johnston
Williams' Battalion: Captain E. F. Kolb

CAVALRY CORPS: Major General Joseph Wheeler

Martin's Division: Major General William T. Martin
Morgan's Brigade: Brigadier General John T. Morgan
Iverson's Brigade: Brigadier General Alfred H. Iverson

Kelly's Division: Brigadier General John H. Kelly
Allen's Brigade: Brigadier General William W. Allen
Dibrell's Brigade: Brigadier General George G. Dibrell
Hannon's Brigade: Colonel Moses W. Hannon

Humes' Division: Brigadier General William Y. C. Humes
Humes' Brigade: Colonel John T. Wheeler
Harrison's Brigade: Colonel Thomas H. Harrison
Grigsby's Brigade: Colonel J. Warren Grigsby

Horse Artillery: Lieutenant Colonel Felix H. Robertson

1st Division, Georgia Militia: Major Gen. Gustavus W. Smith
1st Brigade: Brigadier General Reuben W. Carswell
2nd Brigade: Brigadier General Pleasant J. Phillips

ARMY OF MISSISSIPPI: Lieutenant General Leonidas Polk

Loring's Division: Major General W. W. Loring
Featherston's Brigade: Brig. Gen. W. S. Featherston
Adams' Brigade: Brigadier General John Adams

Scott's Brigade: Brigadier General Thomas M. Scott

French's Division: Major General Samuel G. French
Ector's Brigade: Brigadier General M. D. Ector
Cockrell's Brigade: Brigadier General F. M. Cockrell
Sears' Brigade: Colonel W. S. Barry

Cantey's Division: Brigadier General James Cantey
Quarles' Brigade: Brigadier General William A. Quarles
Reynolds' Brigade: Brigadier General D. H. Reynolds
Cantey's Brigade: Colonel V. S. Murphey

Artillery: Lieutenant Colonel S. C. Williams
Waddell's Battalion: (unknown)
Myrick's Battalion: Major J. D. Myrick
Storrs' Battalion: Major George S. Storrs
Preston's Battalion: Major W. C. Preston

Cavalry Division: Brigadier General W. H. ("Red") Jackson
Armstrong's Brigade: Brigadier General F. C. Armstrong
Ross's Brigade: Brigadier General L. S. Ross
Ferguson's Brigade: Brigadier General S. W. Ferguson
Horse Artillery: Captain John Waties

DEPARTMENT OF ALABAMA, MISSISSIPPI AND EAST LOUISIANA:

Commanding General—Major General Stephen Dill Lee

District of No. Miss. and W. Tenn.: Maj. Gen. N. B. Forrest

Chalmer's (cavalry) Division: Brig. Gen. James R. Chalmers
1st Brigade: Colonel James J. Neely
2nd Brigade: Colonel Robert McCulloch

Buford's (cavalry) Division: Brig. Gen. Abraham Buford
3rd Brigade: Colonel Hylan B. Lyon
4th Brigade: Colonel Tyree H. Bell

5th (cavalry) Brigade: Brig. Gen. Samuel J. Gholson

6th (cavalry) Brigade: Colonel Edmund W. Rucker

Artillery Battalion: Captain John W. Morton

District of Central Mississippi: Brigadier General Wirt Adams
Mabry's (cavalry) Brigade: Colonel Hinchie P. Mabry
Scott's (cavalry) Brigade: Colonel John S. Scott

District of Northern Alabama: Brig. Gen. Philip D. Roddey
Patterson's (cavalry) Brigade: Colonel Josiah Patterson

Johnson's (cavalry) Brigade: Colonel William A. Johnson

District of Central Alabama: Brigadier General Gideon Pillow

District of the Gulf: Major General Dabney H. Maury

District of S.W. Miss. & E. La.: Brig. Gen. George B. Hodge

TRANS-MISSISSIPPI DEPARTMENT:
Commanding General—Lieutenant General Edmund Kirby Smith

District of West Louisiana: Major General Richard Taylor

Louisiana Division: Brigadier General Mouton
Polignac's Brigade: Brigadier General C. J. Polignac
Gray's Brigade: Colonel Henry Gray

Texas Division: Major General John G. Walker
Waul's Brigade: Brigadier General T. N. Waul
Scurry's Brigade: Brigadier General W. R. Scurry
Randal's Brigade: Colonel Horace Randal

Texas Cavalry Division: Brigadier General Thomas Green
Bee's Brigade: Brigadier General H. P. Bee
Major's Brigade: Brigadier General James P. Major
Bagby's Brigade: Brigadier General Arthur P. Bagby

Sub-District of No. La.: Brig. Gen. St. John R. Liddell

District of Arkansas: Major General Sterling Price

Missouri Division: Brigadier General M. M. Parsons
1st Brigade: Brigadier General John B. Clark, Jr.
2nd Brigade: Colonel S. P. Burns

Arkansas Division: Brigadier General Thomas J. Churchill
Tappan's Brigade: Brigadier General John C. Tappan
Hawthorn's Brigade: Brigadier General A. T. Hawthorn
Gause's Brigade: Colonel L. C. Gause

Arkansas Cavalry Division: Brigadier General J. F. Fagan
Cabell's Brigade: Brigadier General W. L. Cabell
Dockery's Brigade: Brigadier General T. P. Dockery
Crawford's Brigade: Colonel W. A. Crawford

Missouri Cavalry Division: Brig. Gen. John S. Marmaduke
Greene's Brigade: Colonel Colton Greene
Shelby's Brigade: Brigadier General Joseph O. Shelby

Maxey's Cavalry Division: Brig. Gen. Samuel B. Maxey
Gano's Brigade: Colonel Charles De Morse

The Choctaw Brigade: Colonel Tandy Walker
The Cherokee Brigade: Colonel Stand Watie
District of Texas: Major General John Magruder

*components of Pickett's Division
+ later added to Hampton's Division
@ sent as reinforcements to Department of So. Va. and N.C.

Appendix C

Bibliography

ESSENTIAL STUDIES

This work would not have been possible in anything like its present form without extensive reference to the following three books:

Matter, William D. *If It Takes All Summer: The Battle of Spotsylvania.* Chapel Hill, 1988.

Robertson, William Glenn. *Back Door To Richmond: The Bermuda Hundred Campaign, April–June 1864.* Newark, 1987.

Steere, Edward. *The Wilderness Campaign.* New York, 1960.

OTHER SECONDARY SOURCES:

Ammen, Daniel. *The Atlantic Coast.* New York, 1883.

Bearss, Edwin C. *Forrest at Brice's Cross Roads.* Dayton, Ohio, 1979.

Boatner, Mark Mayo, III. *The Civil War Dictionary.* New York, 1959.

Carter, Samuel, III. *The Last Cavaliers.* New York, 1979.

Catton, Bruce. *Grant Takes Command.* Boston, 1968.

———. *A Stillness At Appomattox.* New York, 1957.

Coggins, Jack. *Arms and Equipment of the Civil War.* Garden City, 1962.

Cornish, Dudley Taylor. *The Sable Arm.* Lawrence, Kansas, 1957.

Davis, William C. *The Battle of New Market.* New York, 1975.

Dowdey, Clifford. *Lee's Last Campaign.* New York, 1960.

Faust, Patricia L., ed. *Historical Times Illustrated Encyclopedia of the Civil War.* New York, 1986.

Foote, Shelby. *The Civil War: a Narrative.* 3 vols. New York, 1958–1974.

Freeman, Douglas Southall. *Lee's Lieutenants* 3 vols. New York, 1942–1944.

————. *R. E. Lee.* 4 vols. New York, 1934–1935.

Fuller, J. F. C. *Grant and Lee.* Bloomington, Ind., 1957.

Hattaway, Herman. *General Stephen D. Lee.* Jackson, Miss., 1976.

Humphreys, Andrew A. *The Virginia Campaign of '64.* New York, 1883.

Leech, Margaret. *Reveille In Washington.* New York, 1941.

Lewis, Thomas A. *The Guns of Cedar Creek.* New York, 1988.

Long, E. B. *The Civil War Day By Day: An Almanac, 1861–1865.* New York, 1971.

McDonough, James Lee, and James Pickett Jones. *War So Terrible.* New York, 1987.

Miers, Earl Schenck. *The General Who Marched to Hell.* New York, 1951.

————. *The Last Campaign: Grant Saves the Union.* New York, 1972.

Nevins, Allan. *Ordeal of the Union,* 2 vols. New York, 1947.

Newman, Ralph, and E. B. Long. *The Civil War.* 2 vols. New York, 1956.

Pond, George E. *The Shenandoah Valley in 1864.* New York, 1883.

Pullen, John J. *The 20th Maine,* New York, 1957.

Pyne, Henry R. *Ride To War.* New Brunswick, N.J., 1961.

Robertson, James I., Jr. *The Stonewall Brigade.* Baton Rouge, 1963.

Sandburg, Carl. *Abraham Lincoln: The War Years 1864–1865* New York, 1926.

Starr, Louis M. *Bohemian Brigade.* New York, 1954.

Starr, Stephen Z. *The Union Cavalry in the Civil War,* 3 vols. Baton Rouge, 1979–1985.

Trudeau, Noah Andre. *Bloody Roads South.* Boston, 1989.

Urwin, Gergory J. W. *Custer Victorious.* East Brunswick, N.J., 1983.

Williams, T. Harry. *Lincoln and His Generals.* New York, 1952.

Woodward, W. E. *Meet General Grant.* New York, 1928.

PRIMARY SOURCES:

Basler, Roy P., ed. *The Collected Works of Abraham Lincoln.* 8 vols. New Brunswick, N.J., 1953–1955.

Beauregard, G. T. "Four Days of Battle at Petersburg." In *Battles and Leaders of the Civil War,* edited by Robert Underwood Johnson and Clarence Clough Buell, vol. 4, New York, 1887.

"The Capture of Fort Pillow." In *Battles and Leaders,* vol. 4. See Beauregard.

Chestnut, Mary Boykin. *A Diary From Dixie.* Boston, 1945.

Dana, Charles A. *Recollections of the Civil War.* New York, 1963.

Dowdey, Clifford, and Louis H. Manarin, eds. *The Wartime Papers of R. E. Lee.* New York, 1961.

Duke, Basil W. "John Morgan in 1864," *Battles and Leaders,* vol. 4. See Beauregard.

Dyer, Frederick H. *A Compendium of the War of the Rebellion.* 3 vols. New York, 1959.

Gilbert, Elliott. "The First Battle of the Confederate Ram 'Albemarle.' " In *Battles and Leaders,* vol. 4. See Beauregard.

Grant, Ulysses S. *Personal Memoirs of U. S. Grant.* New York, 1886.

Holden, Edgar. "The 'Albemarle' and the 'Sassacus,' " In *Battles and Leaders,* vol. 4. See Beauregard.

Howard, Oliver O. "The Struggle For Atlanta." In *Battles and Leaders,* Vol. 4. See Beauregard.

Irwin, Richard B. "The Capture of Port Hudson." In *Battles and Leaders,* vol. 3. See Beauregard.

———. "The Red River Campaign." In *Battles and Leaders,* vol. 4. See Beauregard.

Jones, John B. *A Rebel War Clerk's Diary.* New York, 1958.

McMahon, Martin T. "The Death of General John Sedgwick." In *Battles and Leaders,* vol. 4. See Beauregard.

Porter, Horace. *Campaigning With Grant.* New York, 1897.

Rodenbough, Theo. F. "Sheridan's Richmond Raid." *In Battles and Leaders,* vol. 4. See Beauregard.

———. "Sheridan's Trevillian Raid." In *Battles and Leaders,* vol. 4. See Beauregard.

Russell, Charles Wells, ed. *The Memoirs of Colonel John S. Mosby,* Bloomington, Ind., 1959.

Sherman, William T. *Memoirs of General W. T. Sherman.* New York, 1891.

Smith, E. Kirby. "The Defense of the Red River." In *Battles and Leaders,* vol. 4. See Beauregard.

Smith, William Farrar. "Butler's Attack on Drewry's Bluff." In *Battles and Leaders,* vol. 4. See Beauregard.

———. "The Eighteenth Corps At Cold Harbor." In *Battles and Leaders,* vol. 4. See Beauregard.

Snead, Thomas L. "The Conquest of Arkansas." In *Battles and Leaders,* vol. 3. See Beauregard.

MAGAZINE ARTICLES:

Ewing, Joseph H. "The New Sherman Letters." *American Heritage* 38, no. 5.

Hufstodt, James T. "Ransom at the Crossroads." *Civil War Times Illustrated,* 19, no. 8.

Klinger, Michael J. "Botched Union Attack." *America's Civil War*, September 1989.

Longacre, Edward G. "Cavalry Clash at Todd's Tavern." *Civil War Times Illustrated* 16, no. 6.

———. "Rescue on the Red River." *Civil War Times Illustrated* 14, no. 6.

Noblitt, Phil. "Heedless Frontal Assault." *America's Civil War*, January 1990.

Pohanka, Brian C. "Not War But Murder," *America's Civil War*, January 1989.

Sloan, W. Eugene. "Goodbye To The Single-Shot Musket," *Civil War Times Illustrated* 23, no. 3.

Index